ISSUES FOR DEBATE
IN CORPORATE
SOCIAL RESPONSIBILITY

SELECTIONS FROM CQ RESEARCHER

Los Angeles | London | New Delhi
Singapore | Washington DC

For information:

SAGE Publications, Inc.
2455 Teller Road
Thousand Oaks, California 91320
E-mail: order@sagepub.com

SAGE Publications Ltd.
1 Oliver's Yard
55 City Road
London EC1Y 1SP
United Kingdom

SAGE Publications India Pvt. Ltd.
B 1/I 1 Mohan Cooperative
    Industrial Area
Mathura Road, New Delhi 110 044
India

SAGE Publications Asia-Pacific Pte. Ltd.
33 Pekin Street #02-01
Far East Square
Singapore 048763

Printed in the United States of America

Library of Congress Cataloging-in-Publication Data

Issues for debate in corporate social responsibility: selections from CQ researcher.
    p. cm.
ISBN 978-1-4129-7756-2 (pbk.)
    1. Social responsibility of business—United States. 2. Corporate culture—United States. I. Sage Publications, inc. II. CQ researcher.
HD60.5.U5.I87 2010
174′.4—dc22   2009023015

This book is printed on acid-free paper.

09   10   11   12   13   10   9   8   7   6   5   4   3   2   1

Acquisitions Editor:	Lisa Cuevas Shaw
Editorial Assistant:	MaryAnn Vail
Production Editor:	Laureen Gleason
Typesetter:	C&M Digitals (P) Ltd.
Cover Designer:	Candice Harman
Marketing Manager:	Christy Guilbault

Contents

Annotated Contents

INTRODUCTION TO CORPORATE SOCIAL RESPONSIBILITY

Corporate Social Responsibility: Is Good Citizenship Good for the Bottom Line?

Corporations across the country are embracing efforts to improve society. Unlike traditional efforts by businesses to appear socially responsible, the current movement emphasizes profit and long-term company success along with good works. Firms such as Whole Foods and Nike strive to make good citizenship a recognized part of their brand. General Electric, Coca-Cola and other more traditional corporations also support corporate social responsibility (CSR), motivated by advocacy group pressures, threatened government regulations and demands from employees, customers and investors. Some conservatives oppose CSR activities, arguing a company's only legitimate purpose is to enhance shareholder value. Some critics from the left label CSR a public relations ploy and say the government should expand corporations' legal responsibility to employees, the public and the environment.

ORGANIZATIONAL ISSUES

Curbing CEO Pay: Is Executive Compensation Out of Control?

This spring's shareholder proxy season promises to trigger fireworks among shareholders. Scores of public companies are under scrutiny from shareholders and politicians for rewarding their chief executive officers with huge pay and severance packages, sometimes despite spectacular management failures. Home Depot's Robert L. Nardelli, for example, received a $210 million severance package in January, while Capital One Financial's Richard D. Fairbank took home $280 million in compensation in 2005. Meanwhile, an investigation is proceeding into the possible manipulation of executive stock options at up to 200 companies. New federal rules requiring companies to disclose once-hidden details of their compensation took effect this year, setting the stage for bitter controversy over corporate pay. A coalition of shareholders is petitioning some 50 corporations for the right to advise their boards on the companies' executive compensation, and the new Democrat-controlled Congress has made moves aimed at curbing pay.

Gender Pay Gap: Are Women Paid Fairly in the Workplace?

More than four decades after Congress passed landmark anti-discrimination legislation —including the Equal Pay Act of 1963—a debate continues to rage over whether women are paid fairly in the workplace. Contending that gender bias contributes to a significant "pay gap," reformists support proposed federal legislation aimed at bringing women's wages more closely in line with those of men. Others say new laws are not needed because the wage gap largely can be explained by such factors as women's choices of occupation and the amount of time they spend in the labor force. Meanwhile, a class-action suit charging Wal-Mart Stores with gender bias in pay and promotions—the biggest sex-discrimination lawsuit in U.S. history — may be heading for the Supreme Court. Some women's advocates argue that a controversial high-court ruling last year makes it more difficult to sue over wage discrimination.

Labor Unions' Future: Can They Survive in the Age of Globalization?

The American labor movement suffered a major blow at its 50th-anniversary convention in Chicago in July. The beleaguered AFL-CIO split nearly in half as seven unions formed the rival Change to Win coalition. The seceding unions argued that the AFL-CIO, led by John Sweeney, had been spending too much time and money trying to get Democrats elected to national office and not enough time recruiting new members. The defections reflect the concern over declining union membership in recent years, due in part to automation and job outsourcing.

Some 3 million U.S. factory jobs alone were lost between 2000 and 2003. As he starts a new term, Sweeney confronts the possibility of more defections, businesses that are aggressively anti-union and unafraid to move operations abroad and a younger generation that knows little about unions. The split also raises questions for the Democrats, who historically derived funding and votes from the labor movement.

ECONOMIC ISSUES

Socially Responsible Investing: Can Investors Do Well by Doing Good?

Socially responsible investing, which combines financial goals with the aim of improving society through stock screening, shareholder activism and other methods, has grown into a multi-trillion-dollar industry. Concerns about climate change, worker rights and other issues are prompting big institutional accounts as well as small investors to put more and more emphasis on social, environmental and corporate governance factors in weighing investment decisions. But critics say stock-screening methods used by mutual funds are subjective and that socially responsible investments tend not to perform as well as conventional ones. Some of the harshest criticism has been directed at public pension funds using social-investing approaches, such as the California State Teachers' Retirement System, which uses a "double bottom line" approach to investing.

Regulating Credit Cards: Are Tougher Regulations Needed to Protect Consumers?

As home refinancing dries up as a source of cash for many Americans, credit card debt is rising faster than ever. Seeking to protect consumers from serious debt trouble, Congress is discussing the first significant legal restraints on credit card issuers imposed in many years — and possibly the toughest ever. The banking industry argues that most people don't get into severe financial distress from credit card spending and that a crackdown on fees and other bank practices could dry up the consumer credit that drives the economy. But some consumer advocates say that the approximately 35 million households behind in payments or over their credit limits demonstrate that tough action is needed—including caps on interest rates. Meanwhile, some economists warn that increasing the earning power of working-class families is the only long-term solution to consumer credit woes.

Fair Trade Labeling: Is It Helping Small Farmers in Developing Countries?

The number of products sold with fair trade labels is growing rapidly in Europe and the United States. Big chains like Wal-Mart, Dunkin' Donuts, Starbucks and McDonald's have begun offering coffee and other items. Fair trade brands hope to raise their profile by targeting consumers who care about the environment, health and fair-labor standards. Fair trade supporters say small farmers in the developing world benefit by receiving a guaranteed fair price, while the environment gets a break from intensive industrial farming. But critics say consumers pay too much and that fair trade's guarantee of a good return — no matter what the market price — sends the wrong economic signal to farmers. When the price of a global commodity like coffee tumbles in response to oversupply, overcompensated fair trade farmers will remain in an uneconomic sector long after they should have switched to some other crop or livelihood, free-market economists argue.

Buying Green: Does It Really Help the Environment?

Americans will spend an estimated $500 billion this year on products and services that claim to be good for the environment because they contain non-toxic ingredients or produce little pollution and waste. While some shoppers buy green to help save the planet, others are concerned about personal health and safety. Whatever their motives, eco-consumers are reshaping U.S. markets. To attract socially conscious buyers, manufacturers are designing new, green products and packaging, altering production processes and using sustainable materials. But some of these products may be wastes of money. Federal regulators are reviewing green labeling claims to see whether they mislead consumers, while some critics say that government mandates promoting environmentally preferable products distort markets and raise prices. Even if green marketing delivers on its pledges, many environmentalists say that sustainability is not a matter of buying green but of buying less.

Consumer Safety: Do Government Regulators Need More Power?

Americans have been alarmed by recent product recalls, including toothpaste containing an ingredient found in antifreeze, tainted pet food and millions of Mattel toys containing toxic lead paint. The recalls — all involving Chinese-made products — prompted government hearings that spotlighted problems at the underfunded and, critics say, overwhelmed Consumer Product Safety Commission. Meanwhile, inspectors found contamination in imported seafood as well as millions of pounds of U.S.-produced ground beef, triggering concerns that the two agencies responsible for food safety —the Food and Drug Administration and the Department of Agriculture — were also understaffed and underpowered. While food and product safety scares are not new, the skyrocketing growth of Asian imports has forced even industry groups to call for stepped-up consumer protection. Consumer advocates salute the trend but warn that some industries may be seeking to regulate themselves in an effort to preempt Congress from passing tougher laws.

Limiting Lawsuits: Is Business Pushing Too Hard to Restrict Litigation?

Business groups are continuing their decades-long war with trial lawyers and consumer groups over the U.S. litigation system. Business lobbies led by the U.S. Chamber of Commerce contend that companies are beset by lawsuits that are often unjustified, jury verdicts that may contradict federal regulations and punitive damage awards that may reach into the tens of millions of dollars. Trial lawyers and consumer groups claim that business interests exaggerate the number of suits and the frequency and size of jury awards. In addition, they contend that companies are simply seeking legal protection for wrongdoing that results in injuries to workers and consumers. The Bush administration has backed business in urging federal preemption of some state court suits in areas regulated by federal agencies, such as drug safety. The administration has been largely unsuccessful in pushing legal reforms through Congress, but President Bush's two Supreme Court appointees have strengthened the court's pro-business tilt on litigation issues.

SOCIETAL ISSUES

The New Environmentalism: Can New Business Policies Save the Environment?

Concern about the environment is intensifying, but new efforts to reduce pollution and save energy differ from past environmental movements. Unable to get much satisfaction from the Republican-dominated federal government, environmental activists have set their sights on businesses — trying to influence corporate behavior and even forming partnerships with companies to confront environmental challenges. A growing number of businesses — including Wal-Mart, the world's biggest retailer — are concluding that saving the environment is good for the bottom line. But some conservative critics charge that such actions actually dilute companies' primary purpose — to increase shareholder value. Meanwhile, in the absence of federal action, state and local governments are instituting policies aimed at weaning industry from fossil fuels. And some environmentalists are even rethinking nuclear power.

Confronting Warming: Can States and Localities Prevent Climate Change?

Growing concern about climate change has led states and cities to adopt new policies to try to conserve energy and reduce emissions of carbon dioxide and other greenhouse gases. California recently adopted new rules that aim to reduce such gases by 30 percent by 2020, while a cap on carbon emissions in the Northeast took effect Jan. 1. But critics say the efforts are more symbolic than substantive, pushing real sacrifices far off into the future. Many business groups, meanwhile, complain that the new rules will increase the cost of energy and hurt the economy —despite current promises that a "Green New Deal" can create jobs. The Obama administration promises to be far more aggressive in addressing global warming than the skeptical Bush White House. Even though the issue is coming to the fore in Washington, states and cities that have filled the policy vacuum in recent years pledge to stay vigilant in addressing the issue.

Carbon Trading: Will It Reduce Global Warming?

Carbon emissions trading — the buying and selling of permits to emit greenhouse gases caused by burning fossil fuels — is becoming a top strategy for reducing pollution that causes global climate change. Some $60 billion in permits were traded worldwide in 2007, a number expected to grow much larger if the next U.S. administration follows through on pledges to reduce America's carbon emissions. Advocates say carbon trading is the best way to generate big investments in low-carbon energy alternatives and control the cost of cutting emissions. But carbon trading schemes in Europe and developing countries have a mixed record. Some industries are resisting carbon regulations, and programs intended to help developing countries onto a clean energy path have bypassed many poor nations, which are the most vulnerable to the impacts of climate change. Some experts argue that there are simpler, more direct ways to put a price on carbon emissions, such as taxes. Others say curbing climate change will require both taxes and trading, plus massive government investments in low-carbon energy technologies.

Ecotourism: Does It Help or Hurt Fragile Lands and Cultures?

In the booming global travel business, ecotourism is among the fastest-growing segments. Costa Rica and Belize have built national identities around their celebrated environmental allure, while parts of the world once all but inaccessible — from Antarctica to the Galapagos Islands to Mount Everest — are now featured in travel guides, just like Manhattan, Rome and other less exotic destinations. Advocates see ecotourism as a powerful yet environmentally benign tool for sustainable economic development in even the poorest nations. But as the trend expands, critics see threats to the very flora and fauna tourists flock to visit. Moreover, traditional subsistence cultures may be obliterated by the ecotourism onslaught, replaced by service jobs that pay native peoples poverty wages. Meanwhile, tour promoters are using the increasingly popular "green" label to lure visitors to places unable to withstand large numbers of tourists.

Philanthropy in America: Are Americans Generous Givers?

Billionaire investor Warren Buffett has a message for wealthy Americans: Give away your money. Last June Buffett announced he was donating 85 percent of his $44 billion fortune, most of it earmarked for a charitable foundation established by Microsoft co-founder Bill Gates and his wife, Melinda. Although Americans donated more than $7 billion for hurricane, tsunami and earthquake relief in 2005, the super-rich, in general, have not stepped up their donations to match the economy's growth. Some in the philanthropy community argue, in fact, that Americans' self-image as uniquely generous is overblown. Meanwhile, the foundations that are a mainstay of U.S. philanthropy need more public oversight, critics say. And some scholars question whether charitable organizations are funding medical and other services that the government should provide.

Preface

Can investors do well by doing good? Is executive compensation out of control? Is fair trade helping small farmers in developing countries? These questions—and many more—are at the heart of corporate social responsibility. How can instructors best engage students with these crucial issues? We feel that students need objective, yet provocative examinations of these issues to understand how they affect citizens and organizations today and will for years to come. This collection aims to promote in-depth discussion, facilitate further research and help readers formulate their own positions on crucial issues. Get your students talking both inside and outside the classroom about *Issues for Debate in Corporate Social Responsibility*.

This first edition includes fifteen up-to-date reports by *CQ Researcher*, an award-winning weekly policy brief that brings complicated issues down to earth. Each report chronicles and analyzes executive, legislative and judicial activities at all levels of government. This collection is divided into three distinct areas—organizational issues, economic issues, and societal issues—to cover a range of issues found in most corporate social responsibility and strategic management or leadership-related courses.

CQ RESEARCHER

CQ Researcher was founded in 1923 as *Editorial Research Reports* and was sold primarily to newspapers as a research tool. The magazine was renamed and redesigned in 1991 as *CQ Researcher*. Today, students are its primary audience. While still used by hundreds of journalists and newspapers, many of which reprint portions of the reports, the *Researcher's* main subscribers are now high school, college and public libraries. In 2002, *Researcher* won the American Bar Association's coveted Silver Gavel award for magazine excellence for a series of nine reports on civil liberties and other legal issues.

Researcher staff writers—all highly experienced journalists—sometimes compare the experience of writing a *Researcher* report to drafting a college term paper. Indeed, there are many similarities. Each report is as long as many term papers—about 11,000 words—and is written by one person without any significant outside help. One of the key differences is that writers interview leading experts, scholars and government officials for each issue.

Like students, staff writers begin the creative process by choosing a topic. Working with the *Researcher's* editors, the writer identifies a controversial subject that has important public policy implications. After a topic is selected, the writer embarks on one to two weeks of intense research. Newspaper and magazine articles are clipped or downloaded, books are ordered and information is gathered from a wide variety of sources, including interest groups, universities and the government. Once the writers are well informed, they develop a detailed outline, and begin the interview process. Each report requires a minimum of ten to fifteen interviews with academics, officials, lobbyists and people working in the field. Only after all interviews are completed does the writing begin.

CHAPTER FORMAT

Each issue of *CQ Researcher*, and therefore each selection in this book, is structured in the same way. Each begins with an overview, which briefly summarizes the areas that will be explored in greater detail in the rest of the chapter. The next section chronicles important and current debates on the topic under discussion and is structured around a number of key questions, such as "Does corporate social responsibility really improve society?" or "Does corporate social responsibility restrain U.S. productivity?" These questions are usually the subject of much debate among practitioners and scholars in the field. Hence, the answers presented are never conclusive but detail the range of opinion on the topic.

Next, the "Background" section provides a history of the issue being examined. This retrospective covers important legislative measures, executive actions and court decisions that illustrate how current policy has evolved. Then the "Current Situation" section examines contemporary policy issues, legislation under consideration and legal action being taken. Each selection concludes with an "Outlook" section, which addresses possible regulation, court rulings and initiatives from Capitol Hill and the White House over the next five to ten years.

Each report contains features that augment the main text: two to three sidebars that examine issues related to the topic at hand, a pro versus con debate between two experts, a chronology of key dates and events and an annotated bibliography detailing major sources used by the writer.

ACKNOWLEDGMENTS

We wish to thank many people for helping to make this collection a reality. Tom Colin, managing editor of *CQ Researcher*, gave us his enthusiastic support and cooperation as we developed this edition. He and his talented staff of editors and writers have amassed a first-class library of *Researcher* reports, and we are fortunate to have access to that rich cache. We also wish to thank our colleagues at CQ Press, a division of SAGE and a leading publisher of books, directories, research publications and Web products on U.S. government, world affairs and communications. They have forged the way in making these readers a useful resource for instruction across a range of undergraduate and graduate courses.

Some readers may be learning about *CQ Researcher* for the first time. We expect that many readers will want regular access to this excellent weekly research tool. For subscription information or a no-obligation free trial of *CQ Researcher*, please contact CQ Press at www.cqpress.com or toll-free at 1-866-4CQ-PRESS (1-866-427-7737).

We hope that you will be pleased by this edition of *Issues for Debate in Corporate Social Responsibility.* We welcome your feedback and suggestions for future editions. Please direct comments to Lisa Cuevas Shaw, Executive Editor, SAGE Publications, 2455 Teller Road, Thousand Oaks, CA 91320, or lisa.shaw@sagepub.com.

—The Editors of SAGE

Contributors

Thomas J. Billitteri is a freelance journalist in Fairfield, Pennsylvania, who has more than 30 years' experience covering business, non-profit institutions and related topics for newspapers and other publications. He has written previously for *CQ Researcher* on teacher education, parental rights and mental-health policy. He holds a BA in English and an MA in journalism from Indiana University.

Marcia Clemmitt is a veteran social-policy reporter who joined *CQ Researcher* after serving as editor in chief of *Medicine and Health,* a Washington-based industry newsletter, and staff writer for *The Scientist.* She has also been a high school math and physics teacher. She holds a bachelor's degree in arts and sciences from St. Johns College, Annapolis, and a master's degree in English from Georgetown University.

Rachel S. Cox is a freelance writer in Washington, D.C. She has written for *Historic Preservation* magazine and other publications. She graduated in English from Harvard College.

Sarah Glazer specializes in health, education and social-policy issues. Her articles have appeared in *The Washington Post, Glamour, The Public Interest* and *Gender and Work,* a book of essays. Glazer covered energy legislation for the Environmental and Energy Study Conference and reported for United Press International. She holds a BA in American history from the University of Chicago.

Alan Greenblatt is a staff writer for Congressional Quarterly's *Governing* magazine. He previously covered elections and military and agricultural policy for *CQ Weekly*. He was awarded the National Press Club's Sandy Hume Memorial Award for political reporting. He holds a bachelor's degree from San Francisco State University and a master's degree in English literature from the University of Virginia.

Kenneth Jost, associate editor of *CQ Researcher*, graduated from Harvard College and Georgetown University Law Center, where he is an adjunct professor. He is the author of *The Supreme Court Yearbook* and editor of *The Supreme Court from A to Z*, both published by CQ Press. He was a member of *CQ Researcher* team that won the 2002 American Bar Association Silver Gavel Award.

Peter Katel is a veteran journalist who previously served as Latin America bureau chief for *Time* magazine, in Mexico City, and as a Miami-based correspondent for *Newsweek* and the *Miami Herald's* Spanish language edition *El Nuevo Herald*. He also worked as a reporter in New Mexico for 11 years and wrote for several nongovernmental organizations, including International Social Service and the World Bank. He has won several awards, including the Interamerican Press Association's Bartolome Mitre Award. He is a graduate of the University of New Mexico in University Studies.

Pamela M. Prah, a former *CQ Researcher* staff writer, is now political editor for Stateline.org. She has also written

for Kiplinger's *Washington Letter* and the Bureau of National Affairs. She holds a master's degree in government from Johns Hopkins University and a bachelor's degree in magazine journalism from Ohio University.

Tom Price is a Washington-based freelance journalist and a contributing writer for *CQ Researcher*. Previously he was a correspondent in the Cox Newspapers Washington Bureau, and chief politics writer for the *Dayton Daily News* and *The Journal Herald*. He is author, with Tony Hall, of *Changing the Face of Hunger: One Man's Story of How Liberals, Conservatives, Democrats, Republicans and People of Faith are Joining Forces to Help the Hungry, the Poor, and the Oppressed*. He also writes two Washington guidebooks, *Washington, D.C., for Dummies*, and the *Irreverent Guide to Washington, D.C.* His work has appeared in *The New York Times, Time, Rolling Stone* and other periodicals. He earned a bachelor of science in journalism at Ohio University.

Jennifer Weeks is a *CQ Researcher* contributing writer in Watertown, Massachusetts, who specializes in energy and environmental issues. She has written for *The Washington Post, The Boston Globe Magazine* and other publications, and has 15 years' experience as a public-policy analyst, lobbyist and congressional staffer. She has an AB degree from Williams College and master's degrees from the University of North Carolina and Harvard.

1

Corporate Social Responsibility

Is Good Citizenship Good for the Bottom Line?

Tom Price

Coca-Cola representatives and villagers in rural Kenya celebrate the soft-drink company's installation of a new well. Traditional U.S. corporations like Coke and General Electric are becoming environmental and social activists in response to advocacy group and consumer pressure and possible government regulations. Corporations say activism builds profits, but critics say it's a public relations ploy of limited value and not in shareholders' best interests.

From *CQ Researcher*, August 3, 2007.

Courtesy Coca-Cola

Scenes from a rapidly growing corporate trend in the U.S.:

- In Washington, D.C., the chief executives of 10 major U.S. corporations — including Alcoa, DuPont and General Electric — gather at the National Press Club to urge the federal government to require companies to reduce their emissions of greenhouse gases. "The science of global warming is clear," Duke Energy's James Rogers tells reporters at the executives' Jan. 22 news conference. "We know enough to act now. We must act now."[1]
- Across the country in Beaverton, Ore., Nike releases an audit that details ways its Third World suppliers mistreat their factory workers and pledges to improve working conditions. "Our greatest responsibility as a global company is to play a role in bringing about positive systemic change for workers within our own supply chain, and in the industry overall," the sports apparel company declares.[2]
- In New York, The Conference Board, a mainstay of the global business establishment, creates the Center for Corporate Citizenship and Sustainability. *Fortune* magazine adds a companion to its well-known list of the world's 500 largest corporations: a ranking of companies by "how well they conform to socially responsible business practices." And the company behind the most famous measure of economic performance — the Dow Jones Industrial Average — creates the Dow Jones Sustainability Indexes, to track the financial performance of companies that practice social and environmental responsibility.

Strong Support for Corporate Citizenship

In a 2005 survey of 1,189 U.S. businesses, 98 percent of large companies — and 81 percent of all companies — said corporate citizenship is a priority. Moreover, 84 percent of large companies report that being socially responsible has increased profits.

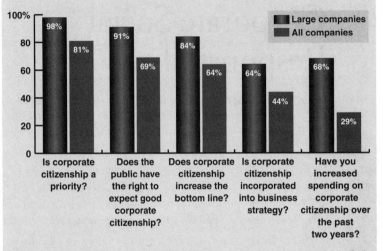

Source: Barbara Dyer, *et al.,* "The State of Corporate Citizenship in the U.S.," Boston College Center for Corporate Citizenship, 2005

Corporate social responsibility (CSR) — along with such variants as corporate citizenship and sustainability — is the new business mantra.

Adam Smith and Milton Friedman must be spinning in their graves.

Self-interest, not good intentions, creates the "wealth of nations," argued Smith, the great Scottish philosopher of the free market.

"It is not from the benevolence of the butcher, the brewer, or the baker, that we expect our dinner," he wrote in 1776, "but from their regard to their own self-interest.[3] By pursuing his own interest [an individual] frequently promotes that of the society more effectually than when he really intends to promote it."[4]

Friedman, a Noble Prize-winning economist and Smith's modern American successor, specifically rejected the notion of corporate social responsibility in a still widely quoted 1970 *New York Times Magazine* piece titled "The Social Responsibility of Business is to Increase its Profits."[5]

Conservative scholars and political activists frequently cite Smith and Friedman today. But it's nearly impossible to find a senior corporate executive who doesn't extol his company's commitment to being socially responsible.

"I'm a businessman and a free market libertarian, but I believe that the enlightened corporation should try to create value for all of its constituencies," said John Mackey, founder and CEO of Whole Foods Market. "At Whole Foods, we measure our success by how much value we can create for all six of our most important stakeholders: customers, team members [employees], investors, vendors, communities and the environment."[6]

From the time Mackey and his girlfriend opened a small natural-foods store in Austin, Texas, in 1978, his business has been about more than profit. But the heads of more traditional corporations also speak Mackey's language.

"The Coca-Cola Company must be both a great business and a great corporate citizen," Coke Chairman and CEO E. Neville Isdell said.[7]

General Electric "must be a great company with the capability, reach and resources to make a difference," GE chief Jeffrey R. Immelt said. "But we must also be a good company, because true impact means defining success in ways that go well beyond the bottom line."[8]

Such comments led Gib Hedstrom, The Conference Board's conference program director, to declare that "the debate is over. Leading companies are making a business out of solving the world's toughest problems. Citizenship is establishing itself as the requisite mindset for doing business in the 21st century."[9]

Corporate philanthropy is nothing new. Companies have been donating to charities, establishing philanthropic foundations and implementing community improvement projects since at least the 19th century. What's different is the way an overwhelming number of executives are accepting a *core corporate duty* to the welfare of "stakeholders" beyond those who own company stock — and also the way they are integrating that concept into their companies' day-to-day operations as a business opportunity. Their goal is to devise business strategies that improve society, protect the environment and increase profits over the long term — the so-called triple bottom line of "people, planet, profit."

A 2005 survey of 1,189 U.S. businesses by the Boston College Center for Corporate Citizenship and the U.S. Chamber of Commerce found that virtually all (98 percent) large companies make corporate citizenship a priority. When smaller companies are added, the figure drops to 81 percent. And two-thirds of large businesses (44 percent overall) incorporate citizenship into their business strategy.[10] (*See graph, at left.*)

The strong commitment reflects factors such as advocacy group pressures, fear of (or efforts to shape) government regulations, recruitment and retention of top-notch employees and efforts to make their companies more attractive to investors and customers.

For instance, after being attacked for buying products from Third World sweatshops, Nike began to publish its supply-chain information — and to engage in other good-citizen activities. Pushed by the Rainforest Action Network, Citicorp, JPMorgan Chase and Goldman Sachs agreed to consider the environmental consequences of their loans and investments.

The Environmental Defense advocacy group has served as a consultant to FedEx, Wal-Mart, DuPont and other corporations trying to improve their environmental records.

Concluding that government regulation of greenhouse gas emissions is inevitable, 30 major corporations formed the United States Climate Action Partnership to campaign for rules that are "environmentally effective, economically sustainable and fair."[11]

Because an African-American employees association at General Electric cared deeply about poverty and disease in Africa, GE applied its business capabilities to help build health facilities there.[12] Needing a highly skilled workforce, Intel spends more than $100 million a year to improve science and mathematics education in more than 50 countries.[13] And because its workers demand quality schools for their children, Intel works to improve the school districts around its facilities, says Intel Corporate Government Affairs Director Richard Hall.

Corporate good citizenship has long been a key marketing component for companies such as Whole Foods and Ben & Jerry's ice cream. Now companies such as GE and even Wal-Mart are advertising their efforts to improve society.

AP Photo/Richard Vogel

Workers assemble shoes at a Nike factory near Ho Chi Minh City, Vietnam, in 2000. After being attacked for using Third World sweatshops, Nike launched a campaign to improve working conditions in its suppliers' factories. "Our greatest responsibility as a global company is to play a role in bringing about positive systemic change for workers within our own supply chain, and in the industry overall," the company says.

In addition to hoping the strategy will lure shoppers into their stores, the companies want to increase their share of the nearly $2.3 trillion invested by socially conscious stockholders in the United States. (*See graph, p. 6.*) Those investments — which represent one-tenth of all professionally managed investments — grew slightly faster than all professionally managed assets between 1995 through 2005, according to the Social Investment Forum, the trade association for socially responsible investment firms.[14] (*See graph, p. 6.*)

Businesses also are finding that social responsibility can cut costs. FedEx's new fuel-efficient hybrid trucks reduce fuel expenses by more than a third while shrinking smog-causing emissions by two-thirds and nearly eliminating particulate emissions, the company reported.[15]

Costco, which offers more-generous employee benefits than other low-price retailers, enjoys half the worker turnover of Wal-Mart and the retail industry as a whole. Recruiting and training new employees is a costly expense that Costco minimizes. John Bowen, an investment manager in Coronado, Calif., said that "happy employees make for happy customers, which in the long run is ultimately reflected in the share price."[16] To measure corporations' reputations, Communications Consulting Worldwide surveyed media reports and rankings — such as lists of best-managed companies and best places to

Environmentalists Shape $45 Billion Energy Deal

Activists' role in TXU takeover "a turning point in the fight against global warming"

When two investment firms set their sights on acquiring Texas' largest electric company, they recruited a pair of surprising partners to their takeover team — the Natural Resources Defense Council and Environmental Defense, two leading advocacy organizations.

The resulting $45 billion takeover proposal in February by Kohlberg Kravis Roberts & Co. and Texas Pacific Group was the largest private buyout bid in history. But it captured even more attention because of what the environmental groups extracted from KKR and TPG, as the takeover firms are commonly called.

If they successfully acquire TXU Corp., KKR and TPG have pledged a long list of changes, including:

- Shrink from 11 to three the number of new coal-fired power plants TXU plans to build in Texas.
- Scrap plans to build new coal plants in Pennsylvania and Virginia.
- Reopen several mothballed natural gas plants, which pollute less than coal.
- Explore the possibility of building a plant that burns coal cleanly.
- Cut carbon dioxide emissions to 1990 levels by 2020.
- More than double TXU's use of wind power.
- Promote consumer use of solar power.
- Double spending to promote energy efficiency among its customers.
- Create a sustainable energy advisory board that includes representatives from national environmental groups.
- Tie executive compensation to climate-change goals.
- Cut some electric rates.
- Support federal legislation to mandate reductions in carbon dioxide emissions.[1]

James Marston, who led Environmental Defense's campaign against the proposed TXU power plants and participated in the negotiations with KKR and TPG, called the bid "a turning point in the fight against global warming."[2] TXU's size would enable it to reshape the power industry in Texas and influence the state's federal lawmakers to support climate-change legislation, he predicted.[3]

"It's one thing for companies in California to take the lead in reducing pollution," Marston said. "But this is Texas."[4]

"To say TXU is just another company," agreed David Hawkins, who represented the Natural Resources Defense Council in the negotiations, "is like saying Muhammad Ali was just another boxer."[5]

TPG Partner William Reilly, who was key to bringing the bidders together with the environmentalists, said the success of those talks "has led us to expect a future that will be collaborative and history-making."[6]

Daniel Esty, director of Yale University's Center for Business and Environment, said the bid demonstrates the "revolution" occurring in contemporary corporate responsibility.

"KKR and TPG most certainly have not gone soft," Esty said. "The masters of the universe have not given in to greenmail in a fit of political correctness. To the contrary, they are super-sophisticated business people who have learned that success in the marketplace now depends on getting corporate environmental strategy right."[7]

The takeover certainly would launch a dramatic makeover of TXU, which has battled environmental groups over its plant-construction plans and other issues. It has been described as leading the power industry in its advocacy of coal.[8] The 11 plants would have added another 78 million tons of carbon dioxide annually, more than doubling TXU's current 55 million.[9] The three plants still in the bidders' plans would increase emissions by nearly 20 percent.[10]

KKR and TPG first told TXU of their designs on the company in November 2006. In February, Reilly called Environmental Defense President Fred Krupp and asked for a

work. The New York firm concluded that if Wal-Mart's reputation rose to match higher-rated Target's, its stock would climb 8.4 percent, or $16 billion.[17]

"People want to work for companies that are socially responsible and that create avenues for them to be as well," says Nathan Garvis, Target's vice president for government affairs.

Companies also realize that "a healthy community is a great place to operate a business, to hire people, to locate a store, a great place for people to come and shop," confidential discussion. Reilly, the first President Bush's Environmental Protection Agency director, wanted help preparing a bid that environmental groups could support. Ironically, TXU Chairman John Wilder earlier had rejected a Krupp request to talk about the power-plant plans.

The two equity firms believed TXU's stock was undervalued because of its dependence on coal. And they already were trying to develop a more promising business plan with their lead financial adviser, Goldman Sachs, which itself works with environmental groups and transports its executives in hybrid limousines.

Marston and Hawkins were assigned to represent their groups in talks with Reilly and other representatives of the equity firms. After a week and a half of phone conversation, Marston flew to San Francisco for the final session, which began at breakfast in San Francisco's luxurious Mandarin Oriental Hotel. With Hawkins participating by telephone the talks finally wrapped up at TPG's offices overlooking San Francisco Bay at 1 a.m. on Feb. 22. Only then did the KKR and TPG representatives fly to Austin to tell Texas government officials of their plans. On Feb 25, TXU's board approved the sale. It still must be submitted to a shareholder vote.[11]

Not everyone is satisfied with the outcome. Some worry that TXU's coal-plant cutbacks would cause an electricity shortage within just a few years and lead to rate hikes. Others plan to keep opposing the three plants that TXU still plans to build. They also worry the new owners might not keep their promises, which are not legally binding.

TXU Mining's Big Brown site, near Fairfield, Texas, provides coal for a nearby coal-fired power plant.

AP Photo/David J. Phillip

"Promises are only promises," said Tim Morstad, advocacy director for AARP-Texas.[12]

[1] "TXU to Set New Direction As Private Company," Kohlberg Kravis Roberts & Co., Feb. 26, 2007, www.kkr.com/news/press_releases/2007/02-26-07.html; "The Facts on the TXU Buyout," *Environmental Defense*, March 6, 2007, www.environmentaldefense.org/article.cfm?contentID=6027; Tom Fowler, "Power Crisis Tune Changes Quickly," *The Houston Chronicle*, Feb. 28, 2007, p. 1; Elizabeth Souder, "Buyers May Go National with TXU," *The Dallas Morning News*, June 25, 2007, p. 1.

[2] Felicity Barringer and Andrew Ross Sorkin, "Utility to Limit New Coal Plants in Big Buyout," *The New York Times*, Feb. 25, 2007, p. A1.

[3] Steven Mufson and David Cho, "Energy Firm Accepts $45 Billion Takeover," *The Washington Post*, Feb. 26, 2007.

[4] Janet Wilson and Peter Pae, "Utility sale is boon for green activists," *Los Angeles Times*, Feb. 26, 2007, p. A10.

[5] *Ibid.*

[6] *Ibid.*

[7] Daniel C. Esty, "When Being Green Puts You in the Black," *The Washington Post*, March 4, 2007, p. B1.

[8] Andrew Ross Sorkin and Clifford Krauss, "At $45 Billion, New Contender for Top Buyout," *The New York Times*, Feb. 24, 2007, p. A1.

[9] David Koenig, The Associated Press, "TXU Board OKs Buyout Offer," *The Houston Chronicle*, Feb. 26, 2007, p. 1.

[10] Mufson and Cho, *op. cit.*

[11] Andrew Ross Sorkin, "A Buyout Deal That Has Many Shades of Green," *The New York Times*, Feb. 26, 2007; Mufson and Cho, *op. cit.*; Heather Green, "How Green Green-Lighted the TXU Deal," *Business Week Online*, Feb. 26, 2007.

[12] Tom Fowler, "Consumer Groups Want Details from TXU," *The Houston Chronicle*, July 17, 2007, Business Section, p. 1.

Garvis says. "The health of the community is an undergirding platform for economic success."

Some scholars and business executives point to one other influence on the rising popularity of corporate social responsibility: An increasing number of senior executives grew up amid the social turmoil of the 1960s and '70s, and they bring values they learned then into their boardrooms and executive offices.

"A generation of people in search of deeper meaning in their lives is now taking over the corporate suites,"

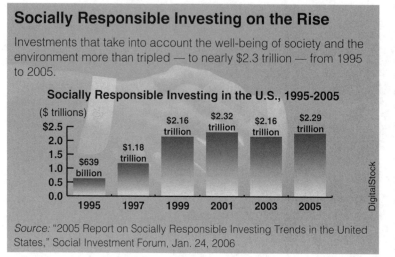

Socially Responsible Investing on the Rise

Investments that take into account the well-being of society and the environment more than tripled — to nearly $2.3 trillion — from 1995 to 2005.

Socially Responsible Investing in the U.S., 1995-2005

($ trillions)

1995	$639 billion
1997	$1.18 trillion
1999	$2.16 trillion
2001	$2.32 trillion
2003	$2.16 trillion
2005	$2.29 trillion

DigitalStock

Source: "2005 Report on Socially Responsible Investing Trends in the United States," Social Investment Forum, Jan. 24, 2006

said Andrew Savitz, former lead partner in Pricewater- houseCoopers' sustainability business services practice.[18]

Asked how he's different from his legendary GE pre- decessor Jack Welch, the 51-year-old Immelt likes to say that he's 20 years younger. That gets a laugh, but it's also a serious answer, according to Robert Corcoran, GE's vice president for corporate citizenship.

"He said, 'Let me explain this,'" Corcoran recalls, describing an Immelt meeting with a group of employees shortly after he assumed the company's top post. "'I grew up and went to high school and college in the '60s and '70s. I grew up with civil rights marches, the Vietnam War, women's liberation, Earth Day, sex, drugs and rock- and-roll. Those issues shaped how I think about and view the world. That's a different set of experiences from someone who grew up 20 years before.'"

These experiences, Corcoran continues, "give this gen- eration of leaders a view of the role of business in the world that's different from what someone might have gotten in the '50s or the '40s."

As activists, executives and investors consider the social role of business in the 21st century, here are some of the questions they're debating:

Do businesses have a responsibility to society beyond turning profits?

While nearly all major American businesses embrace cor- porate social responsibility, conservative critics launch continual — often vehement — attacks on the practice.

They call it a violation of the free- market principles that created and sustain prosperity. They also label it a dangerous transfer to corporations and activist groups of power over social issues that properly belongs to individuals and elected public officials.

"A company's responsibility is to its shareholders," says John Hood, president and chairman of the John Locke Foundation, a conservative think tank in North Carolina. "If managers have a different end than maximizing shareholder value, they're violating their responsibility."

When profit maximization is the goal, Hood says, shareholders have a clear measure of managers' performance. "When you move away from profit maximization and get into these more nebulous corporate social responsibility objec- tives," he adds, "that puts us at sea without a rudder."

Corporate executives and activists who promote cor- porate social responsibility are attempting to "privatize regulatory power" and levy "a hidden tax on corporate shareholders," says Nick Nichols, a senior fellow at the Center for Defense of Free Enterprise who teaches crisis communications at Johns Hopkins University. (*See "At Issue," p. 17.*)

"Power is shifting away from elected officials and regulators toward non-government organizations" that influence corporate policies, Nichols argues. "CSR is an effort by socialists to accomplish in the boardroom what they have failed to accomplish at the ballot box — corporate socialism."

Wal-Mart's adoption of corporate social responsibility policies and cooperation with advocacy groups "pose a significant risk to free markets and limited government," said Tom Borelli, a founder and portfolio manager of the Free Enterprise Action Fund, a mutual fund for conser- vative shareholder activists. "CSR supporters want the company to increase its overhead by paying higher wages, providing health care for all its workers, and guarantee- ing workers' rights by having its employees unionized," Borelli said, calling such proposals "the incremental path to socialism." Referring to the classic paean to individual freedom and laissez-faire capitalism, Borelli said Wal-Mart should "use its marketing muscle to sell Ayn Rand's timeless novel *Atlas Shrugged* into millions of homes."[19]

According to George Mason University economics Professor Russell Roberts, the popularity of corporate social responsibility shows that "most people don't understand how capitalism works — the role that profits played in creating higher standards of living over the last century.

"The implication is a corporation should act something like a non-profit, should not try to make as much money as possible, should pay not what the market will bear to its employees but a fair wage. I think that's not a particularly healthy attitude for companies to have.

"When you're a publicly held company, you're not spending your own money. You're spending the money of shareholders who have entrusted it to you."

GE's Corcoran agrees that "we take other people's money and have an absolute responsibility to use that wisely, invest that in products and people and marketing strategies that will grow the economic value of the shareholders' investment." But, he adds, "the individual who opposes every dollar a company gives away to charity or Katrina relief or helping to address issues of the environment — and thinks every dollar they give away is a dollar that doesn't go back to shareholders — has a very narrow and dangerous and ill-informed interpretation" of a corporation's duties.

Profits are not Whole Foods' primary purpose but rather the "means to the end of fulfilling [the company's] core business mission," Mackey said. "We want to improve the health and well-being of everyone on the planet through higher-quality foods and better nutrition, and we can't fulfill this mission unless we are highly profitable. Just as people cannot live without eating, so a business cannot live without profits. But most people don't live to eat, and neither must a business live just to make profits."[20]

Andrew Shallit, shareholder advocacy director for Boston-based Green Century Capital Management,

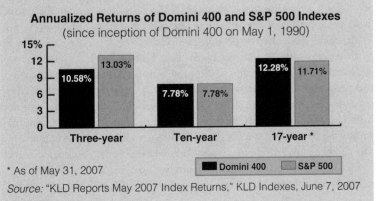

Socially Responsible Investing Pays Off

Companies in the Domini 400 Social Index — which tracks environmentally and socially responsible firms — are performing better over the long term than companies in the S&P 500, although their short-term returns are lower.

Annualized Returns of Domini 400 and S&P 500 Indexes
(since inception of Domini 400 on May 1, 1990)

Three-year: Domini 400 10.58%, S&P 500 13.03%
Ten-year: Domini 400 7.78%, S&P 500 7.78%
17-year *: Domini 400 12.28%, S&P 500 11.71%

* As of May 31, 2007

Source: "KLD Reports May 2007 Index Returns," KLD Indexes, June 7, 2007

defines the market as including "shareholder activists, the communities that are affected by a corporation and ultimately all the people in the world making their demands for what they need for a better life."

Green Century's mutual funds invest in companies that have a positive impact on the world after all their costs are taken into account, Shallit says. That is the proper way to assess a company's responsibility in the market, he argues.

"Is the company having a net negative effect and making a profit based on the fact that these costs are hidden — the pollution is going into the river and someone else is having to pay for that?" he asks. "Or is it in truth adding to the overall health and wealth of the world?"

Corporate social responsibility supporters note that corporations could not exist without the laws and regulations that enable them to do business. This "license to operate" comes with specific legal requirements and an "unwritten bargain with the societies in which they operate," said Allen White, senior adviser to Business for Social Responsibility, a nonprofit association that helps companies develop and implement social responsibility policies.[21]

"Governments grant corporations the license to operate because it is in the public interest to do so," White said, and most companies acknowledge their obligation to take the public's needs into account.

In their statements of corporate purpose, White said, companies commonly include intentions to serve shareholders, employees, customers and society at large. A late 2005 global survey of business executives found more than 80 percent agreeing that "generating high returns for investors should be accompanied by broader contributions to the public good," according to the McKinsey & Co. consulting firm, which conducted the poll. Only one-in-six said that "high returns should be a corporation's sole focus."[22]

British investment manager David Pitt-Watson said widespread stock ownership — through mutual funds and pension plans — creates "enormous overlap" in corporations' responsibility to shareholders and society. The "ultimate shareholder" has become "millions of people" with such investments, said Pitt-Watson, director and former chief executive of Hermes Focus Asset Management, Great Britain's largest shareholder-activist fund. "As a result, social and private interests go together."[23]

Is social responsibility good for the bottom line?

For the Coca-Cola Co., a predicted global water crisis is "a strategic threat to our business," because water is the company's most important raw material, says Jeff Seabright, Coke's vice president for environment and water. "Climate change is going to stress this even further," he adds. As a result, he says, Coke advances its business interests by conserving water at its plants, helping communities manage their watersheds better and reducing the company's contribution to global warming.

Wal-Mart follows advice from environmental organizations to reduce its waste of materials and energy, then helps its suppliers do the same, says Marc Major of Blu Skye Sustainability, a Wal-Mart consultant in Healdsburg, Calif. After that, Major continues, the giant retailer tells the suppliers: "You cut your energy bills, so you can cut the cost of the products you sell to us."

Good schools are needed to supply a qualified workforce, says Weyerhaeuser Co. Foundation President Karen Johnson. The forest products company makes education a key component of its philanthropy, awarding college scholarships to employees' children and helping to improve school districts near its operations.

But critics complain that companies squander shareholders' assets in corporate social responsibility programs.

"The modern corporation, by its very existence, has become a responsible institution at the task it is assigned to do, which is to organize people to create a product at an affordable price [and] to create wealth," argued Fred Smith Jr., president of the Competitive Enterprise Institute, which promotes free markets. "To divert the corporation from that task will weaken the wealth-creation progress that we have seen over the last two centuries, and it would do nothing to achieve these myriad of other goals, because only you and I — only individuals — can pursue the myriad values that a moral society has."[24]

Supporters of corporate social responsibility contend that it actually is good for the bottom line, as demonstrated by the experiences of Coke, Wal-Mart, Weyerhaeuser and many other companies.

Responding to environmentalists' calls to cut waste also cuts costs, they say. Companies need a healthy, well-educated workforce. They need safe and healthy communities in which to locate their retail establishments. Companies that are recognized as good corporate citizens attract investors and consumers — especially upscale consumers — and recruit and retain employees more effectively. Activist groups are less likely to attack those companies, advocates say, and corporate social responsibility policies can ward off government regulation. As companies make their products and seek customers all over the world, they reap benefits by helping to improve conditions in disadvantaged communities.

"Our business will succeed in communities that thrive," says Coke Corporate Responsibility Director Karen Flanders, sounding a theme repeated by many corporate executives.

Critics also charge that if corporate responsibility is good for the bottom line, then it's just smart management and is nothing really new. But supporters say a fundamental change is under way. Companies are discovering new ways to be profitable as a byproduct of seeking to be responsible. Responding to attacks from advocacy groups, companies are forging relationships with unlikely partners and becoming more effective businesses as a result.

"Company executives will say we used to think we had all the info and perspective we needed internally, and now we realize we need to talk to a diverse group of actors outside the company," says Business for Social Responsibility President Aron Cramer.

"You see a lot more dialogue with non-governmental organizations, the environmental community, the human-rights community, community organizations, academic experts, experts from international organizations and multilateral organizations," Cramer continues. "And that really enriches a company's decision making."

Hannah Jones, Nike's vice president for corporate responsibility, says responsibility "can be a vehicle for innovation and growth." Company executives challenged Nike product designers to incorporate environmental concerns into their work, Jones explains, and "it's led to innovation that led us to make better shoes."

Nike's signature "air" soles actually contained the greenhouse gases sulfur hexafluoride and polyfluorene phenylene. While looking for a way to use a benign gas, Jones says, designers discovered how to extend a nitrogen-filled air bag for the full length of the shoe — something they had not been able to do before.

Corporate responsibility also has become "a huge piece of recruitment, retention and motivation" of employees, Jones says. "It's interesting to watch [prospective employees] in interviews, asking about CR and their ability to be engaged in CR through their work."

But David Vogel, a business and political science professor at the University of California at Berkeley, thinks "the business benefits from CSR are often exaggerated."

Most studies have shown the impact to be "fairly modest, either positive or negative," says Vogel, author of *The Market for Virtue: The Potential and Limits of Corporate Responsibility.* Conservation can cut costs, he concedes. He's seen "some examples" of corporate responsibility helping companies deal with governments and advocacy groups. "A lot of circumstantial evidence" indicates it can help recruitment, morale and retention, but he thinks it boosts sales only for some "niche market companies that sell expensive products," such as Whole Foods and Ben & Jerry's.

KLD Research & Analytics, an investment research firm, created six stock market indexes designed to compare the financial performance of companies that have good social responsibility records against traditional indexes, such as the Standard & Poor's 500 and the Russell 3000. Since the indexes were established, between 1990 and 2006, two have outperformed the traditional indexes and four have not.

Advocates say corporate responsibility delivers the most benefit over the long term, and KLD's oldest index — the Domini 400 Social Index, created in 1990, outperformed the S&P 500. (*See graph, p. 7.*) So did the Global Climate 500, which was created in 2005.

All the KLD indexes trailed their traditional counterparts in May, primarily because the environment-friendly indexes contained few energy stocks, which were soaring at the time.[25]

Does corporate social responsibility really improve society?

Companies proclaim that their social responsibility activities protect the environment and improve people's lives around the world.

Impoverished Africans get treatment for HIV/AIDS because major pharmaceutical companies supply drugs at low costs, for instance. Disadvantaged students become employable because Microsoft supports training programs in information technology. Under-equipped law-enforcement agencies track down murderers because Target lets them use sophisticated forensics laboratories it created to deal with crime in its 1,400 stores.

Critics beg to differ. While there may be isolated examples of effective programs, they say, for the most part, corporate responsibility doesn't work.

"Is CSR mostly for show?" *Atlantic Monthly* Senior Editor Clive Cook asked rhetorically in *The Economist,* when he was deputy editor there. "The short answer must be yes.

"For most conventionally organized public companies — which means almost all of the big ones — CSR is little more than a cosmetic treatment. The human face that CSR applies to capitalism goes on each morning, gets increasingly smeared by day and washes off at night. Under pressure, big multinationals ask their critics to judge them by CSR criteria, and then, as the critics charge, mostly fail to follow through."[26]

Businesses aren't qualified for many of the social and environmental tasks they're assigning themselves, according to T. J. Rodgers, president and CEO of Cypress Semiconductor Corp. and an outspoken critic of corporate social responsibility.

"We specialize in doing different tasks, and people who specialize are better at what they do," Rodgers says. "There's no reason to think companies are competent at philanthropy.

"Suppose a convent of nuns decided that high-efficiency automobiles were required to lower greenhouse gases, and they decided they were going to make a 100-miles-per-gallon automobile at a convent. We'd say that's

CHRONOLOGY

Early 1800s *Companies provide for needs of workers in isolated areas.*

Late 1800s-Early 1900s *Industrial barons Andrew Carnegie and John D. Rockefeller give much of their personal wealth to philanthropic causes.*

1881 Carnegie begins to build free public libraries.

1890 Rockefeller finances University of Chicago.

1900 Carnegie Institute of Technology established.

1910 Carnegie Endowment for International Peace created.

1911 Fire at Triangle shirtwaist factory in New York City kills more than 140 workers, calling attention to sweatshops and child labor.

1913 Rockefeller Foundation established.

1915-1940 *Labor unrest and economic collapse press corporations to address public needs.*

1916 Executives from major U.S. corporations establish National Industrial Conference Board, now The Conference Board "to find solutions to common problems."

1919 World War I veterans return to domestic workplaces and begin demanding higher wages, better working conditions and stiffer government regulation of corporations.

1929 Stock market crash marks start of Great Depression, causing public respect for business to crash as well.

1933 Inauguration of President Franklin D. Roosevelt and beginning of New Deal bring increased government regulation of business, along with tax breaks to encourage corporate philanthropy.

1934 General Electric President Gerard Swope says corporate America must "take the lead" in addressing social problems.

1940-1960 *U.S. corporations accept need to help fight World War II and respond to the war's destruction afterwards. Corporate philanthropy grows.*

1960s-1970s *Social action movements — civil rights, women's rights, consumerism, environmentalism, antiwar — challenge traditional corporate practices and spur new government regulation of business.*

1965 Equal Employment Opportunity Commission begins operations.

1970 Environmental Protection Agency and Occupational Safety and Health Administration created.

1972 Consumer Product Safety Commission created.

1980s-2000s *Companies tie grant making to their core business through "strategic philanthropy." Growing number view corporate social responsibility as beneficial to bottom line.*

1992 Executives from 50 socially oriented companies found Business for Social Responsibility to advocate good corporate citizenship.

1994 British consulting firm SustainAbility coins phrase "triple bottom line," contending corporations' long-term success requires attention to society and environment as well to shareholders.

2005 Business Roundtable launches "S.E.E. Change" initiative to encourage companies to adopt policies that improve society, environment and economy.

2007 Conference Board establishes Center for Corporate Citizenship and Sustainability. . . . Equity firms consult environmental advocacy groups before launching the largest private buyout bid in history, for TXU Corp.

pretty stupid. Why don't you stay in the nun business and let the carmakers make cars?"

Communities are better off when individuals, not corporations, decide which social improvement projects to support, George Mason University's Roberts argues.

"I make a lot of donations to charity," Roberts says. "I want to make the decision [on how] to spend my money. Why is it that a shareholder would want to invest in a company that gives employees paid time off to go out and build houses, rather than give directly to Habitat for Humanity, for instance?

"If corporations gave the money back to employees in higher wages, to customers in lower prices, to shareholders in higher dividends, then those individuals would decide what makes the community healthier," he continues.

The John Locke Foundation's Hood criticizes companies that require suppliers to offer better pay and benefits than markets require in poor countries.

"If people are willing in Bangladesh or Malaysia to take jobs at wage rates that appear to us to be astronomically low, they may know something we don't about what their alternative is," Hood says. "Maybe the only option that person has is to work in the field in much less pleasant conditions with much less certainty about the future."

David Baron, a professor of political economy and strategy at Stanford University, agrees that companies should be "maximizing their market value — subject to certain ethical duties." The dilemma, he adds, is "what constitutes an ethical duty."

Giving drugs to poor HIV/AIDS patients "is obviously socially good," he says. "The question is who should be responsible for making them available. Should it be the rich countries that buy the drugs and give it to the poor countries, or should it be the manufacturers themselves?"

Sometimes businesses are best able to address a problem, insists Scott Johnson, vice president for global environment and safety concerns at SC Johnson, manufacturer of iconic household items such as Pledge, Fantastik and Windex.

"When things need to be done on a global basis, business has far more capability to cross borders with programs like our greenhouse gas reduction goals than just about any other organization," he says. "Political organizations are bounded within their localities, but businesses can move where we do business."

Heerad Sabeti, co-founder of a North Carolina company that makes home decorations, rejects the argument that he should maximize profits, then make contributions to charity.

"We want social responsibility to be completely embedded in everything we do" at TransForms, he said. "What good does [contributing to charity] do if I'm using plastic for my packaging and helping to contribute to job losses by manufacturing in China?"[27]

Mathew Nelson, head of corporate foundation services at the Council on Foundations, says many social responsibility programs do work. When he was community relations manager at Ameriprise Financial headquarters in Minneapolis, for instance, the company funded career and college centers at local high schools and encouraged employees to volunteer at the centers.

"The employees were helping the kids to know what it was like in the real world and helping them in making decisions about what careers to go into, as well as being adult mentors, which lots of research has shown is key to the success of youths," Nelson explains.

Microsoft co-founder Bill Gates supports both sides in the debate. His company practices social responsibility, and he has donated billions of dollars of his own money to charity. But he doesn't practice socially responsible investing.

After the *Los Angeles Times* revealed the Bill & Melinda Gates Foundation owns stock in companies whose business practices conflict with the foundation's purposes, foundation Chief Operating Officer Cheryl Scott explained the Gateses' investment philosophy.

Acknowledging that "shareholder activism is one factor that can influence corporate behavior," Scott said the Gateses "have chosen not to get involved in ranking companies based upon factors such as their lending policies or environmental record."

Focusing on programs enables the foundation "to have the greatest impact for the most people," she said. The Gateses "also believe there would be much room for error and confusion in [assessing companies' social responsibility], and that divesting from these companies would not have an effect commensurate with the resources we would divert to this activity."

The foundation does avoid investing in companies whose actions are "egregious," such as tobacco companies, Scott said.[28]

Doing Business at the 'Base of the Pyramid'

SC Johnson sells cleaning supplies in Africa "a squirt at a time"

In three slums of Nairobi, Kenya, young people walk door to door offering to clean homes and eradicate pests with SC Johnson products.

The budding entrepreneurs are part of the home-products manufacturer's efforts to earn profits and do good at the "base of the [economic] pyramid."

While there would not appear to be much business in communities where families survive on less than $4 a day, the manufacturer of Raid, Fantastik and other well-known brands has concluded these potential consumers have much to contribute to the company's long-term growth.

"Historically, large companies focus at the tip of the pyramid," where 10 percent of the world's population consumes 85 percent of the planet's resources, Cornell University Management Professor Stuart Hart says. "But the tip of the pyramid is running out of gas," while enormous potential markets sit untapped throughout the rest of the world.

Some 4.5 billion people reside in the economic pyramid's base, Hart explains, and another 1.4 million in the area between the top and the bottom. In addition, these poor populations are growing faster than those in the developed world, creating what Hart calls "trickle-up opportunity."

A company can't simply start marketing to the poor of Nairobi the way it sells to the middle class in Peoria, however.

Traditionally, Hart says, companies try to sell their products to the poor by finding less expensive means of production, using smaller packages, cutting prices, extending distribution to places previously not served and perhaps working with nonprofit organizations to deliver needed goods to people who had been unable to get them. He calls this strategy "BOP (base of pyramid) 1.0."

BOP 2.0 "has to be about creating new livelihood and wealth, not just selling products to poor people — not just extraction," he says. This requires "engaging the poor, building local capacity, building mutual value."

SC Johnson supports base-of-the-pyramid research at Cornell by Hart and research associate Duncan Dukes and agrees the potential market is "too big to ignore," says Scott Johnson, the company's vice president for global environment and safety concerns. "Millions of poor people live near SC Johnson operations around the world, but we have no business with them." So the company agreed to test the scholars' theories.

The process entailed what the scholars term "deep listening" to the community to identify potential markets, and forming partnerships with potential local entrepreneurs who would sell the company's products there. The goal was to "create something not possible by the multinational corporation or the local community by itself," Hart explains. SC Johnson would increase sales as the local entrepreneurs

BACKGROUND

'Company Towns'

From the early 19th to the early 20th centuries, companies with operations in isolated areas practiced something resembling contemporary corporate social responsibility, building housing for employees and stores where workers could buy necessities. Some businesses added parks and other community amenities.[29]

These "company towns" weren't always so good for the workers, however. Corporations used the towns and company facilities to keep employees in line — evicting strikers, for example. Companies also sometimes banned competing merchants and charged monopoly prices at the company stores.

When railroads began spreading across the country, they contributed to local YMCAs so their itinerant employees would have places to stay. Sears, Roebuck & Co. helped teach farmers better agricultural practices in the belief that more prosperous farm families would buy more from Sears' mail-order catalogs.

In the late 19th and early 20th centuries, Andrew Carnegie and John D. Rockefeller, the kings of steel and oil, gave much of their wealth to humanitarian causes and established institutions that are among the most important nonprofits on Earth today.

Carnegie gave away $350 million — 90 percent of his wealth — and in the process created the Peace Palace at The Hague, where the World Court now sits; the Carnegie Corporation to support education and research;

created businesses that buoyed the local economy.

Realizing that families earning a few dollars a day would be reluctant to purchase products that retail for several dollars a can, the company and the young entrepreneurs decided to use SC Johnson products in a service business. The company trained the young people in such skills as pest management, accounting and marketing, then sent them out on door-to-door sales calls.

They now offer cleaning and pest-control services to homes and businesses, using SC Johnson merchandise such as Windex glass cleaner, Toilet

Cleaning products are delivered by 52 motorcycle riders to small retailers in Nigeria normally left out of the delivery chain.

Duck bathroom cleansers and Baygon insect-control products. Nairobi's poor can afford to buy those products "by the squirt," Johnson says, and get healthier homes and workplaces as a result.

The new tactic represented a fundamental change for both the company and the community, Duke notes. SC Johnson was "moving from a product focus to a service focus" in "a place where there's no service provided to homes."

Success will require patience and flexibility, Duke says, traits that may come easier to privately owned SC Johnson than to a publicly held corporation with shareholders focused on quarterly returns.

"We take the long view on decisions," Johnson explains. At the base of the pyramid, "there's not going to be a short-term success," and the company can live with that. "We believe the long view is simultaneously what's best for our business and for the places where we do business."

While "it's too early to tell" the long-term prospects for the Nairobi project, Johnson says, the company already is reporting success working with small retailers who sell to the poor in Nigeria.

There, SC Johnson employs motorcycle riders to deliver its products to kiosks, roadside hawkers and "others usually not served effectively by other distributors," the company reported. The process is creating "an important new route to market," the company said. The 52 motorcycles operating around the country at the end of last year "have already recouped the capital invested and significantly improved our distribution in key Nigerian markets."[1]

---

[1] "Doing Our Part," SC Johnson, 2007, www.scjohnson.com/community/2007_Public_Report.asp.

---

the Carnegie Endowment for International Peace; the Carnegie Institute of Technology, and some 3,000 libraries around the world.

"The man who dies rich," he said, "dies disgraced."[30]

Rockefeller, who endorsed Carnegie's philanthropic "Gospel of Wealth," created the Rockefeller Foundation, which has given away more than $14 billion. Among his other legacies: the University of Chicago and the Rockefeller Institute for Medical Research, now known as Rockefeller University.

The industrialists' unprecedented philanthropy was "a very positive development," according to Mal Warwick, an adviser to nonprofits and co-founder of Business for Social Responsibility. But "it was a far cry from corporate social responsibility." Their philanthropy was personal, he notes, and their corporations were far from socially responsible.

"Andrew Carnegie gave away hundreds of millions of dollars and built thousands of libraries and deserves much credit for that," Warwick says. "As a corporate leader, [however], his name has gone down in infamy for his exploitative practices and the violence he directed against workers who defied his overseers.

"Rockefeller was certainly a paragon of virtue in many respects. I would not want to detract one bit from his legacy of philanthropy. But, as a businessman, he was ruthless, treated his competition like dirt, was no friend of his employees and was behind some of the violence directed against workers who were rebelling against the direction of his companies."

Industrialist Andrew Carnegie (above) and oil baron John D. Rockefeller gave away much of their wealth to humanitarian causes in the late 19th and early 20th centuries, establishing major philanthropies still influential today. "The man who dies rich dies disgraced," Carnegie once said.

Violence and Turmoil

At about the same time Carnegie and Rockefeller were giving away their fortunes, some active business executives were delving into corporate responsibility. Public confidence in American business was plunging, they realized. Muckraking journalists were exposing hazardous industrial working conditions. Labor and management were locked in heated conflicts, some of which turned violent.

Responding to this turmoil in 1916, a group of executives from major corporations founded the National Industrial Conference Board, now simply The Conference Board. The board was created to be "a respected, not-for-profit, nonpartisan organization that would bring leaders together to find solutions to common problems and objectively examine major issues having an impact on business and society."[31]

Pure corporate philanthropy became widespread during World War I as companies contributed to local Community Chests, the forerunners of United Way. Executives liked the simplicity of making one contribution to an organization thought to understand the top needs of the community.

The ferment that spawned The Conference Board continued after the war, with growing labor militancy and demands for stiffer government regulation of corporations. Major companies — such as GE, Eastman Kodak, National Cash Register, Standard Oil and Goodyear Tire & Rubber — portrayed themselves as socially responsible, with promises of higher wages and better working conditions. They hoped to meet public demands without succumbing to regulation or unionization.

Goodyear became particularly notable for addressing the needs of its employees. "Goodyear has all about her the human quality," P. W. Lichfield, president and/or CEO from 1926 to 1956, said. "And it has been to this human quality, fully as much as to her business methods, that Goodyear owes her meteoric rise in the ranks of American industry."[32]

Presaging criticisms of contemporary corporate social responsibility, some other corporate executives labeled Lichfield a socialist and a Marxist.

The 1929 stock market crash and subsequent Great Depression deepened public antagonism toward business and spurred corporations to make more efforts to appear socially responsible. Most corporate executives worried about the growth of government power during the New Deal, and some feared the very survival of capitalism was at stake.

"Organized industry should take the lead," GE President Gerard Swope said, "recognizing its responsibility to its employees, to the public and to its shareholders, rather than that democratic society should act through its government."[33]

"If the corporate system is to survive," New Deal architects Adolf Berle and Gardiner Means argued, "corporations must balance a variety of claims by various groups in the community and assign to each a portion of the income stream on the basis of public policy rather than private cupidity."[34]

The New Deal also encouraged more business philanthropy by creating tax deductions for corporate giving.

Postwar Stimuli

The U.S. government's leadership in rebuilding Europe following World War II prompted American business executives to recognize "a collective need and obligation to engage in reconstruction of the country and the world," according to Lenny Mendonca, chairman of McKinsey & Company's Global Institute.[35] The postwar economic boom encouraged more corporate philanthropy and the growth of corporate foundations.

The multiple social action movements of the 1960s and '70s — civil rights, women's rights, consumerism, environmentalism, antiwar — challenged traditional corporate practices. Between 1965 and '73, four new federal agencies began regulating business conduct — the Occupational Safety and Health Administration, the Equal Employment Opportunity Commission, the Consumer Product Safety Commission and the Environmental Protection Agency. Companies responded by contributing more to social welfare organizations, increasing their political activity and launching marketing campaigns designed to make them appear more socially responsible.

"The more distant the self-interest, the more altruistic the corporate philanthropy seemed," Sylvia Clark and Kate Dewey wrote in a report for the Council on Foundations. "Consequently, causes contrary to the corporation's interest often were supported."[36]

Melding company interests with broader community needs, much corporate philanthropy in the 1980s focused on quality of life. "In order to recruit and retain employees and customers," Clark and Dewey wrote, "corporations strived to ensure that communities were attractive places to live and work."[37]

During the 1990s, a growing number of corporations began to practice "strategic philanthropy," by which they tied grant making to the company's core business and offered the company's skills to help nonprofits perform their work more effectively. Strategic philanthropy was "steering corporate America into a more powerful and direct social role," Craig Smith, a consultant to The Conference Board, wrote at the time. It had the potential to "make corporate culture more benevolent," he said.[38]

Milestones on the road from strategic philanthropy to contemporary corporate social responsibility included:

- Creation in 1992 of Business for Social Responsibility, to advocate good corporate citizenship and advise businesses on how to achieve it. Founders included executives from 50 socially oriented companies, including Ben & Jerry's ice cream, Patagonia apparel and Tom's of Maine personal-care products.[39]
- Coining the phrase "triple bottom line" in 1994 by SustainAbility, a British consulting firm that specializes in corporate responsibility and sustainable development. The phrase encapsulates the firm's contention that companies need to consider their impact on society and the environment, as well as return to shareholders, if they are to prosper over the long term. The phrase "people, planet, profit" now is widely accepted by major corporations.[40]
- The Business Roundtable's launching in 2005 of the S.E.E. Change initiative to "leverage the power of business as a force for good." The initiative encourages companies to adopt policies that improve society, the environment and the economy (S.E.E.).[41]
- The Conference Board's establishment in early 2007 of the Center for Corporate Citizenship and Sustainability. The center's mission is to help companies make citizenship and sustainability "integral, core business strategies, targeting business opportunities that provide maximum economic, environmental and societal benefit to all."[42]

CURRENT SITUATION

New Approach

Several factors distinguish contemporary corporate social responsibility from its predecessors. One is its emphasis on enhancing society, the environment and shareholder value simultaneously. Another is the overwhelming number of large companies that are integrating the concept into their core business strategy. A third is the contention by advocates that it is not just the morally right thing to do but is necessary for long-term business success.

"It used to be about how much money you give to something," explains Larry Burton, executive director of the Business Roundtable.

Building Global Responsibility

Intel 2006 Corporate Responsibility Report

Courtesy Intel

Like many big U.S. corporations, Intel now issues an annual corporate social responsibility report. The company spends more than $100 million a year to improve science and mathematics education in more than 50 countries.

Now, according to Marian Hopkins, the Roundtable's director of public policy, "it's not charity or humanitarian aid. It's a business proposition that makes sense, a strategic way of looking at things and behaving. It's about being smart as a company."

As Business for Social Responsibility President Cramer puts it: "Corporate social responsibility is about how a company earns its money, not how it gives it away after it's earned it."

Among the corporate CEOs who comprise the Roundtable, the watchword is "sustainability," Burton and Hopkins say.

Environmentalists originated the concept, advocating conduct by individuals, businesses and governments that would sustain life on the planet. For corporate executives it now means sustaining the environment, society and their businesses.

"It's about today, the quarter, the year, the future," Burton says. According to Hopkins, "It's about doing what you need to do today without compromising future generations doing what they need to do."

This requires long-term thinking that's compatible with protecting the environment and building healthy societies that last. It leads to corporate support for education, health care, community improvement projects, economic development in poor nations, and even for stiffening some environmental-protection laws.

"There's a growing understanding at the top of the major corporations that humanity has been a poor steward of our planet, that we are facing resources shortages," says Business for Social Responsibility co-founder Warwick. "We are coming up against the time when it will be impossible for companies to obtain all the materials they need if they keep operating in the way they always have — particularly if they waste such basic resources as water, energy and minerals."

Response to Globalization

Burton notes the growing corporate support for action on global warming, which he terms "the ultimate sustainability question."

Globalization, technology and the increasing importance of businesses — especially large businesses — contribute to a growing public demand for corporate responsibility.

"We've experienced rapid globalization and the rise of market economies in every part of the world," Cramer explains. Because of the Internet and other advanced information technology, "we live in a much more transparent world, so the actions a company takes can be seen and understood by a global community."

An activist, shareholder advocacy director Shallit points out, "can very easily go to China, to a computer dump, where you have children working with hammers and acid baths trying to recover lead from our old computer monitors. The activist takes a picture of a monitor that has a Dell logo, and puts it on a Web site and sends it in an e-mail to Michael Dell. That has an immediate impact in a way that would not be possible" before the Internet.

Executives feel the need to protect their companies against a public that is worried about globalization's impact on jobs, repulsed by working and environmental conditions in developing countries and fearful of climate change, the University of California's Vogel says.

Does corporate social responsibility endanger U.S. prosperity?

YES
Nick Nichols
Crisis Communications Instructor
Johns Hopkins University

Written for *CQ Researcher*, July 2007

The financial well-being of 91 million Americans is tied to the fortunes of publicly traded corporations because half of American households own stock. It does not take an economics guru to conclude that diverting corporate assets away from activities that improve earnings endangers American prosperity.

Corporate executives are responsible for obeying laws and regulations. The corporate social responsibility (CSR) movement, however, is all about spending company resources (a.k.a. other people's money) on social and environmental programs that are not mandated by law. Every buck that is shanghaied from corporate coffers represents a hidden levy on shareholders, undermining their prosperity.

Why would business titans embrace corporate socialism? Some have chosen appeasement in response to activist group pressure. Others have been duped by public relations snake-oil peddlers who claim that jumping on the CSR bandwagon will protect a company from public attacks if something goes wrong.

Look at what happened to British Petroleum (BP) after one of its refineries blew up and its Alaska pipeline started leaking. The poster child for corporate do-gooders was publicly skewered for mismanagement. All those millions that BP spent posing for holy pictures with the likes of Greenpeace paid zero dividends in the court of public opinion as investors watched share values plummet.

A quick Google search suggests that thousands of companies are joining the march toward corporate social responsibility. One critic claims that Nike spends about $10 million a year just staffing its CSR program.

While no one knows how many shareholder dollars are being spent each year on CSR, I suspect the bottom line would impress even the Congressional Budget Office. Think of CSR as the redistribution of prosperity away from those who have invested their savings in the stock market and toward those people or things that the unelected non-government organizations of the world consider worthy.

For those on Capitol Hill who think it is about time corporations got a dose of social responsibility, think again. The CSR movement is not only about redistributing the wealth but also about redistributing political power — away from legislators and regulators and toward non-government organizations that are unaccountable to the public and rarely accountable to government.

You may think it is cute that corporate executives are frolicking with activist groups, but I suspect you will think differently when those same groups determine that you are irrelevant.

NO
Aron Cramer
President and CEO,
Business for Social Responsibility

Written for *CQ Researcher*, July 2007

Corporate social responsibility (CSR) has been embraced by many of the most respected companies in America. CSR means the integration of environmental and social impacts into a company's strategies and operations.

Contrary to what some critics might claim, CSR has little to do with altruism and a great deal to do with enlightened self-interest. This is why companies like General Electric and Wal-Mart have embraced CSR as a way of building and maintaining their business strategies. This is why more than 1,000 multinational companies now produce public CSR reports.

Why is this agenda critical, not only for the U.S. business community but also the American and global economy?

First, there is money to be made from looking at the social and environmental dimensions of business. As GE has made abundantly clear, "Green is Green," as the company has grown its revenues through environmentally beneficial technologies. As natural resources become more scarce, efficiency becomes more important.

Second, in a global economy, companies do not have the luxury of ignoring the way "Brand America" is perceived in the world. As survey after survey indicates that America's reputation is declining in the world, American business takes note. Doing business the right way helps to ensure that American companies are — and are seen to be — good neighbors in an increasingly complex world.

Third, CSR is an essential tool for operating in our global world. As Clyde Prestowitz famously put it in the title of his recent book, there are "three billion new capitalists" in China, India and Russia. They view the world differently from many in the United States, Europe and Japan. CSR helps to build business strategies that generate products and services for the half of the world's population found in those countries.

Finally, CSR helps companies succeed in our increasingly networked and transparent environment. In the You Tube world, anyone can shape a company's reputation — for good or ill. Companies that embrace external dialogue are poised to succeed; those that ignore it do so at their peril.

Some may claim that CSR wastes corporate assets on matters unrelated to core business purpose. This argument is based on a distorted view of CSR. It also begs a more fundamental question: Do opponents of CSR suggest that business should proceed without regard to ethics, social impact or the environment?

There is a reason why America's leading businesses have embraced CSR. It delivers value for their companies, their employees, their consumers and their communities.

CSR is simply good business.

General Electric Chairman Jeffrey Immelt listens to students read at Isaac Sheppard Elementary School in Philadelphia, where GE issued a $250,000 grant to improve city schools. "True impact means defining success in ways that go well beyond the bottom line," he says.

Companies also drive each other to corporate responsibility.

"Wal-Mart throws a huge shadow across the world when it asks for action," notes Daniel Esty, director of Yale University's Center for Business and Environment. "When Wal-Mart is your customer and says it's time to move, you better get moving."

The giant retailer's efforts to protect the environment are driving its suppliers to switch to more environmentally friendly packaging, to make more environmentally friendly products and to ship their products in a more environmentally friendly manner.

"When [Wal-Mart CEO] Lee Scott said you've got to reduce emissions when you deliver to our stores, that got the bottlers' attention," Coca-Cola Corporate Responsibility Director Flanders says.

Indeed, when Home Depot this year announced plans for an "Eco Options" marketing campaign, manufacturers submitted more than 60,000 products for inclusion. Unfortunately, many were not all that eco friendly (plastic-handled paintbrushes were pitched because they saved trees, wood-handled ones because they didn't use the dreaded plastic). Still, the home-improvement retailer found 2,500 items to promote, including solar-powered landscape lighting and low-polluting paint.[43]

Suppliers also are seeking profits by convincing their customers to be socially responsible.

"There is opportunity to sell solutions," Esty says, suggesting that a supplier can "help a customer develop an environmental plan that the supplier can contribute to.

"If you're GE selling jet engines, fuel economy means a lot to airlines. There are very few companies that don't face some environmental pressures."

Last year, BT Americas, British Telecom's operation in the Western Hemisphere, joined the list of corporations with an executive in charge of CSR. Part of the newly created job is facilitating the company's social responsibility policies, such as using green energy, following certain personnel rules and offering pro-bono telecommunications consulting to nonprofits. New CSR Director Kevin Moss also "works with customers to help them identify and implement CSR through our products."

Examples include holding audio- and teleconferences to avoid long-distance travel and using information technology to enable employee telecommuting. Cutting travel reduces the customers' contribution to greenhouse gas emissions, Moss points out. Telecommuting "can increase diversity by making the workplace more accessible to working parents and handicapped workers." Having a dispersed work force "makes your organization less susceptible to disaster," Moss says, "and home workers call in sick less often."

Nike calls the triple bottom line "ROI squared — return on investment squared," says Vice President for Corporate Responsibility Jones. The company is infusing "corporate responsibility thinking across the business model," she says. Executives' performance reviews contain corporate responsibility targets.

On May 31 the company announced business targets for 2011 that include improving labor conditions in its suppliers' factories, shrinking CO_2 emissions throughout its operations, reducing waste in its products and packaging, increasing its use of environmentally friendly raw materials and providing financial support to youth sports programs.

Cutting waste means cutting costs, Jones says, and "that's where the chief financial officer and I become best friends."

OUTLOOK

Government Regulation?

Even most critics concede that corporate social responsibility is likely to be around for the long term. Business executives, activists and scholars expect companies to become more effective at it and for more companies to join the movement. Some activists hope — and conservatives fear — that Congress will require companies to meet certain corporate responsibility standards.

"Corporations will still employ the language of social responsibility to seek competitive advantage and to protect themselves from political risk," the John Locke Foundation's Hood says. "That is a basic behavior in modern corporate life. We shouldn't expect it to go away."

Cypress Semiconductor's Rodgers speculates companies "will drift slowly toward more involvement" as the country becomes wealthier. "As we get richer — which we are because we're competitive — there's more money in total for us to spend, and that means there's more money to spend on good causes."

Hopkins of the Business Roundtable expects companies "will get a lot smarter, better at assessing opportunities and risks and doing smart strategic planning."

Nike's Jones predicts the public will continually raise its expectations for responsible corporate behavior. At the same time, she adds, "you'll increasingly see brands differentiating themselves from the competition through corporate responsibility."

Companies will move beyond "mitigating problems" toward "making positive contributions," according to G.E.'s Corcoran.

Scott Johnson of SC Johnson and Target's Garvis anticipate more creativity.

"Companies will be looking for new ways to do it," Johnson explains. They will become adept at "understanding need gaps and filling them," he says.

"It's not just about giving money away any more," Garvis says. "It's about giving your skill sets away, or your creativity."

A widespread goal and expectation is that companies will integrate social responsibility throughout their basic business operations.

"In 10 years you may not even be talking about it, because it will just be business," Corcoran says.

Johnson looks to the time when corporate responsibility is part of every executive's job description and performance evaluation.

Saying corporations have done a good job promoting diversity and equal opportunity in American workplaces, The Council on Foundations' Nelson foresees an effort to extend that globally.

"Instead of having the perspective that this job has been outsourced to India, a company would be able to value their Indian colleagues and recognize that there are people all over the world who are helping the corporation succeed," he explains. "The next challenge is going to be shifting the conversation from 'Oh my gosh, my job's being outsourced' to 'What a gift it is to be able to partner with all these people over the world, and we ultimately have a better product as a result.'"

Another challenge will be figuring out how to measure the result of corporate responsibility activities, according to Laysha Ward, Target's vice president for community relations.

"It is an emerging school of activity," Garvis says. "Much of what we're talking about is qualitative and not prone to easy measurement, but we know there are elements of value there. As this becomes a more and more important area, there's going to be more activity around capturing what that value is."

At Yale's Center for Business and Environment Esty spots an "emerging concept of extended producer responsibility." That means "you have to watch your supply chain and you have to watch what your consumers do with your products." It's happening today when companies hold suppliers to environmental and workplace standards while offering recycling services to customers.

The Target executives also foresee closer relations between corporations and nonprofit organizations. Companies will offer training to nonprofit personnel and will help the organizations adopt better business practices, Garvis and Ward predict.

Some activists and business executives foresee new forms of businesses and nonprofit organizations springing up.

"There should be another kind of business incorporated into the theory of capitalism — business to do good," said Muhammad Yunus, founder of the Grameen Bank, which makes tiny business loans to the poor. "I call them 'social businesses.' If we had this structural theory that there is a profit-maximizing business, and social businesses, some people would say, 'I'll do both. I'll make money, and I will do social business.'"[44]

Yunus' bank, which began operations in Bangladesh, is an example of a social business, he said. So is a new company he created with French food producer Danone to make yogurt that is specially formulated for malnourished children. The company's business plan calls for it to earn enough money to cover expenses, but it will not pay dividends.

Tweaking the Grameen model, Ben Powell and Ricardo Terán Jr. formed the Agora Venture Fund in 2006 to invest in socially responsible small businesses in developing nations. They want the fund to turn a profit, but they've also created a nonprofit affiliate to provide training and consulting services to those small companies.[45]

In another twist on the model, Peter Drasher and Dawn Edwards established AltruShare Securities in 2006 as a for-profit brokerage firm that will invest two-thirds of its profits in disadvantaged communities.[46]

Jones expects government to require some actions that companies currently take voluntarily through their corporate responsibility programs. Businesses are likely to face new disclosure requirements, she says. She also anticipates mandated curbs on greenhouse gas emissions.

Deborah Doane, chair of the Corporate Responsibility Coalition in Great Britain, hopes for a fundamental rewriting of the purpose of corporations.

Despite corporate social responsibility activities, she argued, "there is often a wide chasm between what's good for a company and what's good for society as a whole.

"Other strategies — from direct regulation of corporate behavior to a more radical overhaul of the corporate institution — may be more likely to deliver the outcomes we seek."

Her group has proposed legislation that would "see company directors having multiple duties of care — both to their shareholders and to other stakeholders, including communities, employees and the environment."[47]

In the United States, an organization called the Great Transition Initiative has drafted a proposed new statement of purpose for corporations. It says the purpose of the corporation is to, among other things, "harness private interests to serve the public interest" and "accrue fair returns for shareholders, but not at the expense of the legitimate interests of other stakeholders."[48]

Nichols at the Center for Defense of Free Enterprise expects "there will be significant efforts on the part of various governments to regulate CSR in the next five to 10 years." He predicts the efforts will backfire on corporate responsibility advocates.

"There will be a significant backlash, because one of the premises of CSR is that it's all voluntary and predictable," he says. "As a result, you're likely to see corporations walking away from this trend."

NOTES

1. H. Josef Hebert, "CEOs Ask Bush to Back Climate Protection," The Associated Press, Jan. 22, 2007. "Major Businesses and Environmental Leaders Unite to Call for Swift Action on Global Climate Change," U.S. Climate Action Partnership, Jan. 22, 2007, www.us-cap.org/media/release.pdf. For background, see the following CQ Researchers: Marcia Clemmitt, "Climate Change," Jan. 29, 2006, pp. 73-96; Mary Cooper, "Global Warming Treaty," Jan. 26, 2001, pp. 41-64; Tom Price, "The New Environmentalism," Dec. 1, 2006, pp. 985-1008; and Colin Woordard, "Curbing Climate Change," CQ Global Researcher, February 2007, pp. 27-50.

2. www.nike.com/nikebiz/nikeresponsibility/#workers-factories/main.

3. Adam Smith, Wealth of Nations, The Harvard Classics, 1909-14, Book 1, p. 3, www.bartleby.com/10/102.html.

4. Ibid., Book 4, p. 9, www.bartleby.com/10/402.html.

5. Milton Friedman, "The Social Responsibility of Business is to Increase its Profits," The New York Times Magazine, Sept. 13, 1970, p. 17.

6. "Rethinking the Social Responsibility of Business," Reason, October 2005, www.reason.com/news/show/32239.html.

7. "Corporate Responsibility Review," The Coca-Cola Co., July 2006, p. 9, www.thecoca-colacompany.com/ourcompany/pdf/corporate_responsibility_review.pdf.

8. "2006 Citizenship Report," General Electric Co., 2006, www.gemoneybank.de/docs/577335_GE_2006_citizen_06rep.pdf.

9. Program for Conference Board's 2007 "Leadership Conference on Global Corporate Citizenship," www.conference-board.org/pdf_free/agendas/b09007.pdf.

10. Barbara Dyer, Stephen Jordan, Steven A. Rochlin and Sapna Shah, "The State of Corporate Citizenship in the U.S.," Boston College Center for Corporate Citizenship, 2005.

11. "About USCAP," United States Climate Action Partnership, www.us-cap.org/about/index.asp.

12. Mark Kramer and John Kania, "Changing the Game: Leading Corporations Switch from Defense to Offense in Solving Global Problems," *Stanford Social Innovation Review*, spring 2006, p. 28.

13. "Intel Education Initiative," www.intel.com/education/index.htm.

14. "2005 Report on Socially Responsible Investing Trends in the United States," *Social Investment Forum*, Jan. 24, 2006, www.socialinvest.org/areas/research/trends/sri_trends_report_2005.pdf.

15. "About FedEx Hybrid Electric Vehicle," www.fedex.com/us/about/responsibility/environment/hybridelectricvehicle.html?link=4.

16. Ann Zimmerman, "Costco's Dilemma: Is Treating Employees Well Unacceptable for a Publicly Traded Corporation?" *The Wall Street Journal*, March 26, 2004.

17. Pete Engardio, Kerry Capell, John Carey and Kenji Hall, "Beyond The Green Corporation," *Business Week*, Jan. 28, 2007; Pete Engardio and Michael Arndt, "What Price Reputation?" *Business Week*, July 9 and 17, 2007. For background, see Brian Hansen, "Big-Box Stores," *CQ Researcher*, Sept. 10, 2004, pp. 733-756.

18. Andrew Savitz, *The Triple Bottom Line* (2006), p. 66.

19. Tom Borelli, "Wal-Mart's Public Policy Dilemma: Turn Right or Left?" *Townhall.com*, June 16, 2007, www.townhall.com/columnists/TomBorelli/2007/06/16/wal-mart%e2%80%99s_public_policy_dilemma_turn_right_or_left.

20. "Rethinking the Social Responsibility of Business," *op. cit.*

21. Allen L. White, "Is It Time to Rewrite the Social Contract?" *Business for Social Responsibility*, April 2007, www.bsr.org/meta/awhite_new-social-contract.pdf.

22. "The McKinsey Global Survey of Business Executives: Business and Society," *The McKinsey Quarterly*, January 2006, www.mckinseyquarterly.com/article_page.aspx?L2=39&L3=29&ar=1741&pagenum=1.

23. Margaret Steen, "What Does Corporate Social Responsibility Mean to You?" *Stanford Business*, May 2007, www.gsb.stanford.edu/news/bmag/sbsm0705/feature_csr.html.

24. Fred L. Smith Jr., "The Irresponsibility of Corporate Social Responsibility," speech to the Acton Institute for the Study of Religion and Liberty, Feb. 15, 2007, www.cei.org/gencon/023,05890.cfm.

25. "KLD Reports May 2007 Index Returns," KLD Research & Analytics, June 7, 2007, www.kld.com/newsletter/archive/press/pdf/200705_Index_Performance.pdf.

26. Clive Crook, "The Good Company," *The Economist*, Jan. 22, 2005.

27. Stephanie Strom, "Make Money, Save the World," *The New York Times*, May 6, 2007, Section 3, p. 1.

28. Cheryl Scott, "Our Investment Philosophy," Bill & Melinda Gates Foundation, Jan. 11, 2007, www.gatesfoundation.org/AboutUs/Announcements/Announce-070109.htm.

29. This historical section draws from the following sources: Kathy Koch, "The New Corporate Philanthropy," *CQ Researcher*, Feb. 27, 1998, pp. 169-192; Sylvia Clark and Kate Dewey, *Organizing Corporate Contributions: Options and Strategies*, Council on Foundations, 1996; "History of The Conference Board," www.conference-board.org/aboutus/history.cfm; Steen, *op. cit.*; Joel Bakan, *The Corporation: Pathological Pursuit of Profit and Power*, Penguin Books Canada, March 2004; Lawrence Boyd, "The Company Town," *Economic History Encyclopedia, 2003*, www.eh.net/encyclopedia/article/boyd.company.town; "Andrew Carnegie," PBS, www.pbs.org/wgbh/amex/carnegie/filmmore/transcript/index.html; "The Rockefeller Foundation: A History," Rockefeller Foundation, www.rockfound.org/about_us/history/timeline.shtml.

30. "Andrew Carnegie," *op. cit.*

31. "History of The Conference Board," *op. cit.*

32. Bakan, *op. cit.*

33. *Ibid.*

34. *Ibid.*

35. Steen, *op. cit.*

36. Clark and Dewey, *op. cit.*

37. *Ibid.*

38. Koch, *op. cit.*

39. "BSR History," Business for Social Responsibility, www.bsr.org/Meta/about/BSRHistory.cfm.

40. "History," Sustainability, www.sustainability.com/about/history.asp.

41. "The Center's Mission," The Conference Board, www.conference-board.org/knowledge/citizenship center/mission.cfm.

42. "Business Roundtable Launches S.E.E. Change Initiative to Spur Sustainable Growth," *Business Roundtable*, Sept. 21, 2005, www.businessroundta ble.org//newsroom/document.aspx?qs=5926BF807 822B0F1AD1438F22FB51711FCF50C8.

43. Clifford Krauss, "Can They Really Call the Chainsaw Eco-Friendly?" *The New York Times*, June 25, 2007, p. 1.

44. Andres Oppenheimer, "Nobel Winner's 'Social Businesses': a Good Idea?" *The Miami Herald*, March 25, 2007, p. 16.

45. Jim Wyss, "A New, Socially Responsible Form of Microinvesting Is Being Tested in Nicaragua," *The Miami Herald*, March 12, 2007, p. G13.

46. Strom, *op. cit.*; Jeff Chernoff, "New Brokerage Firm Donating Profits to Charities," *Pensions & Investments*, Oct. 2, 2006.

47. Deborah Doane, "The Myth of CSR," *Stanford Social Innovation Review*, fall 2005, www.ssireview .org/articles/entry/the_myth_of_csr.

48. Allen L. White, "Transforming the Corporation," Tellus Institute, 2006, p. 12, www.gtinitiative.org/documents/PDFFINALS/5Corporations.pdf.

BIBLIOGRAPHY

Books

Esty, Daniel, and Andrew Winston, *Green to Gold: How Smart Companies Use Environmental Strategy to Innovate, Create Value, and Build Competitive Advantage, Yale University Press*, 2006.
If companies build environmental thinking into their core business strategies, they can cut costs and generate new revenues, according to Esty, director of Yale's Center for Business and Environment, and business consultant Winston.

Hart, Stuart, *Capitalism at the Crossroads: Aligning Business, Earth, and Humanity*, 2nd Edition, *Wharton School Publishing*, 2007.
Drawing examples from some 20 case studies, a Cornell University management professor argues the right business strategy can reduce poverty and generate profits.

Hollender, Jeffrey, *What Matters Most: How a Small Group of Pioneers Is Teaching Social Responsibility to Big Business, and Why Big Business Is Listening, Basic Books*, 2003.
The president of Seventh Generation — maker of environmentally friendly products — provides an insider's look at running a socially responsible business.

Savitz, Andrew W., and Karl Weber, *The Triple Bottom Line: How Today's Best-Run Companies Are Achieving Economic, Social and Environmental Success — and How You Can Too, Jossey-Bass*, 2006.
A business consultant (Savitz) and a writer discuss how companies can profit from responding to social needs.

Smith, Adam, *The Wealth of Nations, Bantam Classics*, 2003.
First published in 1776, philosopher Smith's famous book is still quoted as the classic defense of free markets.

Articles

"Corporate Social Responsibility," *The Economist*, Jan. 22, 2005.
A collection of essays looks at CSR, often skeptically.

Engardio, Pete, *et al.*, "Beyond The Green Corporation," *Business Week*, Jan. 28, 2007.
The authors take a global survey of corporate responsibility.

Friedman, Milton, "The Social Responsibility of Business is to Increase its Profits," *The New York Times Magazine*, Sept. 13, 1970, p. 17.
This classic argument against corporate social responsibility by the conservative Nobel Prize-winning economist is still quoted and debated today.

Greenhouse, Steven, "How Costco Became the Anti-Wal-Mart," *The New York Times*, July 17, 2005.
The low-cost retailer thrives while treating its employees better than Wal-Mart.

Mackey, John, T. J. Rodgers and Milton Friedman, "Rethinking the Social Responsibility of Business," *Reason*, October 2005, www.reason.com/news/show/32239.html.
A leading proponent (Whole Foods chief Mackey) and two leading critics (economist Friedman and businessman Rodgers) debate the merits of corporate social responsibility.

Strom, Stephanie, "Make Money, Save the World," *The New York Times*, May 6, 2007, p. 3-1.
The author discovers an "emerging convergence" between businesses that do good and nonprofits that adopt business tactics to support their activities.

Reports and Studies

"The McKinsey Global Survey of Business Executives: Business and Society," *The McKinsey Quarterly*, January 2006, www.mckinseyquarterly.com/article_page.aspx?L2=39&L3=29&ar=1741&pagenum=1.
A poll finds overwhelming acceptance of responsibility for more than making profits.

General Electric Co., "2006 Citizenship Report," 2006, www.gemoneybank.de/docs/577335_GE_2006_citizen_06rep.pdf.
Reflecting a growing trend, GE publishes a social responsibility report in addition to the traditional annual report.

Price, Tom, "Activists in the Boardroom: How Advocacy Groups Seek to Shape Corporate Behavior," *Foundation for Public Affairs*, 2006.
The author examines how companies use corporate social responsibility to both cooperate with and fend off advocacy groups.

Social Investment Forum, "2005 Report on Socially Responsible Investing Trends in the United States," Jan. 24, 2006, www.socialinvest.org/areas/research/trends/sri_trends_report_2005.pdf.
A biennial report surveys investors who care about more than the bottom line. Its next report is due in January 2008.

White, Allen L., "Is It Time to Rewrite the Social Contract?" *Business for Social Responsibility*, April 2007, www.bsr.org/meta/awhite_new-social-contract.pdf.
A business-responsibility advocate concludes that the traditional definition of a corporation's purpose is "unsuitable to meet 21st-century challenges."

For More Information

Boston College Center for Corporate Citizenship, 55 Lee Road, Chestnut Hill, MA 02467; (617) 552-4545; www.bcccc.net. Researches corporate citizenship.

Business for Social Responsibility, 111 Sutter St., 12th Floor, San Francisco, CA 94104; (415) 984-3200; www.bsr.org. Advocates good corporate citizenship.

Business Roundtable, 1717 Rhode Island Ave., N.W., Suite 800, Washington, DC 20036; (202) 872-1260; www.businessroundtable.org. Organization of corporation chief executive officers that promotes corporate attention to society, environment and economy through its S.E.E. Change initiative.

Competitive Enterprise Institute, 1001 Connecticut Ave., N.W., Suite 1250, Washington, DC 20036; (202) 331-1010; www.cei.org. Think tank devoted to free enterprise and limited government; opposes CSR initiatives.

The Conference Board, 845 Third Ave., New York, NY 10022; (212) 759-0900; www.conference-board.org. Association of major businesses that advises companies on social responsibility through its Center for Corporate Citizenship and Sustainability.

Social Investment Forum, 1612 K St., N.W., Suite 650, Washington, DC 20006; (202) 872-5319; www.socialinvest.org. Trade association for the socially responsible investing industry.

SustainAbility, 20-22 Bedford Row, London WC1R 4EB, United Kingdom; 44-20-7269-6900; www.sustainability.com. Consulting firm that coined the phrase "triple bottom line," for businesses' responsibility to "people, planet and profit."

U.S. Climate Action Partnership, C/O Meridian Institute, 1920 L St., N.W., Suite 500, Washington, DC 20036; www.us-cap.org. Alliance of major corporations and environmental organizations that lobbies for government action against global warming.

Wal-Mart Watch, 1730 M St., N.W., Suite 601, Washington, DC 20036; (202) 557-7440; www.walmartwatch.com. Advocacy group that pressures Wal-Mart on labor, environmental and community-impact issues.

Yale University Center for Business and Environment, 230 Prospect St., New Haven, CT 06511; (203) 432-3736; http://research.yale.edu/cbey. Carries out research and education on business solutions to environmental problems.

2

Curbing CEO Pay

Is Executive Compensation Out of Control?

Thomas J. Billitteri

Robert L. Nardelli was handed a $210 million severance package when he was fired in January as chairman, president and CEO of The Home Depot. Some experts say corporate compensation is out of control, but others say most highly paid CEOs deserve what they get.

From *CQ Researcher*, March 9, 2007.

The door had barely slammed on Robert L. Nardelli, the deposed CEO of The Home Depot, when the howls of indignation began.

The company's board ousted Nardelli in January over poor performance and other issues, but not before handing him a stunning $210 million severance package. The "golden goodbye" was in addition to the almost $64 million Nardelli had reaped in his six years running the big retailer — a period in which the chain's stock price stagnated and its competition gained ground.[1]

"The departure package is an outrage," said Nell Minow, editor of The Corporate Library, a corporate-governance research firm. "He should be giving money back to the company, not taking anything more."[2]

"Obscene," an Atlanta columnist declared.[3]

Nardelli is far from alone. Dozens of big companies have come under fire recently from shareholders, politicians and the media for lavishing their CEOs with colossal pay and severance packages, sometimes despite serious management failures. Meanwhile, scores of companies are being probed for possible manipulation of stock-option grants to enrich corporate officials and directors at sometimes mind-boggling levels.

Often inflated by stock options, the median total compensation among roughly 2,000 CEOs was $2.9 million in 2005, up about 180 percent since 1999, according to The Corporate Library. Meanwhile, at the nation's 100 largest companies, median CEO compensation was $17.9 million in 2005, according to *USA Today*, and a half-dozen chief executives hauled in more than

Several CEOs Earned More Than $100 Million

A handful of American chief executive officers earned more than $100 million in 2005, led by Capital One Financial's Richard D. Fairbank, who took home a phenomenal $280 million. Stock options played a major role in the huge compensation totals.

Company/ Executive	Total Compensation	Salary	Bonus	Option Gains
Capital One Financial Richard D. Fairbank	$280,083,843	$0	$0	$249,267,658
KB Home Bruce Karatz	$163,934,209	$1,091,667	$5,000,000	$118,370,799
Cendant Henry Silverman	$133,261,147	$3,300,000	$12,316,600	$117,644,547
Lehman Brothers R. S. Fuld Jr.	$119,539,850	$750,000	$13,750,000	$74,958,627
Genentech Arthur D. Levinson	$109,431,444	$975,833	$2,000,000	$66,268,100
Occidental Petroleum Ray R. Irani	$106,524,159	$1,300,000	$3,640,000	$37,562,444
Oracle Lawrence J. Ellison	$92,137,389	$975,000	$6,500,000	$66,891,118
Valero Energy William E. Greehey	$89,450,243	$1,400,000	$3,500,000	$55,269,605
Cisco Systems John T. Chambers	$80,707,753	$350,000	$1,300,000	$61,329,110
Morgan Stanley John J. Mack	$68,187,675	$337,534	$0	$30,030,934

Karatz

Fuld

Ellison

Chambers

Total compensation: includes salary, bonuses, stock and incentives, the potential value of stock options and gains from stock options exercised; excludes "other compensation" such as use of company aircraft

Salary: CEO's base pay

Bonus: incentives and performance awards, usually cash

Stock-option gains: Profits realized after exercising options; an option allows the holder to buy shares at a predetermined price

Source: "Special report: Executive compensation," USA Today, April 10, 2006, based on Aon Consulting's eComp Data Services, www.ecomponline.com

$100 million each. (*See chart, p. 26.*) The biggest paychecks went to Richard D. Fairbank of Capital One Financial ($280 million-plus, $249 million of it in stock-option gains); Bruce Karatz of KB Home ($163.9 million, with more than $118 million in option gains) and Cendant's Henry Silverman (more than $133 million, with nearly $118 million in option gains).[4]

Compensation experts offer numerous explanations for the windfalls, including competition for executive talent, the influence of corporate-pay consultants, tax-policy incentives that encouraged stock option grants and the effect of hostile takeovers on the growth of "golden parachutes" for fired executives.

Indeed, intense debate rages over whether corporate compensation is excessive or simply a product of market forces. But most Americans, apparently, have definite opinions: Four in five respondents to a *Los Angeles Times/Bloomberg* poll last year — including 84 percent of investors living in households making at least $100,000 — said most CEOs of large U.S. companies are paid too much.[5]

Experts in business and academe, however, are deeply divided over corporate compensation. Charles M. Elson, director of the Weinberg Center for Corporate Governance at the University of Delaware, thinks it is out of control. "Absolutely, and in a variety of measures [ranging from] the relationship to overall shareholder return to pay equity within the organization," he says. "It's basically a large-scale asset transfer from shareholders to the managers, and it has consequences for the health of the organization and of the investors."

But Roy C. Smith, a professor at New York University's Stern School of Business, contends executive compensation "isn't the sinful overindulgence of greedy executives that it's made out to be. There may be some abuse...but most of the CEOs who receive those huge pay packages not only earn them but also, yes, deserve them."[6]

The sparks flying over executive pay promise to ignite a firestorm of activism in coming months. Beginning with this spring's annual proxy season, new Securities

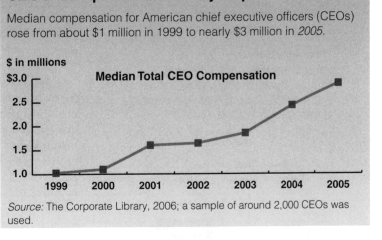

CEOs' Compensation Nearly Tripled

Median compensation for American chief executive officers (CEOs) rose from about $1 million in 1999 to nearly $3 million in *2005*.

Source: The Corporate Library, 2006; a sample of around 2,000 CEOs was used.

and Exchange Commission (SEC) rules require companies to give investors an unprecedented, plain-English look at how much executives are paid. "A lot of things that have not been disclosed before are ending up on proxies, particularly [executives'] perks," Elson says. "It's going to get a lot of people very mad."

Critics have accused the SEC of retreating on the new disclosure rules under pressure from big business. In December, just before the rules took effect, the SEC said companies could spread the value of stock-option grants over a number of years rather than show the much bigger lump-sum value. Even so, the new rules, coupled with simmering dissatisfaction over golden parachutes and outsized CEO paychecks, are expected to help make executive compensation one of the most incendiary policy and political issues of 2007.

In January a broad mix of institutional investors, from the American Federation of State, County and Municipal Employees to the Benedictine Sisters of Texas, announced they were filing a non-binding shareholder resolution — informally called "say on pay" — asking more than 50 U.S. companies to give stockholders an annual advisory vote on executive-compensation packages.

Similar pressure to curb corporate pay is building in the new Democrat-controlled Congress. Rep. Barney Frank, D-Mass., now chairman of the House Financial Services Committee, introduced a bill and scheduled a hearing in March designed to give shareholders a bigger

Executives Earn 195 Times the Average Worker's Wages

The highest-paid American executives made $195 for every $1 earned by the average worker in 2000-2005. The pay gap was four times smaller in 1940–1945.

Executive Pay per $1 Earned by Average Worker*

* Total compensation composed of salary, bonuses, long-term bonuses and stock options.

Source: Carola Frydman and Raven E. Saks, "Historical Trends in Executive Compensation," November 2005; updated in interview

Yet even President George W. Bush, often viewed as friendly to big business, admonished corporate boards this year "to pay attention to the executive-compensation packages that you approve." He added: "You need to show the world that American businesses are a model of transparency and good corporate governance."[7]

Taken together, such developments suggest that corporate pay will be a dominant issue on both the shareholder and policy scene for some time to come. "Anger over pay is at an all-time high in the institutional community and on Main Street," says Patrick McGurn, executive vice president of Institutional Shareholder Services, a Rockville, Md., company that advises investor groups on proxy and corporate-governance issues. "There's no better target right now than fat-cat CEOs at underperforming companies."

Some of the sharpest criticism over pay has been aimed at huge severance packages given to executives pushed out for not delivering on expectations. In addition to Nardelli's deal, the former CEO of Pfizer Inc., forced into early retirement amid a drop in the company's stock price and shareholder anger over his pay, got an exit package worth more than $180 million, including an estimated $82.3 million in pension benefits and about $78 million in deferred compensation.[8] J. C. Penney Co.'s chief operating officer got a severance deal worth $10 million after her termination — and she had been on the job for only about five months.[9]

Some have argued that even though pay and severance packages have soared in recent years, they still represent a fraction of the overall economy and thus have little real impact on the nation's corporate health.

But skeptics say the growth in executive pay has had significant economic repercussions. In a major study of 1,500 top U.S. corporations, Harvard Law School Professor Lucian Bebchuk and Cornell University management Professor Yaniv Grinstein found compensation paid to the top five executives at each firm totaled $350 billion in the 11 years ending in 2003. That compensation, they found, took a bigger and bigger share of total company earnings as the period progressed — about 10 percent in the later years, compared with 5 percent in the early years.[10]

Citing that data, Rep. Frank argued in January that criticism of pay and severance deals isn't just based on jealousy but reflects concern for the nation's economic

voice on executive-compensation plans, an approach used in Britain and Australia that Frank has been championing. Frank has been among the most vocal Democrats on corporate compensation, calling Nardelli's simultaneous dismissal and severance package as "further confirmation of the need to deal with a pattern of CEO pay that appears to be out of control."

The Democrats have linked the pay issue to their appeals for economic relief for working-class Americans. Earlier this year the Senate, in a measure to raise the minimum wage, voted to cap the amount executives can put into tax-deferred plans at $1 million — a move widely seen as an attack on corporate pay practices.

well-being. CEO compensation "has reached a point where it has some macroeconomic significance," Frank said. "When Lee Raymond gets $400 million when he leaves Exxon Mobil, and the pension [fund] is shorted... we're not just talking about envy."[11]

As Congress, corporations and shareholders consider reining in CEO compensation, here are some of the questions they are asking:

Is compensation out of control?

Last year the average CEO of a big company made 411 times the wages of an average worker, according to the Institute for Policy Studies, a liberal Washington think tank. That's roughly 10 times the proportion in 1980, says Sarah Anderson, director of the institute's Global Economy Program.

American CEO pay, she says, "is way out of line compared to what we see anywhere in the world." Typical CEO pay in the United States exceeds that in 25 other locales, according to the latest annual study by the international consulting firm Towers Perrin. In 2005 U.S. chief executives received about $2.2 million compared with roughly $1.4 million for CEOs in Switzerland, $1.2 million in France, the United Kingdom and Germany and less than $550,000 in Japan. (*See sidebar and chart, pp. 36-37.*)

But not all compensation experts agree with Anderson that executive pay in the United States is out of line. "I definitely don't think pay is out of control," says Don Lindner, an executive at WorldatWork, formerly the American Compensation Association and the main trade group for compensation and benefit specialists.

"We see a lot of egregious behavior because it makes the papers, and it should be exposed. But there are a lot of companies that do a very good job of designing plans and building pay packages for the right reasons — to help grow shareholder value and help companies meet their objectives. Most companies do that, and some very well."

The issue turns partly, of course, on which yardstick is used to measure reasonableness of pay. For example, some observers — most notably stockholders — look at the issue in terms of performance: Does the growth in pay track the changes in market value of company shares over time? Trade unions may look at CEO rewards and

Union protesters call Home Depot's then-CEO Robert L. Nardelli an "over paid CEO" during the annual shareholders' meeting on May 25, 2006, in Wilmington, Del. Trade unions oppose high compensation packages for poorly performing CEOs at corporations that are cutting benefits and wages.

Getty Images/William Thomas Cain

contrast them with job and benefit cuts at big corporations. Populists may see the issue in terms of social equity, arguing that those at the bottom of the economic ladder deserve some of the riches going to those at the top. Some may reject outright the notion that any job is worth millions of dollars a year, no matter the circumstances.

Even issues of corporate social responsibility play a role in the pay debate. Recently, big shareholders in the oil giant British Petroleum demanded that a court in Alaska stop Lord Browne, the company's outgoing CEO, from collecting $140 million in pension benefits, bonuses and other compensation while they pursue claims against him and other directors over environmental and safety matters.[12]

While excesses in corporate pay make easy fodder for pundits, some experts stress that compensation defies easy prescription.

"It's a more complicated, more textured story than just saying, 'Gee, aren't they paid a lot compared with what average workers make?' " says Randall Thomas, a professor of law and business at the Vanderbilt University Law School. While acknowledging cases of overpaid CEOs, he says, "You have to differentiate between what's happening on average vs. what's happening at the extreme."

For instance, a 2006 study concluded that the sixfold increase in CEO compensation between 1980 and 2003 "can be fully attributed" to a sixfold increase in market capitalization — the value of outstanding shares — at big U.S. companies during that period.[13]

"Yes, there are numerous examples of corporate malfeasance," Tyler Cowen, an economics professor at George Mason University, wrote in reference to the study. "But it is not obvious that the American system of executive pay — taken as a whole — is excessive or broken."[14]

Last year the Business Roundtable, an association of 160 chief executives of major U.S. companies, found that between 1995 and 2005 CEO compensation at 350 big companies rose 9.6 percent annually, below the 9.9 percent growth in stockholder returns at those companies during that period.[15]

"We wanted to try and promulgate a consistent set of facts because a lot of what we have seen in the media on executive pay we felt was misleading," said the Roundtable's director of public policy, Thomas J. Lehner.[16]

The Roundtable study drew harsh criticism, however, for excluding certain types of compensation, such as dividends on executives' restricted stock, gains from cashing in stock options and restricted stock over the 11 years of the study, pension benefits, deferred compensation and severance pay. The study's author defended his methodology, but another compensation expert called the analysis "disingenuous."[17]

Other researchers have found that not only has executive pay spiraled upward but also the pace of growth has been accelerating sharply.

Carola Frydman, an assistant professor of finance from MIT's Sloan School of Management, and economist Raven E. Saks at the Federal Reserve Board studied the compensation of the three highest paid officers in the 50 largest firms in 1940, 1960 and 1990. They found that the executives' average compensation didn't surpass its Depression-era level of about 63 times average wages until 1987. After that, it exploded, peaking in 2000 at about 317 times average wages.

Frydman noted that the peak was somewhat lower when measured not by the average but by the median, or midpoint, which tends to filter out executives with extremely high or low salaries. The median compensation of the three highest paid officers passed its Depression-era level in 1989 and peaked in 2000 at 119 times average wages.[18]

David Swinford, senior managing director of Pearl Meyer & Associates, a compensation consulting firm, says CEO compensation levels "have been pulling away not only from the masses but from other members of the executive team" as well. Over the last 15 or 20 years, CEO compensation has increased about 9 percent per year, he says, while other executives within large companies saw their compensation increase at more than 3 percent "but certainly less than 9 percent."

Is the link between CEO pay and performance broken?

Some pay experts believe the link — often measured by such things as growth in stock price and earnings per share — is sound. "If you go back 15 years and look at CEO pay and at the wealth that's been produced, it's not way out of balance," says Lindner of WorldatWork.

Others say the link is broken. "I see very few examples of companies where I could say, 'You've got it right in terms of the link between pay and performance,' " says Paul Hodgson, senior research associate for executive and director compensation at The Corporate Library. "Compensation committees need to go back to the drawing board and redesign their pay policies."

Adds McGurn of Institutional Shareholder Services: "There is no question that to a large degree executive compensation is decoupled from companies' performance."

Harvard's Bebchuk and Jesse Fried, a law professor and co-director of the Berkeley Center for Law, Business and the Economy at the University of California, Berkeley, wrote in their influential book *Pay Without Performance* that "most compensation contracts ensure that executives receive generous treatment even in cases of spectacular failure."

They point to Mattel CEO Jill Barad, who "received $50 million in severance pay after being employed for only two years, during which time Mattel's stock price fell by 50 percent, wiping out $2.5 billion in shareholder value." Another example they offer: "Conseco provided $49.3 million to departing CEO Stephen Hilbert, who left the company in a precarious financial situation. The Conseco board then gave incoming CEO Gary Wendt a guaranteed package worth more than $60 million in compensation, even if he failed."[19]

Stock-option gains, in particular, can either tie an executive's fortunes to those of the company or, as Hodgson points out, have little to do with performance at all.

"If you awarded a stock option and your stock price increases in line with the market for seven years, you will make money out of it," he says. "But how much of a company's stock price was due to your running the company, and how much was due to a general rise in the market in that period? In many cases, up to 80 percent of a stock price can be due to a general rise in the market. It is inappropriate for executives to be rewarded for that, particularly when there are tools around that can be used to reward them solely for their input."

In their most elemental form, option grants give the recipient the right — but not the obligation — to buy shares in a company at a set "exercise" price sometime in the future. Typically, that exercise price is the market price of the shares on the day the options are granted. A CEO might receive the option to buy shares of his company's stock four years from now at the $75 per share exercise price it trades at today. If the stock trades at $125 per share four years from now, the CEO can make a tidy profit by selling the stock. The idea, of course, is to give the CEO an incentive to manage the company in a way that its stock price grows, rewarding both the CEO and shareholders.

Options have become controversial, however, partly because they can dilute the value of stock owned by investors by adding to the pool of available shares in a company. In addition, stock options can be manipulated, as evidenced by the unfolding investigation of backdating abuses in which scores of companies are suspected of granting options to executives and backdating the grants to days when their companies' share price was at or near a low, boosting the likelihood of a profit when the options are cashed in.

Options also have come under close scrutiny for their potential to reward executives not for performance but for being lucky during strong bull markets on Wall Street. Indeed, options turned out to be a gold mine for CEOs in the 1990s, when the overall stock market soared far beyond rational expectations.[20]

A Financial Accounting Standards Board rule that took effect last year requires companies to subtract the cost of stock options from their bottom line, something

Rep. Barney Frank, D-Mass., chairman of the House Financial Services Committee, introduced a bill and scheduled a hearing in March designed to give shareholders a bigger voice on executive-compensation plans. Earlier this year, the Senate voted to cap the amount executives can put into tax-deferred plans at $1 million.

Getty Images/Alex Wong

they didn't have to do before. Some observers believe the rule change is inducing companies to shift from options toward other compensation methods, such as performance-based restricted stock, which requires executives to meet specific business targets before they can cash in the stocks.

One thing is clear: The explosion in options in recent years has been widely viewed as a prime culprit in the disconnect between pay and performance.

A solution advocated by some compensation critics is to give executives indexed options, which are calibrated against a broad market basket of stocks. They can filter out the effects of an overall rise on Wall Street and diminish windfalls.

Yet other experts on corporate compensation contend that regular, garden-variety options have been an efficient way of rewarding executives for the value they bring to shareholders and for the risks they take as captains of highly complex enterprises.

"If you want to incentivize managers to worry about what matters to stockholders, which is stock price, you give them options as a way of doing that," says Vanderbilt's Thomas. "What we've done over this period of 1980 to 2006 is try to tie more carefully CEO pay to stock price. CEOs not only are getting paid more but they also are taking on a lot more risk, because stock options don't always pay off."

Moreover, in a complex theory laid out in some of his academic writing, Thomas argues that indexing stock options to the broad market gives executives no greater incentive to perform well than using regular options.[21]

"It would be just the same," he says. "You'd have to pay [the CEO] more to make up for the fact that indexed options are riskier. It's not going to reduce executive pay."

Are new laws needed to regulate executive pay?

When the SEC imposed new disclosure rules on companies beginning with the distribution of corporate proxies this year, it was the most sweeping effort since 1992 to push executive compensation into the sunlight.

The rules require companies to explain to stockholders in plain English the details and rationale for their executive and director compensation plans and to provide a revised summary compensation table. The new law is intended to give investors a more complete picture of what executives are getting than at any time in the past.

Still, the debate continues over whether additional laws are needed to curb the growth in compensation. Not even the harshest compensation critics seem to want to cap pay outright, but many want the full value of compensation to be reported.

Among the critics' targets is a controversial revision to the new SEC disclosure rule adopted in December, which allows companies to spread the value of their options over years rather than showing a lump-sum value. The SEC said it changed the rule in order to better conform to accounting standards governing how stock-option costs are counted on corporate books. But critics said the amendment, announced right before the long Christmas holiday, was little more than a giveaway to big business.

Besides seeking full disclosure of pay practices, some critics also want to limit executives' tax-deferred compensation plans, which typically shelter their income from taxes until retirement. Earlier this year, the Senate approved a provision that would prevent executives from putting more than $1 million a year into deferred-compensation plans.[22]

"For the vast, vast majority of families, there's a limit on [untaxed] deferred compensation . . . of about $15,000" a year, said Finance Committee Chairman Sen. Max Baucus, D-Mont.[23]

If average wage earners can live with a $15,000 deduction, Baucus says, high-earners ought to be willing to accept the $1 million limit on deferred compensation.

It was unclear what would become of the Senate effort to cap deferred compensation because it was not included in the House version of the main bill, which would raise the minimum wage.

Rep. Frank's idea of giving shareholders a vote on executive compensation would also help regulate pay. He has been highly vocal on the issue, complaining that corporate boards "do not provide any real check on CEOs."[24]

In early March Frank introduced a bill (HR1257) that would allow shareholders a non-binding vote on executive compensation plans.[25]

Frank spokesman Steve Adamske said the bill would leave it "up to the corporation to respect" a "no" vote on a pay package "and alter the compensation package or ignore their shareholders."[26]

While Frank's bill calls for an advisory vote, earlier versions ran into stiff opposition from business groups. "In our view, legislative proposals . . . calling for shareholder approval of compensation plans are unwise and ultimately unworkable," Lehner of the Business Roundtable told a House panel last year. "If we adopted a system where small groups of activist shareholders used the process to politicize corporate decision-making, the consequences could very well be destabilizing."[27]

Others in Congress have tried to rein in pay, and even to cap it. Former Rep. Martin Sabo, a Minnesota Democrat who retired in January, promoted a bill that would have prohibited employers from deducting as a business expense any compensation that equaled or exceeded 25 times the lowest compensation paid to any other full-time employee.

Some companies voluntarily regulate their compensation. Last year Whole Foods Market, for example, capped cash compensation for top executives at 19 times the average pay of its full-time workers, or $607,800. What's more, CEO and co-founder John Mackey cut his own salary to $1 beginning this past January and said he would forgo future stock-option awards. Whole Foods' salary cap had risen from a multiple of 10 (or $257,000) in 1999.

But Whole Foods' approach to self-regulation is unusual among corporations. Walter Scott, a professor at Northwestern University's Kellogg School of Management, says it is something "many more could embrace."

While some compensation experts advocate tighter government laws on corporate pay, others — like Smith, the business professor at New York University — reject such an approach. "This essentially is an issue between stockholders and their boards, and it isn't really a concern of government," he says. "This is a private-property issue."

Besides, he says, most stock is owned by institutional investors who already have power over compensation decisions when they elect corporate directors — the people who set the compensation levels. "This is not necessarily a game between little sheep and vicious wolves," Smith says. "This is a game between corporations and sophisticated, well-informed investors."

BACKGROUND

CEO Cult

Big executive paychecks — and the controversy they stir — go back a long way. In 1929 the president of Bethlehem Steel hauled in a $1.6 million bonus on top of his $12,000 salary, becoming the first million-dollar CEO.[28] In 1933 angry stockholders filed what is thought to be the first lawsuit over executive pay after the president of American Tobacco pulled in $1.3 million.[29]

After World War II executive pay gradually rose, and in the 1980s it began climbing sharply. A number of factors account for the meteoric rise.

A wave of hostile takeovers and leveraged buyouts occurred in the 1980s, sweeping aside many old-line executives who had been promoted from within during the 1960s and '70s. Pushing out the old guard was a phalanx of aggressive, risk-taking corporate captains who thought they could provide better returns to shareholders.

The new breed not only negotiated golden parachutes and other big pay deals but also created a mystique of the super-talented CEO — the notion of a rare, highly skilled executive who could move from industry to industry, turn around floundering companies and generate big returns for shareholders. That perceived scarcity of talent helped escalate the level of executive rewards and encouraged the use of performance-based compensation such as stock options and bonuses, say compensation experts.

Other forces have contributed to the boom in executive pay, including the rise of compensation consultants. As the cult of the CEO took hold in the 1980s and '90s, outside pay specialists came on the scene in a big way. Sometimes boards of directors or their compensation committees hired pay consultants, but often it was the CEOs themselves who retained the consultants, putting board members in the position of negotiating with the CEOs' advocates on compensation matters.

Experts say the widespread use of compensation consultants helped raise both the level and complexity of executive pay packages. "Consultants bear some of the blame," says McGurn of Institutional Shareholder Services, adding that he had seen many packages that "look more like a menu in a French restaurant, where you don't know what they are and there's no price tag attached."

"Most compensation specialists use a quartile-ranking system," says Douglas Branson, a law professor at the University of Pittsburgh who studies corporate board and compensation issues. "They ask the compensation committee, 'Do you want your executive to be in the highest [quartile]? Most say 'yes.' " That has created "a constant ratcheting effect" on compensation levels, he explains.

A ratcheting effect also occurs when executives are recruited from other companies. To attract a new CEO, boards often must agree to cover the executive's existing compensation contract — including anticipated proceeds from stock options and other pay deals that the executive might not even have received yet.

Golden parachutes also help ratchet up compensation. CEOs typically negotiate their severance deals before they even walk in the door at a new job, and once they're hired the company may have no choice but to make good on the agreement — even if the CEO stumbles.

That's what happened with Home Depot's Nardelli. Joining the home-improvement retailer in late 2000

CHRONOLOGY

1930s *Growing power of U.S. corporations and their top executives prompts criticism and new calls for oversight.*

1934 Congress creates Securities and Exchange Commission (SEC).

1940s-1950s *Executive compensation declines steeply during the war years and then grows modestly afterwards.*

1950 Revenue Act affords favorable tax treatment for stock options, giving rise to their use as a way to bolster executive compensation.

1960s-1980s *Stock options lose their luster, the result of changes in tax policy, high inflation and Wall Street decline, but corporate takeovers push up CEO compensation.*

1979 *Business Week's* best-paid-executive list marks a first: All 25 earn more than $1 million.

1984 Congress imposes a tax on "golden parachutes," a move that inadvertently encourages higher executive pay packages.

1990s *Booming equity markets and mushrooming use of stock options push CEO compensation to record levels.*

1991 Compensation consultant Graef S. Crystal comes out with his influential book *In Search of Excess: The Overcompensation of American Executives.*

1993 New law prohibits corporations from deducting taxes for executive compensation over $1 million unless it is performance-based.

1995 AT&T plans to cut more than 40,000 jobs, while Chairman Robert E. Allen receives a $16 million compensation package, including stock options valued at more than $10 million.

2000s *Corporate scandals lead to calls for stronger shareholder rights, while growing gap between rich and poor puts new focus on executive pay.*

Sept. 11, 2001 After terrorist attacks on the World Trade Center and the Pentagon, 91 companies that normally did not grant stock options in September did so amid the post-attack market decline, according to a 2006 *Wall Street Journal* analysis. . . . Enron files for bankruptcy in December.

2002 United Kingdom requires annual shareholder votes on executive pay. On July 30, President George W. Bush signs sweeping corporate anti-corruption bill known as the Sarbanes-Oxley Act. . . . On Aug. 29 the law's new two-day filing requirement for stock-option grants takes effect.

2004 New federal rules require companies to subtract the cost of executive stock options from their earnings.

2005 University of Iowa finance Professor Erik Lie publishes a paper in May suggesting some companies might be backdating stock options. . . . In November Rep. Barney Frank, D-Mass., introduces The Protection Against Executive Compensation Abuse Act proposing, among other things, that shareholders be empowered to vote on executive compensation plans.

2006 Federal prosecutors in San Francisco file the first criminal charges on July 20 in a growing scandal over manipulated stock options. . . . SEC unanimously adopts new rules on July 26 requiring greater disclosure of executive compensation. . . . Senate Committee on Banking, Housing and Urban Affairs holds a hearing on Sept. 6 on stock-option backdating. . . . On Dec. 22, SEC amends rules adopted on July 26, giving companies more leeway in how they report stock-option grants.

February 2007 Senate approves measure limiting executives' tax-deferred accounts to $1 million. . . . Aflac becomes the first major U.S. company to voluntarily give shareholders a non-binding vote on executive pay. . . . House Financial Services Committee, led now by Rep. Frank, plans March hearings on empowering shareholders to challenge executive compensation.

from a high-level perch at General Electric, he was a hot property in the CEO talent search. "Nardelli would have been fought over by dozens of companies," says Smith of New York University "but he negotiated a pretty slick deal" with Home Depot. When shareholders sought to block the former CEO's huge exit pay early this year, the company's lawyers said the severance package had been set by Nardelli's employment agreement. A state judge refused to go along with the shareholders, though he gave their lawyers time to collect additional information in the case.[30]

After Nardelli's departure, Home Depot hired from within. The new CEO, Frank Blake, had served as vice chairman of the board and executive vice president of the company. This year he was expected to earn $8.9 million, less than a quarter of Nardelli's $39.7 million paycheck.[31] But it's rarely that easy or cheap to find a replacement for an ousted executive.

"When a stumble happens," says Northwestern University's Scott, "people begin looking outside their organizations to replace that superstar, and to get a superstar they have to pay lavishly to move the person" out of an existing job.

And turnover happens frequently, Scott notes. The average CEO tenure these days is 48 months, compared with a tenure of seven or eight years a decade or two ago, he says.

Undue Influence

Salaries also have shot up, according to Harvard's Bebchuk and UC-Berkeley's Fried, because powerful CEOs have exerted inappropriate influence over boards and compensation committees. "Flawed compensation arrangements have been widespread, persistent and systemic, and they have stemmed from defects in the underlying governance structure that enable executives to exert considerable influence over their boards," they wrote.[32]

"Executives have had substantial influence over their own pay," they wrote. "Compensation arrangements have often deviated from arm's-length contracting because directors have been influenced by management, sympathetic to executives, insufficiently motivated to bargain over compensation or simply ineffectual in overseeing compensation."[33]

Other compensation experts take issue with that view, arguing, for example, that highly skilled managers have so many opportunities open to them that it is reasonable for them to command extraordinarily high salaries.

Pay experts also point out that the role of the corporate CEO has become much more demanding so it is only natural that compensation has grown in step with the increasing complexity of the CEO's job. Others also argue that pay has risen over the years in lockstep with the increase in shareholder value.

But others say market forces are not the main engines driving executive pay.

"I think boards of directors and their compensation committees have been rigged by CEOs," says Branson of the University of Pittsburgh. "Compensation committees generally have been a failure partly because of the excessive size of executive compensation packages. When you look at how the system has been rigged, it tilts the debate against executives and those who say it's just the market at work."

Many cite the recent saga of the Walt Disney Co. as an example of excessive executive influence over board members. In 1997 Disney shareholders went to court to try to recover a $140 million severance payment to former president Michael Ovitz, who had been hired by his then-close friend, CEO Michael Eisner — and then forced out 14 months later by Eisner.

In 2005 a Delaware court upheld the severance payment, dismissing the shareholders' charges that the board had breached its fiduciary duty in Ovitz's hiring and dismissal. But the judge sharply chastised Eisner and his influence over Disney's board.

Eisner had "enthroned himself as the omnipotent and infallible monarch of his personal Magic Kingdom," the judge wrote. Eisner, he added, had "stacked his (and I intentionally write 'his' as opposed to 'the Company's') board of directors with friends and other acquaintances who, though not necessarily beholden to him in a legal sense, were certainly more willing to accede to his wishes and support him unconditionally than truly independent directors."[34]

Rules Backfire

Some blame skyrocketing executive pay in part on the unintended consequences of government efforts to curb

Foreigners Resent U.S. CEOs' High Pay

But defenders say they earn it

Simmering resentment over the gap between American and European CEO pay burst into the open at this year's World Economic Forum in Davos, Switzerland. Skyrocketing CEO pay is a "completely sick" trend that amounts to "theft," said Swiss activist Thomas Minder.

"Managers are employees, too. They are not entrepreneurs," Minder continued, to hearty applause.[1]

American CEOs receive more than their counterparts in other nations, according to Towers Perrin, a U.S. human-resources consulting firm. The typical U.S. chief executive received about $2.2 million in total compensation in 2005, far outstripping his counterparts in other nations. (*See graph, p. 37.*)[2]

"In the United Kingdom, in Canada, everyone involved in the [executive compensation] process is definitely trying to stop the importation of U.S.-style pay practices," says Patrick McGurn, executive vice president of Institutional Shareholder Services, a Rockville, Md., firm that advises institutional investors on corporate-governance issues. "They look at the United States with a certain degree of dread" because of the escalation of pay, the complexity of packages and the layering of compensation methods.

But Bjorn Johansson, chairman of a corporate head-hunting firm in Switzerland, warned that Swiss companies cannot just ignore the trend. "There are very few people who are capable" of leading large corporations, he said. "We can't say to them in Switzerland, 'We do things different.'"[3]

McGurn notes that shareholder advocates have tried to import progressive pay practices common in some other countries, such as giving stockholders an advisory vote on executive compensation.

Theories abound as to why U.S. CEOs make so much more than their global counterparts. Many believe U.S. executives exert excessive power over boards and compensation committees and take advantage of weaknesses in corporate governance to maximize their pay.

But Randall Thomas, a law professor at Vanderbilt University who studies executive compensation, offers a long list of other reasons for the pay gap between U.S. and foreign CEOs.

The quest for the corner office is much less competitive overseas than in the United States, where a "winner take all" culture condones bigger rewards for those who come out on top, he says.

American CEOs also tend to have more opportunities to find other lucrative jobs, Thomas notes. Venture capital for entrepreneurs flows more freely in the United States than overseas, he says, and foreign financial markets are less cohesive and are burdened by more regulation.

American CEOs have more power and more decision-making responsibility than foreign CEOs, Thomas also says. Most *Fortune* 500 CEOs chair their companies' boards, which is uncommon in foreign countries. And in some countries, notably Germany, board authority is shared between a management tier and a supervisory tier made up of banks, creditors and labor.

Moreover, in many foreign countries, particularly in continental Europe, a single shareholder can control 60 percent of a corporation, reducing the CEO's power, Thomas says.

When a single shareholder controls a company, Thomas says, there is little need for incentive pay to keep management on the straight and narrow. "In most of continental Europe," he says, "option pay is unnecessary because [companies] already have somebody who's monitoring management."

American CEOs also have more of their pay at risk in the form of company stock and options, a risk for which they expect to be compensated, Thomas notes.

---

[1] William L. Watts, "CEO Pay Under the Microscope at Davos," *MarketWatch*, Jan. 25, 2007.

[2] Towers Perrin, "2005-2006 Worldwide Total Remuneration." The figures represent typical pay at industrial companies with roughly $500 million in worldwide annual sales.

[3] *Ibid.*

the growth in pay. When the SEC strengthened its disclosure on compensation in 1992, consultants and corporate executives suddenly had more information on what other companies were paying than they had before. Rather than keeping pay at bay, the new disclosure rules gave CEOs and their compensation advisers new ammunition with which to negotiate even higher pay deals.

Likewise, a 1993 law capped the amount of compensation corporations could deduct on their taxes for each of their five highest-paid executives at $1 million unless it was performance-based. Proponents argued that the law would close the gap between executives and those farther down the corporate ladder.

But the law backfired. Rather than curbing compensation growth, it helped propel it forward. For one thing, a $1 million salary suddenly became a floor — rather than a ceiling — for many executives who were making less than that. And because stock options were viewed as performance-based, option grants exploded and their value soared on the winds of the bull market of the 1990s. Some of the biggest option recipients were executives at technology start-up companies that paid lavishly in shares.

"One lesson we've learned, I hope, is that every previous compensation-reform effort has had consequences that in some respects make the whole thing worse than the status quo was before," says Jeffrey Gordon, a Columbia University Law School professor who studies corporate-pay issues.

Ironically, pension funds and other investor groups had pushed for greater stock-option use in the early 1990s, believing options would make executives more accountable for the quality of their management. But that idea also boomeranged. "The institutional shareholder didn't realize how much was being given away and how quickly," says Swinford of Pearl Meyer.

U.S. Leads in CEO Pay

American CEOs of big companies receive an average of nearly $2.2 million in annual compensation, or nearly $1 million more than chief executives in Switzerland, the second-most-generous country.

Typical CEO Compensation

Country	Compensation
India	$290,854
Japan	$543,564
China (Hong Kong)	$651,339
Spain	$697,691
Netherlands	$862,711
Sweden	$948,990
Germany	$1,181,292
United Kingdom	$1,184,936
France	$1,202,145
Switzerland	$1,390,899
United States	$2,164,952

Note: Compensation includes salary, annual bonus, benefits and perquisites, restricted stock, profits on the exercise of stock options and any other long-term incentive payout.

Source: "Managing Global Pay and Benefits," Towers Perrin, 2005-2006

While many factors help explain soaring executive pay, other factors explain why this perennially controversial issue is taking on new urgency now.

Media coverage of enormous severance deals like Nardelli's and annual rankings in the business press of the most highly rewarded corporate elite help fuel the flames. The growing militancy of pension funds and other institutional shareholders also has fanned the fires. Computer power has made it easier for scholars to track and analyze compensation data, and the Internet has helped groups disseminate information about pay, as the AFL-CIO does on its Executive PayWatch Web site.[35]

Accounting scandals at Enron, Tyco International, WorldCom and other companies focused public and government attention on corporate governance, as did the Public Company Accounting Reform and Investor Protection Act of 2002 — known as the Sarbanes-Oxley Act, which cracked down on corporate-governance and financial abuses.[36]

But one of the biggest catalysts for renewed interest in corporate compensation is the "politics of pay" — the contrast between lavish rewards for top managers and the everyday financial struggles of middle-class and poor Americans. "The problem of excessive pay goes beyond being just a shareholder issue," says Anderson of the Institute for Policy Studies. "The broader society is affected when we have so much economic power in the hands of so few."

The level and structure of corporate pay deals can give executives an incentive to boost short-term profits and shareholder returns so the value of their bonuses and stock options goes up, which can have "negative effects" on the broader community, she says, such as deciding to "slash workers, do layoffs and not invest in research and development to create a more environmentally [protective] company."

As a senior policy adviser in the Clinton administration, Paul Weinstein, now chief operating officer of the Progressive Policy Institute, helped to shape the law that capped the deductibility of CEO pay at $1 million but allowed an exemption for performance-based pay, including stock options. Weinstein now says it was a mistake to allow the loophole for performance-based compensation, which helped lead to the stock-option deluge in the 1990s. "Government shouldn't be creating incentives for excessive CEO pay," he says.

Like many others these days, Weinstein is concerned about the gap between rich and poor and what can be done to raise the incomes of middle-income Americans. That concern appears central to the policy agenda of the new Democratic Congress. With middle-class bread-and-butter economic issues such as minimum wage and health-care coverage on the table, and the Bush administration's tax cuts and war expenditures under assault, Washington is talking about linking executive pay and populist causes.

"In the Bush economy it pays to be a CEO," declares a report on executive compensation by the Democratic staff of the House Financial Services Committee. But, "life is not as easy for the rest of America's workers."[37]

CURRENT SITUATION

Backdating Exposed

In the immediate future, no compensation issue looms larger than the unfolding scandal about backdated stock options, which has elicited outrage in Congress and generated heavy news coverage by *The Wall Street Journal*, among others.[38]

Backdating happens when a company retroactively sets the grant date of a stock option to a day when the firm's stock price was at or near a low point. The practice not only increases the chances that an executive will reap a profit when it comes time to exercise the option but also provides accounting and tax benefits for companies.

Option backdating and other forms of option timing are not necessarily illegal but must be disclosed to shareholders and accurately reflected in corporate financial statements and taxes. Option manipulation can be very difficult to detect.

As many as 200 companies are suspected of having practiced backdating, but Erik Lie, the University of Iowa finance professor who helped expose the practice, says he thinks perhaps 2,000 have engaged in backdating. (*See sidebar, p. 40.*) Lie told a Senate hearing last September that, in a survey of nearly 40,000 option grants at almost 8,000 companies between 1996 and 2005, at least 29 percent of firms that granted options to their top executives manipulated one or more of the grants in some way.[39]

Last September, Sen. Charles E. Grassley, R-Iowa, then chairman of the Finance Committee, called backdating "disgusting and repulsive," adding: "It is behavior that ignores the concept of an 'honest day's work for an honest day's pay' and replaces it with a phrase that we hear all too often today, 'I'm going to get mine.' Even worse in this situation, most of the perpetrators had already gotten 'theirs' in the form of six- and seven-figure compensation packages of which most working Americans can only dream."[40]

The Sarbanes-Oxley Act of 2002 made option manipulation more difficult to hide than in the past by requiring companies to disclose option grants to the SEC within two business days rather than up to 45 days after the end of a fiscal year, as was previously allowed. Even so, "It still is possible for companies to inappropriately time option grants around the release of corporate news," noted Institutional Shareholder Services.[41]

Even if few or no companies are still engaged in backdating, the scandal is likely to have a long shelf life. Federal prosecutors, the SEC, the press and shareholder advocates have been aggressively pursuing companies suspected of option manipulation.

For instance, federal prosecutors were investigating technology giant Apple's past options dealings early this year, but company officials say an internal investigation cleared CEO Steve Jobs of any wrongdoing.

The backdating scandal is focusing national attention on the role of corporate directors. One study found that directors who serve on interlocking boards — that is, directors of one company serve on the boards of other companies — have played a significant role in spreading the backdating strategy from one corporation to another.[42]

Another study focused on directors who themselves received favorably timed options. Harvard's Bebchuk and two research colleagues found that between 1996 and 2005 about 9 percent of 29,000 stock-option grants to outside directors at roughly 6,000 public companies were "lucky" — meaning the "grant events" fell on days when a stock price equaled a monthly low.[43]

Institutional Shareholder Services (ISS) warned that the option-timing controversy could have a negative impact on big pension funds and other institutional shareholders. "[I]nvestors can expect to experience significant stock losses as more companies disclose investigations into their option-grant practices and restate financial results," said the firm.

According to ISS, the stock price of UnitedHealth, for instance, dipped nearly 30 percent after disclosure of regulatory probes into the board's award of options to CEO William McGuire and other employees. In October McGuire was forced to resign and give up part of his $1.1 billion in options as a result of a massive revamping of the insurance company's governance.[44] UnitedHealth was plagued by "inadequate" internal controls related to its option-grant practices and other problems, concluded a law firm hired to investigate its stock-option practices.

"An appropriate tone at the top, adequate controls and discipline over the option-granting process and management transparency with the board and its committees on executive compensation matters are basic and critical to the integrity of option grants," concluded the report, which UnitedHealth posted on its Web site. "[T]here here were various failings in these areas."[45]

Courts, Regulators Alerted

It remains unclear how forcefully shareholders, federal criminal authorities and Congress ultimately will respond to the backdating scandal. Stockholders, for example,

Securities and Exchange Commission (SEC) Chairman Christopher Cox presides over a meeting on executive compensation on July 26, 2006. Beginning this spring the SEC will require companies to give investors an unprecedented, plain-English look at how much executives are paid. Even so, critics accused the SEC of retreating on the new disclosure rules under pressure from big business.

could sue companies alleged to have backdated options. In the Apple case, for example, a big New York pension system was lead plaintiff in a shareholder lawsuit accusing the company of illegal backdating.[46]

Pension funds "are completely beside themselves and outraged over the self-dealing that has gone on," said Darren Robbins, a partner in a law firm hired last year by several funds. The goal is "to recover the monies that were diverted from the corporate till."[47]

Iowa Professor Helps Uncover Backdating Scandal

New law helps to prevent the practice

Erik Lie, an associate professor at the University of Iowa's Tippie College of Business, wondered what happens to stock prices around the time that companies grant options to their executives.

After examining nearly 6,000 option grants made from 1992 through 2002, he found that "quite consistently" stock prices would drop "right before the grant date, and then [pick] up dramatically" — sometimes as much as 20 percent — right afterwards.[1] Lie concluded the only explanation for the phenomenon was that companies were backdating the option grants to a day when their stock price was at or near a low point, drastically increasing the potential for big profits on the options.

Lie's study — while not the first — helped shine a nationwide spotlight on questionable options practices occurring at scores of companies before U.S. securities laws were reformed by the Sarbanes-Oxley Act in 2002.[2]

Previously, companies had been allowed to notify the SEC about option grants weeks or more after the grants were actually made, allowing option dates to be manipulated. Sarbanes-Oxley narrowed the filing window to two business days — a change that allowed Lie and colleague Randall Heron, a business professor at Indiana University, to test their backdating theory in a second study.

Lie and Heron examined more than 3,700 option grants made after 2002 and found a much weaker stock-price pattern after the two-day reporting requirement became law. For options filed with the SEC within a day of the grant, the pattern disappeared completely, they found.[3]

Erik Lie helped shine a spotlight on questionable options practices at scores of U.S. companies.

"In theory, stock options can be used to motivate executives and other employees to create value for shareholders," Lie told a U.S. Senate committee last year. "However, they have also been used to conceal true compensation expenses, cheat on corporate taxes and siphon money away from shareholders to option recipients."[4] Lie says the way to eliminate backdating is to require companies to file grants electronically with the SEC on the same day the grants are given, as occurs in Lie's native Norway.

"They haven't had any problems" in Norway with backdating, Lie says. "There, if you get a grant one day, you have to file information with the authorities before the market opens the next day."

Lie says if he'd been an investor in companies that illegally backdated their stock options, "I would be pretty mad just to see these executives are taking my money, and I'm not aware of it," he says. "And as an investor I would want my business to be run in an ethical, socially responsible way."

---

[1] Erik Lie, "On the Timing of CEO Stock Option Awards," *Management Science 51*, May 2005. See www.biz.uiowa.edu/faculty/elie/backdating .htm for background on Lie's work.

[2] See David Yermack, "Good Timing: CEO Stock Option Awards and Company News Announcements," *Journal of Finance*, Vol. 50, No. 2, June 1997.

[3] Randall A. Heron and Erik Lie, "Does Backdating Explain the Stock Price Pattern Around Executive Stock Option Grants," *Journal of Financial Economics 83*, 2007.

[4] Lie, *op. cit.*

Is CEO pay in the United States out of control?

YES

Brandon J. Rees
Assistant Director,
Office of Investment, AFL-CIO

From testimony before Panel on Executive Compensation, House Financial Services Committee, May 25, 2006

CEOs are being paid too much relative to their individual contribution to their companies. No CEO is so talented that his or her compensation should be unlimited. Secondly, executive compensation is poorly disclosed to shareholders. Many forms of CEO pay such as pensions and perks are underreported, and CEO pay-for-performance targets are hidden from shareholders. Thirdly, today's executive compensation packages are creating improper incentives for executives. For example, stock options can create a strong incentive to manipulate company stock prices through creative and even fraudulent accounting.

By any measure, today's CEO pay levels are too high. A reasonable and fair compensation system for executives and workers is fundamental to the creation of long-term corporate value. However, the past two decades have seen an unprecedented growth in compensation only for top executives and a dramatic increase in the ratio between the compensation of executives and their employees....

Executive compensation abuse takes dollars out of the pockets of shareholders, including the retirement savings of America's working families. Union members participate in pension plans with over $5 trillion in assets. Union-sponsored pension plans hold approximately $400 billion in assets, and runaway executive pay has diminished returns for working families' pension funds....

More than any other executive compensation issue, shareholders are concerned about pay-for-performance. Year after year, shareholders learn of record CEO compensation packages that have little connection to executives' individual performance.... To public shareholders, the executive compensation system appears entirely subjective and subject to influence by corporate insiders.... Many CEOs have negotiated retirement benefits that promise a lifetime of income far exceeding what they would be entitled to under the retirement plans of their rank-and-file workers....

Executives have received these extraordinary retirement benefits at the same time workers are being asked to bear increased risk for their retirement security.... [I]ncreasingly, companies are terminating their employees' pension plans and transferring the risk of saving for retirement onto their employees. Many of these same companies have turned their executive-pension plans into CEO wealth-creation devices. As a result, many companies have a two-tier retirement system: one for the CEO and one for everybody else....

NO

Thomas J. Lehner
Director of Public Policy,
Business Roundtable

From testimony before Panel on Executive Compensation, House Financial Services Committee, May 25, 2006

There are over 15,000 publicly traded companies in the United States — and if one believed even a few of the stories written you would think all CEOs make tens, if not hundreds, of millions of dollars each and every year. This is not the case, and we believe this type of sensationalism is damaging to the debate, our corporations and our shareholders....

[M]any ... claim that CEO pay exceeds company performance. In fact, the data does not support this. Research using the Mercer 350 database shows that ... from 1995-2005, median total compensation for CEOs has increased 9.6 percent, while the market cap has increased 8.8 percent, and total shareholder return has increased 12.7 percent.... These numbers show a direct correlation between levels of pay, market increase and shareholder return....

We have identified two flaws that contribute to the erroneous figures that inflame this debate. First, many of the statistics cited are averages, not medians. [T]hese are misleading because of extreme instances of the pay scale [that skew] the average for all. The second involves how stock options are counted. When options are exercised, they often represent a decade worth of accumulated stock [but] in the current debate they are characterized as a single, annual amount of compensation.

Furthermore, when counting options we should use the amount when granted, and not the realized gains when exercised. We should also point out that some of the pension payments highlighted in the media represent 30 years or more of service to the company, and deferred compensation payments also represent amounts CEOs have earned over a lengthy period....

[L]egislative proposals ... calling for shareholder approval of compensation plans [are] unwise and ultimately unworkable. If we adopted a system where small groups of activist shareholders used the process to politicize corporate decision-making, the consequences could very well be destabilizing....

Despite the rhetoric from critics of the current system, we know of no instance where a board is willing to pay a CEO more than they are worth or more than the market price bears....

[W]e are sensitive to extreme cases about CEO compensation reported in the media, and we continue to develop and promote best practices for our members to follow.

Independent boards and shareholders will deal with extreme cases, and we should not ruin our free-market system because of a few rogues.

JetBlue CEO David Neeleman turned down a $75,000 bonus in 2006 after the firm had a bad year. He and the firm's next two top executives receive relatively low base salaries of $200,000. He has received no new stock options since the company went public.

Federal prosecutions also are a possibility, suggested Grassley, now the ranking minority member of the Finance Committee. "Outside the corporate suite, Americans don't get to pick and choose their dream stock price," he said. "The market dictates the price. If the tax laws are inadequate, I want to beef them up. . . . I expect the Justice Department to fully enforce the law."[48]

Lately, the federal government has been proceeding against alleged backdating violators. In February, the SEC announced a $6.3 million settlement with the CEO of a technology company and charged the former general counsel of another.

But some critics complain that enforcement actions have been moving too slowly. What's more, SEC commissioners reportedly have disagreed over penalties for those who backdated options, though SEC Chairman Christopher Cox said no such split exists.[49]

However the scandal eventually plays out, its ramifications are likely to be long-lasting. "It's over, it's not going to happen again, but it [reflects] concern over the stewardship of corporate officers and directors," says Elson of the Weinberg Center for Corporate Governance at the University of Delaware. "It's more fuel to the fire for reform."

New Laws?

The backdating scandal is expected to focus new attention on managerial and board leadership issues and could fuel reform efforts in Congress aimed at curbing pay and empowering shareholders to have more of a say in compensation decisions.

Rep. Frank's idea of letting shareholders have an advisory vote on the compensation of top executives is one potential approach. Frank said he hoped to get a bill passed by mid-year giving shareholders a bigger say on executive compensation and a vote on a provision allowing companies to recover compensation from executives in certain situations.[50]

But Frank's proposal is likely to continue to run into stiff resistance from business groups. "When you're comparing the corporate decision-making process and shareholder votes, it really is apples and oranges when you try to apply a democratic model," Lehner of the Business Roundtable said. In light of the SEC's new disclosure rules, he said, Congress should be careful about making more changes too quickly. "We need to give the SEC changes time to work."[51]

As Congress wrestles with legislation to raise the minimum wage, the Senate proposal to cap tax-deferred income in executive compensation plans is also hitting stiff winds. The provision would raise an estimated $806 million in revenue over 10 years that could be used to help offset the cost to small business stemming from a hike in the minimum wage. But groups such as the Securities Industry and Financial Markets Association have called it a "harmful revenue raiser" that has not been adequately evaluated.[52]

Fallout from the options scandal could also trigger renewed calls to leave Sarbanes-Oxley untouched. Before the scandal broke, several trade groups had proposed softening certain Sarbanes-Oxley provisions, claiming they unduly burden businesses, especially small ones.

But as *The Washington Post* editorialized earlier this year: "[S]ome business lobbyists are aiming to roll back Sarbanes-Oxley, and Treasury Secretary Henry M. Paulson Jr. has made comments that could signal the administration's sympathy for that agenda. The stench from Apple shows the danger of a return to the old system."[53]

Outside of Congress, some want to see companies hold more vibrant shareholder elections for board members by reimbursing shareholders, under certain circumstances, for the expense of putting up their own minority slate of directors.

As things stand right now, "if you put up your own slate, you pay out of your own pocket," says Elson. "One proposal is that if managers can pay to get their viewpoint across, then in certain limited circumstances shareholders should have access to the same" money.

OUTLOOK

Growing Pressure

Eye-popping compensation figures are not likely to end anytime soon, but compensation experts say the pendulum is beginning to swing back from the extremes of recent years.

Corporate boards are becoming more vigilant about their pay practices, according to several experts, hastened by the post-Enron focus on governance failures and the recent option-backdating scandal.

"Boards are more demanding, hiring their own compensation consultation," says Scott of Northwestern University. "Things are happening that are changing the situation very dramatically."

Compensation committees recognize "that they are obligated to ask harder questions, be more persistent about those questions and not accept half-baked answers," says Swinford of Pearl Meyer.

Much of the pressure on boards is coming from institutional shareholders, and that pressure is likely to grow.

In February the insurer Aflac voluntarily became the first big U.S. company to give shareholders a non-binding vote on pay. The company's board agreed that as of 2009 it will give shareholders an advisory vote on the compensation of the company's top five executives.[54] "Our shareholders, as owners of the company, have the right to know how executive compensation works," Aflac's chairman and CEO, Dan Amos, said in a statement. The board set 2009 as the effective date because that will be the first year that compensation tables in Aflac's proxy statement will contain three years of data reflecting the SEC's new disclosure rules.[55]

Shareholders in other companies are pushing to allow similar advisory votes. Timothy Smith, senior vice president at Walden Asset Management, one of the architects of the "say on pay" resolution presented to dozens of big companies this year, calls the quest for advisory votes "one of the top corporate governance issues in the proxy season this spring."

The institutional investors backing "say on pay" manage more than $1 trillion in assets, Smith says, and include the $235 billion California Public Employees' Retirement System, the nation's biggest public pension fund. "Suddenly you have a huge jump in the number of investors involved in this proactive effort, in the range of investors who have filed resolutions and in the number who have not filed yet but think it's a worthy idea," Smith says.

What's more, a dozen companies have said the resolution is a good idea but need time to study how to implement it, Smith says. "Our view is that in three years this will be a norm and that many companies will put this into effect."

NOTES

1. Eric Dash, "An Ousted Chief's Going-Away Pay Is Seen by Many as Typically Excessive," *The New York Times*, Jan. 4, 2007, p. C4.

2. Josh Fineman, "Nardelli Exit Package Called 'Outrage,' May Heighten Pay Debate," Bloomberg.com, Jan. 3, 2007.

3. Jay Bookman, "Nardelli Benefits Grossly from Appalling Standard," *Atlanta Journal-Constitution*, Jan. 4, 2007, p. 17A.

4. Gary Strauss and Barbara Hansen, "CEO pay soars in 2005 as a select group break the $100 million mark," *USA Today*, April 11, 2006, p. 1B.

5. *Los Angeles Times*/Bloomberg Poll on personal finances, investments, housing market, etc., Feb. 25-March 5, 2006.

6. Roy C. Smith, "Worth Every Last Million," *The Washington Post*, Jan. 21, 2007, p. B1.

7. "President Bush Delivers State of the Economy Report," www.whitehouse.gov.

8. Ellen Simon, "Pfizer's McKinnell to Get $180M Package," The Associated Press via *The Washington Post*, Dec. 21, 2006.

9. "Severance For Penney Executive," Bloomberg News, via the *New York Times*, Jan. 6, 2007, p. C2.

10. Lucian Bebchuk and Yaniv Grinstein, "The Growth of Executive Pay," *Oxford Review of Economic Policy*, Vol. 21, No. 2, 2005.

11. "Rep. Barney Frank Delivers Remarks at the National Press Club on Wages," Jan. 3, 2007, CQ Transcriptions, 2007.

12. Jim Pickard, "Pension funds to challenge Browne payout," *Financial Times*, Feb. 9, 2007, www.ft.com.

13. Xavier Gabaix and Augustin Landier, "Why Has CEO Pay Increased So Much?" July 21, 2006, http://ssrn.com/abstract=901826.

14. Tyler Cowen, "A Contrarian Look at Whether U.S. Chief Executives Are Overpaid," *The New York Times*, May 18, 2006, p. C4.

15. Gretchen Morgenson, "Is 'Total Pay' That Tough to Grasp?" *The New York Times*, July 9, 2006, p. C1.

16. *Ibid.*

17. *Ibid.* The study was produced by compensation consultant Frederic W. Cook using data supplied by Mercer Human Resource Consulting.

18. From interview with Carola Frydman; see also Carola Frydman and Raven E. Saks, "Historical Trends in Executive Compensation 1936-2003," working paper.

19. Lucian Bebchuk and Jesse Fried, *Pay Without Performance: The Unfulfilled Promise of Executive Compensation* (2004).

20. For background, see Kenneth Jost, "The Stock Market," *CQ Researcher*, May 2, 1997, pp. 385-408.

21. See, for example, John E. Core, Wayne R. Guay and Randall S. Thomas, "Is CEO Compensation Broken?" *Journal of Applied Corporate Finance*, *Vol. 17*, No. 4, Fall 2005.

22. Lori Montgomery and Jeffrey H. Birnbaum, "Senate Panel Limits Pay Deferrals for Executives," *The Washington Post*, Jan. 18, 2007, p. D1; and Montgomery, "House Advances Minimum Wage Hike," *The Washington Post*, Feb. 17, 2007, p. D1.

23. Montgomery and Birnbaum, *op. cit.*

24. Rep. Barney Frank, remarks to National Press Club, *op. cit.*

25. Michael R. Crittenden, "Frank Pushes Measure Aimed at Letting Shareholders Comment on Executive Pay," *CQ Today*, March 1, 2007.

26. *Ibid.*

27. Thomas J. Lehner, "Written Testimony and Comments for the Record," House Financial Services Committee, May 25, 2006.

28. "George T. Milkovich and Jennifer Stevens, "Back to the Future: A Century of Compensation," Center for Advanced Human Resource Studies, Cornell University, *Working Paper 9 9-08*, July 1999.

29. "Executive Pay Up, Up, and Away," *Business Week*, April 19, 1999, p. 72.

30. "Judge won't block Nardelli's huge severance," Reuters via money.cnn.com, Jan. 22, 2007.

31. Michael Barbaro, "Home Depot Gets a Fresh Coat of Less-Glossy Paint," *The New York Times*, Feb. 8, 2007, p. C1.

32. Bebchuk and Fried, *op. cit.*

33. *Ibid.*

34. Opinion and order, *In Re The Walt Disney Company Derivative Litigation*, Delaware Court of Chancery, Consolidated C.A. No. 15452, Aug. 9, 2005.

35. See www.aflcio.org/corporatewatch/paywatch/.

36. For background, see Kenneth Jost, "Corporate Crime," *CQ Researcher*, Oct. 11, 2002, pp. 817-840.

37. Democratic staff of the House Committee on Financial Services, "Executive Compensation vs. Workers: An Overview of Wages, Pensions and Health Benefits of Rank-and-File Workers and Sky-High Executive Pay," Oct. 24, 2006.

38. See Charles Forelle and James Bandler, "The Perfect Payday," *The Wall Street Journal*, March 18, 2006.

39. Testimony before Senate Committee on Banking, Housing, and Urban Affairs, Sept. 6, 2006.

40. "Grassley Takes Aim at Stock Options Backdating, Executive Compensation Tax Loophole," news release, office of Sen. Grassley, Sept. 6, 2006.

41. Ted Allen, Subodh Mishra, *et al.*, "An Investor Guide to the Stock Option Timing Scandal," Institutional Shareholder Services, 2006.

42. John M. Bizjak, Michael L. Lemmon and Ryan J. Whitby, "Option Backdating and Board Interlocks," http://papers.ssrn.com/sol3/papers.cfm?abstract-id=946787, November 2006. See also Mark Hulbert, "Why Backdated Options Might Be Contagious," *The New York Times*, Jan. 21, 2007, p. C5.

43. Lucian Arye Bebchuk, Yaniv Grinstein and Urs Peyer, "Lucky Directors," *Harvard Law and Economics Discussion Paper No. 573*, December 2006, revised January 2007.

44. Eric Dash and Milt Freudenheim, "Chief Executive at Health Insurer Is Forced Out in Options Inquiry," *The New York Times*, Oct. 16, 2006, p. A1.

45. "Report of Wilmer Cutler Pickering Hale and Dorr LLP to the Special Committee of the Board of

Directors of UnitedHealth Group, Inc.," October 2006.

46. The Associated Press, "N.Y. Pension Fund To Lead Lawsuit Over Apple Options," *The Washington Post*, Jan. 24, 2007, p. D2.

47. Scott Duke Harris, "Pension Funds Sign Up Tech Firms' Legal Nemesis," *Mercury News*, SiliconValley.com, June 14, 2006.

48. *Ibid.*

49. Karen Donovan, "The Slow Pace of Justice On Options Backdating," *The New York Times*, Feb. 23, 2007, p. C2.

50. "U.S. House Panel Sets March 8 Hearing on CEO Pay," Reuters, Feb. 14, 2007.

51. Crittenden, *op. cit.*

52. Caitlin Webber, "HR2," *CQ Bill Analysis*, Jan. 5, 2007.

53. "One Bad Apple," editorial, *The Washington Post*, Jan. 5, 2007, p. A16.

54. Del Jones, "Aflac Will Let Shareholders Vote on Pay for Top Executives," *USA Today*, Feb. 14, 2007, p. 1A.

55. *Ibid.*

BIBLIOGRAPHY

Books

Bebchuk, Lucian, and Jesse Fried, *Pay without Performance: The Unfulfilled Promise of Executive Compensation*, Harvard University Press, 2004.
Law Professors Bebchuk of Harvard and Fried of the University of California, Berkeley, argue in this influential book that managers exert inappropriate influence over their own compensation.

Crystal, Graef, *In Search of Excess: The Overcompensation of American Executives*, Norton, 1991.
Compensation consultant Crystal's influential book landed him on TV's "60 Minutes" as the iconoclastic scourge of overpaid executives. His analysis is colorful as well as technical.

Khurana, Rakesh, *Searching For a Corporate Savior*, Princeton, 2004.
A Harvard Business School professor explores how corporations hire their chief executives and concludes that the market for CEOs is not as rational as it might appear.

MacAvoy, Paul W., and Ira Millstein, *The Recurrent Crisis in Corporate Governance*, Stanford University Press, 2004.
Yale management scholars examine the problems afflicting American corporations and suggest ways to improve board performance.

Articles

"In the Money: A Special Report on Executive Pay," *The Economist*, Jan. 20, 2007, p. 18.
On the whole, the public agrees with activists seeking a general overhaul of corporate governance when it comes to executive compensation.

Barbaro, Michael, "Home Depot Gets a Fresh Coat of Less-Glossy Paint," *The New York Times*, Feb. 8, 2007, p. C1.
As Home Depot's new CEO, Frank Blake is trying to distance himself from the tumultuous reign of his predecessor, Robert Nardelli.

Dash, Eric, "An Ousted Chief's Going-Away Pay Is Seen by Many as Typically Excessive," *The New York Times*, Jan. 4, 2007, p. C4.
Former Home Depot CEO Robert Nardelli's rich compensation and poor performance have long been cited by shareholder activists as a prime example of excessive executive pay.

Jones, Del, "Aflac Will Let Shareholders Vote on Pay for Top Executives," *USA Today*, Feb. 14, 2007, p. 1A.
Responding to the uproar against soaring executive compensation, Aflac plans to become the first major U.S. company to let shareholders vote on CEO pay packages.

Reports and Studies

"Enablers of Excess: Mutual Funds & the Overpaid American CEO," *American Federation of State, County and Municipal Employees, AFL-CIO and The Corporate Library*, March 2006.
The report concludes: "With a few exceptions, the largest mutual-fund families are complicit in runaway

executive compensation because they have not used their voting power in ways that would constrain pay by tying it more closely to individual company performance."

"Interim Report of the Committee on Capital Markets Regulation," 2006.
An independent, bipartisan group of 22 leaders in business, law, academe and the investor community highlights six areas of concern about the competitiveness of U.S. capital markets and offers recommendations on how to improve it.

"An Investor Guide to the Stock Option Timing Scandal," *Institutional Shareholder Services*, **2006.**
A firm that advises investors on corporate-governance issues explores the controversy surrounding the timing of stock-option grants.

"Present Law and Background Relating to Executive Compensation," *Joint Committee on Taxation*, **Sept. 5, 2006.**
This report, related to a September 2006 hearing before the Senate Committee on Finance, lays out with some degree of legal and regulatory complexity the major issues surrounding executive pay.

"2005-2006 Worldwide Total Remuneration," *Towers Perrin*.
This study by the human-resources management consultant focuses on compensation and benefit practices in 26 countries.

Haines, Thomas M., "Reading Proxy Statements: A Guide to the New SEC Disclosure Rules for Executive and Director Compensation," *Worldat Work*, **2007.**
A compensation consultant explains the amended disclosure rules that require companies to provide investors with a fuller picture of compensation than in the past.

Milkovich, George, and Jennifer Stevens, "Back to the Future: A Century of Compensation," *Center for Advanced Human Resource Studies, Cornell University, Working Paper 99-08*, **1999.**
The authors review 100 years of compensation history and offer lessons for shaping compensation strategies in the future.

For More Information

AFL-CIO, 815 16th St., N.W., Washington, DC 20006; (202) 637-5000; www.aflcio.org. Labor organization that maintains the Executive PayWatch Web site, at www.aflcio.org/corporatewatch/paywatch/index.cfm.

American Federation of State, County and Municipal Employees, 1625 L St., N.W., Washington, DC 20036; (202) 429-1000; www.afscme.org. Union that advocates on pension and shareholder issues.

Business Roundtable, 1717 Rhode Island Ave., N.W., Suite 800, Washington, DC 20036; (202) 872-1260; www.businessroundtable.org. Association of CEOs of major corporations.

Committee on Capital Markets Regulation, 1557 Massachusetts Ave., LILC 339, Cambridge, Mass., 02138; (617) 384-5364; www.capmktsreg.org. Bipartisan group that researches regulation of capital markets and shareholder rights.

The Corporate Library, 45 Exchange St., Suite 201, Portland, ME 04101; (877) 479-7500; www.thecorporatelibrary.com. Information source on corporate governance and executive and director compensation.

Institutional Shareholder Services, 2099 Gaither Road, Suite 501, Rockville, MD 20850-4045; (301) 556-0500; www.issproxy.com. Proxy and corporate-governance adviser.

Towers Perrin, One Stamford Plaza, 263 Tresser Blvd., Stamford, CT 06901; (203) 326-5400; www.towersperrin.com. Human-resources management consultant that tracks global executive pay.

Walden Asset Management, One Beacon St., Boston, MA 02108; (617) 726-7250; www.waldenassetmgmt.com. Advocates giving institutional shareholders an advisory vote on executive pay.

WorldatWork, 14040 N. Northsight Blvd., Scottsdale, AZ 85260; (480) 483-8352; www.worldatwork.org. Association for human-resource specialists.

3

Gender Pay Gap

Are Women Paid Fairly in the Workplace?

Thomas J. Billitteri

A suit filed by Betty Dukes, right, and other female Wal-Mart employees accuses the retail giant of sex discrimination in pay, promotions and job assignments in violation of the Civil Rights Act of 1964. The case, covering perhaps 1.6 million current and former Wal-Mart employees, is the biggest class-action lawsuit against a private employer in U.S. history.

AP Photo/Noah Berger

From *CQ Researcher*, March 14, 2008.

An insult to my dignity" is the way Lilly Ledbetter described it.[1] For 19 years, she worked at the Goodyear Tire plant in Gadsden, Ala., one of a handful of women among the roughly 80 people who held the same supervisory position she did. Over the years, unbeknownst to her, the company's pay-raise decisions created a growing gap between her wages and those of her male colleagues. When she left Goodyear, she was earning $3,727 a month. The lowest-paid man doing the same work got $4,286. The highest-paid male made 40 percent more than she did.[2]

Ledbetter sued in 1998, and a jury awarded her back pay and more than $3 million in damages. But in the end, she lost her case in the U.S. Supreme Court.[3]

A conservative majority led by Justice Samuel A. Alito Jr. ruled that under the nation's main anti-discrimination law she should have filed a formal complaint with the federal government within 180 days of the first time Goodyear discriminated against her in pay. Never mind, the court said, that Ledbetter didn't learn about the pay disparity for years.

"The Supreme Court said that this didn't count as illegal discrimination," she said after the ruling, "but it sure feels like discrimination when you are on the receiving end of that smaller paycheck and trying to support your family with less money than the men are getting for doing the same job."[4]

The *Ledbetter* decision has added fuel to a long-burning debate over sex discrimination in women's wages and whether new laws are needed to narrow the disparity in men's and women's pay.

Women Closing the Pay Gap . . . Slowly

More than 40 years after women began demanding equal rights and opportunities, they still earn 77 percent of what men earn. The pay gap has been closing, however, because women's earnings have been rising faster than men's.

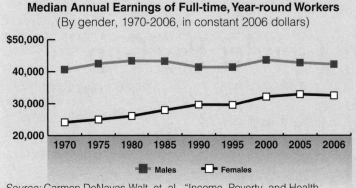

Median Annual Earnings of Full-time, Year-round Workers
(By gender, 1970-2006, in constant 2006 dollars)

Source: Carmen DeNavas-Walt, et. al., "Income, Poverty, and Health Insurance Coverage in the United States: 2006," U.S. Census Bureau, August 2007

wage gap exists between men and women. In 2006 full-time female workers earned 81 percent of men's weekly earnings, according to the latest U.S. Labor Department data, with the wage gap broader for older workers and narrower for younger ones. Separate U.S. Census Bureau data put the gap at about 77 percent of men's median full-time, year-round earnings.[6]

The fundamental issues are why the gap exists, how much of it stems from discrimination and what should be done about it.

Some contend the disparity can largely be explained by occupational differences between women and men, variations in work experience, number of hours worked each year and other such things.

June O'Neill, an economics professor at the City University of New York's Baruch College and former director of the Congressional Budget Office in the Clinton administration, says that the most important factors affecting the pay gap stem from differences in the roles of women and men in family life. When the wages of men and women who share similar work experience and life situations are measured, the wage gap largely disappears, she says. Reasons that the earnings disparity may appear bigger in some research, she says, include the fact that many studies do not control for differences in years of work experience, the extent of part-time work and differences in training and occupational choices. O'Neill notes that Labor Department data show median weekly earnings of female part-time workers exceed those of male part-timers. She also says the wage gap has been narrowing over time as women's work experience, education and other job-related skills have been converging with those of men.

"Large amounts of discrimination? No," she says. "Individual women may experience discrimination, and it's good to have laws that deal with it," she adds. "But those cases don't change the overall picture. The vast majority of employers don't harbor prejudice against women."

"A significant wage gap is still with us, and that gap constitutes nothing less than an ongoing assault on women's economic freedom," declared U.S. Rep. Rosa L. DeLauro, D-Conn., at a congressional hearing on a pay-equity bill she is sponsoring, one of several proposed on Capitol Hill.

But that view is hardly universal. "Men and women generally have equal pay for equal work now — if they have the same jobs, responsibilities and skills," testified Diana Furchtgott-Roth, a senior fellow at the Hudson Institute, a conservative think tank, and former chief economist at the Labor Department in the George W. Bush administration.[5]

The wrangle over wages is playing out not just in Washington but in cities and towns across America. In the biggest sex-discrimination lawsuit in U.S. history, a group of female Wal-Mart employees has charged the retail giant with bias in pay and promotions. The case could affect perhaps 1.6 million women employees of Wal-Mart and result in billions of dollars in back pay and damages. (*See sidebar, p. 60.*)

The enormously complex gender-pay debate encompasses economics, demographics, law, social justice, culture, history and sometimes raw emotion. Few dispute that a

Yet others argue that beneath such factors as occupation and number of hours worked lies evidence of significant discrimination — covert if not overt.

"Women do not realize the enormous price that they pay for gender wage discrimination because they do not see big bites taken out of their paychecks at any one time," Evelyn F. Murphy, president of The Wage Project, a nonprofit organization that works on eliminating the gender wage gap and author of *Getting Even: Why Women Don't Get Paid Like Men and What To Do About It*, told a congressional panel last year.[7]

In her book, she told the hearing, she wrote of employers "who had to pay women employees or former employees to settle claims of gender discrimination, or judges and juries ordered them to pay up. The behavior of these employers vividly [illustrates] the commonplace forms of today's wage discrimination: barriers to hiring and promoting qualified women; arbitrary financial penalties imposed on pregnant women; sexual harassment by bosses and co-workers; failure to pay women and men the same amount of money for doing the same jobs," and "everyday discrimination" marked by "the biases and stereotypes which influence [managers'] decisions about women."

Women's advocates point to a 2003 General Accounting Office (GAO) study concluding that while "work patterns" were key in accounting for the wage gap, the GAO could not explain all the differences in earnings between men and women. "When we account for differences between male and female work patterns as well as other key factors, women earned, on average, 80 percent of what men earned in 2000.... We cannot determine whether this remaining difference is due to discrimination or other factors," the GAO report said.[8]

The study said that in the view of certain experts some women trade promotions or higher pay for job flexibility that allows them to balance work and family responsibilities.

Women's advocates point out that many women have little choice but to work in jobs that offer flexibility but pay less because they typically shoulder the bulk of family caregiving duties. And, they argue further, expectations within companies and society — typically subtle, but sometimes not — often channel women away from male-dominated jobs into female-dominated ones that pay less.

Gap Widens for College Graduates

College-educated women earn only 80 percent of what their male counterparts earn a year after graduation, when both male and female employees have the same level of work experience and (usually) no child-care obligations — factors often used to explain gender pay differences. The gap widens to 69 percent by 10 years after graduation.

Gap in Average Weekly Earnings for Bachelor's Degree Recipients
(For full-time workers)

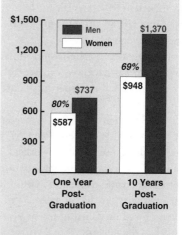

Source: "Beyond the Pay Gap," American Association of University Women, based on data from the "2003 Baccalaureate and Beyond Longitudinal Study," National Center for Education Statistics, U.S. Department of Education

"People who argue that [wage discrimination] is small will say a lot of it is due to women's choices," such as the choice to stay home with the children, work part time or enter lower-paying fields, says Reeve Vanneman, a sociology professor at the University of Maryland, College Park, who studies gender inequality. But, he says, it's misleading to explain most of the wage gap in that way, especially when mid-career and older female workers are concerned.

"Why do women make those choices? Part of the reason is because they are discriminated against in the job. They see men getting rewarded more and promoted more than they are."

Women face unequal work not just on the job but at home, too, Vanneman says, with husbands not picking up their share.

Part of the wage gap stems from weak government enforcement, some argue. A U.S. inspector general's report stated last fall that the Equal Employment Opportunity Commission, which enforces federal employment-discrimination laws, is "challenged in accomplishing its mission" because of "a reduced workforce and an increasing backlog of pending cases." The agency has experienced a "significant loss of its workforce, mostly to attrition and buyouts...offered to free up resources," the report said.[9]

The news on gender discrimination in pay is not all bad. The wage gap has narrowed considerably in recent decades. For example, Labor Department data show that for 35- to 44-year-olds, the earnings ratio of women to men rose from 58 percent in 1979 to 77 percent in 2006. For 45- to 54-year-olds, it went from 57 percent to 74 percent.[10] Among the youngest workers, ages 16 to 24, only about 5 percentage points separated median weekly wages of men and women in 2006.[11]

Still, many experts say the progress of the 1980s and early '90s has slowed or stalled in recent years, with the wage gap stuck in the range of 20 to 24 percent, although it is not entirely clear why. Some argue that entrenched wage discrimination remains a major culprit.

In a study of college graduates last year, the American Association of University Women Educational Foundation found that one year out of college, women working full time earn only 80 percent as much as their male colleagues, and 10 years after graduation the gap widens to 69 percent. Even after controlling for hours worked, training and education and other factors, the portion of the pay gap that remains unexplained is 5 percent one year after graduation and 12 percent a decade afterward, the study found.[12] (See graph, p. 51.)

"These unexplained gaps are evidence of discrimination," the study concluded.

Employer advocates challenge such conclusions, though. Michael Eastman, executive director of labor policy at the U.S. Chamber of Commerce, questions the assumption "that whatever gap is not explained must be due to discrimination. An unexplained gap is simply that — it's unexplained."

Election-year politics and the recent shift toward Democratic control of Congress — along with the Supreme Court's decision in the *Ledbetter* case — have helped to reinvigorate the pay debate. Proposed gender-pay bills have strong support from women's-rights groups and some economists, who argue that the Equal Pay Act and Title VII of the Civil Rights Act of 1964 — the main avenues for attacking wage discrimination — fall short.

Presidential contender Sen. Hillary Rodham Clinton, D-N.Y., is sponsoring the Senate version of the DeLauro bill; another presidential hopeful, Sen. Barack Obama, D-Ill., is one of the 22 co-sponsors, although he didn't sign on to it until more than a month after she introduced it. Among other things, the measure would raise penalties under the Equal Pay Act, which bars paying men and women differently for doing the same job.[13]

Obama is co-sponsoring a more controversial bill, introduced in the Senate by Sen. Tom Harkin, D-Iowa, that advocates the notion of comparable worth; the idea, generally speaking, suggests that a female-dominated occupation such as social work may merit wages that are comparable to those of a male-dominated job such as a probation officer.[14] The Harkin measure would bar wage discrimination in certain cases where the work is deemed comparable in skill, effort, responsibility and working conditions, even if the job titles or duties are different. (See sidebar, p. 58.)

A third effort would undo the Supreme Court's ruling in the *Ledbetter* case.[15] A bill passed the House last summer, and advocates are hoping the Senate version — sponsored by Sen. Edward M. Kennedy, D-Mass., and co-sponsored by Clinton and Obama — moves forward soon. But the Bush administration has threatened a veto, and business interests are vehemently opposed.

As the debate over wage disparities continues, these are some of the questions being discussed:

Is discrimination a major cause of the wage gap?

When economist David Neumark studied sex discrimination in restaurant hiring in the mid-1990s, he discovered something intriguing: In expensive restaurants, where waiters and waitresses can earn more than they can at low-price places, the chances of a woman getting a wait-staff job offer were 40 percentage points lower than those of a man with similar experience.[16]

The study is a telling bit of evidence that the wage gap is real and that discrimination plays a significant part in it, says Vicky Lovell, director of employment and work/life programs at the Institute for Women's Policy Research, an advocacy group in Washington. She estimates that perhaps a third of the wage gap stems from discrimination — mostly "covert" bias that occurs when people make false assumptions about the ability or career commitment of working women.

Lovell has little patience with those who say the wage gap stems from non-discriminatory reasons that simply haven't yet been identified. "That's just specious," she says. "If we can't explain why women on average get paid less, what is the alternative explanation?"

The role of discrimination lies at the heart of the pay-gap debate. Researchers fall into different camps.

Some see little evidence that bias plays a big part in the gap. When adjusted for work experience, education, time in the labor force and other variables, wages of men and women are largely comparable, they contend.

"This so-called wage gap is not necessarily due to discrimination," the Hudson Institute's Furchtgott-Roth said in congressional testimony. "Decisions about field of study, occupation and time in the work force can lead to lower compensation, both for men and women."[17]

What's more, "some jobs command more than others because people are willing to pay more for them,"

Pay Gap Exists Despite Women's Choices

Those who discount the seriousness of gender pay bias often blame differences in men's and women's salaries on women's choices to study "softer" sciences or to have children. But a recent study shows that the pay gap persists even when women choose not to have children and when they choose male-dominated fields of study and occupation — such as business, engineering, mathematics and medicine. The pay gap is greatest in the biology, health and mathematics fields. Women out-earn men only in the history professions.

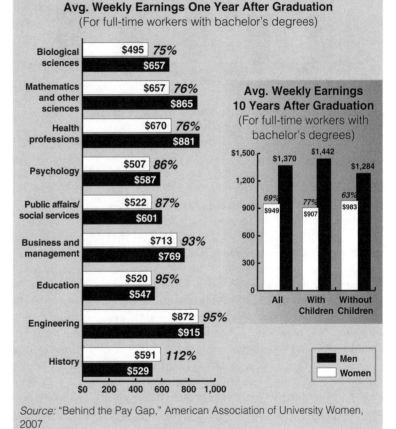

Avg. Weekly Earnings One Year After Graduation
(For full-time workers with bachelor's degrees)

Avg. Weekly Earnings 10 Years After Graduation
(For full-time workers with bachelor's degrees)

Source: "Behind the Pay Gap," American Association of University Women, 2007

she said. "Many jobs are dirty and dangerous.... Other highly paid occupations have long, inflexible hours.... Women are not excluded from these or other jobs but often select professions with a more pleasant environment and potentially more flexible schedules, such as teaching and office work. Many of these jobs pay less."

Wage Disparities Highest Among Asians

The median weekly earnings for women are lower than men's across all ethnic groups. The largest disparity is among Asians, where men earn $183 more on average per week than their female counterparts. The average difference for all groups is $143.

Median Weekly Earnings of Full-Time Workers
(by gender and ethnicity, 2006)

Source: "Highlights of Women's Earnings in 2006," Bureau of Labor Statistics, September 2007

■ Men □ Women

Warren Farrell, who in the 1970s served on the board of the New York City chapter of the National Organization for Women, argues in his 2005 book — *Why Men Earn More: The Startling Truth Behind the Pay Gap — and What Women Can Do About It* — that women pay an economic price by seeking careers that are more fulfilling, flexible and safe. With a stated goal of helping women gain higher pay, Farrell offers 25 "differences in the way women and men behave in the workplace." Those who earn more, he says, work longer hours, are more willing to relocate, require less security and produce more, among other things.

O'Neill, of Baruch College, points out that women are much more likely to go into occupations that will allow them to work part time, and typically "that doesn't pay as well."

She studies data that track the work histories of women and men over a long period of time. "Women have just not worked as many weeks and hours over their lives as men," she says. "When you adjust for that, you explain most of the [pay] difference.... You're still left with a difference, but then there are other things that become harder to measure."

The AAUW study found that even women who make the same choices as men in terms of fields of study and occupation earn less than their male counterparts. A typical college-educated woman working full time earns $46,000 a year compared to $62,000 for college-educated male workers — a difference of $16,000.

"The pay gap between female and male college graduates cannot be fully accounted for by factors known to affect wages, such as experience (including work hours), training, education and personal characteristics," the AAUW study says. "In this analysis the portion of the pay gap that remains unexplained after all other factors are taken into account is 5 percent one year after graduation and 12 percent 10 years after graduation. These unexplained gaps are evidence of discrimination, which remains a serious problem for women in the work force."[18]

"This research asked a basic but important question: If a woman made the same choices as a man, would she earn the same pay? The answer is no," Catherine Hill, director of research at the AAUW, told a House Committee on Education and Labor hearing last year.

Speaking more generally about pay inequity, Linda Meric, national director of 9to5, National Association of Working Women, a Milwaukee-based advocacy group, says that "when you control for all the other so-called factors" that might explain the wage gap, "there is still a gap."

"And many of those so-called factors are not independent of discrimination and stereotypes of women. One is time in the work force. If there aren't policies that allow women to get jobs and maintain and advance in employment at the same time they are meeting their responsibility in terms of family caregiving, that's not an independent factor. It's something that influences the pay gap significantly."

Heather Boushey, senior economist at the Center for Economic and Policy Research, a Washington think tank, noted that time away from the workforce strongly affects lifetime earnings. She said it is a myth that women choose lower-paying occupations because they provide the flexibility to better manage work and family. "The empirical evidence shows that mothers are actually less likely to be employed in jobs that provide them with greater flexibility."[19]

Echoing that sentiment, Beth Shulman, co-director of the Fairness Initiative on Low Wage Work, a public policy advocacy group also in Washington, says, "We have kind of an Ozzie and Harriet workplace, with a full-time worker and the wife at home," but "70 percent of women with children are in the workplace." She adds, "Our structures haven't kept up with that. So women who are primary caregivers get punished."

Schulman, author of *The Betrayal of Work: How Low-Wage Jobs Fail 30 Million Americans*, says that while overt gender discrimination exists in the job market, an equally important contributor to the wage gap is the lack of flexibility for low-income working women with families. For example, she says, female factory employees with family responsibilities often find it difficult to accept better-paying manufacturing jobs because such jobs often require mandatory overtime.

Shulman also says that three-fourths of women in low-wage jobs don't have paid sick days. So when a child is sick or an elderly parent needs help, women may be forced to leave the workforce and then re-enter it — something that has a huge effect on wages over time.

"Low-wage workers get kind of ghettoized into these part-time jobs that have poor wages, poor benefits and less government protection," Shulman says.

In a 1998 study, Cornell University economists Francine Blau and Lawrence Kahn found that 40 percent of the pay gap is unexplained after adjusting for gender differences in experience, education, occupation and industry. Blau cautions that such an estimate is conservative, because variables such as women's choices of occupation or industry and even their education and work experience can themselves be affected by discrimination. On the other hand, she acknowledges that some of the unexplained differences may be due to unmeasured productivity characteristics that increase men's earnings relative to women's earnings.

Applying that 40 percent figure to current government wage-gap data would suggest that 8 to 9 cents of each dollar in wage disparity is unexplained, with an unknown portion of that amount caused by discrimination.

Martha Burk, who directs the Corporate Accountability Project for the National Council of Women's

AP Photo/Ron Edmonds

U.S. Rep. Rosa L. DeLauro, D-Conn., is sponsoring one of several pay-equity bills in Congress. Presidential contender Sen. Hillary Rodham Clinton, D-N.Y., is sponsoring the Senate version of DeLauro's bill; Sen. Barack Obama, D-Ill., is one of the 22 co-sponsors. "A significant wage gap is still with us, and that gap constitutes nothing less than an ongoing assault on women's economic freedom," DeLauro says.

Organizations, a coalition of more than 200 women's groups, says some of the pay gap stems from "historical discrimination" rooted in a time when employers could legally exclude women from certain jobs and pay them less for the kinds of jobs they typically did hold, such as teaching and clerical work.

Burk, who led the fight to open the Augusta (Ga.) National Golf Club to women, says those female-dominated jobs "were systematically devalued, and that has carried through to modern times."

Are new laws needed to close the gender pay gap?

When President John F. Kennedy signed the Equal Pay Act in 1963, he called it "a first step."[20]

Over the decades, the pay gap has narrowed significantly, but the push for new laws to curb gender-pay inequity goes on, fueled in part by the view among women's advocates that progress toward wage equity has slowed or stalled in recent years.

"The best way is for corporations to behave as socially responsible corporate citizens [and] examine their wage practices," says Lovell of Women's Policy Research. "But that is not going to happen. I don't see any reason to think the private sector is going to address this issue on its own. A few will to the extent they can within their own workforces. But if corporations individually or within industry groups aren't going to make this a priority, then that's why we have a government."

Opponents of new laws have sharply different views, though.

Roger Clegg, president and general counsel of the Center for Equal Opportunity, a conservative think tank in Falls Church, Va., says some gender discrimination will always exist but that existing laws can address it. Besides, Clegg says, the amount of gender discrimination that remains in the American work force "is greatly exaggerated by the groups pushing for legislation."

Much of the support for new laws rests on the view that some jobs pay poorly because females historically have dominated them. Jocelyn Samuels, vice president for Education and Employment at the National Women's Law Center, a Washington advocacy group, told a congressional hearing last year that 95 percent of child-care workers are female while the same proportion of mechanical engineers are male.

Moreover, she said, wages in fields dominated by women "have traditionally been depressed and continue to reflect the artificially suppressed pay scales that were historically applied to so-called 'women's work.' " Maids and housecleaners — 87 percent of whom are women — make roughly $3,000 per year less than janitors and building cleaners, 72 percent of whom are men, she said. "Current law simply does not provide the tools to address this continuing devaluation of traditionally female fields."[21]

To attack that situation, some advocates back the comparable-worth theory, arguing that women should be paid commensurate with men for jobs of equivalent value to a company, even if the work is different. But critics argue that such an approach violates the free-market principles of supply and demand for labor and

that it could hurt both the economy and the cause of women.

"The comparable-worth approach has the government setting wages rather than the free market, and a great lesson of the 20th century is that centrally planned economies and centrally planned wage and price systems do not work," Clegg says.

Carrie Lukas, vice president for policy and economics at the Independent Women's Forum, a conservative group in Washington that backs limited government, contends that "government attempts to 'solve' the problem of the wage gap may in fact exacerbate some of the challenges women face, particularly in balancing work and family."

In an opinion column last year, she criticized the Clinton/DeLauro bill, which calls for guidelines to help companies voluntarily "compare wages paid for different jobs...with the goal of eliminating unfair pay disparities between occupations traditionally dominated by men or women." Lukas wrote that the bill would "give Washington bureaucrats more power to oversee how wages are determined, which might prompt businesses to make employment options more rigid." Flexible job structures would become less common, she argued. Why, Lukas wondered, "would companies offer employees a variety of work situations and compensation packages if doing so puts them at risk of being sued?"[22]

Not only might women suffer from new laws, but so would employers, some argue. Washington lawyer Barbara Berish Brown, vice-chair of the American Bar Association's Labor and Employment Law Section, said in a hearing on the Clinton/DeLauro bill that she is "unequivocally committed" to erasing gender-pay bias, but that existing laws suffice.

"All that the proposed changes will do is encourage more employment-related litigation, which is already drowning the federal court docket, and make it much more difficult, if not impossible, for employers, particularly small businesses, to prove the legitimate, nondiscriminatory reasons that explain differences between the salaries of male and female employees," she said.[23]

But longtime activists such as Burk, author of *Cult of Power: Sex Discrimination in Corporate America and What Can Be Done About It*, say existing laws are not effective enough to stamp out wage bias. "It has always been the view of conservatives that if you pay women equally, it's going to destroy capitalism," she says. "So far capitalism has survived quite well."

Is equity possible after the Supreme Court's Ledbetter ruling?

After the Supreme Court ruled in the Goodyear pay-discrimination case, Eleanor Smeal, president of the Feminist Majority, urged congressional action to reverse the decision. "We cannot stand by and watch a Bush-stacked court destroy in less than a year Title VII — the bedrock of women's rights and civil rights protection in wage-discrimination cases," she said.[24]

Yet, such outrage at the Supreme Court is matched by praise from business advocates. "We think the court got it exactly right," says Eastman, the U.S. Chamber of Commerce labor policy official.

In the 5-4 ruling, the court said workers can't sue under Title VII of the Civil Rights Act, the main federal anti-discrimination law, unless they file a formal complaint with the EEOC within 180 days of a discriminatory act. And in Ledbetter's case, the clock didn't start each time a new paycheck was issued. The 180-day timeline applies whether or not the employee immediately spots the discrimination.

Critics argue that because pay decisions are seldom broadcast throughout a company, the ruling makes it difficult — if not impossible — for an employee to detect bias until it may have gone on for years. "The ruling essentially says 'tough luck' to employees who don't immediately challenge their employer's discriminatory acts, even if the discrimination continues to the present time," said Marcia Greenberg, co-president of the National Women's Law Center.[25]

"With this misguided decision, the court ignores the realities of the 21st-century workplace," Margot Dorfman, chief executive officer of the U.S. Women's Chamber of Commerce, told a congressional panel this year. "The confidential nature of employee salary information complicates workers' abilities to recognize and report discriminatory treatment."[26]

Lovell, of the Institute for Women's Policy Research, says the Ledbetter ruling "seems to reflect a complete lack of understanding of the labor market and a complete lack of concern for individuals who are at any kind of disadvantage in the labor market." Workers wouldn't necessarily know right away that they were being

discriminated against, she says. When Congress passed Title VII, it "was trying to establish an avenue for people who are discriminated against to pursue their claims…, not trying to make it impossible."

In a strongly worded dissent to the Ledbetter ruling, Justice Ruth Bader Ginsburg noted that pay disparities often occur in small increments, evidence of bias may develop over time, and wage information is typically hidden from employees. At the end of her dissent she wrote that "the ball is in Congress' court" to correct the Supreme Court's "parsimonious reading of Title VII" in the Ledbetter decision, just as Congress dealt with a spate of earlier Supreme Court decisions with passage of the 1991 Civil Rights Act.

Business groups have stood firm in the face of such impassioned views, though.

An exchange between Eastman of the U.S. Chamber of Commerce and law professor Deborah Brake last fall on the National Public Radio show "Justice Talking" helped underscore how polarizing the Ledbetter decision has been between advocates for women and for employers.[27]

Brake, a professor at the University of Pittsburgh School of Law who once litigated sex-discrimination cases for the National Women's Law Center, said she thought it was questionable whether the ruling was even good for employers.

"What an employee is supposed to do, let's say from the moment in time that they are hired, is search around the workplace and make sure that they're not being paid less if it's a woman than her male colleagues," she said on the radio program.

"If she has the slightest inkling or suspicion that she might be paid less than her male colleagues, she'd better immediately file a pay-discrimination claim. At every raise decision she better be sniffing around to make sure that her raise wasn't less than that of her male colleagues. And if she hears that someone got a higher raise than her who was a male, to preserve her rights under [the Ledbetter ruling] she'd better immediately file an EEOC claim. I don't think that is in the best interest, long-term, of employer or employees."

Eastman, though, said Title VII "has a strong incentive for employees to file claims quickly so that matters are resolved while all the facts and evidence are fresh and in people's minds. And it is very difficult for employers to defend themselves from allegations made many, many years down the line."

Brake said it wasn't the 180-day limit that bothered her. "What I'm objecting to is a ruling that starts the clock running before any employee has enough reason or incentive to even think about filing a discrimination claim," she said.

BACKGROUND

Early Wage Gap

From the republic's beginning, women have played an integral role in American economic growth and prosperity, yet a wage gap has always been present.

During the Industrial Revolution of the 19th century, as the nation's productivity and wealth exploded, young, single women moved from farm to city and took jobs as mill workers, teachers and domestic servants.

The factory work wasn't easy, and owners exploited women and girls as cheap sources of labor. In 1830, females often worked 12 hours a day in "boarding-house mills" — factories with housing provided by mill owners. They earned perhaps $2.50 a week. "Minor infractions such as a few minutes' lateness were punished severely," historian Richard B. Morris noted, and "one-sided contracts gave them no power over conditions and no rewards for work."[28]

Still, young women flocked to manufacturing jobs in the cities. In Massachusetts, among the earliest states to industrialize, a third of all women ages 10 to 29 worked in industry in 1850, according to Harvard University economist Claudia Goldin.[29]

As demand for goods grew along with the nation's population, the wages of women working full time in manufacturing rose slowly as a percentage of men's pay. The wage gap narrowed from about 30 percent of men's earnings in 1820 to 56 percent nationwide in 1885, according to Goldin.[30]

But progress came more slowly, if at all, in ensuing years and decades.

In manufacturing, Goldin noted in a 1990 book on the economic history of American women, "The ratio of female to male wages . . . continued to rise slowly across most of the nineteenth century but reached a plateau before 1900."[31]

As the 20th century dawned, some women's advocates pushed for equal pay for equal work between the sexes. But others questioned the equal-pay idea. In 1891, the British economist Sidney Webb pointed to "the impossibility of discovering any but a very few instances in which men and women do precisely similar work, in the same place and at the same epoch."[32]

By the turn of the 20th century, women's jobs had started growing more diverse. Women found work not only in domestic service and manufacturing but also in teaching, sales and clerical positions. Still, only 21 percent of American women worked outside the home in 1900, and most left the labor force upon or right after marriage.[33]

Women seeking to move up in the business world faced huge cultural hurdles. In 1900 *Ladies' Home Journal* told its readers: "Although the statement may seem a hard one, and will unquestionably be controverted, it nevertheless is a plain, simple fact that women have shown themselves naturally incompetent to fill a great many of the business positions which they have sought to occupy. . . . The fact is that no one woman in a hundred can stand the physical strain of the keen pace which competition has forced upon every line of business today."[34]

Women's labor participation gradually rose in the early decades of the 20th century, fueled in part by World War I, which ended in 1918. By 1920, almost a quarter of all U.S. women were in the labor force, and 46 percent of single women worked.[35]

World War I advanced women's status, historian Michael McGerr noted. "Although the number of employed women grew only modestly during the 1910s, the wartime departure of men for military service opened up jobs traditionally denied to women in offices, transportation and industry. Leaving jobs as domestic servants, seamstresses and laundresses, women became clerks, telephone operators, streetcar conductors, drill press operators and munitions makers. Women's new prominence in the work force led in turn to the creation of a Women's Bureau in the Department of Labor."[36]

In 1920 women gained the right to vote with adoption of the 19th Amendment. Soon afterward, Quaker activist Alice Paul introduced the first version of today's Equal Rights Amendment. In 1982 the amendment fell three states short of ratification, and its passage remains controversial today.[37] (See "At Issue," p. 64.)

CHRONOLOGY

1900-1940 *Women make economic gains but face discrimination.*

1914 Start of World War I marks a period of advancement in the status of women, who go to work in traditionally male jobs.

1919 Women gain the right to vote through the 19th Amendment.

1923 The Equal Rights Amendment is introduced, but it falls three states short of ratification.

1930 Half of single women are in the labor force, and the labor-participation rate among married women approaches 12 percent.

1938 Fair Labor Standards Act establishes rules for a minimum wage, overtime pay and child labor.

1940-1960 *Women make major contribution to wartime manufacturing efforts but don't gain wage equality with men.*

1942 National War Labor Board urges employers to equalize pay between men and women in defense jobs.

1945 Congress fails to approve Women's Equal Pay Act.

1955 Census Bureau begins calculating female-to-male earnings ratio.

1960-1980 *Major anti-discrimination laws helps women to fight pay bias.*

1963 Equal Pay Act bans gender pay discrimination in equal jobs.

1963 *The Feminine Mystique* by Betty Friedan challenges idea that women can find happiness only through marriage.

1964 Title VII of the Civil Rights Act bans job discrimination on the basis of race, color, religion, national origin and sex.

1965 Equal Employment Opportunity Commission founded.

1966 National Organization For Women is formed.

1973 Supreme Court's *Roe v. Wade* ruling overturns laws barring abortion, energizes the women's movement.

1979 National Committee on Pay Equity is formed.

1980-2000 *Gender pay gap continues to narrow, but progress toward wage equality shows signs of slowing in the 1990s.*

1981 Supreme Court ruling in *County of Washington v. Gunther* allows female jail guards to sue for sex discrimination but declines to authorize suits based on theory of comparable worth.

1993 Family and Medical Leave Act requires employers to grant unpaid leave for medical emergencies, birth and care of newborns and other family-related circumstances.

2001-Present *States expand laws to help working families, while several major corporations face gender-bias accusations.*

2001 Wal-Mart employees file for sex-discrimination claim against the retailer, to become the largest class-action lawsuit against a private employer in U.S. history.

2004 California grants up to six weeks partial pay for new parents.

2004 Equal Employment Opportunity Commission and Morgan Stanley announce $54 million settlement of sex-discrimination suit.... Wachovia Corp. agrees to pay $5.5 million in a pay-discrimination case involving more than 2,000 current and former female employees.

2007 San Francisco requires employers to provide paid sick leave to all employees, including temporary and part-time workers.

2007 In *Ledbetter v. Goodyear*, Supreme Court rules that a female worker's pay-discrimination claim was invalid because it was filed after a 180-day deadline.

Debating the Comparable-Worth Doctrine

Would the approach help close the gender gap?

Imagine a company whose employees include a man who supervises telephone linemen and a woman who supervises clerical employees. They oversee the same number of workers, report to the same number of bosses, work the same hours and their jobs have been deemed of equal value to the company. Should their paychecks be the same?

Should the man get extra points for having to work outside in the cold? Should the woman get extra points for having a college degree or more years of experience?

Or, as some argue, should competitive market forces and the laws of supply and demand determine how much the man and woman earn?

Such questions lie at the heart of the debate over "comparable worth." The doctrine argues that when jobs require similar levels of skill, effort, responsibility and working conditions, the pay should be the same — even if the duties are entirely different.

Advocates of comparable worth say the market historically has undervalued jobs traditionally held by women — such as social work, secretarial work and teaching — and that such inequity has been a major contributor to the gender pay gap. If comparable worth were taken into account, they argue, it would even out wage inequality between those working in jobs dominated by women and those traditionally held by men when an impartial evaluation deems the jobs are of equal value to an employer.

Advocates also say neither the Equal Pay Act of 1963 — which bars unequal pay for the same job — nor Title VII of the Civil Rights Act of 1964, which bans discrimination based on race, color, gender, religion and national origin in hiring and promotion, do what the comparable-worth doctrine would do: Root out bias against entire occupations traditionally dominated by females.[1]

Although women began entering non-traditional fields decades ago, Labor Department data show that certain occupations still are filled mostly by females. For example, in 2006, 89 percent of paralegals and legal assistants were women, while only 33 percent of lawyers were women. And only 7 percent of machinists were women, while 84 percent of special-education teachers were female.[2]

"There's a lot of [job] segregation, and the closer you look, the more segregation you find," says Philip Cohen, a sociologist at the University of North Carolina who studies gender inequality. "Under current law, it's very difficult to bring legal action successfully and say the pay gap between men and women is discrimination, because the employer can say 'they're doing different jobs.' "

But critics say comparable worth would disrupt the traditional market-based system of determining wages based on the laws of supply and demand. "You would have people moving into occupations where there was really no shortage" of workers, says June O'Neill, an economist at the City University of New York's Baruch College. "You would have gluts in some [job categories] and shortages in others.

In 2000 testimony before a congressional panel, O'Neill outlined what she saw as the dangers of adopting a comparable-worth approach. Because there is no uniform way to rank occupations by worth, she says, such a policy would "lead to politically administered wages that would depart from a market system of wage determination." Pay in traditionally female occupations would likely rise — appointing people

During the Great Depression of the 1930s, the proportion of single women who were working stayed more or less flat. But the percentage of married women who worked rose to almost 14 percent by 1940 — a jump of more than 50 percent over the 1920 rate.[38] World War II brought millions more women into the labor force, as females — characterized by the iconic image of Rosie the Riveter — took jobs in defense plants doing work traditionally performed by men.

Equal-Pay Initiatives

As women proved their mettle behind the drill press and rivet gun, advocates continued to push for equal pay. In 1942 President Franklin D. Roosevelt had the National War Labor Board urge employers to equalize wage rates between men and women "for comparable quality and quantity of work on the same or similar operations."[39]

In the closing months of the war, the first bill aimed at barring gender pay discrimination came to the floor of favorable to the comparable-worth idea "would all but guarantee that result," she said. But that higher pay would raise costs for employers, leading them to put many women out of work, she suggested. "The ironic result is that fewer workers would be employed in traditionally female jobs."

Not only that, but some employers would respond to the higher wage levels by providing fewer non-monetary benefits, such as favorable working hours, that help accommodate women with responsibilities at home, O'Neill said. "Apart from the inefficiency and inequality it would breed," she concluded, "I find comparable worth to be a truly demeaning policy for women. It conveys the message that some cannot compete in non-traditional jobs and can only be helped through the patronage of a job evaluator."

Critics also say that comparable worth would put the government into the role of setting wages for private business, an idea that is anathema to business interests.

"Who determines what is equal value?" asks Michael Eastman, executive director of labor policy at the U.S. Chamber of Commerce. "Equal value to society? Who's setting wages then? Is the government coming up with guidelines? For example, are truckers equal to nurses, and who's making that comparison? We've never had the government setting private-sector wage rates like that."

Martha Burk directs the Corporate Accountability Project for the National Council of Women's Organizations.

Supporters of comparable worth brush off such concerns. Martha Burk, a longtime women's activist, notes that a bill proposed by Sen. Tom Harkin, D-Iowa, would require companies to disclose how they pay women and men by job categories, a practice that alone would lead to more equitable wages. "What you have is a government solution that is not telling anybody what to pay their employees," she says. It would only "increase the transparency so the company can solve its own problem if it has one."

As to the notion that comparable worth amounts to government intrusion in the private market, Burk says, "Free marketers think anything short of totally unregulated capitalism is interfering in the free market."

"It may be that markets are efficient from the point of view of employers," adds Vicky Lovell, director of employment and work/life programs at the Institute for Women's Policy Research in Washington. "But I don't think they're efficient from the point of view of workers."

[1] For background, see June O'Neill, "Comparable Worth," *The Concise Encyclopedia of Economics*, The Library of Economics and Liberty, www.econlib.org.

[2] "Women in the Labor Force: A Databook," U.S. Department of Labor, Report 1002, September 2007, Table 11, pp. 28-34.

Congress. The Women's Equal Pay Act of 1945 went nowhere, though.[40]

By 1960, more than a third of women were working, and among single, white women ages 25 to 34, the labor participation rate was a then-record 82 percent.[41] But most women continued to work in low-paying clerical, service and manufacturing jobs, and the wage gap between males and females was wide. By 1963, women made only 59 cents for every dollar in median year-round earnings paid to men.[42] Women who tried to break into so-called "men's" occupations faced huge resistance.

That year, after decades of struggle by women's advocates for federal legislation on gender pay equity, Congress passed the Equal Pay Act as an amendment to the Fair Labor Standards Act of 1938. In signing the act, President Kennedy said the law "affirms our determination that when women enter the labor force they will find equality in their pay envelopes."[43]

Did Wal-Mart Favor Male Workers?

Women's suit seeks billions in damages.

Dedra Farmer, the daughter of an auto mechanic, worked in the Tire Lube Express Division of Wal-Mart Stores, the only female in her district who held a salaried manager position in that division. During her 13 years with the retail giant, she told a congressional panel last year, she saw evidence that women — herself among them — earned less than men holding the same jobs.

Farmer said she complained to Wal-Mart's CEO through e-mails, expressed her concern at a store meeting and was assured by the store manager that she'd get a response. "The response I received was a pink slip," she said.[1]

Farmer has joined a class-action lawsuit accusing Wal-Mart of sex discrimination in pay and promotions. The case, which could cover perhaps 1.6 million current and former female employees and result in billions of dollars in damages, is the biggest workplace discrimination lawsuit in the nation's history.

Filed in 2001 by Betty Dukes and five other Wal-Mart employees, the case has gone through a series of legal maneuverings, most recently in December, when a three-judge panel of the U.S. 9th Circuit Court of Appeals reaffirmed its certification as a class-action lawsuit but left the door open for Wal-Mart to ask for a rehearing on that status. If the appeals court does not reconsider the class-action designation, the company reportedly will petition the Supreme Court.[2]

The stakes in the case are high. Goldman Sachs Group last year estimated potential damages at between $1.5 billion and $3.5 billion if the retailer loses, and punitive damages could raise the figure to between $13.5 billion and $31.5 billion.[3]

The company's lawyers have asserted that a class-action suit is an inappropriate vehicle to use because Wal-Mart's employment policies are decentralized, and individual store managers and district managers make pay and promotion decisions.[4]

Theodore J. Boutrous Jr., a lawyer for Wal-Mart, has said that decisions by thousands of managers at 3,400 Wal-Mart stores during six years were "highly individualized and cannot be tried in one fell swoop in a nationwide class action."[5] He has also said the company has a "strong diversity policy and anti-discrimination policy."[6]

But Brad Seligman, executive director of the Impact Fund, a nonprofit group in Berkeley, Calif., representing the plaintiffs, said, "No amount of PR or spin is going to allow Wal-Mart to avoid facing its legacy of discrimination."[7]

A statistician hired by the plaintiffs said it took women an average of 4.38 years from the date of hire to be promoted to assistant manager, while it took men 2.86 years. Moreover, it took an average of 10.12 years for women to become managers compared with 8.64 for men.[8]

The statistician, Richard Drogin, of California State University at East Bay, also found that female managers made an average annual salary of $89,280, while men in the same position earned an average of $105,682. Female hourly workers earned 6.7 percent less than men in comparable positions.[9]

The measure, as finally adopted, stopped short of ensuring the elusive comparable-worth standard that women's advocates had so long sought. Instead, the bill made it illegal to discriminate in pay and benefits on the basis of sex when men and women performed the same job at the same employer.

Under the law, for example, a company couldn't pay a full-time female store clerk less per hour than a male one for doing the same job in stores located in the same city. But the law was silent on situations in which, say, the work of a female secretarial supervisor was deemed to be of comparable worth to that of a male who supervised the same company's truck drivers.

While the Equal Pay Act marked progress, it was far from an airtight guarantee of "equality in . . . pay envelopes." For example, the law initially did not cover executive, administrative or professional jobs; that exemption was lifted in 1972. Yet, one study argues that courts have interpreted the act so narrowly that white-collar female workers have had trouble winning claims through its provisions.[44]

Appellate Judge Andrew J. Kleinfeld has dissented in the case, arguing that certifying the suit as a class action deprived the retailer of its right to defend against individual cases alleging bias. In addition, he argued that female employees who were discriminated against would be hurt by class-action status, because women "who were fired or not promoted for good reasons" would also share in any award if Wal-Mart lost the case.[10]

Business lobbies also have urged that the class-action certification be reversed. An official of the U.S. Chamber of Commerce, which filed a "friend of the court (*amicus curiae*) brief in the case, warned of "potentially limitless claims" against companies "with limited ability to defend against them." He added: "The potential financial exposure to an employer facing a class action of this size creates tremendous pressure to settle regardless of the case's merit."[11]

But women's advocates argue that a class-action approach is appropriate. It "provides the only practical means for most women in low-wage jobs to redress discrimination in pay because of such workers' often tenuous economic status," stated an *amicus* letter written to the appeals court on behalf of the U.S. Women's Chamber of Commerce.[12]

A Wal-Mart store manager reads the store's weekly sales results to other workers. Male hourly workers at Wal-Mart earn 6.7 percent more than women in comparable positions, a pay-equity study contends.

Added Margot Dorfman, chief executive officer of the group: "A woman with family responsibilities often isn't in a position to quit her job or risk antagonizing her employer with a challenge to a bad workplace practice."[13]

---

[1] Statement of Dedra Farmer before House Committee on Education and Labor, April 24, 2007.

[2] Amy Joyce, "Wal-Mart Loses Bid to Block Group Bias Suit," *The Washington Post*, Feb. 7, 2007, p. 1D.

[3] Details of the Goldman Sachs analysis are from Steve Painter, "Judges modify sex-bias decision; Wal-Mart appeal likely to see delay," *Arkansas Democrat-Gazette*, Dec. 12, 2007.

[4] Steven Greenhouse and Constance L. Hays, "Wal-Mart Sex-Bias Suit Given Class-Action Status," *The New York Times*, June 23, 2004.

[5] Joyce, *op. cit.*

[6] Quoted in Bob Egelko, "Wal-Mart sex discrimination suit advances; Appeals court OKs class action status for 2 million women," *San Francisco Chronicle*, Feb. 7, 2007, p. B1.

[7] Joyce, *op. cit.*

[8] *Ibid.*

[9] *Ibid.*

[10] Painter, *op. cit.*

[11] "U.S. Chamber Files Brief in Wal-mart Class Action," press release, U.S. Chamber of Commerce, Dec. 13, 2004, www.uschamber.com/press/releases/2004/december/04-159.htm.

[12] Mark E. Burton Jr., Hersh & Hersh, San Francisco, et al., letter submitted to 9th U.S. Circuit Court of Appeals, March 27, 2007, www.uswcc.org/amicus.pdf.

[13] PR Newswire, "U.S. Women's Chamber of Commerce Joins Fight in Landmark Women's Class Action Suit Against Wal-Mart," March 28, 2007.

Perhaps more significantly, the law gives companies several defenses for pay disparities: when wage differences stem from seniority or merit systems, are based on quantity or quality of production, or stem from "any other factor other than sex."

That last provision, critics say, can sometimes allow business practices that may seem gender-neutral on the surface but discriminate nonetheless.

The Equal Pay Act took effect in 1964, and that same year Congress passed Title VII of the Civil Rights Act of 1964, a broad measure that prohibits employment discrimination on the basis of race, color, religion, national origin and sex, and covers hiring, firing and promotion as well as pay. A measure called the Bennett Amendment, sponsored by Rep. Wallace F. Bennett, a Utah Republican, sought to bring Title VII and the Equal Pay Act in line with each other.

In ensuing years, the overlap of the Equal Pay Act and Title VII created confusion but also helped to animate the battle against wage discrimination. Part of the conflict over pay equity played out in the courts in the 1970s and '80s.

Key Court Rulings

In a case that initially raised hopes for the theory of comparable worth, the U.S. Supreme Court ruled 5-4 to allow female jail guards to sue for sex discrimination. The women, called "matrons," earned 30 percent less than male guards, called "deputy sheriffs."[45] The women argued that while they had fewer prisoners to guard and more clerical duties than the male guards, their work was comparable. An outside job evaluation showed that the women did 95 percent of what the men were doing, but received $200 less a month than the men.[46]

Prior to the Supreme Court's ruling, *The Washington Post* noted at the time, "the only sure grounds for a pay discrimination claim by a woman under federal law was 'unequal pay for equal work' — an allegation that she was paid less than a man holding an identical job. The jail matrons and women's rights lawyers said that lower pay for a comparable, if not equal, job could also be the basis for a sex-discrimination charge."

Justice William J. Brennan wrote that a claim of wage discrimination under Title VII did not have to meet the equal work standards of the Equal Pay Act. Thus, noted Clare Cushman, director of publications at the Supreme Court Historical Society, "a woman employee could sue her employer for gender-based pay discrimination even if her company did not employ a man to work the same job for higher pay."[47]

Still, Cushman wrote, while the court "opened the door slightly for women working in jobs not strictly equal to their male counterparts, it also specifically declined to authorize suits based on the theory of comparable worth."

In 1985 that theory suffered a blow that continues to resonate today, partly because of the personalities who were involved. In *AFSCME v. the State of Washington*, the 9th U.S. Circuit Court of Appeals overturned a lower court's ruling ordering Washington to pay more than $800 million in back wages to some 15,000 state workers, most of them women.[48]

The case turned on the question of whether employers were required to pay men and women the same amounts for jobs of comparable worth, rather than equal wages for the same jobs. It eventually ended in a draw when the state negotiated a settlement with AFSCME (American Federation of State, County and Municipal Employees union).[49]

Judge Anthony M. Kennedy, who now sits on the U.S. Supreme Court and presumably could help decide a comparable-worth case should one arise before the justices, wrote the appellate court's decision. Kennedy wrote: "Neither law nor logic deems the free-market system a suspect enterprise." During this same period, two other personalities who now sit on the high court also expressed negative views on comparable worth. As a lawyer in the Reagan administration, John Roberts, now chief justice, described it as "a radical redistributive concept."[50] And the EEOC, then under Chairman Clarence Thomas, rejected comparable worth as a means of determining job discrimination. "We found that sole reliance on a comparison of the intrinsic value of dissimilar jobs — which command different wages in the market — does not prove a violation of Tile VII," Thomas stated.[51]

The views of Thomas and Roberts reflected the conservative policies of the Reagan administration during the 1980s. Yet despite the political tenor of that era, women made major strides toward workplace equality. From 1980 to 1992, the wage gap in median weekly earnings of full-time female wage and salary workers narrowed from 64 percent to 76 percent after adjusting for inflation. But it shrank only from 77 percent to 81 percent from 1993 — the year that Democratic President Bill Clinton took office and the Family and Medical Leave Act was enacted — to 2006.[52]

Measuring Progress

Experts debate whether and to what degree women's gains may have slowed or stopped in recent years. Some point to huge political gains in this decade, including Sen. Clinton's role in the presidential race and the rise of Rep. Nancy Pelosi, D-Calif., to speaker of the House. Others cite such evidence as a recent study showing that female corporate directors, though a small minority in boardrooms, out-earn male directors.[53]

But many scholars believe women's gains have indeed slowed.

Vanneman, the University of Maryland sociologist, has carefully charted a number of trends linked to the so-called gender revolution, and on his Web site he notes that he and several colleagues are studying the pace of women's progress.

"For much of the last quarter of the 20th century, women gradually reduced gender inequalities on many fronts," he wrote, citing such trends as women entering the labor force in growing numbers, the opening of previously male-dominated jobs to women, the narrowing wage gap, women's role in politics and a growing openness in public opinion about the participation of women in public and community life.

But, he added, "all this changed in the early to mid-1990s." A "flattening of the gender trend lines" is seen in nearly all parts of society, he added: working-class and middle-class, black, white, Asian and Hispanic, mothers with young children and those with older ones, and so on. "All groups experienced major gender setbacks during the 1990s. The breadth of this reversal suggests something fundamental has happened to the U.S. gender structure."

In an interview, Vanneman says he has no theories as to what accounts for that reversal — only hunches — as he continues to study the phenomenon. One hunch is that the flattening started happening in the 1980s but didn't show up in a big way until the 1990s. He also says he suspects the reversal in women's progress gathered momentum in the 1990s as the "culture of parenting" changed. Americans, he says, became less accepting of women trying to balance busy careers with the pressures of motherhood, a shift that has put women in more of a bind than they felt in previous periods. As a result, many women have backed away from high-paying careers and devoted more time to family, he says.

"There's been tremendous growth in expectations of what it means to be a good parent," Vanneman says.

Cornell University economist Blau agrees that progress in women's wages slowed in recent years, though she sees some evidence that the picture has brightened a bit.

One reason for the slowdown in the 1990s, she says, may have been that the increase in demand for white-collar and service workers shifted into a lower gear compared to the 1980s, when many women benefited from a surge in hiring for white-collar jobs, including ones that required computer skills, while blue-collar jobs dominated by men began to wane.

In addition, Blau says that during the eighties, as many women began to stay in the workforce even after marriage and childbirth, employers' view of the value of female workers improved. That, she says, helped narrow the wage gap at a faster pace than in earlier decades.

Blau also sees evidence that men were doing more at home in the 1980s than ever before. That trend didn't go away in the past decade, she says, but it hasn't grown much either.

CURRENT SITUATION

Prospects in Congress

As concerns over the progress of gender equity grow, women's advocates are hoping that the Democrat-controlled Congress will pass new laws this year. But proposed legislation is likely to face stiff opposition.

Reversing the Supreme Court's *Ledbetter* decision seems to have the best chance of making it through Congress. The House passed the Ledbetter Fair Pay Act last July 31 by a 225-199 vote, largely along party lines.[54] A companion bill in the Senate, called the Lilly Ledbetter Fair Pay Restoration Act, had garnered 37 co-sponsors as of early March. Momentum continued this year with a Senate hearing.

In introducing the Senate version of the bill last July, Sen. Kennedy said it "simply restores the status quo" that existed before the *Ledbetter* decision "so that victims of ongoing pay discrimination have a reasonable time to file their claims."[55]

But employer advocates such as the U.S. Chamber of Commerce dispute such descriptions. Pointing to the House version that passed last summer, chamber officials said it would broaden existing law to apply to unintentional as well as intentional discrimination and would lead to an "explosion of litigation second-guessing legitimate employment and personnel decisions."[56]

The Bush administration has threatened a veto, saying last year that if the House bill came to the president, "his senior advisers would recommend that he veto" it.[57] The measure would "impede justice" by allowing employees to sue over pay or other employment-related discrimination "years or even decades after the alleged discrimination occurred," the administration said. Moreover, the House bill "far exceeds the stated purpose of undoing the court's decision" by "extending the expanded statute of limitations to any 'other practice' that remotely affects an individual's wages, benefits, or other compensation in the future."

Is the Equal Rights Amendment to the Constitution still needed?

YES
Idella Moore
Executive Officer, 4ERA

Written for *CQ Researcher*, February 2008

We still need the Equal Rights Amendment (ERA) because sex discrimination is still a problem in our country. Like race or religious discrimination, gender discrimination is intended to render its victims economically, socially, legally and politically disadvantaged. But unlike racism and religious intolerance — whose practice against certain groups is localized within countries or regions — sex discrimination is universal. Why, then, in our court system are race and religious discrimination considered more serious offenses?

Today, American women — of all races and religions — are still fighting to achieve equal opportunity, pay, status and recognition in all realms of our society. At this moment, the largest class-action lawsuit in the history of this country is being argued on behalf of 1.6 million women who were discriminated against purely because of their gender. If the ERA had been ratified back in the 1970s, by now these types of lawsuits would be extinct.

We still need the ERA because ratification of the amendment will elevate "sex" to, in legal terms, a so-called suspect class. A suspect class has the advantage in discrimination cases. Gender, as yet, is not afforded that advantage. As we've seen with race, suspect class status increased the chance of favorable outcomes in discrimination cases. This, in turn, served as a deterrent. Consequently, in our society racism is now socially unacceptable. Sex discrimination, however, is not.

We still need the ERA because the continuing struggle for legal equality for women should be seen as a shameful and embarrassing condition of our society. Yet today lawmakers — sworn to represent all their constituents — proudly voice their objections to granting legal equality to women and without any fear of consequences to their political careers. How different our reactions would be if they were espousing racism.

The Equal Rights Amendment will perfect our Constitution by explicitly guaranteeing that the privileges, laws and responsibilities it contains apply equally to men and women. As it stands today the Constitution is sometimes interpreted that way, but women, as a universally and historically disadvantaged group, cannot rely on such interpretations. We have seen these "interpretations" vary and change, often due to the whims of the political climate. Therefore, without the ERA any gains women make will always be tenuous.

I see the Equal Rights Amendment, too, as a pledge to ourselves and posterity that we recognize that sexism exists and that we as a country are determined to continue perfecting our democracy by proudly and unequivocally guaranteeing that one's gender will no longer be a detriment to achieving the American dream.

NO
Phyllis Schlafly
President, Eagle Forum

Written for *CQ Researcher*, February 2008

The Equal Rights Amendment (ERA) was fiercely debated across America for 10 years (1972-1982) and was rejected. ERA has been reintroduced into the current Congress under a slightly different name, but it's the same old amendment with the same bad effects.

The principal reason ERA failed is that although it was marketed as a benefit to women, its advocates were never able to prove it would provide any benefit whatsoever to women. ERA would put "sex" (not women) in the Constitution and just make all our laws sex-neutral.

ERA advocates used their massive access to a friendly media to suggest that ERA would raise women's wages. But ERA would have no effect on wages because our employment laws are already sex-neutral. The equal-pay-for-equal-work law was passed in 1963, and the Equal Employment Opportunity Act — with all its enforcement mechanisms — was passed in 1972.

Supreme Court Justice Ruth Bader Ginsburg's book *Sex Bias in the U.S. Code* spells out the changes ERA would require, and it proves ERA would take away benefits from women. For example, the book states that the "equality principle" would eliminate the concept of "dependent women." This would deprive wives and widows of their Social Security dependent-wife benefits, on which millions of mothers and grandmothers depend.

Looking at the experience of states that have put ERA language into their constitutions, we see that ERA would most probably require taxpayer funding of abortions. The feminists aggressively litigate this issue. Their most prominent victory was in the New Mexico Supreme Court, which accepted the notion that since only women undergo abortions, the denial of taxpayer funding is sex discrimination.

ERA would also give the courts the power to legalize same-sex marriages. Courts in four states have ruled that the ERA's ban on gender discrimination requires marriage licenses to be given to same-sex couples. In Maryland and Washington, those decisions were overturned by a higher court by only a one-vote margin. The ERA would empower the judges to rule either way.

If all laws are made sex-neutral, the military draft-registration law would have to include women. We don't have a draft today, but we do have registration, and those who fail to register immediately lose their college grants and loans and will never be able to get a federal job.

Eric Dreiband, a former EEOC general counsel in the Bush administration, told this year's hearing on the Senate bill that the measure would subject state and local governments, unions, employers and others to potentially unlimited penalties and could expose pension funds to "potentially staggering liability."[58]

Still, women's advocates remain sanguine about the measure's prospects. "My hope is that the bill will move expeditiously [this] spring" in the Senate and that "the president will reconsider and recognize how important this fix to the law is," says Samuels of the National Women's Law Center.

The other two main bills on gender pay equity could have rougher sledding.

Sen. Clinton's Paycheck Fairness Act is similar to a bill by the same name proposed during her husband's presidential administration. As of early March, the bill had garnered 22 co-sponsors in the Senate and 226 in the House.

Among other things, it would strengthen penalties on employers who violate the Equal Pay Act, make it harder for companies to use the law's defense for wage differences based on factors "other than sex," and bar employers from retaliating against workers who share wage information with each other. It also calls for the Labor Department to draw up guidelines aimed at helping employers voluntarily evaluate job categories and compare wages paid for different jobs with the aim of eliminating unfair wage differences between male- and female-dominated occupations.

The bill has drawn enthusiastic support from some women's advocates, but it also has opponents. Washington lawyer Brown said the goal of the provision on voluntary guidelines was "nothing more than the discredited 'comparable-worth' theory in new clothing."[59]

The Fair Pay Act, proposed by Sen. Harkin and Del. Eleanor Holmes Norton, D-D.C., a former EEOC chair, steps even closer to embracing the comparable-worth theory and thus, many observers believe, is likely to face stiff headwinds. The main ideas have circulated in Congress for years.

As Harkin describes it, the bill requires employers to provide equal pay for jobs that are comparable in skill, effort, responsibility and working conditions, regardless of sex, race or national origin, and it bars companies from reducing other employees' wages to achieve pay equity.[60]

Again, advocates such as Samuels are hopeful Congress will pass both the Paycheck Fairness and Fair Pay Act and that the president won't veto them if they do make it to his desk. "The hope would be that the level of support for these bills both in Congress and among the public is so substantial, and they so clearly are a necessary step toward ensuring true equality of wages, that the president would understand the necessity for them and sign them," she says.

But business opposition is likely to be strong. Eastman at the U.S. Chamber of Commerce lists a variety of complaints about both bills, such as their provisions for punitive damages and their allowances for class-action suits against employers. "The case has not been made that these bills are justified," he says.

State Action

While women's advocates hold out hope for congressional action, they also are turning their attention to the states in hopes of pressing legislatures to stiffen laws on pay equity and make local economies friendlier to gender issues. As of April 2007, all but 11 states and the District of Columbia had laws on equal pay.[61]

Minnesota has had a system of comparable worth, or "pay equity," for public employees since the 1980s, and last year proposals were made to expand the system to private employers that do business with the state. The Minnesota program gave smaller raises to public workers in male-dominated jobs and bigger raises to those in female-dominated ones, according to a former staff member of the Minnesota Commission on the Economic Status of Women. The system shrank the pay gap from 72 percent to nearly equal pay.[62]

A report by the Institute for Women's Policy Research said in 2006 that while women's wages had risen in all states in inflation-adjusted terms since 1989, "in no state does the typical full-time woman worker earn as much as the typical man." It would take 50 years "at the present rate of progress" for women to achieve wage parity with men nationwide, it said.[63]

Some advocates are unwilling to wait that long. In Colorado, for example, a Pay Equity Commission appointed by Donald J. Mares, executive director of the state Department of Labor and Employment, worked since last June to formulate policy recommendations to curb gender and racial pay inequities in the private and public sectors. The 12-member commission includes policy analysts, business and labor union representatives, academics and advocates for women and minorities.[64]

Meric, the 9to5 director and a Colorado resident, said her group was instrumental in getting the state to appoint the commission. Although the panel has no authority to force employers to alter pay practices, Meric hopes the commission's work leads to change. One key recommendation, she says, is that employers do more to create flexible policies so that workers — especially women with caregiving responsibilities — aren't penalized for meeting both work and family responsibilities.

Mares told the Colorado Women's Legislative Breakfast in February that another recommendation calls for making the commission permanent, so it can continue to monitor gender pay equity in the state and help educate businesses on good practices.

In Colorado, he said, the average woman makes 79 cents for every dollar earned by the average man. "Every day you as a community walk in the door," he told the gathering of women, "your pay is being discounted. That's not good."[65]

Better negotiating skills could help narrow the gender wage gap, in the view of women's advocates. The Clinton/DeLauro bill calls for grants to help women and girls "strengthen their negotiation skills to allow the girls and women to obtain higher salaries and the best compensation packages possible for themselves."

It's a talent that many women don't exercise, says Linda Babcock, an economist at Carnegie Mellon University in Pittsburgh and co-author of the recent book *Women Don't Ask: Negotiation and the Gender Divide*. Babcock found in a study of Carnegie Mellon students graduating with master's degrees in public policy that only 12.5 percent of females tried to negotiate for better pay when they received a job offer, while 51.5 percent of males did. Afterward, the females earned 8.5 percent less than the males.

Babcock sees several reasons why women are not inclined to negotiate more, including that they have been socialized by American culture to be less assertive than men. And, she says, women who do try to bargain for better wages often are subjected to "backlash" by employers and peers.

Not that women are incapable of negotiating, Babcock stresses. While they may not always stand up for themselves in seeking higher wages, women outperform men when negotiating on behalf of somebody else, she has found.

"It's really striking," she says. "If we were missing some gene, we wouldn't really be able to turn it on on behalf of somebody else."

OUTLOOK
Pressure for Change

Some women's advocates are not especially sanguine about the possibility of big strides on the gender-wage front, at least in the near future.

"I don't think five years is long enough [for there] to be much change, particularly if we don't see much concerted effort among employers," says Lovell of the Institute for Women's Policy Research.

Big change would require a "push from the federal government" or "some dramatic effort on the part of socially conscious employers," she says. "That hasn't happened before, and I don't think it will in the next few years."

Still, observers believe that social and political shifts will produce new pressure for changes in the way employers deal with wage equity.

Meric says 9to5's "long-term agenda" is to have the theory of comparable worth enshrined in law as well as to have "guaranteed minimum labor standards" for all workers that include paid sick leave and expanded coverage under the Family and Medical Leave Act. In Colorado, she hopes the recommendations outlined by the Pay Equity Commission will serve as a model for other states and "move us closer" to that long-term goal. "Basic protections should apply to workers wherever they live in the United States."

"In the last five or 10 years we have seen progress stall in [achieving] gender equality," says Philip Cohen, a sociologist at the University of North Carolina at Chapel Hill who studies gender inequity. But in coming years, he says he is inclined to think that college-educated women will exert increasing pressure on federal and state lawmakers and employers to make policy changes that can narrow the wage gap.

"If you look back to feminism in the '60s," Cohen says, "a lot of women had college degrees but weren't able to take advantage of their skills in the marketplace, and that became the 'feminine mystique' " explored in Betty Friedan's groundbreaking 1963 book.

Today, "Women are outnumbering men in college graduation rates, and I think we are going to see more and more women looking around for better opportunities. If they don't see gender equality resulting, they're going to be very dissatisfied."

And that dissatisfaction, Cohen says, could well show up in the political arena.

Samuels of the National Women's Law Center hopes the debate in Congress and fallout from the Supreme Court's *Ledbetter* decision will spur further gains in wage equity for women.

"Unfortunately, over the course of the last several years things have pretty much stagnated," she says. "I do hope that the recent public attention paid to wage disparity will cause employers to take a look at their pay scales and try to do the right thing."

NOTES

1. Testimony of Lilly Ledbetter before the Committee on Education and Labor, U.S. House of Representatives, on the Amendment of Title VII, June 12, 2007.

2. Testimony of Lilly Ledbetter before Senate Committee on Health, Education, Labor and Pensions, Jan. 24, 2008.

3. Ledbetter v. Goodyear Tire & Rubber Co. Inc., 550 U.S. __ (May 29, 2007).

4. Ledbetter testimony, op. cit., June 12, 2007.

5. Diana Furchtgott-Roth, testimony on the Paycheck Fairness Act before House Committee on Education and Labor, April 24, 2007.

6. "Highlights of Women's Earnings in 2006," U.S. Department of Labor, September 2007, Table 1, p. 7. Data are for median usual weekly earnings of full-time wage and salary workers ages 16 and older. For the Census Bureau data, see www.census.gov/ compendia/statab/tables/08s0628.pdf. The Census Bureau data represent median full-time, year-round earnings for male and female workers 15 years old and older as of March 2006.

7. Testimony before Senate Committee on Health, Education, Labor and Pensions, April 12, 2007.

8. "Women's Earnings: Work Patterns Partially Explain Difference between Men's and Women's Earnings," U.S. General Accounting Office, October 2003.

9. U.S. Equal Employment Opportunity Commission, Office of Inspector General, "Semiannual Report to Congress," April 1, 2007-Sept. 30, 2007, Oct. 30, 2007, p. 7.

10. "Highlights of Women's Earnings," op. cit., p. 1.

11. Ibid., Table 1, p. 7.

12. Judy Goldberg Dey and Catherine Hill, "Behind the Pay Gap," American Association of University Women Educational Foundation, 2007.

13. Paycheck Fairness Act, HR 1338, S 766.

14. Fair Pay Act, S 1087 and HR 2019, sponsored in the House of Representatives by Del. Eleanor Holmes Norton, D-D.C.

15. Lilly Ledbetter Fair Pay Act, HR 2831 and Fair Pay Restoration Act, S 1843.

16. David Neumark, with the assistance of Roy J. Bank and Kyle D. Van Nort, "Sex Discrimination in Restaurant Hiring: An Audit Study," The Quarterly Journal of Economics, August 1996.

17. Furchtgott-Roth testimony, op. cit.

18. Dey and Hill, op. cit.

19. Testimony of Heather Boushey before House Committee on Education and Labor, April 24, 2007, p. 4.

20. John F. Kennedy, Remarks Upon Signing the Equal Pay Act, June 10, 1963, quoted in John T. Woolley and Gerhard Peters, The American Presidency Project [online], Santa Barbara, Calif., University of California (hosted), Gerhard Peters (database), www.presidency.ucsb.edu/ws/?pid=9267.

21. Testimony of Jocelyn Samuels before Senate Committee on Health, Education, Labor and Pensions, "Closing the Gap: Equal Pay for Women Workers," April 12, 2007, p. 6.

22. Carrie Lukas, "A Bargain At 77 Cents To a Dollar," The Washington Post, April 3, 2007, p. 23A.

23. Testimony of Barbara Berish Brown before Senate Committee on Health, Education, Labor and Pensions, April 12, 2007.

24. Quoted in Justine Andronici, "Court Gives OK To Unequal Pay," Ms. Magazine, summer 2007, accessed at www.msmagazine.com/summer2007/ledbetter.asp.

25. Quoted in Michael Doyle, "Justices Put Bias Lawsuits on Tight Schedule," Kansas City Star, May 30, 2007, p. 1A.

26. Testimony of Margot Dorfman before Senate Committee on Health, Education, Labor and Pensions on the "The Fair Pay Restoration Act: Ensuring Reasonable Rules in Pay Discrimination Cases," Jan. 24, 2008, pp. 2-3.

27. "Employment Discrimination: Post-Ledbetter Discrimination," "Justice Talking," National Public Radio, Oct. 22, 2007, accessed at www.justicetalking.org/transcripts/071022_EqualPay_transcript.pdf.

28. Richard B. Morris, ed., "The U.S. Department of Labor Bicentennial History of the American Work," U.S. Department of Labor, 1976, p. 67.

29. Claudia Goldin, Understanding the Gender Gap: An Economic History of American Women (1990), p. 50.

30. Ibid., Figure 3.1, p. 62, and text pp. 63, 66.

31. Ibid., p. 67.

32. Quoted in ibid., p. 209.

33. Ibid., Table 2.1, p. 17, citing U.S. Census data.

34. "Setting a New Course," CQ Researcher, May 10, 1985, citing Julie A. Matthaei, An Economic History of Women in America (1982), p. 222.

35. Goldin, op. cit., p. 17.

36. Michael McGerr, A Fierce Discontent: The Rise and Fall of the Progressive Movement in America, 1870-1920 (2003), pp. 295-296.

37. For background, see Richard Boeckel, "Sex Equality and Protective Laws," Editorial Research Reports, July 13, 1926; and Richard Boeckel, "The Woman's Vote in National Elections," Editorial Research Reports, May 31, 1927, both available at CQ Researcher Plus Archive, www.cqpress.com.

38. Ibid.

39. American Association of University Women, "A Brief History of the Wage Gap, Pay Inequity, and the Equal Pay Act," www.aauw.org/advocacy/laf/lafnetwork/library/payequity_hist.cfm. For background, see K. R. Lee, "Women in War Work," Editorial Research Reports, Jan. 26, 1942, available at CQ Researcher Plus Archive, www.cqpress.com.

40. Ibid.

41. Goldin, op. cit., Table 2.2, p. 18.

42. Ibid., Table 3.1, p. 60.

43. John F. Kennedy, op. cit.

44. Juliene James, "The Equal Pay Act in the Courts: A De Facto White-Collar Exemption," New York University Law Review, Vol. 79, November 2004, p. 1875.

45. Clare Cushman, Supreme Court Decisions and Women's Rights, CQ Press (2000), p. 146. The case is County of Washington v. Gunther (1981). For background, see Sandra Stencel, "Equal Pay Fight," Editorial Research Reports, March 20, 1981, and R. Thompson, "Women's Economic Equity," Editorial Research Reports, May 10, 1985, both available at CQ Researcher Plus Archive, www.cqpress.com.

46. Deborah Churchman, "Comparable Worth: The Equal-Pay Issue of the '80s," The Christian Science Monitor, July 22, 1982, p. 15.

47. Cushman, op. cit.

48. James Warren, "Fight for Pay Equity Produces Results, But Not Parity," Chicago Tribune, Sept. 8, 1985, p. 13.

49. Judy Mann, "New Victory in Women's Pay," The Washington Post, Aug. 27, 1986, p. 3B.

50. Linda Greenhouse, "Judge Roberts, the Committee Is Interested in Your View On...," The New York Times, Sept. 11, 2005, p. 1A.

51. "Women Dealt Setback on 'Comparable Worth,'" Chicago Tribune, June 18, 1985, p. 1.

52. "Highlights of Women's Earnings in 2006," op. cit., Table 13, p. 28.

53. Martha Graybow, "Female U.S. corporate directors out-earn men: study," Reuters, Nov. 7, 2007. The study of more than 25,000 directors at more than

3,200 U.S. companies was done by the Corporate Library. It found that female directors earned median compensation of $120,000 compared with $104,375 for male board members.

54. Libby George, "House Democrats Prevail in Effort to Clarify Law on Wage Discrimination," CQ Weekly, Aug. 6, 2007, p. 2381.

55. Sen. Edward Kennedy, statement on S 1843, "Statements on Introduced Bills and Joint Resolutions," Senate, July 20, 2007, accessed at www.thomas.gov.

56. U.S. Chamber of Commerce, "Letter Opposing HR 2831, the Ledbetter Fair Pay Act," July 27, 2007, accessed at www.uschamber.com/issues/letters/ 2007/070727_ledbetter.htm.

57. "Statement of Administration Policy: HR 2831, Lilly Ledbetter Fair Pay Act of 2007," Executive Office of the President, Office of Management and Budget, July 27, 2007, accessed at www.whitehouse .gov/omb/legislative/sap/110-1/hr2831sap-r.pdf.

58. Statement of Eric S. Dreiband before Senate Committee on Health, Education, Labor and Pensions, Jan. 24, 2008, pp. 11-13.

59. Barbara Berish Brown testimony, op. cit.

60. Statement of Sen. Tom Harkin at the Health, Education, Labor and Pensions Committee Hearing on Equal Pay for Women Workers, April 12, 2007, accessed at www.harkin.senate.gov/pr/p.cfm ?i=272330.

61. National Conference of State Legislatures, "State Laws on Equal Pay," April 2007.

62. H.J. Cummins, "Legislature will look at closing the gender gap," Star Tribune, April 23, 2007, p. 1D.

63. Heidi Hartmann, Olga Sorokina and Erica Williams, "The Best and Worst State Economies for Women," Institute for Women's Policy Research, December 2006.

64. "Pay Equity Commission holds first meeting," Denver Business Journal, June 26, 2007.

65. Remarks of Donald Mares, Colorado Women's Legislative Breakfast, Feb. 12, 2008, accessed at www.youtube.com/watch?v=UIO0mlHb6b8&featu re=related.

BIBLIOGRAPHY

Books

Cushman, Clare, *Supreme Court Decisions and Women's Rights, CQ Press*, 2000.
In clear prose, the director of publications for the Supreme Court Historical Society covers the waterfront of Supreme Court cases and issues involving women's rights, including those related to pay equity and discrimination in the workplace.

Farrell, Warren, *Why Men Earn More, AMACOM*, 2005.
The only man elected three times to the board of directors of the National Organization for Women's New York chapter argues that the pay gap can no longer be ascribed to discrimination, and he seeks "to give women ways of earning more rather than suing more."

Goldin, Claudia, *Understanding the Gender Gap: An Economic History of American Women, Oxford University Press*, 1990.
A Harvard University economics professor traces the evolution of female workers and gender differences in occupations and earnings from the early days of the republic to the modern era.

Murphy, Evelyn, with E.J. Graff, *Getting Even: Why Women Don't Get Paid Like Men — and What to Do About It, Touchstone*, 2005.
The former Massachusetts lieutenant governor writes in this anecdote-filled book that the "gender wage gap is unfair" and "it's not going away on its own."

Articles

Hymowitz, Carol, "On Diversity, America Isn't Putting Its Money Where Its Mouth Is," *The Wall Street Journal*, Feb. 25, 2008.
Progress for women and minorities in business has stalled or moved backward at many of the nation's largest companies, and the inequality shapes perceptions about who can or should fill leadership roles.

Murphy, Cait, "Obama flunks Econ 101," *Fortune*, CNNMoney.com, June 6, 2007, http://money.cnn .com/2007/06/04/magazines/fortune/muphy_ payact.fortune/index.htm.

The presidential candidate is "flirting with a very bad idea" by co-sponsoring the Fair Pay Act, "a bill that would bureaucratize most of the labor market," Murphy argues.

Parloff, Roger, and Susan M. Kaufman, "The War Over Unconscious Bias," *Fortune*, Oct. 15, 2007.
Wal-Mart and other companies are facing accusations of gender pay bias and other forms of job discrimination, "but the biggest problem isn't their policies, it's their managers' unwitting preferences."

Reports and Studies

Dey, Judy Goldberg, and Catherine Hill, "Behind the Pay Gap," *American Association of University Women Educational Foundation*, April 2007, www.aauw.org/ research/upload/behindPayGap.pdf.
A study of college graduates concludes that one year out of college women working full time earn only 80 percent as much as their male colleagues and that a decade after graduation the proportion falls to 69 percent.

Foust-Cummings, Heather, Laura Sabattini and Nancy Carter, "Women in Technology: Maximizing Talent, Minimizing Barriers," *Catalyst*, 2008, www .catalyst.org/files/full/2008%20Women%20in%20 High%20Tech.pdf.
Technology companies are making progress at creating more diverse work environments, but women in the high-technology field still face barriers to advancement, such as a lack of role models, mentors and access to networks.

Hartmann, Heidi, Olga Sorokina and Erica Williams, *et al.*, "The Best and Worst State Economies for Women," *Institute for Women's Policy Research*, IWPR No. R334, December 2006, www.iwpr.org/ pdf/R334_BWState Economies2006.pdf.
The advocacy group concludes that women's wages have risen in all states since 1989 after adjusting for inflation, but that in "no state does the typical full-time woman worker earn as much as the typical man."

For More Information

Eagle Forum, PO Box 618, Alton, IL 62002; (618) 462-5415; www.eagleforum.org. Conservative social-policy organization opposed to ratification of the Equal Rights Amendment.

4ERA, 4355J Cobb Parkway, #233, Atlanta, GA 30339; (678) 793-6965; www.4era.org. Single-issue organization advocating ratification of the Equal Rights Amendment.

Institute for Women's Policy Research, 1707 L St., N.W., Suite 750, Washington, DC 20036; (202) 785-5100; www .iwpr.org. Research organization that focuses on gender pay as well as other issues affecting women, including poverty and education.

National Committee on Pay Equity, c/o AFT, 555 New Jersey Ave., N.W., Washington, DC 20001-2029; (703) 920-2010; www.pay-equity.org. Coalition of women's and civil rights organizations, labor unions, religious, professional,

legal and educational associations and others focused on pay-equity issues.

National Women's Law Center, 11 Dupont Circle, N.W., Suite 800, Washington, DC 20036; (202) 588-5180; www.nwlc.org. Advocacy group that focuses on employment, health, education and economic-security issues affecting women and girls.

9to5, National Association of Working Women, 207 E. Buffalo St., #211, Milwaukee, WI 53202; (414) 274-0925; www.9to5.org. Grassroots organization focusing on economic-justice issues for women.

U.S. Chamber of Commerce, 1615 H St., N.W., Washington, DC 20062-2000;.(202) 659-6000; www .uschamber.com. Represents business interests before Congress, government agencies and the courts.

4

Labor Unions' Future

Can They Survive in The Age of Globalization?

Pamela M. Prah

New York police officers protest their contract with the city last year. The labor movement suffered a major blow in July when dissident unions formed a rival to the venerable AFL-CIO. Union supporters say all workers have benefited from organized labor's efforts to improve wages and working conditions, but critics argue that unions' spend too much time politicking and not enough organizing. Union membership has plummeted in the past 20 years.

From *CQ Researcher*, September 2, 2005.

Allie Robbins may be just what organized labor needs if unions are to halt their steep decline. Just 22 years old, she's a recent college graduate and a card-carrying union member. Indeed, she's a union recruiter.*

As the national organizer of United Students Against Sweatshops, Robbins addressed the annual AFL-CIO convention in Chicago in July, giving delegates a new vision of unions' future. "I hope many more young people will be involved in all levels of the labor movement," said Robbins, standing nervously before thousands of union members gathered at the Navy Pier.

Robbins may represent labor's future, but she was surrounded by stereotypes of unions' past, including beefy, cigar-smoking men looking for all the world like extras from "The Sopranos," the hit HBO television series about the mob.

"The biggest misconception is that unions are corrupt and unnecessary," Robbins contends. Her organization prods universities to avoid buying their T-shirts, coffee mugs and other logo merchandise from overseas sweatshops.

However, she admits, "It's been a bit of a slow road getting unions to open up to work with younger people. They haven't figured out exactly how to do it yet."

But if unions are going to survive, supporters say, they need to figure it out soon. Labor unions in the 1950s represented about one in three workers, but now it's less than one in eight.

---

* Robbins belongs to the International Federation of Professional and Technical Engineers, which claims a membership of more than 75,000 professional, technical and administrative workers.

Teachers and Police Lead in Union Membership

More than a third of the nation's teachers, librarians, fire fighters and policeman are union members, reflecting the generally high union membership of public-sector workers. By comparison, only about 20 percent of blue-collar professionals in the private sector, such as construction workers and carpenters, belong to unions.

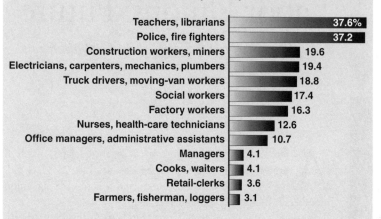

Percentage of Workers Who Are Union Members, by Occupation

Occupation	Percentage
Teachers, librarians	37.6%
Police, fire fighters	37.2
Construction workers, miners	19.6
Electricians, carpenters, mechanics, plumbers	19.4
Truck drivers, moving-van workers	18.8
Social workers	17.4
Factory workers	16.3
Nurses, health-care technicians	12.6
Office managers, administrative assistants	10.7
Managers	4.1
Cooks, waiters	4.1
Retail-clerks	3.6
Farmers, fisherman, loggers	3.1

Source: Bureau of Labor Statistics, Jan. 27, 2005

Union supporters say all Americans, including non-union workers, have benefited from organized labor's efforts over the last 50 years. They point out that union contracts often set the wage scale for non-union workers in a local area, and that labor has been in the forefront of securing workplace safety and anti-discrimination measures that apply to all workers.

"People take for granted what their forefathers fought for all these years," says Linda Dickey, president of Local 419 of the Glass, Molders, Pottery, Plastics and Allied Workers, in Newell, W.Va., during a break at the convention.

But critics argue that unions have outlived their purpose, and that in the age of a globalized work force unions' outdated practices and protection of poor performers encourage employers to shift jobs overseas where there are fewer union protections.

Others complain that unions take members' money to support political causes that many members don't support. "Union members have virtually no say in how their unions spend their hard-earned money," said Linda Chavez, president of the Center for Equal Opportunity, a conservative think tank, and author of the 2004 book, *Betrayal: How Union Bosses Shake Down Their Members and Corrupt American Politics.*[1]

The Chicago convention was supposed to help the union movement figure out how to boost declining membership in the face of hostile business and government actions and mend a split within its own ranks. Instead, the AFL-CIO suffered a bitter and dramatic divorce on the first day of the convention.

The group split nearly in half as seven unions formed a rival labor group called Change to Win. The seceding unions argued that the AFL-CIO had lost its way and was spending too much time and money trying to get Democrats elected to national office and not enough time organizing new members.

The post-split AFL-CIO now embraces 53 unions and 9 million workers, while Change to Win boasts three of the nation's largest unions, representing 6 million workers in the fast-growing service industries.[2]

Andy Stern, president of the Service Employees International Union (SEIU) and a former protégé of AFL-CIO President John Sweeney, led the revolt. His group has organized 900,000 workers in the past nine years, often using unconventional approaches. For example, in 1995 the SEIU blocked bridges leading into Washington, D.C., to call attention to its "Justice for Janitors" campaign.

"Our world has changed. Our economy has changed. Employers have changed, but the AFL-CIO is not willing to make fundamental change as well," Stern said when SEIU and the Teamsters pulled out of the federation, followed a few days later by the United Food and Commercial Workers.

Change to Win had wanted the AFL-CIO to return to the individual unions half the dues money the federation now collects — about $2 billion over the next five years — to fund more organizing. They also wanted to spend $25 million collected from union-backed credit-card purchases to launch a campaign to organize Wal-Mart, the country's largest private employer, which adamantly remains union-free.[3]

The dissenting unions also wanted the 70-year-old Sweeney, who has led the AFL-CIO for a decade, to step aside. He refused, calling the union defections a "grievous insult to all the unions" and a "tragedy for working people."[4]

The split comes at a perilous time for unions. Deregulation, globalization, outsourcing and the information revolution have dealt a staggering blow to the labor movement.

"We got complacent," says Ray Horton, a member of the Tri-County Council of Labor, in Henderson, Ky. "We've had it good for so long, and now we're getting hit from all sides. We need to regroup, re-strategize."

Layoffs in steel and other heavily unionized manufacturing sectors have undercut Sweeney's efforts to bolster labor's sagging membership. The U.S. economy has grown in recent years largely by shifting many unionized manufacturing jobs to Mexico, India, China and other countries with lower labor costs.

Unions also have to fight unscrupulous employers, who hire undocumented workers on the cheap, says Chicago management attorney Jules Crystal. Immigrants can legally join unions even if they are here illegally. But many undocumented workers worry that by joining a union more people will find out that they are here illegally, and some employers threaten deportation if immigrants show interest in joining a union, he says.

"Neither the union nor the employer wants to be basically a party to a fraud upon the government" by knowingly having illegals as members and employees, he says.

Organized labor, nonetheless, has made headway in recruiting immigrants: The number of immigrants in unions increased to 1.8 million in 2003, from 1.4 million in 1996, a 29 percent increase.[5]

Organized labor also is taking a beating from the Bush administration and Congress, according to Richard Hurd, a professor of industrial and labor relations at Cornell University. For example, within months of coming into office, President Bush repealed a Clinton-era ergonomics rule that unions had fought for and eliminated policies that gave unions an edge in some federal contracts.

The current administration is "the most anti-union" in the past 100 years, says Hurd. President Bush and the GOP-controlled Congress "are pursuing policies that make it extraordinarily difficult for unions, and that emboldens employers to pursue anti-union strategies."

In 2004 unions spent heavily to put Democratic presidential candidate John Kerry in the White House in hopes he would roll back Bush policies. Democrats traditionally have favored union interests and enjoyed their heavy backing — in money and votes.

"We should be fighting the Bush administration and corporations, not each other," says Rogelio Flores, a national vice president of the American Federation of Government Employees, the largest union representing federal employees.

The AFL-CIO says politics and organizing go hand in hand. "Political action is certainly a key to workplace rights and probably the No. 1 thing. If you don't elect folks who are sympathetic to the needs of workers, you're only going to lose," says Mike Caputo, a member of the United Mine Workers union and a Democratic West Virginia state legislator.

Many observers say unions need to work on their image as well as their message. "There is still the perception of people at the top feathering their nests at the expense of the lowest-paid workers at the bottom," says Randel Johnson, vice president of labor, immigration and employee benefits for the U.S. Chamber of Commerce.

As unions debate their future, here are some questions being asked:

Do today's workers need unions?

Unions were created in an era before employment laws required safe working conditions, a minimum wage, unemployment benefits or protections against discrimination. Many of those laws were passed in the early 20th century after organized labor demanded them.

Many critics say labor unions today are dinosaurs from a bygone era that are more worried about their own power than workers' needs.

But supporters say unions are critical. "Workers need unions today as much as they ever have," says Robert Korstad, a history professor at Duke University who specializes in labor. Most workers want full-time jobs with health care, retirement and other benefits, he says, but in

Union Participation Has Steadily Dropped

Union membership has decreased by 50 percent over the past 20 years. Labor experts blame a number of factors, including globalization, deregulation, outsourcing and changes in the economy. Critics of unions say their outdated practices, including protection of poor performers, encourage employers to shift jobs overseas. Others complain that unions take members' money to support political causes that many members don't support.

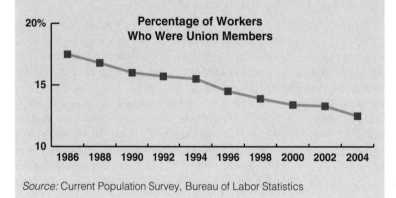

Percentage of Workers Who Were Union Members

Source: Current Population Survey, Bureau of Labor Statistics

today's economy workers can often only find part-time work without benefits. Others work full time to collect "poverty wages" that aren't enough to feed a family, he says.

"Just for financial reasons alone, there are lots of arguments in support of unions," Korstad says.

Union workers' median weekly earnings are 28 percent higher than their non-union counterparts ($781 a week vs. $612).[6] And while only 16 percent of non-union workers have guaranteed pensions, 70 percent of union workers do, according to the AFL-CIO. Moreover, 86 percent of union workers' employers offer health insurance benefits, compared with only 59.5 percent among non-union workers.[7]

Unions also are credited with helping to build America's middle class after the Great Depression and World War II, prodding employers to pay wages high enough so workers could afford to buy the products that many made on the assembly lines.

"If you think back to what made America great 50 years ago, it was because a job at GM, a union job on construction or driving a truck was a job [that allowed] you to own a home, raise a family, have a bridge to the middle class," said SEIU President Stern. Today, "it takes two, three, four Wal-Mart jobs to raise a family, you don't get health care and a Wal-Mart job is a bridge to nowhere." Change to Win unions want to "bring back the GM economy, where work is rewarded," he said.[8]

But Chavez, whose nomination as Labor secretary for President Bush was defeated largely because of union opposition, sees it very differently. "The shift away from unionization in the private sector is a natural one, as private companies have competed for the best workers by offering good wages and benefits, rendering private-sector unions unnecessary in most cases," she writes.[9]

However, Johnson of the U.S. Chamber of Commerce says that even though today's workplace laws "protect workers from the roughest edges of capitalism," unions are not obsolete. "Is there less of a need for unions than there has been in the past? Yes. But that doesn't mean there is no need for unions. If a work force is in the situation in which an employer is truly exploiting them, then the union option is an important one to have."

If unions are still vital, why aren't workers joining them?

Labor supporters cite a 2005 AFL-CIO poll showing that 54 percent of non-union workers would join a union if they had a choice.[10] But unions contend U.S. labor laws are too weak to protect workers who are too frightened to organize for fear they will lose their jobs. The National Labor Relations Act (NLRA) is the main U.S. law meant to protect workers' rights to organize, to bargain collectively and to strike. The Railway Labor Act covers workers in the railroad and airline industries while the Federal Labor Relations Act covers federal government employees' organizing and bargaining rights.

"U.S. labor laws contain weak penalties, are riddled with loopholes and are not effectively enforced," says Carol Pier, labor rights and trade researcher at Human Rights Watch, a New York-based advocacy group.

Workers fired for organizing often wait for years for their cases to be decided by labor boards and courts while employers "pay no price for deliberate delays and frivolous appeals," the group said, citing a report that concluded the "deck is stacked against U.S. workers."[11]

Employers also have the upper hand in organizing drives because they can force workers to attend anti-union meetings, but at the same time prohibit organizers from even distributing union literature in work areas, wrote Andrew Strom, a staff attorney for SEIU Local 32BJ, which represents 75,000 building service workers in New York, New Jersey, Connecticut and Pennsylvania.[12]

Moreover, Strom said, workers who think they were fired for trying to organize a union — a violation of the NLRA — can't sue for discrimination like other workers. Instead, they have to go to the National Labor Relations Board; it can order the employer to reinstate the worker and pay back wages, but there are no fines, penalties or punitive damages. The process can take five years, he says. "No wonder companies regularly fire workers for trying to organize," he wrote.[13]

The business community discounts allegations that the NLRA makes it difficult for workers to join unions. "Nowhere in the [U.S.] Constitution [does] it say union organizing has to be easy," employment lawyer Crystal says. Unions want employers to stay impartial during drives and sign "neutrality" agreements, which he says are a bad idea. "It's a big decision for workers; they should hear both sides."

Pat Cleary, senior vice president for communications at the National Association of Manufacturers (NAM), agrees. If the unions aren't blaming the law, he says, they blame President Ronald Reagan's 1981 firing of striking air-traffic controllers and what they call the "anti-union" policies of the GOP administrations of Reagan, George H. W. Bush and now George W. Bush. But unions' numbers continued to slide under President Bill Clinton, a pro-labor Democrat, Cleary points out. The unions, he says, have "blamed everyone but themselves" for their lagging membership numbers.

"The law is the same as in the 1950s, when unions were riding high," says Johnson, of the U.S. Chamber. "Something else is going on here. Maybe there are other reasons, like their message needs to be changed."

Marick Masters, a professor of business administration at the University of Pittsburgh, says there is an element of truth in all the reasons unions cite for their membership decline, but "the main point is that labor hasn't come up with a model that appeals to most workers."

Others say some workers don't need or want unions and join only because they work in states that require workers to pay union fees. (*See map, p. 77.*)

"Rather than working to preserve and expand their power to order workers to 'pay up or be fired,' unions should try to improve their product in order to attract workers' voluntary support," said Stefan Gleason, vice president of the National Right to Work Legal Defense Foundation, which provides free legal advice to workers who think their rights have been violated by "compulsory unionism abuses."[14]

Are unions protecting U.S. workers from the effects of globalization?

Today's global economy moves products, technology and jobs at lightning speed, shifting millions of unionized jobs to lower-wage countries.[15] Nearly 3 million factory jobs have been lost between 2000 and 2003.[16]

And even jobs that have not been shifted overseas are negatively affected by globalization, say union officials, because domestic employers often feel compelled to reduce pay and benefits for U.S. workers to compete with overseas competitors.

"Corporate greed is driving profit share at the expense of wages, safe workplaces, conditions and entitlements for workers," Sharan Burrow, president of the International Confederation of Free Trade Unions, told the AFL-CIO convention this summer. "Without a global governance architecture that protects the rights of workers and their communities, the corporate law of the jungle grows and so does the dislocation of jobs and the consequent divide between the rich and the poor within and across countries."

But others say labor needs to get off its protectionist bandwagon and join the global market. Today unions that help U.S. employers remain competitive help American workers keep their jobs, says Johnson of the U.S. Chamber. "It's important for unions to approach workers saying, 'We know there are international competitive pressures, but we can find ways to improve your situation and still keep your employer competitive,'" he says.

AFL-CIO President John Sweeney, Secretary-Treasurer Richard Trumka and Executive Vice President Linda Chavez-Thompson put up a united front at the federation's July 24 Unity rally. The next day, the Teamsters and Service Employees International unions broke from the federation, rejecting Sweeney's offer to change policies.

Businesses say labor costs are not the only reason they move their operations, but wages and benefits are a big target since they make up about 70 percent of costs.

For years, the top priority for most unions representing the auto, steel, chemical and other manufacturing sectors was to keep union jobs at home. But in today's globalized labor market, employers say, unions cannot come to the bargaining table with sudden demands and expect the company to stay in business.

Cleary of the NAM says in a changing global marketplace unions' outdated "us vs. them" polarized workplace no longer works. "Today the trend is away from confrontation and toward cooperation . . . the competition is outside the plant, not in it."

In fact, many employers say if they cannot reduce labor costs, they cannot survive. Several iconic American corporations announced steep layoffs this summer, citing global competitive pressures. Eastman Kodak is laying off up to 25,000 workers by 2007; Hewlett-Packard will eliminate 14,500 jobs over the next year and Kleenex-maker Kimberly-Clark plans to cut 6,000 jobs by 2008.[17]

Unions have steadfastly opposed free-trade policies with countries that do not protect workers' rights and safety or provide benefits. Without such protections written into trade treaties, unions say, U.S. businesses are enticed to send jobs to countries where workers often toil for 12 or 15 hours a day in unsafe conditions without health insurance or pensions. The 1993 North American Free Trade Agreement (NAFTA), for example, cost 1 million U.S. jobs, unions say.[18] Unions also opposed the Central American Free Trade Agreement (CAFTA), which Congress approved at the same time the AFL-CIO held its convention.[19]

"CAFTA, like NAFTA, will sell out Americans' jobs," said Linda Chavez-Thompson, executive vice president of the AFL-CIO. "Multinational corporations will speed up their race to the bottom when it comes to wages and workplace protections, driving workers further into exploitation."[20]

Korstad of Duke says unions must build international alliances with other unions and human rights groups in order to improve working conditions in the Third World and to give unions more leverage. "The labor movement can't go it alone."

Charles Kernaghan, executive director of the National Labor Committee, a New York City-based labor-rights advocacy group, agrees. "You're not going to negotiate your way out of a global economy. You're not going to do it alone with individual unions. It's not possible."

Kernaghan's organization has exposed low-wage overseas factories producing goods for Disney, Nike and Target, and in the late 1990s it put a national spotlight on the sweatshops in Honduras that made Kathy Lee Gifford's Wal-Mart clothing line.

"There's been a tremendous turnaround" in U.S. unions' understanding that protectionism is not the answer, but fighting overseas sweatshops is crucial, he says. "Unions now realize they need to be at the table when the global economy is being discussed. We certainly can have more worker-rights standards attached to trade agreements."

The Steelworkers' union was quick to catch on to the need for international alliances, Kernaghan says. The union got its wake-up call in the 1980s after Phelps Dodge broke the union's copper mine strike in Arizona and permanently replaced striking workers. "We had our lunch eaten in the 1980s. We knew we had to change," says Marco Trbovich, assistant to the Steelworkers' president for communications. After striking union members at Bridgestone-Firestone were also fired and replaced in the 1990s, the union launched a series of "strategic alliances with sophisticated militant and reasonably resourced unions" worldwide, says Gerald Fernandez, assistant to the Steelworkers' president for international affairs.

The Steelworkers forged ties with counterparts in Australia, the Czech Republic, Germany, Mexico and Turkey. This past June, for example, some 10,000 unionized workers in Mexico, Peru and the United States protested in support of the Steelworkers' strike against Asarco, owner of several Arizona copper mines.

"Cross-border solidarity is the only way to deal with global companies," Fernandez says.

Both the AFL-CIO and the Change to Win coalition vow to unite workers across borders, and a primary target is Wal-Mart, the nation's largest employer, with 1.2 million U.S. workers.

"Wal-Martization is a global phenomenon, and a global approach is required," Change to Win's Web site explains. The AFL-CIO kicked off a "Wake Up Wal-Mart" campaign that calls for massive effort by organized labor "to help Wal-Mart workers win a voice at work and ensure that Wal-Mart's business model does not spread to other countries."

"We are not against unions," the company said. "They may be right for some companies but there is simply no need for a third party to come between our associates and their managers."[21] The company eliminated the butcher shop at a Texas store in 2000 after local workers voted to unionize, and it closed a store in Quebec, Canada, this year rather than negotiate with workers who voted for a union.[22]

A major union concern is Wal-Mart's health plan. Its high deductibles and other requirements have forced some employees to rely on Medicaid as a safety net. In Florida, for example, Wal-Mart has some 12,300 employees and family members enrolled in Medicaid — more than any company in the state.[23] The company also is facing the country's largest gender-discrimination case, affecting some 1.6 million female workers.

'Right to Work' Laws Enacted in 22 States

Twenty-two states had "right to work" laws in 2004 giving employees the right to join or not join a workplace union. In the remaining states, employees must pay union fees at unionized job sites even if they don't join the union. Unions oppose "right to work" laws because they lower union participation.

Source: National Right to Work Legal Defense Fund

"When Wal-Mart executives calculate that by underpaying employees and providing inadequate health care they can sell a cheaper product, that forces competitors to make the same tough calculations — or go out of business," said AFL-CIO President Sweeney.[24]

Should unions change their focus?

The unions that deserted the AFL-CIO in July said it had spent too much on politics and not enough to organize new members. But the federation says both are equally important.

Other unionists, however, say neither the AFL-CIO nor the dissenting unions quite get it. They say labor needs a new message and a new role in today's high-tech, transient world of work, where jumping from one employer to another is commonplace and where international borders are no obstacle to employers seeking lower wages.

The seven unions in the new Change to Win coalition say organizing is their top priority. Representing 6 million workers, the seven — the Carpenters, Laborers, Service Employees, Teamsters, United Farm Workers, United Food and Commercial Workers and a merged

Georgetown Living Wage Campaign

Georgetown University students protest in February 2005 for living wages for the school's blue-collar workers. Along with students on many other campuses, unions have lobbied for living-wage ordinances in at least 100 cities since 1994. Georgetown raised its hourly rate to $13.

union of hotel and garment workers known as UNITE-HERE — are targeting some 35 million service jobs that cannot be outsourced, such as construction, hospitality and child and health care.

Rather than organize workers by one plant or work site at a time, the coalition plans to try organizing an entire company at once, the way industrial unions organized the auto and steel industries in the 1930s. SEIU, the coalition's lead union, used the strategy in Los Angeles and Washington, D.C., to organize janitors across several employers.

The coalition says its political clout will grow as its membership grows. "We must have more members in order to change the political climate that is undermining workers' rights in this country," Teamsters President James P. Hoffa said when the 1.4 million-member union left the AFL-CIO in July.[25]

However, Change to Win will not be an ATM money machine for Democrats running for election, unlike the AFL-CIO, coalition leaders say. Nearly 90 percent of labor's $61 million in contributions in the 2004 elections went to Democrats, according to the Center for Responsive Politics.[26]

"Over the last several years, we've gotten more and more focused on politics and particularly on Democratic

politics," SEIU's Stern has said. "And I don't think that will grow our labor movement stronger."

The AFL-CIO, on the other hand, says labor needs a united front to fight anti-worker companies and policies, and Sweeney said the federation would focus "on the greedy corporations and the right-wing elected officials who are trying to tear our country apart."[27]

Sweeney also says that despite lagging union membership in recent years, the federation had been able to step up its political influence since he took over as president in 1995. Even though union households constitute only 17 percent of the voting-age population, they represented 24 percent of the 2004 vote, well above the 19 percent of 1992, the AFL-CIO says.[28]

But Sweeny admits that although the AFL-CIO aligns itself primarily with Democrats, 25-30 percent of union members are Republicans. "We have to hold politicians accountable, regardless of the party," he said.

However, says Korstad of Duke, the labor movement must rethink its political strategy. "What's the point of giving money to candidates that your own members won't even vote for?"

The percentage of union households that voted for Republican congressional candidates has stayed in the 30-40 percent range since 1952, and the rates are even higher for GOP presidential candidates.[29] Some 45 percent of union households, for example, voted in 1980 for Republican presidential candidate Ronald Reagan, who historians say successfully appealed to blue-collar laborers' resentment that their tax dollars were being squandered on "welfare parasites."[30]

Labor supporters and opponents agree that unions need to work on their image and their message. Unions need a new message other than just saying, " 'Employers are bad, and you need unions to protect you,'" says Johnson of the U.S. Chamber. "I don't think that sells anymore."

The University of Pittsburgh's Masters says today's workers "look at unions as providing rigid work rules and conflictual types of relationships that don't have much appeal to them." Workers, and young people in particular, "have no more interest in being represented by a stodgy bureaucratic organization than they do in going to work for one. And that's the problem with labor's image."

Masters suggests unions provide services for both workers and employers, such as employee training or group health insurance, he says, so individual employers don't have to carry all the health-care costs.

Nelson Lichtenstein, a history professor at the University of California, has suggested turning union "hiring halls" into job centers for today's programmers, consultants and other professionals who change jobs frequently.[31] "The idea of collective bargaining between one union and one employer is clearly an antique notion," he wrote in his 2002 book, *State of the Union: A Century of American Labor.*

Cornell's Hurd says workers are more individualistic than 50 years ago, when they wanted union protection. "Unions need to find a way to connect with workers," he says, particularly professional, technical and low-wage workers. "It may require something totally different from what unions have offered in the past," such as continuing education to help technical workers stay on top of their game.

Moreover, says Korstad of Duke, "The labor movement needs to really think about its public relations, how it convinces members of the American middle class that people working in the service sector deserve the kinds of benefits and opportunities that the United States has to offer."

BACKGROUND

Birth of the Movement

When the labor movement was born in the 1880s, most Americans — including children — worked 14-hour days, six days a week, often in dangerous conditions for little pay. Overtime and sick pay were non-existent.

Machines were just starting to replace the workers who knitted stockings, stitched dresses and cut leather for shoes. But the pace was fast and furious for the new machine operators. Children in cotton mills put in 14-hour shifts for seven cents a day, or toiled in coal mines wearing harnesses that enabled them to drag buckets or carts of coal.[32]

At first, labor's future appeared to lie with the Knights of Labor, one of the first large unions.[33] But the organization of skilled and unskilled workers, farmers and small-business men, floundered in the face of competition from the American Federation of Labor, which targeted only skilled workers, such as carpenters and printers.

However, it took several years for the AFL's dominance to emerge. In 1881 leaders of local craft unions created the Federation of Organized Trade and Labor Unions, which five years later morphed into the AFL. Samuel Gompers, the leader of a cigar-making union, became its first president in 1896.

In the 1890s bitter labor strikes occurred at Homestead Steel in Pennsylvania (1892) and the Pullman railway car company in Illinois (1894). Both led to riots that killed several workers. In both cases, the federal and state governments helped end the strikes by sending in thousands of troops.

For a brief time, radical elements in the labor movement contributed to the public's perception that anarchists or socialists dedicated to the destruction of the free-enterprise system ran the unions. For instance, the International Workers of the World (IWW), or Wobblies, called on workers to take over factories, but their movement fizzled in the face of severe opposition, particularly after they called for a strike in industries manufacturing war goods during World War I.

Meanwhile, hundreds of IWW leaders were found guilty of sedition, swept up along with other dissidents during an anti-communist "red scare" that gripped the country in 1919. In some cases, mobs beat, tarred-and-feathered and lynched IWW members.[34]

Although unions were regarded with suspicion, labor's legislative agenda won support from populists and progressives in the late 19th and early 20th centuries.

Protecting Labor

In the early 1900s, the labor movement helped gain passage of state wage and hour laws, aided by the imfamous Triangle Shirtwaist Fire, which killed 146 young women and girls working in a New York City garment factory. The tragedy led to new factory-inspection laws and improved safety conditions. It also boosted the International Ladies' Garment Workers Union. A year later, Congress created the U.S. Department of Labor.

However, when the Great Depression began in 1929, workers still lacked federal laws allowing them to form or join a union or establishing a minimum wage or maximum workweek. That changed with the election of Franklin D. Roosevelt as president. In 1935, FDR proposed the National Labor Relations Act, also known as the Wagner Act for its chief sponsor, Sen. Robert F. Wagner, D-N.Y.

CHRONOLOGY

Before 1900 *Workers start to organize into unions as the country industrializes and moves westward.*

1886 Unionization of skilled "trade" workers such as printers and cigar makers leads to founding of the American Federation of Labor (AFL).

1890s Bitter strikes at Homestead Steel (1892) in Pennsylvania and the Pullman railway car company in Illinois (1894) lead to riots, killing several workers.

1900-1940s *New laws provide tools to settle workplace problems.*

1935 National Labor Relations Act gives workers the right to join unions while prohibiting employers from using "unfair labor practices."

1938 Differences between the "trade" unions of the AFL and industrial unions lead to a formal split in the AFL and creation of the Congress of Industrial Organizations (CIO).

1947 Congress passes the Taft-Hartley Act outlawing the practice of hiring only union members, known as "closed shops."

1950s-1970s *Links between unions and organized crime are discovered. George Meany, a fervent anti-communist, becomes AFL president in 1952 and heads AFL-CIO until 1979.*

1955 AFL-CIO is created, representing some 15.5 million workers.

1959 Congress passes Landrum-Griffin Act to root out organized crime in labor unions; unions must file annual financial reports showing how union dues are spent.

1977 Congress rejects unions' bids for stiffer penalties for employers who break the law when workers try to organize and speedier union-representation procedures

1980s-1990s *Union membership drops amid increasing global competition.*

1981 President Ronald Reagan fires 11,000 striking air-traffic controllers and decertifies their union, signaling to private-sector employers that they can hire permanent replacements during work stoppages.

1984 Unions help Walter F. Mondale win Democratic presidential nomination, but he loses in a landslide to Reagan as union members deliver votes to the GOP.

November 1993 Congress and President Bill Clinton override labor's opposition and approve the North American Free Trade Agreement (NAFTA).

November 1994 Republicans capture both chambers of Congress for the first time since 1954, undercutting organized labor's political agenda.

October 1995 John Sweeney, head of the Service Employees International Union, replaces Lane Kirkland as head of the AFL-CIO.

March 1996 Top AFL-CIO leaders endorse President Clinton for re-election and OK increasing dues to help build a $35 million political fund to target House Republicans.

2000s *Several unions split off from the AFL-CIO to create the Change to Win coalition to focus more on organizing.*

2001 Newly elected President Bush repeals a Clinton-era ergonomics rule that unions had sought for more than a decade.

June 2005 Dissident AFL-CIO unions form the Change to Win coalition and threaten to pull out of the federation, arguing it is not spending enough time on organizing.

July 2005 Two of the AFL-CIO's largest unions — the Service Employees International Union and the Teamsters — pull out of the AFL-CIO on the first day of the federation's convention in Chicago, followed by the United Food and Commercial Workers Union. Four other unions make up the coalition: Carpenters, Farm Workers, Laborers and UNITE-HERE. The AFL-CIO and the coalition both vow to step up organizing and to target non-union companies such as Wal-Mart.

The Wagner Act still guarantees most private-sector workers the right to join unions and prohibits employers from "unfair labor practices" that discriminate against workers trying to unionize. It also requires employers to bargain in good faith with unions. The Railway Labor Act of 1926 provided similar protections for railroad workers; it was amended in 1936 to cover airline workers.

In 1938 the federal Fair Labor Standards Act outlawed child labor and established the first minimum wage — 25 cents an hour — and a 40-hour workweek.

But even as the reforms made it easier for workers to join unions, labor leaders bickered over how best to organize workers. The dispute led to the creation in 1935 of the Committee for Industrial Organizations (CIO) within the AFL. The dispute centered around whether the labor movement should target workers with specific crafts or trades — the AFL's strategy — or go after unskilled workers, the strategy advocated by the CIO.

The AFL said any attempt to organize workers in an entire factory had to recognize separate "crafts." So, for example, workers in a car plant who painted the cars could join the Painters union while workers who made the cars could join the Machinists union. The CIO, led by firebrand John L. Lewis, wanted all the workers in the plant to belong to the same union, contending that the AFL's craft classifications were irrelevant in an economy that by the 1930s was becoming dominated by mass-production industries.

The CIO didn't wait for the AFL's blessing. It proceeded to organize the steel, auto, glass and rubber sectors and quickly enlisted more new members than the AFL. It broke away from the AFL in 1938, but its acronym now stood for Congress of Industrial Organizations.

Mafia Ties

Alarmed by a series of strikes in the 1940s, business and conservative leaders pressed Congress in 1947 to pass the Taft-Hartley Act limiting unions' powers. Enacted over the veto of President Harry S Truman, the law, still in effect today, outlawed closed shops, or workplaces that hired only union members.

The law also allowed states to pass "right to work" laws, which give employees the right to decide not to join a union. The measure also required a mandatory

cooling-off period in any strike deemed by a president to constitute a "national emergency."

The 1950s kicked off a period of relative labor peace, as the country basked in a robust postwar economy. A twist of fate in 1952 found both the AFL and CIO needing new leaders when the presidents of both groups died within two weeks of one another. The new leaders — AFL's George Meany and CIO's Walter Reuther — agreed to bury the hatchet. In 1954 the two federations signed a "no-raiding" pact and reunified the following year. The new AFL-CIO represented some 15.5 million workers, its all-time high.

In 1950-51, televised Senate hearings chaired by Sen. Estes D. Kefauver, D-Tenn., exposed the darker, organized-crime side to some unions. Then in 1957, McClellan committee investigators, led by Chief Counsel Robert F. Kennedy, discovered that the Mafia had infiltrated the Teamsters union.

Over the next two decades, the U.S. economy shifted from union mining, manufacturing and transportation jobs to non-union service and retail jobs. In the 1970s, the Northeast and Midwest — the epicenters of unionized, industrial jobs — were devastated by increased competition from Asian producers of steel, ships and automobiles.

Yet organizing was not a high priority for AFL-CIO President Meany, who remained steadfastly committed to the increasingly divisive Vietnam War. It was not uncommon to see unionized workers wearing hard hats and waving American flags beating up anti-war demonstrators.[35]

During the 1970s, the AFL-CIO enjoyed a mixed legislative record. Congress enacted worker-protection measures in the Occupational Safety and Health Act and approved minimum standards for workers' pension plans under the Employee Retirement Income Security Act in 1974.

When Democrat Jimmy Carter won the presidency in 1976, labor hoped it had a better chance to stiffen penalties against employers who block union organizing efforts and to speed up the NLRB union-representation procedures. But vehement business-community opposition killed the effort in 1977.

Busting Unions

The legislative defeat was a harbinger of what was to come during the Reagan and Bush administrations in the

Married to the Mob?

Nicodemo "Little Nicky" Scarfo, Vincent "Chin" Gigante and Anthony "Gaspipe" Casso are just some of the mobsters who have been involved with organized labor.

Scarfo, serving a 69-year prison sentence for racketeering, extortion and murder, ran the Hotel and Restaurant Employees union in the late 1980s. Genovese crime boss Gigante — who had allegedly infiltrated the International Longshoreman's Association — was later convicted of racketeering. And Casso — former underboss of the Luchese crime family and now serving a life sentence after admitting to 36 murders — was accused in 2001 of taking money to influence several construction unions, including a local of the Laborers' International Union of North America.[1]

Several major U.S. Senate investigations beginning in the 1950s have documented organized crime's involvement with unions. Live telecasts of 1950-51 hearings of a special Senate panel chaired by Sen. Estes Kefauver (D-Tenn.) were credited with increasing the public's awareness of organized crime and the breadth of its stranglehold on unions and their pension funds. In a book about his committee's work, Kefauver wrote, the Mafia "is no fairy tale" and is engaged in "almost every conceivable type of criminal violence, including murder…smuggling…kidnapping and labor racketeering."[2]

Another probe, conducted in 1957-58 by the Senate Select Committee on Improper Activities in the Labor or Management Field, found "systemic" racketeering in both the International Brotherhood of Teamsters and the Hotel Employees and Restaurant Employees (HERE) union.[3] The federal government took over both unions in the late 1980s and early '90s — the most drastic step it could take — to weed out mob influence.

In 1959 Congress passed the Landrum-Griffin Act, which requires that unions file annual financial reports showing how union dues are spent. Congress then passed the Racketeer Influenced and Corrupt Organizations Act of 1970 — the so-called RICO act — which allowed the Justice Department to go after unions with mob ties.

In 1986, the President's Commission on Organized Crime reported that the Laborers' International Union was dominated by organized crime.[4] In the early 1980s, former Gambino family boss Paul Castellano was overheard saying, "Our job is to run the unions," according to the FBI, which had planted bugs in Castellano's house in 1983.[5] Castellano was shot and killed in front of a steakhouse on New York's East Side in 1985 on the orders of future Gambino crime boss John Gotti.

According to federal authorities, union and mob bosses often team up to demand kickbacks from union members in return for prime job assignments. Crime families also have been known to demand money from contractors in exchange for "labor peace." And contractors on union projects sometimes must pay salaries for "ghost" employees — crime family members who either don't show up or show up but do not work.

Prosecutors say union corruption in New York City inflates the already high cost of building union projects in Manhattan by $200 million to $500 million a year, an amount prosecutors sardonically call the "mob tax."[6]

By 2004, the Labor Department's inspector general had 359 pending labor racketeering investigations, of which more than a third involved organized crime.[7] Internal affairs of the "big four" unions — Teamsters, HERE, Laborers' and International Longshoreman's Association — still make up a significant portion of the Labor Department's racketeering investigations, the department said.

Union pension funds are a tempting target for labor racketeers. Union officials with mob ties have been found diverting union pension funds for their own personal use or investing the money in mob-tied businesses. Money from the Teamsters pension fund, for example, reportedly financed 85 percent of the casino hotels that appeared on the Las Vegas Strip in the late 1970s.[8]

Three major unions with longtime corruption problems are still trying to rid their unions of corruption:

International Brotherhood of Teamsters — To many observers, the Teamsters is the poster boy for mob-run unions. The federal government deems the union so corrupt that it took over the union in 1989 and continues to oversee its operation.

The legendary Jimmy Hoffa, president of the Teamsters from 1957-71, was convicted of attempted bribery of a grand juror in 1967 and sentenced to 15 years in prison. In 1971, however, President Richard M. Nixon commuted his sentence to time served on the condition he not participate in union activities for 10 years.

Hoffa disappeared in 1975, never to be found, after leaving for a lunch with men linked to the Mafia. His son, James P. Hoffa, a labor lawyer, is now president of the 1.3-million-member union. He took over as president in 1998 after federal investigators discovered that union funds were being diverted to support President Ron Carey's 1996 re-election. Carey never served jail time, but some of his associates did. Last year, former federal prosecutor Edwin Stier, whom the Teamsters hired to clean up the union, resigned, saying Hoffa — who has vowed to get rid of federal oversight of the Teamsters — was retreating from his anti-corruption pledges.[9]

Laborers' International Union — The federal government also keeps close tabs on the 800,000-member Laborers' union, which represents construction, maintenance and food service workers, but the union isn't in trusteeship. In 1995, the Justice Department decided not to pursue formal criminal charges but retained the right to file a racketeering suit if the union didn't clean up its act. In 2000 the union reached an agreement with the Justice Department after promising to retain "anti-corruption" reforms through 2006.[10] The union has removed at least 226 corrupt officials, including 125 who were linked to organized crime.[11] President Arthur A Coia Jr., a fund raiser for the Democratic Party and a visitor to the White House during Clinton's presidency, pleaded guilty in 2000 to a felony tax-evasion charge and was banned for life from holding any positions of power within the union. However, he was allowed to collect his $250,000 salary as "general president emeritus."[12] Terrence O'Sullivan, a top aide to Coia, took over as president in 2000.

HERE-UNITE — The 2004 merger of the hotel workers union and the Union of Needletrades, Industrial and Textile Employees created HERE-UNITE, which represents nearly 450,000 hotel, casino and garment workers. In the 1930s, organized crime was linked to HERE locals in New York City and in the 1970s to locals in Florida.[13] In 1991, the Justice Department took control of HERE's Local 54 in Atlantic City, N.J., which represented hotel and casino workers and reportedly had ties to organized crime figures in Philadelphia.[14] In 1995, the Justice Department asked the courts to take over the entire HERE union, maintaining that the union was run by organized crime.[15] It was

Former Teamsters union President James R. Hoffa testifies in 1957 before the Senate Rackets Committee. He disappeared in 1975, presumably killed by former Mafia associates.

Getty Images/Al Muto

the first time the government resorted to such drastic action since it took over the Teamsters in 1989. The federal government oversaw the union until 2000, when the Justice Department determined the organization had largely purged its ties with organized crime.[16]

[1] George McEvoy, "Mob Influence Checked in Some Years Ago," *Palm Beach Post*, Aug. 30, 1995, p 1A; Carl Horowitz, "Union Corruption in America: Still a Growth Industry," National Institute for Labor Relations Research, p. 36; and U.S. Department of Labor press release: "Scalamandre Brothers Plead Guilty to Mob Payoffs in Exchange for Labor Peace," Oct. 31, 2001.

[2] Estes Kefauver, *Crime in America* (1952).

[3] FBI Investigative Programs, *Organized Crime*, available at www.fbi.gov/hq/cid/orgcrime/lcn/laborrack.htm.

[4] President's Commission on Organized Crime, Report to the President and the Attorney General, "The Edge: Organized Crime, Business and Labor Unions," U.S. Government Printing Office, March 1986.

[5] FBI Investigative Programs, *op. cit.*

[6] Steven Malanga, "How To Run the Mob Out of Gotham," *City Journal*, winter 2001.

[7] Office of Inspector General, U.S. Department of Labor, "The Evolution of Organized Crime and Labor Racketeering Corruption," November 2004.

[8] "Heroes of Law Enforcement: Peter Wacks, Retired FBI Special Agent," *Illinois Police & Sheriff's News*, available at www.ipsn.org/wacks.htm, updated Aug. 9, 2005.

[9] Steven Greenhouse, "Citing Pullback, Antigraft Team Quits Teamsters," *The New York Times*, April 30, 2004, p. A1.

[10] Press release, U.S. Department of Justice, "Justice Department Announces New Agreement Continuing Laborers Union Reforms Until 2006," Jan. 20, 2000.

[11] Carl Horowitz, "Union Corruption in America: Still A Growth Industry," National Institute for Labor Research, 2004, p. 17.

[12] Mike Stanton, "Coia enters guilty plea to felony fraud charge," *The Providence* [Rhode Island] *Journal*, Feb. 1, 2000, p. B1.

[13] McEvoy, *op. cit.*

[14] Press release, "Casino Workers' Union Officers to Step Down," April 12, 1991, released by PR News Wire; Horowitz, *op. cit.*

[15] McEvoy, *op. cit.*

[16] Steven Greenhouse, "U.S. Agrees to End Oversight of Hotel-Restaurant Union," *The New York Times*, Dec. 3, 2000. Section 1, p. 47.

Getty Images/Bob Strong

Vincent "Chin" Gigante, former boss of the powerful Genovese crime family in New York, was convicted of labor racketeering in 1997 and sentenced to 12 years in prison. Federal prosecutors say some unions still have ties to organized crime.

1980s and early '90s. Reagan, a former head of the Screen Actors Guild, won the presidency in 1980 and again four years later, in part, by winning over conservative union voters. Yet he set an anti-union tone for his presidency in 1981 when he fired striking air-traffic controllers — government employees represented by the Professional Air Traffic Controllers' Organization (PATCO) — and decertified the union. Reagan said the strike was illegal.

To labor's horror, most Americans endorsed Reagan's take-charge handling of the strike. In the coming years, Reagan and other Republicans increasingly cast organized labor as a selfish special interest unconcerned about ordinary citizens' needs.[36]

Reagan's actions signaled to employers in the private sector that it was OK to hire permanent replacements during work stoppages — as Reagan had done. Over the next few years, several major companies, including Greyhound, Phelps Dodge and Eastern Airlines, followed suit.

Moreover, in the first full year after PATCO, the number of major strikes fell from several hundred a year to less than 100 and has continued to fall ever since. The federal government in 2004 recorded only 17 major strikes or lockouts involving at least 1,000 workers.[37]

In the 1984 presidential election, unions played a big role in winning the Democratic presidential nomination for Walter F. Mondale, only to see their candidate lose in a landslide, as many union members — dubbed "Reagan Democrats" — delivered votes to the GOP.

Organized labor hoped that Democrat Bill Clinton's election as president in 1992 would change its political fortunes. In 1993, Clinton pushed through the labor-backed Family and Medical Leave Act, a success for labor. But that same year, the Democratically controlled Congress approved the North American Free Trade Act despite labor's concerns it would cost U.S. jobs — and thus union members.

Labor's political hopes were dashed, however, in 1994, when Republicans captured control of both chambers of Congress — for the first time since 1954. Since FDR, unions have tied their fate to that of the Democrats, although there have been exceptions. The Teamsters, for instance, endorsed Reagan for president and have reached out to Republicans and business on issues such as drilling in the Arctic National Wildlife Refuge in Alaska.[38]

AFL-CIO activists demanded a change, charging that Lane Kirkland — who had replaced Meany in 1979 — wasn't doing enough to help U.S. workers. SEIU head Sweeney ousted Kirkland in 1995.

Sweeney came in promising to organize more workers and boost unions' influence.[39] He aggressively confronted business, rallied workers and joined forces with students and community activists. In 1996, the AFL-CIO launched "Union Summer" to train student activists in organizing picket lines and holding demonstrations. Then in 2000, the group unveiled "Seminary Summer" to involve religious leaders in workplace issues. The groups fanned out to campuses and cities to protest overseas sweatshops and promote "fair trade" policies that incorporate labor protections in trade treaties.

Unions also have lobbied for so-called living-wage ordinances in nearly 100 cities since 1994. The laws require companies that receive tax breaks or contracts from cities to pay workers more than the federal minimum wage.[40] In 2003 the AFL-CIO created a

Student Activists Fight for Workers' Rights

On campuses across the country, student activists have teamed up with unions and nonprofit groups to prod universities to pay "fair" wages to their low-level workers and to shun firms that treat overseas workers inhumanely. They also are encouraging university workers to join unions. But whether the activists themselves will join unions after graduation remains uncertain.

- At Georgetown University, for example, 22 students went on a hunger strike in March, demanding that the university pay its workers a "living wage" of $15/hour, compared to the $6.60 some custodial and dining hall workers earned. The university now pays a minimum of $13 per hour.[1]

- Students from Duke, the University of North Carolina-Chapel Hill, Florida State, Michigan State and other schools supported the AFL-CIO's Farm Labor Organizing Committee's efforts to win better pay and conditions for 8,000 migrant cucumber pickers at the Mt. Olive Pickle Co. in North Carolina. The contract that resulted provides for a union hiring hall in Mexico for recruiting workers, among other benefits.[2]

- Student activists also encouraged 191 colleges and universities to join the Washington-based Fair Labor Association (FLA), created in 1999 after a White House initiative on sweatshops launched by President Bill Clinton. Schools affiliated with FLA promise to promote "fair and decent conditions in the production of goods bearing their logo" and to disclose factory locations where licensed products are manufactured.

- Students joined in boycotting Taco Bell restaurants on 21 campuses over allegations the company bought tomatoes from suppliers who paid substandard wages to farmworkers. The Coalition of Immokalee Workers ended the boycott in March after Taco Bell agreed to

work with the coalition to improve pickers' working conditions.[4]

The question remains, however, whether campus labor activism will convert young people into union members after they graduate and enter the work force. Only 4.7 percent of workers ages 16 to 25 were union members in 2004.[5]

"Recruiting young people is key to the future of the labor movement," says Mike Caputo, a member of the United Mine Workers and a Democratic lawmaker in the West Virginia legislature. "The key is bringing young people into the labor movement and constantly reminding them why they have what they have and what they stand to lose if they don't get involved," which he says includes dignity on the job, workplace safety, wages and benefits.

Allie Robbins, national organizer of the United Students Against Sweatshops, says unions haven't done enough to attract young people but are beginning to with programs such as paid internships that some unions offer and the AFL-CIO's "Union Summer," which hires student interns to work with unions.

"A lot of people don't understand what a union does, or why they would need a union in the workplace," she says.

---

[1] Dan DiMaggio, "Student-Labor Activism Spreading," *Justice*, No. 43, May-June 2005, the newspaper of Socialist Alternative.

[2] Press release, Farm Labor Organizing Committee, "Precedent Setting Agreement Reached, Mt. Olive Pickle Boycott Over," Sept, 16, 2004, and Steven Greenhouse, "Growers' Group Signs First Union Contract for Guest Workers," *The New York Times*, Sept. 17, 2004, p. A16.

[3] Evelyn Nieves, "Florida Tomato Pickers Still Reap 'Harvest of Shame'; Boycott Helps Raise Awareness of Plight," *The Washington Post*, Feb. 28, 2005, p. A3.

[4] Press statement, "Comments by Coalition of Immokalee Workers Co-Director Lucas Benitez at Press Conference Announcing Settlement of the CIW's Taco Bell Boycott," March 8, 2005.

[5] Press release, "Union Members in 2004," U.S. Bureau of Labor Statistics, Table 1, Jan. 27, 2005.

---

community affiliate called Working America, through which non-union workers can get involved in labor issues. By July 2005 the group had 1 million members and hoped to have 2 million by 2006. Unions have also invested pension funds in corporations as leverage to curb executive pay and to promote global labor codes of

conduct. In 2004, unions submitted fully 43 percent of all "corporate governance" proposals, many of which target pay for top CEOs.[41]

Politically, labor stirred up Republicans in 1996 with a plan to spend $35 million to defeat House Republicans. But the plan failed, only to be followed by the controversial 2000 presidential election, when labor's candidate, Al Gore, had the popular votes but lost the election to Republican Bush.[42]

Within months of coming into office, Bush:

- Rescinded a Clinton-era ergonomics rule on repetitive workplace injuries, which unions had worked on for a decade;
- Required employers to post notices informing workers of their right to avoid unionization and union dues used for political activities;
- Revoked Clinton's policy encouraging federal contractors to pay union wages; and
- Dissolved the National Partnership Council, which Clinton used to try to improve relations between unions and federal agencies.[43]

Bush also targeted the unions' stronghold: government-employee unions. After the Sept. 11, 2001, terrorist attacks on New York and the Pentagon, Bush insisted that the new Department of Homeland Security operate outside civil-service rules — a move that "unilaterally canceled the collective bargaining rights of 170,000 workers," unions said.[44]

Then in 2003, the president unveiled plans to make it easier for private companies to compete for 850,000 federal jobs.[45]

Moreover, Clinton-era pro-labor regulatory rulings were reversed by Bush appointees to the National Labor Relations Board (NLRB). Bush's NLRB also has issued rulings that unions say threaten new recruiting tactics. The board also ruled that graduate assistants, who often teach college courses, are students — not employees — and therefore cannot join a union.[46] The ruling was a blow to the United Auto Workers, which had begun organizing at Columbia, Brown and other top universities.[47]

Finally, AFL-CIO activists said they had had enough. Under Sweeney's watch, they complained, union numbers had continued to slide, and labor-backed presidential candidates had lost twice. It was time for change.

CURRENT SITUATION

Change to Win

Ten years after Sweeney became AFL-CIO leader, seven unions complained that the federation's failure to boost union membership was costing labor clout at the bargaining table and in Congress.

"We're not trying to divide the labor movement, we're trying to rebuild it," the SEIU's Stern said in July. "When you're going down a road and it's headed in the wrong direction . . . you got to get off the road and walk in a new direction."[48]

But the 70-year-old Sweeney refused to step down. "That's been the issue from the beginning," said Sheet Metal Workers International President Michael Sullivan at the convention.[49] "It's not about organizing; we're all interested in organizing."

The convention was supposed to celebrate the 50th anniversary of the merger of the AFL and the CIO, but after the SEIU and Teamsters pulled out, the United Food and Commercial Workers followed suit.

The Carpenters union, which had quit the AFL-CIO in March 2001, also has joined Change to Win. "The AFL-CIO continues to operate under the rules and procedures of an era that passed years ago, while the industries that employ our members change from day to day," Carpenters President Douglas McCarron said in pulling out.[50]

Besides asking Sweeney to return some $2 billion in dues money over the next five years, the dissenting unions also wanted the federation to earmark $25 million in yearly profits from a union-backed credit card program to organize Wal-Mart. Instead, the AFL-CIO decided to devote $22 million to organizing.

Cornell's Hurd is among the labor observers who see the recent defections as historic. "The last time we saw a major split in the national labor movement was in the mid-1930s," Hurd says, when John L. Lewis left the AFL to form the CIO.

The disagreement today is the same: How best to organize workers in the economy's growth sectors. In the 1930s, the CIO wanted to organize workers in the emerging, mass-producing steel, auto and rubber industries. The Change to Win coalition wants to organize workers in growing industries such as construction, child and health care and hospitality.

"The CIO did not organize one Ford plant; they organized Ford," Stern said in July. "The only way to rebuild this labor movement is . . . to organize all of a company at one time, not one plant, one shop, one work site at a time."[51]

Will the split in the AFL-CIO revive the labor movement?

 YES
Robert Reich
Former Secretary of Labor
Professor of social and economic policy,
Brandeis University

 NO
Richard W. Hurd
Professor of Labor Studies
Cornell University

Written for the *CQ Researcher*, August 2005

Forty years ago, over a third of the American work force belonged to a labor union. Today, it's fewer than 8 percent of private-sector workers. What happened?

First came global competition. Then technology, which automated lots of jobs. Mega-retailers like Wal-Mart forced thousands of suppliers to become even leaner and meaner. Meanwhile, privatization and deregulation allowed lots of new entrants into government services.

Wages and benefits typically account for 70 percent of a company's total costs. So as companies have scrambled to cut costs, they've done everything possible to cut the wages and benefits — and numbers — of their employees. One method, of course, has been to fight unions.

Industrial workers have been hardest hit. Deficit-ridden federal and state governments also have cut costs by trimming payrolls and outsourcing to the private sector. Not surprisingly, workers want to hold on to what they have left. Unions that represent them constitute the core of the AFL-CIO. While they're interested in gaining new members, they see their primary mission as preserving the good jobs and relatively high incomes of their members in the face of these fierce headwinds.

Their future depends largely on what happens in Washington. They're using what's left of their political muscle to fight trade agreements, oppose privatization and deregulation, join with their companies to get government contracts and preserve their members' health and pension benefits.

Contrast them with the other blue-collar workers who inhabit the local service economy. Their jobs can't be outsourced, and most won't be automated. In fact, these jobs keep growing. Their problem is low wages and few benefits. Most of these jobs have never been unionized. If they were, these workers might have more bargaining clout with their employers.

By and large, the unions who look out for these workers are the ones now leaving or threatening to leave the AFL-CIO. They see their mission less as preserving good jobs in danger of disappearing and more as boosting the prospects of people trapped in lousy ones. They're less interested in gaining political clout because the fate of their members is not closely tied to votes taken in Washington. Their future depends instead on how many other local service workers become union members, and how quickly. That's why organizing is of such central importance to them.

Given the evolution of the American economy, it's just possible that the split in the AFL-CIO will mark a rebirth — or at least the rejuvenation — of organized labor.

Written for the *CQ Researcher*, August 2005

The fissure in the AFL-CIO has little to do with the key challenges facing the labor movement. Prior to secession, the unions in the Change to Win coalition promoted an aggressive restructuring plan and a streamlined, central federation. They argued that by concentrating resources in 15 or so national unions in core industries, and by committing substantial resources to organizing, labor could simultaneously increase bargaining leverage and reverse the slide in membership.

It is hard to imagine how a divided labor movement could stimulate growth. Instead of consolidating and uniting behind an organizing priority, the split actually achieves the opposite. Now it appears that there will be two federations with different foci, and it would not be surprising to see direct competition for members, especially in growth industries like health care.

In order to re-establish a powerful presence in the private economy, unions will need to adapt to globalization and the changing workplace. Twenty-first century labor markets do not match the experience of organizations long associated with job security, seniority and the protection of domestic production. There is little practical incentive for workers to embrace organizations whose culture and strategic perspective are captive to an historical framework that is no longer operational.

There are three key challenges:

- If unions hope to recruit successfully in the low-wage service sector, they must transform internally to build social-movement zeal that embraces the culture of service workers — predominately women, African-Americans and immigrants from Latin America and Asia.
- Unions must simultaneously connect with the expanding professional and technical work force. These workers' identity is occupational, and they are most likely to be drawn to new forms of representation that operate beyond the framework of traditional collective bargaining.
- Globalization presents what is probably the greatest paradox for unions accustomed to operating almost exclusively within the confines of the United States. The new, corporate world order mandates global labor alliances that go well beyond contemporary practice.

The split in the AFL-CIO detracts attention from challenges that will ultimately determine labor's future. As the feuding continues, unions lose precious time, and the chances for revival diminish. Hope now rests with grass-roots activists and strong leaders of individual national unions, who must rise above the internecine squabbling and show that a new form of unionism can emerge from the ashes of the old.

Striking Northwest Airlines mechanics picket at O'Hare International Airport in August 2005. When the mechanics struck, the airline already had temporary workers lined up to replace the strikers. The mechanics' union is not a member of the AFL-CIO or the Change to Win coalition and is getting little support from the labor community.

The Change to Win unions also had argued for a "one-union per industry" approach that would curb the competition among unions for the same workers. Health-care workers, for example, are divided into more than 30 unions. The dissenting unions argue bigger unions would have more leverage at the bargaining table. Sweeney agrees but says the unions themselves must decide to consolidate.

Anti-Union Climate

Washington's attitude toward unions today is starkly different from the 1930s, says the University of Pittsburgh's Masters. Unions were growing then, not declining, he points out, and a wave of legislation gave workers the right to organize. "Today, any sort of pro-worker legislation is far off the radar screen on Capitol Hill," Masters says.

Indeed, Cornell's Hurd calls the Bush administration one of the most anti-union in history. Besides rolling back policies important to unions, he says, the administration and Congress are trying to block an organizing strategy unions have used in recent years to recruit up to 550,000 new members.[52]

The new approach, called "card-check recognition," allows unions to bypass the NLRB. Essentially, workers convince employers to voluntarily accept a union if enough workers sign cards saying they want a union. Unions want to avoid the NLRB because the formal process is time consuming and because the board has become a "deathtrap" for union organizers, rather than the impartial referee for union and management disagreements it was supposed to be, according to Andy Levin, director of the AFL-CIO's Voice at Work organizing campaign.

Arguing the technique allows union organizers to intimidate workers into signing the cards, business wants Congress to outlaw card-check and President Bush to appoint new NLRB members who oppose the policy.

Meanwhile, the Labor Department also has increased its scrutiny of union finances. In 2003 it updated regulations requiring unions to show how they spend their money. The AFL-CIO called the proposal a "huge tangle of red tape" that would cost unions $1 billion a year to comply.[53] The new regulations went into effect this year.

While the Labor Department is spending more time inspecting unions' books, labor says the Bush administration is giving employers a pass when it comes to enforcing wage and hour and safety laws. At current staffing and inspection levels, for example, it would take the U.S. Occupational Safety and Health Administration (OSHA) 108 years to inspect each workplace under its jurisdiction just once, the AFL-CIO said in a 2005 report, "Death on the Job."[54]

In addition to the ergonomics rule, unions also say the Labor Department rolled back other important workplace rules, including new regulations in 2004 that unions say "robbed" 6 million workers of the right for overtime pay.

And while the Labor Department says it was not involved, unions fault the Bush administration's Immigration and Customs Enforcement (ICE) agency for using the pretext of an OSHA meeting and free coffee and doughnuts to lure about 50 immigrant construction workers in North Carolina to a location where they were handcuffed and taken into custody for allegedly using false documents.[55]

"Instead of scaring workers into silence by these types of immigration enforcement actions, the Bush administration should be focusing on crafting real solutions to our broken immigration system," AFL-CIO Executive Vice President Chavez-Thompson said.

The mechanics' strike against Northwest Airlines Corp. that began on Aug. 20 this year shows how labor unions have lost the strike as a threat against management. When the mechanics walked off the job, the airline already had temporary workers lined up to replace the strikers, which is legal. While the airline and union offer different reports of the strike's effect, the airline is still running.

"If a corporation can eliminate an entire work force and bring in replacement workers, it has ramifications for every other unionized company," said Steve MacFarlane, a spokesman for the Aircraft Mechanics Fraternal Association (AMFA).[56]

Although Northwest is seeking more than $100 million in concessions, AMFA says the issue isn't money but job security.[57]

AMFA is not a member of the AFL-CIO or the Change to Win coalition and is getting little support from the labor community. The lack of union solidarity is due in large part to AMFA's reputation for recruiting other workers from other unions to join AMFA, what other unions call raiding or poaching.

To some, the Northwest strike also illustrates organized labor's fragmentation. "The AMFA strike has all the issues that should excite the labor movement into mass demonstrations," Gary Chaison, a professor of industrial relations at Clark University in Worcester, Mass., told National Public Radio. "It [the strike] has outsourcing of union jobs, it has employer pressure to reduce wages and it has the use of striker replacements. The labor movement is so in disarray and confused about its priorities right now, it really doesn't know how to react to this."[58]

Legal Action

A bright spot for labor came in August when a district court in Washington, D.C., prevented the administration from implementing portions of its new personnel rules for the Department of Homeland Security, which scrapped certain collective-bargaining protections.[59]

"This is a truly astronomical win," said Mark Roth, general counsel for the American Federation of Government Employees.[60] The ruling could prevent the administration from making similar changes for civilian workers at the Defense Department.

Organized labor says governors and businesses are taking their cues from Washington and going after unions. Republican Govs. Mitch Daniels of Indiana and Matt Blunt of Missouri both used executive orders to wipe out the collective-bargaining rights of some 50,000 state workers shortly after taking office in 2005.[61] They followed the lead of Republican governors in California, Kentucky, Maryland and Massachusetts. Federal labor laws protect the collective-bargaining rights of private-sector employees, but it's up to the individual states to pass laws providing protection for state and local public employees. Twenty-five states have such laws on the books. The governors who rescinded public-sector bargaining did so by executive order, not by repealing any laws.

Gerald McEntee, president of the American Federation of State, County and Municipal Employees (AFSMCE), said these actions "are a coordinated assault by right-wing forces on a part of the union movement that is growing." Government workers are the nation's most unionized. Less than 8 percent of private workers are organized, compared with 36 percent of government workers.[62]

In California, Republican Gov. Arnold Schwarzenegger is pursuing what labor calls an anti-union agenda, backing a ballot initiative this November to prohibit public unions from collecting dues for political purposes without first obtaining the workers' written permission. He also has rankled nurses' unions by trying to block new rules that would require hospitals to have more nurses. But a court intervened, and the rules went into effect.[63]

Schwarzenegger was thwarted in another anti-union effort. He was forced to drop a controversial bid to revamp the pension plan for state workers that would have forced state employees to use a 401(k)-style benefit rather than the current system, which pays set benefits.

"The governor's not only attacked teachers but he's attacked the entire core of California," said Barbara Kerr, president of the California Teachers Association. "He's attacked firefighters, he's attacked police officers, teachers and state workers. We are the people that make this state run."[64]

OUTLOOK

Recruiting Push

Employers expect a burst of organizing activity in the coming months as the two rival labor groups vie for the same workers to join their ranks. But the picture is less clear on Capitol Hill and in statehouses, where politicians and lobbyists are still trying to figure out what the labor split means for them.

Harvard University economist James Medoff called the breakup "good news for the corporations and political conservatives. A divided labor movement is a weaker labor movement, and employers know this very well."[65]

Masters of the University of Pittsburgh doesn't agree. "This notion that labor has to be united in the form of all standing behind the AFL-CIO in lockstep is just nonsense." But Masters says labor desperately needs to quickly score major organizing successes. A breakthrough at Wal-Mart or Comcast "would go a long way in justifying the need for the split that has taken place," he says.

Labor has already been using some non-traditional tactics to attack anti-labor practices at firms like Wal-Mart. Among other things, unions have initiated "corporate campaigns" that attack a company's labor practices through negative ads, consumer boycotts and legal action, such as lawsuits against the company for allegedly breaking wage and safety laws. Businesses can expect more of those tactics from unions, says Charles S. Birenbaum, a San Francisco labor attorney.

Activist unions also are vowing to step up efforts to organize and bargain globally. In August, SEIU joined forces with unions representing service workers across the globe to help organize cleaners in the Netherlands and security officers employed by multinationals in India, Germany, South Africa and Poland.[66]

"It's much easier to change the behavior of a company that's unionized at an 80 percent level globally than it is when it's unionized at 10 percent," said SEIU President Stern.[67]

"We need a global strategy to hold global employers accountable to the public they serve and to their employees," said Philip Jennings, general secretary of the Swiss-based Union Network International (UNI), a global coalition of 900 national unions representing service workers. Among other things, UNI wants to end what it calls "union busting" in Britain and the United States by T-Mobile, a subsidiary of Deutsche Telecom.[68]

However, back at home, unions are already fighting over workers, including some who are unionized, and the infighting could get worse. Stern of SEIU, who leads Change to Win, has promised not to poach other unions' members, but some expect a free-for-all. "When [Stern] says he is not going to raid other unions, he is lying," AFSCME member Mike Fox said at the convention. Fox charged that SEIU is trying to steal 10,000 home-care providers in Riverside County, Calif., whom AFSCME represents.

Business groups are not convinced the renewed attention on organizing will translate into more union members. "Just putting more organizing troops on the ground isn't going to change the equation," Johnson of the U.S. Chamber says.

Politically, the rift could affect which candidate and policy get labor's support. "I think it's a disaster for Democrats," said Steve Elmendorf, a senior adviser to Sen. John Kerry during the 2004 campaign.[69]

Democrats, whom unions of both camps complain have taken their votes and political donations for granted, may have to work harder to win labor's support. Sweeney vowed to make Democrats who voted against labor in the recent CAFTA trade legislation pay the consequences for their "sell-out votes." The Change to Win coalition promises to hold Democrats accountable for their vote but also plans to reach out to Republicans.

"We absolutely believe the AFL-CIO has become too much in the back pocket of Democrats," said coalition Chairwoman Anna Burger.[70]

The AFL-CIO, which used to be the one organization that spoke for all of organized labor, now has competition when it goes to Capitol Hill and statehouses to lobby its causes. Johnson says the split is advantageous to the business community and will hurt organized labor's political agenda, but only in the short term. "Although they are divided, they will get their house together," he predicts.

NOTES

1. Linda Chavez, "A tough year for the AFL-CIO," July 20, 2005, available at www.lindachavez.org.

2. Fact sheets from AFL-CIO at www.afl-cio.org/aboutus/faq/ and Change to Win, www.changetowin.org, August 2005.

3. For background, see Brian Hansen, "Big-Box Stores," *CQ Researcher*, Sept. 10, 2004, pp. 733-756.

4. Keynote address of AFL-CIO President John Sweeney, AFL-CIO convention, July 25, 2005 at www.afl-cio.org/mediacenter/prsptm/sp07252005a.cfm.

5. Migration Policy Institute, "Immigrant Union Members, Numbers and Trends," May 2004.

6. Bureau of Labor Statistics, "Median weekly earnings of full-time wage and salary workers, annual averages 1983-2004."

7. AFL-CIO Fact Sheet, "The Union Difference."

8. "All Things Considered," National Public Radio, July 25, 2005.

9. Linda Chavez and Daniel Gray, *Betrayal: How Union Bosses Shake Down Their Members and Corrupt American Politics* (2005), p. 16.

10. Peter D. Hart Research Associates, "The Public View of Unions," February 2005.

11. Statement, "Deck is stacked against U.S. workers," Human Rights Watch, Aug. 31, 2000.

12. Andrew Strom, "How the United States' stacked labor laws make it nearly impossible for workers to gain union representation," *Dollars & Sense Magazine*, No. 249, September/October 2003.

13. *Ibid.*

14. Press release, National Right to Work Legal Defense Foundation, July 25, 2005.

15. For background, see Mary H. Cooper, "Exporting Jobs," *CQ Researcher*, Feb. 20, 2004, pp. 149-172.

16. *Ibid*, p. 152.

17. Company news releases: "Kodak Accelerates Digital Transformation Strategy," July 20, 2005; "HP Unveils Targeted Program to Streamline Company, Reduce Costs, Drive Greater Customer Focus," July 19, 2005, available at www.hp.com/hpinfo/newsroom/press/2005/050719a.html; and "Kimberly Clark Announces Second Quarter Results And Initiatives to Further Improve Competitive Position," July 22, 2005.

18. For background, see Mary H. Cooper, "Rethinking NAFTA," *CQ Researcher*, June 7, 1996, pp. 481-504.

19. Robert E. Scott and David Ratner, "NATFA's Cautionary Tale," Economic Policy Institute, *Issue Brief 214*, July 20, 2005.

20. Linda Chavez-Thompson, "To boost workers, turn down CAFTA," *San Antonio Express-News*, May 15, 2005.

21. Wal-mart statement, www.walmartfacts.com/keytopics/unions.aspx.

22. Doug Struck, "Wal-Mart Leaves Bitter Chill," *The Washington Post*, April 14, 2005, p. E1.

23. Sydney P. Freedberg and Connie Humburg, "Lured employers now tax Medicaid," *St. Petersburg Times*, March 25, 2005.

24. John Sweeney, "Wal-Mart leads way in lowering standards for employees," *Detroit Free Press*, Feb. 25, 2005.

25. "Statement of James P. Hoffa on the Teamsters' Disaffiliation from the AFL-CIO," July 25, 2005.

26. "Business-Labor Ideology Split in PAC and Individual Donations to Candidates and Parties," Center for Responsive Politics, based on data released by the FEC, March 28, 2005.

27. Remarks by John J. Sweeney, president of the AFL-CIO, Building and Construction Trades Department Convention, Boston, Aug. 9, 2005.

28. Fact Sheet, "AFL-CIO Political Program Gives Working Families A Voice," July 2005.

29. "National Election Survey," University of Michigan's Center for Political Studies.

30. Foster Rhea Dulles and Melvyn Dubofsky, *Labor in America: A History* (Fifth ed.), 2004, p. 392.

31. Nelson Lichtenstein, *State of the Union: A Century of American Labor* (2002).

32. For background, see Charles S. Clark, "Child Labor and Sweatshops," *CQ Researcher*, Aug. 16, 1996, pp. 721-744.

33. Dulles & Dubofsky, *op. cit.*, p. 120.

34. *Ibid*, p. 213.

35. *Ibid*.

36. *Ibid*, p. 392.

37. U.S. Bureau of Labor Statistics, "Major Work Stoppages in 2004," April 8, 2005. Major strikes peaked in 1952 at 470, according to federal data that go back to 1947.

38. John Cochran and Rebecca Adams, "Fresh From a Set of Hill Victories, Can Labor Keep the Momentum?" *CQ Weekly*, Sept. 1, 2001.

39. For background, see Kenneth Jost, "Labor Movement's Future" *CQ Researcher*, June 28, 1996, pp. 553-576.

40. For background, see Jane Tanner, "Living Wage Movement," *CQ Researcher*, Sept. 27, 2002, pp. 769-792.

41. AFL-CIO Fact Sheet, "What's Wrong With Executive Pay — And What Union Funds Are Doing About It," 2005; www.afl-cio.org/corporatewatch/ paywatch/retirement-security/index.cfm.

42. For background, see Kenneth Jost and Gregory L. Giroux, "Electoral College," *CQ Researcher*, Dec. 8, 2000, pp. 977-1008.

43. Rebecca Adams, "GOP-Business Alliance Yields Swift Reversal of Ergonomics Rule," *CQ Weekly*, March 10, 2001.

44. AFL-CIO, "BushWatch," May 2003.

45. Office of Management and Budget, Revision to Office of Management and Budget Circular No. A-76, "Performance of Commercial Activities," May 29, 2003. Available at www.whitehouse.gov/omb/ fedreg/rev_a76_052903.html.

46. National Labor Relations Board decision, *Brown University and International Union, United Automobile, Aerospace and Agricultural Implement Workers of America, UAW, AFL-CIO*, Case No. I-RC-21368, July 13, 2004.

47. Jennifer John and Mike Rosenbaum, "Graduate Student Workers Need More Than Prestige," United Auto Workers, *Solidarity*, January/February 2002.

48. Steven Greenhouse, "Two Large Unions Say They Are Leaving the AFL-CIO," *The New York Times*, July 25, 2005.

49. Michael Bologna, "AFL-CIO's Sweeney Angered by Defection of Dissident Unions as Convention Kicks Off," *BNA Daily Labor Report*, July 26, 2005.

50. "Carpenters union pulls out of AFL-CIO," *Northwest Labor Press*, April 6, 2001, www.nwlaborpress .org/2001/4-6-01Carpenters.html.

51. "Future of the US labor movement," "Talk of the Nation," National Public Radio, July 19, 2005.

52. Peter Szekely, "Labor Board Ruling Threatens Union Recruiting," Reuters, June 10, 2004.

53. Statement by AFL-CIO President John J. Sweeney on New Regulations for Union Reporting, Dec. 23, 2002.

54. For background, see David Hatch, "Worker Safety," *The CQ Researcher*, May 21, 2004, pp. 445-468.

55. For background, see Peter Katel, "Illegal Immigration," *The CQ Researcher*, May 6, 2005, pp. 393-420.

56. Keith L. Alexander, "Northwest Says It's Prepared for Strike; Airline Taking Tough Stance With Mechanics," *The Washington Post*, Aug. 19, 2005, p. D1.

57. Statement, Aircraft Mechanics Fraternal Association, Aug. 24, 2005.

58. National Public Radio, "All Things Considered," Aug. 23, 2005.

59. *National Treasury Employees Union v. Michael Chertoff, Department of Homeland Security*, Civil Action No. 05-201 (RMC), U.S. District Court for the District of Columbia.

60. American Federation of Government Employees, press release, "Labor unions win case against agency's proposed regulations," Aug. 14, 2005.

61. Kathleen Hunter, "GOP governors trim state employees' bargaining clout," *Stateline.org.*, Feb. 25, 2005.

62. Bureau of Labor Statistics, "Union Members in 2004," Jan. 27, 2005.

63. *California Nurses Association vs. Schwarzenegger* (Case No. 04CS01725) www.saccourt.com/courtrooms/ trulings/dept16/d16-04cs01725-06.07.05.doc.

64. BBC, "Fight looms over Schwarzenegger plans," Aug. 10, 2005, http://news.bbc.co.uk/2/hi/americas/ 4136128.stm.

65. Alonso Soto, "Weakened AFL-CIO pledges to organize workers," Reuters, July 26, 2005.

66. Press release, "Groundbreaking Union Alliance to Help Raise Standards in Global Service Industries," Service Employees International Union, Aug. 25, 2005.

67. Harold Meyerson, "Workers of the World Uniting," op. ed. column, *The Washington Post*, Aug. 27, 2005, p. A17.

68. Press release, "UNI global union targets global corporations," Union Network International, July 18, 2005.

69. "Labor split could hurt Democrats' Campaigns," *The Seattle Times*, July 26, 2005.

70. Jeanne Cummings, "Unions Recast Their Political Role," *The Wall Street Journal*, July 27, 2005, p. A4

BIBLIOGRAPHY

Books

Brody, David, *The American Labor Movement*, University Press of America, Reprint edition, 1985.
Essays by various authors look at trade unionism, socialism, unions and the black community and other issues that shaped the U.S. labor movement. Brody is professor emeritus of history at the University of California at Davis.

Chavez, Linda, and Daniel Gray, *Betrayal: How Union Bosses Shake Down Their Members and Corrupt American Politics*, Three Rivers Press, 2005.
Chavez, president of the Center for Equal Opportunity, a conservative think tank, recommends that unions be prevented from spending members' dues on politics without their permission.

Dubofsky, Melvyn, and Foster Rhea Dulles, *Labor in America: A History* [7th edition], *Harlan Davidson*, 2004.
The authors trace U.S. labor history from Colonial times. Historian Dulles wrote the first three editions, beginning in 1949 and Dubofsky, a professor of history at the State University of New York at Binghamton, has updated the book since.

Geoghegan, Thomas, *Which Side Are You On? Trying To Be for Labor When It's Flat on Its Back*, Plume Books, 1992.

A labor lawyer employed by Chicago-area local unions concludes that steel-mill closings, leveraged buyouts and Third World competitive labor have contributed to the decline of organized labor.

Lichtenstein, Nelson, *State of the Union, A Century of American Labor*, Princeton University Press, 2002.
A professor of history at the University of California provides historical analysis of labor since the New Deal. He concludes that a larger, more powerful labor movement is central to the health of American democracy.

Articles

Benenson, Bob, and John Cochran, "Breakaway Labor: A Fragile Unity," *CQ Weekly*, Aug. 1, 2005, pp. 2092-2093.
Veteran political writers look at how both hope and doubt greet the dissident unions that pulled out of the AFL-CIO and how Democrats weigh the impact of the split.

Bernstein, Aaron, "The House of Labor Divides," *Business Week*, July 26, 2005.
A labor reporter recaps the infighting that led to the historic breakup of the AFL-CIO.

Fields, Gary, *et al.*, "Reinventing the Union," *The Wall Street Journal*, July 27, 2005, p. B1.
Fields looks at labor's new strategies in the face of factory job losses, outsourcing and the growth of domestic service jobs.

Fine, Janice, "Debating Labor's Future," *The Nation*, Aug. 1/8, 2005, pp. 15-22.
Fine poses questions about the future of organized labor to leaders of the AFL-CIO and the newly formed Change to Win coalition, including AFL-CIO President John Sweeney and Andy Stern, president of the dissident Service Employees International Union.

Greenhouse, Steven, "Democrats Concerned by Prospects of a Labor Schism," *The New York Times*, July 24, 2005, Section 1, p. 19.
Greenhouse looks at the impact the labor split may have on the Democratic Party, which has relied heavily on unions for donations and get-out-the-vote drives.

Hirsch, Stacey, "2 once-close labor leaders take diverging paths," *The Baltimore Sun*, July 27, 2005, p. D1.

Hirsch looks at the two main labor leaders involved in the split, John Sweeney, president of the AFL-CIO, and Andy Stern, president of the Service Employees International Union, and their relationship.

Paulson, Amanda, "Unions look ahead — and inward too," *The Christian Science Monitor,* **July 6, 2005, p. 1.** Paulson presents a balanced look at the issues facing organized labor in the 21st century.

Reports and Studies

Masters, Marick, *et al.,* **"The Divided House of Labor: A Report on Competing Proposals to Reform the AFL-CIO,"** *Center on Conflict Resolution and* *Negotiations, Katz Graduate School of Business, University of Pittsburgh,* **July 14, 2005.** The director of the Katz school concludes that the Change to Win coalition may be a step toward developing a new vision for unions.

Scott, Robert E., and David Ratner, "NAFTA's Cautionary Tale," *Economic Policy Institute,* **July 20, 2005.** Two economists from the left-leaning think tank provide a state-by-state estimate of jobs lost to Canada and Mexico, concluding that the trade pact cost the United States 1 million jobs.

For More Information

AFL-CIO, 815 16th St., N.W., Washington, DC 20006; (202) 637-5000; www.afl-cio.org. A federation representing 9 million U.S. workers in 53 unions.

Change to Win, c/o Service Employees International Union, 1313 L St., N.W., Washington, DC 20005; (202) 898-3200; www.changetowin.org. A new coalition of seven unions representing 6 million workers.

Economic Policy Institute, 1600 L St., N.W., Suite 1200, Washington, DC 20036; (202) 775-8810; www.epi.org. A labor-backed think tank that researches labor conditions, jobs, trade and globalization.

National Association of Manufacturers, 1331 Pennsylvania Ave., N.W., Washington, DC 20004; (202) 637-3000; www .nam.org. An influential lobbying group representing small and large manufacturers.

National Right to Work Legal Defense Foundation, 8001 Braddock Road, Suite 600, Springfield, VA 22160; (703) 321-8510; www.nrtw.org. A nonprofit providing free legal aid to workers who feel their rights have been violated by "compulsory unionism abuses."

U.S. Bureau of Labor Statistics, 2 Massachusetts Ave., N.E., Washington, DC 20212; (202) 691-5200; www.bls .gov. A Department of Labor agency providing information about wages, work stoppages, collective bargaining and unionization rates.

U.S. Chamber of Commerce, 1615 H St., N.W., Washington, DC 20062; (202) 659-6000; www.uschamber .org. An influential business-lobbying group representing 3 million businesses and 2,800 state and local chambers.

5

Socially Responsible Investing

Can Investors Do Well by Doing Good?

Thomas J. Billitteri

Solar panels generate electricity from the roof the state capitol in Salem, Ore. Many socially responsible investors seek out firms that address environmental concerns, such as climate change and energy conservation. But critics say social investments tend not to perform as well as traditional ones.

From *CQ Researcher*,
August 29, 2008.

W hen Ann B. Alexander and her husband sold their natural-foods store in Durham, N.C., they pocketed a tidy sum. But they didn't want their profits to simply sit in a typical investment fund, even if they did grow in value. They also wanted their money to do good.

So the Alexanders chose a financial adviser who specializes in "socially responsible investing," an increasingly popular approach that combines investors' financial goals with a desire to improve society and hold corporations accountable.

"To have these corporations pay attention and be more responsible, it's good for all of us — not just the people who have money," Mrs. Alexander says.

She's not alone in that view. Socially responsible investing — sometimes called "sustainable investing," "ethical investing" and simply SRI — involves screening investments according to social or environmental, as well as financial, criteria, plus other strategies.

From a small niche of the financial world during the protest era of the 1960s and '70s, SRI has evolved into a complex and controversial trillion-dollar global industry spanning mutual funds, pension plans and big institutional and private holdings.

Many investors are attracted to social investing for moral or ethical reasons stemming from such concerns as climate change, workers' rights, workplace diversity, skyrocketing CEO pay and corporate political influence. Others may choose it out of a practical belief that companies that treat their employees well and protect the environment will be more profitable, more open about their operating methods and less prone to lawsuits and regulatory sanctions.

Social Investments Did Well Over Long Term

Over its 18-year life span, the Domini 400 Social Index (DS400) — composed of companies regarded as socially responsible — has outperformed the Standard and Poor's 500 (S&P 500). At one-, three-, five- and 10-year intervals, however, the DS400 lagged behind the S&P.*

DS400 Performance Statistics

	Total returns as of July 31, 2008							
	July 08	Last Qtr	Year to Date	One Year	Three Year	Five Year	10 Year	Since 5/1/90
KLD's DS400 Index	0.24%	-3.84	-12.67	-11.49	1.32	5.49	2.46	10.40
S&P 500	-0.84%	-2.73	-12.65	-11.09	2.85	7.03	2.91	9.91

* The S&P 500 is a broad stock market index (indicator) representing 500 publicly traded companies.

Source: KLD Research and Analytics

But the SRI movement also has vocal critics. They argue that stock-screening methods used by SRI mutual funds are ill-defined and highly subjective, that social investments tend not to perform as well as traditional ones and that SRI techniques have no place in the public pension world, where money managers have a fiduciary duty to maximize investment returns. (*See "At Issue," p. 111.*)

Despite the controversy, the movement is growing.

According to the Social Investment Forum, the industry's main trade group, assets under management using at least one of three core SRI strategies — investment screening, shareholder advocacy and "community investing" in areas underserved by traditional financial institutions — totaled $2.71 trillion last year, more than four times the amount in 1995 and about one of every nine dollars under professional management in the United States.[1]

As it has grown, social investing has evolved from its roots of simply avoiding tobacco, alcohol and other so-called sin stocks. It is placing more and more weight on companies that pay close attention to environmental, social and corporate-governance issues — "ESG" factors in investing parlance.

That emphasis is spreading to the broader financial world. For example, Goldman Sachs Group developed a 179-page report last year that recommended

44 companies based on a formulation that included ESG performance.[2] Most SRI assets — an estimated $1.9 trillion, according to the forum — are in accounts professionally managed for big institutional and high-net-worth clients.[3] Institutions embracing the responsible-investing approach include religious groups, private foundations, hospitals and labor unions and some of the nation's biggest public pension funds.

"In the old days, most people associated with SRI were just taking tobacco, alcohol and gambling stocks out of portfolios," says Paul Hilton, director of advanced equities research at the Calvert Group, a major SRI mutual fund company. "More recently, there's an understanding that what we're trying to do is use environmental, social and governance factors as another way to identify risk and better-quality management. That's getting through to institutional investors in a way that it hasn't before."

Even so, some critics argue that social investments have tended to produce mediocre returns compared to the broader stock market, causing investors to give up potential profits. The Domini 400 Social Index, a main SRI benchmark, has lagged the broader Standard & Poor's 500 index at the last one-, three-, five-, and 10-year intervals, although it is ahead of the S&P 500 over its entire 18-year life. (*See chart above.*)[4]

The use of socially responsible investing approaches in public pensions has been especially controversial. In California, which adopted a so-called double-bottom-line approach eight years ago, the $239 billion California Public Employees' Retirement System — the nation's largest pension fund — missed $400 million in gains by forgoing investments in China and other countries, according to *Business Week.* And a ban on tobacco stocks cost the $172 billion California State Teachers' Retirement System $1 billion, though returns for both pension funds still outpaced the S&P 500 over the past five years, the magazine said.[5]

California's pension system reportedly is considering reversing its tobacco policy, which critics of socially responsible investing say could undermine support for the movement.[6] (*See "Current Situation," p. 110.*)

And while the SRI mutual fund industry's stock-picking methods have become more refined over the years, they have occasionally led to stumbles. This summer Pax World Management Corp., a venerable SRI firm founded in 1971, settled charges with the Securities and Exchange Commission that it violated its own guidelines against buying shares in such businesses as alcohol, gambling, tobacco and defense.[7]

The company agreed to a $500,000 fine. The actions took place from 2001 through 2005 in two Pax funds, though not in its World Balanced Fund, which held over 90 percent of Pax World assets at the time, the company said.[8]

"We regret and take full responsibility for what occurred," said Joseph F. Keefe, who became CEO in 2005 after the SEC began its investigation.

Despite such missteps, supporters say responsible investing is fast moving into the mainstream. While investors may be attracted to it for different reasons, "the remarkable thing is the coming together of these investors with literally, now, trillions of dollars to press companies, or encourage companies, to act in a responsible way," says Timothy Smith, senior vice president of the environment, social and governance group at Walden Asset Management, an SRI firm in Boston.

Concerns over global climate change and natural-resource sustainability have provided perhaps the biggest impetus for the recent growth. So-called green funds new to the market include the Global Alternative Energy fund, started by the Calvert Group in May 2007, the Winslow Green Solutions Fund, started last November, and the five-month-old Global Green Fund, part of Pax World Funds.

Climate concerns are heavily reflected not only in mutual funds but also in shareholder activism. In this year's proxy season, 54 global-warming resolutions were filed with U.S. companies by public pension funds, labor and religious groups, and other institutional investors, according to the *Environmental Leader*, an online trade publication. Many of the investors belong to the Investor Network on Climate Risk, an alliance of 60 institutional investors with combined assets of more than $5 trillion.[9]

Also driving the responsible-investing movement are concerns about corporate behavior. Scandals at Enron

and Tyco International earlier this decade, outrage over child exploitation in overseas sweatshops making goods for the West, and corporate links to human-rights hotspots like Sudan have led some investors to look carefully at which companies are in their stock portfolios.

Social investing is getting a boost, too, from the ongoing intergenerational transfer of wealth that is putting unprecedented sums of inherited money into the hands of baby boomers — a group weaned on '60s-era activism.[10]

"More and more and more people are asking themselves the question: What do I want to profit from?" says Cliff Feigenbaum, managing editor of the *Green Money Journal*, a Santa Fe, N.M., publication that promotes social and environmental values in investing.

As socially responsible investing attracts more followers and gains more scrutiny, here are some key questions that proponents and skeptics are asking:

Do socially screened investment funds perform as well as regular ones?

Meir Statman, a professor of finance at Santa Clara University in California, has done several studies examining the performance of socially responsible mutual funds and ones that don't apply social screens.

"The performance is about the same," he says. "Not better or worse."

Scores of other studies have reached similar conclusions. Yet they have not convinced everyone.

"The use of social criteria may be fine for the affluent who gamble their own money as a feel-good, vanity investment — but for those who can't afford to take a chance, SRI is a bad bet," argues Jon Entine, an adjunct fellow at the conservative American Enterprise Institute and a longtime critic of socially responsible investing.[11]

But Mercer, the international consulting firm, along with the United Nations Environment Program Finance Initiative, said last year after reviewing 20 academic studies on the subject, "Investors incorporating environmental, social and corporate-governance factors within their investments don't have to give up returns." Mercer formed a "Responsible Investment" business unit in 2004.[12]

Likewise, researchers at Lehigh University in Pennsylvania studied SRI-screened portfolios and concluded that "there is no cost to being good."[13]

Community Investing Continues to Expand

The amount of money that social investors directed to communities that are underserved by traditional financial services grew sixfold since 1995, and 32 percent from 2005 to 2007.

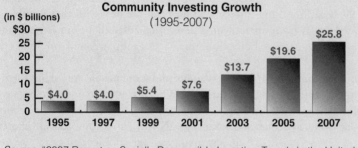

Community Investing Growth
(1995-2007)

(in $ billions)

1995	1997	1999	2001	2003	2005	2007
$4.0	$4.0	$5.4	$7.6	$13.7	$19.6	$25.8

Source: "2007 Report on Socially Responsible Investing Trends in the United States," Social Investment Forum Foundation, 2008

And Alex Edmans, a finance professor at the University of Pennsylvania's Wharton School, found that stocks of companies on *Fortune* magazine's "Best Companies to Work For" list robustly outperformed the overall market.[14]

Yet, other evidence has fed doubts about the correlation between socially responsible investing and stock performance. Robert F. Stambaugh, a finance professor at Wharton, and two colleagues found that when returns are adjusted for risk, index-style investors don't give up much when they use socially responsible funds, but investors who select actively managed funds can lose more than 3.5 percentage points of return a year.[15]

"Sometimes being socially responsible is costly, and sometimes it isn't," Stambaugh said. "It depends on what kind of investor you are."[16]

And research published in the *Harvard Business Review* this year found only a minor correlation between corporate social responsibility and good financial results.[17]

Some of the most spirited debate over social investing has involved SRI barometers like the benchmark Domini 400 Social Index. The index limits or avoids stocks in some industries that have performed well in recent years, such as gambling and military weapons, and is significantly weighted in industries like banking and information technology that hit rough patches.

Peter D. Kinder, president of KLD Research & Analytics, a Boston SRI research firm that owns the Domini 400 Social Index, says a key reason the index has lagged the S&P 500 is that it generally excludes stocks in companies that extract natural resources, such as oil-drilling and mining. Those sectors have soared recently.

"When industries we typically either exclude or underweight are doing very well, we will perform less well," Kinder says. On the other hand, "we are going to perform better relative to the broad market indexes when these companies underperform."

Amy Domini, who as a KLD partner helped develop the index before starting her own company, Domini Social Investments, says social investing has been hurt by market shifts stemming from the post-Sept. 11 "war economy."

"People look for hard assets — gold, copper, oil — and those are not very robust for social investment funds to find opportunities in," she says.

Domini's flagship Social Equity Fund was down nearly 12 percent for the year ending July 31 and, partly because of the bursting of the tech bubble earlier this decade, has lagged the S&P 500 over time.

Amy Domini has felt the pressure that so-so stock performance can bring to bear. Since the Social Equity Fund's inception in 1991 it had tracked the Domini 400 index, but two years ago she changed that strategy. Now the fund is actively managed through a computer-driven stock-picking strategy.

"Emotionally, this is difficult," Domini said in 2006, after making the hard decision to change the fund's management approach. "But I can't ask my shareholders to be patient forever."[18]

Entine argues that the lag in benchmarks like the Domini 400 Social Index points to a larger flaw in the social-investment approach. To avoid investing in defense, energy and tobacco — areas viewed negatively in the SRI world but that have soared in recent years — social funds made unwise bets on banking and technology, only to be slammed by speculative bubbles, he charges.

"They overweighted based on social prejudices, not on metrics," he says. And "when you overweight, essentially you're gambling with someone's money."

Squabbling over SRIs' performance compared with conventional investments isn't likely to be settled soon. "This debate is going to continue," insists Walden Asset Management's Smith, a 40-year veteran of SRI. "There's no definitive knockout blow on either side."

Are screening methods used by mutual funds sound?

Walden Asset Management bills itself as "a leader in socially responsive investing," but that doesn't mean it shuns one of the world's most controversial industries. For years Walden has owned shares in British Petroleum (BP).

Smith calls the company a "work in progress" on health and safety issues and expresses discouragement over a deadly BP refinery explosion in Texas in 2005 and an oil spill in Alaska in 2006. Still, he says, the company continues to be a leader among energy producers on the climate-change issue.

"In some industries, companies stand out, and therefore there are some positive reasons to approach them," he says.

Walden's approach is known as "best in class," one of the strategies that SRI funds use to choose which stocks fit their missions.

The Domini Social Equity Fund holds stock in McDonald's — a company that, over the years, has been accused of everything from destroying rainforests for food production to polluting the environment with packaging waste. But Amy Domini says McDonald's has answered the critics, setting standards for beef production, addressing the packaging issue and participating in a coalition to improve international labor standards.

"Am I going to throw out the company that has been highly responsive to consumers and third parties time after time?" she asks.

Screening industries and companies has always been tricky for social investors, leaving the field open to charges that it compromises too much, lacks uniform screening standards and uses methods that are confusing or even misleading to people who want to invest with a conscience.

Cold cash totaling $12 million awaits the winner of the World Series of Poker main event at Harrah's in Las Vegas. Investment funds that screen for gambling stocks had more than $41 billion in assets under management in 2007.

The research can be "shoddy," Entine charges, adding, "It depends on how well companies manage their reputations, more or less."

Social-investment advocates strongly disagree, however. "We are more sophisticated than we've ever been, and we'll be more sophisticated tomorrow," says the *Green Money Journal's* Feigenbaum. "We're screening as thoroughly as we possibly can."

When it comes to SRI mutual funds, investment companies use different approaches to decide which industries and stocks to avoid, embrace or include with reservations.

In *Socially Responsible Investing: Making a Difference and Making Money,* a 2001 overview of the field, Domini noted that "[r]esponsible investors struggle with how best to deal with . . . troubling industries. Many have come down on the side of avoiding problematic industries completely. Others decide to underweight some industries while avoiding others."[19]

Social funds may also use their shares to exert pressure on companies through shareholder resolutions or direct talks. "There are companies that we invest in that on balance have a positive record but still have some problems, and then we use our shareholder voice to engage those companies and urge them to change," Smith says.

In addition, SRI portfolios may shift to keep up with changing times or circumstances.

Last November *The Wall Street Journal* reported that Pax World discontinued its policy of rejecting alcohol- and gambling-related investments after the policy led it three years ago to divest from Starbucks Corp. — widely regarded as socially progressive — for licensing the Starbucks name to a coffee liqueur. "Now, while they still decline to invest in weapons and tobacco makers, portfolio managers . . . weigh potential investments based on a mix of financial and ESG metrics, including corporate governance, community relations, product integrity, human rights and climate change," the newspaper said.[20]

The Calvert Group, based in Bethesda, Md., traditionally has avoided the nuclear-power industry. But Hilton, the advanced equity research director, says the company's two newest funds — Global Alternative Energy and International Opportunities — are willing to invest in certain companies that have existing nuclear plants but are doing excellent work in wind or solar power. "That's not so much of an endorsement of nuclear as the fact that we want to invest in companies pushing ahead in alternative energy," he says.

SRI proponents regard such attempts at nimbleness as signs that the SRI field is maturing. But the field's methods have also invited sharp criticism, some of it from people dedicated to the cause of sustainability and social responsibility.

In 2004, environmentalist and entrepreneur Paul Hawken — cofounder of the Smith & Hawken garden- supply business and executive director of the Natural Capital Institute, a research group in California — wrote a stinging critique of the SRI mutual-fund industry, saying he wanted to help it better respond to investors seeking "to invest with a conscience and a purpose."[21]

Hawken charged, in part, that SRI mutual funds lack common standards, definitions and codes of practice; that taken as a whole, the investment portfolio of the combined SRI fund industry "is virtually no different" than that of conventional mutual funds and that the field is marred by a "lack of transparency and account- ability in screening and portfolio selection." He also said the language used to describe social-investment mutual funds is "vague and indiscriminate" and that "fund names and literature can be deceptive."

This year he was quoted in a British newspaper as saying that "the situation has not got better. [Financial]

performance has become the primary driver. They [ethi- cal funds] are doing everything they can to be acceptable to the broadest possible clientele, and with that has come dilution of meaning and standards."[22]

Julie N. W. Goodridge, president of Northstar Asset Management, a Boston social-investment firm, wants the SRI industry to adopt stronger disclosure policies to give investors a better understanding of what funds are investing in, and why.

"The consumer doesn't necessarily know that differ- ent funds do different things," she says. "I worry that consumers . . . find that Coca-Cola is sitting right smack in the middle of their fund, and they would never pur- chase the product, let alone invest in it."

Many social investors have avoided Coke for reasons as varied as its use of precious water resources in develop- ing countries and its sponsorship of this year's Olympics in China, which has been accused of human-rights abuses.

Joe Nocera, a business columnist for *The New York Times*, last year criticized KLD Research & Analytics, upon whose analysis many SRI funds rely for guidance. Nocera said KLD had only two dozen researchers moni- toring 3,000 companies and that they relied on media reports, blogs, interactions with activist groups and con- versations with companies themselves. "That hardly seems like enough to make a decision on whether a com- pany is good or bad," Nocera wrote.[23]

But Kinder, KLD's president, says his company "takes full advantage of Internet tools" to research companies and that "companies don't fundamentally change that often.

"We've been looking at these companies for 20 years. I feel as confident as any researcher can be in our research."

Can socially responsible investors influence corporate behavior?

Last year, activists led by Christian Brothers Investment Services — an investment advisory firm for Catholic dioceses, hospitals and other organizations — put forth a shareholder resolution seeking an independent exami- nation of the environmental and social impact of Newmont Mining Co.'s operations around the globe.

But the Denver-based gold-mining company didn't fight the resolution — in fact, it endorsed it before the shareholder vote was taken.[24]

Social-investment proponents point to that endorsement as a sign of the SRI movement's growing influence, although the resolution's ultimate effect on Newmont's operations remains to be seen.

"It's hard to say at this point what the results will be," says Julie Tanner, assistant director of socially responsible investing at Christian Brothers and a member of a panel reviewing the issue. "We look forward to the board's recommendations," due before Newmont's 2009 annual meeting, she says.

As the SRI movement matures, it has shifted more and more of its focus toward engaging companies directly on a variety of issues, ranging from CEO pay to human rights in overseas factories.

"Responsible investors are no longer simply avoiding stocks in companies they have problems with," says Smith of Walden Asset Management. "They are, with trillions of dollars behind them, engaging companies, writing letters, talking with them, voting their proxies, filing shareholder resolutions and voting and debating at stockholder meetings. These are not investors that are seeking an illusory, pure corner of the marketplace, they are investors who are engaged in the [real] marketplace."

Shareholder resolutions are the most visible manifestation of that engagement. From 2005 through the first half of 2007, a total of 1,065 resolutions were filed on social, environmental and governance issues. Support for resolutions filed in the first half of 2007 stood at 15.4 percent of votes cast, compared with 9.8 percent in 2005 and 13.3 percent in 2006.[25]

Even so, shareholder activism can be a tough road. Companies often resist resolutions, especially those that are costly or disruptive. Even resolutions that pass may not lead to real change.

"A company can do something because of a shareholder resolution," says Tanner, "but the real question is,

Socially Responsible Investments Near $3 Trillion

The amount of money in socially responsible investments (SRI) in the United States has increased more than fourfold since 1995, to $2.7 trillion. The number of funds offering SRI has also increased from 55 in 1995 to 260 in 2007 (not shown).

Socially Responsible Investing in the United States, 1995-2007
(in $ billions)

Year	Social screening	Shareholder advocacy	Community investing	Total*
1995	$162	$473	$4	$639
1997	$529	$736	$4	$1,185
1999	$1,497	$922	$5	$2,159
2001	$2,010	$897	$8	$2,323
2003	$2,143	$448	$14	$2,164
2005	$1,685	$703	$20	$2,408
2007	$2,098	$723	$26	$2,711

* The sum of the three columns for each year is less than the total shown because overlapping assets involved in screening and advocacy are subtracted to avoid double counting.

Source: "2007 Report on Socially Responsible Investing Trends in the United States," Social Investment Forum Foundation, 2008

how robust and substantive is the company's implementation going to be?"

SRI advocates often prefer to try engaging in direct talks with management on issues of concern before going the resolution route. "The preferable outcome is negotiated settlement," says KLD's Kinder. "It doesn't start with a proxy resolution. A proxy resolution in the context of socially responsible investing typically represents failed negotiations."

In the Newmont Mining case, Tanner says, "We were in dialogue with the company, we had been speaking to them for a while; it wasn't necessarily that we were having a failed negotiation [but] I don't think things had gotten to where the company was going to take action to the extent we wanted them to."

Jeanne M. Logsdon, a professor of business ethics, and Harry J. Van Buren III, an assistant professor of business and society, both at the University of New Mexico, study shareholder activism. In one study they classified more than 1,700 shareholder resolutions filed over seven years with companies listed on the New York Stock Exchange by members of the Interfaith Center on Corporate Responsibility (ICCR), an association of 275 faith-based institutional investors. More than 40 percent of the resolutions — 707 in all — related to "justice" issues, with employment and economic-development concerns the most prevalent.[26]

Logsdon says that while few such resolutions are approved by the majority of a corporation's stockholders, they can be effective in raising the public profile of an issue.

"You don't do it because you're going to win, you do it to bring attention to an issue — to take a stand and to signal to corporate leaders that the companies should be dealing with the issue."

Van Buren, who engages in shareholder activism on behalf of the Episcopal Church, says the church doesn't do much stock screening but has been an active filer of shareholder resolutions.

For years, he says, the church has been raising red flags about predatory and sub-prime lending, issues now at the center of Wall Street upheaval. "If you look at shareholder resolutions that are being filed today, in many cases they represent leading-edge issues that corporations or other stakeholders pick up in years to come," Van Buren says.

In a study published this summer, Logsdon and Van Buren looked at how social activists influence companies through direct dialogues with management. They studied nearly 1,200 new and ongoing dialogues initiated by ICCR members from 1999 through 2005 with such firms as Citigroup (20 dialogues), Wal-Mart Stores (19), Coca-Cola (15) and Bank of America and Target (14 each).[27]

Van Buren says no researchers have systematically tracked whether shareholder activists are getting concrete results from such talks. But one "imperfect" measure of such progress, he says, is the number of shareholder resolutions that are withdrawn. Such withdrawals may occur if a company makes enough of an effort to change to satisfy the concerns of activists.

"The real work of shareholder activism gets done in ongoing corporate dialogue," Van Buren says. "You file a resolution, you may withdraw the resolution, but with a condition of withdrawal the company will agree to do something."

According to the Social Investment Forum, of the 1,065 resolutions filed from 2005 to mid-2007, 319 were withdrawn, and 561 were voted on.[28]

BACKGROUND

Early Activism

Socially responsible investing boasts a venerable history. In an 18th-century sermon titled "The Use of Money," Methodism's founder, Anglican minister John Wesley, warned against engaging in liquor production, industries that pollute, such as tanning, and practices such as bribery.[29] "We ought not to gain money at the expense of life," he declared.[30]

Quakers and Methodists in early America refused to invest in ways that might help the slave trade.[31] And during the 19th century, many religious investors refused to put money into such activities as liquor and tobacco production, gambling and weapons manufacturing.

Mutual funds that practice social screening emerged in the 20th century. The Pioneer Fund began screening out "sin" stocks in 1950 to serve Christian investors.[32] Then, in 1971, two United Methodist Church activists in peace, housing and employment issues started the Pax World Fund, which the company calls the first broadly diversified, publicly available mutual fund to use social as well as financial criteria in making investment decisions.[33]

During the late 1960s and early '70s intense social activism by advocacy and religious groups began placing more and more emphasis on corporate responsibility.

The Interfaith Center on Corporate Responsibility (ICCR) was founded in 1971 partly as a result of opposition to the Vietnam War. Progressive clergy questioned whether churches were profiting from the war, such as by holding the stocks of arms manufacturers. The questioning spread further, to such issues as production of nuclear weapons, sale of military goods abroad, creation of space weapons and apartheid in South Africa.[34]

"One of the things our founding members looked at was, if we're going to be endowed institutional investors, do we choose to own companies that make money on some of the precise social ills we're trying to counteract?" says Laura Berry, executive director of the ICCR.

South Africa's system of racial separation was becoming a highly visible cause among many socially conscious investors during this period. In 1971 the Episcopal Church filed the first church-sponsored shareholder resolution, which called on General Motors (GM) to close down operations in South Africa because of the government's apartheid policy.

That same year, Leon Sullivan, an African-American Baptist minister, was elected a GM director. He used his influence on the GM board to campaign against apartheid and later in the decade developed a code of conduct for companies doing business in South Africa, known as the Sullivan Principles.

By the 1980s, growing anti-apartheid fervor, including pressure from Sullivan, helped lead a number of churches, pension plans and other institutional investors to either divest themselves of stock in U.S. corporations operating in South Africa or use their shares to urge companies to withdraw from the country. By the end of the 1980s scores of companies were leaving South Africa.

"The anti-apartheid campaigns of the 1980s provided a galvanizing moment in the history of SRI," according to the Social Investment Forum.[35]

Apartheid was not the only concern that led social investors to examine their stock portfolios. Environmental catastrophes such as a poison-gas leak at a Union Carbide factory in Bhopal, India, that killed thousands in 1984, a nuclear disaster in Chernobyl, in what is now Ukraine, in 1986 and the *Exxon Valdez* oil spill in Alaska in 1989 "served as flashpoints for investor concerns over pollution and corporate responsibility," the forum noted.[36]

By the 1990s and early 2000s, social investing had percolated into the mainstream investment world, leading to the creation of an entire infrastructure of investing vehicles.

Tobacco and Alcohol Are Top Social Screens

Among funds that screen for social and environmental concerns, tobacco is the most prevalent criterion incorporated into portfolio management. It was employed by 166 of the 260 funds identified, with more than $174 billion in total net assets under management, or more than 86 percent of the total assets of socially screened funds. Alcohol is the second most predominant social screen, with more than $158 billion managed by 125 funds.

Total Net Assets of Socially Screened Funds by Category, 2007

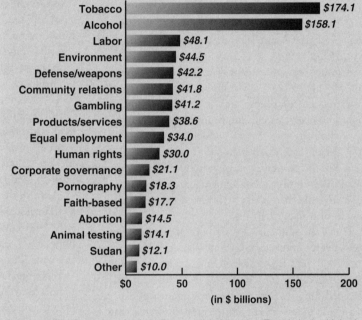

Category	(in $ billions)
Tobacco	$174.1
Alcohol	$158.1
Labor	$48.1
Environment	$44.5
Defense/weapons	$42.2
Community relations	$41.8
Gambling	$41.2
Products/services	$38.6
Equal employment	$34.0
Human rights	$30.0
Corporate governance	$21.1
Pornography	$18.3
Faith-based	$17.7
Abortion	$14.5
Animal testing	$14.1
Sudan	$12.1
Other	$10.0

Source: "2007 Report on Socially Responsible Investing Trends in the United States," Social Investment Forum Foundation, 2008

SRI indexes — for example, the Domini 400 Social Index, Dow Jones Sustainability Indexes (started in 1999) and London-based FTSE4Good indexes (2001) — have helped track the financial performance of companies and provided yardsticks for corporations to measure their social progress against their peers.

And as social investing grew, it also evolved and diversified. "We started looking for positive things to invest in," says Goodridge of Northstar Asset Management, "and we then moved into shareholder activism in a big way, and then into community investing."

Key Rulings

Several key government rulings have added to the movement's momentum.

In 2003, the Securities and Exchange Commission (SEC) required all mutual funds to disclose their proxy votes on corporate issues — the kind of disclosure that had long been sought by social investors.[37] In 1999 Domini Social Investments says it became the first mutual fund manager to publicly disclose its proxy votes.

Critics of the SEC decision said it would be costly for shareholders and wouldn't help them much, but SRI proponents hailed the new regulation. "What [mutual funds] are really worried about is the end of all their conflicts of interest," said Tim Grant, then-president of Pax World Funds.[38]

Another key government decision involved the question of whether company-sponsored "defined contribution" retirement plans, such as 401(k) plans, could include socially responsible funds among their investment choices.

A decade ago, many plan administrators shied away from SRI investments out of concern that they would violate the Employee Retirement Income Security Act (ERISA) rule that assets be invested for the exclusive benefit of plan participants.[39]

However, William M. Tartikoff, general counsel of the Calvert Group, requested an advisory opinion from the Labor Department, which said in a May 1998 letter that ERISA's fiduciary standards don't rule out socially screened funds as long as "the investment was expected to provide an investment return commensurate to investments having similar risks."[40]

"The letter gave us great optimism," Tartikoff said on the 10th anniversary of the opinion. "It gave us comfort and validated what we were doing and what we were saying was correct and that, in fact, there was no inherent reason for Calvert's socially screened funds not to be chosen on a 401(k) platform and as a plan option."[41]

SRI has made inroads into the retirement-plan field since then. A survey last year by Mercer found that 19 percent of defined-contribution retirement-plan sponsors had an SRI option, and an additional 41 percent expected to be doing so within three years.[42]

As the responsible-investing movement moves more and more into the mainstream, investors and money managers are increasingly using environmental, social and corporate governance factors — or ESG principles — to guide their investment decisions, a trend driven in no small way by concern over climate change.

Traditional investing firms have picked up on the trend. For instance, State Street Global Advisors has been using some ESG-applied research over the past couple of years, according to *The Wall Street Journal.* "We are seeing these factors start mainstreaming," said William Page, chairman of State Street's ESG Team. He said the team uses ESG research for accounts of some wealthy investors and private institutional investors.[43]

While ESG principles are consistent with the traditional moral or ethical impulses that have long driven the SRI movement, many institutional investors are embracing them because they help shape financial performance.

In 2006, the United Nations issued a set of voluntary "Principles for Responsible Investment" that aimed to help institutional investors and others integrate environmental, social and governance factors into their investment decisions and ownership practices with the goal of improving long-term returns.

As of this past May, the principles had garnered 362 signatories, with European investors leading the way with 148 signatories representing $9.7 trillion in assets under management. North America counted 70 signatories with $2.3 trillion.[44]

"The great majority of new signatories continue to be mainstream pension funds, insurance companies and investment managers, with a minority coming from the dedicated socially responsible investment sector," according to the latest progress report on the effort.[45]

The U.N. principles are not the only effort to frame investment decisions around corporate responsibility. For example, the Carbon Disclosure Project, a British nonprofit group, serves institutional investors with some $57 trillion in assets under management globally. It analyzes how major companies around the world are responding to climate change and examines the commercial risks and opportunities it presents to corporations. This year it sought emissions data from 3,000 companies.

Investment-consulting firms also are adopting ESG principles in their work. For example, Mercer's "responsible investment" unit employs 16 people around the world

C H R O N O L O G Y

1700s-1950 *Roots of socially responsible investment movement are developed.*

1700s Methodism founder John Wesley warns against making money "at the expense of life."

1800s Religious investors shun liquor and tobacco production, gambling and weapons-making.

1950 Pioneer Fund becomes first mutual fund to screen for "sin" stocks.

1970s *Opposition to South African apartheid and Vietnam War helps establish social-investing practices.*

1971 Interfaith Center on Corporate Responsibility is founded. . . . Pax World launches nation's first publicly available socially responsible investment fund. . . . Episcopal Church files first church-sponsored shareholder resolution.

1977 African-American pastor Leon H. Sullivan develops code of conduct on human rights and equal opportunity for companies operating in South Africa, eventually helping to dismantle apartheid; in the late 1990s Sullivan announces successor set of principles for industries worldwide.

1980s-1990s *Anti-apartheid campaigns help spur companies to leave South Africa, and socially responsible investing moves increasingly into the mainstream investment world.*

1982 Calvert Social Investment Fund becomes the first U.S. mutual fund to prohibit investments in companies doing business in South Africa.

1985 Social Investment Forum launched.

1989 Ceres, a national network of investors and others addressing environmental sustainability, is formed.

1990 Domini 400 Social Index, first index to measure performance of broad group of socially responsible stocks in the U.S., is created.

1998 U.S. Department of Labor tells Calvert Group federal law doesn't preclude use of "socially responsible" funds in retirement plans.

1999 Domini Social Investments becomes first mutual fund manager to publish its proxy-voting record. . . . Dow Jones Sustainability Indexes are launched.

2000-Present *Public pensions impose tobacco and other screens; climate change rises as social-investment priority.*

2000 Nation's largest pension fund, the California Public Employees' Retirement System (CalPERS), announces it will sell its tobacco holdings.

2001 London-based FTSE4Good indexes begin tracking social investing.

2003 Securities and Exchange Commission requires mutual funds to disclose proxy votes.

2004 Environmentalist and entrepreneur Paul Hawken issues report critical of the socially responsible investment mutual fund industry, arguing it "has no standards, no definitions and no regulations other than financial regulations." . . . Mercer, a worldwide consulting firm, starts a "responsible investment" unit.

2006 United Nations launches "Principles of Responsible Investment" to help large investors integrate environmental, social and governance factors into their investment decisions. . . . Sudan Divestment Task Force established to persuade states, universities and other groups to restrict Sudan-linked investments.

2007 Mercer survey finds that 19 percent of defined-contribution retirement plans include a social-investment option, and 41 percent plan to add one over the next three years. . . . *Los Angeles Times* publishes stories critical of investment policy of Bill & Melinda Gates Foundation.

2008 California public pensions reportedly re-examining policy on tobacco investments. . . . New Hampshire orders its public pensions to divest Sudan-related investments, sparking resistance from pension officials. . . . Social Investment Forum identifies $2.7 trillion in assets under management using socially responsible investing strategies.

Big Financial Institutions Are Going 'Green'

Investors say profits and principles go together.

Climate change may be bad for planet Earth, but it's good for the bottom line, Deutsche Bank decided last fall, launching its new "climate change investment initiative."

The big German-based institution was one of the latest mainstream financial institutions and socially responsible investment companies to focus on issues like global warming, renewable fuels and environmental sustainability.

"Companies and investors are quickly realizing that climate change is not merely a social, political or moral issue — it is an economic and business issue as well," declared Kevin Parker, Deutsche Bank's global head of asset management.[1]

Environmental funds have been attracting stronger investor interest lately than some other social-investing vehicles. Inflows of money into so-called green funds totaled $766 million for the year ending May 31, compared with net outflows among religion-based funds of $37 million for that 12-month period, according to Morningstar, which tracks both categories under the heading of socially responsible investing.[2]

"It's not just tree huggers" who are concerned about global warming, Holly Isdale, managing director and head of wealth advisory at Lehman Brothers, the big New York investment bank, told *The Wall Street Journal* last year. "There's money to be made, and people want to know how to make it."[3]

New green funds have sprouted at longtime social-investment companies such as Pax World, whose five-month-old Global Green Fund invests in companies focused on "mitigating the environmental impact of commerce," and Calvert, which launched the Calvert Global Alternative Energy Fund last year and plans to launch a Global Water Fund later this year.[4]

And new funds are popping up at traditional financial firms in Europe, the United States and elsewhere.

"In a little more than two years," Parker of Deutsche Bank wrote in March, "we estimate retail investors all over the world have pumped around $66 [billion] into more than 200 newly launched mutual funds and exchange-traded funds investing in companies that help to mitigate or adapt to climate change."[5]

Last November Deutsche Bank, through its U.S. retail unit, launched the DWS Climate Change Fund, which focuses on alternative energy, energy-efficient products and companies that deal with damage to the environment.

One overarching factor is behind the growth in socially responsible investing, says Peter Kinder, president of KLD Research & Analytics, a social-investing research firm: "There's always more than one answer [but] the short answer is, global warming is driving this. There is in my mind no question that is true."

who rate institutional money managers according to how they use environmental, social and governance factors in their investment decisions. That information helps guide Mercer clients, such as pension-plan administrators and private foundations, in selecting investment managers.

"It's a big growth area for us," says Craig Metrick, U.S. head of responsible investments for Mercer Investment Consulting. "Increasing numbers of institutional investors are coming to look at social responsibility as way to manage risk and look for opportunities in their portfolios long term."

Sharp Critiques

As responsible investing has become a more prominent part of the investing scene, it also has invited sharp critiques — particularly where mutual funds and stock screening are concerned.

In his 2004 report, for example, environmentalist Hawken took issue with screening methods among SRI funds, saying they "allow practically any publicly held corporation to be considered as an SRI portfolio company."[46] The single most important criterion for a company, he argued, is whether "its services and products [are] helpful to the world we inhabit. . . . What does it matter if one fast-food company is singled out as 'best in its class. . . ?" he posited. ". . . [I]f you are going the wrong way, it doesn't matter how you get there."[47]

In his influential book *The Market for Virtue: The Potential and Limits of Corporate Social Responsibility,*

KLD's Global Climate 100 Index, which the company bills as the first global index focused on climate change, marked its third anniversary this summer. It holds companies engaged in renewable energy, clean technology and "future fuels."[6]

In an analysis of social-screening trends among all investment funds, the Social Investment Forum found that environmental concerns were more frequently incorporated into fund management than either labor-friendly criteria or alcohol restrictions, though the 146 funds that incorporate environmental criteria managed fewer assets overall than either labor-friendly or alcohol-restricted funds.[7]

As environmental issues heat up, social investors are joining with others in public-policy advocacy efforts.

This summer, for example, an investor group that includes officials from a number of social-investment companies, pension funds, foundations and other organizations, called on the U.S. Senate to extend tax credits for renewable energy and energy-efficiency projects that are set to expire at the end of the year.[8] In May investors urged senators to enact legislation dealing with global warming.[9]

The efforts were organized by Ceres, a 19-year-old Boston-based network of investors, environmental groups and other public-interest groups, and its Investor Network on Climate Risk, made up of more than 70 institutional investors with roughly $6 trillion in assets.

Ceres also started the Global Reporting Initiative, based in Amsterdam, which provides a framework for companies and other organizations to report their environmental, social and governance performance. The framework is used by more than 1,200 companies worldwide.[10]

"While U.S. policy makers are running in place on climate change," Ceres President Mindy S. Lubber wrote in a blog this month, "global investors are moving quickly to make money from its far-reaching risks and opportunities."[11]

[1] Deutsche Asset Management, "Investing In Climate Change," October 2007, p. 1.

[2] Elizabeth O'Brien, "Green Investing — The Gold Rush," *Financial Planning*, Aug. 1, 2008.

[3] Jilian Mincer, "Why 'Green' Investing Has Gained Focus," *The Wall Street Journal*, June 21, 2007.

[4] O'Brien, *op. cit.*

[5] Kevin Parker, "Investment is key in climate change battle," *Financial Times*, March 24, 2008.

[6] "KLD Global Climate 100 Index Marks Three Year Anniversary," www.kld.com/newsletter/archive/press/pdf/1216311527_GC100%20 3rd%20Anniv%20release_Final%20(2).pdf.

[7] Social Investment Forum, "2007 Report on Socially Responsible Investing Trends in the United States," p. 11.

[8] Ceres, "Investors with $1.5 Trillion in Assets Call on Congress to Extend Renewable Energy and Energy Efficiency Tax Credits," press release, July 29, 2008, www.ceres.org/NETCOMMUNITY/Page.aspx? pid=923&srcid=705.

[9] Ceres, "Investors Managing $2.3 Trillion Call on Congress to Tackle Global Climate Change," press release, www.incr.com/NET COMMUNITY/Page.aspx?pid=900.

[10] Ceres, www.ceres.org/NETCOMMUNITY/Page.aspx?pid=415& srcid=552.

[11] Mindy S. Lubber, "Climate Change: Investors' Next Global Mega-Trend? Harvard Business Publishing, Aug. 1, 2008, http://blogs.harvard business. org/leadinggreen/2008/08/climate-change-investors-next.html.

David Vogel — a professor of both business ethics and political science at the University of California, Berkeley — questioned some of the underlying tenets of the SRI movement.

Vogel noted, for example, "that the social-investment community was no more able than any other investors to identify the failures of corporate governance that created such massive shareholder losses at the beginning of the twenty-first century." He pointed out that Enron and WorldCom, among other troubled companies, were widely held by SRI funds.[48]

"Implicit in the very existence of SRI is the claim that it is possible to identify which firms are more or less responsible," Vogel also wrote. "Not only is this claim questionable, but the selection criteria employed by SRI fund managers and researchers can be criticized on several grounds."[49]

In *The Atlantic* magazine last fall, former Wall Street stock analyst Henry Blodget concluded, in the words of the article's subtitle, that "socially responsible investing is neither as profitable nor as responsible as advertised."[50]

Blodget himself is no stranger to Wall Street controversy, as he acknowledges in the article. In 2003 regulators banned him from the securities industry and fined him $4 million for putting out misleading stock research in violation of federal laws.[51] He has since become a prominent financial writer.

In *The Atlantic* article Blodget argued that "the central dilemma for most socially responsible investors" is that "virtue can cost you."

Should Foundations Screen Their Investments?

Some experts question the benefit to society.

With some $39 billion in assets, the Bill & Melinda Gates Foundation is the nation's largest private foundation — and a revered leader in global philanthropy. But early last year, the Los Angeles Times questioned the huge philanthropy's investment practices.

The newspaper concluded that the foundation "reaps vast financial gains every year from investments that contravene its good works" and had holdings in companies that had "failed tests of social responsibility because of environmental lapses, employment discrimination, disregard for worker rights, or unethical practices."[1]

In one example, it noted that the foundation had spent $218 million on polio and measles immunization and research worldwide, including in the Niger Delta, but that it had invested $423 million in companies responsible for most of the oil-plant flares that spew pollution in the delta.[2]

The articles touched off a spirited debate in philanthropy circles about whether foundations, which together control some $670 billion in assets, should do more to align their investments with their charitable missions.[3]

"Creating an immutable firewall between investments and grants is nonsensical, a strategy worthy of ostriches, not leaders," Allison H. Fine, a senior fellow at Demos: A Network for Ideas and Action, said at a panel discussion last year prompted by the articles on the Gates Foundation.[4]

But some philanthropy experts question whether efforts by foundations to screen their investment holdings can do very much to help society.

"There is definitely a virtue to aligning the investments of the foundation with its mission," says Mark Kramer, founder and managing director of FSG Social Impact Advisors, a nonprofit consulting organization in Boston. But, he adds, while shareholder advocacy "can absolutely have a demonstrable impact" on companies, "it's not clear that screening public equities has any demonstrable social impact."

"It would be very hard to have enough volume [of shares] to truly affect the [stock] price of a large publicly traded company, and even if you did, in a sense what you might be doing is simply giving a better investment to someone who's less ethically inclined because they can pick up a valuable stock at a lower price.

"So there is something around the advocacy piece — the pressure that . . . foundations can put on companies — but whether they are not buying tobacco stocks, or are buying stocks in companies they believe are more sustainable, it's a good thing to do in terms of aligning your values, but it's not clear that it's a high impact strategy."

Gates keeps its grant making and investment management separate. It says Bill and Melinda Gates guide the foundation's endowment managers in voting proxies in a manner "consistent with the principles of good governance and good management" and that "they have defined areas in which the endowment will not invest, such as companies whose profit model is centrally tied to corporate activity that they find egregious." The foundation singles out tobacco stocks.[5]

On the issue of investments in Sudan, the foundation says the Gateses have directed the investment team "to be consistent with the approach taken by the endowment managers for Harvard, Yale and Stanford universities." The Gates endowment "no longer has any holdings in the companies identified by these institutions in their investment policy statements on Sudan."

If Gates does not apply broader screens to its investments, it is hardly alone among foundations. A *Chronicle of Philanthropy* survey of the 50 wealthiest private foundations in 2006 found that 34 applied no screens or declined to comment. At least 13 foundations said they screened for tobacco, and several of those screened other investments, such as those in alcohol, firearms or gambling.[6]

The newspaper also found that most foundations don't do much to influence shareholder votes. The survey found that 30 of the 50 big foundations allow their money managers to make all decisions about proxy voting.[7]

Even so, some foundations are strengthening efforts to bring their philanthropic aims into closer alignment with their endowments.

A study last year of 92 foundations by FSG Social Impact Advisors found that the number of philanthropies involved in mission-related investing doubled in the previous decade. Making loans to charities, a process known as program-related investments, was the most common approach.[8]

The F. B. Heron Foundation, Annie E. Casey Foundation and Meyer Memorial Trust have challenged other grant makers to dedicate at least 2 percent of assets to mission-related investments.[9]

Also, the W.K. Kellogg Foundation last year earmarked $100 million for social and mission-driven investments in Africa and the United States. "Few foundations have fully realized the potential of what is commonly referred to as 'double-bottom-line investing,' " Sterling Speirn, the foundation's CEO, said. "We want to maximize our social return on the investment front."[10]

The John D. and Catherine T. MacArthur Foundation formalized a policy for voting shareholder proxies "to reduce or eliminate a substantial social injury caused by a company's actions," according to the *Los Angeles Times*.[11]

The William and Flora Hewlett Foundation screens tobacco stocks from its portfolio but says it generally is not attracted to investment screening. Instead, it is attracted to proxy voting, which "appears to be having an increasing influence on management decisions" and "is unlikely to degrade investment returns."

"We believe that we can be most effective in voting proxies that implicate climate change or forestry practices," the foundation says, adding that it "may selectively choose to exercise proxies when doing so is seen to have a particularly beneficial impact."[12]

Philanthropy experts say that actions like proxy voting remain the exception rather than the rule among philanthropies, though.

"Proxy voting is a basic first step in aligning investments and mission," according to As You Sow, a nonprofit shareholder-advocacy organization in San Francisco engaged in social and environmental issues. Yet, it adds, "when it comes to using the proxy process, most foundations still passively follow management recommendations even when they are not aligned with the foundations' own mission and values."[13]

Bill and Melinda Gates, with investor Warren Buffett, don't invest in companies whose profit is tied to "egregious" corporate activity, such as tobacco production.

Still, Larry Fahn, the group's executive director, says that "slowly but surely," more and more foundations are trying to align their investments with their missions by voting their proxies, engaging companies in dialogue on social and environmental issues and publishing information showing which proxy issues are important to them and how they are voting.

He says that while a foundation may dedicate its annual payout, typically 5 percent of assets, to a mission-related cause, what is needed is a "95 percent solution" in which the rest of the assets are used "proactively" through shareholder engagement.

---

[1] Charles Piller, Edmund Sanders and Robyn Dixon, "Dark cloud over good works of Gates Foundation," *Los Angeles Times*, Jan. 7, 2007.

[2] *Ibid.*

[3] Figure based on Foundation Center data.

[4] Ian Wilhelm, "Philanthropy Experts Debate Merits of Socially Responsible Investments," *The Chronicle of Philanthropy*, Feb. 22, 2007. The panel was organized by the Hudson Institute's Bradley Center for Philanthropy and Civic Renewal.

[5] Bill and Melinda Gates Foundation, "Our Investment Philosophy," www.gatesfoundation.org/AboutUs/OurWork/Financials/RelatedInfo/OurInvestmentPhilosophy.htm.

[6] "Stock-Investment Policies at the 50 Wealthiest Private Foundations," *The Chronicle of Philanthropy*, May 4, 2006.

[7] Harvy Lipman, "Meshing Proxy With Mission," *The Chronicle of Philanthropy*, May 4, 2006.

[8] Ian Wilhelm, "Foundations Seek to Tie Investments to Their Charitable Missions," *The Chronicle of Philanthropy*, April 19, 2007. The study is Sarah Cooch and Mark Kramer, "Compounding Impact: Mission Investing by US Foundations," Social Impact Advisors, March 2007, www.fsg-impact.org/images/upload/Compounding%20Impact(5).pdf.

[9] Social Investment Forum, "2007 Report on Socially Responsible Investing Trends in the United States," 2008, p. 22.

[10] "W.K. Kellogg Foundation Launches Mission-Driven Investing," press release, Oct. 23, 2007, www.wkkf.org.

[11] Charles Piller, "Foundations align investments with their charitable goals," *Los Angeles Times*, Dec. 29, 2007.

[12] "The William and Flora Hewlett Foundation Social Investment Policy," www.hewlett.org.

[13] Michael Passoff, "Proxy Season Preview 2008," As You Sow, www.asyousow.org.

Noted shareholder activist Evelyn Davis addresses Ford directors at the company's annual meeting in Wilmington, Del., on May 8, 2008. Agenda items included discussion of a proposed report on global warming sought by the Free Enterprise Action Fund, which owns Ford shares. Many socially responsible investors seek to influence workplace and corporate governance issues.

He points out that an investor who put $1,000 in the S&P 500 in 1957 would have ended up with $124,000 in 2003, but about 5 percent less than that amount if tobacco company Philip Morris (now Altria) — the index's single best-performing stock for 46 years through 2003 — had been excluded. If the investor had put the entire $1,000 into Philip Morris alone, the ending figure would have been $4.6 million.

Blodget's critique touched on a litany of other points as well, but ended on a conciliatory note.

"[S]ocially responsible investing certainly deserves to go mainstream," he wrote. "Capital allocation decisions *can* help shape behavior. Even with different investors emphasizing different priorities, there is usually some common ground. And we need to stop insisting that SRI should be both socially *and* financially superior to traditional alternatives. It is unlikely to be both. . . .

"A lifetime of investing in SRI funds might cost you a lot more than organic milk and hybrid cars," he concluded.

"But as SRI investors become both cannier and more numerous, the sacrifice involved need not amount to the 5 percent you might have lost by boycotting Philip Morris. Perhaps, even if SRI returns are no higher than can be achieved through traditional investing — or even a bit less — the practice can be its own reward."

CURRENT SITUATION

Taking Stock

Generalizing about the performance of the SRI field in this year's volatile stock market is difficult, partly because of the field's broad array of holdings and investment strategies.

"Socially responsible funds are such a diverse group that it's hard to make a judgment on how well they do," David Kathman, an analyst at Morningstar who follows SRI mutual funds, noted earlier this year. "Comparisons are not all that helpful."[52]

The Domini 400 Social Index provides at least a clue, though. Through the first seven months of 2008 the 400 corporations charted by the Domini index performed about the same as the S&P 500 — roughly a negative 12.7 percent for the period. The Domini index did better than the S&P 500 in July, rising 0.24 percent compared with a 0.8 percent decline in the broader index.

Business Week noted this spring that some socially responsible funds were seeing inflows of money as investors shifted out of riskier investments and looked for ways to make money in energy.[53]

SRI managers didn't think the market downturn had shaken investor confidence in socially responsible investing, the magazine said. Geeta Aiyer, a portfolio manager at Boston Common Asset Management, said a bigger test of investors' willingness to stick with SRI has occurred during the past five years, as energy-extraction and defense stocks — shunned by social investors — have been among the strongest categories.

"For years we've been addressing the opportunity costs — what you give up by being a social investor," Aiyer said. "Now we see there's opportunity from being a social investor."[54]

Still, this year's collapse of financial stocks has left the social-investing field open to sharp criticism from those who argue that it has put too much faith in banking stocks, just as it invested heavily in technology shares early this decade.

Almost every company "that went south in the '01 collapse [in communication technology], and almost every major financial company that has imploded during the current bubble was ranked high by social investors," says Entine at the American Enterprise Institute (AEI).

AT ISSUE

Should public pensions engage in socially responsible investing?

YES
Timothy Smith
Senior Vice President,
Walden Asset Management

Written for *CQ Researcher*, August 2008

Public pension funds have a fiduciary duty to protect the financial interests of their beneficiaries and are obliged to keep their eye on that target. However, a responsible fiduciary is also obliged to consider a range of non-financial factors that can and do affect shareholder value.

Increasingly, it is understood that environmental, social and governance (ESG) issues have a bottom-line impact. Thus, it would be a limited and ideologically rigid perspective to flatly state these ESG issues have no place in the investment process because they are "social." In fact, pension funds around the globe increasingly have integrated ESG as a necessary ingredient, not as an afterthought.

Investment responsibility, as practiced by pension funds with literally trillions of dollars under management, includes a wide variety of strategies. Critics often define ESG or Responsible Investing as "all about screening" — thus setting up a convenient but historically inaccurate premise.

In fact, active, responsible investors are involved in:

- Voting their proxies thoughtfully and conscientiously;
- Discussing issues with companies seeking forward-looking policies and practices;
- Filing shareholder resolutions urging companies to improve environmental, social or governance practices; and
- Integrating ESG into their investment process.

Globally, investors managing more than $14 trillion in assets have endorsed the U.N.'s "Principles for Responsible Investing," which hold that part of an investor's fiduciary duty is making ESG a part of their investment process. Several issues are before such pension funds, including:

- Governance Reforms — Pension funds from unions to states and cities promote governance reforms as a means of building accountability to investors and improving value for investors.
- Climate Change — Future global devastation from climate change is well documented. As a result, investors globally with more than $50 trillion in assets under management have supported the Carbon Disclosure Project, which urges companies to reveal and reduce their carbon emissions. Hundreds of companies have stepped up as climate leaders — not for narrow, "green" reasons but because it makes long-term business sense.

Should responsible pension funds engage in ESG investing? If hundreds of companies agree that it is in their business interests to be good corporate citizens, forward-looking pension funds are simply ensuring this is reflected in their investment philosophy.

NO
Alicia H. Munnell
Director, Center for Retirement
Research, Boston College

Written for *CQ Researcher*, August 2008

Social investing by public pension plans is generally ineffective and potentially dangerous. Federal law prohibits private plans from introducing social considerations into their investment decisions. And the case for public plans is even stronger.

Advocates suggest that screening out, say, tobacco stocks will hurt tobacco companies, thereby reducing cigarette supplies. But the evidence suggests the opposite. With efficient capital markets, the price of the stock is equal to the present discounted value of future cash flows. Boycotting tobacco stocks may result in a temporary fall in the stock price, but as long as some buyers remain they can swoop in, purchase the stock and make money. So ridding portfolios of "sin" has no impact on the targeted firm.

The same is true for stock prices of "good" companies. But how does one identify desirable firms? Corporations that pass ideological litmus tests today with respect to good governance, protecting the environment or having diverse workforces may turn into tomorrow's disasters. Enron had independent directors; Arthur Andersen prided itself on quality. And Odwalla was dedicated to producing healthy juices, but flaws in its systems led to injuries and a death.

Private pension plans hold virtually no investments in companies that have been screened for either "good" or "bad" characteristics. From the beginning, the Department of Labor has stringently enforced the duties of loyalty and prudence set by ERISA (Employee Retirement Income Security Act). In 1994, the Labor Department reminded fiduciaries that they are prohibited from "subordinating the interests of participants and beneficiaries . . . to unrelated objectives." And the department has just reiterated this warning, so social investing remains a public pension fund phenomenon.

But public pension funds are particularly ill-suited to social investing. First, in many instances, the environment surrounding public pension fund investing is politically charged, and encouraging fund trustees to take "their eyes off the prize" of the maximum return for any given level of risk is asking for trouble. Public pension funds have made serious mistakes in the past when they have introduced social concerns into their investment decisions. Second, the decision-makers and the stakeholders are not the same people. The decision-makers are either the fund boards or the state legislatures. The stakeholders are tomorrow's beneficiaries and/or taxpayers. If social investing produces losses either through higher administrative costs or lower returns, tomorrow's taxpayers will have to ante up, or future retirees will receive lower benefits. Public plans should just say "No" to socially responsible investing.

Walden Asset Management, which calls itself "a leader in socially responsive investing," owns shares of British Petroleum despite its mixed environmental record. Walden says BP has been a leader among energy producers on the climate-change issue. Above, BP's refinery in Grangemouth, Scotland.

Yet some SRI managers did see trouble coming. *Business Week* noted that Patrick McVeigh — president of Boston-based Reynders, McVeigh Capital Management, which engages in social investing — sent a letter to *Business Ethics* magazine back in 2004 after it named government-supported mortgage-funding provider Fannie Mae the most socially responsible company that year. The letter attacked Fannie Mae for having become a big hedge fund by taking on piles of debt as it grew into new markets, *Business Week* said. Fannie's stock has plummeted this year amid huge credit losses.

"*Business Ethics* said Fannie was in the business of building dreams," McVeigh said. "We said they're in the business of building nightmares by putting people in homes they can't afford."[55]

As the SRI movement becomes larger and more prominent, it can expect to become a bigger target for critics, including those who do not think it belongs in the pension world.

AEI's Entine is among the most vocal. "In some states and municipalities, including California, New York and New York City, elected and appointed politicians responsible for overseeing public retirement funds are embracing highly controversial social and environmental criteria to decide on which companies to invest in or publicly lobby against," he wrote in a 2005 book examining public pensions and socially responsible investing.[56]

He went on to say that "social investors and advocacy groups have allied themselves with union leaders and sympathetic politicians, introducing ideology into the management of public pension funds with a stated goal of more directly influencing corporate and public policy."

The California Public Employees' Retirement System (CalPERS) and State Teachers' Retirement System (CalSTRS) have been under scrutiny for a "double bottom line" approach to investing that was introduced in 2000 by former state Treasurer Philip Angelides. His idea, according to *Business Week*, was to take pension fund money out of two asset classes that were performing poorly back then — tobacco stocks and emerging markets — and reinvest in businesses and real estate in low-income California neighborhoods. The aim was to produce both a social return and a healthy financial return.[57]

But a recent CalSTRS report revealed that the $172-billion fund would have had $1 billion more had it not shunned tobacco stocks, *Business Week* said. What's more, real estate investing by the $239 billion CalPERS has been "particularly painful," it said, adding: "Among other bad deals, it faces a loss of nearly $1 billion on one land investment alone."

"The performance of the double bottom line plan illustrates the potential drawbacks of socially responsible investing," *Business Week* wrote. "While it's fine for individual investors to vote their conscience by putting money into the growing number of socially responsible mutual funds, they should know that it could lead to weaker investment performance. . . . Like it or not, people do gamble, smoke and buy expensive nuclear-powered war machines."

Pension Problems

How long the California public pension system plans to stick with its investing approach is in question, however. The system reportedly is considering reversing its anti-tobacco policy. The State Teachers' Retirement System could vote on such a move as early as this fall, and the California Public Employees' Retirement System is also monitoring the issue, according to a report in August in *The New York Sun*.[58]

Entine at AEI says a retreat by the California funds would be a "watershed" event and a sign that "from a fiduciary standpoint [SRI] doesn't hold water."

In New Hampshire the legislature passed a law requiring its two public pension systems to sell its investments supporting Sudan, which has been accused of genocide, but pension officials said the law may be unconstitutional, The Associated Press (AP) reported in August.[59] Pension officials were studying whether to challenge the law after Democratic Gov. John Lynch refused a request to veto the bill.

In a letter obtained by the AP, a pension system lawyer told Lynch the divestiture provision violated the state constitution "because it would require the board to make investment decisions for [a] purpose other than providing benefits to members and beneficiaries and divest assets in order to further the foreign policy objectives of the New Hampshire legislature."

Public-pension squabbles aren't alone in stirring up controversy on the social-responsibility front. Shareholder activism by religious investors and union pension funds also has been controversial.

Last year the Securities and Exchange Commission asked for public comment on proposals to limit the right of shareholders to file proxy resolutions and participate in nominating corporate board members. The curbs were supported by business groups and opposed, in part, by thousands of investors through a Web site formed by the Social Investment Forum and Interfaith Center on Corporate Responsibility (ICCR).[60] The SEC dropped the proxy-resolution idea, but the board-nomination proposal remains on hold, according to Smith at Walden Asset Management.

Meanwhile, the SEC, in a shift of policy, told corporations this year they have to let shareholders vote on a proposal for universal health insurance coverage — a topic of great concern to many social investors.[61] The proposal, backed by such groups as the ICCR, urges companies to adopt "principles for comprehensive health-care reform" such as those reported by the Institute of Medicine, part of the National Academy of Sciences.

The SEC said it was appropriate for shareholders to tell companies what they think by voting on "significant social policy issues" that go beyond day-to-day business matters.[62]

Religious groups and labor unions have submitted the same basic health-care proposal to several dozen corporations, according to *The New York Times.* "We are working for a national policy that provides universal access to health care, and we do hold more than 30,000 shares of General Electric stock," Barbara Kraemer, a Roman Catholic nun who is national president of the School Sisters of St. Francis, told the newspaper. "As we pursued the proposal with G.E., the company requested a dialogue in lieu of the shareholder resolution, so we withdrew it. The dialogue was productive, resulting in G.E.'s public endorsement of the Institute of Medicine principles."[63]

A shareholder campaign by the AFL-CIO that includes the health-care proposal has met stiff resistance from the U.S. Chamber of Commerce. Last year the chamber asked the Labor Department to weigh in on whether a shareholder campaign by the labor group on health care and other issues was in line with ERISA, the federal retirement-security law. The opinion, issued in December, said pension trustees risk running afoul of their fiduciary duty when they "attempt to further legislative, regulatory or public policy issues through the proxy process when there is no clear economic benefit to the plan."[64]

> The integration of environmental, social and governance standards into investment analysis is already widespread in Europe, and many SRI advocates believe the approach will continue to gain favor in the United States among professional money managers.

The letter "sends a clear message that union pension trustees need to put workers' retirement security first, instead of any political agenda," Chamber President Thomas J. Donohue said. "Union pension savings belong to beneficiaries and retirees and must not be tapped to advance goals other than the economic enhancement of those funds."[65]

But Daniel Pedrotty, director of the AFL-CIO's Office of Investment, argues that the advisory opinion broke no new ground and does not preclude investor groups proposing shareholder resolutions that affect their members and beneficiaries.

That, he says, was borne out by the SEC's recent change in policy allowing shareholders to vote on the health-care principles.

"The No. 1 competitive concern for companies is the cost of health care," he says. "We felt like it was a legitimate issue."

OUTLOOK

Continued Growth?

As global warming, health-care access, employee rights in overseas factories and other issues continue to emerge on the public-policy scene, the appeal of socially responsible investing seems likely to grow.

But the sector also faces challenges in convincing skeptics that its screening methods are sound and that financial returns on social investments are at least competitive — if not superior — to those found in conventional ones.

The integration of environmental, social and governance standards into investment analysis is already widespread in Europe, and many SRI advocates believe the approach will continue to gain favor in the United States among professional money managers.

"To the degree that we can demonstrate that this integration approach can improve performance, that's where you're going to attract more investors" to SRI, says Hilton of the Calvert Group. "In some ways, if we're successful, it will almost put us out of a job, meaning if we're really good at integrating ESG performance and we have better performance, then at some point everybody's going to start doing that."

SRI advocates point to the fact that progress reports on environmental sustainability have become standard among many of the nation's biggest corporations as climate and energy issues have gained prominence. While some of those companies may engage in "greenwashing" — substituting public relations spin for substance in promoting their environmental efforts — the reports are nonetheless significant, SRI advocates say.

"Yes, [the corporate sustainability reports] might not be as honest as they could be," the *Green Money Journal's* Feigenbaum says. But "they're putting it in print, they're putting themselves out there in a way they have never done before. There is an unstoppable movement [among] every board in this country" to address the sustainability issue.

Besides environmental issues, a range of other concerns is likely to animate the SRI movement in coming years, either through investing practices or shareholder activism. Those issues range from excessive CEO pay, which many SRI proponents see as a social as well as governance concern, to divestment in stocks of companies profiting from commerce in Sudan.

As advocates of socially responsible investing look back on the movement's early roots, they express the hope that it continues to move into the mainstream.

"This industry is a lot like the natural-foods industry," says Alexander, the former grocery store owner in Durham, N.C. "When we started, people thought we were just a bunch of wacko hippies. Twenty or 25 years later, at the convenience store they're selling soy milk. I'm hoping socially responsible investing is like that."

NOTES

1. Social Investment Forum, "2007 Report on Socially Responsible Investing Trends in the United States," 2008, p. iv.

2. Carolyn Cui, "For Money Managers, A Smarter Approach to Social Responsibility," *The Wall Street Journal*, Nov. 5, 2007.

3. Social Investment Forum, *op. cit.*, p. v.

4. KLD Research & Analytics Inc., www.kld.com/indexes/ds400index/performance.html.

5. Christopher Palmeri, "CalPERS: The Price of Good Intentions," *Business Week*, Aug. 11, 2008, p. 54.

6. Julie Satow, "Big Funds Eye Reinvesting in Tobacco Firms," *The New York Sun*, Aug. 14, 2008.

7. John Hechinger, "Pax Funds Strayed From Its Mission," *The Wall Street Journal*, July 31, 2008, p. 1C.

8. Pax World, "A Letter From the President and CEO of Pax World Funds," http://paxworld.com/homepage/2008/07/30/a-letter-from -the-president-and-ceo-of-pax-world-funds.

9. "Investors File 54 Global Warming-Related Shareholder Resolutions," *Environmental Leader*, March 9, 2008. Investors withdrew 14 of the 54 resolutions after the companies agreed to disclose potential impacts from emerging climate regulations and strategies for curbing greenhouse-gas emissions, *Environmental Leader* said.

10. For background, see Alan Greenblatt, "Aging Baby Boomers," *CQ Researcher*, Oct. 19, 2007, pp. 865-888.

11. Jon Entine, "Delusional Goodwill," in "The Debate Room: SRI: Invest With Your Heart and Soul," *Business Week*, July 2007, www.businessweek.com/debateroom/archives/2007/07/invest_with_you.html.

12. "Responsible investment doesn't hurt returns: UNEP & Mercer report reveals," Oct. 24, 2007, www.mercer.com. University of California, Berkeley, "New Study on Employee Satisfaction and Long-Run Stock Performance Wins 2007 Moskowitz Prize for SRI Research," Nov. 5, 2007.

13. Ann-Marie Anderson and David H. Myers, "The cost of being good," *Review of Business*, fall 2007.

14. Alex Edmans, "Does the Stock Market Fully Value Intangibles? Employee Satisfaction and Equity Prices," 2008, http://papers.ssrn.com/sol3/papers.cfm?abstract_id=985735.

15. Knowledge@Wharton, "Risks and Costs of Socially Responsible Investing," Aug. 13, 2003, http://knowledge.wharton.upenn.edu/article.cfm?articleid=831. The study is Christopher Geczy, Robert F. Stambaugh and David Levin, "Investing in Socially Responsible Mutual Funds," *Social Science Research Network*, July 22, 2003, revised, Feb. 15, 2006, http://papers.ssrn.com/sol3/papers.cfm?abstract_id=416380.

16. Knowledge@Wharton, *ibid.*

17. Joshua D. Margolis and Hillary Anger Elfenbein, "Do Well by Doing Good? Don't Count on It," *Harvard Business Review*, January 2008, pp. 19-20.

18. Lauren Young, "A Social Fund's Strategic Shift," *Business Week*, May 26, 2006.

19. Amy Domini, *Socially Responsible Investing: Making a Difference and Making Money* (2001), p. 57.

20. Cui, *op. cit.*

21. Paul Hawken and the Natural Capital Institute, "Socially Responsible Investing: How the SRI industry has failed to respond to people who want to invest with conscience and what can be done to change it," 2004.

22. Proinsias O'Mahony, "Ethical living: Profits and principles," *The Guardian*, Feb. 21, 2008, p. 18.

23. Joe Nocera, "Well-Meaning but Misguided Stock Screens," *The New York Times*, April 7, 2007.

24. Ben Arnoldy, "US mining company agrees to 'green' review," *The Christian Science Monitor*, April 26, 2007.

25. Social Investment Forum, *op. cit.*, p. 27. Data source is RiskMetrics Group.

26. Jeanne M. Logsdon and Harry J. Van Buren III, "Justice and Large Corporations," *Business and Society*, online publication, May 2, 2008.

27. Logsdon and Van Buren, "Beyond the Proxy Vote: Dialogues Between Shareholder Activists and Corporations," *Journal of Business Ethics*, online publication, June 18, 2008.

28. Social Investment Forum, *op. cit.* Data source is RiskMetrics Group.

29. Domini, *op. cit.*, p. 29.

30. *Ibid.*, p. 28.

31. Social Investment Forum, *op. cit.*, p. 4.

32. *Ibid.*

33. Pax World Funds, www.paxworld.com/about/pax-history.

34. "About ICCR: FAQ," Interfaith Center on Corporate Responsibility, www.iccr.org/about/faq.php.

35. Social Investment Forum, *op. cit.*

36. *Ibid.*

37. Jonathan Glater, "S.E.C. Adopts New Rules For Lawyers and Funds," *The New York Times*, Jan. 24, 2003.

38. *Ibid.*

39. Jennifer Byrd, "Socially conscious investing blossoms with DOL's blessing," *Investment News*, June 23, 2008.

40. *Ibid.*

41. "Calvert Celebrates 10-Year Anniversary of DOL letter," Calvert Group, www.calvertgroup.com.

42. "U.S. Defined Contribution & Socially Responsible Investing Survey," Mercer, June 5, 2007, www.mercer.com.

43. Cui, *op. cit.*

44. United Nations, "Principles for Responsible Investment Report on Progress 2008," www.unpri .org/report08, p. 4.

45. *Ibid.*

46. Hawken, *op. cit.*, p. 18.

47. *Ibid.*, p. 27.

48. David Vogel, *The Market for Virtue* (2005), p. 38.

49. *Ibid.*, p. 39.

50. Henry Blodget, "The Conscientious Investor," *The Atlantic*, October 2007.

51. Clark Hoyt, "Taint by Association," *The New York Times*, Nov. 11, 2007

52. Nancy Stancill, "Investing with Conscience," *Charlotte Observer*, May 11, 2008.

53. David Bogoslaw, "Socially Responsible Funds Hang Tough," *Business Week*, May 14, 2008.

54. *Ibid.*

55. *Ibid.*

56. Jon Entine, ed., *Pension Fund Politics* (2005), pp. 1-2.

57. Christopher Palmeri, "The Golden State's not-so-golden goose," *Business Week*, July 16, 2008.

58. Satow, *op. cit.*

59. Norma Love, "NH funds mull Sudan divestment," The Associated Press, Aug. 11, 2008, www.boston.com.

60. www.SaveShareholderRights.org.

61. Robert Pear, "S.E.C. Backs Health Care Balloting," *The New York Times*, May 27, 2008.

62. *Ibid.*

63. *Ibid.*

64. Letter from Robert J. Doyle, director of regulations and interpretations, U.S. Department of Labor, to Thomas J. Donohue, president and CEO, U.S. Chamber of Commerce, Dec. 21, 2007, and Pear, *ibid.*

65. U.S. Chamber of Commerce, "Chamber Applauds DOL Union Proxy Activity Decision," Jan. 3, 2008.

BIBLIOGRAPHY

Books

Domini, Amy, *Socially Responsible Investing: Making a Difference and Making Money,* **Dearborn Trade, 2001.**
The founder of Domini Social Investments writes, "by integrating deeply held personal or ethical concerns into the investment decision-making process, investors can bring about a world that values and supports human dignity and environmental sustainability."

Entine, Jon, ed., *Pension Fund Politics: The Dangers of Socially Responsible Investing,* **AEI Press, 2005.**
Five critics, including Alicia H. Munnell, director of the Center for Retirement Research at Boston College, analyze the history, strategy and risks of retirement-fund involvement in socially responsible investing.

Vogel, David, *The Market for Virtue: The Potential and Limits of Corporate Social Responsibility,* **Brookings Institution Press, 2005.**
A professor of business ethics and political science at the University of California, Berkeley explores the corporate-responsibility movement, including the claims and performance record surrounding socially responsible investing.

Articles

Blodget, Henry, "The Conscientious Investor," *The Atlantic,* **October 2007.**
A former securities analyst argues that socially responsible investing is not as profitable as many advocates contend.

Chatterji, Aaron, and Siona Listokin, "Corporate Social Irresponsibility," *Democracy,* **winter 2007, www.democracyjournal.org/article.php?ID=6497.**
Only governments and multilateral agreements can solve social injustices, and progressives should "end their fixation with corporate social responsibility."

Feigenbaum, Cliff, "Essays on the Future: Looking Ahead," *GreenMoneyJournal.com,* **www.greenmoney-journal.com/index.mpl?newsletterid=41.**
A publication focusing on environmental sustainability presents essays from key figures in the SRI movement.

Nocera, Joe, "Well-Meaning but Misguided Stock Screens," *The New York Times,* **April 7, 2007, http://select.nytimes.com/2007/04/07/business/07nocera .html.**
A business journalist analyzes socially responsible investing, including the work of KLD Research & Analytics, a Boston company that constructs widely used SRI

indexes, and says social investing "oversimplifies the world."

Palmeri, Christopher, "CalPERS: The Price of Good Intentions," *Business Week*, Aug. 11, 2008.
The SRI strategy of the California Public Employees' Retirement System and the California State Teachers' Retirement System has hurt fund returns, even though the funds have outpaced the S&P 500 over the past five years.

Piller, Charles, Edmund Sanders and Robyn Dixon, "Dark cloud over good works of Gates Foundation," *Los Angeles Times*, Jan. 7, 2007, www.latimes.com/ news/nationworld/nation/la-na-gatesx07jan07,0, 6827615.story.
Part of a series on the Bill & Melinda Gates Foundation, the article says the nation's biggest private foundation invested "in many companies that have failed tests of social responsibility because of environmental lapses, employment discrimination, disregard for worker rights or unethical practices."

Satow, Julie, "Big Funds Eye Reinvesting in Tobacco Firms," *The New York Sun*, Aug. 14, 2008, www .nysun.com/business/big-funds-eye-reinvesting-in-tobacco-firms/83867/.
A newspaper says California's public system is considering reversing its policy of shunning tobacco stocks, in what could be a "potentially devastating blow" to the socially responsible investing movement.

Reports and Studies

"The language of responsible investment," *Mercer LLC*, Jan. 3, 2008, www.mercer.com/ridictionary.
An international business-consulting firm offers a guide to key organizations in the SRI field and defines such insider terms as "eco-efficiency" ("the ratio between goods produced or services rendered and the resources consumed or waste produced").

"2007 Report on Socially Responsible Investing Trends in the United States," *Social Investment Forum*, 2008, www.socialinvest.org/pdf/SRI_Trends_ ExecSummary_2007.pdf.
Socially responsible investing is growing at a faster rate than the broader universe of investment assets under professional management, says this biennial report from the trade group of the social-investing field.

Hawken, Paul, "Socially Responsible Investing: How the SRI industry has failed to respond to people who want to invest with conscience and what can be done to change it," *Natural Capital Institute*, 2004, www .responsibleinvesting.org/database/dokuman/SRI% 20Report%2010-04_ word.pdf.
An ecologist and entrepreneur offers a stinging critique of the socially responsible mutual fund industry, arguing among other things that it lacks transparency and that the language surrounding socially responsible investing is vague.

For More Information

American Enterprise Institute, 1150 17th St., N.W., Washington, DC 20036; (202) 862-5800; www.aei.org. A private, nonpartisan, not-for-profit institution dedicated to research and education on issues of government, politics, economics, and social welfare.

As You Sow, 311 California St., Suite 510, San Francisco CA 94104; (415) 391-3212; www.asyousow.org. Shareholder advocacy group that seeks to bring about change within public companies.

Calvert Group, 4550 Montgomery Ave., Suite 1000N, Bethesda, MD 20814; (800) 368-2748. Mutual fund company engaged in socially responsible investing.

Ceres, 99 Chauncy St., 6th Floor, Boston, MA 02111; (617) 247-0700; www.ceres.org. Coalition of investors, environmental organizations and other public-interest groups working with companies and investors to address "sustainability" issues such as climate change.

Domini Social Investments, P.O. Box 9785, Providence, RI 02940; (800) 762-6814; www.domini.com. Mutual fund company engaged in socially responsible investing.

Interfaith Center on Corporate Responsibility, Room 1842, 475 Riverside Dr., New York, NY 10115; (212) 870-2295; www.iccr.org. Association of 275 faith-based institutional investors.

KLD Research & Analytics, 250 Summer St., 4th Floor, Boston, MA 02210; (617) 426-5270; www.kld.com. Independent investment research firm focusing on social investing.

Natural Capital Institute, 3 Gate Five Road, Suite A, Sausalito, CA 94965; (415) 331-6241; www.naturalcapital .org. Research group on social responsibility, corporate accountability and environmental issues.

Pax World Funds, 30 Penhallow St., Suite 400, Portsmouth, NH 03801; (800) 767-1729; www.paxworld.com. Mutual fund company engaged in socially responsible investing.

Social Investment Forum, 1612 K St., N.W., Suite 650, Washington, DC 20006; (202) 872-5361; www.social invest.org. Trade group for socially responsible investment industry.

Walden Asset Management, One Beacon St., Boston, MA 02108; (617) 726-7155; www.waldenassetmgmt.com. A division of Boston Trust & Investment Management Co. that specializes in socially responsive investments.

Regulating Credit Cards

6

Are Tougher Regulations Needed to Protect Consumers?

Marcia Clemmitt

Washington State University student Brea Thompson thinks college students use their credit cards when cash runs low. Card debt hits low-income and young Americans the hardest, and today at least 35 million U.S. households are behind in payments or over their spending limits. Consumer advocates say tighter restrictions on cards are needed, but the industry says their benefits outweigh the problems and that serious misuse of cards affects relatively few people.

From *CQ Researcher*, October 10, 2008.

AP Photo/Joe Barrentine

"As I was growing up, I always thought, 'I don't want a credit card; if I don't have the money, I just won't buy,'" says Edwin Lindo, a senior business major who is student body president at the University of the Pacific in Stockton, Calif. He'd seen his family struggle with some debt and didn't want to repeat those experiences.

But early in his college career, he faced some big purchases — a laptop computer, for example, and about $500 for books each semester — that changed his mind. Quickly, Lindo found himself with three cards — only one of which he actually intended to apply for — and rising debts. "For a while, I was using all three, but when I got the bills and realized I was paying more for things than I would have paying cash, I didn't like it at all and realized I was in a very bad position," says Lindo.

"Right now," working a part-time campus job that pays $9.50 an hour, "all the money I earn, I'm using to pay off my credit cards," he says. But Lindo says he worries that his combined student loans and credit card debt will constrict his career dreams. He hopes to attend law school and would like to go into public service, but he fears he'll have to take a job in a private firm, instead, just because of the better pay.

Consumer debt increasingly plagues Americans, and credit card debt makes up a large portion of that. Between 1980 and 2005, Americans' annual credit card purchases jumped 25-fold — from $69 billion to $1.8 trillion.[1] And along with the increase have come calls to regulate the credit card industry and end some industry practices that can transform moderate debt into a crushing burden for unwary consumers. Congressional bills introduced this year

Alaskans Had the Most Credit Card Debt

The average borrower in Alaska had nearly $3,400 in credit card debt in 2006 — more than any other state and triple the rate among Mississippians, who had the least credit card debt.

State	Median credit card debt per borrower
Ten States with Most Credit Card Debt, 2006	
Alaska	$3,384
New Hampshire	$2,109
Connecticut	$2,094
Maryland	$2,042
Colorado	$2,030
Nevada	$1,994
Virginia	$1,983
Delaware	$1,960
Washington	$1,941
Massachusetts	$1,937
Ten States with Least Credit Card Debt, 2006	
Nebraska	$1,388
Oklahoma	$1,364
Kentucky	$1,357
Arkansas	$1,313
South Dakota	$1,304
Louisiana	$1,285
North Dakota	$1,258
West Virginia	$1,237
Iowa	$1,135
Mississippi	$1,098

Source: Americans for Fairness in Lending

University of Illinois, total annual personal income in the United States "was less than our total household debt," including both mortgage debt and consumer debt such as credit cards. In other words, "if everybody in the country devoted their entire incomes to repayment of our personal debt, we still wouldn't be able to retire it," he says.

Moreover, while mortgages make up the biggest chunk of personal debt, in the past two years — as housing prices have dropped and home-equity-backed consumer loans have dried up — credit card debt rose four times as fast as it did between March 2001 and March 2006, says Tim Westrich, a research associate at the liberal think tank Center for American Progress.

Among the approximately 80 percent of U.S. households with at least one credit card, outstanding credit card debt now averages $10,000, says Ronald J. Mann, a professor at Columbia Law Schools in New York City. And only households earning more than $200,000 a year could comfortably pay off that amount of debt in the next billing cycle, he says. Thus, many are carrying so much credit card debt that their ability to respond to sudden needs is limited.

Americans' median debt levels — the level at which half have more debt and half less — range from Mississippi's low of $1,098 per individual borrower to Alaska's whopping $3,384. (*See box, at left.*)[2]

And many can't keep up with those payments. At least 35 million U.S. households are either behind in payments or over the limit on at least one card, says Christopher Viale, president of the Cambridge Credit Counseling Corp. in Massachusetts.

Credit card debt is also instrumental in pushing more low- and moderate-income people into bankruptcy, says

and in 2007 would ban, among other things, such bank practices as increasing credit card interest rates without notice. For its part, the banking industry argues that only a small percentage of people get into severe financial distress from credit card spending and that the benefits of cashless transactions outweigh the problems.

Overall personal debt — including credit card debt — has risen substantially in recent years. By 2006, says Robert M. Lawless, a professor of law at the

Lawless, who estimates 1.1 million American families will file for bankruptcy this year.

Filmmaker Danny Schecter, whose 2006 documentary "In Debt We Trust" traces the web of debt in American society, often asks college audiences how many are in credit card debt. Usually, no one raises a hand at first, he says. Eventually a student will admit to a few thousand in debt, and "suddenly there are topper stories all around the room," he says. " 'I've got $10,000.' 'I've got $100,000.' "

But many analysts point out that having readily available portable credit is a boon in many ways. "We could not have the kind of society we have" — with the ability to travel and engage in business everywhere and the "flexibility to make quick decisions and act on them financially" — without the current credit card system, says Jeffrey I. Langer, a partner at Chicago-based financial-services law firm Chapman and Cutler.

Credit cards are a big help to merchants, freeing them from the dangers of handling large amounts of cash, for example, he says. And a hotel will accept a credit card rather than a wad of cash for a room because "they can put a hold on your card for a significant amount more than the actual room charge to protect themselves from your unexpectedly using a lot of paid services that run the bill from $400 to $900," he says.

Indeed, some analysts say, Congress risks mucking up the credit card market with ill-considered regulations.

Free competition, largely unfettered by prescriptive rules, has

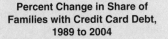

Debt Grew Fastest Among the Vulnerable

Credit card debt increased the most among minority families and the poor and young from 1989 to 2004.

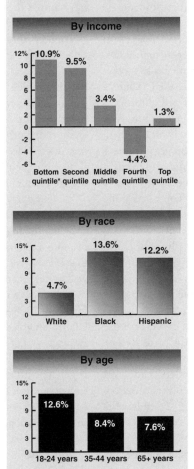

Percent Change in Share of Families with Credit Card Debt, 1989 to 2004

By income

- Bottom quintile*: 10.9%
- Second quintile: 9.5%
- Middle quintile: 3.4%
- Fourth quintile: -4.4%
- Top quintile: 1.3%

By race

- White: 4.7%
- Black: 13.6%
- Hispanic: 12.2%

By age

- 18-24 years: 12.6%
- 35-44 years: 8.4%
- 65+ years: 7.6%

* A quintile equals one-fifth of the population.

Source: Christian E. Weller, "Pushing the Limit: Credit Card Debt Burdens American Families," Center for American Progress, July 2006

allowed the industry to develop cards that consumers want, says Langer. People who pay late, for example, have seen their penalties rise from around $10 a decade-and-a-half ago to $35 to $40 today, but raising those fees has allowed companies to reduce charges elsewhere, such as lowering interest rates for people who pay on time, he argues.

But others say current card practices allow or even encourage too many people to get into trouble. "Right now there is virtually no regulation of the substantive terms of credit cards," says Adam Levitin, an associate professor of law at Georgetown University.

Industry practices that consumer advocates call troublesome include:

- charging customers with late fees for payments that arrive on the due date but after an arbitrary cutoff hour, which can be as early as 9 a.m.;
- raising interest rates suddenly and with no stated reason for customers in good standing;
- applying new higher interest rates to existing balances, not just future purchases; and
- requiring customers to bring disputes before professional arbitrators rather than the courts — even when the disputed debt may have resulted from identity theft.

"Arbitrators have a strong financial incentive to rule in favor of the companies . . . because they can make hundreds of thousands of dollars a year conducting arbitrations," according to the consumer group Public Citizen.[3]

Card issuers and free-market economists generally prefer greater disclosure of credit terms instead of more rules. But "the evidence [shows] disclosure is just not working," says Lawless, who recommends "substantive" regulation. "We need to look seriously at some form of interest-rate cap," he says, similar to the 36 percent cap on consumer-loan interest that Congress approved for the military in 2006.[4]

The more vulnerable segments of the population — the poor and unsophisticated borrowers such as students — increasingly are offered credit cards.

The use of credit cards has steadily increased, with most of the recent jump occurring in lower-income households. "Credit card companies have become really good at exploiting people's irrationality," says Michelle J. White, a professor of economics at the University of California at San Diego. "They know that if they get the card into your pocket, you'll use it, even if you think you won't." Then, "once you do something like pay late, you get put into a riskier group," your interest rate and fees rise, and the debt becomes much more difficult to repay, she says.

Extending more credit to poorer people has gone hand in hand with another troubling trend, says White. "People filing for bankruptcy have become poorer and poorer," she says. "The average person filing for bankruptcy now is well below median income," a significant change from 20 years ago. "And that's not surprising, with more credit available. Once you've built up a big balance, you can't pay it off."

But others dispute that expansion of credit card use has harmed low-income groups. If credit cards weren't easily accessible, many would borrow anyway, using far riskier loan sources, such as payday lenders, said Todd Zywicki, a professor at George Mason University School of Law, in Fairfax, Va. The percentage of the lowest-income households "in financial distress" has been largely constant since 1989, he said.[5]

Here are some of the key questions being debated by lawmakers and consumer advocates:

Should Congress crack down on credit card industry practices?

Consumer advocates call for a crackdown on credit card industry practices, but other analysts say lenders' freedom from restrictive laws has allowed them to develop popular products.

Penalty fees have risen over the past two decades, but if the increases "were part of some abusive pricing scheme to take advantage of customers, one would expect issuer profits to have risen accordingly" — but they haven't, said economists Jonathan M. Orszag and Susan H. Manning in a report for the American Bankers Association, which represents card-issuing companies.[6]

Even if some abusive actions do occur, no congressional action is needed because courts and regulators have ample tools "to attack deceptive and fraudulent practices on a case-by-case basis," said Zywicki.[7]

Tighter rules could have a substantial impact on so-called securitization of credit card debt — banks' ability to package and "sell" credit card debt to investors as a way of bringing in extra funds so they can continue lending to consumers, says Eric Higgins, an associate professor of finance at Kansas State University. Up to now, credit card issuers have been able to repeatedly shift pricing, interest, fees and other card terms to ensure a solid return on such securities, but tightened rules would threaten that ability, he says.

Langer particularly opposes a proposal to exempt a consumer's existing card balance from interest-rate hikes, applying the higher interest only to new purchases. "If I become a greater payment risk," for whatever reason, that higher risk will "affect my outstanding balance" as well as new charges, he says.

Perhaps the riskiest proposal is the Credit Card Fair Fee Act of 2008, sponsored by House Judiciary Committee Chairman John Conyers Jr., D-Mich., says David S. Evans, author of *Paying With Plastic: The Digital Revolution in Buying and Borrowing*. It would allow merchants to negotiate with credit card issuers collectively on the per-transaction fees that merchants pay the credit card companies. "We know from the experience of other countries," such as Australia, that when merchants' fees go down card fees and interest for consumers go up, he says.

But other analysts say many credit card practices should be reined in.

For instance, the idea that card issuers need complete flexibility to price credit cards according to people's relative risk doesn't hold water, Georgetown's Levitin said. There is "no empirical evidence connecting the advent of risk-based pricing to lower costs of credit to creditworthy consumers or greater credit availability to subprime borrowers," he said.[8]

Banks' generally lower cost of borrowing money also could explain the lower interest rates the most creditworthy customers have seen over the past two decades, said Levitin. In addition, banks' ability to "securitize" credit card debt and sell it as investments — securitization — "is at least as good of an explanation" as risk-based fees for banks' willingness to offer credit cards to low-income people — dubbed "subprime" cards for their similarity to mortgage loans made to poor people, he said.

If federal rules banning some credit card industry practices were established, then the whole industry would have to make changes at once, says A. Mechele Dickerson, a professor of bankruptcy law at the University of Texas at Austin. A single company can't risk taking big pro-consumer steps on its own, since it would risk being run out of business by other companies in the very competitive market, she says.

The fact that credit card late fees have risen much faster than inflation — from an average $12.83 in 1995 to $33.64 in 2005 — shows that some card provisions are unreasonable and should be challenged, said Curtis E. Arnold, author of *How You Can Profit from Credit Cards: Using Credit to Improve Your Financial Life and Bottom Line.*

Arnold also thinks another common practice should be banned — applying payments only to the low-interest portions of a credit card bill. Card companies often offer low introductory interest rates on purchases during the first few months, and then higher rates thereafter, but the consumer's payments are applied only to the lower-interest balance. Such practices increase the total interest the cardholder pays and the time it will take to discharge the debt. "I sincerely hope this practice will be outlawed, and payments will have to be credited against the balance with the highest rate" in order to cut consumer costs, Arnold said.[9]

Nevertheless, even those who advocate action caution that Congress should consider its next move carefully. "The biggest risk is that we'll do things that sound good and accomplish nothing," says Columbia Law School's Mann. "It's a bad idea" to simply "ban the most egregious things," because it risks companies finding clever ways around the bans that lawmakers hadn't anticipated, he says.

He recommends requiring a standardized credit card agreement, with standard definitions for all allowable

AFP/Getty Images/Robyn Beck

The nation's housing crisis has driven up credit card use. As housing prices dropped and home-equity-backed consumer loans have dried up, credit card debt rose four times as fast in the last two years as it did between March 2001 and March 2006. Americans' annual credit card purchases jumped from $69 billion to $1.8 trillion between 1980 and 2005. Above, a foreclosed house for sale in the city of Rialto in Southern California on Feb. 26, 2008.

terms, and then allowing companies to compete based on interest rates and other terms that people can understand. All other consumer financial products, from apartment leases to mortgages, he points out, have standardized contracts. And while "a mortgage is so huge that you might actually read the contract" before signing it, credit card terms may be overlooked until it's too late, he says.

Levitin says better disclosure of credit card terms can help but is not enough. "Disclosure could work if we can simplify credit card pricing so the consumer can see" the exact differences between cards, he says. "We could probably boil down to three" the important disclosures — the annual fee, the interest rate and the per-purchase transaction fee, he says.

Currently, merchants pay the transaction fees in the form of so-called interchange fees, and they aren't allowed to pass the fees on to individual purchasers, he says. But Levitin would like to see consumers pay those fees instead, to "lessen the cross-subsidization" of heavy users by lighter users.

Certain specific points of "coherent disclosure would be useful," Dickerson says. For example, credit card bills should state that, as of the current date, "if you pay the minimum each month and charge nothing else, this is how long it will take to pay off" your debt, a provision that was proposed and rejected during congressional debate of the 2005 bankruptcy-law overhaul. This would show consumers the consequences of their debts and payment practices, she says.

Lawless prefers returning more power to the states instead of tightening federal law. States should regulate card terms for their own consumers without being preempted by federal law or any other single standard, he says. States could experiment with interest-rate caps and other rules and potentially hit upon good solutions, he says.

A credit card safety rating system would supplement information disclosure, as would, potentially, a legal ban on some abusive practices, says Christian E. Weller, an associate professor of public policy at the University of Massachusetts in Boston and senior economist at the Center for American Progress. Similar to the five-star crash-test rating for new cars, the system would award stars to credit cards based on their consumer-friendliness.

Have credit card issuers unfairly targeted vulnerable populations?

Advocates of more government oversight say card issuers play on inexperience and financial vulnerabilities to sign people up for cards that expose them to damaging amounts of debt. But others argue that current law has helped many low-income people borrow money they need.

So, far from being abusive, card issuers' marketing efforts to young people and the poor have provided necessary access to credit, according to economists Orszag and Manning. "Increased lending to consumers at lower incomes has . . . allowed millions of Americans to take advantages of the benefits of credit," they wrote.[10]

"A lot of people are savvier than we give them credit for," George Mason University's Zywicki says. "People do dumb things, and maybe they make a mistake with credit when they're in college, but people eventually figure out what they're doing," and shouldn't be denied credit, because handling it requires a learning process, he says.

Few people actually get into severe debt, a fact that demonstrates credit card issuers aren't unfairly targeting the vulnerable, says *Paying With Plastic* author Evans. "My guess is that a smaller proportion of credit card users" become severely debt-ridden than the proportion of "social drinkers who become alcoholics," he says.

Other analysts say aggressive marketing of credit cards to young people and low-income people exposes consumers to serious risk.

"Entering college students are bombarded with an average of eight credit card offers during their first week," wrote Creola Johnson, a professor at Ohio State University's Moritz College of Law.[11] She found that most Ohio State students who sign up for cards do so because they want the free gifts offered by card companies and that few fully understand the consequences, such as the

---

Average Undergrad Owes $2,200

Credit card companies began aggressively targeting college students in the 1990s. Today:

- Credit cards are held by 41 percent of all college students.
- The average undergrad has $2,200 in credit card debt.
- About 65 percent of college students with credit cards pay their bills in full every month, a rate higher than the general population.

Source: Ben Woolsey and Matt Schulz, "Credit card industry facts, debt statistics 2006-2008" (using statistics from Nellie Mae, "Undergraduate Students and Credit Cards in 2004: An Analysis of Usage Rates and Trends" and "Student Monitor Annual Financial Services Survey," 2008), www.creditcards.com/credit-card-news/credit-card-industry-facts-personal-debt-statistics-1276.php.

fact that "a tarnished payment history" can lead to wide-ranging troubles, including in landing a job.[12]

Companies also offer students more credit than they can handle, mailing "unsolicited blank checks and uni-laterally increasing a student's line of credit, even though the companies have scant information" and no "proof of ability to repay a higher debt load," said Johnson, offer-ing the cards "in hopes that students will persuade their parents to repay the debt."[13]

Students approached on campus often "mistakenly believe that their school" supports the cards or "screens credit card companies that solicit on campus," Benjamin Lawsky, deputy counsel to the New York State attorney general, told the House Committee on Financial Services in June.[14]

Credit card marketing campaigns on campus often "extol the benefits of 'responsible use'" but don't tell stu-dents how to accomplish it or explain the downsides, wrote Robert D. Manning, a professor of consumer finance at the Rochester Institute of Technology in New York. "The credit card industry knows exactly what it is doing" when it markets excess credit to naïve students, said a debt-burdened college student Manning inter-viewed. "Let's face it, how can these banks justify giving me 11 credit cards" — including a Gold American Express and Platinum Visa cards — "on an annual income of only $9,000."[15]

A former call-center worker from the large credit card issuer MBNA recently told CNN the company practiced aggressive selling, including pushing large cash advances that would get customers to max out their cards. Workers were trained to look for "trigger words like 'I'm in finan-cial difficulty' or 'I can't make my payments'" and push large cash advances to those customers in particular, said Kathy Ellingwood, who worked in the Belfast, Maine, MBNA center for a year and a half.[16]

Some studies suggest that credit card companies mar-ket heavily in low-income neighborhoods. In a study of 50 low-income women, of whom about half lived in pub-lic housing and half in government-subsidized (Section 8) housing, more than 90 percent said they received credit card offers on a regular basis and several said they got offers daily, according to Angela Littwin, an assistant professor at the University of Texas Law School.[17]

But credit cards are a dangerous form of payment, because of flaws in human reasoning that we all share,

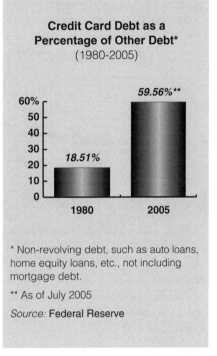

Card Debt Has Tripled

Credit card debt now amounts to nearly 60 percent of non-credit card debt within American households — three times what it was in 1980.

Credit Card Debt as a Percentage of Other Debt*
(1980-2005)

* Non-revolving debt, such as auto loans, home equity loans, etc., not including mortgage debt.

** As of July 2005

Source: Federal Reserve

and they pose serious danger to low-income people who can't afford to make financial mistakes, Littwin wrote. Humans tend to weigh near-term events most heavily in their calculations and seriously discount events in the distant future, she said.

"A common story was that a participant obtained a credit card with no intention of borrowing on it," plan-ning to use it only in case of emergency, "but she would quickly find herself charging on it with regularity" and running up debt, even though she'd never intended to, Littwin said.[18]

Credit cards are directly at odds with bill-paying strategies used by low-income people to survive — identifying which bills can be paid late while still avoid-ing immediate catastrophe, said Littwin. Using that sensible strategy for managing scarce funds, credit cards look ideal "because lateness will not result in an

Credit Card Spending Rising Abroad

Americans have traditionally spent more on credit cards than consumers in other industrialized countries, with credit card spending per capita reaching $6,700 in 2005 in the United States. But since 2003, credit card use has been on the rise in other countries, where debit cards generally had been preferred over credit cards in the past. Among a select group of nations, Australia had the highest increase of 157 percent.

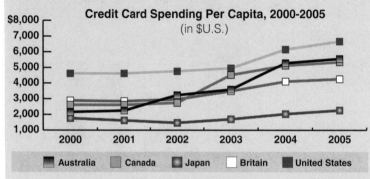

Credit Card Spending Per Capita, 2000-2005
(in $U.S.)

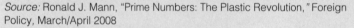

Source: Ronald J. Mann, "Prime Numbers: The Plastic Revolution," *Foreign Policy,* March/April 2008

immediate eviction notice or shutting off of the electricity," but in fact paying them late "is the precise behavior that can cause a family to become mired in debt over time," she said.[19]

Is credit card debt bad for the country?

Supporters of greater regulation argue that cards' very nature creates a risk of overindebtedness, but others argue that the advantages of credit generally outweigh the risk.

Even as credit card use expanded to lower-income consumers, Americans' financial stability has remained stable, said economists Orszag and Manning. Between 1995 and 2004, the proportion of households that could be considered in financial distress — those dedicating 40 percent or more of monthly income to paying off debts — remained "relatively stable," they said.[20]

George Mason's Zywicki says that total consumer debt has remained equal to about 4 percent of household wealth for 50 years.

Credit cards have helped give small businesses a level playing field with big business, something they didn't have in the days when installment credit was offered on a business-by-business basis, says Zywicki. "Sears, J.C.

Penney, Wal-Mart and companies like that are big enough to run an in-house credit operation, but for small companies that's not an option."

Although banks sell credit card debt in "securitized" form to investors in the same way as mortgage debt is sold, investments that consist of bundled credit card receivables — the payments consumers make on credit card accounts over time — don't pose the same threat to financial markets that mortgage-backed investments have, says Mann.

Credit card issuers "are totally not at fault" in the current meltdown in financial markets, says Columbia Law School's Mann.

That's mainly because "the credit card market is a lot simpler than the mortgage market" — with fewer intermediate players such as mortgage brokers — and both the banks that sell and investors that buy the securities better understand the risks, Kansas State University's Higgins says. While investors in mortgage-backed securities were buying very-long-term risky loans, the "average life of a credit card receivable is 60 to 90 days," Higgins says. As a result, new cards are continually added to an investment pool as debts are paid off, and this "replenishment gives it a little more stability," in part because banks can and do "replenish the pool with really good risks or at a discount" to improve the investment, he says.

Current levels of credit card borrowing pose other serious risks, however, many analysts say.

Simply having a credit card in your wallet makes it likely you will spend and borrow more, said Mann. Credit cards are unique contributors to the overindebtedness problem, he said. And "in a country in which the level of overall consumer borrowing remains constant, an increase of about $100 per capita in annual credit card debt is associated with an increase in bankruptcy filings two years later of about 200 per million people," Mann said.[21]

Data from the United States and four other countries show that credit card spending by itself is related to increased consumer debt, and because the data are international, they "strongly undermine the idea that problems that credit cards might cause are limited to their use by Americans, infected by the 'consumerist' values that so many decry here and abroad," said Mann.[22]

"Just a generation ago, the average family simply couldn't get into the kind of financial hole that has become so familiar today" because "a middle-class family couldn't borrow very much money," wrote Harvard Law School Professor Elizabeth Warren and her daughter, business consultant Amelia Warren Tyagi, in their book, *The Two Income Trap: Why Middle-Class Mothers and Fathers Are Going Broke.* Credit card practices such as "offers to 'consolidate' all . . . debt by moving it from one credit card to another" contribute to the growing indebtedness, they said.[23]

Credit cards have nearly become the nation's currency, and leaving such control in the unchecked hands of businesses is a mistake because "control of the currency is a mark of control over the country," says Georgetown's Levitin.

With credit cards used virtually everywhere — and merchants barred by credit card companies from passing their per-purchase fees along to individual credit card customers — all customers share in paying those fees, whether they use credit cards or not, Levitin says. This constitutes a "hidden tax" on cash buyers — who often have low incomes — forcing them to subsidize purchases by the usually higher-income card users, without any consumers being aware of the fact, Levitin says.

Meanwhile, although card issuers might not have caused the current financial crisis, some financial analysts think they could be caught up in it.

"I used to think that they'd be OK until we saw a rise in default rates" on cards, says Susan Menke, a financial-services analyst for Mintel International, a Chicago-based market-research firm. "But it's all based on confidence, and now I think it could happen sooner" if panic sets in. "We have a precedent from the mortgage markets showing that if there's any bad news at all, people will stop buying," she says. If banks can't find investors, they must stop offering credit.

Fees and Penalties on the Rise

The average credit card late fee more than doubled — from $13 to $28 — between 1995 and 2007, with some reaching as high as $39 per incident, according to a survey of 83 credit cards issued by 20 banks. And an increasing number of companies are imposing significantly higher "penalty" interest rates — which average 24.5 percent but can top 32.2 percent — on consumers who miss a payment or a deadline, even by a few hours. By 2007, 85 percent of credit card companies were imposing "penalty" rates on late-paying consumers — up from 79 percent of companies in 2005.

Source: "2007 Credit Card Survey," Consumer Action News, May 23, 2007, www.consumer-action.org/news/articles/2007_credit_card_survey/#Topic_02.

Individuals, businesses, financial institutions and the government all have too much debt, and credit card debt is part of the problem, warns Addison Wiggin, author of the 2008 book *I.O.U.S.A.: One Nation. Under Stress. In Debt.*

Decades ago, Americans checked their bank-account balances to see whether they could afford a wanted item, but today "we check our credit card limits," which measure not what we can afford but what the credit card issuer will offer us, Wiggin says. Often, credit cards are issued with limits that have no relation to what the cardholders can actually afford, based on their earnings, as with many of the cards carried by college students, for example, he says.

Carrying large credit card balances makes it "impossible for people to adjust when something bad happens," such as a health crisis, and "now we have a generation who doesn't even think about savings, who don't even know what savings is but look to the credit card limit" as their sole spending standard, says Wiggin.[24]

BACKGROUND

Nation of Debtors

Debt has been around as long as civilization, and American society, in particular, has been built on debt from the earliest days.[25]

"Why do you think people left Europe to come to the United States? . . . We like to describe it as, 'Oh, it was about religious freedom.' No . . . They were looking for

CHRONOLOGY

1940s-1960s *General purpose credit cards are introduced.*

1946 Flatbush National Bank in Brooklyn, N.Y., launches the first bank credit card.

1950 New York-based Diners Club becomes the first independent credit card company.

1958 American Express, Chase Manhattan Bank of New York and the Bank of America launch their first credit cards. Bank of America's AmeriCard will later become Visa.

1960 Sen. Paul Douglas, D-Ill., introduces the "truth-in-lending" act.

1968 Truth in Lending Act is enacted, requiring credit card issuers to disclose annual interest rates and other fees in standardized terms.

1970s-1980s *Credit card regulation is eased.*

1970 Congress bans the mailing of unsolicited credit cards as marketing.

1974 After women complain they can't get consumer credit, Congress prohibits card issuers from discriminating on the basis of sex or marital status.

1978 In *Marquette v. First of Omaha*, the Supreme Court allows credit card issuers to bypass state usury laws and charge nationally the highest interest rate allowed by their home states. Previously, 37 states capped interest rates, most at under 18 percent annually.

1980 Most major credit card issuers have moved their headquarters to Delaware and South Dakota, which don't cap interest rates.

1988 Congress requires all credit card promotional material to prominently display a standardized list of a card's terms, including annual fees, annual interest, late-payment and cash-advance fees in legible type.

1990s-2000s *Credit card use expands to most of the adult population.*

1991 Senate passes bill to cap credit card interest rates at 14 percent, but banks protest and the measure fails.

1993 Credit card companies send 1.52 billion offers to American households.

1996 In *Smiley vs. Citibank*, the Supreme Court ends state caps on credit card fees.

2000 On average, a credit card sale costs a retailer 72 cents, compared to 36 cents for a check transaction and 12 cents for a cash sale.

2001 Credit card issuers mail out over 5 billion new-card offers.

2002 Credit card late fees generate $7.3 billion in revenue for card issuers, up from $1.7 billion in 1996.

2003 U.S. Second Circuit Court of Appeals rules that MasterCard and Visa can't bar their member banks from issuing other cards.

2004 Credit card fees generate $24 billion in revenues for card issuers, up from $8.3 billion in 1995.

2005 "Rewards" cards make up 58 percent of new credit cards offered — up from 24 percent in 2001.

2006 As home-equity loans dry up, credit card debt begins to climb steeply. . . . Congress caps interest on consumer loans to members of the military at 36 percent.

2007 After Democrats become the majority in the House and Senate, bills are introduced to regulate credit card industry practices. . . . Federal Reserve Board solicits public comments on a plan to tighten credit card regulations.

2008 House approves the Credit Cardholders' Bill of Rights to prohibit practices like raising interest rates without notice or imposing late fees on customers who pay on the due date. . . . The House Judiciary Committee approves allowing small businesses to negotiate jointly for credit card transaction fees. . . . Congressional hearings highlight the risks of debit cards that draw on consumers' retirement accounts. . . . U.S. credit card debt reaches a record high of $1 trillion.

a way to escape their debts," Harvard Law School's Warren told PBS.[26]

Starting out as a farm economy meant that most Americans were in frequent debt, even after they arrived in the new land. Farmers needed cash to get crops started but earned no money until, and if, those crops came in, many months later. For local merchants, extending credit to farmers to buy spring seed and other agricultural necessities was a vital investment to keep their communities — and their own stores — going.

By the time American colonies were establishing their governments, Europe had long allowed money lending while attempting to ban usury — a term that originally meant taking money in return for a loan but came to mean taking excessive money in return for lending. In 1545, King Henry VIII of England legalized charging interest on loans of up to 10 percent. But by 1714 England's top legal interest rate had dropped to 5 percent.

Twelve of the original American colonies — New Hampshire was the exception — set their own maximum legal interest rates in the 18th century but made them just enough higher than 5 percent to entice British citizens to invest their money in colonists' enterprises.

Meanwhile, waves of new immigrants kept up the need for credit, including in the cities, where many 19th-century immigrants settled, says Zywicki of George Mason University "You'd see small lenders and pawnshops set up" to fund immigrants' new start and tide them over in months when their temporary or seasonal jobs weren't available, he says.

Debates over interest rates also began early. Farmers, in particular, wanted cheaper money, but American lenders — originally mostly merchants whose customers bought on the installment plan — chafed against interest caps. As early as 1834, some 200 Boston businessmen staged a protest to end rate ceilings.

Legal interest rates were lowered over time in many states, but another world of lending grew up outside the law, with high-interest pawnbrokers and loan sharks becoming a common source of credit by the late 1800s.

By then, the industrial era was producing not only new, more expensive consumer goods like washing machines but also workers who earned enough to consider buying beyond bare necessities.

The Singer Sewing Machine Co. is said to have extended credit to consumers as early as 1850. Before the home sewing machine arrived, it took about 14 hours to make a man's shirt by hand, and homemakers spent days each month making and mending families' clothes, often paying a dressmaker to help out. A machine could slice shirt-making time to about an hour and a quarter and also dispensed with the need to pay a dressmaker.[27]

By 1925, a dollar's worth of merchandise out of every seven sold in America was purchased on credit through installment-type plans, including 80 percent of phonographs and 85 percent of furniture.

In 1922, a skeptical Federal Trade Commission found that "the most frequent form of installment contract is the lease, in which a customer who defaults finds that he has been merely 'renting' and has nothing to show for his payments." The commission found that installment-plan prices averaged 16 percent higher than cash prices.[28]

But many economists credited consumer debt with lifting the country out of economic slumps. "Think of what the government...might have had to do if consumer credit and the related expansion in the automobile ...and...housing [industries] hadn't stepped into the breach" to lift the country out of a post-Korean War recession in 1953 by stimulating sales and perking up businesses and employment, said Geoffrey H. Moore, an economist at the National Bureau of Economic Research who pioneered the study of business cycles.[29]

Paper or Plastic?

The ancestors of today's ubiquitous plastic credit cards were credit tokens that late-19th-century merchants issued to customers with store charge accounts. The tokens sped up counter transactions since clerks could simply record a token number rather than laboriously looking up the customer's account.[30]

In the 1920s, somewhat more portable credit became available when oil companies and hotel chains issued cards allowing purchases at all their outlets. But true credit cards — that allow users to accumulate open-ended debt with a variety of merchants — became available only in the mid-20th century, after banks and financial companies began offering consumer credit.

In 1946, banker John Biggins of the Flatbush National Bank in Brooklyn, N.Y., invented the "Charge-It" card program — the first bank credit card — which allowed

Using Credit Cards Wisely Isn't Easy

"Reality hit me like a ton of bricks."

By the time Curtis E. Arnold finished graduate studies at the University of Texas at Dallas, his credit card debt had climbed to $45,000. The looming debt put him under "unbelievable" stress, says Arnold, the founder of Little Rock, Ark.-based CardRatings.com, a consumer-education site that compares credit cards.

Today, credit cards are a ubiquitous — and often welcome — feature of the daily lives of most Americans. But the very nature of credit cards can make them debt traps for low-income people and unwary consumers of all economic levels.

Over-optimism about one's own earning ability can be a trap, says Arnold. "I bought into some lies as an undergraduate, like that I was going to make six figures when I got out of college and that my debt was temporary," he recalls. "Every college in America has 'increasing your salary' as one of its talking points," but that pitch — while true in the long run — ignores the fact that new grads start out in entry-level positions.

Arnold started off in a $25,000-a-year spot as a local bank manager and was in no position to pay off that "temporary" debt quickly, he says. The "debt happened so gradually, like a snowball rolling downhill, and I thought — I'm going to a good school, and as long as I make those minimum payments, I'm fine." But minimum payments "spread out over a number of cards" quickly mounted up to over $100 a month, and Arnold's debt didn't get any smaller.

"Reality hit me like a ton of bricks," he says. 'This is not going to be temporary. You've deceived yourself."

Today, almost anyone can get a credit card, but analysts agree that, most likely, not everyone should, although getting along without one is tough in today's society.

"When you go to the video store, for God's sake, they want a credit card," said one low-income woman interviewed by Angela Littwin, an assistant professor at the University of Texas Law School.[1] Nevertheless, most women in Littwin's study were shocked that they could get cards. "I sent [the application] in, and they actually sent [a card] to me, and I was in shock. I was like, 'Who the hell would give me a credit card?' " one said.

Arnold says that some people with low incomes, such as students, should avoid cards completely if they can.

"Not everyone can handle a credit card," says Arnold. "I'm generally pro-credit but with a bunch of caveats," mainly because "study after study has shown people spend more on a credit card [than without one] and even more on a rewards card," he says. "If that reward card will cause you to get another airplane ticket, then don't use that card." Otherwise, "you're digging yourself into a deeper and deeper hole."

"I would say, don't get a credit card until you're a junior," says Edwin Lindo, a senior business major and student body president at the University of the Pacific in Stockton, Calif., who's currently digging out from under his own credit card debt.

local merchants to send sales slips for cardholders' purchases to the bank, which would bill the customers.[31]

In 1950, three New York City businessmen, Frank X. McNamara, Ralph Schneider and Casey R. Taylor, formed the first independent card company, Diners Club, which allowed high-end consumers to make charge-card purchases at a network of merchants that quickly spread nationwide.

In a business structure similar to today's credit cards, Diners Club charged merchants who accepted the card — mostly in the entertainment and travel industries — 7 percent of each transaction. Diners Club would pay the merchant, and the cardholder would repay the club. Merchants agreed to the fees because accepting the cards

brought them more, higher-spending customers. Diners Club originally issued charge — not credit — cards, on which users were required to pay their bills in full each month.[32]

Credit cards — allowing open-ended long-term borrowing — soon replaced most charge cards. In 1958, American Express launched its first credit card, and the Bank of America issued BankAmericard, now Visa, in California. By 1965, 1.25 million Californians — one in 14 — carried a BankAmericard, and the bank began developing a nationwide network of retailers.

By the late 1960s, card issuers began mailing unsolicited credit cards — not credit card applications — to

That's partly because temptations to spend are all around. "There's a perception that as college students, we hang on by threads, are minimalist, live on ramen [noodles], but that's just not realistic," Lindo says. Like other Americans, "we're surrounded by media" and advertising exerting constant — if largely unconscious — pressure to spend. And the nature of credit cards is such that "you don't realize what you're spending because you don't see the bill until later," and, even then, the bill won't clearly show the additional amounts you'll pay in interest, on top of the cost of your purchases, he says.

Worsening the peril is that, today, credit card bills and contracts inform users of some of the most dangerous provisions only in complex, legal language and small print.

A 2006 Government Accountability Office report found that cardholder contracts are written at a reading level that "50 percent of Americans can't understand," making it extremely difficult for many people to grasp the rules of the cards they hold, such as what the fees are and when those fees will be imposed, says Tim Westrich, a research associate at the Center for American Progress.

A few rules are very important to keep in mind, says Arnold. First, "be very aware of universal default" — the card industry's practice of sharply increasing your card's interest rate if you make a mistake on any bill, such as paying rent or phone bills late, bouncing a check or going over the credit limit on another card, he says. To avoid triggering high default rates — which can be as high as triple your previous interest — it's vital to pay all your bills on time, he says.

It's also crucial to be aware of your credit limit and keep your balance as far under it as possible to help your credit score — the number banks and other lenders use to determine your personal creditworthiness for loans and favorable interest rates, says Christopher Viale, president of the Cambridge Credit Counseling Corp. in Massachusetts. A full 30 percent of your credit score "is based on how close you are to your credit limit," says Viale.[2]

Don't use special cards like store and gas cards, even if you think they'd be good for travel, says Viale. "It's way too difficult to navigate their promotional discounts," he says.

Be especially cautious with medical expenses, as well, Viale says. In a medical emergency, it's natural to panic and charge hospital or doctor bills on a credit card, but that's a huge mistake, he says. "You can work the charges out with hospitals, and as long as you didn't put it on a credit card, you won't be charged interest, just some collection fees." But once a medical bill is on a credit card, paying interest is inevitable unless you can pay it off in the first billing cycle, he says.

If you decide to get a card, don't just take the first offer, look around to "find the card that's right for you," says Arnold. "If you pay off your balance" each month, get a card without an annual fee, and "look at how you can maximize rewards" on a card whose rewards match spending you'd do anyway. "If you have a balance to pay down, don't look for rewards, look for the best interest rate," he says.

---

[1] Angela Littwin, "Beyond Usury: A Study of Credit Card Use and Preference Among Low-Income Consumers," forthcoming, *Texas Law Review*, 2008, http://papers.ssrn.com/sol3/papers.cfm?abstract_id=968330.

[2] For background, see *Your Credit Scores*, Consumer Federation of America/Fair Isaac Corporation, www.pueblo.gsa.gov/cic_text/money/creditscores/your.htm.

consumers, in an attempt to convince retailers that enough people held the cards to make it worth their while to join the network. Congress banned the risky practice in 1970.[33]

Today's consumer-credit system is dominated by banks, but bank cards took a while to take off. Banks didn't profit at first because there were large start-up costs, and they found it hard to earn money from the many "convenience" card users who paid off their bills each month and thus paid no interest. Nevertheless, banks were afraid to remain outside the new system because it was widely viewed as the forerunner of an all-electronic, cashless society that many believed was just over the horizon.

Growing Profits

In their early years, credit card companies were constrained by state usury laws that strictly capped interest, which held down profits, especially during the inflationary 1970s, when the rates banks themselves paid to borrow money were rising. Some banks actually reported losing money on their Visa and MasterCharge — now MasterCard — programs.

Nevertheless, card use kept growing. Then in 1978 the game changed in card issuers' favor, after state usury laws capping credit card interest rates were essentially removed by the U.S. Supreme Court's decision in *Marquette National Bank v. First of Omaha Corp.* The case began in 1971, when Iowa resident Fred Fisher filed a complaint

All Plastic Is Not Created Equal

Some economists question 401(k) debit cards.

Credit cards aren't the only cards out there. Far from it. Paying with plastic is an ever-growing phenomenon worldwide, and cashless payment takes a variety of forms. While credit cards are most common in the United States, Europeans, for example, typically use debit cards — which allow users to tap a bank balance without carrying around cash.[1]

Here are some alternative forms of plastic payment beyond the credit card:

- **Charge Cards.** The oldest form of payment card, charge cards have been around since the early 20th century, mostly offered by merchants rather than banks. Like credit cards, they're essentially a loan from a business to a consumer. Merchants may issue charge cards for purchases in their own stores.

  Unlike credit cards, charge cards offer only a very short-term loan, usually of about a month, and must be paid in full at the end of that period. Card users don't have to pay interest on the brief loan — sometimes called a "float" — but failing to pay off the balance at the end of the month usually brings a large late fee and possible cancellation of the card.

  Today, many high-end retailers offer charge cards to customers, even in the United States, and around the world banks, major credit card companies like Visa and other businesses all offer charge cards.

- **Prepaid Cards.** A fast-growing phenomenon, prepaid cards are most familiar in the form of phone cards that allow users to deposit money with the phone company, then make calls until that amount has been exhausted.[2] Today, however, many retailers and even banks issue prepaid cards. Unlike retailers' cards, prepaid bank cards can be used anywhere a credit card is used.

  For banks and merchants, prepaid cards are a boon, since they never need to worry that the bills will not be paid.

  Prepaid cards allow consumers with bad credit to participate in some credit card-only transactions, such as reserving rental cars and hotel rooms, and prepaid card holders will never find themselves paying high interest on an impulse purchase. However, prepaid cards can't be used for monthly withdrawal-type bills like Internet subscriptions or phone bills, since the businesses have no guarantee you'll have enough cash in your account when the bill comes due. In addition, consumers pay a fee to open an account for a card and an additional fee each time they deposit more cash.

- **Debit Cards.** Although credit cards are fast making inroads overseas, debit cards have long been the most popular form of plastic overseas.[3]

  Banks issue debit cards to people with checking accounts, who can use them in two ways. By signing your name or in some cases entering a PIN — personal identification number — into a card-swiping machine, you can use the card to pay for retail purchases. You can also use a debit card to make purchases over the phone or the Internet, without using

after the First National Bank of Omaha, Neb., sent him an unsolicited credit card carrying an interest rate that was legal in Nebraska but too high under Iowa's usury law.

Fisher's case ended up in the Supreme Court, which ruled unanimously in 1978 that, while "exportation" of interest rates "may impair the ability of states to maintain effective usury laws," the National Bank Act of 1864 clearly intended nationally chartered banks to be regulated only by the federal comptroller of the currency and the bank's home state. "Any correction of that situation would have to be achieved legislatively" by Congress, wrote Justice William Brennan in the decision.[34]

Quickly, banks went in search of states with no interest caps that would invite the banks to operate there, since federal rules stated that a bank couldn't relocate outside of its original home state unless the new state's either your PIN or your signature, just as with a credit card. The PIN also allows you to use the card to withdraw cash at an ATM or request "cash back" when you make a store purchase.

Retailers generally prefer the PIN payment method, which debits the customer's bank account immediately. Banks, however, encourage customers to sign a sales slip, often offering mileage points or other awards for doing so. Signature payments take a day or two to clear, and merchants must pay a higher fee for processing signature payments than PIN payments.

As with credit cards, some retailers to whom you present your debit card — such as hotels — may ask the bank to authorize a bigger payment than the current bill, in case the card holder ends up running a bigger charge by staying a second night or making heavy use of a minibar. It's vital to realize that the amount the merchant requests to be held in your account will decrease the account balance you have available for additional purchases, until your bill is finalized.

Debit cards have other pitfalls. If another person makes unauthorized use of your credit card, you're liable for only $50 of the unauthorized charges. But if your debit card or PIN is stolen, you can be liable for $500 or more in losses if you don't report the problem within two business days of discovering it.

Debit cards also make it fatally easy to run up overdraft charges on checking accounts. Before 2003, banks routinely turned down debit card purchases or ATM withdrawals that exceeded the balance in the customer's account. Since then, however, many banks have begun paying out the money without alerting the cardholder that he's passed the limit and

socking the customer with high overdraft fees as a result.

- **401(k) Debit Cards.** This controversial new form of debit card allows users to take out money from their employer-sponsored 401(k) retirement accounts, instead of from a checking account.[4]

Card users withdraw money from a 401(k) account up to an amount approved by their employer, and that money is deposited into another account, which can then be tapped for purchases with the debit card. The catch is that the withdrawals constitute a loan from the 401(k) account, which, by law, must be paid back with interest. A consumer will also pay fees to set up and maintain the new account and to make cash withdrawals.

Companies that offer the retirement-account debit cards tout their convenience, but some economists say the price of convenience is far too high if it means depleting retirement accounts. Legislation has been introduced in Congress to ban debit cards that tap retirement accounts.

---

[1] For background, see Arnold Rosenberg, *Better Than Cash? Consumer Protection and the Global Debit Card Deluge*, Thomas Jefferson School of Law Research Paper Series, 2005, http://papers.ssrn.com/sol3/papers.cfm?abstract_id=740528.

[2] For background, see Julia S. Cheney and Sherrie L. W. Rhine, *Prepaid Cards: An Important Innovation in Financial Services*, Federal Reserve Bank of Philadelphia, July 2006, www.consumerinterests.org/files/public/Rhine_PrepaidCardsAnImportantInnovationinFinancial Services.pdf.

[3] For background, see "The Dark Secrets of Debit," ConsumerReports.org, 2007, www.consumerreports.org.

[4] For background, see "401(k) Debit Cards: Think Before You Swipe," Financial Industry Regulatory Authority Web site, www.finra.org/Investors/ProtectYourself/InvestorAlerts/RetirementAccounts/P038556.

---

legislature invited it to enter. South Dakota, seeking to stimulate its economy, was the first state to eliminate its usury laws and extend a legislative invitation — to then-New-York-based Citibank, which had tried but failed to persuade New York to dump its usury law. By 1980, Citibank had moved its credit card processing facility to Sioux Falls, which picked up 3,000 white-collar jobs in the deal.

Delaware quickly followed suit, and the two states soon became home to most of the nation's largest banks, now free to charge credit card interest at any levels they chose.

Ironically, "a lot of the deregulation" of credit cards "has been done in what I would call accidental policy decisions," not through deliberate actions by policymakers, says Lawless of the University of Illinois. In the *Marquette* decision, for example, "the court was interpreting

Financial Illiteracy Is Widespread

Women, minorities and the elderly have the lowest levels of financial literacy, according to a 2007 study. Those with lower levels of debt literacy tend to incur more fees and have difficulty paying off debt.

Among those surveyed:

- Only 36 percent could correctly perform an interest-rate calculation.
- Only 35 percent understood that making minimum payments equivalent to the interest payment on outstanding credit card debt will never eliminate the debt.
- Only 7 percent responded correctly to a question requiring an understanding of the notion that the longer it takes to pay off an interest-bearing loan, the more the loan costs.

Groups with the lowest levels of financial literacy included:

- The elderly (those older than 65) — who displayed the least knowledge about interest compounding; more than 30 percent could not answer a question about credit card debt.
- Women — whose correct-response rate was often 20 percentage points lower than that of men.
- Minorities — particularly African-Americans and Hispanics.
- Those who are divorced/widowed/separated.
- Those with low income and fewer financial assets.

Source: Annamaria Lusardi and Peter Tufano, "Debt Literacy, Financial Experience, and Overindebtedness," draft paper, May 9, 2008, www.rand.org/labor/aging/rsi/rsi_ papers/2008/lusardi3.pdf.

a Civil War-era" statute, not actually ruling on the merits of arguments related to credit cards, he says.

A 1996 Supreme Court case completed the deregulation of credit card charges.

A California woman, Barbara Smiley, had brought a class-action lawsuit against Citibank, charging that its late-payment fees violated California consumer laws. This time a unanimous Supreme Court accepted Citibank's argument that the fees could be considered "interest" and thus, as in the *Marquette* ruling, regulated by the bank's home state, not the consumer's.[35]

The ability to raise fees has significantly lowered interest rates for most card users, said economists Orszag and Manning in their report for the American Bankers Association (ABA). Before 1990 most cards charged fixed interest rates of around 20 percent to all consumers, but by 2005 "80 percent of cardholders paid interest rates lower than 20 percent."[36]

In 2005, Congress took direct action to assist credit card companies. After several years of debate, it passed new bankruptcy legislation recommended by the card industry to close loopholes that card companies said allowed well-off, opportunistic consumers to run up big bills, then walk away from the unpaid debts.[37]

The bill, which Congress debated for several years before approving, has helped the companies, says White of the University of California. "The harder it is to file for bankruptcy, the better it is for the companies, who have more months to call you, garnish your wages" and take other actions to get their money, she says.

But White argues that it is low-income debtors who are most constrained by the new law, not the wealthy debtors that card issuers accused of waltzing away from bills. "The basic change the bill made — though this was not stated, but concealed — was to make it a lot more expensive to file for bankruptcy," and the legislation "just about doubled the cost of filing," she says. The legislation "put in lots of new rules for bankruptcy lawyers, adding requirements that you have a financial management course," and similar provisions, which is a "much bigger burden for people who are poor."

New Regulations

Efforts to tighten regulation of credit cards have been relatively few, but the 1960s and '70s saw congressional requirements for credit card issuers to disclose the financial terms of their contracts, standardize how interest is calculated and protect cardholders against large losses when cards are used fraudulently.

In 1960, Sen. Paul Douglas, D-Ill., an economist, introduced a "truth in lending" bill to require merchants and lenders to disclose the cost of the consumer credit they offered, such as by disclosing annual interest rates. Many members of Congress and President John F. Kennedy endorsed the bill as good consumer protection.[38]

However, small loan companies, car dealers and furniture stores who offered credit fiercely opposed the measure, which they believed would push interest rates down by forcing lenders to compete on cost. Eventually, the ABA and the U.S. Chamber of Commerce also joined the opposition.

After years of struggle, the Truth in Lending Act — requiring standardized disclosure of interest rates and other charges — was finally enacted in 1968; it remains the federal law that governs credit cards.

Over the years, Congress added some protections, including in 1970 limiting cardholders' maximum liability for unauthorized use to $50, and in 1974 banning issuers from discriminating on the basis of sex or marital status, when divorced and single women complained they couldn't get credit.

In 1988, Sen. Charles Schumer, D-N.Y., sponsored a successful amendment requiring that basic costs such as annual fees, annual interest rate and late-payment and cash-advance fees be listed in legible type and standard terms on all promotional material.

In 1991, senators failed in an attempt to cap credit card interest nationally. In a bid to increase consumer spending and stave off recession, senators voted 74 to 19 to cap rates at 14 percent, but after banks protested loudly and the George H. W. Bush administration threatened a veto, the provision was abandoned.[39]

In recent years, merchants and consumer groups have filed numerous class-action lawsuits against credit card practices they call abusive and anticompetitive, and card issuers have lost several decisions.

In a 2003 federal district court settlement, for example, Visa and MasterCard agreed to pay merchants $3 billion, lower some per-transaction fees paid by retailers and exempt debit cards from the Visa/MasterCard policy of requiring merchants who accepted any Visa or MasterCard to accept all kinds of cards that carry those logos. Merchants had argued that because debit cards have high transaction fees yet don't offer merchants the ability to extend consumers credit, the accept-all-cards rule was unfair.[40]

In a 2007 settlement, Visa, MasterCard and Diners Club agreed to pay millions of consumers at least $25

each for currency-conversion fees the companies had imposed without notice for a decade on all overseas credit card transactions.[41]

CURRENT SITUATION
Bill of Rights

Soon after Democrats took control of both houses of Congress in January 2007, they introduced several proposals to crack down on credit card industry practices that have been a thorn in the side of some consumers and retailers and convened a series of hearings. (*See "At Issue," p. 136.*)

The House passed the Credit Cardholders' Bill of Rights (HR 5244) by a 312-112 vote on Sept. 23, and similar legislation has been introduced in the Senate. However, definitive action on new credit card rules will have to wait until at least 2009. Congress has been focused on other pressing matters, including the worsening financial crisis, and lawmakers want to adjourn this month to campaign for reelection.

Congressional hearings and legislative proposals this year are mainly a warm-up for definitive action that Democrats hope to take in January, if Sen. Barack Obama, D-Ill., wins the November election, says Columbia Law School's Mann. Consumer advocates and many Democrats "were really angry about the bankruptcy bill," and are eager to "get back against the credit card companies," who they believe rammed through unneeded bankruptcy-law changes that have harmed low-income people while not imposing any restraints on their industry, Mann says.

Among other provisions, the Bill of Rights legislation would:

- Ban universal cross-default — imposing high penalty interest rates on trustworthy cardholders who are believed to have defaulted on a bill to some other creditor;
- Require 45 days' notice before an interest-rate hike;
- Ban late fees for customers whose payments arrive before 5 p.m., Eastern time, on the due date; currently, some card issuers consider payments late if they arrive after noon or even 9 a.m. on the due date;

Should Congress ban specific credit card industry practices?

YES
Rep. Carolyn B. Maloney, D-N.Y.
Chairman, House Financial Services Subcommittee on Financial Institutions and Consumer Credit

From testimony before House Financial Services Committee, July 31, 2008

This is the first time Congress has ever considered credit card reform, and it is high time. Americans are falling further and further into credit card debt — almost a trillion dollars and rising exponentially.

I believe in personal responsibility, but unfair and deceptive credit card practices have made it literally impossible for consumers to borrow only what they can repay. . . .

After I introduced the Credit Cardholders' Bill of Rights, the Federal Reserve, the Office of Thrift Supervision, and the National Credit Union Administration proposed rules to eliminate the same credit card practices that my bill addresses. The rules strengthen the case for this bill — they declare that the practices the bill seeks to eliminate are unfair and deceptive. . . .

As Federal Reserve Chairman Ben Bernanke said about credit cards to this committee, "The market will actually work better and produce more credit in situations where there is not so much distrust and confusion about what it is exactly that is in the contract."

Some members of Congress are considering a substitute that would replace this bill with a sense of Congress supporting the proposed Fed rule. But many issuers oppose the rule on the grounds that enacting these reforms as a rule rather than a law could create serious retroactive liability problems for the credit industry, creating uncertainty in the markets. This bill does not raise that issue.

Without legislation, lucrative, abusive practices will continue, and issuers who give them up will lose profits. We need legislation to level the playing field for consumers and issuers, so that the normal forces of the free market can work again.

This bill targets specific abusive practices:

- Retroactive rate increases that trap cardholders with unexpected debt;
- Double-cycle billing that charges interest on balances already paid;
- Payment allocation that prevents cardholders from paying down high-rate balances;
- Due-date gimmicks that trick people into paying late and getting hit with retroactive rate increases, penalty interest rates, late fees and a finance charge;
- Multiple over-limit fees for one over-limit charge;
- Subprime cards whose annual fees alone eat up most of the credit line before a single charge is made.

Another provision bars credit cards to minors.

NO
Oliver L. Ireland
Partner, Morrison & Foerster LLP

From testimony before House Financial Services Subcommittee on Financial Institutions and Consumer Credit, March 13, 2008

As a result of the convenience, efficiency, security and access to credit that credit cards provide, credit cards have become a driving force behind the consumer spending upon which our national economy is largely based.

Despite the benefits, in recent years credit card practices have been criticized as unfair to consumers in large part because these practices are inconsistent with consumers' expectations. These criticisms call into question whether the current credit card disclosure regime has kept up with the market. It has not.

Recognizing this, in June 2007 the Federal Reserve Board proposed a comprehensive revision to the credit card provisions of its Regulation Z, which implements the Truth in Lending Act. It is premature to address credit card practices in legislation until these regulatory initiatives are completed. The risks of unintended consequences are significant.

The Credit Cardholders' Bill of Rights (H.R. 5244) would significantly curtail the ability of credit card issuers to accurately price for risk on existing accounts, substantially reducing their ability to modify pricing to reflect changes in the creditworthiness of borrowers and changing market conditions.

Current credit card pricing is based on individual risk factors, allowing a card issuer to provide cards with lower rates to lower-risk cardholders while still providing cards at higher rates to higher-risk consumers who otherwise might be unable to obtain credit. Under H.R. 5244, the current pricing model is likely to be restructured to one in which cardholders with good credit histories would subsidize higher-risk cardholders. It is also likely to lead to a tightening of credit availability for lower-income cardholders, or for those in acute financial stress, since many issuers may simply avoid offering credit to this segment of the market rather than increasing costs to others.

The bill would prohibit increases in interest rates that are based on negative information that is not directly related to account performance. This would encourage card issuers to charge higher rates initially in order to take into account the potential deterioration in cardholder creditworthiness.

H.R. 5244 would prohibit the application of interest to credit card balances that have been paid within the so-called "grace period," if the credit card issuer provides such a grace period — a practice that the bill refers to as "double-cycle billing." This provision would discourage credit card issuers from providing grace periods for anyone, i.e., eliminate the interest-free loan aspect of credit cards even for those that pay on time and in full.

- Require mailing of statements at least 25 days before the due date;
- When interest rates are raised, allow consumers to cancel the card and pay off the balance at the current rate; and
- Require card issuers to report their profits, fees and interest rates to Congress annually.

Banking-industry supporters say banks would make consumer credit much harder to get if the rules were enacted.

"While well-intentioned," the legislation "will increase the cost of credit for consumers and small businesses . . . , result in less access to credit . . . and may further roil the securities markets — all at a time when our economy can least afford it," said Edward Yingling, president and CEO of the ABA.[42]

"Passing legislation like this will discourage lending," said Rep. Pete Sessions, R-Texas. "It's not wise policy to create a consumer credit crunch at the same time that our economy is experiencing a commercial credit crunch."[43]

But some industry analysts castigate the financial industry for opposing regulation at the same time they are looking for a taxpayer bailout.

"While banks say they would be tanking without taxpayer money, here comes a bill that would help taxpayers, and the banks say it isn't right. I'm amazed that there's not more humility at a time like this," said Bill Hardekopf, chief executive officer of LowCards.com, which tracks credit card rates.[44]

In May 2007, the Federal Reserve Board, which oversees U.S. banks, proposed revisions to its credit card rules similar to provisions in HR 5244. With the revised "Regulation Z" expected by year's end, the White House argues that legislation is inappropriate at this time. "Regulations are better suited to addressing these problems than legislation because they can be adapted more readily to changes in market conditions," said a Sept. 22 Bush administration statement.[45]

But the bill's sponsor, House Financial Services Subcommittee on Financial Institutions and Consumer Credit Chair Rep. Carolyn B. Maloney, D-N.Y., countered that rules are easier to evade than laws.

"Without legislation, regulation can be stopped or scaled back and lucrative abusive practices can continue," she said.[46]

Other Measures

Congress also is mulling other credit card rules.

In July, on a 19-16 vote, the House Judiciary Committee approved legislation (HR 5546) to allow business owners to negotiate jointly with credit card issuers to set merchants' fees, something that they're barred from doing under antitrust law.

Committee Chairman Conyers says fees are currently too high, but small business owners can't refuse them because they need to accept Visa and MasterCard payments or lose customers. Large businesses have the clout to demand more favorable terms, but small businesses don't, he said.[47]

The banking industry calls the bill an unacceptable form of price controls. "There is no evidence that demonstrates that such price controls will result in savings passed along to consumers," said MasterCard in a statement.[48]

In 2007, Sen. Ron Wyden, D-Ore., introduced the Credit Card Safety Star Act, which would authorize the Federal Reserve to award each credit card a rating of between one and five stars, with five-star cards judged safest for consumers.[49] Cards with straightforward terms that informed consumers in clear language about rules, fees and interest rates would get the highest ratings, and the ratings would be prominently displayed on cards and marketing material.

Government safety ratings for financial products like credit cards make sense, says Harvard's Warren. "In the U.S. today it is not possible to buy a toaster that has a one-in-five chance of bursting into flames and burning down a customer's home" or to see the "price on a washer and dryer" change after they're purchased, wrote Warren. "But it is possible to triple the price of the credit used to finance the appliances long after the papers have been signed," or unwittingly sign up for other equally dangerous financial products because they lack the regulatory safeguards Congress has enacted for consumer products, she said.[50]

"Why not create a Financial Product Safety Commission," modeled on the Consumer Product Safety Commission, to review products and establish safety guidelines? Warren proposes.[51]

But banking industry analysts say that financial education to make Americans financially savvy enough to

AP Photo/Ed Betz

Bridget Glover sorts out her bills at home in Wheatley Heights, N.Y. With money tight, the mother of two found her credit card bills exploding, and she considered bankruptcy. Instead, a nonprofit credit counseling agency helped Glover work out a debt repayment program.

shun bad credit deals and other risky financial behavior is the best answer. "Advancement in society occurs through the gaining of knowledge," says Chicago financial-service attorney Langer. "Congress could decide that as a result of the current financial crisis, financial education is so important that we should pay for it."

OUTLOOK
Plastic Future

There's little evidence that credit cards will be used any less in the future, and even today credit card use is rapidly expanding around the globe. But some economists warn that consumer credit will be highly risky any time

workers' earnings don't give them a solid chance to improve the average family's standard of life.

Already, students "live in something pretty close to a cashless society," says George Mason University's Zywicki. "The younger generation doesn't have checks, doesn't use cash, relies entirely on a credit card or debit card," he says.

Card technology will soon link up with other high-tech wizardry to revolutionize the commercial world, says business consultant Evans. For example, in the next decade, a marriage of global-positioning-satellite technology, electronic payment systems and mobile phones will allow merchants to locate potential customers on the street, then send targeted advertising right to their mobile phones, such as an electronic coupon for 50 cents off a frappucino at the coffee bar you're passing, Evans says. "That's a benefit to you and to Starbuck's," he says.

Today, the world's economies tremble in a global credit crisis. Too much debt on too many levels has left some individuals, businesses and financial institutions financially shaky and unable to absorb new shocks. And the shakiness of some has led to distrust by many, with banks reluctant to lend money in the form of mortgages, business loans or consumer credit.

The freeze is beginning to affect credit card users and will continue to do so, says Weller of the Center for American Progress.

"Credit card companies are becoming much more cautious about lending, and consumers are becoming much more cautious about borrowing," he says. And both these trends "will put another damper on consumer spending," which has been a major driver of economic prosperity, Weller says.

The freeze in credit cards will have its largest effect on the parts of the economy that depend on credit purchases by families with incomes just below median income, says Weller. "The Wal-Marts of this world will be the ones suffering."

The only solution to the problem long term is for individual workers at all economic levels to be in a strong enough financial position to spend, says Steven Fazzari, a professor of economics at Washington University in St. Louis. "Sustainability of demand growth will require income growth," but average incomes have been stagnating, he says.

To create an economy that has long-term strength and where consumer credit is viable will require attention to some neglected issues, including stemming health-care cost inflation, extending health-care coverage universally, "leveling the playing field for workers to join unions" and exercising fiscal responsibility in government, says Weller. Without those steps, credit card regulation, no matter how good, won't ward off future consumer-debt problems because the average citizen's financial position will be too weak, he says.

NOTES

1. Jonathan M. Orszag and Susan H. Manning, "An Economic Assessment of Regulation Credit Card Fees and Interest Rates," paper commissioned by the American Bankers Association, October 2007, www.aba.com/aba/documents/press/regulating_credit-card_fees_interest_rates92507.pdf. Orszag and Manning are economic consultants at Cambridge, Mass.-based Competition Policy Associates.

2. "Credit Card Debt: Where Does Your State Rank?" Credit Card Action Center Web site, Americans for Fairness in Lending, July 29, 2008, www.affil.org.

3. *The Arbitration Trap: How Credit Card Companies Ensnare Consumers*, Public Citizen, September 2007, p. 2, www.citizen.org/documents/ArbitrationTrap.pdf.

4. For background, see Karen Jowers, "With Interest-Rate Cap in Place, Focus Turns to Enforcement," *Army Times*, Oct. 4, 2007, www.armytimes.com/news/2007/10/military_paydayloans_071001w/.

5. Todd J. Zywicki, testimony before House Financial Services Subcommittee on Financial Institutions and Consumer Credit, April 26, 2007, http://mason.gmu.edu/~tzywick2/Credit%20Card%20Testimony.doc.

6. Orszag and Manning, *op. cit.*

7. *Ibid.*

8. Adam Levitin, "The Credit Cardholders' Bill of Rights," Credit Slips blog, Feb. 25, 2008, www.credititslips.org/creditslips/2008/02/the-credit card.html.

9. Curtis E. Arnold, *How You Can Profit from Credit Cards: Using Credit to Improve Your Financial Life and Bottom Line* (2008), p. 18.

10. Orszag and Manning, *op. cit.*, p. 13.

11. Creola Johnson, "Maxed Out College Students: A Call to Limit Credit Card Solicitations on College Campuses," No. 77, *Public Law and Legal Theory Working Paper Series*, Ohio State University Center for Interdisciplinary Law and Policy Studies, August 2006.

12. *Ibid.*

13. *Ibid.*

14. Testimony before House Financial Services Subcommittee on Financial Institutions and Consumer Credit, June 26, 2008.

15. Quoted in Robert D. Manning, *Credit Card Nation* (2001), p. 175.

16. Quoted in *ibid.*

17. Angela Littwin, "Beyond Usury: A Study of Credit Card Use and Preference Among Low-Income Consumers," forthcoming, *Texas Law Review*, 2008, http://papers.ssrn.com/sol3/papers.cfm?abstract_id=968330.

18. *Ibid.*

19. *Ibid.*

20. Orszag and Manning, *op. cit.*, p. 16.

21. Ronald J. Mann, "Optimizing Consumer Credit Markets and Bankruptcy Policy," *Law and Economics Working Paper No. 059*, University of Texas School of Law, September 2006, www.utexas.edu.

22. Ronald J. Mann, "Credit Cards, Consumer Credit & Bankruptcy," The University of Texas School of Law and Economics Research Paper No. 44, March 2006, http://papers.ssrn.com/sol3/papers.cfm?abstract_id=690701.

23. Elizabeth Warren and Amelia Warren Tyagi, *The Two-Income Trap: Why Middle-Class Mothers and Fathers Are Going Broke* (2003), p. 127.

24. For background see Mary H. Cooper, "Retirement Security," *CQ Researcher*, May 31, 2002, pp. 481-504.

25. For background, see the following in *Editorial Research Reports*, which are available in CQ Researcher Plus Archive: "Installment Buying in the United States," April 6, 1926, Vol. II; C.E. Noyes, "Restriction of Consumer Credit," Aug. 9, 1941,

Vol. II; D. Boorstin, "Consumer Credit Economy," April 11, 1975, 1975 Vol. I; and Barbara Mantel, "Consumer Debt," *CQ Researcher*, March 2, 2007, pp. 193-216.

26. "Interview: Elizabeth Warren," in "Secret History of the Credit Card," "Frontline," www.pbs.org/wgbh/pages/frontline/shows/credit/interviews/warren.html.

27. "History of the Sewing Machine," Museum of American Heritage Web site, www.moah.org/exhibits/virtual/sewing.html.

28. Quoted in "Installment Buying in the United States," *op. cit.*

29. Quoted in M. Packman, "Consumer Credit," *Editorial Research Reports*, Feb. 10, 1956, available in *CQ Researcher Plus Archive*, www.library.cqpress.com.

30. "History of Credit Cards," "The History of Credit & Debt," Myvesta Foundation, http://myvesta.org.

31. Mary Bellis, "Who Invented Credit Cards?" Inventors, About.com Web site, http://inventors.about.com/od/cstartinventions/a/credit_cards.htm.

32. "History of Credit Cards," *op. cit.*

33. D. Boorstin, *op. cit.*

34. *Marquette National Bank v. First of Omaha Corp.*, 439 U.S. 299 (1978).

35. *Smiley v. Citibank* (South Dakota), 517 U.S. 735 (1996).

36. Orszag and Manning, *op. cit.*

37. For background, see M. H. Cooper, "Bankruptcy's Thriving Business," *Editorial Research Reports*, Nov. 18, 1983, in *CQ Researcher Plus Archive.*

38. Julius Duscha, "Your Friendly Finance Companies and Its Friends on Capitol Hill," *Harper's*, October 1962, pp. 75-78.

39. Robin Stein, "The Ascendancy of the Credit Card Industry," in "Secret History of the Credit Card," *op. cit.*

40. "Visa, MasterCard to Pay $3 Billion in Credit Card Suit," consumeraffairs.com Web site, May 1, 2003, www.consumeraffairs.com/news03/debit_suit.html.

41. "In re Currency Conversion Fee Antitrust Litigation (MDL 1409)," Currency Conversion Fee Antitrust Litigation Web site, www.ccfsettlement.com.

42. Quoted in Connie Prater, "House Passes Credit Cardholders' Bill of Rights Bill," CreditCards.com Web site, Sept. 23, 2008.

43. Quoted in *ibid.*

44. Quoted in David Lazarus, "Banks Love Bailout, Hate Credit Card Curbs," *Los Angeles Times*, Sept. 28, 2003.

45. Quoted in Prater, *op. cit.*

46. Quoted in *ibid.*

47. Joanna Anderson and Adrianne Kroepsch, "House Committee Approves Bill Intended to Open Credit Negotiations," *CQ Today*, July 16, 2008, www.cq.com.

48. Quoted in Adrianne Kroepsch, "Bill Would Open Negotiations on Credit Fees," *CQ Today*, July 15, 2008.

49. For background, see Tim Westrich, "Credit Card Crash Test," *The Washington Post*, March 13, 2008.

50. Elizabeth Warren, "Make Credit Safer: The Financial Product Safety Commission," The Tobin Project, May 6, 2007, www.tobinproject.org.

51. *Ibid.*

BIBLIOGRAPHY

Books

Arnold, Curtis E., *How You Can Profit From Credit Cards: Using Credit to Improve Your Financial Life and Bottom Line, FT Press,* **2008.**
The founder of a Web site (www.cardratings.com) that compares credit card terms explains who should and shouldn't use credit cards and how to avoid consumer-credit mistakes.

Evans, David S., and Richard Schmalensee, *Paying With Plastic: The Digital Revolution in Buying and Borrowing, The MIT Press,* **2005.**
An economist (Evans) and a professor of management and economics at the Massachusetts Institute of Technology trace the growth of the credit- and debit-card industries.

Mann, Ronald J., *Charging Ahead: The Growth and Regulation of Payment Card Markets Around the World, Cambridge University Press,* **2007.**

A law professor from Columbia University explains how credit cards have affected the U.S. and other economies.

Articles

"Customers' Fixation on Minimum Payments Drives Up Credit Card Bills," *Science Daily Web site*, Oct. 6, 2008, www.sciencedaily.com/releases/2008/10/081006130542.htm.
A British researcher finds that credit cards that list a minimum monthly payment cause borrowers to pay less on their bill each month than they would if no minimum payment were listed.

Morgenson, Gretchen, "Given a Shovel, Americans Dig Deeper Into Debt," *The New York Times*, July 20, 2008.
Health crises, overspending, risky mortgages and complex credit card terms combine to thrust more Americans deep in debt.

Weiss, Gary, "Don't Get Clobbered by Credit Cards!" *Parade*, Aug. 10, 2008, p. 4.
A veteran business reporter describes credit card industry practices he says are plunging more Americans into severe personal-debt crises.

Reports and Studies

"The Arbitration Trap: How Credit Card Companies Snare Consumers," *Public Citizen*, September 2007, www.citizen.org/documents/ArbitrationTrap.pdf.
A consumer-advocacy group argues that cardholders lose out when credit card disputes are referred to arbitration.

"Credit Cards: Increased Complexity in Rates and Fees Heightens Need for More Effective Disclosures to Consumers," *Government Accountability Office*, September 2006, www.gao.gov/new.items/d06929.pdf.
Congress' nonpartisan auditing office finds that credit card terms have become much more complicated over the years.

Draut, Tamara, and Heather C. McGhee, "Retiring in the Red: The Growth of Debt Among Older Americans," *Demos*, February 2004, www.demos-usa.org/pubs/Retiring_In_The_Red_WEB.pdf.
Analysts for a centrist-left think tank find that credit card debt has been rising among elderly Americans.

Draut, Tamara, and Javier Silva, "Generation Broke: The Growth of Debt Among Young Americans," October 2004, www.demos.org/pubs/Generation_Broke.pdf.
Analysts find that credit card debt and the proportion of income devoted to interest payments have been rising steadily among younger Americans.

Fellowes, Matt, and Mia Mabanta, "Borrowing to Get Ahead, and Behind: The Credit Boom and Bust in Lower-Income Markets," *The Brookings Institution*, May 2007, www.brookings.edu/papers/2007/0511metropolitanpolicy_fellowes.aspx.
Analysts for a centrist think tank finds that more low-income households are in debt than two decades ago.

Levitin, Adam J., "A Critique of the American Bankers Association's Study of Credit Card Regulation," *Georgetown University Law Center Public Law and Legal Theory Working Paper No. 11044327*, Aug. 18, 2008, http://papers.ssrn.com/sol3/papers.cfm?abstract_id=1029191.
A Georgetown University associate professor of law argues that credit cards aren't generally priced based on cardholders' riskiness as borrowers, as the banking industry claims.

Orszag, Jonathan M., and Susan H. Manning, "An Economic Assessment of Regulating Credit Card Fees and Interest Rates," *Compass/American Bankers Association*, October 2007, www.aba.com/aba/documents/press/regulating_creditcard_fees_interest_rates92507.pdf.
In a study commissioned by the banking industry, economic analysts argue that freedom from excessive regulation has allowed the credit card industry to develop consumer-loan products that benefit people across the economic spectrum.

Westrich, Tim, and Christian E. Weller, "House of Cards: Consumers Turn to Credit Cards Amid the Mortgage Crisis, Delaying Inevitable Defaults," *Center for American Progress*, February 2008, www.americanprogress.org/issues/2008/02/pdf/house_of_cards.pdf.
Analysts for a liberal think tank say the home-foreclosure crisis and the dwindling of home-equity loans are leading to potentially dangerous increases in credit card debt.

For More Information

American Bankers Association, 1120 Connecticut Ave., N.W., Washington, DC 20036; (800) 226-5377; www.aba .com. Provides information and advocacy on government policy related to banks, including credit card policy.

Card Hub, www.cardhub.com. Allows users to search for credit cards matching personal criteria, including credit scores and various fees.

CardRatings.com, U.S. Citizens for Fair Credit Card Terms, 143 Crestview Dr., North Little Rock, AR 72116; (501) 663-0314; www.cardratings.com. Posts consumer-written reviews of credit cards and a searchable database of credit card terms and fees.

Center for Responsible Lending, 302 West Main St., Durham, NC 27701; (919) 313-8500; www.responsible lending.org. Nonpartisan research and policy group that seeks to eliminate abusive lending practices.

Credit.com, 550 15th St. #37, San Francisco, CA 94103; (415) 901-1550; www.credit.com. Provides information about consumer-credit problems and credit card terms.

CreditBloggers, www.creditbloggers.com. News and analysis on consumer debt posted by a panel of consumer-finance experts.

Credit Card Nation, www.creditcardnation.com. Web site maintained by professor of consumer finance; includes quizzes to assess and build financial literacy and a calculator for figuring how long it will take to pay down credit card debt.

Credit Slips Blog, www.creditslips.org. Attorneys and law professors post news and analysis on credit- and bankruptcy-related events.

Jump$tart Coalition for Personal Financial Literacy, 919 18th St., N.W., Suite 300, Washington, DC 20006; (888) 453-3822; www.jumpstartcoalition.org. Provides tools and curriculum-support material to build young people's financial literacy.

LowCards.com, 2070 Valleydale Road, Suite #2, Birmingham, AL 35244; www.lowcards.com. A credit card comparison Web site operated by a marketing company.

Myvesta, www.myvesta.org. Provides a history of debt and credit, financial calculators and educational articles on credit.

Fair Trade Labeling

Is It Helping Small Farmers in Developing Countries?

Sarah Glazer

Starbucks is one of several big U.S. chains that sells fair trade coffee and other products. The fair trade label signifies that farmers in the developing world received a fair price for their crops. Only 20 percent of coffee-drinking Americans are familiar with the fair trade label, compared to more than half of British consumers.

From *CQ Researcher*, May 18, 2007.

At the upscale London supermarket chain Waitrose, the smiling faces of small farmers from Africa and Latin America lend a human touch to coffee packages bearing a distinctive green and blue "Fairtrade" label.[1]

In testimonials, the farmers say the fair trade company they deal with, Cafédirect, pays them better than competing coffee buyers and helps them preserve the environment. But Cafédirect coffee costs more than the competing brand, posing a dilemma for shoppers: Is it worth the extra cost, and do the farmers really benefit?

The answer for many British shoppers is apparently yes, judging from galloping sales of fair trade products, which have doubled every two years since 2002.[2]

The Fairtrade label, which signifies that farmers in the developing world received a fair price for their crops, now covers some 2,500 retail and catering lines in Britain, including fresh fruit, tea, chocolate and baby food.[3] Sainsbury's, a supermarket chain, sells fair trade bananas exclusively. Marks & Spencer, a major department store, touts its commitment to fair trade cotton T-shirts and underwear with full-page newspaper ads.

Britons now spend about five times more per capita on fair trade items than Americans. But U.S. sales of fair trade items have also grown rapidly — averaging an estimated 50 percent annually since 2001 — and some experts predict the United States could soon overtake Britain in per capita spending on fair trade products.[4] Coffee represents the lion's share of fair trade products, and U.S. fair trade coffee consumption alone already dwarfs any other nations' total retail spending on fair trade. (*See graph, p. 147.*)

Fair Trade Imports by U.S. Increase

U.S. importation of fair trade-certified coffee, tea and cocoa has risen significantly in recent years. Coffee imports alone have increased by over 850 times since 1998.

Imports of Fair Trade-Certified Products, 1998-2006
(in pounds)

Year	Coffee	Tea	Cocoa
1998	76,059	N/A	N/A
1999	2,052,242	N/A	N/A
2000	4,249,534	N/A	N/A
2001	6,669,308	65,261	N/A
2002	9,747,571	86,706	14,050
2003	19,239,017	95,669	178,888
2004	32,974,400	180,310	727,576
2005	44,585,323	517,500	1,036,696
2006	64,774,431	629,985	1,814,391

Source: "Fair Trade Almanac 1998-2006," TransFair USA

At the same time, awareness of fair trade products is far lower in the United States than in Europe. Only 20 percent of coffee-drinking Americans are familiar with the fair trade label, compared to more than half of British consumers.[5] The U.S. selection of fair trade items is also more limited — the most common items are coffee, chocolate, tea and bananas — and they often are available only in health food or gourmet stores.

Fair trade brands hope to raise their profile by gunning for the market niche known as "conscious consumers" — those who care about the environment, health and fair-labor standards. Big chains like Wal-Mart, Dunkin' Donuts, Starbucks and McDonald's have begun offering fair trade coffee and other items.

Sam Magona, a Ugandan coffee farmer, says his revenues have more than tripled since he started selling under the fair trade banner in 1998. Until farmers organized into cooperatives — a requirement of fair trade certification — exploitative middlemen were taking "most of the profits," says Magona, chairman of the Gumutindo cooperative union, which represents about 3,000 small farmers in Uganda.

Many families in his village could not afford to send their children to school and needed them to work in the fields. And when the world price of coffee dropped precipitously in 2001-2004, coffee farmers who sold on the open market could not even cover their costs, Magona recalls. By contrast, selling fair trade products guarantees a minimum price, insuring farmers against disaster when the price of coffee, traded on international markets, drops.

Now, children in the Gumutindo community are attending school. "People have a roof instead of grass thatch," Magona says, and "they eat more meat now after selling the coffee." But when Magona factors in how much it would cost to pay the family members who donate their labor for free, he says he is just "nearly breaking even."

Experts say this is the reality of subsistence farming in developing countries — farmers live on the margins, fair trade or not. At the same time, the fair trade system often pays up to one-third more than farmers would get on the open market, according to Christopher Himes, chief financial officer of TransFair USA, the leading labeling organization that certifies fair trade goods sold in the United States.

But some consumers may be disturbed to learn that as little as 10 percent of the extra price they pay for a fair trade cup of coffee goes to the grower, according to some estimates. That's because wholesalers, processors, branders and retailers each take a little of the extra price for themselves. TransFair has no control over those extra dips into the profit chain, Himes responds; it merely guarantees that a fair price was paid to the grower.

Some critics say fair trade's guarantee of a good return — no matter what the market price — sends the wrong economic signal to farmers. When the price of a commodity like coffee, which is traded on world markets, tumbles in response to global oversupply, over-compensated fair trade farmers will remain in an uneconomic sector long after they should have switched to some other livelihood, free-market economists argue.

"If there's an artificial inducement — like fair trade — to stay in the market, then that retards the exit process [of farmers] needed to rebalance supply and demand," and encourages more farmers to enter the market, driving down the world price for everyone else, says Brink Lindsey, vice president for research at the conservative Cato Institute in Washington, D.C.

And, critics add, fair trade doesn't help the very poorest farmers, those who don't own land or aren't members of a growers' co-op, because the movement aims primarily to help small land-owning farmers. Large coffee plantations and their workers are barred from certification. "The cooperative system can end up discriminating against people who uphold the values of the fair trade movement but who happen to be part of bigger farms, or just don't want to join a cooperative," according to Lawrence Solomon, director of the Energy Probe Research Foundation, a Toronto firm that analyzes trade and consumer issues.[6]

Responding to free-marketers, other analysts say fair trade is sending an accurate market signal: Some consumers are willing to pay more for a product when they know the producer is paid fairly. The movement has been savvy enough to focus on the fastest-growing slice of the coffee market — the gourmet sector — and recently has been winning awards at international tasting competitions.

When Britain's Twin Trading Ltd. first started marketing fair trade coffee, the product had a reputation for poor quality, and "everyone laughed at us," says Communication Manager Simon Billing. "Now everyone's talking about its chocolaty, velvety flavors," he says at the firm's London headquarters, as a white-coated quality-control taster swishes samples of Peruvian coffees in his mouth and spits them into a bowl.

"If you talk to gourmet coffee or chocolate companies, they will say there's not enough good-quality coffee or chocolate out there," says sociologist Laura T.

How Fair Trade Guarantees Safety Net

Fair trade certification guarantees coffee farmers a minimum price of $1.26 per pound — $1.21 per pound plus a five-cent "social premium" to fund community projects (dotted line). When the world market price of coffee plummets, as in 2001-2002, the fair trade price remains stable and can be twice the market price. If the market price rises above $1.21, as it did last January, the fair trade minimum meets it, plus pays the social premium.*

(Price in $) **Fair Trade Price vs. Market Price, Arabica Beans, 1997-Present**

Market price
Fair trade price

* Under new rules starting June 1, 2007, the social premium rises to 10 cents per pound.

Source: TransFair; Market prices are from New York Board of Trade for Arabica beans, the type imported to the United States under fair trade.

Raynolds, co-director of Colorado State University's Center for Fair and Alternative Trade Studies. "Fair trade is bolstering the capacity of producers to enter into this stronger specialty market." Indeed, as fair trade growers continue to improve their coffee beans, gourmet brands could lure them away with even higher prices than fair trade buyers offer.

Since 1997, the fair trade movement has been overseen by Fairtrade Labelling Organizations International (FLO), a Bonn, Germany-based association of 20 national labeling organizations like TransFair. FLO sets minimum prices and standards and monitors sites wherever fair trade products are grown and produced. Organizations like TransFair USA — the national labeling organization for North America — license and certify the actual buying and selling of fair trade products bearing their black-and-white label.

Most experts prefer the FLO system, with its independent inspectors, over efforts by corporate growers to create their own "fair trade" labels. Yet the *Financial Times* last year found seasonal workers for fair trade growers in Peru were paid below minimum wage and questioned whether the inspection system could keep up with growing demand for fair trade products.[7] (*See sidebar, p. 148.*)

Fair trade's roots can be traced in part to the broader "trade justice" movement, which seeks to reform world trading rules seen as discriminating against poor countries. Massive demonstrations at World Trade Organization meetings have been among the most widely publicized protests against the current "free trade" regime, which critics say favors wealthy countries' markets at the expense of developing countries.

For Americans who are not likely to protest arcane trade rules, fair trade products are another way of reaching them, says Laura Rusu, a spokeswoman for Oxfam America, a leader in the trade justice movement. Her organization is currently lobbying to reduce the billions of dollars in federal agricultural subsidies coming up for a vote later this year in the U.S. farm bill. Government subsidies to American farmers encourage overproduction of products like cotton, driving down the world price and putting farmers in Africa out of business, Oxfam charges.

"If we look at only one thing to achieve change for most farmers — it's definitely through changing the rigged rules at the international level," says Rusu. Fair trade certification is "something in the meantime where we can make a change."

Yet with multilateral trade talks at a stalemate and wealthy countries reluctant to give up their subsidies and trade protections, some academics agree with activists that fair trade labeling may be a faster way to achieve some of those goals. The labeling scheme "is essentially an end-run around the government; it doesn't rely on policy makers making politically risky decisions," says Michael J. Hiscox, a political economist at Harvard University. Ironically, even though the labeling initiative grew out of a left-leaning movement hostile to free-market ideology, it has turned out to be a "market-based solution that relies on good information," he observes.

When it comes to international trade talks, "we're not holding our breath," confirms Himes of TransFair USA. "We're taking an approach that allows us to assist growers right now and raise society's awareness as we do that."

As the market for fair trade products continues to grow, here are some of the questions being debated among consumers, activists and the international community:

Does fair trade certification improve life significantly for small farmers in developing countries?

The face of Nicaraguan coffee farmer Melba Estrada darkens when she recalls 2001, the "sad and difficult" year when the world coffee price fell to a historic low of 49 cents a pound. After Estrada had paid the half-dozen seasonal workers who helped harvest the coffee on her three-acre family farm, "there was not enough money for our own food," recalls the widowed mother of six.

The major standard-setting body for fair trade, FLO, aims to keep small farmers like Estrada afloat during those difficult times by setting a floor price calculated to cover the farmer's costs and provide a decent standard of living.

Currently, the basic minimum price FLO guarantees for coffee from Central America, Africa and Asia is $1.21 per pound, plus a five-cent "social premium" for community projects the growers' cooperative chooses, such as schools or clinics. If the world coffee price rises above the minimum, the fair trade price rises to meet it, and the fair trade importer must pay that price plus the social premium.

For example, on Jan. 4, the world price was $1.25 per pound.[8] So the lowest an importer could have paid for fair trade coffee was $1.30 (the world price plus the social premium).

While the five-cent premium may not seem like much when the coffee price is high, as it is now, fair trade farmers say the guarantee can mean having enough to eat in lean years when the price drops precipitously, as it did between 2001 and 2004. (*See graph, p. 145.*) During those years, fair trade farmers could sell their coffee at more than double the street price paid by local "coyotes" — or middlemen.[9]

Indeed, while small coffee farmers around the world received an additional $17 million in income last year as a result of U.S. fair trade sales, they received an even bigger premium of $26 million in 2004, when world prices were at a low point, even though they exported half as many beans.[10]

But how much does that improve individual farmers' lives? Estrada, who started selling to fair trade six years ago, says the extra income allowed her to convert her dirt-floor adobe hut into a cement home and make investments on her farm to improve the quality of her coffee.

Fair trade provides credit in cash-poor seasons, better information about current world prices and bargaining power, advocates say, especially for farmers like Estrada who live in remote areas and used to sell to exploitative itinerant buyers.

"We were fairly impressed by the range of benefits," says Douglas L. Murray, co-director of the Center for Fair and Alternative Trade Studies, who directed a two-year study of fair trade's impact on farmers in Mexico and Central America. "But," he adds, "our conclusion was most of the benefits were beyond income."

Murray found that fair trade cooperatives gave growers technical skills to convert to more profitable organic coffee, developed marketing strategies to enter the gourmet market and helped farmers diversify into other products they could sell in slack seasons. "The social premium in some cases resulted in some fairly nice benefits, from health clinics and schools," he adds.

Yet those benefits only reach a minority of farmers and farmworkers. Only about 30 percent of the world's small-scale coffee producers are linked to fair trade networks.[11]

In addition, fair trade growers generally receive only a small fraction of the extra margin consumers pay. Take the fair trade cup of coffee sold at Costa, a London coffee bar. For several years, Costa charged an extra 20 cents a cup. But when *Financial Times* writer Tim Harford analyzed the costs, he found that more than 90 percent of that premium did not reach the farmer. The extra cost to Costa of buying free trade coffee beans should have translated to a cost increase of only 2 cents a cup, Harford calculated, since it only takes a quarter-ounce of coffee to make a cappuccino. The other 90 percent, he figured, went to Costa's bottom line.

"The truth is that fair trade coffee wholesalers could pay two, three or sometimes four times the market price for coffee in the developing world without adding anything

U.S. Leads in Fair Trade Sales

With $499 million worth of Fair Trade Certified coffee alone in 2005, the United States leads the world in the retail value of Fair Trade Certified products. The United Kingdom is second, with a value of $351 million.

Retail Value of Fair Trade-Certified Products, 2005
(in millions of dollars)

United States	$499*
United Kingdom	$351
Switzerland	$182
France	$138
Germany	$90
Canada	$44
Italy	$36
Japan	$4
Australia and New Zealand	$3

* Only includes Fair Trade Certified coffee. Figures for other countries also include other products such as tea, cocoa, rice, sugar and fruit.

Source: "Fair Trade Almanac 1998-2006," TransFair USA

noticeable to the production cost of a cappuccino, because coffee beans make up such a small proportion of the cost," Harford writes in his new book, *The Undercover Economist.* So why was Costa charging so much more? Harford's answer: fair trade coffee "allowed Costa to find customers who are willing to pay a bit more if given a reason to do so."[12]

Even analysts sympathetic to fair trade estimate that only five cents of an additional 20 cents the shopper pays for a pound of fair trade bananas would go to the farmers, largely because wholesalers and retailers all ratchet up their mark-ups.[13] Fair trade labeling organizations also charge fees to co-ops and wholesalers for their services — like inspecting farms — which are reflected in the price.

Defenders of fair trade say this is the way the free enterprise system works, and fair trade is no different. "This is a business, not a charity," says Billing, at Twin Trading in London. "We have no way of controlling the margins beyond what we're paying growers."

Even Harford acknowledged that at the time of his Costa study, the extra 80 cents-$1.10 a pound that fair trade was paying farmers could still nearly double the

Is Fair Trade Monitoring Adequate?

Financial Times *uncovers problems in Peru*

Some critics have suggested the monitoring system run by Fairtrade Labelling Organizations International, or FLO, may be inadequate, or even weakened by corruption. A *Financial Times* reporter wrote last year that four out of five fair trade-certified farms he visited in Peru paid summer coffee pickers below minimum wage, despite FLO standards requiring payments in line with minimum-wage laws.[1]

"Our standards for small-farmer co-ops don't cover their payments to seasonal workers," responds Ian Bretman, vice chairman of the Fairtrade Foundation, Britain's labeling organization, partly because it's "nearly impossible to verify" at every farm.

Bretman stresses that monitoring is aimed primarily at verifying the price paid to small growers — the main group the movement is trying to help. While small farmers are encouraged to pay decent wages, they're not subject to the rigorous inspections carried out at larger plantations with many full-time workers, according to Bretman.

Officers with the labeling organizations also point out that the farmworkers interviewed by the *Financial Times* were still being paid more than the prevailing local wage. "Certification isn't a guarantee that nothing bad ever happens; it's a guarantee there are repercussions when bad things happen," says Christopher Himes, chief financial officer of TransFair USA, the leading labeling organization that certifies fair trade goods sold in the United States. "The *Financial Times* article was interviewing groups we were in the process of decertifying."

While FLO does annual inspections of cooperatives when they're first certified, its visits become more infrequent once a co-op is established after several years. In a cooperative of 1,000 farmers, only 10-15 of the farms might be visited, according to Bretman, so certifiers won't necessarily catch every violation.

In a written response to the *Times*, the Fairtrade Foundation said that of the Peruvian cooperatives mentioned in the article, one group sold only 10 percent of their beans on fair trade terms; another 15 percent. "This means they remain heavily at the mercy of the conventional market, often forced to sell for less than the cost of production" and "are often still very poor themselves."[2]

The *Times* reporter also quoted industry insiders saying non-certified coffee was being falsely exported under a fair trade label. The Fairtrade Foundation responded that FLO audits "had already identified irregularities in the supply chain in Peru" and had scheduled an inspection for the week following the appearance of the article.

Nevertheless, industry observers have questioned the ability of certifiers to keep up with growing demand for ethically grown coffee — possibly creating an incentive to misleadingly export non-certified coffee. Some also questioned the independence of the certifiers. FLO answers that inspections are conducted by FLO-CERT, a company owned by FLO but operated independently.

[1] Hal Weitzman, "The Bitter Cost of 'Fair Trade' Coffee," *Financial Times*, Sept. 8, 2006, at www.ft.com.

[2] "Fairtrade Foundation Briefing on *Financial Times* Article," at www.fairtrade.org.uk.

income of a farmer in Guatemala, where the average income is less that $2,000 a year.[14]

Still, some critics consider fair trade pricing deceptive for the consumer who thinks the extra cost is going entirely to the farmer. "It may be more efficient to provide that help by supporting a charity than it is to pay 40 pence (80 cents) more for your coffee when you don't know what happens to the 40 pence," says Philip Booth, editorial and program director at the Institute of Economic Affairs, a conservative London think tank.

"Only a very small percent of all the people who buy fair trade coffee would ever write a check to [a charity like] Oxfam," TransFair USA's Himes retorts. "For all the people who don't have writing a check to farmers on their top 10 list of things to do today, what we're talking about here is millions of consumers in tens of thousands of outlets."

Moreover, the money farmers get is helping them develop a business; a charity check is merely a handout, Himes adds.

The extra cost of fair trade products can also reflect the fees fair trade labeling organizations like TransFair charge to farmers and wholesalers, which Booth criticizes as excessive. But if consumers want the fair trade label to be trustworthy, Murray notes, labeling organizations need to conduct inspections, and charge fees to cover the cost.

Some critics question the fair trade premise that farmers should stay on the soil, where they're only earning a few pennies more — rather than improving their lot through education and city jobs. "Fair trade is about Western feel-good rather than transforming people's lives," says Ceri Dingle of WORLDwrite, a London cultural exchange organization. The fair trade movement's encouragement of organic methods means farmers are doing more weeding by hand and don't have access to modern agricultural methods, she charges, encouraging manual toil.

Indeed, free-market economists like Booth argue that fair trade doesn't work as a large-scale development strategy; usually it takes urbanization and industrialization to accomplish that. For farmers like Estrada, the most dramatic change from fair trade may occur in the next generation, when children leave the farm. Her eldest daughter is studying medicine — the first in her community to attend college — under a scholarship funded by fair trade social premiums.

Surprisingly, some leaders of the movement agree their effect on people's lives is modest. Ian Bretman, vice chairman of the Fairtrade Foundation, Britain's labeling organization, calls the experience of Uganda's Magona "very typical" for subsistence farmers. "They're barely getting by," he concedes. "It's almost utopian to think we can transform that position in such a short period of time." With fair trade, he says, "We hope people don't fall below the level where they can sustain a decent lifestyle."

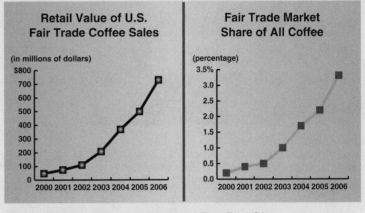

Fair Trade Coffee Sales Rise

Since 2000, the retail value of fair trade coffee sales in the United States has increased dramatically (left). As a percentage of all U.S. coffee sales, the market share of fair trade coffee rose from 0.20 percent in 2000 to 3.31 percent in 2006 (right).

Retail Value of U.S. Fair Trade Coffee Sales
(in millions of dollars)

Fair Trade Market Share of All Coffee
(percentage)

Source: "Fair Trade Almanac 1998-2006," TransFair USA

Does fair trade certification distort markets, ultimately hurting some small producers?

Some free-market economists have suggested that the fair trade approach could ultimately hurt most farmers, especially those not fortunate enough or savvy enough to join co-ops that sell to higher-paying fair trade buyers.

In a widely quoted report last December, the weekly British newsmagazine *The Economist* took up that argument. "By propping up the price, the Fairtrade system encourages farmers to produce more of these commodities rather than diversifying into other crops and so depresses prices — thus achieving, for most farmers, exactly the opposite of what the initiative is intended to do," the magazine editorialized.[15]

In the case of coffee, the propped-up price encourages more producers to enter the market and drives down the price of non-fair trade coffee even further, "making non-Fairtrade farmers poorer," the magazine said.[16]

But fair trade coffee is still such a small part of the U.S. market — less than 4 percent — that the idea it could sway world prices is almost laughable to those active in the movement.[17]

Ugandan coffee farmer Sam Magona proudly holds a bag of Mt. Elgon coffee produced by his cooperative of 3,000 farms on fair trade terms. Magona was visiting the London office of Twin Trading Ltd., which buys his coffee beans for Cafédirect, a fair trade company.

"If we did get to that [influential] level of market share, fair trade is flexible enough that we can change the standards," says Charlotte Opal, chair of FLO's Standards Committee, which sets minimum prices.

And some economists say fair trade coffee beans are essentially a different market from the world commodity market, which determines pricing for run-of-the-mill blends for consumers looking for the lowest-cost product.

"They're two different products and have a different demand-and-supply curve. To the extent that the signal is, 'Consumers want more fair trade coffee,' the effect should be to get more producers to grow fair trade coffee," says Harvard political economist Hiscox. "And that is the correct signal."

Studies by Hiscox and others have shown that consumers of fair trade products are willing to pay a higher price for the assurance that growers are paid fairly. (*See sidebar, p. 159.*)

Yet skeptics like Booth at the Institute of Economic Affairs doubt consumers would be willing to keep paying a premium if the world coffee price sends competitive brands plummeting. Could wholesalers sell enough fair trade coffee to keep farmers afloat in a glutted supply market? he asks.

"Absolutely, we'll be able to sell," responds Rick Peyser, director of social advocacy and coffee-community outreach at Green Mountain Coffee Roasters in Waterbury,

Vt., a wholesaler of fair trade and other specialty coffees. That situation "already happened in 2001," he says, when world coffee prices hit bottom. "That's when our fair trade sales started to skyrocket," as customers' sympathies were roused by news stories about the thousands of poor coffee farmers being driven out of business.

Some critics say fair trade unfairly creates insiders — those inside the fair trade co-ops who get superior prices — and outsiders, who are still beholden to market prices. "Whether it brings significant net benefits to the poor in general is questionable," the Institute of Economic Affairs' Booth concludes in an upcoming article.[18]

The poorest farmers are the least likely to benefit from fair trade, co-author Booth says, because they're not organized in co-ops and can't afford the certification fees charged to co-ops by labeling organizations.

"My concern is that the improvement for a small number of growers comes at a price — in particular restricting the corporate forms of the organizations involved by requiring them to be cooperatives," says Booth. He argues that co-ops are prone to corruption and mismanagement because there are no clear lines of authority.

Supporting that concern, a recent study of Latin American coffee cooperatives at Colorado State University found rather than democratically choosing a community project to fund from the five-cent-per-pound social premium, cooperative leaders have at times "made the unilateral decision to use the premium to cover operational costs."[19]

So why are co-ops a requirement? They provide the kind of central management crucial to checking that fair trade standards are actually being met, explains TransFair's Himes, and he says fair trade pricing provides incentives for small farmers to join them. "Dealing with the absolutely poorest unaffiliated farmer — that's not what fair trade does right now," he acknowledges.

Although cooperatives don't always live up to the vision of democratic institutions, Murray at the Center for Fair and Alternative Trade Studies says companies are equally prone to flaws in how management decisions are made.

Opal maintains that even farmers who don't sell to fair trade can benefit from a fair trade cooperative in their community. "We see prices for non-fair trade coffee going up" in those localities, she says, because "there's more information, and farmers in the village know what they should be earning." And projects funded by fair trade's social premiums, such as new roads, schools, clinics and wells, often benefit everyone in the village, she notes.

In the long run, the *Financial Times'* Harford speaks for many free-market believers when he concludes that "fair trade cannot fix the basic problem: Too much coffee is being produced." As long as growing coffee looks economically attractive, he argues, "it will always be swamped with desperate people who have no alternative."[20]

But it's hard to expect a coffee farmer, who must wait four years for trees to bear and who may farm on soil unsuitable for anything else, to turn on a dime in response to dropping world prices. "A coffee farmer who loses his land won't become a software engineer," observes Himes. More likely he'll join the illegal immigrants seeking work in some North American city, suggests Billing at Twin Trading.

Meanwhile, and somewhat contrary to classical economics, the gourmet retailers who buy from Green Mountain are willing to pay more in low-priced cycles to tide over farmers of specialty beans so they can ensure a continuing supply of high-quality coffee, Peyser says.

Would trade reforms help small farmers more than fair trade certification?

If buying fair trade cappuccino at your local Starbucks is not the answer to addressing poverty, in the eyes of free-market economists, what is? It's something that's "less fun than shopping," suggests *The Economist* in a widely cited editorial.

"Real change will require action by governments," the editors wrote, including "reform of the world trade system and the abolition of agricultural tariffs and subsidies, notably Europe's monstrous common agricultural policy, which coddles rich farmers and prices those in the poor world out of the European market."[21]

Similar U.S. government subsidies for crops like cotton and rice have been assailed by economists for encouraging overproduction of unprofitable crops, driving their prices so low that poor rice farmers in Ghana, for example, have been forced out of business.

Although they may disagree on the precise solutions — free-marketers want to remove all trade barriers, liberals generally want to keep some for poor countries — some prominent liberal economists agree that the current world-trade regime benefits rich countries at the expense of poor countries.

Since World War II, writes Nobel Prize-winning economist Joseph E. Stiglitz in his book *Fair Trade for*

All, developed countries like the United States have been "somewhat duplicitous" in advocating that other nations reduce their tariffs and subsidies for goods in which the rich nations have a comparative advantage. At the same time, rich countries have been reluctant to open up their own consumer markets when it comes to goods where developing countries have an advantage.[22]

If governments really want to "make poverty history," as some British Labor Party leaders have pledged, they would change the way that world trade currently contributes to poverty, Stiglitz wrote in the *London Daily Telegraph*. Rich nations currently cost developing countries three times as much with their protectionist trade policies as they give them in aid each year, he estimated. A mere 1 percent increase in Africa's share of world trade would bring it some $60 billion, he calculated.[23]

In light of these huge monetary inequities, the relatively small fair trade movement may be a distraction from efforts to make trade agreements more equitable between rich and poor countries, some liberal economists worry.[24]

Oxfam America, which is lobbying to reduce some $4 billion in cotton subsidies to American farmers, calculates such a reform could increase the world price of cotton by as much as 20 percent. "When you look at a farmer earning a little over $100 a year on his farm in West Africa, an extra 20 dollars a year could mean his or her daughter going to school or a successful village effort at getting a well," says Oxfam America spokeswoman Rusu.

Recent multilateral trade rounds have continued to give the advantage to developed countries, which keep their protectionist trade barriers while persuading developing countries to drop theirs, according to Stiglitz.[25] The 2003 trade meeting in Cancun, Mexico, for example, ended in a walkout after many participants accused the United States and Europe of reneging on their promises over agricultural reform.

But even some advocates of trade reform doubt there's any life left in multilateral trade talks. "The Doha Round is in a coma right now, and it's unknown whether it will ever revive," says the Cato Institute's Lindsey, an advocate for reductions in U.S. tariffs.* "The outlook isn't promising for putting real discipline on our subsidies," either, he predicts.

---

* The so-called Doha Round in Doha, Qatar, in 2002 launched a new round of multilateral trade talks focusing on aiding poor countries.

That gloomy political outlook is one reason Harvard's Hiscox has become enthusiastic about fair trade as an alternative to trying to insert labor standards in trade agreements — for manufacturing as well as farming. Historically, poor countries have opposed such standards for fear they'll lose their cheap-labor advantage when it comes to exporting goods. And inserting economic penalties for countries that violate labor standards could ultimately hurt poor farmers in those countries and stifle economic growth, he points out.

On the other hand, if higher fair trade prices actually compensated firms for their higher labor costs, "everyone could win," he writes, and "it could be possible to improve working conditions without adversely affecting investment and growth in developing countries."[26]

Trade justice activists, as advocates for reform of international trade rules are known, are reluctant to admit to internal tension within their movement caused by fair trade activists, but there are some differences. "You can admit fair trade is part of a solution to a much bigger problem — one way of addressing poverty, but it's not a panacea and will not fix the problem overall," says Amy Barry, trade spokeswoman for Oxfam International, a leader in the trade justice movement and a founder of Fairtrade International, the British fair trade labeling organization.

Leaders of the fair trade movement in both Britain and America say they're linked in principle to the goals of the larger trade justice movement. But they say fair trade offers a market solution right now while the prospects for trade reform look dim. And, Oxfam's Rusu agrees, "given that it will take some time to get to a fair international-trading system, fair trade-certified products encourage consumers to use their dollar to choose products that are more fair."

The big question, according to Colorado State sociologist Raynolds, is: "Does an initiative like fair trade heighten awareness of inequalities in our current trade system so we can start to get the consensus and effort to get some significant reforms?"

BACKGROUND

Rise of Fair Trade

The roots of fair trade can be traced to projects initiated by churches in North America and Europe in the late 1940s to provide relief to refugees and other poverty-stricken communities by selling their handicrafts to wealthier markets.

In Western Europe, just after World War II, charities began to import handicrafts from impoverished Eastern Europe to promote economic development.[27] In the United States, around the same time, the Mennonite Central Committee began to develop a market for embroidery from Puerto Rico by creating a crafts-selling organization that would become known as Ten Thousand Villages.

By the 1960s, these initiatives had evolved into "world shops," marketing goods from the developing world. Their goal was to eliminate middlemen and return more of the profits to Third World craftsmen. Oxfam led this effort with its "helping by selling" program in 1965, marketing imported handicrafts in its charity shops in England.[28]

The first independent fair trade labeling initiative began in the Netherlands in 1988, when world coffee prices started to plunge. The Max Havelaar Foundation began marketing coffee under its own label, certifying that a guaranteed minimum price was being paid to the farmers.

Oxfam followed in 1992, joining with four other British philanthropic groups to establish the Fairtrade Foundation, Britain's third-party auditor of fair trade practices. Today, affiliated fair trade certifying organizations are active in Europe, Australia, New Zealand, Canada, Japan, Mexico and the United States.

In 1997, the Fairtrade Foundation joined with other national initiatives to form the umbrella Fairtrade Labelling Organizations International (FLO), to pool certification and marketing efforts. The FLO subsequently established detailed standards for certified commodities governing pricing and labor standards. It monitors producer and trader groups to ensure compliance and may de-certify groups for failing to meet the criteria.[29]

To ensure fair prices, producers must receive a guaranteed minimum price and an additional "social premium" for community projects, set separately for each product by FLO.

FLO has developed specific standards for coffee, tea, cocoa, quinoa, bananas, cane sugar, rice, cotton, wine grapes, nuts and oil seeds, dried fruit, fresh fruit and vegetables, fruit juices, herbs and spices, flowers and plants.

CHRONOLOGY

1940s–1960s *Churches and philanthropies sell Third World handicrafts, returning profits directly to craftsmen. Post–World War II attempts to liberalize trade begin.*

1948 U.N.'s General Agreement on Tariffs and Trade (GATT) is set up, begins "rounds" of negotiations to reduce trade barriers.

1965 British humanitarian organization Oxfam starts "helping by selling" program, leading to sales of Third World crafts.

1980s *World coffee prices plunge, impoverishing thousands of small farmers; early fair trade labeling efforts start to pick up steam.*

1986 Equal Exchange, a worker-owned cooperative in the United States, begins importing and roasting only "fairly traded" coffee.

1988 The Max Havelaar Foundation in the Netherlands begins marketing coffee under its own label, certifying that a guaranteed minimum price is being paid to the farmers.

1990s *Fair trade labeling efforts start in England and United States; international umbrella group formed to set fair prices and inspect farms; EU expresses support; coffee becomes dominant product.*

1992 Oxfam and other philanthropic groups in England establish the Fairtrade Foundation, Britain's third-party auditor of fair trade practices.

1997 Fairtrade Foundation and labeling groups in other countries form Fairtrade Labelling Organizations International (FLO), to set prices.

1998 TransFair USA, the lead certifying organization in the United States, is founded.

1999 TransFair begins serious labeling effort; fair trade coffee sales begin average annual growth of 79 percent.

2000s *Major U.S. chains start selling fair trade coffee and other items; U.S. fair trade sales average 50 percent growth annually; activists demonstrate at international trade talks.*

2000 Starbucks introduces fair trade coffee.

2001 Demonstrators charging that trade rules hurt poor countries stall World Trade Organization (WTO) talks in Seattle.

2002 WTO launches new trade talks in Doha, Qatar, known as the "Doha Round," focusing on development of poor countries.

September 2003 Trade talks in Cancun, Mexico, end as walkouts charge rich countries reneged on reducing farm subsidies; first fair trade fair held at talks. . . . Green Mountain Coffee Roasters in Waterbury, Vt., begins producing fair trade coffee for supermarket chains.

2004 Fair trade organizations from 30 countries sign declaration at Conference on Trade and Development in Sao Paulo, Brazil, calling for fair prices for small farmers. . . . Wal-Mart begins selling fair trade coffee. . . . Starbucks quadruples purchases of fair trade coffee over 2001.

2005 McDonald's begins serving fair trade coffee blend in New England, Albany, N.Y.

2006 European Parliament calls for European Union to support the fair trade movement . . . The number of certified fair trade producer organizations reaches 586 by year's end in 58 nations in Africa, Asia and Latin America. . . . Awareness of fair trade label among U.S. coffee drinkers rises to 20 percent from 7 percent in 2003.

Feb. 14, 2007 On Valentine's Day Divine Chocolate, a U.S. fair trade chocolate, is launched.

March 2007 Whole Foods Market chain announces it will sell TransFair-labeled products, with 10-year goal of making half of imported foods from the developing world fair trade. . . . TransFair announces more than 600 U.S. businesses carry fair trade products in about 40,000 retail outlets. . . . Fair trade coffee, fastest-growing segment of U.S. specialty market, sells $730 million retail in 2006.

Fair Trade Towns Boost Consumer Awareness

Business picks up too in British, Pennsylvania towns

Outside Bar 19 in England's Avon River Valley, a chalkboard proudly proclaims the "Fair Trade" menu. Inside, lunchtime tables filled with parents and children on Easter break testify to the restaurant's successful transformation from a seedy bar to popular — and socially conscious — family spot.

In 2003, when Richard Smith reopened the café with blond wood paneling in the picturesque town of Keynsham, he advertised it as an "alternative" venue featuring organic and local products and the first smoke-free dining environment in town. But he was reluctant to load the menu with fair trade items, fearing customers would think "they're overpaying for poor quality foods."

Confidence replaced reluctance a year later, when Keynsham, nestled in an agricultural river valley between Bath and Bristol, started a campaign to become a "fair trade town." The town council passed a unanimous resolution pledging to serve fair trade tea and coffee at town functions, encourage businesses to sell fair trade products and promote the concept of fair trade in the schools and local media. To qualify, the town of 15,000 residents had to satisfy the Fairtrade Foundation, Britain's lead fair trade labeling and certifying organization.

The proliferation of fair trade towns — at last count 262 in the U.K. — helps explain the rapid growth in British consumption of fair trade goods, some activists believe. The movement started in 2000 when Garstang, a small market town in Northern England, declared itself "fair trade." A year

Richard Smith finds that patrons willingly accept fair trade products at his Bar 19 in Keynsham, in England's Avon River Valley.

CQ Press/Sarah Glazer

later, 71 percent of the town's residents recognized the "Fairtrade" label, compared to about 20 percent nationally. Today, more than half of adults in Britain recognize the label.[1]

Keynsham's campaign made it possible for Smith to do "a lot less advertising" to convince customers fair trade foods could be good quality and well-priced. Smith started promoting fair trade wines from South Africa and rum from Paraguay, which he features in the café's rum cake. (The tea, coffee and even pineapple juice are fair trade, too.) If anything, fair trade helped his business grow, he says.

"This is a good example of where fair trade has added to the business and is part of its identity," says Rachel Ward, a Keynsham official who kick-started the campaign. "Fair trade is a way of telling people this is a place worth shopping." Local officials hope fair trade status will help revive the main shopping street of the historic market town and even draw some of the tourists who flock to nearby Bath.

Across the "pond," attracting visitors and shoppers also figured in support for turning Media, Pa. into the first — and so far the only — fair trade town in the United States. When Media resident Elizabeth Killough pitched the idea to the local business association, she says, "They got it right away" as a way to attract "conscious consumers" — the well-heeled niche that goes for organic and fair trade products. Though Media has only 5,000 residents, restaurants and shops on its quaint Main Street compete for a daytime population of around 25,000 who converge on the county seat.

The idea was the brain-child of local tour magnate Hal Taussig, whose Untours Foundation makes low-interest loans abroad to create jobs and support fair trade products. "My own interest is to get all the merchants in Media to sell fair trade goods so when you walk down the street and ask people, 'What is Fair Trade?' they'll know what it is," says Taussig who donates the profits of his tour company to the foundation.

Media's town fathers decided to adopt the same criteria used in Britain after they learned how Garstang had pioneered the concept.

Local official Rachel Ward, right, helped turn Keynsham into one of Great Britain's 262 fair trade towns.

"As far as bringing people to Media, anything we can do to promote our town in a positive way is a bonus. And we're getting recognition around the country from other towns," says Media Borough Councilwoman Monica Simpson.

Media's restaurants were surprisingly resistant to serving fair trade coffee, because they usually rely on a single distributor for pre-measured coffee and urns, says Killough, associate director of the Untours Foundation. A supplier was finally located who had started offering fair trade coffee to compete for contracts at college campuses, where students demanded it.

Similarly, when Keynsham approached its largest employer, Cadbury Chocolate, about serving fair trade products in its employee canteen, the company resisted on the grounds its food supplier didn't offer them, town officials say. It's no small irony that the work force at the chocolate plant has been decimated as Cadbury jobs have migrated overseas to low-wage countries.

The chocolate giant does not carry the fair trade label on most of its products although it says on its Web site that it pays its growers a fair return. [2] But local employees still decided to put in a vending machine featuring fair trade hot drinks at the social club on the plant's campus.

In Garstang, the inspiration for fair trade germinated in 1999, when veterinarian Bruce Crowther attended workshops by the British charity Oxfam on Third World poverty, which condemned unfair trade practices. "They drew my attention to the realization that a child is dying somewhere in the world every two to three seconds because of poverty," he recalls. "That statistic totally horrified me."

Crowther draws a direct line from his activism as coordinator of Britain's fair trade towns initiative to 19th-century abolitionists, who campaigned against the slavery on sugar plantations with brochures asking, "What price is your sugar?"

"It's absolutely the same argument today," Crowther says, for products that rich countries can buy cheaply because they pay Third World farmers so poorly. "It's morally unacceptable that people should suffer in order for us to get sugar for a cheap price," he declares.

Garstang is mirroring the slave triangle of more than 200 years ago — but in a reverse, fair trade image. In the 1800s, the triangle connected neighboring Lancaster, Britain's fourth-largest slave-trading port; Ghana, the source of the slaves; and the former American colonies where slaves were shipped. Since 2002, Garstang has forged a cultural exchange with a town in Ghana, New Koforidua, home to cocoa farmers selling to fair trade. In March, Garstang also accepted an invitation to become a twin town with Media, once an important stop for runaway slaves on the Underground Railroad.

---

[1] Elisa Arond, "The Fairtrade Towns Initiative: Lessons from across the Ocean," May 2006, Oxfam America, pp. 15, 40.

[2] "Fairtrade is not the only way to ensure farmers receive a fair return for their crops," the Web site notes, since many farmers are not in cooperatives as required by the Fairtrade Foundation. See www.cadburyschweppes.com/EN/EnvironmentSociety/EthicalTrading/fair_trade.htm.

Until the recent introduction of fair trade cotton goods, sports balls were the only manufactured item certified by FLO.

For coffee, the main fair trade product, FLO requires that producers be small, family-based growers organized into politically independent democratic organizations — cooperatives — and that they limit the use of environmentally harmful chemicals. FLO has developed separate standards for operations employing large numbers of workers, such as farms growing tea, bananas and other fruit.

Importers of fair trade products must comply with another set of FLO standards aimed at giving cash-poor farmers, often beholden to extortionate money-lenders, credit at reasonable rates: Buyers must agree to long-term purchasing agreements (beyond one year) and provide advance financing to farmers.

By the end of 2006, there were 586 certified fair trade producer organizations in 58 developing nations in Africa, Asia and Latin America.[30]

U.S. Enters Market

As the fair trade market picked up steam through the 1980s, coffee quickly became the dominant product.[31] In the United States, the pioneer in the market was Equal Exchange, a worker-owned cooperative in West Bridgewater, Mass., which began importing and roasting only "fairly traded" coffee in 1986.

TransFair USA, the lead American certifying organization, opened in 1998 and began a serious labeling effort the following year. Since then, fair trade coffee sales have grown an average of 79 percent annually, according to TransFair, and coffee remains the dominant crop.

In addition to coffee, TransFair introduced fair trade-certified tea and cocoa to the U.S. market. Sugar, rice and vanilla recently came under its label. Flowers, wine and nuts are new products on the horizon, according to Chief Financial Officer Himes.

Total U.S. sales of fair trade-certified products grew by 350 percent between 2001 and 2005 and by 60 percent between 2004 and 2005, estimates Harvard's Hiscox.[32] Today, more than 600 U.S. businesses carry fair trade products in about 40,000 retail outlets, according to TransFair USA. (For a list of stores, go to www.transfairusa.org.)

Much of the rapid U.S. growth is due to the "mainstreaming" of fair trade beginning in 2000, when Starbucks introduced fair trade coffee. In 2003, Green Mountain Coffee Roasters began producing fair trade coffees for large supermarket chains, and in 2004, Wal-Mart began selling it. Starbucks quadrupled its purchases of fair trade coffee between 2001 and 2004.[33]

In 2005, McDonald's introduced a fair trade coffee blend created for it by Green Mountain and Newman's Own Organics, which the chain now serves in 650 restaurants in New England and Albany, N.Y. But McDonald's doesn't tell customers the coffee — the only kind served in those restaurants — is fair trade. Indeed fair trade was not the main reason behind McDonald's choice. According to McDonald's USA spokeswoman Danya Proud, the "main impetus" was that "Green Mountain is a name well-known in that part of the country, and the quality of the coffee is high."

The United States currently accounts for almost a third of global fair trade sales, and Europe almost two-thirds.[34] The enormous scale of the American consumer market, especially for coffee, makes the United States the largest single consumer of fair trade goods. But as individuals, European consumers spend far more per person than the average American. Swiss consumers spend about 20 times more on fair trade and Britons almost five times more than the average American.[35] In 2003, the average Swiss spent 19 Euros ($26), the Briton $7, and the average American $1.60 on fair trade products.

Awareness of fair trade labels among American consumers remains far behind their European counterparts, although it is rising. A recent survey of the nation's coffee consumers — those most likely to have seen fair trade coffee in coffee bars — showed awareness grew from 7 percent in 2003 to 20 percent in 2006.[36] By contrast, more than half of British consumers recognize the label.

Fair trade became well-known in the United Kingdom partly because nonprofits like Oxfam, with hundreds of thousands of subscribers, had been conducting campaigns about injustices they perceived in the world trading system some 25 years before they started the labeling system.

"By doing that work for so long, you have quite a lot of the population that knows something about it in quite a detailed way," says Sophie Tranchell, managing director of Divine Chocolate Ltd., a fair trade company in England. The development of fair trade brands like

Divine Chocolate and Cafédirect, exclusively for fair trade coffee, and their growing presence in British supermarkets also contributed to rapid sales growth.

Trade Justice Movement

The growth of the fair trade movement coincided with growing concern and activism over trade inequities for poorer countries amid expanding globalization. Widespread attempts to liberalize world trade and bring the benefits of trade to all countries began after World War II. In 1948, the General Agreement on Tariffs and Trade (GATT), set up under the auspices of the newly formed United Nations, attempted to arbitrate international trade disputes through a series of "rounds" of negotiations designed to eliminate trade barriers between countries.

Since those initial efforts, the world has been moving toward reduced tariffs and restrictions on trade. For example, between 1960 and 1980, lending by the International Monetary Fund and the World Bank was often tied to requirements that developing countries drop their trade barriers.[37]

GATT and its successor, the World Trade Organization (WTO), succeeded in generating more free trade; total trade in 2000 was 22 times that in 1950. "Global inequality has also grown," however, note two advocates of fair trade, citing figures showing that the share of the world's income among the poorest 10 percent fell during this period, while the richest 10 percent got wealthier.[38]

As developing countries continued to liberalize their trade barriers, wealthy nations like the United States were increasingly reluctant to drop their protections for products for which developing countries had an advantage, writes economist Stiglitz. "As a result, we now have an international trade regime which, in many ways, is disadvantageous to the developing countries," he concludes.[39]

These tensions came to a head in September 2003, when a series of multilateral meetings in Cancun, Mexico, ended abruptly without any agreement on the major issues. The meetings were intended to follow up on a declaration made at the WTO's meeting in Doha, Qatar, in 2002. The so-called Doha Round launched a new round of multilateral trade talks focusing on aiding poor countries. But the Cancun talks fell apart in large measure because many participants felt the United States had reneged on its promises, particularly pledges to reduce its own agricultural subsidies.[40]

TransFair USA is the leading third-party certifier of Fair Trade products in the United States (left). Fairtrade Labelling Organizations International (FLO) is the worldwide fair trade standard-setting and certification organization (right).

Philanthropic groups focusing on Third World poverty, like Oxfam, have become increasingly convinced over the last decade that "trade not aid" is the best route to alleviating poverty in the developing world.[41]

Meanwhile, college-student activists concerned about overseas sweatshops and child labor have at times merged with anti-globalization activists, whose sentiments culminated in violent demonstrations at the WTO talks in Seattle in 2001.[42]

Supporting a wider campaign for global trade reform and trade justice is one of three aims of the fair trade movement — in addition to alleviating poverty and empowering small farmers — write fair trade activists Charlotte Opal and Alex Nicholls in their book *Fair Trade*. "Fair Trade began as a campaigning issue driven by activists and maintains a powerful international network of lobbyists," they write.[43]

The movement's growing political impact, the authors claim, could be seen in 2004 at the U.N. Conference on Trade and Development in Sao Paulo, Brazil, which generated a declaration signed by more than 90 fair trade organizations from 30 countries calling for greater trade price stability and fair prices for small farmers in developing countries.[44]

An evaluation by researchers at the London School of Economics found no "direct impacts" on WTO rules could be attributed to the fair trade movement but noted its increasing lobbying presence at international meetings, including a trade fair at the Cancun meeting.[45]

Poverty activists' increased interest in fair trade has been sparked by the perception that international aid, the main alternative to the fair trade movement, "often seems to have had little long-term effect," note Nicholls and Opal. While aid can alleviate sudden world crises like famines, they argue, it "often fails to offer a developmental path for the poor out of poverty and dependence on outside support."[46]

CURRENT SITUATION

Government Support

Governments and political leaders in the United Kingdom and throughout Europe and have given the fair trade movement considerably more support than it has received in the United States, where politicians are more likely to scratch their heads over the meaning of the term.

In 2006, the European Parliament, in a largely symbolic move, unanimously adopted a resolution that called for a European Union-wide approach to supporting the movement. In previous resolutions in 1997 and 1998, it called on the European Commission to support importers of fair trade bananas and other goods.

The commission issued a declaration of support for fair trade with developing nations in 1994. And the 2000 Cotonou trade agreement between the European Union and African, Caribbean and Pacific nations called for the promotion of fair trade initiatives.[47] Several European governments also provide grants to cover the costs of certification for producers in developing countries.[48]

In 2000, government agencies in several European nations began purchasing fair trade-certified coffee and tea to serve in government offices, including the European Parliament building. The European Commission has co-financed a project securing commitments from policy-makers to include fair trade criteria in public-procurement legislation.

Serving fair trade coffee, tea and biscuits in government offices can have a big ripple effect, says Divine Chocolate's Tranchell. "It's difficult for small fair trade product companies to get on the list of big catering companies," she says. "So if key accounts like government departments start to ask for products, then they're on the menu and other people can buy them too."

In Britain, the government has provided loan guarantees to help fair trade start-up companies like Divine Chocolate and has made grants to educate schoolchildren about how fair trade products help Third World families.

As Tranchell explains, the lure of chocolate "gives us an in" with kids. Divine Chocolate has used grant money it received with a nonprofit partner to set up a Web site named after its "Dubble" chocolate bar, where 50,000 young people have signed up as "a Dubble agent" to change the world "chunk by chunk." Another Web site provides teaching materials teachers can download.

More than 260 towns in the U.K. have passed resolutions declaring themselves Fair Trade Towns, a designation that requires the town's governing body to commit to serve fair trade products at town functions and to encourage local business to sell the products. Some activists think the designation helps explain the movement's rapid growth and high level of public recognition. Inspired by the British example, Media, Pa., dubbed itself the first U.S. Fair Trade Town. (*See sidebar, p. 154.*)

On Valentine's Day, Divine Chocolate introduced its brand to the United States. It set up headquarters in Washington, D.C., because "Divine Chocolate's mission is to be a highly visible and vocal advocate for better conditions in the chocolate industry," according to Erin Gorman, U.S. CEO. At a briefing on Capitol Hill, "there was clear interest on the part of Hill staffers about how the U.S. government might follow the example of the U.K. in supporting fair trade companies such as Divine," Gorman says.

However, some leaders of the movement say they're leery of government involvement, particularly since, in their view, interest-group lobbying has watered down the organic food standards set by the U.S. Agriculture Department. "I don't think we would look for legislation or even necessarily standardization," says TransFair's Himes. "It introduces complexity and politicking."

Coming in for criticism was a recent $8.6 million grant from the U.S. Agency for International Development (AID) to the Rainforest Alliance, an international environmental group based in New York, to certify products from more than 300,000 acres of forest and farmland as well-managed environmentally. The

Consumers Say They Will Support Fair Trade

But what do they do at the mall?

A majority of American consumers say in surveys they would pay more for clothes and other products if they knew they weren't made in sweatshops. But do they?

In a 2002 experiment, University of Michigan sociologists placed two groups of identical athletic socks in a department store, labeling only one group as being made under "Good Working Conditions."[1]

About a quarter of the consumers were willing to pay more for the labeled items — far fewer than the 70-80 percent who tell survey takers they will pay extra.[2]

More recently, a Harvard study at ABC Carpet in New York City found that more consumers bought towels and candles promising "fair labor conditions" than similarly priced products without the label. Intriguingly, when researchers raised prices of the fair trade products 10 percent above the competition, sales rose even more. When they raised prices 20 percent, they rose higher yet.

"It was more believable that standards were higher if the price was higher," suggests Harvard political economist Michael J. Hiscox, whose team created the label, "Fair and Square," and presented it as ABC's own for the experiment. His tentative conclusion: Retailers could increase their sales and their profits by charging 10-20 percent more for fair trade-labeled goods. (Another possibility is that consumers think there's some hidden quality advantage in a higher-priced item. Hiscox is designing new experiments to tease out that question.)

But Hiscox cautions that shoppers with less money are less likely to behave like ABC's customers, who are generally "well-to-do New Yorkers with a taste for contributing to social causes."

Hiscox has become an enthusiast for fair trade labeling because he thinks it might be able to achieve what the World Trade Organization has not — better labor standards abroad. Unions and activists have lobbied for including such standards in international trade agreements, but developing countries like China and India have resisted for fear they'd lose their cheap-labor advantage in their exported goods.

So far, sports balls are the only manufactured item certified by TransFair USA, the lead fair trade labeling organization in the U.S., which focuses on paying small farmers fairly. Cotton goods are the newest product to win fair trade labeling in Britain, but the label only guarantees that a fair price is paid to cotton growers in poor countries, not to makers of the garment.

No cotton goods are certified fair trade in the U.S. because of TransFair's concerns that it can't guarantee workers' conditions all the way up the manufacturing chain — from sewers to zipper makers. "Although African cotton farmers have a compelling story, that's not where the concern is in the U.S.," says Christopher Himes, chief financial officer of TransFair. "The sweatshop issue is very important to us. We want to make that the core mission of fair trade cotton garments in the U.S. We think we will do fair trade garments eventually, but we're not there yet."

Whether factory-made goods can be included in the existing fair trade labeling scheme — and inspected and certified in a way that's credible to consumers — is "the big enchilada," Hiscox says, if fair trade goods are to become a major player in this country's retail market and ultimately affect working conditions on a large scale.

"There are a lot of consumers that would like to advance [fair labor] causes while they're shopping," he says, "but we don't know how big a [group] that is and how much they're willing to pay extra."

---

[1] The study, by Howard Kimeldorf, *et al.*, is cited in Michael Hiscox and Nicholas F.B. Smyth, "Is There Consumer Demand for Improved Labor Standards? Evidence from Field Experiments in Social Labeling."

[2] A study by Marymount University Center for Ethical Concerns found 86 percent of those surveyed in a 1999 poll said they would be willing pay $4 more for a $20 garment made under good conditions. A 1999 poll by the National Bureau of Economic Research found about 80 percent of those surveyed would be willing to pay more. See *ibid.*, p. 8.

Is fair trade the best way to help poor farmers?

YES

Charlotte Opal
Chair, Standards Committee,
Fairtrade Labelling Organizations (FLO)
Co-author, Fair Trade:
Market-driven Ethical Consumption

Written for *CQ Researcher,* May 2007

To many poor farmers in developing countries, the free market is a distant dream. There are no roads connecting their farms to market, so they are dependent on middlemen to come to their farm and buy their crops. They do not have access to price information, so they don't know how much the middlemen should be paying them. They can't take out loans to improve the quality of their products, build roads to access more buyers or switch to a more profitable crop.

Fair trade turns this reality on its head by ensuring farmers the income and organization they need to make the market work for them. In the fair trade system, small farmers are organized into cooperatives that pool their income to buy their own trucks to deliver product to the market, apply for low-interest loans or hire experts to help them diversify their crops. Individual small farmers living hand to mouth cannot access these free-market instruments — but once they are earning enough to live on and are organized into a cooperative, the benefits of a properly functioning free market are finally available to them.

Guaranteeing that the extra money consumers pay for fair trade-certified products actually goes to the farms with the best living and working conditions requires audits and inspections, some of which are paid for by companies, and some by the farmers themselves. Companies that carry the Fair Trade Certified label must pay a nominal fee for auditing to a nonprofit certifier. In the United States, this certifier is TransFair USA, and each $1 of its budget guarantees an extra $7 in income to fair trade farmers and workers — quite a strong return on a social investment.

Farms must also pay an inspection fee, although it is much lower than the fees they pay for organic, food safety and other certifications. As fair trade is the only system that guarantees farmers more money, it is no wonder that more than 1 million farming families are willing to pay for these inspections to gain access to the fair trade market.

If we believe the free market is the best way to relieve poverty for the rural poor, fair trade is the only mechanism consumers have for making sure the free market actually reaches small farmers. American families who buy coffee, tea, bananas, vanilla, and other tropical products every day want to know that their purchases are empowering, not impoverishing, farmers and workers. Fair trade certification gives them that guarantee.

NO

Philip Booth
Editorial and Program Director,
Institute of Economic Affairs,
London

Written for *CQ Researcher,* May 2007

The best way to improve the lives of the poor is to ensure that the necessary preconditions for development exist. These include good governance, a favorable business climate and free trade. These three conditions are mutually reinforcing. One of the biggest sources of corruption in developing countries is the regulation of trade. The fair trade movement in Europe has the potential to do considerable harm through its campaigning for the restoration of trade regulation in the coffee market, though its position on the regulation of the cotton trade is more sensible.

The movement should stick to its basic business principles, the application of which can help some farmers in particular conditions. Fair trade can help farmers by providing credit facilities, contracts with price guarantees and business facilities and information sharing in unsophisticated markets.

But fair trade has its downsides, too. There is considerable reliance on inefficient and unaccountable cooperative structures. The fair trade price promise is not quite what it seems to well-meaning and possibly naïve Western consumers. The various fair trade organizations do not promise to buy the farmers' produce at the price. They buy at a fixed price only what the market demands. In poor market conditions, there is a risk of "insider/outsider" markets where those who are able to sell at the price do very well at the expense of others.

Western consumers are probably also not aware that organizations charge wholesalers for the use of the fair trade label and that a huge proportion of this charge, in the U.K. at least, goes simply into marketing the brand. It is no wonder we only hear good things about fair trade! I doubt, too, that consumers know organizations charge producers to join up and that the fee is about 10 times the annual income of the average Kenyan.

Different business models have different disadvantages. There are, of course, costs and benefits of all ways of doing business, so the above points are not intrinsic criticisms of fair trade. In international development policy, we are used to important people campaigning for politicians to pull big levers. The reality is that once certain preconditions for development are in place, prosperity comes as a result of lots of people doing small things in the business economy. The fair trade organizations can help this process. But they should be modest in their economic claims and very cautious regarding their ethical claims.

Rainforest Alliance label, which also pledges good working conditions, would apply to 90 million boxes of certified bananas and 30,000 tons of certified coffee through partners including Chiquita and Kraft Foods.

But the certification project could lead to an "undermining" of fair trade standards, according to Colorado State University researchers, because the Rainforest label is focused primarily on environmental management, and brings fewer benefits to small farmers and less reliability in monitoring them than TransFair's certification.[49]

Proliferating Labels

Competition from the Rainforest Alliance and other labels pledging good working conditions poses a challenge to the fair trade movement. Some advocates worry proliferating labels could lead to consumer confusion or distrust, especially if they dilute the TransFair standards. The Rainforest label, for example, avoids Transfair's fees since the organization doesn't have to pay for such extensive monitoring, critics say.

But some proponents of alternative labels say TransFair doesn't have a moral monopoly on judging labor standards. The Organic Consumers Association has campaigned against Starbucks, charging that by buying only a small percentage of its coffee from farmers certified by TransFair, the company has not made a good-faith effort to help farmers in developing nations. According to Starbucks' annual report, 6 percent of the coffee beans it purchased in 2006, some 18 million pounds, were certified by TransFair.[50]

Cooperative Coffees, a group of 21 small coffee companies committed to selling only fair trade beans, uses a different label — the insignia of the Fair Trade Federation — to distinguish themselves from competitors that sell only a minority of fair trade coffee. "Many companies use a few token Fair Trade items as a marketing tool to give the impression of being a fair trade company," says the group on its Web site. By contrast, each of the 21 companies claims to sell 100 percent fair-traded coffee, although not all of it has been certified by FLO.[51]

"The argument of the '100 percenters' is that someone like Green Mountain Coffee Roasters takes your customer account away by offering cheaper prices. And the reason they can do that is that most of their purchases are

Fair trade bananas are grown at the Juliana Jaramillo Cooperative in the Dominican Republic. Big banana growers are permitted to take part in the fair trade scheme, but big coffee growers and other large operations currently are not included.

© 2003 Fairtrade Foundation

much cheaper coffee, because they're not paying the fair trade price on 100 percent of their products," says Organic Consumers Association National Director Ronnie Cummins. Fair trade products are about one-quarter of Green Mountain's total sales.

In an e-mail, TransFair's Himes responds that for growers, Starbucks' purchase of 18 million pounds at fair trade prices is "extremely significant." TransFair just certifies the product being sold, not the company, he stressed. "If we took the company-certification approach," he adds, "we'd have very few partners, and very few people would have heard of or been able to buy fair trade products."

Some activists also have expressed impatience with the slowness of TransFair to certify manufactured goods like organic cotton clothing, a market that is booming. TransFair has decided not to certify cotton now because it is not yet capable of ensuring no sweatshops are involved in production, according to Himes.

The Organic Consumers Association has joined some 80 groups and companies participating in the Domestic

Fair Trade Working Group, which is developing a new label that would certify products as both organic and fair trade.

"If we want consumers to be able to tell that the garment was not made in an exploitative factory, we need a label," says Cummins. "And we can't wait around for TransFair to decide it's a priority." Although TransFair encourages its growers to farm organically and guarantees a premium for organically grown products, not all of its products have government-certified organic status.

As for the proliferation of labels, some observers see it as a positive sign — that the marketplace is increasingly recognizing consumer demand for fair working conditions.

OUTLOOK

Growth Potential

How much further can the fair trade market grow? The American fair trade market is now only about one-fortieth the size of the organic market, which attracts similar consumers. If fair trade sales continue growing at their current rate, by 2012 they should match today's $15 billion-plus organic market, predicts Harvard political economist Hiscox.[52]

A major factor in determining how big the market grows will be whether large coffee farms, some owned by multinationals, will be allowed to enter the fair trade scheme. It currently bars them from FLO certification on grounds that the movement is trying to help the most disadvantaged growers. But some observers think big producers eventually will be included, as banana growers already are.

Market growth could also be held back by limited demand for fair trade products. Fair trade cocoa producers in Ghana, for example, could sell only 8 percent of their crop to fair trade, and fair trade coffee producers in Tanzania sold only 10 percent, one study found.[53]

By emphasizing high-quality products, however, the market will have a better chance of attracting new consumers, some observers believe. Fair trade-certified coffee is now the fastest-growing segment of the $11 billion U.S. specialty coffee market.[54] Yet as small farmers grow savvier about the market, they may take different avenues

to capturing more of the final retail value of their gourmet coffees and chocolates.

Ugandan coffee farmer Magona says his cooperative would like to capture more of the profit margin taken by wholesalers and retailers for his prized high-altitude Mt. Elgon coffee — by processing the beans in Uganda instead of abroad. The Ethiopian government, meanwhile, has been trying to obtain trademark status from the U.S. Patent Office for three specialty coffees, an alternative approach that would allow Ethiopian farmers to keep more of the profit margin now charged by Starbucks, says Oxfam's Rusu.

But trade barriers blocking the importation of processed goods, opposition by established companies in consuming countries and the practical difficulties of developing a new industry in a poor country could hinder those kinds of efforts. If fair trade makes consumers more aware of trading inequities between countries, it might increase pressure for more equitable trading agreements, removing barriers to growers' efforts to do more of the processing and branding themselves.

As fair trade grows, another challenge for certifying organizations will be keeping up with the need to monitor more farms. Reports last year in Peru of some farmers selling non-fair-trade beans at fair trade prices might be a sign of the movement's growing pains.[55]

If fair trade is to make a major dent in the consumer market, some observers say, it will have to start including manufactured products, like cotton clothing, as Britain has already done. But experts inside and outside the movement agree it will be much harder to monitor sweatshops in the apparel industry, which often employs numerous subcontractors in a variety of countries before finishing a garment.

As savvy growers learn more about the value of their products, they may be lured into selling to high-end companies that aren't necessarily part of the fair trade system.

Would that necessarily be a bad thing? It might be if those companies abandoned growers during cycles of excess supply and plummeting prices — just the time fair trade helps them most.

On the other hand, some advocates say, the ultimate goal for the fair trade movement is to put itself out of business: When all products become fairly traded.

NOTES

1. In Britain, the label promoted by the lead certifying organization, The Fairtrade Foundation, spells the term as one word. In the United States the equivalent label, with a black-and-white symbol, approved by TransFair, is two words: "fair trade."

2. Fairtrade Foundation press release, "Boost for Farmers," Feb. 26, 2007; www.fairtrade.org.uk.

3. *Ibid.* The full range of Fairtrade products is: coffee, tea, chocolate, cocoa, sugar, bananas, pineapples, mangoes, oranges, satsumas, clementines, lemons, avocados, lychees, grapes, apples, pears, plums, fruit juices, smoothies, quinoa, peppers, green beans, coconuts, dried fruit (apricots, mango, raisins, dates), herbal teas, rooibos tea, green tea, ice-cream, cakes, biscuits, honey, muesli, cereal bars, jams, chutney, sauces, herbs, spices (vanilla pods, cinnamon sticks, ground ginger, ground turmeric, black pepper, cloves, nutmeg), nuts (brazils, cashews, peanuts), nut oil, wine, beer, rum, rice, yoghurt, baby food, flowers, sports balls, sugar body scrub, cotton wool and other cotton products.

4. Michael J. Hiscox, "Fair Trade as an Approach to Managing Globalization," memo prepared for the Conference on Europe and the Management of Globalization, Princeton University, Feb. 23, 2007, p. 7. Between 2001 and 2005, the average annual growth rate was around 50 percent; between 2005 and 2006 the market grew by over 60 percent.

5. More than 50 percent of adults in the U.K. recognize the Fairtrade mark. See Elisa Arond, "The Fairtrade Towns Initiative: Lessons From Across the Ocean," Oxfam America, May 2006, p. 40. Twenty percent in the U.S. recognized the Fair Trade Certified label in 2006. See Transfair USA, *Fair Trade Almanac*, 1998-2006, p. 18.

6. Sam Kornell, "The Pros and Cons of Fair Trade Coffee: Bean Counting," *Santa Barbara Independent*, April 5, 2007.

7. Hal Weitzman, "The Bitter Cost of 'Fair Trade' Coffee," *Financial Times*, Sept. 8, 2006; www.ft.com.

8. This is the world price for Arabica, the type of beans TransFair USA imports to the United States. The $1.21 fair trade floor price is for Arabica.

9. Douglas L. Murray, *et al.*, "The Future of Fair Trade Coffee: Dilemmas Facing Latin America's Small-Scale Producers," *Development in Practice*, April 2006, pp. 179-192.

10. TransFair USA, *op. cit.*, pp. 4, 7.

11. Murray, *et al.*, *op. cit.*, p. 182.

12. Tim Harford, *The Undercover Economist* (2007), pp. 33-34. At the end of 2004, following Harford's questioning, Costa began to offer fair trade coffee for no extra cost. The 40 British pence additional cost reported by Harford has been converted to U.S. currency using current exchange rates.

13. Hiscox, *op. cit.*, p. 5.

14. Harford, *op. cit.*, p. 33.

15. "Good Food? Ethical Food," *The Economist*, Dec. 9, 2006.

16. "Special Report: Voting with Your Trolley-Food Politics," *The Economist*, Dec. 9, 2006.

17. In 2006, fair trade coffee accounted for 3.31 percent of all coffee sold in the United States. See TransFair USA, *op. cit.*, p. 15.

18. Philip Booth and Linda Whetstone, "Half a Cheer for Fair Trade," *Economic Affairs* (forthcoming) June 2007.

19. Murray, *et al.*, *op. cit.*, p. 188.

20. Harford, *op. cit.*, p. 232.

21. "Good Food? Ethical Food," *op. cit.*

22. Joseph E. Stiglitz and Andrew Charlton, *Fair Trade for All: How Trade Can Promote Development* (2005), p. 12.

23. Joseph Stiglitz and Andrew Charlton, "The Way to Help Ourselves by Helping Others," *Daily Telegraph* (London), Dec. 12, 2005, p. 8. The estimate of $60 billion for Africa is an approximate equivalent of the 30 billion British pounds cited in this article. For background see Peter Katel, "Ending Poverty," *CQ Researcher*, Sept. 9, 2005, pp. 733-760.

24. Hiscox, *op. cit.*, p. 10. Hiscox cites economist Dani Rodrik.

25. Stiglitz and Charlton, *op. cit.*, Dec. 12, 2003, p. 6.

26. Michael J. Hiscox and Nicholas F.B. Smyth, "Is there Consumer Demand for Improved Labor Standards?

Evidence from Field Experiments in Social Labeling," (unpublished paper), p. 2.

27. Alex Nicholls and Charlotte Opal, *Fair Trade: Market-Driven Ethical Consumption* (2005), p. 21.

28. Hiscox, *op. cit.*, p. 8.

29. See www.fairtrade.net.

30. Hiscox, *op. cit.*, p. 4.

31. Murray, *et al.*, *op. cit.*, p 181.

32. Hiscox, *op. cit.*, p. 8. Total U.S. retail sales figures for 2006 were not available at press time, but according to TransFair, total U.S. fair trade coffee sales reached $730 million in 2006.

33. Hiscox, *op. cit.*, p. 8.

34. *Ibid.*

35. *Ibid.*

36. TransFair USA, *op. cit.*, p. 18. Statistics are from National Coffee Association.

37. Nicholls and Opal, *op. cit.*, p. 17.

38. *Ibid.*, p. 18.

39. Stiglitz and Charlton, *Fair Trade for All*, *op. cit.*, p. 13.

40. *Ibid.*, p. 4.

41. Nicholls and Opal, *op. cit.*, p. 22.

42. For background, see Brian Hansen, "Globalization Backlash," *CQ Researcher*, Sept. 28, 2001, pp. 761-784.

43. Nicholls and Opal, *op. cit.*, p. 22.

44. *Ibid.*, pp. 26-28.

45. Philip Riedel, *et al.*, "Impacts of Fair Trade," Trade and Market Linkages; Proceedings of the 18th International Symposium of the International Farming Symposium, Oct. 31-Nov. 3, 2005, p. 15; www.fao.org/farmingsystems/pdf/IFSA/Theme2_Trade_and_Markets.pdf.

46. Nicholls and Opal, *op. cit.*, p. 30.

47. Hiscox, *op. cit.*, p. 9.

48. *Ibid.*

49. Murray, *et al.*, *op. cit.*, p. 187.

50. Starbucks Corporation, "Social Responsibility-Fiscal 2006 Annual Report," p. 4; www.starbucks.com/aboutus/csrannualreport.pdf.

51. See "Frequently Asked Questions," www.coopcoffees.com.

52. Hiscox, *op. cit.*, p. 7.

53. Riedal, *et al.*, *op. cit.*, p. 7.

54. Fair trade-certified coffee grew an average of nearly 80 percent every year since 1999, according to TransFair.

55. Weitzman, *op. cit.*

BIBLIOGRAPHY

Books

Harford, Tim, *The Undercover Economist*, Abacus, 2006.
Financial Times columnist Harford downplays benefits of fair trade and says only a small fraction of the extra price consumers pay for fair trade coffee reaches small farmers.

Nicholls, Alex, and Charlotte Opal, *Fair Trade: Market-Driven Ethical Consumption*, Sage Publications, 2005.
Two fair trade advocates take a comprehensive look at fair trade's history, inner workings and impact on the market.

Raynolds, Laura, *et al.*, *Fair Trade: The Challenges of Transforming Globalization*, Routledge, 2007.
Researchers from Colorado State University explore the rapid growth of fair trade and future challenges, emphasizing the tensions of a movement working both in and against the market.

Stiglitz, Joseph E., and Andrew Charlton, *Fair Trade for All: How Trade Can Promote Development*, Oxford University Press, 2005.
Nobel Prize-winning economist Stiglitz and Charlton, a scholar at the London School of Economics, trace how international trade rules have disadvantaged poor countries and lay out their program for fairer trade rules.

Articles

"Good Food? Ethical Food," *The Economist*, Dec. 9, 2006.

A widely cited editorial charges the fair trade system could depress prices and leave farmers worse off by encouraging them to grow too much coffee and other crops.

"Voting with Your Trolley-Food Politics," *The Economist*, Dec. 9, 2006.
A special report lays out economists' arguments against fair trade.

Baggini, Julian, "Free Doesn't Mean Unfair," *The Guardian* (London), March 5, 2007, p. 9.
This editorial response by the editor of *Philosophers' Magazine* to *The Economist's* criticism of fair trade (see above) argues that "fair trade is a triumph of the free market."

Booth, Philip, and Linda Whetstone, "Half a Cheer for Fair Trade," *Economic Affairs* (forthcoming, June); www.iea.org.uk.
The authors criticize fair trade from a free-market and moral perspective; Booth is editorial and program director at the Institute of Economic Affairs, a conservative London think tank.

Hiscox, Michael J., and Nicholas F.B. Smyth, "Is there Consumer Demand for Improved Labor Standards? Evidence from Field Experiments in Social Labeling"; www.people.fas.harvard.edu/%7Ehiscox/papers.html.
Harvard political economist Hiscox finds sales rise when prices of fair trade goods go up.

Ickle, Louise, "Graduate: Fairtrade for Fashionistas," *The Guardian* (London), March 3, 2007, p. 28.
Fair trade cotton clothing, which is certified in Britain, has attracted major department stores as buyers.

Murray, Douglas L., Laura T. Raynolds and Peter L. Taylor, "The Future of Fair Trade Coffee: Dilemmas Facing Latin America's Small-Scale Producers," *Development in Practice*, April 2006, pp. 179-192; www.colostate.edu/Depts/Sociology/cfats/research .html.
After two years of researching Mexican and Central American farmers growing coffee for the fair trade market, Colorado State University sociologists lay out the challenges they see for future successful growth of the fair trade movement.

Taylor, Jerome, "Café Society: The Rise of Consumers with a Conscience," *The Independent*, Feb. 12, 2007; www.independent.co.uk.
A journalist reports on how fair trade has changed the lives of Nicaraguan coffee farmers.

Weitzman, Hal, "The Bitter Cost of 'Fair Trade' Coffee," *Financial Times*, Sept. 8, 2006; www.ft.com.
A reporter finds fair trade farms in Peru paying below minimum wage and coffee beans falsely sold as fair trade. A response by the Fairtrade Foundation is at www.fairtrade .org.uk.

Reports and Studies

Arond, Elisa, "The Fairtrade Towns Initiative: Lessons from Across the Ocean," *Oxfam America*, May 2006.
A report looks at the British fair trade towns movement, its role in raising awareness of fair trade and how it might be duplicated in the United States.

Quigley, Maureen, and Charlotte Opal, "Fair Trade Garment Standards: Feasibility Study," prepared for *TransFair USA*, July 2006; www.transfairusa.org/pdfs/ FT%20Garment%20Standards%20Feasibility%20 Study.pdf.
The authors conclude the complexity of the garment-supply chain means "much more work needs to be done" to decide if a stringent fair trade garment standard is feasible to develop in the United States.

***TransFair USA*, "TransFair Almanac 1998-2006"; www.transfairusa.org/pdfs/2007FairTradeAlmanac .pdf.**
The lead fair trade-labeling group in the United States presents the latest statistics about the fair trade market.

For More Information

Center for Fair and Alternative Trade Studies, Department of Sociology, Colorado State University, B258 Clark Building, Fort Collins, CO 80523-1784; (970) 491-6044; www.colostate.edu/Depts/Sociology/cfats/index.html. A research group at Colorado State University that studies fair trade.

Cooperative Coffees, 302 W. Lamar St., Suite C, Americus, GA 31709; (229) 924-3035; http://coopcoffees.com. A group of 20 small U.S. and Canadian coffee roasters committed to selling 100 percent of their coffee fair trade.

Fairtrade Foundation, Room 204, 16 Baldwin's Gardens, London EC1N 7RJ, United Kingdom; +44-(0)20-7405-5942; www.fairtrade.org.uk. The leading labeler of fair trade goods in the United Kingdom.

Fairtrade Labelling Organizations International, Bonner Talweg 177, 53129 Bonn, Germany; +49-228-949230; www.fairtrade.net. FLO is an umbrella organization for 20 fair trade-labeling organizations around the world that sets prices and monitors transactions for fair trade-certified products.

Institute of Economic Affairs, 2 Lord North St., Westminster, London SW1P 3LB, United Kingdom; +44-(0)20 7799 8900; www.iea.org.uk. A free-market think tank that has been critical of the fair trade movement.

Organic Consumers Association, 6771 South Silver Hill Dr., Finland, MN 55603; (218) 226-4164; www.organic-consumers.org. A consumer association that has been critical of Starbucks' level of commitment to fair trade coffee.

Starbucks, 2401 Utah Ave. South, S-NV1, Seattle, WA 98134; 1-800-235-2883; www.starbucks.com. Perhaps the largest purchaser of fair trade coffee, although it has been criticized for its level of commitment.

TransFair USA, 1500 Broadway Ave., Suite 400, Oakland, CA 94612; (510) 663-5260; www.transfairusa.org. The lead labeling group in the United States for fair trade goods certified by FLO (see above).

Actor Brad Pitt is spearheading the construction of 150 "affordable and sustainable" homes in hurricane-battered New Orleans. Activists say the key to protecting the environment is "buying green" — choosing products designed to reduce pollution and waste. Consumer spending accounts for about two-thirds of the $14 trillion U.S. gross domestic product, making eco-consumerism a potentially powerful influence on policy and the economy.

AP Photo/Alex Brandon

From *CQ Researcher*, February 29, 2008.

8

Buying Green

Does It Really Help the Environment?

Jennifer Weeks

During Lent, many Christians commemorate the time that Jesus spent fasting and praying in the desert, according to the Bible, before taking up his ministry. Most churchgoers mark Lent by giving up alcohol, red meat or other luxuries. But this year two prominent British bishops called on the faithful to sacrifice something else: carbon emissions. Through steps such as insulating hot-water heaters, sealing drafts in their houses and changing to energy-efficient light bulbs, the church leaders urged observers to reduce their carbon footprints — the greenhouse gases (GHGs) emitted from human activities that contribute to global climate change. "We all have a pivotal role to play in tackling the stark reality of climate change," said Richard Chartres, Bishop of London. "Together we have a responsibility to God, to future generations and to our own well-being on this earth to take action."[1]

Although they may not cast the issue in religious terms, Americans are increasingly willing to take personal action to protect the environment. And while conservation has long been associated with sacrifices, such as driving smaller cars and turning down the heat, today some advocates argue that a comfortable lifestyle can be eco-friendly. The key, they say, is "buying green" — choosing products designed to reduce pollution, waste and other harmful impacts.

Activists have long recognized that consumer spending, which accounts for about two-thirds of the $14 trillion U.S. gross domestic product, can be a powerful influence on national policy. Consumer campaigns often stigmatize a product to highlight suppliers' unacceptable behavior. For example, civil rights activists in the 1950s and '60s boycotted segregated buses in Montgomery, Ala., and held sit-ins at lunch counters that refused to serve African-Americans.

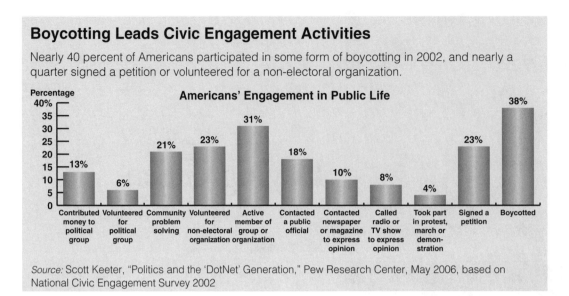

Boycotting Leads Civic Engagement Activities

Nearly 40 percent of Americans participated in some form of boycotting in 2002, and nearly a quarter signed a petition or volunteered for a non-electoral organization.

Americans' Engagement in Public Life

Percentage

	Percentage
Contributed money to political group	13%
Volunteered for political group	6%
Community problem solving	21%
Volunteered for non-electoral organization	23%
Active member of group or organization	31%
Contacted a public official	18%
Contacted newspaper or magazine to express opinion	10%
Called radio or TV show to express opinion	8%
Took part in protest, march or demonstration	4%
Signed a petition	23%
Boycotted	38%

Source: Scott Keeter, "Politics and the 'DotNet' Generation," Pew Research Center, May 2006, based on National Civic Engagement Survey 2002

Both strategies drew national attention to segregation in the South and built support for new civil rights laws.

Consumers can also reward positive behavior with their dollars. In the 1970s, the garment workers' union urged Americans to "Look for the union label" that identified clothing made in the United States instead of choosing products from low-wage foreign sources. Today eco-conscious shoppers are buying organically grown food, fuel-efficient cars and shares in socially responsible investment funds that target companies with strong environmental records.

According to the annual Green Brands Survey, U.S. consumers will spend about $500 billion on environmentally friendly products and services in 2008, double last year's amount.[2] A typical American family spends roughly $50,000 each year on food, clothing, shelter, transportation, health care, entertainment and other items.[3] (*See graph, p. 169.*) And consumers frequently use buying power to communicate their opinions: Boycotting or "buycotting" (deliberately choosing) products for political or ethical reasons are among the most common ways in which Americans express political views.[4] (*See graph, above.*)

"The consumer movement has quietly become part of the fabric of American society," says Caroline Heldman, an assistant professor of politics at Occidental College in Los Angeles and author of a forthcoming book on consumer activism. "Environmental concerns are the most important motives that drive people to engage

in consumer activism, and with concern about global warming so high, the public is primed to act if environmental groups can find tangible things for people to do."

However, not all green products deliver on their promises. Since it first issued guidelines for environmental marketing in 1990, the Federal Trade Commission (FTC) has acted against 37 companies for misleading consumers with green claims.[5] A recent survey by TerraChoice, an environmental marketing firm, suggests that "greenwashing" — making misleading environmental claims about a company or product — is becoming more pervasive as companies bring new green products to market. In a review of 1,108 consumer products that made environmental claims, TerraChoice found that all but one provided some form of false or misleading information. (*See sidebar, p. 177.*)

"Green labeling today is where auto-safety information was in the 1950s. Standards and certification programs are still emerging," says TerraChoice Vice President Scot Case. "This is unexplored territory, so marketers may be stretching the truth unintentionally. We think that the sudden interest in green just caught a lot of people off guard, and marketers were busy slapping buzzwords on packaging. But FTC's guidelines are clearly 15 to 20 years out of date."

Many issues are spurring interest in green products. In 2007 the Intergovernmental Panel on Climate Change, an international scientific association created to advise national governments, called global warming unequivocal and concluded with at least 90 percent certainty that human activities since 1750 had warmed the planet.[6] Repeated warnings about climate change are prompting many companies and individuals to shrink their carbon footprints. New products like renewable energy certificates and carbon offsets, which allow buyers to pay for green actions that happen elsewhere, make this task easier. (*See glossary, p. 171.*) But critics say that these commodities are feel-good gestures and do not always promote new, clean technologies.

Recent cases of contaminated food and toxic ingredients in common household products like pet food and toothpaste also are spurring consumers to seek out green alternatives.[7] Green consumption is a logical response to environmental threats, but Andrew Szasz, a sociologist at the University of California, Santa Cruz, believes that it could actually threaten environmental progress if consumers see it as a substitute for political action.

"A lot of people get environmentally conscious enough to get worried. Then they go buy everything green that they can afford and move on to something else," says Szasz, who calls the trend an example of "inverted quarantine" — citizens protecting themselves from danger by building barriers instead of organizing to reduce the threat. "Pressure from social movements to take toxic substances out of our water and air will create more progress than individual consumer actions," he argues.

Eco-consumption mirrors a similar trend in the business sector. Many U.S. companies are working to green their operations, both to appeal to the fast-growing market and because leaders are finding that environmental strategies can help cut costs and make their operations more efficient.[8] Many large corporations that have clashed with environmentalists in the past, such as DuPont, Monsanto and Waste Management, Inc., now highlight their commitments to environmental stewardship and sustainability.[9]

Average Household Spends Nearly $50,000

The average household spent $48,398 in 2006, including more than one-third on housing and 18 percent on transportation. According to a recent survey, U.S. consumers will spend about $500 billion on environmentally friendly products and services in 2008, double last year's amount.

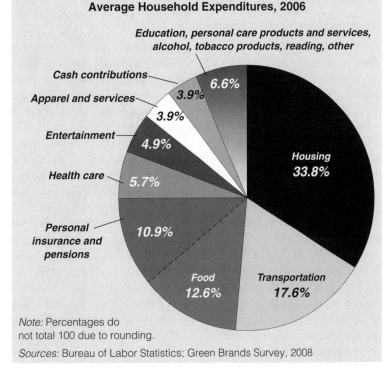

Average Household Expenditures, 2006

Education, personal care products and services, alcohol, tobacco products, reading, other — 6.6%
Cash contributions — 3.9%
Apparel and services — 3.9%
Entertainment — 4.9%
Health care — 5.7%
Personal insurance and pensions — 10.9%
Food — 12.6%
Transportation — 17.6%
Housing — 33.8%

Note: Percentages do not total 100 due to rounding.

Sources: Bureau of Labor Statistics; Green Brands Survey, 2008

In a notable sign of corporate greening, the U.S. Climate Action Partnership (a coalition including Alcoa, General Electric, Shell and Xerox) called in early 2007 for prompt mandatory limits to slow and reverse the growth of GHG emissions. Many large companies have opposed mandatory GHG limits in the past, arguing that putting a price on carbon emissions would drive up energy costs.[10] However, U.S.-CAP members contended that addressing climate change "will create more economic opportunities than risks for the U.S. economy."[11]

Corporate greening appears to be widespread but hard to measure because there is no authoritative definition of a green business. A recent report by Greener World Media found that green businesses are making progress toward some milestones, such as disclosing their carbon emissions and investing in new clean technologies. It also judged, however, that corporate America is treading water or falling behind on other targets, such as using more renewable energy and emitting fewer GHGs per unit of economic activity. "Green business has shifted from a movement to a market. But there is much, much more to do," the authors asserted.[12]

As environmentalists, business executives and consumers ponder what buying green can accomplish, here are some issues they are considering:

Do carbon offsets slow climate change?

Curbing climate change is difficult because greenhouse gases, especially carbon dioxide (CO_2), are produced from many routine activities like powering appliances and driving cars. Every year the average American generates roughly 10 to 20 metric tons of CO_2 through day-to-day activities, mainly through home energy use and transportation.[13]

Consumers can shrink their carbon footprints through steps such as adding insulation to their houses, buying more energy-efficient appliances and using public transit for some trips instead of cars. But if people want to do more, or have carbon-intensive lifestyles because they own large homes or travel frequently, they can buy carbon offsets from brokers, who use the money to fund projects elsewhere that reduce GHG emissions. Pollution offsets date back to the mid-1970s, when the Environmental Protection Agency (EPA) allowed industries to build new emission sources in regions with serious air pollution if they made larger reductions at existing sources nearby. This policy was written into the Clean Air Act in 1977 and later expanded to let companies earn and trade emission-reduction credits if they cut emissions below thresholds required by law.

"Offsets have an important role to play as we try to shrink our carbon footprint," says Mike Burnett, executive director of the Climate Trust, an Oregon nonprofit created to implement a 1997 state law that requires new power plants to offset some CO_2 emissions. The trust invests money from power plants, as well as businesses and individuals, in energy efficiency, renewable energy and other low-carbon projects to offset clients' emissions. "Oregon has pledged to reduce its GHG emissions 75 percent below 1990 levels by 2050. Investing in high-quality offsets can help us address climate change at the lowest overall cost, which will leave more money for other priorities," says Burnett.

The Climate Trust uses strict criteria to screen potential investments. Emission reductions must be rigorously quantified, and sponsors have to show that offset projects would not happen without funding from the trust — a concept called "additionality" to indicate that resulting GHG reductions must be additional to business as usual. For example, although installing underground systems at landfills to capture methane (a potent greenhouse gas produced when waste decomposes) is a popular type of offset, the trust would not invest in a methane-capture project if regulations already required the landfill operator to control methane emissions.

Not all providers are as strict. A 2006 study commissioned by Clean Air-Cool Planet (CACP), a New England nonprofit group, found that the market for voluntary carbon offsets was largely unregulated and had no broadly accepted standards for defining or measuring offsets. Prices to offset a ton of carbon varied widely, as did the types of offsets available and the amount of information companies provided to customers.[14]

"There clearly are good offsets and not-so-good ones on the market, so the problem for buyers is finding the good ones," says CACP Chief Executive Officer Adam Markham. "If they don't buy good ones, they're not making a difference, and they're wasting their money."

A popular strategy that has raised questions is paying to plant trees. Growing plants absorb CO_2 from the atmosphere to make plant tissue, and trees also offer many other benefits, such as stabilizing soils and providing habitat for animals and birds. Movie stars Brad Pitt and Jake Gyllenhaal, along with Home Depot, Delta Airlines and other corporations, have funded tree-planting projects from suburban Atlanta to Bhutan.

But trees don't always help the environment. Planting non-native species can soak up local water supplies and replace other valuable ecosystems such as prairie grassland. Moreover, calculating how much carbon various types of forests take up is an inexact science. And since trees eventually release carbon when they die and decompose (or are logged or burned down), they cycle carbon quickly and only remove it from the atmosphere for a matter of decades. In contrast, today's oil, coal and natural gas supplies represent much more permanent carbon reserves that formed when carbon-based plant materials were compressed in ancient, underground fossil beds. Burning these fossil fuels permanently releases carbon stores that have been sequestered for thousands of years and will not be recreated in the foreseeable future.[15]

"Forest offsets tend to be more risky because we know less about how much carbon they displace than we do

A 21st-Century Carbon Glossary

The pollutant plays a key role in today's environmental efforts.

Carbon footprint — The sum of all greenhouse gas (GHG) emissions caused during a specified time period by a person's activities, a company's operations or the production, use and disposal of a product.

Carbon neutral — Operating in a way that does not produce any net addition of GHGs to the atmosphere. For both businesses and individuals, becoming carbon neutral typically involves two steps: reducing GHG emissions that they generate directly, through steps such as conserving energy; and buying carbon offsets that equal whatever direct GHG emissions they cannot eliminate.

Carbon offset — An activity that reduces GHG emissions, such as planting trees to take up atmospheric carbon dioxide or producing energy from carbon-free fuels like wind and solar energy. Buying carbon offsets is a way of contracting out GHG emission reductions, typically because the offset project can reduce emissions more cheaply than the buyer can.

Carbon trading — Buying and selling GHG emission allowances (government permits to release a specific quantity of pollution) or emission-reduction credits, which may be issued by government under mandatory regulations or created by companies and individuals through voluntary trading schemes.

Greenhouse gases (GHGs) — Heat-trapping gases that absorb solar energy in the atmosphere and warm earth's surface. Six major GHGs are controlled under the Kyoto Protocol, but since carbon dioxide (CO_2) is the most abundant and causes the most warming, companies and governments convert their total emissions into CO_2 equivalents.

Renewable energy certificates (RECs) — Certificates that represent the environmental attributes of electricity produced from renewable sources and can be sold separately from the electricity itself. Investors can buy RECs to support green energy whether or not they are located close to the source. Some companies may market themselves as "powered by green energy," even though they use electricity from coal- or gas-fired power plants, because they buy RECs to equal their total electric power usage (thus helping to put that amount of carbon-free energy into the electric power grid).

---

for energy projects, and they're less likely to be permanent," says Markham. Instead, he prefers energy projects because it's easier to quantify the emissions that they displace and demonstrate additionality. "Wind power and methane-capture projects tend to be pretty high-quality investments," Markham says.

But nothing is guaranteed. After the for-profit broker TerraPass provided offsets to help green the 2007 Academy Awards ceremony, an investigation by *Business Week* magazine found that six projects that generated TerraPass offsets would have taken place in any case. One, a methane-capture system installed by Waste Management, Inc. at an Arkansas landfill, was initiated in response to pressure from state regulators. TerraPass's investment was "just icing on the cake" for another project, a county official in North Carolina told *Business Week*.[16]

"There are a lot of new entrants into the market, so some offerings probably aren't as robust as others, and it's causing some confusion," says Burnett. "If this sector doesn't become more standardized within the next five years, government will have to step in. We don't necessarily need a single federal scheme, but it would be very useful to have a federally sanctioned panel of experts who could review offset products."

Beyond the characteristics of specific projects, some critics argue that carbon offsets don't reduce climate change because they let people keep doing high-carbon activities, which the offsets counterbalance at best. Worse, offsets may serve as cover for carbon-intensive activities. For example, a recent report from the Transnational Institute in Amsterdam, the Netherlands, points out that British Airways offers passengers an option to buy carbon offsets for their flights but is also pushing to expand British airports and short-haul flights, which will increase the company's total GHG emissions.[17]

"Offsets may be tarnished by revelations of practices that aren't credible. That would be a problem, because these tools can be quite useful if they're applied effectively," says Thomas Tietenberg, a professor of economics at Colby College in Waterville, Maine. "The consumer offset market is facing an important moment in terms of its credibility. It needs to get some agreement about what the standards are."

Should government require green purchases?

Government officials often want to boost demand for green products, even if they cost somewhat more, because these goods reduce pollution, conserve energy or keep waste out of landfills. One option is to mandate the use of green goods and services. But critics argue that government interference distorts markets and that setting environmental performance standards may deliver inferior products.

Renewable energy is perhaps the most widely mandated green commodity. As of January 2008, 26 states and the District of Columbia had adopted renewable portfolio standards (RPSs) requiring electricity suppliers to generate certain fractions of their power from renewable fuels like wind, solar energy and biomass.[18] Advocates would like to see a national renewable-energy requirement, but so far Congress has failed to enact one.

Most recently, in 2007 the House passed an energy bill that included a 15 percent RPS requirement by 2020, with utilities allowed to meet up to 4 percent of their targets through energy conservation. Supporters argued that the measure would reduce air pollutants and greenhouse gas emissions from fossil fuel combustion and spur the growth of a domestic renewable-energy industry. But the provision was dropped after critics charged that it would raise electricity prices and penalize regions with fewer renewable resources. (See "At Issue," p. 183.)

"The market should be allowed to work things out. We don't support having the government impose a mandate that says, "Thou shalt do this," says Keith McCoy, vice president for energy and resources policy at the National Association of Manufacturers. "Utilities and regulators in RPS states are looking at the right fuel mixes for their regions, but we need to take into account what's possible in different parts of the country."

RPS advocates want a national standard to push states that have been less aggressive in developing renewable energy. A national RPS "is absolutely achievable," said Rep. Tom Udall, D-N.M., a sponsor of the measure, during House debate. "[B]ut the full potential for renewable electricity will be left unrealized without the adoption of a federal program to enhance the efforts of these states."[19]

Governments can also ensure that products are at least somewhat green by establishing content or performance requirements. Measures such as building codes and energy-efficiency standards for appliances are one way to remedy a common problem: Many buyers don't know much about products, so it's hard to choose the best even if they want to. "If you're walking around a house looking at it, you have no idea what kind of insulation is in the walls or how efficient the heating system is, but building codes set some basic thresholds for performance," says Colby College economist Tietenberg.

Forcing manufacturers to comply with new standards may spur technical advances, but it can also challenge businesses to meet the new goals. When new energy-efficiency standards for top-loading washing machines went into effect in 2007, *Consumer Reports* gave low performance ratings to the first models that it tested. The Competitive Enterprise Institute (CEI), a think tank that opposes excessive regulation, accused the Energy Department of ruining a once-dependable home appliance. "Send your underwear to the undersecretary," CEI urged dissatisfied consumers.[20]

"If these technologies really are that good, we shouldn't need laws to force them down people's throats," says CEI General Counsel Sam Kazman. "We don't think that promoting energy efficiency is an appropriate role for government, but if that's the goal, the way to do it is with an energy tax, which would reduce energy use and create incentives to develop energy-saving technologies. One big attraction of regulations is that the public doesn't see them as tax increases — people perceive them as relatively cost-free."

Today, however, those energy-efficient washers look better. "What a difference a year makes," *Consumer Reports* commented in February 2008. The best high-efficiency top-loading washers were performing better, testers found, and *CR* pointed out that high-efficiency models could end up costing the same or less than standard machines over their lifetime when energy savings were factored in.[21]

Posing the issue as a choice between a free market or regulations is misleading, says Bill Prindle, deputy director of the American Council for an Energy-Efficient Economy (ACEEE). "The real issue is what the rules should be for market players. When you set boundaries and targets, manufacturers come up with very ingenious solutions that give customers great value," Prindle contends. He also notes that manufacturers and conservation advocates have negotiated some two dozen energy-efficiency standards since 2005 that subsequently were enacted into law. "These are largely consensus-based agreements. They wouldn't have passed otherwise," Prindle argues.

Another way to promote green technologies is through voluntary labeling programs that identify environmentally preferable products. The Energy Star program, administered by EPA and the Department of Energy, was launched in 1992 in response to a Clean Air Act provision directing EPA to find non-regulatory strategies for reducing air pollution. Energy Star defines superior energy efficiency standards for more than 50 types of residential, commercial and industrial equipment, including consumer electronics, heating and cooling systems and lighting.[22] EPA estimates that over 2 billion products with Energy Star labels were sold in 2006, saving 170 billion kilowatt-hours of electricity, or enough to power more than 15 million average American households for a year.[23]

Another program, Leadership in Energy and Environmental Design (LEED), was developed by the U.S. Green Building Council to identify highly energy-efficient buildings with extremely healthy indoor environments.[24] More than 800 buildings in the U.S. and worldwide have received LEED certification by scoring points on a fixed scale for features like energy and water conservation and indoor air quality. Many large corporations and universities have built LEED buildings to demonstrate environmental commitments.

Labeling programs complement requirements to use green products, says Tietenberg. "Mandates make sense as a floor, but you don't want to stop there. Labels like LEED provide something that performs above the minimum," he says. "They let buyers know that they are

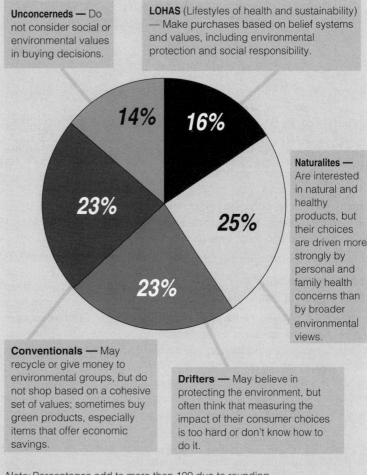

Some Buyers Are Greener Than Others

A 2006 study by the Natural Marketing Institute classified adult U.S. consumers into five categories based on their attitudes toward ethical consumption.

Unconcerneds — Do not consider social or environmental values in buying decisions.

LOHAS (Lifestyles of health and sustainability) — Make purchases based on belief systems and values, including environmental protection and social responsibility.

14%   16%   25%   23%   23%

Naturalites — Are interested in natural and healthy products, but their choices are driven more strongly by personal and family health concerns than by broader environmental views.

Conventionals — May recycle or give money to environmental groups, but do not shop based on a cohesive set of values; sometimes buy green products, especially items that offer economic savings.

Drifters — May believe in protecting the environment, but often think that measuring the impact of their consumer choices is too hard or don't know how to do it.

Note: Percentages add to more than 100 due to rounding.

Source: LOHAS Forum, "Understanding the LOHAS Consumer: The Rise of Ethical Consumerism," www.lohas.com

getting a certain value for their investment and communicate that fact to other people."

CEI's Kazman argues that green labeling programs can also be problematic. "Consumers don't get the full story if labels omit repair issues and the risk that very new technologies will have problems," he says. "And

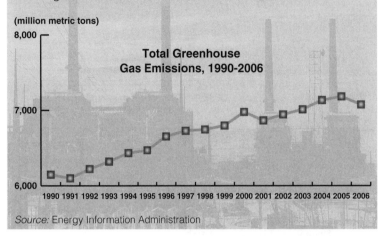

GHG Emissions Still Rising

Greenhouse gas emissions have risen by 15 percent since 1990, reaching over 7 billion metric tons in 2006.

Total Greenhouse Gas Emissions, 1990-2006

(million metric tons)

Source: Energy Information Administration

to sustain it," said entrepreneur and satellite radio host Josh Dorfman, the self-styled "Lazy Environmentalist," in a 2007 interview. "As a nation, we don't really want to deal with [global warming]. We have neither the political leadership nor the political will, which is why I think that for now the environmental solutions presented have to be both effective and painless."[25]

This is a new perspective for the environmental movement, which has long argued that rampant economic growth and high consumption are root causes of environmental harm. Not all environmentalists agree that so-called checkbook environmentalism can save the planet. For one thing, critics argue, the green product boom has had little impact so far on U.S. greenhouse gas emissions. Since 1990 the emissions intensity of the U.S. economy (the amount of GHG emissions produced for every dollar of economic activity) has declined, but total GHG emissions have increased nearly every year due to overall economic growth. (*See graph, at left.*)

"True, as companies and countries get richer they can afford more efficient machinery that makes better use of fossil fuel, like the hybrid Honda Civic I drive," writes bestselling author Bill McKibben. "But if your appliances have gotten more efficient, there are also far more of them: The furnace is better than it used to be, but the average size of the house it heats has doubled since 1950. The 60-inch TV? The always-on cable modem? No need for you to do the math — the electric company does it for you, every month."[26]

Complicating the issue, many green living guides fail to distinguish between actions that have a major impact, like insulating your house, and those with smaller effects such as buying a natural-fiber shower curtain or dog leash. "People tend not to sort through which choices are important and which are insignificant. They view most actions as equally important," says Warren Leon, coauthor of *The Consumer's Guide to Effective Environmental Choices* and director of the Massachusetts Renewable Energy Trust.[27] (*See sidebar, p. 179.*) "I worry about products that are sold as green, often by promoters who

once items earn stars, there's a risk that the next step will be to mandate them. But we'd rather have government give advice and make recommendations than impose mandates."

Is buying green better for the environment than buying less?

Most observers agree that today's green consumption boom signals the mainstreaming of environmental values. In the 1980s eco-friendly products like soy milk and recycled paper were of uneven quality and were viewed as niche goods for a small subset of dedicated customers. Today megastores like Wal-Mart and Target offer green cleaning supplies, organic food and energy-efficient light bulbs.

"We've seen green waves before, but today there's better understanding of environmental issues, higher quality products and more consumer understanding," says Case at TerraChoice Environmental Marketing. "This issue has penetrated the heads of the average consumer and business executive."

With more consumers buying more earth-friendly products, some advocates say that environmental protection no longer has to mean scaling back affluent lifestyles. Instead, they assert, we can shop our way to sustainability. "We all need to be presented with better product choices that enable us to maintain the way of life to which we're accustomed without overtaxing the planet's ability sincerely believe in them, but that either don't work well or don't have a serious impact. Mediocre or trivial green products will turn consumers off in the long run," he warns.

"Greenwashing" further undercuts the impact of buying green by marketing products with vague claims like "All Natural," "Earth Smart" and other labels that are too general to document whether goods will help the environment or not. Some consumers analyze these slogans critically, but many are likely to take them at face value. According to a 2006 study by the Natural Marketing Institute, LOHAS (Lifestyles of Health and Sustainability) buyers, who make purchases based on belief systems and values, including environmental protection and social responsibility, account for only about 16 percent of U.S. consumers. (*See graph, p. 173.*)

Although LOHAS consumers are a relatively small segment of the market, green business experts say that they have significant influence. "LOHAS consumers push the envelope. They're always testing the boundaries, and they make decisions for the sake of the mission," says Ted Ning, who directs an annual business gathering in Colorado called the LOHAS Forum. "Once their items become mainstream, they move on to the next issue. For example, instead of just buying organic food or locally grown food, now they're choosing food based on its carbon footprint."

LOHAS buyers also size up companies critically, says Ning. "They expect a lot of in-depth information to show whether products are authentic. Blogs and Web sites give people lots of ways to communicate, so if companies don't make that data available, there's an assumption that they have something to hide. And LOHAS consumers are evangelists, so they're proud to share their information. If you get on their wrong side, they'll badmouth you to death."

Businesses are keenly interested in LOHAS consumers, who represent an estimated $209 billion market for goods including organic food, personal and home care products, clean energy technologies, alternative transportation and ecotourism.[28] But it's not clear that this group's preferences can steer the entire U.S. economy toward sustainability.

"Consumers are most interested in high-quality, affordable products. That's still a larger driver than other environmental considerations, although green aspects

Growing numbers of eco-conscious shoppers are buying organically grown food today. Demand for organic and natural groceries has made Whole Foods the nation's largest natural food market chain.

often are tie-breakers," says TerraChoice's Case. Recent polls show that while Americans are increasingly willing to make lifestyle changes to protect the environment, they prefer easy actions like recycling over more demanding steps like reducing their carbon footprints.[29]

"Green labeling and marketing are market-based instruments that can be adopted quickly as our environmental knowledge grows, but in the long term they'll be seen as transitional steps," says Case. "Ultimately, we'll address these issues with other mechanisms like cap-and-trade systems and taxes."

BACKGROUND

Conservation Focus

Before the United States was a century old, early conservationists began to warn about threats to precious lands and resources. In his 1854 classic *Walden*, Henry David Thoreau decried loggers and railroads that encroached on his forest retreat. In 1876 naturalist John Muir wrote that California's forests, which he called "God's first temples," were "being burned and cut down and wasted like a field of unprotected grain, and once destroyed can never be wholly restored even by centuries of persistent and painstaking cultivation."[30]

Congress began putting lands under federal protection with the creation of Yellowstone National Park in 1872. It also established scientific agencies to manage

CHRONOLOGY

1960-1980 *Environmentalists use lobbying, litigation and citizen action to curb pollution....Congress imposes new regulations on businesses.*

1967 Congress enacts Clean Air Act.

1969 Congress passes National Environmental Policy Act, requiring environmental-impact studies for federal projects with potentially significant effects on the environment.

1970 Millions of Americans celebrate Earth Day on April 22....Congress establishes Environmental Protection Agency and expands Clean Air Act.

1973 Endangered Species Act enacted.

1974 Safe Drinking Water Act enacted.

1978 Homeowners in New York's Love Canal neighborhood force federal government to pay for evacuating them from houses built atop toxic-waste dump.

1979 Three Mile Island nuclear power plant in Pennsylvania partially melts down, stalling the growth of nuclear energy.

1980 Superfund law assigns liability and fund cleanup at hazardous-waste sites....Ronald Reagan is elected president on platform calling for reducing government's role.

1980-2000 *Global climate change emerges as major environmental issue.*

1987 Twenty-four nations initially sign Montreal Protocol, pledging to phase out chemicals that deplete Earth's ozone layer; dozens more sign in subsequent years.

1989 *Exxon Valdez* runs aground in Alaska, contaminating more than 5,000 kilometers of pristine coast with oil and killing thousands of animals and birds.

1990 Congress creates market-based allowance trading system to reduce emissions that cause acid rain....Federal Trade Commission (FTC) brings first enforcement case against deceptive green marketing, challenging claims for "pesticide free" produce sold by Vons supermarkets.

1992 Delegates to the Earth Summit in Rio de Janeiro, Brazil, adopt first international pledge to cut greenhouse gas (GHG) emissions....FTC issues marketing guides for green products and services.

1997 International conference approves Kyoto Protocol requiring GHG reductions but lets wealthy nations meet some of their obligations with offset projects in developing countries; U.S. signs but fails to ratify pact.

1998 U.S. Green Building Council launches Leadership in Energy and Environmental Design (LEED) program for rating energy-efficient, healthy buildings.

2000 British Petroleum re-brands itself BP and pledges to go "Beyond Petroleum" by investing in clean energy.

2001-2007 *As environmental concern grows, more companies offer eco-friendly products. Skeptics warn of "greenwashing."*

2000 Department of Agriculture issues final rule for certifying organic food.

2001 President George W. Bush rejects mandatory controls on GHG emissions....Following the Sept. 11 terrorist attacks, Bush urges Americans to shop to help fend off economic recession.

2005 General Electric launches "Ecomagination" advertising campaign to demonstrate its environmental commitment....Kyoto Protocol enters into force, including credits for carbon offset projects in developing countries....European Union members begin trading carbon credits.

2006 Democrats recapture control of Congress, increasing support for policies to boost renewable energy and curb greenhouse gas emissions.

2007 FTC initiates review of green marketing guidelines and environmental products, including carbon offsets....Toyota Prius hybrids surpass top-selling sport-utility vehicles.

The Six Sins of 'Greenwashing'

Misleading environmental claims are common.

A perfectly green product may not exist, but some certainly are much greener than others, according to a recent study by Pennsylvania-based TerraChoice Environmental Marketing.[1] It examined 1,018 consumer products that made a total of 1,753 environmental claims and found that every product but one offered false or misleading information. The firm identified six broad categories of misleading environmental claims, or "greenwashing":

- **The hidden trade-off:** Marketing a product as eco-friendly based on a single green attribute like recycled content, without addressing other issues such as where its materials come from or how much energy is required to produce it.
- **No proof:** Making environmental claims without providing information backing them up at the point of purchase or on the manufacturer's Web site.
- **Vagueness:** Touting products based on claims that are too vague to have any real meaning, such as "Non-Toxic," "All Natural" or "Earth-Friendly."
- **Irrelevance:** Offering a claim that is true but not important or helpful to consumers. For example, some products are labeled "CFC-Free," but ozone-destroying chlorofluorocarbons (CFCs) have been outlawed in the U.S. for several decades.
- **Lesser of two evils:** Selling a product with an environmental label even though it belongs to a class of goods that is generally bad for consumers' health or the environment, such as organic cigarettes.
- **Fibbing:** Providing false information or claiming a certification, such as USDA Organic, that the product has not actually earned.

Greenwashing matters for several reasons, the study contends. First, consumers will waste money and may conclude that environmentally friendly products do not work. Second, greenwashing takes business away from legitimate green products. This makes it harder for honest manufacturers to compete and slows the rate at which high-quality products penetrate the market.

Indeed, greenwashing was a factor in the demise of an early wave of green consumerism in the 1980s, says TerraChoice Vice President Scot Case, but more scrutiny this time may deter cheaters. "We'll know if things are improving when we repeat the study in a few months," says Case. "We're hopeful that attention from the media and the Federal Trade Commission [FTC] will help."

Consumers who want to ensure that they are getting green products have several options. First, they can look for seals of approval from organizations such as EcoLogo and Green Seal, both of which certify green products based on multiple criteria.[2] These eco-labeling programs are standardized under a set of principles developed by the International Organization for Standards.

Consumers also can check product labels and manufacturers' Web sites for information that supports green marketing claims. "Companies should be very careful not to claim that things are green, only that they are greener," says Case. "They shouldn't suggest that just because they've addressed one issue, it's a green product." The FTC has published guidance to help consumers sort through green advertising claims.[3]

Although greenwashing may be pervasive today, TerraChoice argues that green marketing can be a positive force. "[G]reen marketers and consumers are learning about the pitfalls of greenwashing together," the report states. "This is a shared problem and opportunity. When green marketing overcomes these challenges, consumers will be better able to trust green claims, and genuinely environmentally preferable products will penetrate their markets more rapidly and deeply. This will be great for consumers, great for business and great for the planet."[4]

---

[1] TerraChoice Environmental Marketing, "The 'Six Sins of Greenwashing," November 2007, www.terrachoice.com.

[2] For more information see www.ecologo.org and www.greenseal.org.

[3] U.S. Federal Trade Commission, "Sorting Out 'Green' Advertising Claims," www.ftc.gov/bcp/edu/pubs/consumer/general/gen02.pdf.

[4] TerraChoice, *op. cit.*, p. 8.

natural resources, including the U.S. Fisheries Commission (later the Fish & Wildlife Service) in 1871 and the U.S. Geological Survey and Division of Forestry (later the Forest Service) in 1879.

But politicians mainly sought to develop and use resources, not to protect them in their natural states. To settle the West, Congress passed laws like the 1872 Mining Law, which allowed prospectors to buy mining rights on public lands for $5 per acre, and the 1878 Timber and Stone Act, which made land that was "unfit for farming" available for $2.50 per acre for timber and stone resources. These statutes often allowed speculators and large corporations to exploit public resources at far less than fair market value.[31]

Environmental advocates formed many important conservation groups before 1900, including the Appalachian Mountain Club, American Forests and the Sierra Club. Their members, mainly affluent outdoorsmen, focused on preserving land for hunting, fishing and expeditions. One notable exception, the Massachusetts Audubon Society, was founded in 1896 by two Boston society women who opposed killing exotic birds to provide feathers for fashionable ladies' hats. Within a year the group persuaded the state legislature to ban commerce in wild bird feathers. Its work later spurred Congress to pass national legislation and support a treaty protecting migratory birds.[32]

Although early groups won some notable victories, most conservation work was mandated by the federal government. Congress and Presidents Theodore Roosevelt (1901-1909) and William Howard Taft (1909-1913) set aside many important tracts of land as parks and monuments. Congress created the National Park Service in 1916 to manage these new preserves. But national policy also spurred harmful development, such as federally funded irrigation projects to help settlers farm in dry Western states. With government agencies urging them on, farmers plowed up the Great Plains, destroying their natural grass cover and helping to create the Dust Bowl when drought struck in the 1930s.

During the long tenure of President Franklin D. Roosevelt, (1933-1945), several important conservation programs were launched even as Western dam building accelerated. The Civilian Conservation Corps (CCC), also known as "Roosevelt's Tree Army," hired more than 3 million unemployed Americans to build fire towers, plant trees and improve parks across the nation. More than 8 million people worked for the Works Progress Administration on projects including roads, bridges and park lodges.

These were top-down programs, writes anthropologist Michael Johnson: "The federal government defined the problems, defined the solutions and then 'fixed' the problems by employing lots of people . . . the average citizen had an almost blind trust in the federal definition of problems and solutions." Moreover, while the CCC and other initiatives treated symptoms such as soil erosion, they failed to address human actions like plowing and over-grazing that caused the problems.[33]

Environmental Awakening

As the economy grew rapidly after World War II, human impacts on the environment became obvious. Pollutants from power plants, factories and passenger cars mixed in the atmosphere to create toxic smog. Offshore oil-drilling platforms appeared along California's scenic coastline. And Rachel Carson's 1962 book *Silent Spring* warned that widespread use of pesticides threatened ecosystems and human health.

Alarmed environmentalists began fighting back. In 1955 they rallied against a hydropower dam that would have flooded part of Dinosaur National Monument in Utah. A decade later, a coalition led by the Sierra Club helped to block a dam that would have inundated the Grand Canyon. Conservationists won a big victory in 1965 when a federal court allowed them to sue against a proposed electric power plant on Storm King Mountain in New York's Hudson Valley.[34] Courts previously had decided such siting issues on narrow technical grounds but in this case held that groups not directly involved in development projects could intervene to protect scenic resources. Litigation quickly became an important tool for environmental advocates.

Congress passed several key environmental laws in the 1960s, including the Wilderness Act (1964), which created a process for protecting land permanently from development, and the National Environmental Policy Act (1969), which subjected major federal actions such as building dams to environmental-impact studies. But new disasters spurred calls for further action. In 1969 an offshore oil well near Santa Barbara, Calif., ruptured and spilled oil along 30 miles of coastline. Five months later

Guidelines for Eco-minded Consumers

Here's how to have the most impact.

For many consumers, the biggest challenge of buying green is not finding earth-friendly goods but figuring out which choices have the biggest environmental impact. Green buying choices can be complicated, and green products often cost more than conventional alternatives.

Moreover, as journalist Samuel Fromartz observes in his history of the organic food business, few shoppers buy everything from premium suppliers like Whole Foods. Instead, regardless of income level, they buy organic in categories that matter to them, such as milk for their children, and choose other items of lower concern from conventional or discount stores.[1]

To help eco-minded consumers focus on purchases with the biggest environmental impact, *The Consumer's Guide to Effective Environmental Choices* identifies the biggest environmental problems related to household consumption: air and water pollution, global warming and habitat alteration. Then, by quantifying environmental impacts and linking these impacts to consumer products and services, authors Michael Brower and Warren Leon identify three household activity areas that account for most of these impacts: food, household operations and transportation.

To address these issues, Brower and Leon urge consumers to take steps such as driving fuel-efficient, low-polluting cars, eating less meat and making their homes energy-efficient.[2]

"A green purchase can have at least three results," says Leon. "First, it can favor a lower-impact product over conventional options. Second, it may allow you to consume fewer resources over the lifetime of the product. That's why energy choices are important — not only does energy use have significant environmental impacts, but you will use less energy every time you turn that appliance on."

As another example, consider a gardener who spends several hundred dollars on outdoor furniture. If she chooses items made from sustainably harvested wood, she may preserve several trees in a threatened forest. But if she uses the same money to buy a backyard composting bin, she can divert hundreds of pounds of food waste from landfills

Installing compact fluorescent light bulbs is one of several tips for responsible consumption recommended by the Center for a New American Dream.

Getty Images/Steve Wisbauer

(which produce greenhouse gases as wastes break down and can leak and contaminate groundwater) during the years that she uses the bin.

Third, Leon argues, some green purchases can favor new environmentally friendly technologies or industries with big growth potential. "By joining the early adapters who reinforce demand for a new product, you can help create a perception that it's a success," he says. However, it is important to note that some products will never become market phenomena because they have small niche markets. Only a small fraction of the Americans who drink wine will buy organic wine, but nearly everyone has to clean a bathroom at some point, so green cleaning supplies have a bigger prospective market.

The nonprofit Center for a New American Dream, which advocates for responsible consumption, offers a similar list of personal steps to "Turn the Tide":

- Drive less.
- Eat less feedlot beef.
- Eat eco-friendly seafood.
- Remove your address from bulk mailing lists.
- Install compact fluorescent light bulbs.
- Use less energy for home heating and cooling.
- Eliminate lawn pesticides.
- Reduce home water usage.
- Inspire your friends.

"None of Turn the Tide's nine actions involve drastic changes in your life, yet each packs an environmental punch," says the center. "In fact, every thousand participants prevent the emission of 4 million pounds of climate-warming carbon dioxide every year."[3]

---

[1] Samuel Fromartz, *Organic, Inc.: Natural Foods and How They Grew* (2006), pp. 248-53.

[2] Michael Brower and Warren Leon, *The Consumer's Guide to Effective Environmental Choices* (1999), pp. 43-85.

[3] Center for a New American Dream, "Turn the Tide," www.newdream.org/cnad/user/turn_the_tide.php.

Ohio's Cuyahoga River caught fire when flammable chemicals on its surface ignited.

On April 22, 1970, the first Earth Day, more than 20 million Americans attended rallies and teach-ins designed to force environmental issues onto the national agenda. Activists followed up with lobbying and lawsuits. In response Congress passed a flurry of new laws, including an expanded Clean Air Act (1970), the Endangered Species Act (1973), the Safe Drinking Water Act (1974), the Resources Conservation and Recovery Act (1976) and the Clean Water Act (1977).

"Citizens across the country became aware of what was happening to their physical surroundings," writes journalist Philip Shabecoff. "Equally important, they also acquired a faith — not always requited — that in the American democracy change was possible, that they could act as individuals and communities to obtain relief from the environmental dangers with which they were threatened."[35] Slogans like "Reduce, reuse, recycle" and "Think globally, act locally" underlined the importance of personal action.

While national groups pressured Congress and the new EPA, grassroots activists attacked local problems. In 1978 residents of the Love Canal neighborhood in upstate New York, led by housewife Lois Gibbs, forced the federal government to pay for moving them out of homes that had been built on top of an industrial-waste site. Groups with names like the Abalone Alliance sprang up to oppose new nuclear power plants, blocking some and delaying others.

Businesses and free-market advocates pushed back. President Ronald Reagan was elected in 1980 on a platform that called for reforming regulation and ensuring that benefits from environmental controls justified their costs.[36] During the campaign Reagan argued that air pollution had been "substantially controlled" in the United States and that laws like the Clean Air Act were forcing factories to shut down.[37] When he installed anti-regulation appointees like Interior Secretary James G. Watt and EPA Administrator Anne Gorsuch, many environmentalists worried that their recent victories would be reversed.

Working With Markets

As the Reagan administration learned, most Americans did not support a broad rollback of environmental laws. Public backlash against proposals such as selling off millions of acres of public lands drove Watt and Gorsuch from office. But environmentalists still faced a Republican administration and Senate majority that opposed new controls.

In response some groups began working with the private sector and developing market-based policies. Proponents of this environmental "third wave" contended that if regulations were more cost-effective and flexible, industries could be persuaded to cut pollution instead of having to be forced.

Their most visible success was promoting tradable permits to cut pollution. EPA had started experimenting in the 1970s with programs that allowed companies to earn and trade credits for reducing air pollutants such as carbon monoxide and particulates. Business leaders preferred this approach because instead of mandating specific control technologies, it let them decide how and where to make reductions. For example, instead of installing pollution controls a company might make its operations more efficient or switch to cleaner methods or products.

When Congress amended the Clean Air Act in 1990, some environmentalists supported a cap-and-trade system to reduce sulfur dioxide (SO_2) and nitrogen oxide emissions that caused acid rain. This approach set an overall cap on emissions and issued a fixed number of tradable emission permits to sources. Factories emitting less pollution than their allotments could sell extra permits to other sources — giving polluters an economic incentive to clean up, advocates asserted.[38]

The SO_2 trading program went into effect in 1995 and expanded in 2000. Many supporters praised it for cutting SO_2 releases sharply at a lower cost than industry had predicted.[39] However, acid rain remained a problem in areas located downwind from major pollution sources, such as the Adirondack Mountains, and emissions trading did not prove to be a panacea for other U.S. air pollution problems.[40]

During the 1990s some economic experts began to argue that going green made sound business sense. By reducing pollution, the theory held, companies would make their operations more efficient, which meant that they would use less energy and waste fewer raw materials. "Innovation to comply with environmental regulation often improves product performance or quality," business professors Michael Porter and Claas van der Linde asserted in 1995.[41]

As one step, some companies forged relationships with large environmental groups.[42] McDonald's worked with Environmental Defense to design a paperboard alternative to its polystyrene "clamshell" hamburger package, and the Rainforest Alliance helped Chiquita Brands develop social and environmental standards for its banana farms in Latin America.[43] However, critics argued that by accepting corporate donations and putting business executives on their boards of directors, environmentalists risked becoming too sympathetic to private interests.[44]

Some smaller groups stuck to more aggressive tactics. San Francisco's Rainforest Action Network carried out scrappy direct-action campaigns that persuaded Burger King to stop using beef raised on former rainforest lands and Home Depot to sell only sustainably produced wood. The Earth Island Institute used negative publicity and a consumer boycott to make tuna companies adopt fishing practices that avoided killing dolphins in tuna nets. And major groups continue to vilify companies like oil giant Exxon/Mobil, whose opposition to action on global warming and support for oil drilling in the Arctic National Wildlife Refuge made it a prime environmental target.[45]

The 1997 Kyoto Protocol applied offsets to climate change in a provision called the Clean Development Mechanism (CDM), under which developed countries could meet part of their commitments by paying for projects that reduced GHG emissions in developing countries. This process was designed to reduce costs by letting industrialized nations cut GHG emissions in locations where environmental upgrades were cheaper. (GHGs dissipate widely throughout the atmosphere, so eliminating a ton of CO_2 emissions has the same impact on climate change wherever it occurs.)

Shopping for Change

National environmental policy became more contentious after George W. Bush was elected president in 2000 with strong support from energy- and resource-intensive industries. Many administration appointees pushed to loosen environmental regulations, and President Bush reversed a campaign pledge to limit greenhouse gas emissions that caused global warming, arguing that doing so would hurt the economy.[46]

Stymied at the federal level, environmentalists looked for other ways to leverage public support for green policies. Many advocacy groups deepened ties with businesses to influence corporate policies and earn political support from the private sector. They also urged members to target their buying power toward green goals. "People got tired of the gloom and doom approach. They wanted to hear about solutions," explained Bud Ris, executive director of the Union of Concerned Scientists from 1984 through 2003.[47]

Even as scientific consensus increased that human actions were causing global climate change, President George W. Bush opposed calls for mandatory controls on U.S. GHG emissions. Instead, in 2002 Bush pledged to reduce U.S. GHG emissions per dollar of economic activity by 18 percent by 2012. "This will set America on a path to slow the growth of our greenhouse gas emissions and, as science justifies, to stop and then reverse the growth of emissions," Bush said. However, many analysts noted, even if the American economy became 18 percent less carbon-intensive, its total GHG emissions would increase during that time as a result of normal economic growth.

Many corporations joined voluntary initiatives, however, like EPA's Climate Leaders program or the privately funded Pew Center on Global Climate Policy, both to show stockholders that they were paying attention to the environment and to discuss what kind of climate change policies would be most workable for businesses.[48] These partnerships required companies to measure their GHG emissions and develop strategies for reducing them. Companies also began exploring options like renewable energy certificates (RECs) and carbon offsets to reduce their carbon footprints.

Some companies turned growing concerns about pollution and climate change to their advantage with products that were both high-quality and green. Toyota's gas-electric hybrid Prius hatchback, which promised drivers 60 miles per gallon in city driving, debuted with limited sales in U.S. markets in 2000. By 2005 the Prius had become a symbol of green chic, and Toyota was selling 100,000 per year. And after the U.S. Department of Agriculture finalized standards for certifying organic food in 2000, Whole Foods rode growing demand for organic and natural groceries to become the largest natural food market chain in the nation.

CURRENT SITUATION

Keeping Standards High

As consumer interest in green products rises, regulators and environmentalists are taking a critical look at definitions and marketplace practices. Strong standards are needed, observers say, to prevent a new wave of greenwashing and help consumers avoid wasting money.

"The nature of marketing is to puff up products. That's why we have labeling laws, and there are struggles over who regulates what," says University of California sociologist Szasz. "The first struggle is over how regulated a product like organic food will be and who will do it. Then once the rules are written, debate over practices like greenwashing takes place within those boundaries."

In late 2007 the Federal Trade Commission (FTC) announced plans to review its green marketing guidelines and new green products such as carbon offsets.[49] FTC's guidelines offer advice for manufacturers on a variety of green products, but the commission may issue specific guidance on carbon offsets and RECs.

"We want to learn more about what these products are, how they work and how much activity is going on in the marketplace. We're also exploring how marketers are substantiating their claims and what consumers need to know about these products that we can provide," says FTC attorney Hampton Newsome.

The FTC is not an environmental agency, so it will not set specifications for individual products. Rather, it considers questions such as whether labels provide enough clear information for consumers to make judgments. For example, according to agency guidelines, a bottle labeled "50% more recycled content" would be ambiguous because the comparison could refer to a competing brand or to a prior version of the product. A label reading "50% more recycled content than our previous package" would be clearer.[50]

"Marketers have to substantiate express or implied marketing claims with competent and reliable evidence," says Newsome. "How consumers understand the claim is key, because that determines their purchasing decisions, not what the seller intended." Under the Federal Trade Commission Act, which outlaws unfair and deceptive trade practices, companies that make false or misleading claims could face penalties including injunctions or forfeiture of profits.

Many organizations are working to help standardize carbon offsets and define high-quality versions. There are a number of issues to consider, says Colby College's Tietenberg. "Quantification is important. The fact that something reduces greenhouse gases is useful, but you need to quantify how much it reduces them," he says. "You need to ensure that the initial reductions prevail through the life of the offset — for example, if you plant trees and the forest burns down, you don't get the offset. And you need a tracking system to keep people from selling the same offsets to multiple buyers."

Advocates also want to make green certification programs more rigorous. Some have criticized the LEED rating system for green buildings, saying that its checklists are simplistic and give too much weight to small steps, like installing bicycle racks, and not enough to bigger ones, such as renovating a historic building instead of razing it.[51] But the green building movement remains strong: By 2010, trade publications estimate that about 10 percent of commercial construction starts will be green projects (not all of which may seek LEED ratings).[52]

Watchdogs also see room for improvement in the Energy Star program. In 2007 EPA's inspector general reported that the agency was not doing enough to confirm that Energy Star products (which are tested by manufacturers, not EPA) performed at the promised level, or to prevent unqualified products from being labeled as Energy Star models.[53] The Government Accountability Office also criticized relying on manufacturers to test products and urged EPA and the Energy Department to look more closely at issues such as how many products are purchased because of Energy Star ratings.[54]

More Mandates?

Congressional supporters of a national renewable electricity portfolio standard have pledged to bring RPS legislation up again this year. Countering the argument that this policy would penalize some states, a study by the American Council for an Energy-Efficient Economy (ACEEE) projects that electricity prices would be lower across the U.S. in 2020 and 2025 under a standard like that passed by the House in 2007 (combining renewable electricity and conservation) than without an RPS. A more aggressive standard that met 15 percent of electricity demand with renewable fuels and 15 percent through conservation would push prices even lower, ACEEE found.[55]

Does the United States need a national renewable electricity portfolio standard?

YES — Gov. Bill Ritter, Jr., D-Colo.

From testimony before House Select Committee on Energy Independence and Global Warming, Sept. 20, 2007

It has been our experience that [a renewable electricity portfolio standard] creates new jobs, spurs economic development and increases the tax base all while saving consumers and businesses money and protecting our environment. In 2004, following three years of failed legislative efforts, the people of Colorado placed the nation's first citizen-initiated renewable portfolio standard (RPS), Amendment 37, on the ballot. While the effort was opposed by virtually all Colorado utilities, including the state's largest utility — Xcel Energy — the effort passed by a wide margin. The Colorado RPS established a goal of 10 percent renewable resources by 2015 for Xcel Energy (along with the other Colorado Public Utilities Commission-regulated utility, Aquila).

In 2004, 10 percent was an ambitious goal: a little over 1 percent of Xcel's electricity was generated from renewable sources at that time. Today, it is the country's leading provider of wind energy. Xcel will meet the 10-percent-by-2015 goal at the end of 2007 — nearly eight years ahead of schedule.

Xcel has done what all successful businesses do — it adapted. While Xcel originally viewed the RPS as a burden, it soon recognized it as an opportunity, and the utility is now a great example of the successes that will come from our New Energy Economy. . . .

Renewable energy development of the future is not limited to wind. In Colorado, we are fortunate to have a broad mix of renewable resources, including wind on our Eastern Plains, solar in the San Luis Valley and southwest part of the state and geothermal all along our Western Slope. . . .

The committee has asked how a national renewable electricity standard will impact technologies in Colorado. Developments in wind technology have led the industry to be cost competitive with fossil fuel generation, but we need similar developments in both solar electric as well as concentrated solar technology. With the appropriate leadership from the federal government, these resources have the opportunity to join wind as a primary source of renewable power. . . .

As we saw with the RPS in Colorado — we encouraged the market through the RPS, and the market has responded. Investment, research and development are following the establishment of the RPS. A federal RPS provides more markets for renewable energy, prosperity for Americans in the heartland and a more responsible energy future for our nation.

NO — Chris M. Hobson
Senior Vice President, Research and Environmental Affairs, Southern Company

From testimony before House Select Committee on Energy Independence and Global Warming, Sept. 20, 2007

Southern Company opposes a national renewable-energy mandate. We believe that mandates are an inefficient and potentially counterproductive means of increasing the production of cost-effective, reliable electric power from renewable sources. We prefer to seek cost-effective additions to our generation portfolio based on technological maturity, technical performance, reliability and economic cost. . . .

Our estimates show that a 15 percent federal renewable-energy mandate would far exceed the available renewable resources in the Southeastern region. To replace 15 percent of the nation's retail energy by 2020 would require approximately 80,000 wind turbines of 2 megawatt capacity each, or 2,200 square miles of land — an area larger than Delaware — for solar photovoltaic arrays, or 87,000 square miles of switch grass fields — an area the size of Minnesota. To replace 15 percent of just Southern Company's retail energy by 2020 would require approximately 6,900 wind turbines of 2 megawatt capacity each, or 200 square miles of land for solar photovoltaics, or 6,000 square miles of switchgrass fields — an area the size of Connecticut. . . .

Because the renewable resources that would be required to comply with a 15 percent mandate are not available in the Southeast, Southern Company would be required to comply largely by making alternative compliance payments to the federal government. . . . Because of the limited availability of renewable resources in our region and the fact that most of what is available will likely be more expensive than the 3 cents/kilowatt-hour price cap, the majority of the $19 billion cost to our customers will simply be payments to the federal government. Thus a nationwide [renewable portfolio standard] mandate could cost electricity consumers in the Southeast billions of dollars in higher electricity prices, with no guarantee that additional renewable generation will actually be developed. . . .

Not every technology will be well-suited to every region of the country. We do believe that the use of renewable energy to produce electricity can be increased, and we intend to play a key role in the research and development needed to reach such an objective. This is best reached by the enhancement of current strategies to provide incentives for the R&D as well as the use of renewable energy as compared to the adoption of a federal mandate for a single standard across the country.

Many grocery stores have begun selling reusable shopping bags as an alternative to environmentally unfriendly plastic bags.

"Including energy efficiency brings down wholesale prices," explains ACEEE Deputy Director Prindle. Efficiency and renewables also complement each other, he says, because conservation projects can be put in place more quickly while new renewable energy projects are sited and built.

But opponents are likely to fight any new RPS proposals in 2008. Energy producers in the Southeast maintain that a national RPS will penalize their region, and the White House threatened to veto the 2007 energy bill over its RPS requirement. "A federal RPS that is unfair in its application, is overly prescriptive in its definition by excluding many low-carbon technologies and does not allow states to opt out would hurt consumers and undercut state decisions," National Economic Council Chair Allan Hubbard wrote to congressional leaders in late 2007.[56]

First Congress may have to revisit another controversial green mandate — the Renewable Fuels Standard (RFS), enacted in 2005 and expanded in 2007, which promotes bio-based transportation fuels like ethanol and biodiesel.[57] The original RFS, which was adopted to reduce U.S. dependence on imported oil and cut pollution from transportation, required refiners to use 5.4 billion gallons of renewable fuels (mostly blended with conventional gasoline) in 2008, rising to 7.5 billion gallons by 2012. The new law mandates 9 billion gallons in 2008, increasing to 36 billion gallons by 2022.

Most biofuel sold in the United States is ethanol made from corn, although researchers are starting to make ethanol from cellulosic sources (crop wastes and woody plants), which have a higher energy content and require fewer resources to produce. For the moment, however, much support for the RFS comes from farm-state lawmakers and agribusinesses invested in corn ethanol.

Many observers believe that the RFS is poorly designed and is producing unintended consequences. Two recent studies suggest that the push to expand biofuel crops may trigger such widespread land clearing that it increases climate change (by destroying forests that take up carbon) instead of reducing it.[58] And by driving up demand for corn, which also is used in animal feed and processed foods, critics say the mandate is increasing food prices.[59]

"The RFS has a narrow focus on a particular technology, and it doesn't strike a balance between demand and supply," says Prindle. "Also, it will take a lot of new capacity to meet the targets, including inputs like water and electricity as well as grain. You have to develop a massive new infrastructure across the middle of the country [where most corn is grown]." Colby College's Tietenberg seconds this perspective. "Mandates should be performance-based instead of requiring a specific input," he says. "You want to make sure the standard is clear but that there are flexible options for meeting it."

Green Is Red-Hot

Amid these debates, green marketing is spreading across much of the nation's economy. Today green labeling is most commonly found on office products, building materials, cleaning products and electronics. "In the 20 years between the last green bubble and this one, the only people who expressed strong interest in green products were large institutional purchasers like government agencies, colleges and hospitals, so green labeling had a very business-centric focus," explains TerraChoice's Case.

But now the message is penetrating into new sectors. Transportation, for example, accounts for about 27 percent of U.S. GHG emissions and is a major contributor to regional air pollution. A decade ago gas-guzzling sport utility vehicles (SUVs) and light trucks dominated the U.S. auto market, but in 2007 sales of gas-electric hybrid Toyota Prius hatchbacks surpassed the Ford Explorer, long the top-selling SUV.[60]

Now, with gas prices high and new fuel-efficiency standards signed into law, U.S. automakers are terminating some SUV lines, converting others to smaller "crossovers" and putting more money into alternative vehicles. In 2007 General Motors unveiled a concept model of the Chevrolet Volt, a plug-in electric car that uses a small gasoline engine as a generator to charge its batteries. GM is still designing the Volt but hopes to have it on the market by late 2010.[61] Other companies, including Toyota and Ford, are developing plug-in hybrids that can be recharged at standard 120-volt outlets.

Home and personal care products are also becoming increasingly green, in response to consumer alarm over recent reports describing toxic, hazardous and untested ingredients in common consumer goods. For example, laboratory testing carried out for the Campaign for Safe Cosmetics in 2007 found detectable levels of lead, a neurotoxic chemical, in many brand-name lipsticks.[62] Another recent study found increased levels of phthalates (chemical softeners that have been linked to reproductive problems and are banned from personal care products in the European Union) in infants who were treated with baby lotions, powders and shampoos.[63] Toys, food and beverage containers, upholstery, and other goods have also been found to contain compounds known or suspected to be hazardous to human health.

But this area is a major greenwashing zone, with marketers often relying on slogans that have no standard meaning. "While splashy terms and phrases such as 'earth-friendly,' 'organic,' 'nontoxic,' and 'no harmful fragrances' can occasionally be helpful, the ugly truth is in the ingredients list," the environmental magazine *Grist* advises in its green living guide.[64]

OUTLOOK

Focus on Carbon

Whichever party wins the White House in 2008, it appears likely that the United States will adopt binding GHG limits sometime after a new president takes office in 2009. All of the front-runners for president, including Democrats Hillary Rodham Clinton and Barack Obama and Republican John McCain, support cap-and-trade legislation that would sharply reduce U.S. emissions by 2050 — a timetable that many scientists believe is needed to avert catastrophic global warming.[65]

Many companies can read the writing on the wall and are working to turn the issue to their advantage. "The business community sees tremendous opportunity in green products. It's a chance for companies to push technology and come up with innovative solutions," says the National Association of Manufacturers' McCoy. "We're on the cusp of some fascinating discoveries that could help solve our energy needs. We need to consider what research and development incentives government can offer to facilitate that, with manufacturers and the business community involved." Even Exxon/Mobil, long one of the strongest foes of binding GHG limits, has started to discuss what national controls should look like.[66]

With mandatory GHG limits in place, will green consumerism still have a role to play? Many observers see buying green as an important piece of the larger solution. "The reality is that we consume products every day. This is not going to change any time soon," says Dorfman, the "Lazy Environmentalist." "So we have to find more environmentally conscious ways to consume if we want to maintain our quality of lives and not see them degraded by climate change. . . . However, the solutions have to fit our lifestyles or the great majority of us won't even consider them."[67]

But green consumption and business/environment partnerships are not substitutes for political action, says Colby College's Tietenberg. "You need policies to level the playing field. If some firms are out there doing more and it costs more, they may have trouble competing and lose market share," he argues. "But if government sets rules that create a level playing field, business will take the ball and run with it. Many businesses are asking for national standards now."

Consumers who want to make a serious impact with their purchases need to learn which steps make the most difference. "People have a limited understanding of their carbon footprints," says Climate Trust Director Burnett. "They don't necessarily know what kind of fuel generates their electricity, or how significant airplane flights are." And comparing products' full life-cycle impacts can get complicated. For example, today many consumers are debating whether it is preferable to buy organically grown food that is shipped over long distances to market (generating GHG emissions in the process) or locally grown food that has been raised using less earth-friendly methods.[68]

"Wisdom is a curse — once you learn about these issues, you can't overlook them," says LOHAS Forum Director Ning. "But as we confront more problems like environmental toxins that stem from manufacturing processes, people are becoming more aware of design impacts. They're trying to understand more about how products work, and producers are trying to learn more about sustainability. Now that these ideas are becoming part of school curriculums, and people are talking about them more, our consciousness is only going to grow."

NOTES

1. Tearfund, "Senior Bishops Call For Carbon Fast This Lent," Feb. 5, 2008, www.tearfund.org.

2. Penn, Schoen, & Berland Associates, "Consumers Will Double Spending on Green," Sept. 27, 2007.

3. U.S. Bureau of Labor Statistics, Consumer Expenditure Survey, 2000-2006, www.bls.gov/cex/2006/standard/multiyr.pdf.

4. Karlo Barrios Marcelo and Mark Hugo Lopez, "How Young People Expressed Their Political Views in 2006," Center for Information & Research on Civic Learning & Engagement, University of Maryland, November 2007; Scott Keeger, "Politics and the 'DotNet' Generation," Pew Research Center, May 30, 2006; Lori J. Vogelgesang and Alexander W. Astin, "Post-College Civic Engagement Among Graduates," Higher Education Research Institute, University of California, Los Angeles, April 2005.

5. U.S. Federal Trade Commission, "The FTC's Environmental Cases," www.ftc.gov/bcp/conline/edcams/eande/contentframe_environment _cases.html.

6. Intergovernmental Panel on Climate Change, *Climate Change 2007: The Physical Science Basis, Summary for Policymakers* (2007), pp. 3, 5. For background, see Marcia Clemmitt, "Climate Change," *CQ Researcher*, Jan. 27, 2006, pp. 73-96, and Colin Woodard, "Curbing Climate Change," *CQ Global Researcher*, February 2007, pp. 27-50.

7. For background see Peter Katel, "Consumer Safety," *CQ Researcher*, Oct. 12, 2007, pp. 841-864, and Jennifer Weeks, "Factory Farms," *CQ Researcher*, Jan. 12, 2007, pp. 25-48.

8. For background see Tom Price, "The New Environmentalism," *CQ Researcher*, Dec. 1, 2006, pp. 985-1008, and Tom Price, "Corporate Social Responsibility," *CQ Researcher*, Aug. 3, 2007, pp. 649-672.

9. For details on these companies' pledges, see www.dupont.com/Sustainability/en_US/; www.monsanto.com/who_we_are/our_pledge.asp; and www.think green.com.

10. For background see Marcia Clemmitt, "Climate Change," *CQ Researcher*, Jan. 27, 2006, pp. 73-96.

11. U.S. Climate Action Partnership, *A Call for Action* (2007), p. 3, www.us-cap.org/USCAPCallForAction.pdf.

12. Joel Makower, *et al.*, *State of Green Business 2008* (2008), p. 3, www.stateofgreenbusiness.com/.

13. CarbonCounter.org, www.carboncounter.org/offset-your-emissions/personal-calculator.aspx; Union of Concerned Scientists, "What's Your Carbon Footprint?" www.ucsusa.org/publications/greentips/whats-your-carb.html.

14. *A Consumer's Guide to Retail Carbon Offset Providers* (2006), www.cleanair-coolplanet.org/ConsumersGuidetoCarbonOffsets.pdf.

15. Ted Williams, "As Ugly As a Tree," *Audubon*, September/October 2007.

16. Ben Elgin, "Another Inconvenient Truth," *Business Week*, March 26, 2007.

17. Kevin Smith, *The Carbon-Neutral Myth: Offset Indulgences for Your Climate Sins* (2007), pp. 10-11, www.carbontradewatch.org.

18. Federal Energy Regulatory Commission, "Electric Market Overview: Renewables," updated Jan. 15, 2008, www.ferc.gov/market-oversight/mkt-electric/overview/elec-ovr-rps.pdf.

19. *Congressional Record*, Aug. 4, 2007, p. H9847.

20. "Send Your Underwear to the Undersecretary," Competitive Enterprise Institute news release, May 16, 2007.

21. "Washers and Dryers: Performance For Less," *Consumer Reports*, February 2008.

22. For details see www.energystar.gov.

23. U.S. Environmental Protection Agency, "Energy Star and Other Climate Protection Partnerships 2006

Annual Report," September 2007, p. 15, www .energystar.gov/ia/news/downloads/annual_report_2006 .pdf. According to the Department of Energy, the average U.S. household uses about 11,000 kilowatt-hours of electricity annually; see www.eere.energy .gov/consumer/tips/appliances.htm.

24. For details see www.usgbc.org.

25. Jenny Shank, "An Interview With 'Lazy Environmentalist' Josh Dorfman," July 2, 2007, www .newwest.net/topic/article/an_interview_with_lazy_ environmentalist_josh_dorfman/C39/L39/.

26. Bill McKibben, "Reversal of Fortune," *Mother Jones*, March/April 2007.

27. Michael Brower and Warren Leon, *The Consumer's Guide To Effective Environmental Choices* (1999).

28. LOHAS Forum, "About LOHAS," www.lohas.com/ about.htm.

29. Patrrick O'Driscoll and Elizabeth Weise, "Green Living Takes Root But Habits Die Hard," *USA Today*, April 19, 2007; Anjali Athavaley, "A Serious Problem (But Not My Problem), *Wall Street Journal Classroom Edition*, February 2008.

30. John Muir, "God's First Temples: How Shall We Preserve Our Forests?" reprinted in John Muir, *Nature Writings* (1997), p. 629.

31. For background see Tom Arrandale, "Public Land Policy," *CQ Researcher*, June 17, 1994, pp. 529-552.

32. Massachusetts Foundation for the Humanities, "Mass Moments," www.massmoments.org/moment .cfm?mid=262.

33. Michael D. Johnson, "A Sociocultural Perspective on the Development of U.S. Natural Resource Partnerships in the 20th Century," USDA Forest Service Proceedings (2000), p. 206.

34. *Scenic Hudson Preservation Conference v. Federal Power Commission*, 354 F. 2d 608 (1965).

35. Philip Shabecoff, *Earth Rising: American Environmentalism in the 21st Century* (2000), p. 7.

36. Republican Party Platform of 1980, adopted July 15, 1980, online at The American Presidency Project, www.presidency.ucsb.edu/showplatforms .php?platindex=R1980.

37. Joanne Omang, "Reagan Criticizes Clean Air Laws and EPA as Obstacles to Growth," *The Washington Post*, Oct. 9, 1980.

38. See "Acid Rain: New Approach to Old Problem," *CQ Researcher*, March 3, 1991.

39. Environmental Defense, *From Obstacle to Opportunity: How Acid Rain Emissions Trading Is Delivering Cleaner Air* (September 2000); Robert N. Stavins, "Experience with Market-Based Environmental Policy Instruments," Discussion Paper 01-58, Resources for the Future, November 2001, pp. 27-29.

40. See Charles T. Driscoll, *et al.*, *Acid Rain Revisited: Advances in Scientific Understanding Since the Passage of the 1970 and 1990 Clean Air Act Amendments* (2001); Mary H. Cooper, "Air Pollution Conflict," *CQ Researcher*, Nov. 14, 2003, pp. 965-988; and Jennifer Weeks, "Coal's Comeback," *CQ Researcher*, Oct. 5, 2007, pp. 817-840.

41. Michael E. Porter and Claas van der Linde, "Toward a New Concept of the Environmental-Competitiveness Issue," *Journal of Economic Perspectives*, vol. 9, no. 4, fall 1995, p. 99.

42. For background see Tom Price, "The New Environmentalism," *CQ Researcher*, Dec. 1, 2006, pp. 985-1008.

43. Daniel C. Esty and Andrew S. Winston, *Green to Gold: How Smart Companies Use Environmental Strategy to Innovate, Create Value, and Build Competitive Advantage* (2006), pp. 70-71.

44. Mark Dowie, *Losing Ground: American Environmentalism at the Close of the Twentieth Century* (1995), pp. 114-124.

45. For details see "Exxpose Exxon," www. exxpose-exxon.com.

46. See Mary H. Cooper, "Energy Policy," *CQ Researcher*, May 25, 2001, pp. 441-464, and Mary H. Cooper, "Bush and the Environment," *CQ Researcher*, Oct. 25, 2002, pp. 865-896.

47. Steve Nadis, "Non-Government Organizations (NGOs) Mini-Reviews," New England BioLabs, www.neb.com.

48. For more information, see www.epa.gov/stateply/ index.html and www.pewclimate.org/companies_ leading_the_way_belc.

49. For more information see www.ftc.gov/bcp/workshops/carbonoffsets/index.shtml.

50. U.S. Federal Trade Commission, "Complying With the Environmental Marketing Guides," www.ftc.gov/bcp/conline/pubc/buspubs/greenguides.pdf.

51. Auden Schendler and Randy Udall, "LEED Is Broken; Let's Fix It," *Grist*, October 26, 2005; Stephen Del Percio, "What's Wrong With LEED?" *Green Building*, spring 2007.

52. McGraw Hill, *Green Building Smart Market Report 2006*, cited in "Green Building by the Numbers," U.S. Green Building Council, February 2008.

53. U.S. Environmental Protection Agency, Office of the Inspector General, "Energy Star Program Can Strengthen Controls Protecting the Integrity of the Label," Aug. 1, 2007, www.epa.gov/oig/reports/2007/20070801-2007-P-00028.pdf.

54. U.S. Government Accountability Office, "Energy Efficiency: Opportunities Exist for Federal Agencies to Better Inform Household Consumers," GAO-07-1162 (September 2007).

55. American Council for an Energy-Efficient Economy, "Assessment of the Renewable Electricity Standard and Expanded Clean Energy Scenarios," Dec. 5, 2007, http://aceee.org/pubs/e079.htm.

56. The full letter is posted online at http://gristmill.grist.org/images/user/8/White_House_letter_on_CAFE.pdf.

57. For background see Peter Katel, "Oil Jitters," *CQ Researcher*, Jan. 4, 2008, pp. 1-24, and Adriel Bettelheim, "Biofuels Boom," *CQ Researcher*, Sept. 29, 2006, pp. 793-816.

58. Joseph Fargione, *et al.*, "Land Clearing and the Biofuel Carbon Debt," *Sciencexpress Report*, Feb. 7, 2008; Timothy Searchinger, *et al.*, "Use of U.S. Croplands for Biofuels Increases Greenhouse Gases Through Emissions from Land Use Change," *Sciencexpress Report*, Feb. 7, 2008.

59. Randy Schnepf, "Agriculture-Based Renewable Energy Production," Congressional Research Service, Oct. 16, 2007, pp. 16-20; Colin A. Carter and Henry I. Miller, "Hidden Costs of Corn-Based Ethanol," *The Christian Science Monitor*, May 21, 2007; "Food Prices: Cheap No More," *The Economist*, Dec. 6, 2007.

60. Bernard Simon, "Prius Overtakes Explorer in the U.S.," *Financial Times*, Jan. 11, 2008.

61. "Chevy Volt FAQs," www.gm-volt.com/chevy-volt-faqs.

62. Campaign for Safe Cosmetics, "A Poison Kiss: The Problem of Lead in Lipstick," October 2007, www.safecosmetics.org.

63. Sheela Sathyanarayana, *et al.*, "Baby Care Products: Possible Sources of Infant Phthalate Exposure," *Pediatrics*, February 2008.

64. Brangien Davis and Katharine Wroth, eds., *Wake Up and Smell the Planet: The Non-Pompous, Non-Preachy Grist Guide to Greening Your Day* (2007), p. 20.

65. "Compare the Candidates," *Grist*, www.grist.org/candidate_chart_08.html.

66. Jeffrey Ball, "Exxon Mobil Softens Its Climate-Change Stance," *The Wall Street Journal*, Jan. 11, 2007.

67. Jenny Shank, *op. cit.*

68. For example, see Mindy Pennybacker, "Local or Organic? I'll Take Both," *The Green Guide*, September/October 2006, www.thegreenguide.com/doc/116/local, and John Cloud, "Eating Better Than Organic," *Time*, March 2, 2007.

BIBLIOGRAPHY

Books

Brower, Michael, and Warren Leon, *The Consumer's Guide to Effective Environmental Choices*, Three Rivers Press, 1999.
Although somewhat dated, this guide prioritizes consumer actions according to the scale of their environmental impacts based on extensive data and analysis. Brower and Leon, both senior environmental experts, draw on research by the Union of Concerned Scientists, a national environmental advocacy group.

Esty, Daniel C., and Andrew S. Winston, *Green To Gold: How Smart Companies Use Environmental Strategy to Innovate, Create Value, and Build Competitive Advantage*, Yale University Press, 2006.

Two Yale experts on business and the environment show how green strategies can help companies manage environmental challenges and gain an edge over competitors.

Szasz, Andrew, *Shopping Our Way to Safety: How We Changed from Protecting the Environment to Protecting Ourselves*, University of Minnesota Press, 2007.
Szasz, a sociologist, warns that the current green consumption boom could have negative impacts if it turns people away from broader political action.

Articles

"Climate Business/Business Climate," *Harvard Business Review*, October 2007.
A special report on the business challenges posed by climate change offers views from a dozen corporate and academic experts.

Davenport, Coral, "A Clean Break in Energy Policy," *CQ Weekly*, Oct. 8, 2007.
A national renewable electricity portfolio standard would trigger widespread changes in the ways that utilities produce power and state regulators oversee them.

Elgin, Ben, "Little Green Lies," *Business Week*, Oct. 29, 2007.
Auden Schendler, environmental director for Aspen Skiing Co., argues that many corporate greening actions are misleading and empty feel-good gestures.

Farenthold, David A., "Value of U.S. House's Carbon Offsets is Murky," *The Washington Post*, Jan. 28, 2008.
Critics say Congress wasted money by buying carbon offsets that funded activities already occurring.

Finz, Stacy, "Food Markets Getting Greener, More Sensual," *San Francisco Chronicle*, Jan. 27, 2008.
Consumers want healthier food raised using eco-friendly methods, and the grocery industry is responding.

Koerner, Brendan I., "Rise of the Green Machine," *Wired*, April 2005.
Koerner explains how Toyota made it cool to own a hybrid car.

Lynas, Mark, "Can Shopping Save the Planet?" *The Guardian* (United Kingdom), Sept. 17, 2007.

Numerous corporations are entering the green product market, but observers argue that at heart green marketing is all about sales, not sustainability.

Schultz, Abby, "How To 'Go Green' on a Budget," *MSN Money*, June 29, 2007.
Many green products are more expensive than conventional options, but consumers can make a difference if they choose their purchases carefully.

Underwood, Anne, "The Chemicals Within," *Newsweek*, Feb. 4, 2008.
Many common household products contain chemicals that could be harmful to humans. Concerns about health effects are driving many shoppers to seek alternatives.

Williams, Alex, "Don't Let the Green Grass Fool You," *The New York Times*, Feb. 10, 2008.
Many suburban Americans would like to shrink their carbon footprints, but skeptics argue that a lifestyle centered on big houses and multiple cars is inherently unsustainable.

Reports and Studies

A Consumer's Guide to Retail Carbon Offset Providers, **Clean Air-Cool Planet**, 2006, www.cleanair-cool-planet.org/ConsumersGuidetoCarbonOffsets.pdf.
An advocacy group that helps businesses, universities and cities and towns reduce greenhouse gas emissions describes key factors that contribute to the quality of carbon offsets and identifies some of the most credible offset providers.

Makower, Joel, *et al.*, *State of Green Business 2008*, January 2008, www.stateofgreenbusiness.com.
A report on the spread of green business practices finds that companies are gradually becoming more eco-friendly, but economic growth is offsetting many of the gains, and that the trend is very hard to quantify.

TerraChoice Environmental Marketing, **"The Six Sins of Greenwashing," November 2007, www.terrachoice .com/Home/Six%20Sins%20of%20Greenwashing.**
A study of environmental claims in North American consumer markets finds that virtually all purportedly eco-friendly products mislead consumers to some degree. More accurate green marketing, it asserts, will benefit consumers, businesses and the environment.

For More Information

American Council for an Energy-Efficient Economy, 1001 Connecticut Ave., N.W., Suite 801, Washington, DC 20036; (202) 429-8873; www.aceee.org. Supports energy-efficiency measures to promote economic prosperity and environmental protection.

Clean Air-Cool Planet, 100 Market St., Suite 204, Portsmouth, NH 03801; (603) 422-6464; www.cleanair-coolplanet.org. A nonprofit organization that partners with businesses, colleges and communities throughout the Northeast to reduce carbon emissions and educate the public and opinion leaders about global warming impacts and solutions.

Climate Trust, 65 SW Yamhill St., Suite 400, Portland, OR 97204; (503) 238-1915; www.climatetrust.org. Created to implement an Oregon law that requires new power plants to offset some of their carbon emissions, the Climate Trust produces greenhouse gas offset projects for energy companies, regulators, businesses, and individuals.

Competitive Enterprise Institute, 1001 Connecticut Ave., N.W., Suite 1250, Washington, DC 20036; (202) 331-1010; www.cei.org. A public policy research center dedicated to advancing the principles of free enterprise and limited government.

Consumers Union, 101 Truman Ave., Yonkers, NY 10703; (914) 378-2000; www.consumersunion.org. A nonprofit expert group that promotes a fair and safe market for all consumers; activities include testing and rating products and publishing *Consumer Reports* magazine, as well as Greener-Choices.org, a Web site focusing on green products.

Federal Trade Commission, 600 Pennsylvania Ave., N.W., Washington, DC 20580; (202) 326-2222; www.ftc.gov. Protects consumers' interests, promotes competition and advises businesses on eco-labeling; it is currently reviewing its green marketing guidelines.

LOHAS Forum, 360 Interlocken Blvd., Broomfield, CO 80021; (303) 822-2263; www.lohas.com. An annual business conference focused on the marketplace for goods and services related to health, the environment, social justice, personal development and sustainable living.

National Association of Manufacturers, 1331 Pennsylvania Ave., N.W., Washington, DC 20004; (202) 637-3000; www.nam.org. Promotes legislation and regulations conducive to economic growth and highlights manufacturers' contributions to innovation and productivity.

TerraChoice Environmental Marketing Inc., 1706 Friedensburg Road, Reading, PA 19606; (800) 478-0399; www.terrachoice.com. Conducts market research and advises on strategy, communication and policy issues.

9

Consumer Safety

Do Government Regulators Need More Power?

Peter Katel

Labels taped to a wall indicate the heights for impact-testing toys at the Consumer Product Safety Commission. "That is a piece of our toy testing facility," the commission's acting chairwoman, Nancy A. Nord, told skeptical lawmakers in September, after conceding the entire lab was in bad shape. The hearing followed calls for stricter federal safety enforcement in the wake of recent product recalls of toys with lead paint and tainted pet food, toothpaste and ground beef.

From *CQ Researcher*,
October 12, 2007.

Office of Sen. Richard J. Durbin, D-Ill.

A steady stream of toy recalls and pet-food scares this summer had Americans on edge. Then a photograph on the front page of *The New York Times* seemed to confirm consumers' worst fears.[1]

The photo of the Consumer Product Safety Commission toy-testing office looked more like the set for a "Saturday Night Live" parody of the beleaguered agency. The only visible measuring devices were pieces of paper taped on the wall — so the tester knew how far toys were falling as he dropped them to the floor.

"Could you explain to me . . . what this reflects in terms of the toy safety inspection capacity of the Consumer Product Safety Commission?" Assistant Senate Majority Leader Richard J. Durbin, D-Ill., asked acting CPSC Chairwoman Nancy A. Nord, at a Sept. 12 hearing.[2]

"That is a piece of our toy testing facility," Nord replied, after conceding that the entire lab was in sorry shape. The tester "basically spends his time doing small-parts testing, drop-testing. If there are other issues dealing with toys, for example, lead testing or electrical testing, there are, obviously, other people in the laboratory that do all that, but Bob's our small-parts guy."

A week later, Nord upbraided reporters and politicians. "While I'm a firm believer in the freedom of the press, I'm also a believer in the responsibility of the press," she told toymakers and safety experts meeting in Washington. But most toy recall stories hadn't noted that "none of the recalls included any report of an injury."

As for politicians, Nord said, "There are a number of new members of Congress who don't understand our agency."

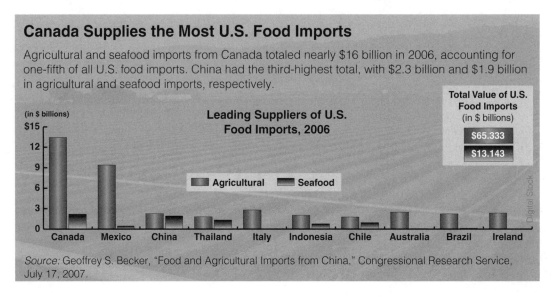

Canada Supplies the Most U.S. Food Imports

Agricultural and seafood imports from Canada totaled nearly $16 billion in 2006, accounting for one-fifth of all U.S. food imports. China had the third-highest total, with $2.3 billion and $1.9 billion in agricultural and seafood imports, respectively.

Leading Suppliers of U.S. Food Imports, 2006

Total Value of U.S. Food Imports (in $ billions)
$65.333
$13.143

Source: Geoffrey S. Becker, "Food and Agricultural Imports from China," Congressional Research Service, July 17, 2007.

But the uproar over consumer safety involves more than questions about the CPSC, Durbin says. "In the pet-food crisis, we were dealing with a vulnerable population who were considered defenseless victims — and China was behind it," he says "And now toys — once again, defenseless victims were being threatened by products from China. And all of a sudden this issue reaches an emotional level it's never had before."

Tamara Fucile, a parent in Washington, D.C., says her daughter had played with one of the recalled toys, a Thomas & Friends train decorated with lead paint.

"I just sort of assumed there were inspections of products," says Fucile. "Did I think that every single item was tested? No. But I thought there was enough random testing that products coming through were safe. This opened my eyes."

Fucile, it turns out, is a legislative assistant for first-term Sen. Amy Klobuchar, D-Minn., who uses that very train — complete with teeth marks — to demonstrate the potential dangers of lead paint.

Holding up the train, former prosecutor Klobuchar asked Nord: "Do you know what percentage of the toys get tested now?"[3]

"No, I don't," Nord replied.

In fact, manufacturers are responsible for ensuring that their goods meet federal safety standards. The CPSC's mission is testing products that consumers have complained about and spot-checking for adherence to safety standards. But former commission staffers have said for years that the lab can't even fulfill that role. "The problem isn't new at all," says Pamela Gilbert, the agency's executive director from 1995-2001. "We asked almost every year when I was at the agency for $1 million to improve the lab, and we never got it."

Now, Durbin and other lawmakers have proposed legislation ratcheting up CPSC funding and making it easier for the commission to warn consumers about potentially dangerous products without getting prior consent from the company. The toy industry opposes that measure, as does Nord, calling it "counterproductive" because she says it would discourage companies from reporting product problems voluntarily.[4]

The recall crisis began in June, when RC2 Corp. of Oak Brook, Ill., recalled 1.5 million Thomas & Friends train sets because of the lead paint, which is banned in the United States. Three more major recalls followed by Mattel, the world's biggest toymaker.

All the toys came from China, which makes more than three-quarters of the world's toys.[5] China also produced most of the other recalled or banned products this year. Last year, however, it was a U.S. product — California spinach tainted with *E. coli* bacteria — that caused the deaths of five people. And late this summer, questions were raised about whether a timely recall was launched in New Jersey for millions of pounds of frozen hamburger patties potentially infected with *E. coli.*[6]

But most of the safety questions have centered on China, amplifying longstanding fears about America's growing dependence on Chinese imports as well as concerns over the effectiveness of government regulatory agencies.[7]

The CPSC now has about 420 employees, roughly half the number it had before cuts that began during the Reagan administration. Since then, China's share of U.S. consumer imports has expanded significantly — jumping 300 percent just from 1997 to 2004. Last year, China accounted for $246 billion worth of consumer products, or 40 percent.[8]

With politicians and consumer advocates aroused, regulators and business trade groups are pushing safety-upgrade proposals critics say are efforts to forestall action by lawmakers. Like the toymakers, the Grocery Manufacturers/Food Producers Association is promoting a proposal requiring the Food and Drug Administration (FDA) to work with food-exporting countries to meet tougher quality standards. Nord, meanwhile, is promoting a proposal that she says would beef up regulatory oversight. And Klobuchar proposes expanding the ban on lead paint in children's products to lead in all products — partly in reaction to the 2006 death of a Minneapolis boy who swallowed a heart-shaped lead charm from a Reebok sales promotion.[9]

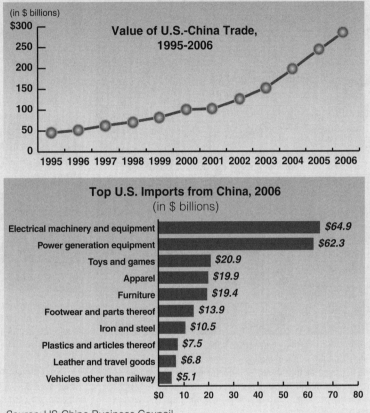

Chinese Exports to U.S. Rising Dramatically

The value of China's trade with the United States reached nearly $300 billion in 2006, a 500-plus percent increase since 1995 (top). More than $60 billion came from machinery (bottom).

Value of U.S.-China Trade, 1995-2006
(in $ billions)

Top U.S. Imports from China, 2006
(in $ billions)

Electrical machinery and equipment	$64.9
Power generation equipment	$62.3
Toys and games	$20.9
Apparel	$19.9
Furniture	$19.4
Footwear and parts thereof	$13.9
Iron and steel	$10.5
Plastics and articles thereof	$7.5
Leather and travel goods	$6.8
Vehicles other than railway	$5.1

Source: US-China Business Council

Consumer advocates reject manufacturers' complaints that the pending bills would set off a wave of government intrusion in business. "These bills would reinstate the necessary authority so the CPSC can enforce the law; they would not impose a command-and-control bureaucracy," says Edmund Mierzwinski, consumer program director for the U.S. Public Interest Research Group. (*See "At Issue," p. 207.*)

Meanwhile, food regulators have their own problems. In a January 2007 report, the Government Accountability Office (GAO) underscored the complexity of federal food-safety regulation, calling it a "high-risk" issue. For example, the agency noted, "Which agency has responsibility for the safety of a ham-and-cheese sandwich depends on whether it's made with one slice of bread or two. [The U.S. Department of Agriculture] inspects manufacturers of packaged open-face meat or poultry sandwiches (e.g., those with one slice of bread), but [the Food and Drug Administration] inspects manufacturers of packaged closed-face meat or poultry sandwiches (e.g., those with two slices of bread)."[10]

The USDA and FDA are among 15 agencies that administer at least 30 laws related to food safety, leading the GAO to note the "patchwork nature of the federal food-oversight system calls into question whether the government can plan more strategically to inspect food production processes, [and] identify and react more quickly to outbreaks of contaminated food."[11]

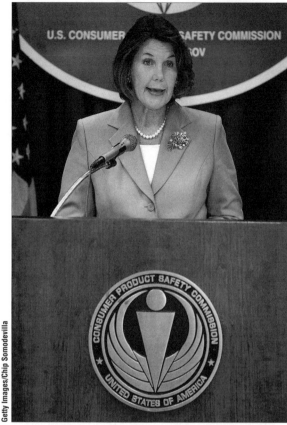

Nancy A. Nord, acting chairwoman of the U.S. Consumer Product Safety Commission, announces yet another toy recall on Aug. 14. She has been on the hot seat for months due to an ongoing controversy over her agency's efforts to ensure the safety of consumer products. Nord is proposing beefing up the agency's regulatory oversight.

Los Angeles veterinarian Pedro Cisneros examines Pebbles, a Yorkshire terrier battling kidney failure after eating tainted dog food made in China. The product killed up to 4,000 animals in the United States last spring.

Events this year have lent urgency to questions about the safety of food and product imports. In March, contaminated wheat gluten in cat and dog food from China caused as many as 4,000 U.S. pet deaths. That discovery sparked a series of recalls involving products for humans. First, Chinese-made toothpaste for sale in Panama, the Dominican Republic and Australia was found to contain diethylene glycol, a toxic antifreeze ingredient that killed 100 Panamanians in 2006 when it was mixed into medicine.[12] This time, no one was killed. But toxic toothpaste turned up in June in New York, New Jersey, Pennsylvania, Maryland and Florida, in some cases counterfeited as Colgate.[13]

Soon afterward, the FDA barred Chinese shrimp, catfish, basa, dace and eel imports after test samples turned up contamination with illegal antibiotics and other chemicals.[14]

The discovery dramatized for many consumers that China exports far more than just toys and appliances. In fact, after Canada, China was America's second-largest source of seafood last year. (*See graph, p. 192.*) All told, the value of all Chinese food imports skyrocketed by 375 percent between 1996 and 2006 — from $880 million to $4.2 billion.[15]

"The food safety process in China is broken," said a report by A.T. Kearney, a global management-consulting firm.[16]

Moreover, China's product-safety bureaucracy appears riddled with corruption. On July 10, the government executed the former chief of the State Food and Drug Administration, Zheng Xiaoyu, after he confessed to taking $832,000 in bribes from drug companies that produced unsafe medicines for China's domestic market.[17]

Although no U.S. recalls were involved, China's harsh response was seen as a signal to export clients that it was taking product safety problems seriously. Chinese officials also met with Nord to assure her China had inaugurated a "zero-tolerance" policy on lead paint.[18] But Nord conceded under questioning by Sen. Durbin that the new policy merely restated existing Chinese law.

"We've got a fistful of promises from the Chinese on safety, and they don't seem to do anything," said House Energy Chairman John D. Dingell, D-Mich. The comment reflected what consumer advocates see as a promising political environment for tougher government supervision of food and product safety.

As the debate over product and food safety heats up, here are some of the issues being debated:

Does the current regulatory system protect consumers?

U.S. consumer-safety laws are far more complicated than most Americans realize. For instance, two different agencies — the USDA and the FDA — share major responsibility for ensuring that food is safe. The USDA's powers include authority to certify foreign meat-processing plants as compliant with U.S. standards, but the FDA, which is responsible for seafood imports, has no such authority over seafood-processing operations abroad.

Perhaps more surprising to most consumers, neither the USDA nor the FDA can recall contaminated foodstuffs. Instead, both agencies work informally with companies to encourage them to initiate a recall.[19] Similarly, the CPSC is prohibited from publicly disclosing the existence of an investigation of possible safety hazards — a provision consumer advocates say puts companies in control of the amount of publicity about safety recalls.

Manufacturers say these voluntary recalls allow speedier action because they avoid legal battles between companies and regulators. But consumer advocates say the simple question remains: Are regulatory agencies ensuring the safety of U.S. foods?

This year's events have raised serious questions about the government's ability to do that, as evidenced by the GAO's "high-risk" designation for food safety problems.

On the product front, the Mattel recalls have led to questions about how manufacturers can ensure safety standards are being met when products are made in remote factories in China or in other developing countries.

Sen. Amy Klobuchar, D-Minn., holds up a recalled Thomas toy train during a Sept. 12 congressional hearing on product-safety agencies and the millions of toys contaminated with lead paint.

Getty Images/Chip Somodevilla

"These recalls should never have happened, especially at Mattel," the company's CEO, Robert Eckert, told the House Energy and Commerce Subcommittee on Commerce, Trade and Consumer Protection on Sept. 19. "Our standards were ignored and our rules were broken. We were let down, and we let you down."[20]

Afterwards, Eckert explained, Mattel hired more inspectors, ensuring full-time supervision in all production plants and requiring that each batch of products be tested for lead before being put on sale. The company also formed a new safety unit, reporting directly to Eckert, and commissioned a third-party review of all safety procedures.

To James L. Gattuso, senior research fellow in regulatory policy at the Heritage Foundation, Mattel's response — and widespread consumer participation in the recalls — show the current system is working. "The market has responded, both manufacturers and consumers — most strongly, consumers. I don't know of any parent of a 5-year-old who has Thomas trains and who doesn't know about this. Millions of trains are being dumped every day."

Gattuso concedes that some parts of the system failed — or the products containing lead paint never would have entered the supply chain. "But once the problem was discovered, the system worked. You are going to have problems occur. The test is whether you have consumer and market reaction; that has clearly happened."

Consumer advocates argue that parental response to recalls of toys may make them a special case. Most recalls bring very few consumers marching back to stores with problematic products. "You get 3-4 percent if you're lucky," says Sally Greenberg, executive director of the National Consumers League. "You put something in the market and it's gone." Greenberg is former senior product safety counsel at Consumers Union.

Greenberg and other critics of the regulatory system have been arguing for years that Congress should ratchet up fines on manufacturers whose products violate standards, and pursue criminal prosecutions as well. "We've been saying all along that there have got to be some penalties for those who don't comply with the law," Greenberg says.

But Frederick Locker, a lawyer for the Toy Industry Association, argues that the Mattel recalls grew out of "human error in China," which allowed some batches of toys to slip through what was already an extensive lead-testing system.

And that system, Locker adds, is why Mattel caught the lead paint in the first place. "There's never been so much lead testing going on. And, keep in mind, this is not government coming to companies and saying you should do this."

Greater harmony exists among consumer advocates and industry officials concerning the state of the food-safety system — which both sides agree has failed to keep up with the times.

"Clearly, FDA's capacity has not kept pace with rising imports," says Scott Faber, vice president of federal affairs for the Grocery Manufacturers/Food Products Association. "And Congress has not provided FDA with the resources needed to respond to dramatic changes in what we eat and where we get our food."

In taking that position, the trade association finds itself in unusual agreement with traditional opponents. (*See sidebar, p. 206.*) "There are a lot of holes and problems with the current system," says Christopher Waldrop, director of the Consumer Federation of America's Food Policy Institute. "There is a huge resource need, particularly on the FDA side. It hasn't been able to keep up with all its responsibilities, which puts consumers at risk."

Do government agencies need stronger regulatory powers?

With food scares, toothpaste panics and successive toy recalls dominating the headlines, politicians, trade associations and consumer groups are scrambling to promote solutions to widely acknowledged problems in the regulatory process.

"Process" may be a misnomer, which itself is part of the problem. Several processes are in place, with different systems covering different kinds of food, for example, while consumer products are the province of yet a third (not counting safety procedures governing automobiles and pharmaceuticals, among other goods).

The existence of different systems reflects the number of laws creating the various arms of the regulatory complex. The nonpartisan Congressional Research Service cites a GAO report that named 15 federal agencies that are enforcing at least 30 laws on food safety alone.[21]

The Federal Meat Inspection Act of 1906, for example, requires all livestock to be inspected during slaughtering and processing. But inspection requirements are lighter for other kinds of foods. Indeed, a food manufacturing plant is likely to get an unannounced visit from an FDA inspector only about once every five years — in contrast to the daily visits to meat plants by USDA inspectors.[22]

The food safety agencies' counterpart is the CPSC, which enforces standards developed by manufacturers, aided in some cases by the American Society of Testing and Materials.

Advocates and officials on all sides of the safety issue acknowledge that industry and consumer-advocacy NGOs (non-governmental organizations) have forged an unusual alliance, especially on food safety matters. Caroline Smith-DeWaal, food safety director at the Center for Science in the Public Interest, typically an industry critic, calls a new proposal by the Grocery Manufacturers/Food Products Association "quite progressive."

As for product regulation, the Mattel recalls have led the Toy Industry Association to devise a plan for mandatory safety inspections, as well as development of a system to ensure that the entire industry complies with American safety standards.

Nevertheless, skepticism still runs deep among advocacy organizations that specialize in product-safety matters. "This is huge that an industry is asking for regulation," says E. Marla Felcher, author of a 2001 book on the marketing of unsafe baby products.[23] "I am obviously suspicious of that. We want to trust these companies, but we can't. Their goal is to make money; my job is as a consumer advocate." Felcher, a former marketing professor at Northwestern University, is an adjunct lecturer on public policy at Harvard University's John F. Kennedy School of Government.

Felcher and others on her side of the debate advocate eliminating a provision that restricts the CPSC from disclosing the names of companies whose products are under investigation for possible safety violations without their consent.

"We call it a gag rule," says the Public Interest Research Group's Mierzwinski, who says the provision effectively requires company consent to all circumstances of a recall. "We've got manufacturers driving the recall train. Look at the roadblocks that the manufacturer can put in front of the CPSC, then you'll see why there are so many voluntary recalls."

Locker of the Toy Industry Association argues that the provision encourages companies to report safety hazards. "You can reassure companies that report [problems] that their proprietary and confidential information will be maintained. If you eliminate that protection, you create a disincentive to reporting."

In addition, Locker notes, the provision allows the CPSC to go public with a company's safety problems when the products in question are "imminently hazardous." Hence, he argues, the commission has no legal barriers to acting more aggressively. "The issue comes down to will and resources."

An ideological difference underlies the dispute. Consumer advocates would give government agencies more power to wield over manufacturers and sellers, a strategy that business views as misguided. "Legislative micromanagement of agencies has historically been a poor way to regulate," Locker says. "We want mandatory regulations to be in place on big generic issues — such as lead. But when you're getting into very product-specific issues, you should let experts develop the standards and have the ability to review them, should technology change."

On the food side of the safety debates, the coalition-building between traditional adversaries hasn't erased all conflicts. Waldrop of the Consumer Federation of America calls the absence of mandatory recall powers for the FDA and USDA a big hole in the food-security net. "Right now, it's a voluntary system — they have to work out agreements with companies, which can be a long, convoluted process," he says. "The agencies don't have the teeth they need."

Waldrop says mandatory recalls wouldn't be necessary in most cases. When food-contamination cases arise, "most companies cooperate" on voluntary recalls, he says. "It's in their interest." But consumer advocates and some lawmakers have long held that the agencies need to have mandatory recall power in reserve, for cases in which the voluntary system fails.

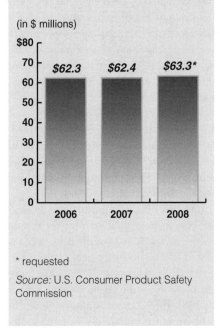

CPSC Funding Remains Stagnant

The budget for the U.S. Consumer Product Safety Commission has not significantly increased since 2006. The administration's 2008 budget would total just over $63 million, less than a $1 million increase from the amount it was allotted two years earlier.

U.S. Consumer Product Safety Commission Budget, 2006–2008

(in $ millions)

* requested

Source: U.S. Consumer Product Safety Commission

In fact, says Faber of the Grocery Manufacturers/Food Producers, the voluntary system has proved its effectiveness. "The food companies have an enormous incentive to recall and eliminate health threats posed by contaminated products."

Faber argues, in fact, that mandatory recall power is a two-edged sword, because any company resisting a recall would have the ability to challenge the order in court — a danger that the present voluntary system bypasses by substituting cooperation for potential litigation.

"Certainly there's no evidence that food companies are dragging their feet when it comes to recalls," Faber says. But he argues that the potential exists. "Mandatory recall and the due-process protections that accompany it could unintentionally slow down recalls when dealing with a bad actor."

Is more funding the answer?

Questions about government services inevitably come down to whether public agencies have enough money to do their job. In the consumer safety debates, most of the non-governmental players agree that government agencies should receive more money. What's in dispute is whether more "resources" would resolve most of the burning questions about the effectiveness of the safety regulatory system.

The position of executive branch players seems to be more delicate. Political appointees represent the Bush administration, which has made a point of not recommending real increases in regulatory agency budgets.

Nevertheless, Congress, not the executive branch, decides how much money agencies should get. And that money has not always been forthcoming, as a veteran lawmaker recently acknowledged. "I am pained to note this morning that it appears that all of us have been derelict in this matter," House Energy Chairman Dingell told a hearing of the House Subcommittee on Commerce, Trade and Consumer Protection. "It is the responsibility of this committee, the subcommittee and, very frankly, the federal government to determine the resources that are available and the sources of the lapse that have taken place, and to take all necessary steps to correct it."[24]

Dingell was alluding to the relatively low budget levels at which safety-regulating agencies have been working since the 1981-1989 Reagan administration. The CPSC budget, for instance, reportedly suffered a 30 percent budget cut during the Reagan administration. The George H.W. Bush and Bill Clinton administrations that followed didn't take steps to make up for that reduction.[25]

Food-safety regulation hasn't fared much better. The Congressional Research Service reported that the Food and Drug Administration's food-safety budget now stands at about one-quarter of its 1971 size. Over the past five years alone, Assistant Commissioner William Hubbard told the House Energy and Commerce Committee's Subcommittee on Oversight and Investigations in July, the FDA's headquarters staff of scientists dropped from about 1,000 scientists to fewer than 800. The "field force" of inspectors and import specialists fell from more than 4,000 to about 3,300.[26]

But, Hubbard says in an interview, increased funding alone wouldn't make up for deficiencies in the food-safety system. "They're not going to be able to inspect every single product," Hubbard says. "You could double their food [regulation] budget and they'd still be underfunded."

In recent months, toy-recall headlines have forced lawmakers to focus greater attention on the CPSC budget. In response, Acting Chairwoman Nord has been calling — though cautiously — for a funding increase for her agency, which now runs on fewer than half the approximately 900 staffers who were on the payroll in 1980.[27]

Nord was asked directly by Rep. Cliff Stearns, R-Fla., whether her agency had "enough people to enforce the mission of the Consumer Product Safety Commission, in your opinion?"

"I would always like more," she replied.

"So you don't have enough people, is what you're saying," Stearns continued.

"I would prefer to have more people," Nord said.[28]

Nord's seeming reluctance to take on that issue may have been explained by an earlier exchange with the hard-charging Dingell. Under his questioning, she acknowledged that the administration's official CPSC budget request for the 2008 fiscal year was based on a 2 percent increase in funding, which, because of inflation, would require a payroll cut from 420 to 401 employees.

Nord told Dingell that she couldn't remember her own request to the administration's Office of Management and Budget, which prepared the recommendation for further paring down of the agency.

For Greenberg, at the National Consumers League, Nord's apparent unease over budget questions has a simple explanation. "It's one of those silly Washington games; they've been told by the Office of Management and Budget that they can't ask for more money, but it's clear that they can't do their job because of cutbacks in staff and resources."

CPSC-regulated companies, meanwhile, walk a line between supporting increased funding and maintaining their preference for a "voluntary" regulatory system, in which companies develop and enforce safety standards mostly on their own. The Toy Industry Association's Locker takes on that task by advocating some modernization and the stanching of further staff losses.

"We've always supported the existence of the agency," Locker says. But, "We don't think necessarily that bigger is better. It's always about doing things in a smarter way. Clearly, they do need updating in the lab, and they do need to retain staff."

By contrast, consumer advocates might be expected to argue the CPSC needs massive infusions of funds. But some argue the commission's limitations aren't fundamentally a matter of money.

"The current problems at CPSC are not primarily resource problems," testified Michael Green, executive director of the Center for Environmental Health, in Oakland, Calif. "Our experience suggests that often CPSC's bias is to protect industry at the expense of the health of America's children."[29]

A similarly nuanced view comes from the Kennedy School's Felcher, also a critic of the CPSC, who advocates tougher penalties for companies that violate safety standards. "Money helps," she says. "It's not just money — that's a necessary but not a sufficient condition."

BACKGROUND

Scandal and Reform

As the United States began to come into its own as a food exporter in the late 1800s, customers abroad began to sound the alarm over U.S. products. In 1879, several countries refused to keep buying American pork after Germany reported contamination with trichinosis and cholera. American beef was also said to be diseased.[30]

Another international uproar arose over "oleo-margarine," which U.S. manufacturers tried to pass off as the real thing, writes Stephen Mihm, a historian at the University of Georgia. Its ingredients included beef fat and ground cow stomach and hog and ewe udders. Not surprisingly, European importers quit buying American butter. Moreover, it turned out that U.S. lard shipped to Britain had been filled out with cottonseed oil.[31]

American consumers, meanwhile, were getting the same shoddy products. By the time the United States

became an exporting nation, Mihm notes, merchants and manufacturers already had developed a culture of disregard for consumers' health as well as for anything approaching truth in labeling.

"Candy was found to contain arsenic and dyed with copper chloride; conniving brewers mixed extracts of 'nux vomica,' a tree that yields strychnine, to simulate the bitter taste of hops," Mihm writes, summarizing the findings of an 1859 report on American food. "Pickles contained copper sulphate, and custard powders yielded traces of lead. Sugar and flour were blended with plaster of Paris. Milk had been watered down, then bulked up with chalk and sheep's brains. Hundred-pound bags of coffee labeled Fine Old Java turned out to consist of three-fifths dried peas, one-fifth chicory and only one-fifth coffee."[32]

The Civil War and its aftermath may have stilled whatever chorus of consumer indignation the report's authors may have hoped to provoke. After the war, however, sentiment began building for federal regulation of food and pharmaceuticals.

But a massive outcry didn't erupt until 1906, when muckraking author Upton Sinclair's novel *The Jungle* revealed flagrant abuses in the meatpacking industry. Sinclair's exposé provoked such outrage that Congress was prompted to pass the Food and Drug and Meat Inspection acts, which President Theodore Roosevelt signed in 1906.

The Food and Drug Act authorized seizures of misbranded foods and foods adulterated with harmful or spoiled ingredients; violators could be fined and sent to prison. Meanwhile, the Bureau of Animal Industry, established in 1884, was ordered to enforce the Meat Inspection Act, which required livestock inspections before and after slaughter and set sanitary standards for slaughterhouses.

Product Safety

In 1920, an avian flu outbreak in New York highlighted the absence of any regulation on poultry. At the time, raising, slaughtering and selling poultry was only starting to become an industry. Congress didn't step into the picture, but many cities and counties began poultry-inspection programs.

During World War II, the U.S. military began requiring inspections for poultry bought for troops. Demand

CHRONOLOGY

1890s-1950s *The industrializing United States moves into the age of consumer protection.*

1906 Crusading journalist Upton Sinclair's novel *The Jungle* portrays filthy conditions in meatpacking plants, leading to the Pure Food and Drug and Federal Meat Inspection acts.

1920 Avian flu outbreak in New York leads to local poultry inspections.

1930 Food and Drug Administration (FDA) is established.

1938 Food, Drug and Cosmetic Act requires FDA to inspect seafood, cheese and other foods.

1957 Poultry Products Inspection Act imposes first national regulatory system for food products.

1958 Amendment to Food, Drug and Cosmetic Act prohibits cancer-causing additives in processed foods.

1960s-1970s *Consumer-protection movement strengthens, but product regulation soon falters.*

1965 Lawyer/activist Ralph Nader's best-selling *Unsafe at Any Speed* virtually launches consumer movement.

1968 President Lyndon B. Johnson establishes Commission on Product Safety.

1972 Congress passes the Consumer Product Safety Act, establishing the Consumer Product Safety Commission (CPSC).

1976 General Accounting Office criticizes CPSC for lax enforcement.

1980s-1990s *Reagan administration launches fight against consumer movement, which it considers meddlesome interference with business.*

1981 President Ronald Reagan's first Office of Management and Budget director vows to cut CPSC "to the bone."

1982 Presidential task force on "regulatory reform" reports that a decrease in enforcement actions saved companies about $2 billion.

1989 Reagan-era cutbacks shrink CPSC budget by $6.5 million; FDA loses about 1,000 employees.

1993 *E. coli*-infected hamburgers kill three children and sicken 300 people in Seattle and elsewhere in the Pacific Northwest.

1996 Clinton administration orders tougher inspection of meat and poultry.

1998 Parents launch campaign for better recall notices after their 17-month-old son dies when his portable crib collapses; little notice had been given that the crib had been recalled.

2000s *Bush administration adopts hands-off policy toward business regulation, but a spate of safety recalls spurs lawmakers to action.*

2002 President George W. Bush's first nominee for CPSC chair is rejected because of her anti-regulation ideology; Senate confirms second candidate with similar views, less stridently expressed.

2004 China's share of U.S. consumer product imports grows to $246 billion, a 300 percent increase from 1997.

2006 Minneapolis boy dies after swallowing lead trinket.... Value of Chinese seafood imported by U.S. has increased by 375 percent in 10 years.

2007 Bush nominates Michael E. Baroody, a lobbyist for the National Manufacturers Association as CPSC chairman. He withdraws after reports the association planned to grant him a $150,000 "severance payment" if he took the post.

2007 Safety scares halt sales or imports of pet food, spinach, seafood and toys. . . . Pet owners report thousands of deaths from contaminated pet food. . . . RC2, maker of Chinese-made Thomas & Friends toy trains, recalls 1.5 million sets. . . . Mattel announces three successive recalls of products, including Barbie play sets, all made in China. . . . Lawmakers propose legislation to toughen product-safety regulation and expand the food-safety system. . . . New Jersey-based Topps Meat Co. closes in October after issuing second-largest beef recall in U.S. history.

for poultry remained high after the war, when the rise of supermarkets vastly expanded the scale of every stage of the food production process. In 1957, Congress passed the Poultry Products Inspection Act.

Poultry products in interstate commerce had to be inspected before and after slaughter, and before processing. Imported birds had to be examined upon entry into the United States. Inspection was also required for chicken plants.

The existence of looser requirements for meat and poultry that wasn't sold across state lines ended in 1967 and 1968, respectively, when Congress passed the Wholesome Meat and Wholesome Poultry Products acts, which mandated state inspection programs at least as rigorous as the federal models.

But as new food-regulation laws were added, the system became increasingly unwieldy and — at times — short on common sense. For instance, the USDA certifies foreign meat and poultry processors, holding them to the same standards as American operations. But the FDA, which is responsible for all other imported foods, such as cheeses, fresh produce and seafood, lacks the authority to grant seals of approval to foreign exporters.

Tougher regulation of meat and poultry marked only one stage of a broad-based campaign for more government supervision of consumer-products manufacturers.

The push for product safety legislation began in 1965 with a campaign for automotive safety by a recent Harvard Law School graduate named Ralph Nader, who went on a lifelong career as a crusader against corporate interests. Nader's challenge to car manufacturers led to seatbelt requirements and other protective measures. "A great problem of contemporary life is how to control the power of economic interests which ignore the harmful effects of their applied science and technology," Nader wrote in his 1965 best-seller, *Unsafe At Any Speed: The Designed-In Dangers of the American Automobile*.[33]

The first federal standards for automobiles were enacted in 1966. Two years later, Congress approved President Lyndon B. Johnson's request to form a seven-member Commission on Product Safety to examine the hazards in such common household items as kitchen appliances, power tools and lawnmowers.

With consumer demand rising for tougher oversight of manufacturers, politicians who fought calls for more regulation found themselves in the minority, like Rep.

H. R. Gross, R-Iowa, who opposed forming the commission. Upon being told that children were getting their fingers caught in washing-machine wringers, Gross replied: "If a few more women would stay home and take care of their children, there wouldn't be so many of them getting their fingers in a wringer."[34]

After two years of investigating, the commission recommended in 1970 that Congress pass a law authorizing mandatory product-safety standards and setting up an executive-branch agency to enforce them. Two years later, Congress passed the Consumer Product Safety Act, which embodied those recommendations. Above all, the law established the CPSC, which by 1980 boasted more than 900 employees.[35]

But even as the commission staff expanded, the agency was coming under fire. A 1976 report by the General Accounting Office (GAO) criticized the CPSC for not ensuring that safety requirements were enforced, thereby allowing unsafe products on store shelves, and for dropping planned criminal cases against manufacturers and retailers. "The commission has not been timely and systematic in assuring industry compliance with safety requirements," the GAO reported.[36]

Some of those who had most strongly supported the CPSC's creation expressed their regret in the strongest terms. The agency's work added up to "a miserable record," Rep. John E. Moss, D-Calif., told *The New York Times* in 1978. "It's been one of my disappointments."[37]

Reagan's Revolution

When President Ronald Reagan took office in 1981, he made deregulation a cornerstone of his administration. Reagan and his big-business backers had held for years that regulators were weakening the economy and unconstitutionally interfering with business' rights. In keeping with that view, Reagan's first director of the Office of Management and Budget promised to cut the CPSC "down to the bone." The new president's special assistant for consumer affairs, Virginia H. Knauer, argued that the administration's doctrine was really pro-consumer. "The general public is now aware that there is a cost to be paid for consumer protection, in some cases a very big cost for very little protection."[38]

By the end of Reagan's first year in office, his Task Force on Regulatory Relief — headed by Vice President George H. W. Bush — reported that the administration's

Cutting Corners: A Great American Tradition

Will China follow in U.S. reform footsteps?

A rising industrial superpower — bent on ramping up its exports — cuts corners in safety and quality along the way. Critics say that aptly describes today's China.

But it also describes 19th-century America, says Stephen Mihm, an assistant professor of history at the University of Georgia.

The examples he cites aren't pretty — "butter" exported to Europe that was actually made from beef fat and stomach and cow, hog and ewe udders, and sausage made from tuberculosis-infected pork.[1]

Such incidents bring to mind recent reports of Chinese exports of diseased seafood, contaminated pet food and lead-tainted toys. "The parallels are really hard to miss, even though they're separated by two centuries and involve two different kinds of societies," Mihm says.

Mihm's recent book, *A Nation of Counterfeiters: Capitalists, Con Men, and the Making of the United States*, focuses on another activity popular in China today — production of fakes. As they say in Shaghai, "We can copy everything except your mother."[2]

Certainly the United States of today bears little resemblance to the young nation of the 1800s, Mihm says. And though he acknowledges that late-19th-century reformers played a key role in arousing public indignation and advocating regulation of manufacturing and food processing, he says there was also another engine of progress — "raw, naked self-interest."

Those who haven't looked closely enough at the past might miss the latter element, he argues. "We like to view these things as having come about because people identified a wrong and rectified it."

The Consumer Product Safety Commission (CPSC) — one of the federal agencies that have come under intense scrutiny during the scandal over unsafe Chinese-made goods — is trying to convince Chinese officials it's in their best interest to develop better enforcement of safety standards. The CPSC describes its so-called China Program as a "cooperative dialogue . . . to reduce the risk of injury to American consumers from Chinese imports."[3]

But it's unclear whether self-interest as a motive has kicked in yet among the Chinese, Mihm says. China hasn't

actions, including a deliberate decrease in enforcement actions against companies, had saved businesses about $2 billion. Those savings would be passed on to consumers, the task force said. Consumer advocate Nader said that, in fact, consumers were paying a price in decreased safety. He cited decisions not to adopt proposals that would have required safer airline seats and airline tires, as well as the administration's endorsement of legislation to loosen food-safety rules.[39]

Reagan and his appointees applied his anti-regulatory doctrine to virtually all industries, including mining, oil exploration and production and transportation, in addition to the consumer-product sector. But product issues often drew the most attention, sometimes prompting successful opposition.

In 1987, a Riverside, Calif., father whose 7-year-old daughter had been killed by a metal-tipped "lawn dart" thrown innocently into the air by her brother launched a one-man campaign that exposed CPSC failure to enforce a rule that was supposed to keep the darts away from children.[40]

That failure was rooted in the "voluntary" approach to regulation taken by CPSC Chairman Terry Scanlon. A congressionally prompted investigation by the commission itself of how it had handled lawn dart regulation showed the tragic results of the CPSC strategy: The toys were widely sold in stores' children's sections; roughly half of the dart packages didn't contain a required warning against children playing with the darts; and 6,100 people had gotten emergency-room treatment for dart injuries in 1978-1986. In 1988, the commission finally issued an outright ban on lawn darts.[41]

By the time Bush became president in 1989, funding for regulatory agencies had been slashed. CPSC staff was cut from 975 to 519, and the agency's budget shrank from $42 million to $34.5 million.[42]

The Food and Drug Administration lost about 1,000 employees between 1994 and 2005 (not including staffers whose salaries are paid by drug makers' user fees and who are assigned exclusively to pharmaceutical issues).[43]

gone through a test experienced by all capitalist societies sooner or later — an economic crash.

"Britain, the United States and other countries went through cataclysmic panics — the growing pains that come with speculative capitalism being unleashed," he says. These led to financial-system reforms, such as establishment of the Securities and Exchange Commission.

In any event, the major difference between the young United States and today's China isn't economic but political, he says. "China is not a democracy, and the United States in the 19th century was, to some extent," Mihm says. "So you don't have the same pressure for change."

On the other hand, a non-democratic system finds ways to deal with scandal that a democratic country would shy away from. For example, China responded to drug-safety problems this year by executing the corrupt head of China's FDA counterpart.[4]

"If the head of the drug agency is corrupt," said James J. Shen, a longtime industry analyst in Beijing, "you can imagine how corrupt the whole system is."[5]

University of Georgia historian Stephen Mihm.

AFP/Getty Images/Jaime Reina

Even so, tracing the parallels kindles more hope than despair for Mihm. "Reform did arrive in the United States in various stages, at various times, even if they were driven by the profit motive," he says. "It makes me more optimistic about China."

---

[1] For further details, see Stephen Mihm, "A nation of outlaws — a century ago, that wasn't China — it was us," *Boston Globe*, Aug. 26, 2007, Ideas Section, p. 1.

[2] Quoted in, "The sincerest form of flattery," *The Economist*, April 24, 2007, www.economist.com/business/displaystory.cfm?story_id=8961838. A vast literature has arisen on counterfeiting. For an introduction, see Ted Fishman, *China Inc.: How the Rise of the Next Superpower Challenges America and the World* (2005), pp. 231-255; Daniel C.K. Chow, "Counterfeiting and China's Economic Development," June 8, 2006 (testimony to U.S.-China Economic and Security Review Commission), www.uscc.gov/hearings/2006hearings/written_testimonies/06_06_08wrts/06_06_7_8_chow_daniel.pdf.

[3] See "International Consumer Product Safety Program 2007, China Program Plan," Consumer Product Safety Commission, 2007, www.cpsc.gov/BUSINFO/intl/china07.pdf.

[4] See David Barboza, "A Chinese Reformer Betrays His Cause, and Pays," *The New York Times*, July 13, 2007, p. A1.

[5] Quoted in *ibid*.

Bush lacked Reagan's passion for deregulation — despite his involvement in the cause as vice president. In any event, during his single term, marked above all by the Persian Gulf War, the long-running fight over regulation mostly simmered.

Political Shifts

The arrival of the Democratic Clinton administration was seen as a sign that tough oversight of business was imminent. "The assault on deregulation is under way," said Brink Lindsey, regulatory affairs director at the Cato Institute, a libertarian, anti-regulation, think tank. "It is entirely likely that we will have substantial new regulatory burdens imposed on business."[44]

That prediction proved exaggerated. While Bill Clinton showed more sympathy to the consumer-advocate community, his major domestic priorities proved to be welfare reform and business expansion.

However, a scare over contaminated meat in the Pacific Northwest that killed three children and sickened 300

people led to an outcry for improved meat inspection. Those stricken had eaten fast-food hamburgers that hadn't been thoroughly cooked, thereby allowing the survival of harmful *E. coli 0157:H7* bacteria that had infected the meat.

Under sudden pressure from frightened consumers, government officials resisted the temptation to simply blame restaurants for not raising cooking temperature to the bacteria-killing temperature of 155 degrees. For one thing, Douglas L. Archer, deputy director of the FDA's Center for Food Safety and Applied Nutrition, told the Senate Agriculture Subcommittee in February 1993, "Even this higher temperature is insufficient to kill high numbers of *E. coli 0157:H7*. . . . The emphasis should not be on changing cooking temperature times; the emphasis must be placed on improving raw ingredients."[45]

Yet, H. Russell Cross, administrator of the U.S. Department of Agriculture (USDA) Food Safety and Inspection Service, told lawmakers: "We do not have the authority to detain or condemn raw meat that is contaminated with bacteria."[46]

Three years later, Clinton announced adoption of more rigorous inspection and control procedures for meat and poultry. Old rules had limited inspectors to the "poke and sniff method" to detect contamination in raw meat. Under new rules, processing plants were required to perform microbial tests for *E. coli*, and inspectors would run tests for another potentially deadly bacterium — salmonella. Food processors also were required to set up detailed plans to control contamination at each stage of their work.[47]

The administration presented the rules as a modern form of regulation that made industry and inspectors partners. "This is an attempt to get away from government micromanaging the process and instead saying to the regulated entity, 'You figure out how to do it, you're responsible, and we'll do some testing to make sure there are performance standards,'" said Sally Katzen, information and regulatory affairs administrator at the Office of Management and Budget.[48]

The 1990s also saw public attention start to focus on an issue that had gotten little attention — notification to consumers who had bought recalled products. In Chicago, the parents of 17-month-old Daniel Keysar helped spotlight the problem after their son died when his Playskool Travel-Lite crib collapsed, choking him.

After 17-month-old Daniel Keysar of Chicago choked to death in the rails of his defective Playskool crib, he became the poster child for a movement to improve safety standards and consumer product recall procedures. His parents, both University of Chicago professors, later learned the crib had been recalled five years earlier after three children had died in the same way. But the recall had gotten little publicity.

The Keysars, both University of Chicago professors, discovered the crib had been recalled five years previously, after three other children had died in the same way. But the recall got little notice.[49]

Manufacturers Hasbro of Rhode Island and Kolcraft Enterprises of Chicago later paid the Keysars a $3 million settlement. They kept up their campaign to force product sellers to keep records of buyers, in case of recalls.[50]

Pendulum Swings

George W. Bush left no doubt of his stance on business regulation when he became president in 2001. The Bush administration recruited from industry and pro-industry lobbying ranks for high-level jobs throughout government that involved supervising business, illustrating his belief that companies had been suffering from overregulation.[51]

Bush suffered a rare defeat, however, in his nomination of an ardently pro-business and anti-regulation member of the CPSC as commission chairwoman. Mary Sheila Gall was rejected for the post when the Senate Commerce Committee voted her down on a party-line vote, at a time when Democrats controlled the Senate. They objected, among other things, to her votes against safety standards for baby walkers and baby bath seats. She had argued unsuccessfully that deaths and injuries involving the devices were the result of adult inattentiveness, not design flaws.[52]

Bush gained approval for his next chairman nominee, Hal Stratton, a former New Mexico state attorney general. Before he resigned in 2006, Stratton earned support from toy manufacturers and other industries. "He's gone out there and tried to stress that the agency is not one to be feared but one to work with," said Locker of the Toy Industry Association.[53]

In one of his closely followed actions, Stratton pushed successfully for adoption of a federal anti-flammability standard for mattresses. But the rule also had the effect of preventing state-court lawsuits by consumers.

Thomas H. Moore, a Democratic commission member, criticized the new standard, saying that lawsuits would be a sign that the rule wasn't effective. Stratton responded, "It doesn't make a lot of sense for our staff to work for 10 years and then have a jury which has no expertise come up with a separate rule for each state."[54]

Stratton also earned criticism for opposing budget increases for the agency and for heavy traveling — about 48 trips in two years — often to industry meetings, with some of the costs borne by trade associations. "Rather than regulate or use the agency as a bully pulpit to promote product safety, Stratton spends his time on airplanes," said Gilbert, who served as the agency's executive director under Stratton's Democratic predecessor. "Does he care about its mission? He likes the trappings and lets the agency putter along with no new advances."[55]

An agency spokesman defended the chairman's travels as part of a strategy "to develop better working relationships with CPSC stakeholders."[56]

In May 2007, Bush's nominee for CPSC chairman withdrew from consideration. Michael E. Baroody, a lobbyist for the National Association of Manufacturers, pulled back after Democrats questioned the propriety of a $150,000 "severance payment" that Baroody would have received from the industry trade group if he had quit to go to the commission.[57]

CURRENT SITUATION

Product Safety Legislation

Action is expected before the end of the year on legislation designed to step up the CPSC's enforcement power and to begin steadily increasing the agency's budget. The goal of increasing funding is to reverse the steady decrease in the CPSC staff that has marked the commission's past 25 years.

The CPSC Reform Act of 2007, introduced by Sen. Mark Pryor, D-Ark., chairman of the Consumer Affairs, Insurance and Automotive Safety Subcommittee, incorporates proposals by Assistant Senate Majority Leader Durbin and Sen. Klobuchar.

As in all regulatory issues, debate and the eventual fate of the legislation are likely to hang on fine distinctions over details.

Major provisions of the bill, however, are simple. They would:

- raise the present limit on CPSC fines to manufacturers;

- give the CPSC greater latitude in publicly disclosing information on companies whose products present safety hazards; and
- ban lead — not simply lead paint — in all children's products.

The lead provision seemed unlikely to provoke major opposition; nor did the proposed budget increase. Pryor's bill would lift the present budget of $63 million to $70 million for the 2008 fiscal year. The goal, a Democratic Senate staffer said, is to appropriate $100 million by 2012, though the bill in its present form would appropriate $106.4 million by then.[58]

Whatever amount is eventually agreed on, the goal of Durbin and his colleagues is to raise the CPSC's staff level from its present 400 to about 500, a staffer said.

In any event, the proposed budget increase is less controversial and complicated than provisions on company secrecy and financial penalties that the CPSC can impose on companies.

Present law authorizes fines of up to $1.8 million for violating commission rules on product safety. Consumer advocates have long called that amount far too low for multibillion-dollar corporations. First of all, says Rachel Weintraub, product safety director for the Consumer Federation of America, fines only rarely reach the maximum amount. More important, she says, "Compliance with CPSC regulations has to be paramount. Fines can't be part of the cost of doing business."

The bill as it now stands would raise the stakes considerably — to a maximum of $100 million per fine.

Nord argues that the possibility of a fine in that amount would have the perverse effect of overloading the commission with company reports of possible safety problems "because in an abundance of caution they [firms] don't want to face a $100 million fine."

The acting chairwoman has proposed raising the fine amount to $10 million. "That would give good incentives but would not unduly overwhelm the agency with meaningless information."

Not surprisingly, the toy industry also objects to the proposed $100 million maximum. But, somewhat surprisingly, Locker echoes consumer advocates in noting that fines have never reached even 70 percent of the present $1.8 million maximum. "You have to wonder, why do you need an increase?" he asks.

Strange Bedfellows Support Product Safety

Both sides want more government spending.

Nothing brings mortal enemies together in Washington faster than sick puppies, tainted food or children being endangered by defective toys.

Witness the strange political bedfellows who have joined forces to respond to the recent series of food and consumer-product recalls: The Grocery Manufacturers/Food Producers Association and other industry lobbies that normally oppose government regulation have linked arms with pro-regulatory groups like the Consumer Federation of America and the Center for Science in the Public Interest.

Former Food and Drug Administration (FDA) Assistant Commissioner William Hubbard first witnessed this sudden blossoming of bipartisanship during a meeting on the status of FDA enforcement.

"The data were even worse than they thought," says Hubbard. "They sat there and said, 'We disagree about almost everything, but we ought to lock arms on this.' "

Scott Faber, the food producers' vice president of federal affairs, says the decision to join with the consumer groups wasn't difficult. "There's widespread agreement that the FDA gold standard — which has really been the international standard for food safety — had lost some of its luster. We've seen that total funding has declined, staff has declined and scientific capacity has declined." Consumer and industry advocates alike agree that a stronger FDA with more inspectors, better scientific capabilities and an improved ability to communicate risk, "is the foundation of a safe food supply."

The trade association has proposed requiring food importers to meet FDA safety and quality standards. "Effective regulation and oversight by federal regulatory agencies such as the FDA are critical and complementary elements of the fabric of consumer protection," the proposal says.[1]

Christopher Waldrop, director of the Consumer Federation of America's Food Policy Institute, gives qualified praise to the proposal. "It's a new recognition by the food industry that a weakened regulatory system doesn't really benefit them or consumers," he says. "It's interesting that they're recognizing the need to ensure that the supply chain is safe."

Indeed, the business lobby generally greeted President Ronald Reagan's anti-regulatory, pro-budget-cutting doctrine in the early 1980s with wild applause — an attitude some businesses still maintain. But amid recent safety scares over consumer products and foods, the food industry's proposal — and its role in forming the pro-FDA alliance — signal a larger shift.

"I have never before seen so many industries joining a push for regulation," said Rick Malberth, director of regulatory policy at OMB Watch, a Washington nonprofit that monitors federal policy. "What we need to watch closely is if this will achieve a real increase in standards and public protections or simply serve corporate interests."[2]

Malberth isn't the only skeptic. "Beware of industry lobbyists," says Edmund Mierzwinski, consumer program director for the U.S. Public Interest Research Group. "Their damage-control guys say, 'We've got to appear to be for reform because we'll have more control over reform.' I've never seen industry seek regulation except when it's in their own best interests."

Members of the pro-FDA coalition, for their part, don't agree on everything. The food industry opposes giving the FDA authority to order food recalls on its own — a power consumer advocates favor.

But the coalition has kept the alliance's objectives simple. "The principal goal is to lobby Congress and the administration to convince them that budget cuts are hurting everyone," Hubbard says. "The FDA has gotten so weak now that it can't do its job effectively."

---

[1] See "A Commitment to Consumers to Ensure the Safety of Imported Foods: Four Pillars of Public-Private Partnership," GMA/FPA, 2007, www.bipac.net/gma/Four_Pillars_Combined_FINAL.pdf.

[2] Quoted in Eric Lipton and Gardiner Harris, "In Turnaround, Industries Seek U.S. Regulations," *The New York Times*, Sept. 16, 2007, p. A1.

Do regulators need expanded authority over consumer goods?

YES
Edmund Mierzwinski
Consumer Program Director,
U.S. Public Interest Research Group

Written for *CQ Researcher*, October 2007

Most Americans would be surprised to learn the Consumer Product Safety Commission (CPSC) does not test products before they are offered for sale. It's left to manufacturers, importers and retailers to guarantee that their products meet all mandatory and voluntary safety standards.

Of course, the commission could never test each of the 15,000 different products — from toasters, escalators and snowmobiles to chainsaws, Barbie dolls and playpens — that it regulates. What the CPSC is supposed to do is enforce the law when companies break it.

But the CPSC is the little agency that couldn't. It's bad enough the commission's current budget of $63 million is woefully inadequate. And with only 15 of its 400-person staff on duty as import inspectors at hundreds of ports of entry, it cannot be expected to stop every lead-laden toy.

Most important, corporations don't fear the commission because its powers to hold them accountable are weak. Companies are more afraid of Wal-Mart's insistence on low prices than on CPSC safety laws.

To better protect consumers, especially children, the CPSC needs, in addition to more money and staff:

- Tougher penalties. Companies view the $1.8 million maximum civil penalty as a cost of doing business, not a deterrent to illegal or unsafe practices.
- More power to force recalls and inform the public about dangerous products. The commission's enabling legislation gives manufacturers and retailers too much control over recalls, including what the agency can say about a product. Thus, many recalls are either "non-recall recalls," where dangerous products are left on shelves, or repair recalls, where consumers must first find out about a recall — which is often poorly promoted — then obtain a repair kit and make repairs on their own.
- Stronger hazard-notification rules. Too many manufacturers are wiggling out of current weak requirements.
- Stronger rules on import safety. Manufacturers have actively promoted third-party testing of imports. Consumer groups don't disagree, provided any third-party certification does not provide immunity for lawsuits brought under state consumer laws. Imported products should also be subject to greater traceability and labeling requirements.

Our society can and should do a better job of protecting the least among us — children — from preventable hazards. These changes would be a start.

NO
James L. Gattuso
Senior Research Fellow,
Regulatory Policy, Heritage Foundation

Written for *CQ Researcher*, October 2007

As the parent of a 5-year-old boy, it was impossible to miss the news. Within hours of the announcement that certain Thomas toy trains were being recalled, our family began to get calls and e-mails from other concerned parents. "Did you hear?" "What are you going to do?" "Should we throw them all away?"

The Thomas recall — triggered when the manufacturer, RC2, found during a routine test that the paint used by its Chinese subcontractor had excessive lead content — was one of many such recalls this year of products (primarily from China) ranging from toys to toothpaste.

The extent of the problem is unclear. Millions of products have been recalled, but there have been no reports of consumer injuries. Injury rates from consumer products have been heading down, and cases of lead poisoning in children are at historic lows. Still, the recalls may be a sign of real problems, especially in China.

But is increasing the power of regulators the solution? Easy answers, such as increasing the number of federal inspectors, may sound good but have little real effect, given the billions of products sold each year. Others, such as empowering state attorneys general to sue, could create a tort nightmare for U.S. companies, raising prices for American goods while not affecting foreign manufacturers beyond legal reach. Still other answers, such as requiring manufacturers to prove financial responsibility, might simply discourage small businesses while benefiting only large corporations.

The best answer to the problems, in fact, may not lie with Congress at all but with consumers, including the informal network of concerned Thomas parents that seemed to spring up in our neighborhood. We didn't throw our Thomas trains away, but many parents across the country did, and many others will be buying far fewer of the little engines and railcars in the future. This affects the bottom line — RC2's market value is down about a third this year. And, while consumers may not deal directly with factories in China and elsewhere, manufacturers do. With their brand names at risk, companies such as Mattel have already acted to strengthen their oversight of offshore manufacturers.

There is a role for regulation. But consumers, acting in the marketplace, provide the strongest, most effective protection against poor quality and unsafe goods. As Sir Topham Hatt (the railroad chief in the Thomas stories) would put it, the marketplace is a really useful engine after all.

Durbin originally proposed a $20 million maximum fine. A Democratic Senate staffer predicts that the present $100 million maximum will be whittled down in negotiations.

The Pryor bill would also set up a procedure under which independent "third party" laboratories would certify the safety of children's products. The toy industry supports the idea.

If the proposed CPSC revamping passes the Senate, it could be combined in the House with smaller-scale measures that are wending their way through the committee process. Among them is a bill by Rep. Jan Schakowsky, D-Ill., that would require makers of cribs, high chairs, strollers and related products to keep contact information for buyers. That way, they could be notified if a product they've bought has been recalled.[59]

The bill is named for Keysar, the Illinois child who died in a crib that his parents hadn't known had been recalled. "How are we going to get the word out? That is the point of this law," Schakowsky said.[60]

Food Safety Legislation

The food-safety system would seem to affect more people than the product-safety regulatory process. But the course of legislation designed to revamp the system is likely to be lengthier than its counterpart on the product-safety side.

However, a few provisions of a new comprehensive bill on the FDA are designed to beef up control of food producers. The measure, which combined several pieces of House and Senate legislation, cleared Congress in late September; President Bush signed it on Sept. 27.[61]

The new provisions, inserted by Durbin, would require food producers to report contamination within 24 hours. And, in the wake of this year's pet-food crisis, the legislation would set pet-food standards and create a warning system when contamination is spotted.

Durbin, a longtime food-safety specialist (as a college student, he worked in a slaughterhouse), has goals that reach beyond the new FDA bill. Speaking in Washington in late September to the Consumer Federation of America's annual food safety conference, Durbin announced that he plans to propose termination of all 12 of the present-day food safety agencies in two years. "That will give us one year to plan a better system, and one year to put the system in place," he said, adding

sardonically, "If the new system isn't any better, we can always go back to the broken system we have now."[62]

But the goal of one big agency may be several years away. In the meantime, Durbin is proposing some patchwork changes.

His Imported Food Security Act of 2007 proposes increasing the number of FDA inspections of food imports by charging fees to importers. The rationale is that the federal government couldn't otherwise afford expanded inspections.

The user-fee strategy would borrow from the FDA's system for evaluating pharmaceuticals for approval. User fees paid by drug manufacturers allowed the FDA to speed up drug studies. The median time per drug approval dropped from 29 months to seven months, Durbin said.

But the food industry — whose members would be paying the new fees — argues that there's a difference between them and drugmakers. "A user fee is a payment for a government service when the benefits of government service accrue narrowly to a particular person or organization," says Faber of the Grocery Manufacturers/ Food Products Association. Food inspection "is a classic case of a benefit that accrues to the public at large and not a particular industry."

Faber agrees that the food-safety system needs expanding. But the industry shouldn't have to pay the price for past inaction, he argues. "Congress has been penny-wise and pound-foolish when it comes to food safety for years and years," he says.

Durbin's bill would cap fees at $20 per imported food product. Revenue would go into research as well as inspections. Research would be aimed at developing new ways to quickly detect contaminants.

However, the food industry has an unlikely ally in its objection to user fees. "We believe that food inspection is a public health service and should be paid for by the federal government," says Waldrop of the Consumer Federation of America's Food Policy Institute, outlining his organization's longtime position. "We don't want to get into the position where the regulated industry is paying for regulation. A natural conflict of interest could pop up."

Waldrop acknowledges that present budgetary circumstances have led him to soften that stance, in light of Durbin's proposal. "There's little chance Congress is going to come up with money to pay for the inspectors we need for the massive amount of imports we have." As a result, he says that he's open to talking with Durbin's staff. User fees "probably need to be explored," he says.

Durbin, for his part, shows little sympathy for consumer advocates' standard anti-user-fee argument. "Don't tell me how much you're for reform if you're not wiling to pay for it," he says. "This is a pay-as-you-go world."

OUTLOOK

'Good Opportunity'?

In a political environment dominated by intense debate over complicated details, some participants in the safety-regulation conflicts seem to have a hard time looking ahead very far. When they do, they're not always cheerful.

"If things keep going the way they are — with the FDA inspecting seven-tenths of 1 percent of imported food now — the FDA will evaporate," says Hubbard, the agency's former assistant commissioner. "As the volume of imports increases, the FDA will go from nothing to less than nothing."

Hubbard puts his hopes in increased congressional funding. "I don't think you're talking about billions of dollars," he says, sounding a note of optimism. "You're talking about an hour's worth of the war in Iraq. A day of the war in Iraq would fund modernization and more inspectors for many years."

Locker of the toy manufacturers predicts a "more invigorated" CPSC in 10 years. "Hopefully, it will be one that is globally engaged." He foresees the negotiation of more safety agreements between the CPSC and foreign governments.

Demands for upgrading of the CPSC — which the toymakers support, he says — are likely to bear fruit. That could enable the CPSC to broaden its scope beyond the industry he represents. "Technically, they have jurisdiction over 15,000 types of consumer products, yet what you hear about is toys, toys, toys."

By contrast, the Heritage Foundation's Gattuso argues that major expansion of the CPSC is unlikely, because it wouldn't be justifiable. "I think there's been a record of success with the present system, relying primarily on markets. The CPSC, especially over the past few years,

AP Photo/Mike Derer

Topps Meat employee Oscar Pachas leaves the plant on Oct. 5 for the last time. The New Jersey meatpacker closed six days after issuing the second-largest beef recall in U.S. history. At least 30 people in eight states were sickened after eating Topps meat tainted with E. coli bacteria.

has been playing a very sensible role in not focusing on new rules and mandates but on consumer education."

Similarly, the food-safety regulatory system shows no need for a major buildup, Gattuso says, because food producers and sellers simply can't stay in business by selling contaminated goods. "These companies have brand names, reputations, and every incentive in the world to protect these reputations by providing consumers what they demand, and their No. 1 demand is safe food. There's no surer way to sink a company than to violate that trust."

But DeWaal of the Center for Science in the Public Interest says that the recent spate of food recalls, coupled with reports of the vastly expanding import market for food sets the stage for major support by politicians and the public for increasing the reach and the capabilities of the food-safety system. "I think we've got a very good opportunity to get comprehensive legislation through Congress in the next year or two."

Durbin, the leading congressional advocate of a reorganized and expanded food-safety system, also sounds an optimistic note. "I believe we have an historic opportunity — now, while people are focused on food safety," he said in a September speech, "to create a strong system that sets the gold standard for food safety worldwide....a 21st-century American food-safety system."[63]

For his part, Faber of the Grocery Manufacturers/ Food Products Association says that the most important element of the new food-safety environment is globalization, which is certain to expand even more over the next decade, promising better food-safety regulation worldwide.

"We'll be importing more food, we'll be exporting more food." As a result, "Food companies are going to be demanding more from their suppliers — more audits, more testing, state-of-the-art food-defense programs," he says. Given that push, "We will have developed new testing capabilities — technological breakthroughs that will make it easier to detect public health threats."

While Faber forecasts these developments as market-driven responses to a new environment, Mierzwinski of the Public Interest Research Group says the present environment also includes a regulatory system that has fallen far behind the demands now placed on it — a circumstance that he says the public now recognizes.

"The way things work around here," he says of Washington, "the pendulum swings, and the pendulum has swung too far toward globalization. There's been a massive push by these corporations for no regulation. We argue that if you're going to be part of this global economy, you've got to respect strong protections for workers, consumers and the environment. Look where just going for the lowest price got us."

NOTES

1. For photo in question see Eric Lipton, "Safety Agency Faces Scrutiny Amid Changes," *The New York Times*, Sept. 2, 2007, p. A1.

2. See "Senate Appropriations Subcommittee on Financial Services and General Government Holds Hearing on Toy Safety Standards," *Congressional Transcripts*, Sept. 12, 2007.

3. *Ibid.*

4. See Annys Shin, "Head of CPSC Opposes Measure," *The Washington Post*, Oct. 5, 2007, p. D1.

5. For toy statistic, see David Barboza, "Owner of Chinese Toy Factory Commits Suicide," *The New York Times*, Aug. 14, 2007, p. C3.

6. See Elizabeth Weise and Julie Schmit, "5 faces. 5 agonizing deaths. 1 year later," *USA Today*, Sept. 21, 2007, p. B1; Kareen Fahim and Andrew Martin, "Food Safety Officials to Review Procedures After Lapses in Recall of Tainted Beef," *The New York Times*, Oct. 5, 2007.

7. See Peter Katel, "Emerging China," *CQ Researcher*, Nov. 11, 2005, pp. 957-980.

8. See "Testimony of the Honorable Nancy A. Nord Acting Chairman, U.S. Consumer Product Safety Commission to the Subcommittee on Financial Services and General Government, United States Senate," Sept. 12, 2007, www.cpsc.gov/pr/nord091207.pdf.

9. See Eric Lipton and Louise Story, "Bid to Root Out Lead Trinkets Falters in U.S.," *The New York Times*, Aug. 6, 2007, p. A1.

10. See "High-Risk Series: An Update," Government Accountability Office, January 2007, p. 27, www.gao.gov/new.items/d07310.pdf.

11. *Ibid.*, p. 4. See also David M. Walker, "Federal Oversight of Food Safety: High-Risk Designation Can Bring Needed Attention to Fragmented System," GAO, Feb. 8, 2007, p. 1, www.gao.gov/new.items/d07449t.pdf.

12. See Walt Bogdanich, "As F.D.A. Tracked Poisoned Drugs, a Trail Went Cold in China," *The New York Times*, June 17, 2007, p. A1; and Walt Bogdanich, "Wider Sale is Seen for Toothpaste Tainted in China," *The New York Times*, June 28, 2007, p. A1; "Key Dates," *op. cit.*; Elizabeth Weise and Julie Schmitt, "Chinese import alert widens," *USA Today*, May 1, 2007, p. A1; Abigail Goldman and Don Lee, "Reported Pet Deaths at 8,500, FDA says," *Los Angles Times*, May 4, 2007, p. C3; Nicholas Zamiska, "Invoice Links Two Chinese Firms To Bad Pet Food," *The Wall Street Journal online*, May 7, 2007.

13. *Ibid.*

14. See "Key Dates," *op. cit.*

15. See Geoffrey S. Becker, "Food and Agricultural Imports From China," Congressional Research Service, updated July 17, 2007, p. 1, www.fas.org/sgp/crs/row/RL34080.pdf. Also, Nelson D. Schwartz, "Chinese Goods Face More Tests By U.S. Firms," *The New York Times*, July 1, 2007, p. A1.

16. See "China Prospers . . . How Do You Get Your Share? The Critical Role of Food Safety," A.T. Kearney, June 21, 2007, pp. 2, 10, www.atkearney.com/res/shared/pdf/ChinaFoodPres.pdf.

17. See Joseph Kahn, "China Quick to Execute Drug Official," *The New York Times*, July 11, 2007, p. C1.

18. See David Barboza, "China Says It Does Care About Product Safety," *The New York Times*, Aug. 18, 2007, p. C3; "Senate Appropriations Committee . . .," *op. cit.*

19. See Lawrence J. Dyckman, "Federal Food Safety and Security System: Fundamental Restructuring Is Needed to Address Fragmentation and Overlap," General Accounting Office, March 30, 2004, p. 2, www.gao.gov/new.items/d04588t.pdf.

20. See "House Energy and Commerce Subcommittee on Commerce, Trade and Consumer Protection Holds Hearing on Lead in Imported Children's Products," Congressional Transcripts, Sept. 19, 2007.

21. See Geoffrey S. Becker and Donna V. Porter, "The Federal Food Safety System: A Primer," Congressional Research Service, updated Feb. 20, 2007, p. 2, http://ncseonline.org/NLE/CRSreports/07March/RS22600.pdf.

22. *Ibid.*, p. 3.

23. See E. Marla Felcher, *It's No Accident: How Corporations Sell Dangerous Baby Products* (2001).

24. See "House Energy and Commerce Subcommittee on Commerce, Trade and Consumer Protection Holds Hearing on Lead in Imported Children's Products," *op. cit.*

25. For budget reduction statistic, see Cindy Skrzycki, "Under Reagan, Scrutiny of Rules Became the Rule," *The Washington Post*, June 8, 2004, p. E1.

26. For Hubbard testimony, see "Safety of Food Supply," House Energy and Commerce Committee, Subcommittee on Oversight and Investigations, *Congressional Transcripts*, July 17, 2007. Also, Geoffrey S. Becker, "Food Safety: Selected Issues and Bills in the 110th Congress," Congressional Research Service, Sept. 4, 2007, p. 14, http://opencrs.cdt.org/rpts/RL34152_20070904.pdf.

27. For statistic on CPSC staffing, see Sen. Richard J. Durbin, D-Ill., opening statement, "Senate Appropriations Subcommittee on Financial Services and General Government Holds Hearing on Toy Safety Standards," *Congressional Transcripts*, Sept. 12, 2007.

28. For dialogue, see "House Energy and Commerce Subcommittee," *op. cit.*

29. *Ibid.*

30. Except where otherwise indicated, material in this subsection is drawn from "About FSIS," Food Safety and Inspection Service, U.S. Department of Agriculture, last modified April 6, 2006, www.fsis.usda.gov/About_FSIS/Agency/History/index.asp; and John P. Swann, "History of the FDA," U.S. Food and Drug Administration, undated, www.fda.gov/oc/history/historyoffda/default.htm; James Harvey Young, "The Long Struggle For the 1906 Law, U.S. Food and Drug Administration, June 1981, www.cfsan.fda.gov/~lrd/history2.html; "Celebrating 100 Years of FMIA," Food Safety and Inspection Service, U.S. Department of Agriculture, May 15, 2006, www.fsis.usda.gov/About_FSIS/100_Years_FMIA/index.asp.

31. See Stephen Mihm, "A Nation of Outlaws," *The Boston Globe*, Aug. 26, 2007, Ideas Section, p. 1.

32. *Ibid.*

33. See www.autolife.umd.umich.edu/Design/Gartman/Books/BK_Unsafe_Any_Speed.htm.

34. Quoted in "House Backs Panel on Product Safety," *The New York Times*, The Associated Press," Nov. 7, 1967. Also see John D. Morris, "Now, Let the Seller Beware," *The New York Times*, Jan. 8, 1968; and John D. Morris, "Safety Standards for Home Devices Urged on Congress," *The New York Times*, June 24, 1970.

35. See Morris, "Safety Standards Urged on Congress," *ibid*. Also see M. Costello, "Toy Safety," *Editorial*

Research Reports, Nov. 15, 1972, available in *CQ Researcher Plus Archives*, http://www.cqpress.com.

36. See "Better Enforcement of Safety Requirements Needed by the Consumer Product Safety Commission," GAO, July 26, 1976, p. i, http://archive.gao.gov/f0202/093698.pdf.

37. Quoted in Jo Thomas, "Performance of Consumer Agency Disappoints Its Early Supporters," *The New York Times*, Jan. 30, 1978.

38. Stockman quoted in Sari Horwitz, "Consumer Agency Faces An Uncertain Future After Tumultuous Week," *The Washington Post*, Jan. 18, 1985, p. K1. Knauer quoted in Michael deCourcy Hinds, "Laissez-Faire Consumerism," *The New York Times*, Aug. 21, 1982, p. A9.

39. See Michael deCourcy Hinds, "Reagan's Drive To Cut Rules: Impact Depends on Industry," *The New York Times*, Jan. 23, 1982, p. A1.

40. See Bob Baker, "Demands Ban on Lawn Darts," *Los Angeles Times*, Sept. 27, 1987, p. A1.

41. *Ibid.* Also, "CPSC Bans Lawn Darts," (official announcement), undated, effective date Dec. 18, 1988, www.cpsc.gov/CPSCPUB/PUBS/5053.html.

42. See Dale Russakoff, "The Little Agency That Can't," *The Washington Post*, Feb. 2, 1989, p. A23.

43. See William K. Hubbard, testimony before House Energy and Commerce Subcommittee on Oversight and Investigations, July 17, 2007.

44. Quoted in Jube Shiver Jr., "Regulators Likely To Be Busy in Clinton Era," *Los Angeles Times*, Nov. 13, 1992, p. D1.

45. Quoted in Daniel P. Puzo, "Meat Inspection: 'No Longer Adequate,' " *Los Angeles Times*, Feb. 11, 1993, p. H2. Also see Mary H. Cooper, "Food Safety," *CQ Researcher*, June 6, 1993, pp. 481-504.

46. *Ibid.*

47. See Todd S. Purdum, "Meat Inspections Facing Overhaul, First in 90 Years," *The New York Times*, July 7, 1996, p. A1.

48. *Ibid.*

49. See Diana Digges, "Turning grief Into a grass-roots movement," *Christian Science Monitor*, July 3, 2001, p. A20; Bruce Mohl and Patricia Wen, "Are Consumers Getting Enough Protection?" *Chicago Tribune*, July 30, 1998, p. A3.

50. See "Playpen makers agree to pay $3 million," *Chicago Tribune*, Dec. 7, 2001, p. A3.

51. See Mary H. Cooper, "Bush and the Environment," *CQ Researcher*, Oct. 25, 2002, pp. 865-896; Peter Katel, "Lobbying Boom," *CQ Researcher*, July 22, 2005, pp. 613-636; Stephen LaBaton, "Bush Is Putting Team in Place for a Full-Bore Assault on Regulation," *The New York Times*, May 23, 2001, p. C1; Joel Brinkley, "Out of Spotlight, Bush Overhauls U.S. Regulations," *The New York Times*, Aug. 14, 2004, p. A1.

52. See Caroline E. Mayer, "Bush Nominee Puts Safety First," *The Washington Post*, April 26, 2002, p. E1.

53. Quoted in Caroline E. Mayer, "Critics Doubt Safety Chief's Priorities," *The Washington Post*, Oct. 30, 2004, p. E1.

54. Quoted in Caroline E. Mayer, "CPSC Passes Mattress Standard That Should Limit Consumer Suits," *The Washington Post*, Feb. 17, 2006, p. D2.

55. Quoted in Mayer, "Critics Doubt . . .," *op. cit.*

56. *Ibid.*

57. "Agency nominee withdraws," *Los Angeles Times*, The Associated Press, May 24, 2007, p. A19.

58. See "S. 2045, Introduced in Senate Sept. 12, 2007," http://thomas.loc.gov/cgi-bin/query/z?c110:S.2045.

59. See Rebecca Kimitch, "Product Safety Bills Would Require Notification, Boost Fines," *CQ Weekly*, Oct. 1, 2007, p. 2868.

60. Quoted in *ibid.*

61. See Drew Armstrong, "FDA Bill Clears After Intense Negotiation," *CQ Weekly*, Sept. 24, 2007, p. 2766.

62. The text of Durbin's speech was supplied by his staff.

63. *Ibid.*

BIBLIOGRAPHY

Books

Felcher, E. Marla, *It's No Accident: How Corporations Sell Dangerous Baby Products, Common Courage Press*, **2001.**

A marketing professor says baby-product manufacturers and the Consumer Product Safety Commission (CPSC) are not protecting consumers.

Schlosser, Eric, *Fast-Food Nation, Harper Perennial*, 2005 (reissue).
A journalist exposes unsafe practices in a signature American industry.

Articles

Barrionuevo, Alexei, "Ingredients Come From All Over, but Are They Safe?" *The New York Times*, June 16, 2007, p. C1.
A business journalist explores the little-known world of globalized ingredients in factory-made foods.

Bogdanich, Walt, "The Everyman Who Exposed Tainted Toothpaste," *The New York Times*, Oct. 1, 2007, p. A1.
A journalist tracks down the humble Panamanian who found the toxic toothpaste ingredient — by reading the label.

Casey, Nicholas, *et al.*, "Mattel Seeks to Placate China With Apology," *The Wall Street Journal*, Sept. 22-23, 2007, p. A1.
Mattel has had to simultaneously deal with American politicians and Chinese officials.

Goldman, Abigail, "Think outside toy box to find hazards," *Los Angeles Times*, Sept. 23, 2007, p. C1.
Children are at greater risk from lead paint on walls and from swallowing small toys than from toys painted with lead.

Lipton, Eric, "Safety Agency Faces Scrutiny Amid Charges," *The New York Times*, Sept. 2, 2007, p. A1.
The CPSC is inadequate on every front, former staffers and consumer advocates tell the *Times*' regulatory-affairs reporter.

Lipton, Eric, and Gardiner Harris, "In Turnaround, Industries Seek U.S. Regulations," *The New York Times*, Sept. 16, 2007, p. A1.
Responding to safety scares and recalls, industries preempt calls for stepped-up regulation by making their own proposals.

Lipton, Eric, and Louise Story, "Bid to Root Lead Trinkets Falters in U.S.," *The New York Times*, Aug. 6, 2007, p. A1.
An in-depth report finds that charms and other children's jewelry made of lead and potentially fatal if swallowed remain widely available.

Pierson, David, and Tiffany Hsu, "Food from China scares some, tantalizes others," *Los Angeles Times*, Aug. 24, 2007, p. B1.
Reporters venture into Los Angeles' Asian-ingredients universe to chronicle the effects of reported contamination of Chinese products.

Schmit, Julie, "U.S. food imports outrun FDA resources," *USA Today*, March 19, 2007, p. B1.
The lead federal regulator of imported food safety can't keep up with the growing volume of food from abroad, a consumer-affairs specialist reports.

Reports

Keithley, Carter, "Testimony to the Senate Committee on Appropriations, Subcommittee on Financial Services and General Government," *Toy Industry Association*, Sept. 12, 2007, www.toyassociation.org/ AM/Template.cfm?Section=Home&CONTENTID=3 073&TEMPLATE=/CM/ContentDisplay.cfm.
The president of the major trade association involved in the recent spate of recalls testifies that the organization is upgrading safety regulation.

Morrison, Wayne M., "Health and Safety Concerns Over U.S. Imports of Chinese Products: An Overview," *Congressional Research Service*, Aug. 28, 2007, www.opencrs.com/rpts/RS22713_ 20070828.pdf.
Researcher Morrison provides a dispassionate overview of safety issues in Chinese imports.

"Scientific Criteria to Ensure Safe Food," *National Research Council*, 2003, http://books.nap.edu/open-book.php?isbn=030908928X.
An excerpt from a book-length study by a leading nongovernmental group argues the food-safety system needs upgrading.

"USDA and FDA Need to Better Ensure Prompt and Complete Recalls of Potentially Unsafe Food,"

Government Accountability Office, October 2004, www.gao.gov/highlights/d0551high.pdf.
The GAO casts a critical eye on how the major food-safety agencies operate when contamination emergencies arise.

Walker, David M., "Federal Oversight of Food Safety: High-Risk Designation Can Bring Needed Attention

to Fragmented System," *Government Accountability Office*, Feb. 8, 2007, www.gao.gov/new.items/d07449t .pdf.
The head of the GAO reports on his agency's effort to raise the level of concern about erosion of the food-safety system.

For More Information

Center for Science in the Public Interest, 1875 Connecticut Ave., N.W., Suite 300, Washington, DC 20009; (202) 332-9110; www.cspinet.org. Maintains an active food-safety advocacy division.

Coalition for a Stronger FDA, 1333 New Hampshire Ave., N.W., Suite 429, Washington DC, 20036; (202) 887-4211; www.fdacoalition.org. Alliance of industry and consumer groups that joined forces to lobby for more funding for the main food-safety regulating agency.

Consumer Federation of America, 1620 I St., N.W., Suite 200, Washington, DC 20006; (202) 387-6121; www .consumerfed.org. The federation's Food Policy Institute promotes legislation to improve food inspections.

Consumer Product Safety Commission, 4330 East-West Highway, Bethesda, MD 20814; (301) 504-7921; www.cpsc .gov. Enforces safety standards on toys, appliances, tools and a wide variety of other items.

Consumers Union, 101 Truman Ave., Yonkers, NY 10703-1057; (914) 378-2000; www.consumersunion.org. Advocates

state and federal consumer-protection measures; publishes Consumer Reports.

Grocery Manufacturers/Food Products Association, 1350 I St., N.W., Suite 300, Washington DC 20005; (202) 337-9400; www.gmabrands.com. The food industry's leading trade association is pushing for legislation to improve food-safety regulation.

National Consumers League, 1701 K St., N.W., Suite 1200, Washington DC 20006; (202) 835-3323; www.nclnet. org. Advocates tougher regulatory enforcement in food and product safety.

Toy Industry Association, www.toyassociation.org. A leading trade group that is developing its own program to improve safety inspections of toys made in China.

U.S. Public Interest Research Group, Federal Advocacy Office, 218 D St., S.E., Washington, DC 20003-1900; (202) 546-9707; www.uspirg.org. Advocates stiffer consumer-safety laws.

10

Limiting Lawsuits

*Is Business Pushing
Too Hard to Restrict Litigation?*

Kenneth Jost

Vermont musician Diana Levine now uses a prosthetic arm following a tragic medical mistake that led to the amputation of her lower arm after she was given a drug manufactured by Wyeth Pharmaceuticals. Levine sued Wyeth and won a nearly $6.8 million award, which Wyeth appealed to the U.S. Supreme Court. The closely watched case, argued on Nov. 3, will determine whether federal law protects drugmakers against state court suits by patients injured by use of their medications.

From *CQ Researcher*,
December 19, 2008.

Diana Levine went to her doctor's office in the rural Vermont town of Plainfield on April 7, 2000, just as she had done many times before, for treatment of a migraine headache. A physician's assistant gave Levine the same medicine she had received before: two shots in the butt, one with the pain-reliever Demerol and the other with an anti-nausea drug marketed by Wyeth Pharmaceuticals as Phenergan.

When the pain and nausea did not go away, Levine, a professional pianist and guitarist and composer of children's songs, returned to the clinic that afternoon. This time, the physician's assistant made a terrible mistake. To get the two drugs into Levine's bloodstream faster, she used a technique known as an "IV-push injection." But the needle went into an artery instead of a vein, causing an infection that eventually led to gangrene and amputation of Levine's right arm up to the elbow.

Levine won a nearly $6.8 million judgment against Wyeth after a state court jury agreed with her that the giant drugmaker had failed to adequately warn patients about the dangers from an IV-push injection of Phenergan.

Wyeth is now asking the Supreme Court to throw out the judgment and gut Levine's case on the ground that federal law bars — or preempts — state court "failure to warn" suits against drugmakers. The closely watched case will determine whether federal law gives pharmaceutical manufacturers broad protection against state court suits by patients injured by use of their medications.

New Jersey-based Wyeth contends that the federal Food and Drug Administration (FDA) approved the warning about IV push included in Phenergan's label and information sheet and that the

Majority of States Limit Punitive Damage Awards

At least 37 states have enacted laws since the late 1980s limiting punitive damage awards either with mathematical caps or tightened evidentiary standards, according to the American Tort Reform Association.

The mathematical caps enacted in 20 states typically limit punitive damages to no more than two or three times the compensatory award in the case. Among the laws in the 17 other states, most require "clear and convincing" evidence of wrongdoing for a punitive damage award — a higher standard than required for a compensatory award; one of those laws (Kentucky's) was later struck down by the state's supreme court. Three of the states passed laws specifying that a portion of any punitive damage award be paid to the state.

Four states do not permit punitive damage awards. The tort reform association lists no new limits on punitive damage awards in the nine other states and the District of Columbia.

Punitive Damage Policies in the U.S.

Punitive Damages
- Not allowed
- Amount capped
- Other limits on awards
- Unlimited

Source: American Tort Reform Association (www.atra.org/reforms/)

company of the big tobacco company Philip Morris USA was seeking to block a broad class-action suit in Maine state courts charging the company with fraud in the marketing of so-called "light" cigarettes.

Preemption is a long-settled legal principle extended within the past two decades to limit state court suits in areas covered by federal law. It is one of three major battlegrounds today in the decades-long war over personal-injury suits waged by the business community and conservative critics of litigation on one hand and trial lawyers and consumer groups on the other.[2]

Business groups suffered a setback on preemption issues when the Supreme Court voted 5-4 on Dec. 15 to allow the Maine smokers to proceed with their suit charging Philip Morris with violating the state's deceptive-practices law. The majority held that the federal law regulating cigarette labeling and advertising does not bar the suit. The three smokers who filed the suit claim the description of Marlboro Lights and Cambridge Lights as having "lowered tar and nicotine" is misleading because Philip Morris knows that smokers typically compensate by inhaling more deeply (*see p. 229*).

In a related area, business groups are also continuing to urge courts and state legislatures to rein in punitive damages — the penalties that judges or juries can tack on to compensatory awards in civil suits in order to punish companies for especially wrongful or harmful conduct. In one protracted legal battle, the justices heard arguments on Dec. 3 in Philip Morris' effort to set aside a $79.5 million punitive damage award won by the widow of a long-time smoker who died of lung cancer in 1997.

Business groups also want courts to help enforce clauses in business-consumer contracts that channel

company would have run afoul of federal law with any additional information.[1] (*See sidebar, p. 226.*)

The case — *Wyeth v. Levine* — was argued on Nov. 3, a little more than eight months after the Supreme Court had ruled on similar preemption grounds that federal law blocks state court suits for injuries caused by FDA-approved medical devices. In a second important preemption case before the justices this fall, the parent disputes out of the courts and into a non-judicial dispute-resolution system known as arbitration. Business lobbyists have helped bottle up bills aimed at limiting arbitration backed by trial lawyers and consumer groups, who say businesses enjoy critical advantages over consumers in arbitration. (*See sidebar, p. 230.*)

The U.S. Chamber of Commerce's Institute for Legal Reform showcased the three topics in a full-day session in Washington on Oct. 29, on the eve of the presidential election. "If we hope to fully restore our economy, we cannot allow lawsuits to siphon off money that should be used to help our country recover," U.S. Chamber President and CEO Tom Donohue said in opening the conference.

Only a few days earlier, the Chamber had sent an e-mail "blast" blaming the legal system for the current financial crisis. Across town, the American Association for Justice (AAJ) — formerly the Association of Trial Lawyers of America — countered with a press release accusing the Chamber of seeking "to protect only negligent corporations, regardless of the consequences to small businesses, investors and American families."

The war of words comes even though business groups acknowledge a change in legal culture wrought by their campaign stretching over four decades to reform the tort system — the branch of law dealing with personal injury suits. "It's been a period of great accomplishment," says Sherman "Tiger" Joyce, president of the American Tort Reform Association.

"The climate has improved with regard to the types of litigation and the level [of litigation]," says Institute President Lisa Rickard. "There's a much greater sensitivity among Americans about the abuses that we've seen in our litigation system."

Over the years, plaintiffs and consumer groups have resisted the tort reform efforts in Congress and state legislatures as well as in state and federal courts. Today, they deny that U.S. business is being hurt by a

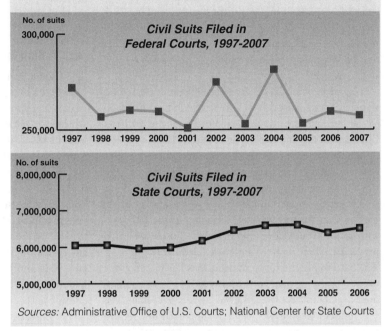

Number of Civil Suits Stayed Flat

The number of civil suits filed in both state and federal courts changed little in the past decade, reflecting the generally held view that overloaded courts are not a problem to the U.S. legal system.

Civil Suits Filed in Federal Courts, 1997-2007

No. of suits

Civil Suits Filed in State Courts, 1997-2007

No. of suits

Sources: Administrative Office of U.S. Courts; National Center for State Courts

flood of lawsuits or a host of big damage awards. "I don't see an uptick at all in the number of suits that are being filed or the remedies being awarded," says Linda Lipsen, the AAJ's director of communications. (*See graphs, above.*)

"Tort reform has been enacted all over the country," Lipsen continues. "The amount of compensation is going down. I see lawyers all over the country not taking cases because the climate is so unfavorable."

"There's no empirical evidence" of business being hurt by large numbers of frivolous lawsuits, says Brian Wolfman, director of the Public Citizen Litigation Group, part of the Washington-based consumer advocacy organization founded by Ralph Nader. Wolfman notes that plaintiffs or lawyers can be penalized by courts for filing frivolous lawsuits and lawyers have a financial disincentive not to take losing cases on a contingency-fee basis.

The late 20th-century changes in the legal climate came after a nearly century-long period of expansion of legal remedies, according to Richard Nagareda, a professor at Vanderbilt Law School and director of the school's program on litigation and dispute resolution.

"There's no doubt that not only did our civil justice system recognize through common law but also through significant national statutes many additional rights of action that were not in place at the beginning of the 20th century," Nagareda says. "We've seen in the late part of the 20th century some skepticism about the difficulties that have come up in a system that facilitates litigation to such a degree."

Nagareda says U.S. courts are more open to litigation than legal systems in other countries, including industrialized democracies in Western Europe and elsewhere. But he adds that the United States also relies more heavily than those countries on the legal system and less on government agencies to compensate individuals for injuries and to regulate products in the market.

Litigation issues have split the two major political parties since the tort wars began raging in the 1970s — with most Republicans supporting the business-backed proposals to limit lawsuits and many Democrats opposed. The pattern of campaign contributions has matched the parties' opposing stands. Business groups have contributed heavily to Republicans, trial lawyers to Democrats.

President George W. Bush has supported tort reform ever since his first campaign for governor of Texas in 1994. As president, Bush pushed tort reform proposals with limited results in Congress but somewhat greater success in getting federal agencies to support preempting state court suits. His two appointees to the Supreme Court — Chief Justice John G. Roberts Jr. and Justice Samuel A. Alito Jr. — have joined in decisions limiting civil lawsuits. (*See chart, pp. 219-220.*)

President-elect Barack Obama's likely stance on the litigation issue and the orientation of the fortified Democratic majority in Congress are viewed hopefully by trial lawyers and consumer groups and warily by the business community. But one litigation expert says debates over the next few years will be shaped not so much by politicians' views as by the public's reaction to unsettling economic conditions.

"In difficult economic times, the people in the business community aren't making money for all of us," says J. David Prince, a professor at William Mitchell College of Law in St. Paul, Minn., and co-author of a blog on product-liability law. "Times are not so good. That lends itself to a more widespread doubt about the business community's motivation and their ability to do the right thing, to make good judgments."

As the battles over civil justice continue, here are some of the major questions on the table:

Should federal preemption be used to limit lawsuits in state courts?

The Canadian Pacific (CP) freight train that derailed in Minot, N.D., on Jan. 18, 2002, released a cloud of 220,000 gallons of caustic anhydrous ammonia into the air, caused one death and hundreds of injuries and led to legal battles still being fought in state and federal courts nearly seven years later. CP and its Minneapolis subsidiary Soo Line Railroad — which was responsible for maintaining the tracks — have paid out undisclosed millions of dollars to settle tens of thousands of claims, with several hundred cases still pending.[3]

Among the issues in the litigation was whether federal law regulating railroads preempted claims based on state law. State and federal courts disagreed on the question. Eventually, Congress passed a law in summer 2007 specifically authorizing federal court remedies in derailment cases and retroactively applying the law to the Minot incident.[4]

Now, a new regulation issued by the Transportation Security Administration (TSA) on Nov. 26 appears to preempt future state law claims against railroads arising from transportation of hazardous materials. In issuing the rule, the TSA said that subjecting railroads to "different regulations in different jurisdictions" could require "a multitude" of different operating procedures and "likely would place a substantial burden on interstate commerce."[5]

The trial lawyers group is denouncing the rule along with some 20 other "midnight regulations" being considered by the Bush administration in its final weeks in office to protect federally regulated industries from claims based on more open-ended state law requirements. "If these regulations are issued within the next few weeks, countless numbers of customers are going to lose their ability to hold manufacturers accountable, and these manufacturers are going to have complete immunity given to them by the Bush administration," says Gerie Voss, AAJ's director of regulatory affairs.

Business groups, on the other hand, applaud the administration's record on preemption issues. "In circumstances where there needs to be a unified rule or statute in place, they're not afraid of making it clear that federal law is going to prevail and trump potentially conflicting state laws," says Matt Webb, senior vice president for legal reform policy at the Chamber of Commerce's Institute for Legal Reform.

Webb sees nothing improper in the administration's final push to put preemptive language into federal regulations. The rules "have been in the pipeline" and available for comment for the appropriate time, Webb says. "They've complied with all the applicable requirements."

Federal preemption of conflicting state laws is a fundamental constitutional principle. The Constitution's Supremacy Clause declares that the Constitution and all federal laws and treaties are "the supreme Law of the Land" (Art. VI, cl. 2). Until the 1990s, however, the Supreme Court's federal preemption decisions centered on how to determine whether a state law directly conflicted or improperly interfered with federal law.

Beginning in the 1990s, the court also ruled that jury verdicts returned in state courts were subject to federal preemption principles. The rulings came in business-backed appeals of jury verdicts in product-liability cases holding companies liable for injuries to consumers based on state, not federal law.

"If it wasn't for the outcry of the business community, it's not clear that these issues would percolate up to the highest court in the land," says Nagareda, the Vanderbilt professor. "It has changed the agenda."

Roberts, Alito Join in Pro-Business Rulings

The Supreme Court has issued at least nine decisions making it harder for plaintiffs to win business-related suits in the two full terms since President George W. Bush's two appointees, Chief Justice John G. Roberts Jr. and Justice Samuel A. Alito Jr., joined the court. Some of the rulings have been by one-sided votes; others were closely divided. Roberts and Alito have voted with the business defendants in all of the cases with the exception of one in which Alito was recused. The decisions are listed in chronological order.

[Photos enlarged of justices voting with the majority]

Breyer **Thomas Kennedy** Stevens **Roberts Scalia** Souter Ginsburg **Alito**

Philip Morris USA v. Williams **(Feb. 20, 2007) 5-4**
Limits punitive damages for harm to parties not before court

Breyer **Thomas Kennedy** Stevens **Roberts Scalia Souter** Ginsburg **Alito**

Bell Atlantic Corp. v. Twombly **(May 21, 2007) 7-2**
Tightens pleading requirements in restraint-of-trade antitrust suits

Breyer **Thomas Kennedy** Stevens **Roberts Scalia** Souter Ginsburg **Alito**

Ledbetter v. Goodyear Tire & Rubber Co., Inc. **(May 29, 2007) 5-4**
Strictly enforces time limits for claims of pay discrimination

Breyer Thomas Kennedy **Stevens Roberts Scalia Souter Ginsburg Alito**

Credit Suisse Securities (USA) LLC v. Billing **(June 18, 2007) 7-1**
Bars antitrust suits against underwriters of initial public stock offerings

Tellabs, Inc. v. Makor Issues & Rights, Ltd. (June 21, 2007) 8–1
Tightens pleading requirements in securities fraud suits

Leegin Creative Leather Products, Inc. v. PSKS, Inc. (June 28, 2007) 5–4
Limits antitrust suits for minimum-pricing agreements

Stoneridge Investment Partners, LLC v. Scientific-Atlanta, Inc.
(Jan. 15, 2008) 5–3
Limits securities fraud suits against companies with indirect connection to
illegal conduct

Riegel v. Medtronic, Inc. (Feb. 20, 2008) 8–1
Bars state-court suits for injuries caused by FDA-approved medical devices

Exxon Shipping Co. v. Baker (June 25, 2008) 5–3
Limits punitive damages in federal maritime cases, slashing penalty for
Exxon Valdez oil spill

Source: Kenneth Jost, The Supreme Court Yearbook, CQ Press (annual
series)

Tort-reform advocates say juries have neither the authority nor the expertise to find companies liable if they have complied with federal regulations. "It's really not for an individual or a jury or a state court to second-guess or overturn the decisions of a regulatory agency," says Joyce at the American Tort Reform Association. "That violates the Supremacy Clause. If that's an area that Congress decides to occupy, that's the end of the discussion."

Trial lawyers and consumer groups counter that state court lawsuits strengthen the enforcement of federal regulations. "I think the tort system more often complements the federal system," says Public Citizen's Wolfman. Lipsen of the trial lawyers' group says weakening state court suits hurts consumers. "If companies are off the hook when their products cause injury or death, there are going to be more dangerous products in the marketplace," she says.

Nagareda says both sides make valid points in the debate. "The plaintiffs bar raises genuine concern about the ability of centralized administrative agencies to engage in enlightened regulation," he says. "We know that regulation does not function at all perfectly.

"At the same time, the business community is right to raise concerns about the decision-making of civil juries," Nagareda continues. Like business groups, Nagareda stresses that juries see "only one side" of a case — the injury to the plaintiff — without considering the overall benefits of a product or the costs of additional regulation. "These are really, really hard trade-offs to make," he concludes.

Should Congress limit mandatory arbitration agreements for business-consumer disputes?

When Hattie Miller was admitted to the Guadalupe Valley Nursing Center in Seguin, Texas, after suffering a stroke, one of her daughters was asked to sign what the staff described as standard forms necessary for admission. Months later, after her family filed suit for injuries Miller sustained while in the center, they learned that the supposedly routine papers required that any dispute be handled not in a court of law but through arbitration.

"We couldn't believe that after the way my grandmother was treated, we didn't have the right to try our case to a jury," Linda Stewart, one of Miller's granddaughters, told a House subcommittee in June. But Stewart said the family decided to settle the case after the company that owned the nursing home said it would fight to enforce the arbitration agreement up to the Texas Supreme Court.[6]

Arbitration began to gain acceptance in the United States early in the 20th century as a method for resolving disputes between businesses. Today, mandatory arbitration agreements are standard in all sorts of consumer contracts. "We're talking about me and my landlord, me and the phone company, me and my health-care provider," says Nicholas Pace, a behavioral scientist with the RAND Corporation's Institute for Civil Justice in Santa Monica, Calif. "They're just everywhere."

Businesses say the agreements give consumers a quick, efficient and inexpensive way to settle disputes. "It enables complaints to be dealt with swiftly, much more swiftly than litigation," says the Chamber of Commerce's Rickard. "And it takes a lot of transaction costs out of the system."

Attorneys for plaintiffs — the so-called plaintiffs' bar — and consumer groups say they do not oppose arbitration in general. But they criticize what they say are common provisions in arbitration agreements that work to consumers' disadvantage. As one example, Lipsen of the trial-lawyers' group points to provisions requiring arbitration far from the consumer's home.

More broadly, Public Citizen's Wolfman notes that many arbitration agreements effectively block small consumer complaints by preventing the consolidation of claims into class actions. "In ordinary, individual

A Canadian Pacific freight train that derailed near Minot, N.D., in 2002 released 220,000 gallons of toxic anhydrous ammonia, causing one death and hundreds of injuries. The resulting legal battles are still being fought in state and federal courts nearly seven years later. Among the issues in the litigation was whether federal law regulating railroads preempted claims based on state law.

AP Photo/Minot Daily News/Heidi Weiss

consumer lawsuits, you can't arbitrate because you have to aggregate the claims," Wolfman says.

In addition, a recent Public Citizen report pointed to many built-in advantages for businesses over consumers in arbitration. Arbitration agreements are confidential, but as repeat users of arbitration, businesses know more than consumers about the procedures. In addition, the report argues that private arbitration organizations have an inherent bias in favor of businesses because companies can steer work away from arbitrators sympathetic to consumers. "It's an honest, historical fact that consumers don't fare very well in arbitration," Wolfman says.[7]

Without seeking to prohibit arbitration, the trial lawyers and consumer groups have been pushing legislation to restrict "mandatory predispute arbitration" — that is, standing agreements in business-consumer contracts that commit the parties to arbitrate any dispute before one arises. "If the companies think it's so great, just let consumers choose it," says Lipsen. "But you don't do it at the point of contract. You do it at the point of injury."

Rickard counters that without standing agreements fewer disputes would be arbitrated. "Once you have a conflict that has arisen, people dig in on both sides, and the ability to get something resolved through arbitration deteriorates quickly," she says.

Joyce also claims that consumers are satisfied with the mandatory arbitration clauses. "I just don't think that most people when they purchase a cell phone contract or take out a credit card are necessarily worried that they might not be able to take their case to the United States Supreme Court," he says. But Pace says it is "nonsense" to think consumers can reject mandatory arbitration clauses. "The next time you get a credit-card offer from Citibank, you try to negotiate the offer," he says.

The most far-reaching of the arbitration bills in Congress — the Arbitration Fairness Act — would have prohibited the enforcement of predispute arbitration agreements in any employment, consumer or franchise dispute or any civil rights or contract dispute between parties with "unequal bargaining power." Vanderbilt law Professor Nagareda calls the bill "overkill." Other bills would have limited arbitration in specific economic sectors. Only one made it into law: a 2008 farm bill provision prohibiting mandatory arbitration in livestock or poultry contracts.

Stewart's testimony about her grandmother's treatment came during a June 12 hearing by the House Judiciary Subcommittee on Commercial and Administrative Law on the Fairness in Nursing Home Arbitration Act, which would have prohibited nursing homes from requiring residents to agree in advance to arbitrate disputes. The bill won subcommittee approval on July 15; the Senate Judiciary Committee approved the counterpart bill on Sept. 11. But neither proposal was brought up for a floor vote.

The nursing-home industry opposed the bills but says nursing homes should not require an arbitration agreement as a condition of admission. The Guadalupe Valley Nursing Center says it offers arbitration, but the patient or family is free to accept or reject the arbitration clause. "We have honored this choice in the past and will continue to honor it in the future," says Kelly Delk, president of the home's governing body.

Should the Supreme Court set additional limits on punitive damages?

Mayola Williams' husband Jesse died of lung cancer in 1997 after having smoked cigarettes for more than 40 years. After his death, Williams sued Philip Morris — maker of Jesse's favored brand, Marlboro — claiming that the nation's largest tobacco company had knowingly lied about the link between cigarettes and disease.

An Oregon jury awarded Williams compensatory damages of about $821,000 and a whopping $79.5 million in punitive damages.

Twice, the U.S. Supreme Court has told Oregon courts to reconsider the award in the light of rulings that limit the discretion that state court judges or juries have to impose punitive damages. Twice, the Oregon Supreme Court has reaffirmed the award. Now, Philip Morris' lawyers are back before the U.S. Supreme Court, accusing the Oregon justices of using a somewhat technical procedural rule to deliberately thumb their nose at the nation's highest court.*[8]

The case — *Philip Morris USA v. Williams* — comes nearly two decades after the Supreme Court first hinted that the 14th Amendment's Due Process Clause might impose constitutional constraints on punitive damage awards in state courts. Industry groups have been pressing appeals at the high court at the same time business and tort reform advocates have been successfully lobbying state legislatures to cap punitive damages or impose stricter requirements for such awards.

Throughout the debate, plaintiffs' lawyers and consumer advocates have been insisting that punitive damages are actually rare and large penalties rarer still. "Punitive damages are awarded in so few cases," says the American Association for Justice's Lipsen.

Academic experts generally agree on the relative infrequency of punitive damage awards. RAND researcher Pace, who has been involved in extensive studies on jury verdicts in civil cases, also sees no evidence of an increase in the number of punitive awards or the size of the median award. On the other hand, Pace says researchers generally agree that the "outliers" — outsized awards like the one in Williams' case — are getting bigger.

Business groups say the extreme awards demonstrate the need for the Supreme Court to set limits on punitive awards. "They're frequent enough and they're large enough and they're unreliable enough to continue to be a problem for the business community," says Robin Conrad, senior vice president of the National Chamber Litigation Center, the U.S. Chamber's litigating arm.

Consumer groups counter that the unpredictability of punitive-damage awards contributes to their intended

---

* With interest, the award is now more than $145 million, according to Williams' attorneys. Under Oregon law, 60 percent of any punitive damage award is paid to the state.

purpose: deterrence. "The fact that they're a bolt out of the blue is actually a positive attribute for the system," says Public Citizen's Wolfman. "If you could plan for them, you wouldn't get the deterrence that they're expected to provide."

The court in separate decisions in 1996 and 2003 laid down criteria for state courts to use in considering punitive damages and then suggested a 1-to-1 ratio as a usual upper limit for the ratio between compensatory and punitive damages. Four years later, the court slashed by nearly 80 percent the $2.5 billion punitive damage award for the 1989 *Exxon Valdez* oil spill by establishing a 1-to-1 ratio for federal maritime cases.[9]

In Williams' case, the justices ruled, 5-4, that punitive damages cannot be used to punish companies for harm caused to anyone other than the plaintiffs before the court. But the court also said that the total harm caused by a company's conduct could be considered in weighing its "reprehensibility" — one of the three criteria permitted under the 1996 ruling.

Tort reform advocates applaud the rulings. "The Supreme Court has pretty clearly articulated what we have already advocated: that punitive damages cannot be unlimited, that they have to be tethered in some respect to the underlying harm," says Joyce at the American Association for Tort Reform.

At the same time, the *Williams* ruling has left many lawyers and court-watchers puzzled about how to instruct jurors on how far they can go in punishing a company for the overall harm caused by its product. "It's kind of a fine distinction to say you can take that into account for some purposes but not for others," says Vanderbilt Professor Nagareda.

In the new appeal, Philip Morris claims to have been surprised by the Oregon Supreme Court's use of a procedural rule on jury instructions to turn aside the Supreme Court's directive to reconsider the punitive damage award. Conrad says the court's constitutional authority is at stake. "You can't even be certain that when the Supreme Court issues a mandate the state court is going to follow it," she says.

The trial lawyers organization, in a friend of the court brief joined by anti-tobacco groups, claims instead that Philip Morris is seeking a special exemption from the state's established procedural rule. The brief accuses the company of "exploiting litigation cost and delay . . . to punish and deter plaintiffs in smokers' actions."

For his part, Prince at the Mitchell College of Law views the entire debate as exaggerated. "The business community talks as though they can't walk out the door and cross the street without being run over by a punitive damages vehicle," Prince says. "The plaintiffs' bar talks about how critical it is for punitive damages to be available to deter corporate behavior. Both sides are overblowing the arguments."

BACKGROUND

New Openness

The United States moved in the 20th century from a legal system with many substantive and procedural obstacles to lawsuits by injured workers and consumers to one more open to claims against employers and manufacturers for workplace and marketplace injuries. The new receptiveness to legal remedies emerged from laws passed by Congress and state legislatures and changes in court-made common law in state and later in federal courts. The changes contributed to the creation of an entrepreneurial-minded plaintiffs' bar, which in turn helped push courts and legislatures through the 1960s and '70s to continue expanding workers' and consumers' ability to gain compensation for injuries.[10]

Legal doctrines that prevailed through the 19th century posed nearly insurmountable obstacles for most injured consumers or workers. Injured consumers generally were prevented from suing manufacturers by a doctrine called "privity of contract," which limited them to seeking damages from the dealer or retailer that actually sold the product. The "fellow servant" rule prevented injured workers from recovering compensation if the injury resulted at least in part from a co-worker's negligence. In addition to those substantive rules, procedural rules — such as a requirement to set out a claim in detail in an initial complaint — also created difficult hurdles for many plaintiffs.

As Stanford University legal historian Lawrence Friedman explains, the industrial revolution that the United States underwent in the late 19th century compelled changes in tort, or personal-injury, law. "For the first time in history, injury to the body caused by machines became a major social problem," Friedman writes in his history, *American Law in the 20th Century*. As a result,

C H R O N O L O G Y

Before 1960 *Legal system opened to suits by injured workers, consumers.*

1906 Congress passes Federal Employers' Liability Act to permit federal court suits by injured railroad workers.

1916 New York court ruling eases suits by injured consumers against manufacturers of defective products.

1925 Federal Arbitration Act requires courts to honor agreements to arbitrate disputes.

1960s-1970s *More favorable changes for plaintiffs in suits against employers, manufacturers.*

1965 American Law Institute's *Restatement (Second) of Torts* recommends "strict liability" for manufacturers for injuries caused by defective, dangerous products; becomes prevailing rule in courts.

1966 *Federal Rules of Civil Procedure* revised to facilitate "class action" suits, consolidating similar claims by large numbers of plaintiffs.

1973 Federal court ruling allows workers to sue insulation manufacturer for workplace exposure to asbestos.

1980s *State tort reforms limit personal injury suits, awards.*

1984 Supreme Court rules arbitration clauses must be enforced in state as well as federal courts.

Mid-1980s First state laws cap or raise standards for punitive damages.

Late 1980s Plaintiffs' success rate in product liability suits said to be dropping because of state laws tightening rules for claims.

1989 Supreme Court hints that Due Process Clause may limit punitive damage awards in state courts.

1990s *Supreme Court hands down first rulings to control punitive damages, apply federal preemption to limit state court suits.*

1992 Fractured ruling by Supreme Court preempts some state court suits against tobacco companies (*Cipollone v. Liggett Group*); majority of justices agree that preemption applies to state jury verdicts.

1995 Gov. George W. Bush, R-Texas, signs omnibus tort reform law, capping punitive damages.

1996 President Bill Clinton vetoes product liability reform bill (May 2). . . . Supreme Court establishes criteria for state court use in evaluating punitive damage awards, including ratio of punitive to compensatory awards (*BMW v. Gore*) (May 20). . . . Supreme Court says federal law does not preempt state court suits over medical devices that bypass Food and Drug Administration (FDA) approval process (*Medtronic v. Lohr*) (June 26).

2000-Present *Bush administration tilts federal agencies toward backing preemption of state court suits; two Bush appointees to Supreme Court fortify pro-business stance.*

2003 Supreme Court says punitive damages should be no greater than 10 times the compensatory award (*State Farm v. Campbell*).

2005 President Bush signs Class Action Fairness Act, aimed at shifting class actions from state to federal courts.

2006 FDA adopts regulations aimed at preempting state court suits over drug labeling issues.

2007 Supreme Court says state juries can impose punitive damages only for harm caused to plaintiff, not to others (*Philip Morris USA v. Williams*).

2008 Supreme Court backs administration on preemption of state suits over FDA-approved medical devices (*Riegel v. Medtronic*) (Feb. 20). . . . Farm bill bars mandatory arbitration clauses in livestock, poultry contracts (May 22); other anti-arbitration bills fail in Congress. . . . Supreme Court slashes punitive damages for *Exxon Valdez* oil spill (*Exxon Shipping v. Baker*) (June 25). . . . Supreme Court rules, 5-4, that federal cigarette labeling act does not preempt suits under state deceptive-practices laws (*Altria Group v. Good*) (Dec. 15).

"the old tort system was completely dismantled," and "a whole new body of law . . . was constructed."[11]

The emerging labor movement won the first important breakthrough when Congress in 1906 passed the Federal Employers' Liability Act making railroads liable in federal court for workplace injuries attributable to employers' negligence. The Supreme Court ruled the law unconstitutional the next year, but Congress enacted a new version in 1908 that was later upheld. The law was a double-edged sword, however. In 1917, the court ruled, 7-2, that the federal act preempted state laws making railroads liable for workplace injuries if no negligence was shown.[12]

Today, workplace injuries are typically covered by state worker-compensation laws that compensate workers through an administrative system instead of court suits. States began enacting such laws in the 1920s — with support of employers interested in limiting potential awards. By 1950, more than three-fourths of the nation's workforce was covered. The earlier federal act, however, remains on the books and now covers airline industry workers as well. In addition, the Jones Act — passed in 1920 — provides federal-court remedies for injured seamen.

The obstacles to product-liability suits began to fall with an influential decision in 1916 by New York's highest court that undercut the "privity of contract" doctrine. The ruling in *MacPherson v. Buick Motor Company*, written by the later Supreme Court justice, Benjamin Cardozo, allowed an injured automobile owner to sue the manufacturer after an accident caused by a defective wheel. Three decades later, another leading jurist, California Supreme Court Justice Roger Traynor, proposed — in a concurring opinion — a strict rule to hold manufacturers liable for injuries caused by a defective product, whether or not negligence was shown. The "strict liability" rule was eventually endorsed by the influential American Law Institute in its *Restatement (Second) of Torts* in 1965 and is the generally prevailing rule for product-defect cases in state and federal courts today.[13]

The scope of product- and workplace-related lawsuits has expanded since the 1960s, thanks in large part to the adoption in the *Federal Rules of Civil Procedure* of Rule 23, facilitating the consolidation of multiple, similar claims into so-called "class action" suits. The federal rules, first adopted in 1938, had already helped plaintiffs by easing initial pleading requirements and allowing pre-trial discovery of evidence from defendants and others. Rule 23 transformed civil litigation by helping plaintiffs lawyers to combine thousands of otherwise insubstantial individual claims into giant lawsuits with potential awards in the millions of dollars. The possibility of huge recoveries allowed plaintiffs' attorneys to spend the time and money needed to wage a protracted legal fight; defendant businesses also had reasons in some instances to negotiate settlements to limit their own expenses and exposure to bad publicity and huge court awards.[14]

The procedural changes combined with the growing recognition that consumers and workers could be injured, sickened or killed not only by machines but also by chemicals found in workplaces, products and the environment. The era of mass toxic torts can be dated from 1973, when the federal appeals court for Texas ruled that asbestos manufacturers could be held liable for injuries to workers who developed asbestosis or other lung diseases as a result of exposure to asbestos. The ruling gave workers a way to circumvent the limits on recoveries through worker compensation and set the stage for the multibillion-dollar asbestos litigation still ongoing today.

The 1970s also witnessed the birth of the first, giant consumer class action: claims by thousands of women against the manufacturer of the Dalkon Shield, an intra-uterine contraceptive device blamed for causing miscarriages, congenital birth defects, infections, sterility and in some instances even death. The company eventually put billions of dollars into a trust to settle the claims.[15]

Tort Reform

The expansion of legal remedies produced a backlash by the late 1970s from business groups and business-minded critics. They blamed what they called a liability or litigation crisis for rising insurance rates, declining product innovation and failing companies. Despite ambiguous statistical evidence, they succeeded in persuading state legislatures to pass so-called tort reform laws that, for example, limited awards in medical malpractice cases or punitive damage awards in civil suits generally.[16]

Tort reform advocates also won Supreme Court rulings beginning in the 1990s to require constitutional scrutiny of punitive damage awards and to limit on

Drugmaker Seeks Limit on State Court Suits

Wyeth says warnings adequate for federal law

Wyeth Pharmaceuticals wants the Supreme Court to overturn the multimillion-dollar damage award that a Vermont jury awarded to Diana Levine because of allegedly inadequate warnings about the risks of its anti-nausea drug, Phenergan. The company's case depends on a theory of federal preemption that most courts have rejected and that the Bush administration adopted over the objections of career officials in the Food and Drug Administration (FDA).

Levine, a professional musician, had her right forearm amputated after suffering a gangrenous infection from a medical mistake: an "IV-push" injection of Phenergan into an artery instead of a vein. The FDA-approved labeling that Wyeth provides with the drug included a warning — with an upper-case heading — about the risk of "gangrene requiring amputation" from "inadvertent intra-arterial injection."

Wyeth, the nation's 10th-largest drug company, with $22 billion in sales in 2007, argued at trial and in subsequent appeals that it could not change or add to the warnings as approved by the FDA. On those grounds, Wyeth said, federal law preempted, or barred, a suit like Levine's claiming a violation of a duty to warn based on state law.

The Vermont jury awarded Levine $7.5 million, which was later reduced by the amount of her $700,000 settlement with the clinic where she was treated. In upholding the award, the Vermont Supreme Court rejected the drug company's preemption argument.

Wyeth "could have warned against IV-push administration without prior FDA approval," the court said in a 4-1 decision. "Federal labeling requirements," the majority said, "create a floor, not a ceiling for state regulation." In a lone dissent, Chief Justice Paul Reiber wrote, "It would be impossible for defendant Wyeth to comply with the requirements of both state and federal law."[1]

The Vermont court's ruling was in line with the vast majority of state and federal courts that have considered whether federal drug law preempts personal injury suits based on state law — either state statutes or judge-made common law. In asking the U.S. Supreme Court to review the ruling, Wyeth's lawyers cited only three decisions from federal trial courts upholding preemption arguments. Wyeth also pointed to what it called Reiber's "strong" dissent in Levine's case.

For years, the FDA had also taken the position that federal law did not preempt state court suits over drug safety. Instead, the agency viewed state court suits as a complement to its own regulatory efforts. The Bush administration changed the agency's position. In 2004, for example, it filed a brief in a pending federal case arguing that the 1976 law regulating medical devices preempted state court suits over devices specifically approved by the FDA.

The FDA rewrote drug labeling regulations in 2006 and 2008 and included in the new rules specific language aimed at preempting state court suits. Career FDA officials

preemption grounds state court suits in some federally regulated areas. Despite some successes in Congress, however, they failed in their major push for a federal bill limiting product-liability suits.

Litigation critics succeeded in implanting in the public mind the belief that civil-suit caseloads were spiraling upwards along with average jury awards and typical punitive damage awards. Plaintiffs' lawyers and consumer advocates generally discounted the extent of the increases in caseloads or awards. Studies by independent researchers often found the evidence of a crisis exaggerated. For example, a 40-year study of civil-jury verdicts by the RAND Institute for Civil Justice, published in

2004, found a "substantial" increase in average jury awards but attributed the increase to a declining number of auto-accident cases — with typically lower awards — and the general increase in health-care costs, often the principal component of jury awards.[17]

From the 1980s on, state legislatures enacted a host of tort reform laws raising substantive or procedural requirements for recovery, limiting awards or both. Doctors and medical insurers had the greatest success. By 2007, more than 30 states had enacted some monetary limits on damage awards in medical malpractice cases, according to the National Conference of State Legislatures.[18]

opposed the change, according to a report by the Democratic staff of the House Committee on Oversight and Government Reform.

The report, released in October not long before the Supreme Court's argument in Levine's case, quoted memos by FDA officials lamenting the agency's inability to effectively regulate drug warning labels. In one of the memos, John Jenkins, described as the highest official in FDA's drug-review process, wrote, "It is unwise to suggest that FDA-approved labeling is always up-to-date and always contains a full and complete listing of all pertinent risk information."[2]

After Levine's lawyers filed the report with the Supreme Court, Wyeth's lawyers submitted a reply. They claimed that Jenkins' comments had been taken out of context and he in fact favored FDA preemption. But Jenkins was also quoted as saying that drugmakers can add new drug-safety information to labels without FDA approval.

At the Supreme Court, Levine's lawyer, Washington attorney David Frederick, argued that Wyeth had known for at least 40 years of the risk of amputation

Vermont musician Diana Levine plays the guitar with a prosthetic arm after a medical mistake involving the nausea drug Phenergan led to gangrene and the amputation of her arm.

AP Photo/Toby Talbot

from inadvertent arterial injection of Phenergan. He also emphasized that in addition to the usual intramuscular injection, the drug could also be safely administered intravenously by a conventional IV drip instead of an IV injection.

Representing Wyeth, Washington lawyer Seth Waxman countered that the label "plainly" warned about the risks of IV-push injection. A stronger warning, he said, would have gone too far in discouraging use of the technique. "Taking options away from a physician isn't always better," he told the justices.

The justices are expected to decide the case this spring, sometime before taking a recess at the end of June.

---

[1] *Levine v. Wyeth*, 2006 Vt. 107 (Oct. 27, 2006), http://libraries .vermont.gov/sites/libraries/files/supct/current/op2004-384.txt. For other materials in the case, see the legal blog SCOTUSWiki, www .scotuswiki.com/index.php?title=Wyeth_v._Levine.

[2] "FDA Career Staff Objected to Agency Preemption Policies," U.S. House of Representatives, Committee on Oversight and Reform, Majority Staff Report, October 2008, http://oversight.house.gov/ documents/20081029102934.pdf.

Business groups enjoyed somewhat less success in winning passage of laws limiting punitive damage awards generally. A compilation by the American Tort Reform Association shows 20 states that limit punitive damage awards. The laws generally permit a penalty of some multiple of the compensatory award or some specified six-figure amount, whichever is greater. Many of the laws also set heightened evidentiary standards or require separate proceedings for punitive damages. In addition, at least three states require a percentage of any punitive award to be paid to the state.[19]

Tort reform advocates had limited success on Capitol Hill. Congress did pass two significant measures in 1995

and 1998 that financial industries pushed to limit securities-fraud suits. It also passed a law in 1995 to limit litigation by prison inmates. But Congress repeatedly allowed federal medical malpractice legislation to die. And tort reform advocates failed in repeated efforts to win passage of federal product-liability legislation. In the closest attempt, the Republican-controlled Congress passed legislation in 1996 to limit punitive damage awards in product suits to the greater of two times compensatory damages or $250,000; penalties could have been increased for "egregious" conduct. President Bill Clinton, a Democrat, vetoed the bill, saying it would not have done enough to protect consumers. Two years later, the House, still under GOP control, passed a somewhat similar bill, but it died in the Senate.[20]

Meanwhile, the Supreme Court gave tort reform advocates some help in their efforts to rein in punitive damages. The court in 1996 set out due-process guidelines to be used to throw out "grossly excessive" punitive awards. The criteria included the "reprehensibility" of the defendant's conduct and the ratio between the punitive and compensatory awards. The court applied those guidelines in a 2003 decision that threw out a punitive damage award in a bad-faith insurance case that was 145 times greater than the compensatory amount. The ruling suggested that anything over a "single-digit" multiplier — that is, a 10-1 ratio or higher — was constitutionally suspect. Four years later, the justices also held in the *Williams* case that a state court could not punish a company for harm caused to consumers outside the state.[21]

The court's initial rulings in preemption cases rejected industry pleas for wholesale protection from state court suits but nevertheless set the stage for more favorable decisions later. In 1992, a fractured decision barred state court suits against tobacco manufacturers for failing to warn consumers of health hazards but allowed suits for fraudulent advertising or conspiracy to conceal health risks. Four years later the court ruled, 5-4, that the 1976 federal law regulating medical devices did not completely preempt defect or failure-to-warn suits in state courts. In both cases, however, a majority of justices recognized that federal preemption principles applied not only to state legislation but also to state court decisions, including jury verdicts.[22]

Later cases applied that principle again, with mixed results. In 2000, for example, the court said state courts could not enforce their own standards for safety warnings at railroad crossings. By contrast, the court in 2002 allowed a state court wrongful-death action against a recreational boat manufacturer for failing to install a safety device not required under federal law.

Bush's Initiatives

President Bush supported tort reform efforts throughout his eight years in office but won only one victory in Congress: a business-backed bill passed in 2005 aimed at shifting class actions from state to presumably less sympathetic federal courts. With less fanfare or attention,

however, the administration used its executive powers to adopt rules or take legal positions invoking federal preemption to limit state court suits in some areas — notably, drugs and medical devices regulated by the FDA. Meanwhile, the Supreme Court was giving business-minded litigation critics victories in a number of areas, including the two decisions in 2008 limiting punitive damages in federal maritime cases and barring state court suits over FDA-approved medical devices.

Bush had supported tort reform proposals since first entering politics. In his first months as governor of Texas in 1995, he pushed through the state legislature a bill aimed at curbing what he called "junk lawsuits" by capping punitive damages at relatively low levels and eliminating duplicate recoveries in cases with multiple defendants. He repeatedly endorsed tort reform in his 2000 presidential campaign and mentioned the issue in his first — and every subsequent — State of the Union address. But tort reform took a back seat to other issues early in 2001 and receded further after the Sept. 11, 2001, terrorist attacks.

As part of a concentrated push at the start of 2003, Bush called for federal legislation to cap damages in medical malpractice cases and to settle asbestos claims through an administrative compensation system. Those proposals went nowhere while Republicans controlled Congress and had even less life after Democrats gained majorities in the House and Senate after the 2006 elections.

Bush's only success in Congress on tort reform issues came in February 2005 with passage of the Class Action Fairness Act.[23] The bill — passed with strong bipartisan majorities in the first full month of the new Congress — gave federal courts jurisdiction over class actions with more than $5 million in dispute and more than two-thirds of plaintiffs from states different from the defendant's. Federal judges were to apply substantive state law but to use federal procedural rules regarded as less favorable to plaintiffs. The bill, strongly backed by business and opposed by trial lawyers and consumer groups, had passed the House three previous times. It overcame Democratic roadblocks in the Senate thanks to the increased GOP majority after the 2004 elections. The 18 Democratic senators voting for the bill included then-Sen. Obama and then-Sen. Joseph R. Biden Jr., D-Del., the vice president-elect.

Even before the major tort reform initiatives, the administration had started to use federal preemption as a way to limit state court suits. As early as 2002, the Justice Department reversed the FDA's previous stance by arguing in a pending case that the agency's regulatory authority barred state court suits for FDA-approved medical devices. By 2006, the administration had extended to other agencies what supporters and opponents alike were calling a "silent tort reform" movement. As one example, the Consumer Product Safety Commission adopted a rule in February 2006 barring state court suits for injuries arising from mattresses that caught fire. Defending the trend, a spokesman for the Office of Management and Budget told *The New York Times* that federal agencies rather than courts were "often in the best position" to make determinations about how to protect public safety.[24]

The administration's strategy bore fruit with the Supreme Court's ruling on Feb. 20, 2008, barring state court suits challenging the safety or effectiveness of FDA-approved medical devices. For the majority, Justice Antonin Scalia relied on an express preemption provision in the 1976 law regulating medical devices. But he also said state court suits could disrupt the federal agency's judgment about how best to balance the benefits of a device against potential risks. In the lone dissent, Justice Ruth Bader Ginsburg noted that up until the Bush administration the FDA had supported state court suits as an aid to its regulatory powers. Scalia said the agency's discarded position carried no weight.

Four months later, the court gave litigation critics another victory with the 5-3 decision cutting the punitive damage award for the *Exxon Valdez* oil spill to $500 million — one-fifth of the $2.5 billion approved by lower federal courts. Writing for the majority in the June 25 ruling, Justice David H. Souter said that jury instructions or appellate review were inadequate mechanisms to control the "unpredictability" of punitive damage awards. Instead, the majority adopted a 1-to-1 ratio for compensatory and punitive damages in maritime cases as long as the defendant's conduct was not "malicious" or motivated by financial gain. Conrad at the National Chamber Litigation Center predicted the ruling could have an effect "far beyond" maritime law.

The court gave litigation critics more encouragement by teeing up three more appeals by business defendants for the new term that was to begin on Oct. 6. A challenge by the Altria Group, the parent company of Philip Morris USA, to the Maine suit claiming fraud in marketing of low-tar cigarettes was to be heard on the court's first day back. Wyeth's appeal of the $6 million award in Diana Levine's failure-to-warn suit was set for argument on Nov. 3. And Philip Morris was set to argue on Dec. 3 in its effort to overturn the Oregon Supreme Court's decision reinstating the $79.5 million award won by Mayola Williams for her husband's death after decades of cigarette smoking.

CURRENT SITUATION
Watching the Court

Trial lawyers are hailing and business groups criticizing a Supreme Court ruling clearing the way for smokers to sue tobacco companies for fraud in marketing "light" cigarettes. Meanwhile, the opposing sides in the litigation wars are still waiting for the justices to decide whether federal law protects drug manufacturers from state court suits for allegedly failing to give adequate warnings about the risks of their medications.

The court's 5-4 ruling on Dec. 15 rejected the appeal by the Altria Group, which cited federal preemption to try to block three Maine smokers from charging the company with violating the state's unfair trade practices act. The plaintiffs claimed that the company's advertising of Marlboro Lights and Cambridge Lights as having "lowered tar and nicotine" was misleading because habitual smokers compensate by inhaling more deeply.

The decision in *Altria Group, Inc. v. Good* did not rule on the plaintiffs' allegations but upheld the argument urged by trial lawyers and anti-tobacco groups that the state-law claim was not preempted by the Federal Cigarette Labeling and Advertising Act. The act, passed in 1965, required warning labels on cigarette packages and advertising and went on to prohibit the states from any additional regulation of cigarette marketing "based on smoking and health."

In the majority opinion, Justice John Paul Stevens said the act had no effect on state law fraud claims. "The Labeling Act does not pre-empt state-law claims . . . that are predicated on the duty not to deceive," Stevens wrote. The opinion was joined by the court's other liberal

Claims About Arbitration Hard to Evaluate

Few states require public disclosure of results.

Hundreds of thousands of consumer, employment and other business-related disputes are handled every year by an alternate, dispute-resolution system that operates largely out of public view.

Arbitration funnels cases away from crowded court dockets to be decided by law-trained arbitrators in streamlined proceedings that supporters say are quicker and cheaper than court trials for all concerned — and just as fair. But critics say the small-print mandatory-arbitration clauses inserted by companies into a host of consumer contracts deny rank-and-file customers their day in court and shunt them into an unfamiliar system with the deck stacked in businesses' favor.

The same groups that have been waging war over lawsuits for decades fight just as fiercely over arbitration. Critics, led by the American Association for Justice (AAJ), the national trial lawyers' lobby, want Congress to prohibit mandatory arbitration in employment, consumer or franchise disputes.

"Mandatory-arbitration clauses are one-sided, preemptive and non-consensual," AAJ says on its Web site. Since the clauses "are presented on a take-it-or-leave-it basis, people have no choice but to waive their rights" to resolution in courts of law.

Business groups, including the U.S. Chamber of Commerce and its Institute for Legal Reform, say arbitration provides "well recognized" benefits to consumers and employees as well as to businesses and society at large. "Without arbitration," the institute says on its Web site, "many consumers and employees will have little recourse — they simply will not be able to afford to go to court."

Private arbitration associations sound the same notes. Arbitration presents "the only viable access to justice" for most consumers and workers, Richard Naimark, senior vice president of the industry-leading American Arbitration Association, told a House subcommittee in fall 2007. Naimark said rules developed over the past 80 years ensure a "level playing field" "in business disputes with customers or employees.[1]

"By all measures, arbitration is the best option for consumers and for most entities alike," says Aimee Egan, vice president for communications at the National Arbitration Forum. "It's as simple as that."

With little information on the public record, the contesting claims are difficult to evaluate. Only three jurisdictions — California, Maine and the District of Columbia — have laws requiring disclosure of arbitration

justices — David H. Souter, Ruth Bader Ginsburg and Stephen G. Breyer — and by Justice Anthony M. Kennedy, who often casts the pivotal vote in closely divided rulings.

For the dissenters, Justice Clarence Thomas argued that the suit was "expressly pre-empted" by the 1965 law. He warned that the decision would leave state and lower federal courts in "confusion" about how to decide whether to allow state suits to proceed. The other dissenters included Justice Antonin Scalia and President Bush's two appointees: Chief Justice John G. Roberts Jr. and Justice Samuel A. Alito Jr.

Les Weisbrod, president of the American Association for Justice (AAJ), the trial-lawyers' group, called the ruling "a victory for consumers." The decision "affirms that cigarette manufacturers cannot claim immunity from

consumer fraud when they claim their products have lowered tar and nicotine levels, even though they do not," Weisbrod said.

From the opposite side, business advocates are disappointed. "It's a bit of a setback," said Conrad at the National Chamber Litigation Center. Alan Untereiner, a business lawyer in Washington and expert on preemption, said the decision is "a step backward from the trend of bringing greater consistency to preemption law."

Both Conrad and Untereiner say, however, that the ruling does not signal the justices' likely stance in the court's other preemption case: Wyeth's appeal of the nearly $6.8 million award (with interest, now over $10 million) that musician Levine won in Vermont courts. The Nov. 3 arguments in the case pitted two top Supreme Court advocates: Seth Waxman, a former proceedings. (The D.C. law has yet to go into effect.) Even caseload statistics are secret. Egan estimates that arbitrators handle 500,000 to 1 million cases a year, but she declines to provide specific figures about the NAF's caseload. "As a private company, National Arbitration Forum does not discuss claim volumes publicly," she says.

The consumer advocacy group Public Citizen used California's disclosure law to gather data used in a highly critical study of arbitration of credit-card disputes. The October 2007 study — "The Arbitration Trap: How Credit Card Companies Ensnare Consumers" — found that NAF-appointed arbitrators favored businesses in 94 percent of the more than 19,000 cases studied.

The report claimed that arbitrators have "a strong financial incentive" to rule in favor of credit-card companies and other "repeat players" because the companies or the arbitration firms themselves can steer cases away from arbitrators who rule in consumers' favor. The report also depicted arbitrations as more expensive than supporters depict and the procedural informality as more likely to benefit businesses familiar with the system than consumers who are not.[2]

In a study commissioned by the Chamber, law professor Peter Rutledge sharply disputed the Public Citizen critique. Rutledge — now at the University of Georgia Law School in Athens — disputed the significance of the finding that credit-card companies won the vast majority of cases. Most of the disputes, he said, were essentially collection cases with little dispute about the card-carriers' liability.

More broadly, Rutledge argued that arbitration does cost less after taking account of attorneys' fees in court cases. Complaints about secrecy and confidentiality are "overblown," he said, while the supposed incentive for arbitrators to favor businesses is unproven.[3]

Public Citizen countered with a rebuttal — issued in July 2008 just as the House Judiciary Committee was taking up a bill to limit mandatory arbitration. The group accused Rutledge of changing his views from previous law journal articles on arbitration. [4] Today, Rutledge denies changing his views and charges Public Citizen with taking some of his quotes from earlier writings out of context. But he says he agrees with Public Citizen and other arbitration critics that more empirical research is needed about how the system operates.

---

[1] Testimony before House Judiciary Subcommittee on Commercial and Administrative Law, Oct. 25, 2007.

[2] "The Arbitration Trap: How Credit Card Companies Ensnare Consumers," Public Citizen, September 2007, www.citizen.org/publications/release.cfm?ID=7545. John O'Donnell, senior researcher with Public Citizen's Congress Watch, is identified as principal author.

[3] Peter B. Rutledge, "Arbitration — A Good Deal for Consumers: A Response to Public Citizen," U.S. Chamber Institute for Legal Reform, April 2008, www.instituteforlegalreform.org/issues/docdetails .cfm?docid=1091.

[4] Public Citizen, "The Arbitration Debate Trap: How Opponents of Corporate Accountability Distort the Debate Over Arbitration," July 2008, www.citizen.org/publications/release.cfm?ID=7589. Taylor Lincoln and David Arkush are identified as authors.

U.S. solicitor general in the Clinton administration, for Wyeth; and David Frederick, a veteran plaintiffs' lawyer in Washington who had earlier argued for the plaintiffs in the smoking case.

Waxman argued that federal law regulating drug labels implicitly preempts any state court suits over the adequacy of its warnings about Phenergan. Frederick countered that Wyeth should have added to the FDA-approved warning because it had additional information about the "catastrophic" risks of gangrene and amputation from improperly administering Phenergan through an IV-push injection.

In his argument, Waxman claimed that Wyeth had provided "ample warnings." Stricter warnings, he said, would discourage doctors from a potentially valuable form of treatment. Justice Scalia, who wrote the Feb. 25

decision preempting state regulation of FDA-approved medical devices, appeared to agree. "The name of this game is balancing benefits and costs," Scalia said. "If you simply eliminate drugs which people have real desperate need for," he continued, "you're not benefiting the public."

Justice Ginsburg, the lone dissenter in the earlier decision, disagreed. "No matter what benefit there was, how could the benefit outweigh that substantial risk?" she asked Waxman.

In a third case, the justices grappled on Dec. 3 with the procedural maze created by the Oregon Supreme Court's decision to reaffirm the punitive damage award in Williams' case after a remand by the high court. The Supreme Court in 2007 had ordered the Oregon justices to reconsider the award against Philip Morris in the light

Are lawsuits hurting American business?

YES
Tiger Joyce
President, American
Tort Reform Association

Written for *CQ Researcher*, December 2008

In Washington's world of competing statistics and sometimes childish "Does not! Does, too!" bickering on cable TV, it's easy to be confused about whether America's world-leading volume of civil litigation affects our economy negatively or positively. (Believe it or not, some folks actually argue that the nation suffers from too few lawsuits.)

But to free one's mind of so-called statistics and various talk-show biases, consider this simple, commonsense fact: Every dollar that businesses large and small are forced to spend defending themselves against speculative, often frivolous lawsuits is a dollar that won't be spent on research and development, capital investment, productivity-enhancing technologies, worker training and benefits, or new job creation.

When framed in such self-evident context, it becomes quite clear to any objective observer that abuse of our civil justice system inures only to the benefit of plaintiffs' lawyers. And in stressed economic times like those we all currently face, this self-evident truth should be all that much more compelling.

All of that said, it should be stipulated that civil justice in the United States is the envy of the world, and appropriately so. The overwhelming majority of judges bring considerable integrity and character to their jobs and work very hard for modest pay to ensure, as promised by the principle engraved above the entrance to the Supreme Court, "Equal Justice Under Law."

By that it is meant that all parties, plaintiffs and defendants, are to be treated fairly and equitably in unbiased searches for truth that lead to those who have been injured being lawfully and justly compensated by those whose negligence or recklessness precipitated such injuries.

But as everyone knows, there are a few judges who ignore principle and precedent and sometimes seek to curry favor with lawyers who practice before them and sometimes write sizable checks to their reelection campaigns. These judges are at the dark heart of what my organization calls "judicial hellholes" — some of the most unfair civil court jurisdictions in the nation.

This year's edition of our annual "Judicial Hellholes" report was just released on Dec.16 (see full text, www.atra.org), and it documents at some length many outrageously adjudicated lawsuits during the past year that, in addition to posing an obvious threat to economic growth at state and national levels, also dangerously erode both the notion of personal responsibility and the respect for the rule of law that have helped make America great.

NO
Les Weisbrod
President, American Association for Justice

Written for *CQ Researcher*, December 2008

After eight years of the Bush administration working to restrict the rights of consumers across the board, the big-business lobby wants to ensure that these rights are not restored by the Obama administration.

For years, big business has argued that lawsuits are hurting American businesses and the economy, in order to restrict consumers' access to the civil justice system. Not only is this assertion totally false and not backed up by data, but it doesn't hold water in the current economic crisis, in which businesses have had less regulation and less oversight.

As a result, Americans have faced dangerous drugs, toxic toys and tainted food. Instead of focusing on how businesses can make their products and services safer, more efficient and better for the environment, the big-business lobby wants to focus on protecting corporations that endanger consumers.

In looking at what businesses say are their top concerns, it seems as if the business lobby is completely out of sync with its members. Study after study conducted by businesses themselves shows that litigation costs rank at the bottom of overall concerns for small businesses. In a National Federation of Independent Business survey of the biggest threats facing small-business owners, cost and frequency of lawsuits ranked 65th out of 75 possible concerns among 3,000 business owners surveyed.

And lawsuits were not a top concern among big American manufacturing companies, according to a survey by the National Association of Manufacturers. When asked to rate several factors in terms of their negative impact on their company, manufacturers ranked "fear of litigation" well below many other issues, including non-wage compensation, materials, energy prices and taxes.

Clearly, the big-business lobby is not only failing the consumers that its members serve but also is failing the businesses it claims to represent.

Our current economic crisis has shown that putting profits over protecting consumers hasn't worked. Businesses should understand that producing safe products and services is a key part of restoring consumers' faith in the market and improving the economy.

Protecting consumers must be a multifaceted effort. It will take the business community, the regulatory system and the legal system to ensure that consumers can rely on the products they purchase. Instead of pushing to limit lawsuits, the business lobby should listen to its members and consumers and work to address the pressing issues facing our global economy.

of its holding that a defendant can be punished only for the harm Williams suffered, not for the harm to others.

The Oregon Supreme Court responded, however, by ruling that Philip Morris was not entitled to challenge the jury's verdict. The state high court said that the company had lost the right to challenge the jury instructions used by the trial judge because its own proposed instruction was not "clear and correct in all respects," as required by Oregon rules.

Representing Philip Morris, Chicago attorney Stephen Shapiro called the Oregon court's decision an "ambush." Robert Peck, a lawyer with the AAJ-affiliated Center for Constitutional Litigation, insisted that the Oregon justices had applied a "traditional" state procedural rule in rejecting Philip Morris' appeal.

With several justices voicing concern about how to exercise authority over state courts, Roberts tentatively suggested that the high court skirt the procedural issue by deciding on its own whether the punitive damage award was or was not consistent with its 2007 ruling. That unusual move would require a new round of legal briefs and arguments, but the case presumably could still be decided — along with the *Wyeth* case — before the justices take their summer recess at the end of June.

Waiting for Obama

Trial lawyers and consumer advocates are hoping the Obama presidency will bring a change of climate on civil justice issues in executive branch agencies and improved prospects for favorable legislation in a Congress with an enhanced Democratic majority. From the opposite side, business groups acknowledge that they will have to play defense on litigation issues at both ends of Pennsylvania Avenue for at least the next two years.

"The very first order of business is to restore balance and give consumers and workers a way to hold corporate wrongdoers responsible," says Lipsen at the American Association of Justice. "Some of that can be done by executive order; some has to be done legislatively."

Rickard, of the Chamber of Commerce's legal reform arm, expects the political climate in Washington to be "quite challenging" once the new Congress convenes on Jan. 6 and Obama is inaugurated on Jan. 20. "The trial bar has teed up their issues very well in this Congress," Rickard says. "This was just a dress rehearsal for what they're going to pursue in the next Congress."

The AAJ lobbied for an array of proposals aimed at expanding or protecting civil litigation over the past two years when both houses of Congress had Democratic majorities for the first time during the George W. Bush presidency. Four became law: three dealing with federal preemption and the measure prohibiting mandatory-arbitration clauses for livestock or poultry contracts.

The trial lawyers' most recent success came in August with congressional agreement on reauthorization of the Consumer Product Safety Commission (CPSC). The bill included language specifying that several federal consumer protection laws enforced by the agency do not preempt damage claims under state statutory or common law. The measure also authorized state attorneys general to enforce federal consumer protection laws independently of the agency. The trial lawyers succeeded in removing a business-backed provision that would have barred state attorneys general from retaining private attorneys in such actions.

A year earlier, trial lawyers had also successfully pushed for the provision in the Federal Rail Safety Improvement Act that barred federal preemption of state law claims for railroad accidents and retroactively applied the provision to permit the Minot derailment suit to proceed. Bush signed the bill into law in August 2007.

Trial lawyers had a more tenuous victory with a bill that Bush signed a month later. The FDA Amendments of 2007 includes an obscurely worded provision in one section that trial lawyers say eliminates federal preemption on the basis of FDA-approved labeling. Industry groups dispute that interpretation and stress that a broadly phrased anti-preemption provision was stripped from the bill.

The other AAJ-backed bills that did not become law covered a wide range of litigation-related topics. Among the unsuccessful bills were measures to authorize class action suits for back pay by employees of cruise lines and shipping companies and to expand the scope of private "whistleblower" suits against government contractors for defrauding the federal government. Another bill would have limited the use of so-called protective orders in civil litigation — judicial orders typically sought by defendants to keep documents in civil suits out of public files.

In the November elections, Democrats picked up 21 seats in the House to gain a 257-178 majority over Republicans and six Senate seats to give them a

57-41 edge over Republicans with two seats — including Obama's Illinois seat — to be filled.*

In addition to the Democratic gains, trial lawyers and consumer advocates cheered a significant leadership change when California Rep. Henry A. Waxman ousted Michigan's John D. Dingell as chairman of the powerful House Energy and Commerce Committee. Waxman, a veteran liberal lawmaker, had been one of several members of Congress who had introduced bills aimed at overturning the Supreme Court's decision preempting state court suits against makers of FDA-approved medical devices.

FDA preemption was expected to be one of the first issues for the business and trial lawyers' lobbies to fight over in the new Congress. "It's clear that there are elements up on the Hill that have issues with preemption," says Webb at the Chamber's Institute for Legal Reform.

Lipsen is cautious over what to expect from the Obama administration. "We're not taking anything for granted," she says. But Public Citizen's Wolfman says the election results signal a shift on civil justice issues. "We had a national election in which the party that is less hostile to litigation and less hostile to ordinary citizens being able to adjudicate their claims in court swept into office pretty dramatically," he says.

Business groups are basing their hopes in part on an expectation that President Obama will be focused on other issues for the time being. "I don't get the sense that this new administration is going to go out of its way to push initiatives that will have a demonstrably poor impact on business at a time when the economy is clearly not robust," says American Tort Reform Association President Joyce. "When I look at what they've said and done so far, their focus is elsewhere."

OUTLOOK

Faces of Litigation

The giant retailer Wal-Mart is getting ready to pay $54 million to settle a civil suit in Minnesota charging the

---

* The Minnesota election between Republican incumbent Norm Coleman and Democratic challenger Al Franken was undecided pending a recount as of mid-December. Obama resigned his seat on Nov. 13. The appointment of a successor was thrown into disarray on Dec. 9 when Illinois Gov. Rod Blagojevich, a Democrat, was arrested on federal corruption charges stemming from alleged efforts to sell Obama's seat.

company with violating state wage and hour laws by failing to credit workers for hours spent in training courses and then failing to correct the practice once it was discovered. Two years earlier, a jury in Pennsylvania had awarded $78 million to Wal-Mart workers in a similar suit over rest breaks and off-the-clock work.[25]

Nancy Braun, one of the original plaintiffs in the case, had testified that managers at the company's Apple Valley store had refused to allow her bathroom breaks while she was working as the sole cook and waitress at the in-store restaurant. Managers were under pressure to keep payrolls down, Braun said, and the store was understaffed.

The Wal-Mart settlement, announced on Dec. 9, made news just as the U.S. Chamber of Commerce's Institute for Legal Reform was unveiling its latest critique of civil justice in the United States. The institute's Web site, www.FacesofLawsuitAbuse.org, highlights a batch of believe-it-or-not lawsuits that have bedeviled small-business owners over the past few years.

The first of the stories features the owners of a small pool-maintenance company in Rockville, Md., who had to defend a slip-and-fall suit filed by a woman who fell after she was startled by a honking male goose as she walked by the store. Owner Howard Weiss said federal bird-protection laws had prevented him from shooing the gander and its mate away after the birds decided to nest just outside his store.

A state court jury ruled in the store's favor, but Weiss saw the verdict as a sort of Pyrrhic victory because of the time taken away from running his business. A large verdict against him, he added, might have forced him out of business.

"Many people have the perception that lawsuits are primarily the concern of faceless, 'deep-pocket' corporations, yet small businesses and average families are also victims of these abusive suits," institute President Rickard said in announcing the new site.

The trial lawyers' group mocked the Chamber's claimed solicitude for small businesses. "When you're bankrolled by giant, multibillion-dollar corporations, it's laughable to claim you're also protecting the interests of small business," said Jon Haber, chief executive officer of the American Association for Justice. He said the Chamber's campaign reflected "their longstanding credo: negligent corporations should never be held accountable."

The rhetorical back and forth illustrates what civil justice expert Prince at William Mitchell law school calls the overblown arguments that the combatants in the civil litigation wars have been making over the past four decades. The political climate in Washington may be changing, but the rhetoric on civil justice issues seems unlikely to be any less heated in the near future.

Trial lawyers are continuing to depict the preemption, arbitration and punitive damages issues as nothing more than efforts by big corporations to gain immunity for wrongdoing. Business groups counter by treating the trial lawyers' stances as nothing more than ambulance chasing and fee grabbing at a macro level. AAJ's press releases are as oblivious to the practical problems faced by business as the Chamber's press releases are to the plight of consumers injured or killed by companies' products.

Business groups expect mainly to hold on to gains they have made in the states and in federal courts. "Our opportunities are going to be fewer," says American Tort Reform Association President Joyce. AAJ spokeswoman Lipsen also expects tort reform will not be a high priority for the near future. But she adds, "I don't expect the business lobby to go away."

Meanwhile, amputee Levine and Wyeth are waiting for the Supreme Court to decide the fate of her multi-million-dollar judgment against the pharmaceutical company for an allegedly inadequate warning about the risks of IV-push injection of Phenergan. In the courtroom, attorney Waxman argued that the FDA-approved labeling in fact warned of the risk of infection from IV-push injection of the medication. A stronger warning, he said, would have gone too far in steering doctors away from a method of treatment useful in some cases.

Outside the court, Levine found no comfort in Wyeth's arguments. Had she known of the risks of losing her arm, she would have tried to cope with the nausea that the Phenergan was designed to relieve. "The company took my arm," she told reporters. "They need to take responsibility for that."[26]

NOTES

1. Legal materials can be found on the blog SCOTUSWiki, www.scotuswiki.com/index.php?title=Wyeth_v._Levine.

2. For background, see Kenneth Jost, "Too Many Lawsuits," *CQ Researcher*, May 22, 1992, pp. 433-456.

3. Background drawn from an excellent overview, Dan Browning, "When Justice Knows No Timetable," *Star Tribune* (Minneapolis), Jan. 23, 2008, p. 1B.

4. The 8th U.S. Circuit Court of Appeals upheld the constitutionality of the law and its application to the Minot derailment litigation in a 2-1 decision on July 2: *Lundeen v. Canadian Pacific Railway Company*, www.ca8.uscourts.gov/opns/opFrame.html.

5. See Transportation Security Administration, Dept. of Homeland Security, "Rail Transportation Security: Final Rule," 19 C.F.R. parts 1520 & 1580, *Federal Register*, Vol. 73, No. 229, pp. 72129-72180 (Nov. 26, 2008), http://frwebgate6.access.gpo.gov/cgi-bin/TEXTgate.cgi?WAIS docID =77152043735+2+1+0&WAISaction=retrieve.

6. Stewart's testimony on June 12, 2008, was before the House Judiciary Subcommittee on Commercial and Administrative Law.

7. See Public Citizen, "The Arbitration Trap: How Credit Card Companies Ensnare Consumers," September 2007, www.citizen.org/publications/release.cfm?ID=7545. For a response, see Institute for Legal Reform, U.S. Chamber of Commerce, "Arbitration — A Good Deal for Consumers: A Response to Public Citizen," April 2008, www.instituteforlegalreform.com/issues/docdetails.cfm?docid=1091.

8. For background, see Kenneth Jost, *Supreme Court Yearbook, 2006-2007*.

9. The decision is *Exxon Shipping Co. v. Baker*, 554 U.S — (2008). For background, see Kenneth Jost, *The Supreme Court Yearbook, 2007-2008*.

10. Background drawn in part from Lawrence M. Friedman, *American Law in the 20th Century* (2002).

11. *Ibid.*, p. 349.

12. The preemption decision is *New York Central R.R. Co. v. Winfield*, 244 U.S. 147 (1917). The plaintiff in the case lost an eye from what the Supreme Court majority called "one of the ordinary risks" of railroad work: while the worker was repairing track, his tool dislodged a pebble, which rebounded and struck his eye.

13. The *McPherson* case is at 217 N.Y. 382 (1916); Traynor's opinion came in *Escola v. Coca Cola Bottling Co. of Fresno*, 27 Cal.2d 453 (1944). Traynor served on the California Supreme Court from 1940-1970, including six years as chief justice.

14. See Friedman, *op. cit.*, pp. 252-256.

15. The asbestos decision is *Borel v. Fibreboard Paper Products Corp.*, 493 F.2d 1076 (5th Cir. 1973). For background, see Kenneth Jost, "Asbestos Litigation," *CQ Researcher*, May 2, 2003, pp. 393-416.

16. For background, see Kenneth Jost, "Medical Malpractice," *CQ Researcher*, Feb. 14, 2003, pp. 129-152.

17. See Seth A. Seabury, Nicholas M. Pace and Robert T. Reville, "Forty Years of Civil Jury Verdicts," *Journal of Empirical Legal Studies*, vol. 1, no. 1 (March 2004), pp. 1-25.

18. See National Conference of State Legislatures, www.ncsl.org/standcomm/sclaw/StateMedliablitylaws2007.htm.

19. See American Tort Reform Association, www.ncsl.org/standcomm/sclaw/StateMedliablitylaws2007.htm.

20. See "House Sustains Product Liability Veto," *CQ Almanac 1996*; "Product Liability Overhaul Dies in Senate," *CQ Almanac 1998*.

21. The decisions are *BMW of North America v. Gore*, 517 U.S. 559 (1996); *State Farm Mutual Automobile Insurance Co. v. Campbell*, 538 U.S. 408 (2003); and *Philip Morris U.S.A. v. Williams*, 549 U.S. 346 (2007).

22. The decisions are *Cipollone v. Liggett Group, Inc.*, 505 U.S. 504 (1992); and *Medtronic, Inc. v. Lohr*, 518 U.S. 470 (1996). For background, see Kenneth Jost, "Closing In on Tobacco," *CQ Researcher*, Nov. 12, 1999, pp. 977-1000.

23. "Limits on Class Action Lawsuits Enacted," *CQ Almanac 2005*.

24. Quoted in Stephen Labaton, " 'Silent Tort Reform' Is Overriding States' Powers," *The New York Times*, March 10, 2006, p. C5. Some other background comes from the article.

25. See Steven Greenhouse, "Wal-Mart to Pay $54 Million to Settle Suit Over Wages," *The New York Times*, Dec. 10, 2008, p. B7.

26. Quoted in Jerry Markon, "High Court Case Looms Large for Drugmakers," *The Washington Post*, Nov. 4, 2008, p. D1.

BIBLIOGRAPHY

Books

Cooter, Robert, and Thomas Ulen, *Law and Economics*, Addison-Wesley, 2007.
This law school textbook by two leaders of the "law and economics" movement includes extensive discussion of the tort system. Cooter is a professor at the University of California-Berkeley School of Law, Ulen at the University of Illinois College of Law. An online supplement provides a classroom-oriented overview of selected issues, including punitive damages (www.cooter-ulen.com/wp/?page_id=90).

Friedman, Lawrence M., *American Law in the 20th Century*, Yale University Press, 2002.
The distinguished Stanford University legal historian provides a succinct overview of 20th-century developments in tort law. Includes detailed notes. For more detail on 19th-century developments, see his earlier book, ***A History of American Law*** (Simon & Schuster, 1973; 3d ed., 2005).

McGarity, Thomas O., *The Preemption War: When Federal Bureaucracies Trump Local Juries*, Yale University Press, 2008.
A professor at the University of Texas School of Law analyzes the legal and policy issues surrounding federal preemption along with a focus on individuals in lawsuits where defendants raised preemption as a defense. Includes detailed chapter notes.

Untereiner, Alan, *The Preemption Defense in Tort Actions*, U.S. Chamber Institute for Legal Reform, 2008.
A Washington, D.C., business lawyer details the history and current status of preemption doctrine and gives

attorneys detailed instructions on how to use preemption as a defense in product liability suits by injured consumers.

Articles

Denniston, Lyle, "A new day on punitive damages law," *SCOTUSBlog*, **June 25, 2008, www.scotusblog.com/ wp/analysis-a-new-day-on-punitive-damages-law/.**
The veteran Supreme Court correspondent examines the implication of the court's decision to set a 1-to-1 ratio for punitive-to-compensatory damages in federal maritime cases.

Mundy, Alicia, "Plaintiffs' Lawyers Fight Restrictions on Product Liability Suits," *The Wall Street Journal*, **Aug. 13, 2008, p. A3.**
The story gives a good overview of the effort by plaintiffs' lawyers to oppose the business-backed campaign to use federal preemption to limit state court suits.

Reports and Studies

American Association for Justice, **"Debunking the Myths," www.justice.org/cps/rde/xchg/justice/hs .xsl/2011.htm (visited December 2008).**
The Web site page seeks to refute "myths" — purportedly generated by business interests — about the incidence of lawsuits in the United States and the costs of litigation borne by consumers. Includes annotations.

Council of Economic Advisers, **"Who Pays for Tort Liability Claims? An Economic Analysis of the U.S. Tort Liability System," April 2002.**
The 19-page report by President Bush's Council of Economic Advisers estimates the annual direct costs of the U.S. tort system at $180 billion — or 1.8 percent of gross domestic product — which the council says is more than double the average cost in other industrialized nations.

Eisenberry, Ross, "Tort Costs and the Economy: Myths, exaggerations, and propaganda," *Economic Policy Institute*, **Nov. 2, 2006.**
The eight-page briefing paper from the progressive think tank argues that the most common claims about the economic costs and impacts of the U.S. tort system "have little or no basis in reality." Eisenberry is the institute's vice president, a lawyer and former policy director of the federal Occupational Safety and Health Administration (OSHA).

Funk, William, Sidney Shapiro, David Vladeck and Karen Sokol, "The Truth about Torts: Using Agency Preemption to Undercut Consumer Health and Safety," *Center for Progressive Reform*, **September 2007, www.progressiveregulation.org/articles/Truth_ Torts_704.pdf.**
The 20-page "white paper" critically examines what the authors call the Bush administration's "unprecedented, aggressive campaign to persuade the courts to preempt state tort [personal injury] actions." Funk, Shapiro and Vladeck are professors, respectively, at Lewis & Clark Law School, Wake Forest University School of Law and Georgetown University Law Center; Sokol is a policy analyst at the Center for Progressive Reform. The center, founded in 2002, has also published *The Truth about Torts: Regulatory Preemption at the National Highway Traffic Safety Administration* (July 2008).

U.S. Chamber Institute for Legal Reform, **"Faces of Lawsuit Abuse.org" (visited December 2008).**
The Web site maintained by the legal-reform lobbying arm of the U.S. Chamber of Commerce features text and video narratives of more than a dozen lawsuits described as "abuses" by the defendants — most of them small-business operators. The site includes updated links to news stories and other materials.

For More Information

American Arbitration Association, 1633 Broadway, 10th Floor, New York, NY 10019; (212) 716-5800; www.adr.org. Provides dispute resolution for individuals and organizations who want to resolve conflicts out of court.

American Association for Justice, 777 6th St., N.W., Washington, DC 20001; (202) 965-3500; www.justice.org. Works to ensure that those injured via misconduct or negligence can obtain justice in U.S. courtrooms.

American Tort Reform Association, 1101 Connecticut Ave., N.W., Suite 400, Washington, DC 20036; (202) 682-1163; www.atra.org. Seeks to increase fairness, predictability and efficiency in the civil justice system.

National Arbitration Forum, P.O. Box 50191, Minneapolis, MN, 55405-0191; (952) 516-6400; www.adrforum.com. Helps resolve commercial and civil disputes.

Public Citizen, 1600 20th St., N.W., Washington, DC 20009; (202) 588-1000; www.citizen.org. Nonprofit consumer advocacy organization representing consumers' interests in Congress, the executive branch and the courts.

RAND Institute for Civil Justice, 1776 Main St., P.O. Box 2138, Santa Monica, CA 90407; (310) 393-0411; www.rand.org/icj. Analyzes trends and policy options to help make the justice system more efficient and equitable.

U.S. Chamber Institute for Legal Reform, 1615 H St., N.W., Washington, DC 20062; (202) 463-5724; www.instituteforlegalreform.org. Founded by the U.S. Chamber of Commerce to improve the nation's legal system on behalf of the business community and others.

The New Environmentalism

Can New Business Policies Save the Environment?

Tom Price

Huge windows reduce energy bills at the experimental Wal-Mart Super Store that opened in Aurora, Colo., in November 2005. The eco-friendly store uses recycled materials for construction and solar and wind power to supplement standard power sources. Wal-Mart and many other businesses are jumping on the conservation bandwagon, joining environmental groups they once fought with.

From *CQ Researcher*,
December 1, 2006.

A cross the globe, evidence abounds of a rising concern for protecting the planet.

But the new concern about the environment is not your father's environmental movement. Corporate executives, investors, conservative Christians, labor unions and others not traditionally associated with the cause have joined the intensifying campaign to save the Earth. There's even a handful of environmentalists who are promoting nuclear power.

• Environmental Defense, a leading advocacy group, hires a director of corporate partnerships and begins helping businesses "go green." Among the many fruits of these collaborations: fuel-efficient hybrid FedEx delivery trucks, reusable UPS shipping envelopes and measures to cut greenhouse-gas emissions at DuPont facilities that saved the company $325 million in one year.[1]

• The National Association of Evangelicals — known for conservative politics — proclaims a "sacred responsibility to steward the Earth," urging governments to "encourage fuel efficiency, reduce pollution, encourage sustainable use of natural resources and provide for the proper care of wildlife and their natural habitats."[2]

• British chemist and environmentalist James Lovelock — famous for arguing that Earth acts as a self-sustaining organism — says building more nuclear power plants is "the only green solution" to the threat of global warming.[3]

In the burgeoning, new environmental movement, a growing number of people are perceiving threats to the environment,

Public Support for Environment Is Up

Support for the environment is up after taking a big dip beginning in 2000. Pro-environment respondents outnumbered pro-economy respondents by 17 percentage points in 2005 and 15 points this year.

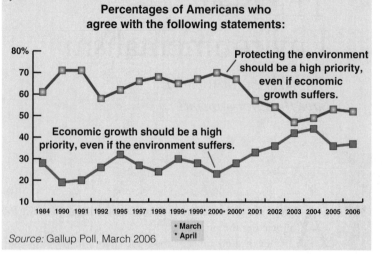

Percentages of Americans who agree with the following statements:

Protecting the environment should be a high priority, even if economic growth suffers.

Economic growth should be a high priority, even if the environment suffers.

• March
* April

Source: Gallup Poll, March 2006

businesses are jumping on the conservation bandwagon and environmentalists are joining hands with groups they once crossed swords with.

"We're seeing the environmental movement getting deeper and broader at the same time," says Rainforest Action Network Executive Director Michael Brune. "We're seeing an increase in straight-up, old-school, traditional grassroots activists wanting to get involved. We're also seeing genuine interest from the business community, evangelicals, labor and other non-traditional allies."

In the words of Oklahoma State University sociology Professor Riley Dunlap, who has studied public opinion about the environment for 40 years and is the Gallup Organization's environmental scholar, "These local government initiatives, state initiatives, corporate initiatives represent a different kind of environmentalism."

The broadening consensus has been spurred mainly by concerns that global warming poses a real and potentially catastrophic threat to life on Earth but that a conservative federal government refuses to act.

"There's undoubtedly a buzz about global warming that wasn't there a year ago," says David Yarnold, executive vice president of Environmental Defense. "The sense

of urgency has grown. And the more people learn about climate change, the more they want to know what they can do."

In a July poll by the Pew Research Center, 70 percent of Americans said there is "solid evidence" for global warming, and 74 percent said it constitutes a serious or somewhat serious problem. In a measure of public confusion about the topic and what should be done, however, 59 percent who believed in global warming thought human activity is the cause, while 30 percent blamed natural climate patterns.[4]

In another poll last January, Pew found that nearly 60 percent of Americans wanted the federal government to make energy and the environment top priorities, the highest percentage since 2001.[5] A Harris Poll last year found three-quarters of Americans feel "protecting the environment is so important that requirements and standards cannot be too high, and continuing environmental improvements must be made regardless of cost."[6]

Despite public support, "there's been an appalling vacuum of leadership coming from within the [Washington] Beltway — on both sides of the aisle," Brune says. "The current administration and [Republican-controlled] Congress can't be accused of being environmental leaders, but even most Democrats haven't been stepping up and showing an appropriate level of response to the environmental threats we face."

In the absence of action in Washington, he adds, "You're seeing a lot of others trying to show leadership."

Although environmentalists were heartened by the Democratic capture of Congress in the November 2006 elections, they're not expecting revolutionary changes in federal policies. President George W. Bush has two more years in office, Democrats hold only a slim majority in the Senate and not all Democrats are environmentalists. For instance, Rep. John D. Dingell, D-Mich. — the presumptive chair of the Energy and Commerce Committee, whose district includes Detroit — has opposed raising automobile gas-mileage requirements.

The most that U.S. Greenpeace Executive Director John Passacantando expects out of the Democrats are "some baby steps." So environmentalists aren't about to change the strategy they've developed since Republicans seized control of Congress in 1994: influencing corporations and state and local governments.

Environmental Defense presents itself to businesses essentially as a consulting firm, offering advice on how they can increase profits by adopting green business practices. The more aggressive Rainforest Action Network (RAN) also enters partnerships — but usually only after businesses succumb to public protests.

"We're not as confrontational as some other groups," says Gwen Ruta, Environmental Defense's corporate partnership director. "We've had pretty good success in going to companies in the spirit of cooperation and saying, 'This is what we want to do.'"

RAN usually stages public demonstrations to "get on the radar screen," says Ilyse Hogue, who manages the organization's campaign to promote green banking, or socially responsible investing. Once a bank agrees to work with her organization, she says, "the intellectual capital at these institutions is so vast that it's fun to participate in the dialogue. These are very bright people who just never really looked at these issues."

Investors also are pressuring companies to adopt green business practices, using tactics such as proposing policy resolutions at shareholders' meetings or investing only in corporations with positive environmental records. How-to guides to shareholder activism have been published both by Friends of the Earth and a partnership of the As You Sow Foundation and Rockefeller Philanthropy Advisors.[7]

"Not to engage the private sector is to miss a huge opportunity to have a positive impact on global warming," says Rockefeller Senior Vice President Doug Bauer.

Some investors band together to increase their clout. Through the Carbon Disclosure Project, for instance, major global investors each year ask about 2,000 companies — including the world's largest 500 — to reveal their impact on greenhouse-gas emissions. In 2006, 225 investors with $31.5 trillion in assets made the request — up from 143 investors the year before. Nearly three-quarters of the largest 500 companies responded this year, up from just under 50 percent in 2005.[8]

The project aims to spur companies to reduce emissions after they've compiled the information needed for

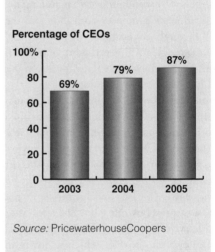

Most CEOs Support Sustainability

The percentage of corporate chief executives in 43 countries who support sustainability has increased nearly 20 percentage points from 2003 to 2005.

CEOs who say environmental sustainability is important to profits

Percentage of CEOs

- 2003: 69%
- 2004: 79%
- 2005: 87%

Source: PricewaterhouseCoopers

the report. Wal-Mart's experience indicates that's happening. In preparing its report, Wal-Mart discovered that refrigerants used in its grocery stores caused more of the company's "greenhouse-gas footprint" than its truck fleet did. Wal-Mart said it is acting on that discovery. (*See sidebar, p. 244.*)

Complaining that the federal government is not acting effectively, cities and states are adopting their own environmental-protection programs — forcing nationwide companies to cope with a patchwork of environmental regulations.

Nearly half the states are requiring that power plants use at least some renewable fuels, and California just mandated cuts in motor vehicles' carbon dioxide emissions. If that law withstands the auto industry's challenges, other states are prepared to act. Meanwhile, just as they did in striving to reduce acid rain, Northeastern states are establishing a consortium to set limits on greenhouse-gas emissions, distribute emission allowances to plants and permit cleaner plants to sell their allowances to dirtier facilities. Western states are crafting a similar agreement.[9]

Gov. Arnold Schwarzenegger, R-Calif., reached across the Atlantic to explore global-warming strategies with British Prime Minister Tony Blair. Former President Bill Clinton is discussing emission-reduction efforts with leaders of the world's 22 largest cities.[10]

Labor unions — which in the past clashed with environmentalists — have joined the new movement through the Apollo Alliance for Good Jobs and Clean Energy.[11] Named for the project that put man on the moon, the alliance promotes both jobs and the environment through government incentives for high-mileage autos, clean and efficient manufacturing, green buildings, renewable energy, public transportation and hydrogen-fuel technology.[12]

Environmentalism has become such a popular topic that it turned former Vice President Al Gore into a best-selling author and movie star while inspiring a real movie star — Leonardo DiCaprio — to try to take environmentalism to television. Gore's book about the threat of global warming, *An Inconvenient Truth*, made *The New York Times* best-seller list, and his movie of the same name was a surprise box-office hit. DiCaprio is teaming up with "Survivor" producer Craig Piligian to create a "reality" television show in which a down-and-out American town gets re-made into a healthy green community. DiCaprio and Piligian are shopping the concept, tentatively titled "E-topia," to networks and sponsors. Instead of just upgrading a wardrobe or a room, as other such shows do, "E-topia" will "take an American town that has been destroyed and bring it back to its former glory and then some," Piligian said. "This town will be reborn as the prototype for the future."[13]

As activists and business executives confront environmental challenges, here are some of the questions they're trying to answer:

Is going "green" good for the corporate bottom line?

A growing number of companies are adopting environmental-protection policies they say are good for business. Some conservative critics contend, however, that such actions actually dilute companies' primary — some say only — purpose: to increase shareholder value.

Corporate executives say they implement green practices for a variety of reasons: to attract more customers, cut costs, drive up the value of their companies' stock, recruit and retain high-quality employees and assure their companies' long-term health.

"Increasingly, suppliers and customers are demanding greater devotion to the environment," says Douglas Pinkham, president of the Public Affairs Council, the professional association for public affairs officers. Employees prefer environmentally friendly corporations because "nobody wants to work for a company that's known as an environmental pirate."

But companies are not going green "just because it helps their reputation," Pinkham adds. "Companies are saying we can make a buck by being environmentally sustainable."

And that goes beyond short-term profit-and-loss calculations, says business consultant Margery Kraus. "I heard an executive comment once that you can't have a successful business in a failed world," explains Kraus, head of APCO Worldwide, an international consulting firm. "I think that says it all." (*See "At Issue," p. 256.*)

According to Oklahoma State's Dunlap, American businesses are beginning to practice "what people in Europe call ecological modernization."

"You don't hear much talk about business vs. environment there," Dunlap explains. "They've adopted the approach that what's good for the environment is good for the economy, and I think we're seeing America kind of struggling to do the same.

"In the old days, it was easy to blame industry for 'greenwashing,' " or trying to appear more environmentally active than they really are. "But I'm increasingly convinced that we're seeing industries realize they have to integrate environmental concerns into their bottom line if they're to be successful."

A 2005 PricewaterhouseCoopers survey of chief executives in 43 countries found 87 percent saying environmental sustainability is important to company profits. That represented a rapid rise from 79 percent in 2004 and 69 percent in 2003.[14] (*See graph, p. 241.*)

Cost-saving is the most obvious benefit of greening a business. As Wal-Mart Chief Executive Lee Scott put it, when a company doesn't recycle, "We pay twice — once to get it, once to have it taken away."[15]

Wal-Mart expects to save $2.4 million a year by shrinking packaging for one private-label toy line, $26 million by cutting delivery-truck idle time and $28 million by recycling plastic in its stores. For really big savings, the giant retailer plans to reduce its stores' energy use by 30 percent and cut its trucks' fuel consumption by 25 percent in three years and 50 percent within 10 years.[16]

DuPont has already saved more than $3 billion by cutting energy use by 7 percent.[17] FedEx is deploying hybrid trucks that reduce fuel costs by more than a third.[18] PNC Financial Services Group is building green bank branches that use 45 percent less energy than standard structures.[19]

General Electric is betting billions that environmentalism sells as well as saves. In mid-2005, the global conglomerate launched its "Ecomagination" initiative to develop products and services that address environmental challenges. GE Chairman and CEO Jeff Immelt announced the company will produce improved technology in solar energy, hybrid locomotives, fuel cells, low-emission aircraft engines, light and strong materials, efficient lighting and water purification.

GE will invest $1.5 billion in research and development in those technologies by 2010 — up from $700 million in 2004 — "and we plan to make money doing it," Immelt said. Moreover, the company intends to double its revenues in those areas, from $10 billion in 2004 to at least $20 billion in 2010 and substantially more later.[20]

Potlatch Corp. Public Affairs Vice President Mark Benson isn't as precise about his forest-products company's future earnings, but he agrees it makes sense to prepare for a green marketplace. Potlatch seeks to distinguish itself from competitors by complying with all of the American Forest and Paper Association's environmental guidelines and then earning certification from the environmental movement's Forest Stewardship Council as well. As a result, Benson says, "we've positioned ourselves so, if that [green] market takes off, we're going to be there to serve it."

Retailers are discovering that "dedication to the environment makes them more attractive to consumers — especially if they're trying to appeal to an upscale audience," Pinkham says. Potlatch's policies also may make it more attractive to green investors, a group that is growing in numbers and influence, Benson says.

Assets devoted to so-called socially responsible investing (SRI) — of which green investing is a part — have grown slightly faster than other kinds of investing over the last decade, according to the Social Investment Forum, the SRI industry's trade association. SRI investments now represent 9.4 percent of all professionally managed assets tracked in Nelson Information's *Directory of Investment Managers.*[21]

Among SRI investors, 37 percent consider companies' environmental records when making investment decisions, the forum reported. Many also attempt to influence corporate environmental policy by introducing resolutions at shareholders' meetings.

Investors are proposing a growing number of resolutions, according to a report from the As You Sow Foundation and Rockefeller Philanthropy Advisors. Investors' proposals have addressed the environment more than any other issue in recent years, the report said, and the number of environmental resolutions proposed has increased faster than most other topics.[22]

But not everyone is bullish on green business.

Jerry Taylor, a senior fellow at the libertarian Cato Institute, suggests that talk of consumers' and companies' concern about the environment is overblown. "Public demands have always been for bigger and bigger and bigger homes," he notes. "How do you square that with the rise of environmentalism? And if consumers are looking at more fuel-efficient cars, I think that has more to do with the price of gas than anything else." If gas prices drop, Americans might go right back to their big SUVs, he says.

Businesses may find conservation economical now, he adds, but if energy prices drop, companies might find it less expensive to use more energy than to buy energy-efficient equipment, he says. Competition could force companies to enlarge packaging to catch consumers' eyes, he says, even if that uses more materials.

While executives contend they adopt green policies to boost the bottom line, Competitive Enterprise Institute President Fred Smith Jr. charged the policies usually are intended "to appease [a business's] critics, to apologize for past mistakes, to bribe its opponents."

"The modern firm solves one — but only one — of the major problems of mankind: the creation of wealth," Smith said. "That wealth then allows individuals in their various roles the opportunity to protect values they care about."[23]

Wal-Mart Sets Ambitious 'Green' Goals

Wal-Mart, the world's largest retailer, wants to be the greenest as well. President and Chief Executive Officer Lee Scott laid out the corporation's ambitious long-term goals a year ago: to use only renewable energy, to create no waste and to sell products that "sustain our resources and environment."

He also established specific short-term goals:

- increase truck fuel efficiency by 25 percent in three years and 100 percent in 10;
- cut store energy consumption by 30 percent and reduce facility greenhouse-gas emissions by 20 percent in seven years;
- reduce solid waste at stores by 25 percent in three years;
- establish a program within 18 months that gives preference to suppliers that "aggressively" reduce their greenhouse-gas emissions, and
- increase sales of organic food and other environmentally friendly products.

"Environmental problems are *our* problems," Scott told employees at the company's Bentonville, Ark., headquarters. Solving them is good for humanity, he said, and it's good for business.[1]

During 2005, Wal-Mart opened two experimental stores — in McKinney, Texas, and Aurora, Colo. — to test green technology.

Highly efficient light-emitting diodes — or LEDs — illuminate exterior signs and interior display cases. Heating systems burn cooking oil and motor oil from the stores' restaurants and auto repair shops. Heat is recovered from refrigerators and freezers, and solar collectors and wind turbines supply electricity. Doors were installed on refrigerated cases that usually are left open, and their lights brighten and dim as shoppers open and close the doors. The restrooms have water-conserving sinks, and the men's rooms use waterless urinals. Countertops are made with recycled glass and concrete.

Outside, drought-tolerant vegetation cuts the water needed for irrigation. Food waste is composted and sold. Roads are paved with recycled materials, and concrete is mixed with fly ash from burned coal and slag from steel production.[2]

Some of the innovations were immediate hits, the company reported in a one-year review, while others "still need to be refined." Some of the earliest successes — the lighting, landscaping, sinks and urinals — will begin showing up in other Wal-Marts in 2007. The company hopes the other innovations will prove themselves over the next two years.

"Due to our size and scope, we are uniquely positioned to have great success and impact in the world, perhaps like no company before us," Scott said.

Seemingly small changes, when Wal-Mart makes them, can save millions of dollars.

Because its truck fleet travels a billion miles a year, for instance, raising fuel efficiency by just one mile per gallon would save the company more than $52 million annually at current fuel prices, Scott said. Meeting his goal of doubling efficiency by 2015 would jump that savings to $310 million.

If the company could sell one compact fluorescent light bulb to each of the 100-plus million shoppers who walk into Wal-Mart stores every week, those customers' electric bills would drop a collective $3 billion. If the company succeeds in encouraging green practices by its 60,000 suppliers and 1.3 million employees, environmental benefits will ripple around the world.[3]

Known primarily for its low prices, Wal-Mart confronts a stiff challenge in selling green products that often cost more than their non-green counterparts.

Is more federal action needed to encourage energy efficiency?

Almost everyone agrees Americans would be better off if they used energy more efficiently. Even those who don't fear global warming see benefits in reducing U.S. dependence on energy sources from unstable regions of the world, such as the Middle East. Most also agree that only federal action could spur significant gains in efficiency.

But there is disagreement over whether the desire for efficiency warrants government intervention and which measures would be most effective. Most environmental organizations advocate government mandates. Many businesses prefer incentives for voluntary action.

"We cannot solve these issues without the active participation of the federal government," says the Rainforest Action Network's Brune.

"We've seen that if a green product costs the same, it's a runaway success," Vice President Andrew Ruben says. "If it costs a little more, it can be successful. Above that, we've got to do things in a smarter way" to try to bring the price down. The company's goal is to price organic products no more than 10 percent above their conventional counterparts.

Environmentalists and organic-farming advocates give Wal-Mart's plan mixed reactions.

The company has consulted with the World Wildlife Federation, the Natural Resources Defense Council, Greenpeace and other environmental organizations. Environmental Defense, another Wal-Mart advisor, opened a Bentonville office so it could dispatch a representative to corporate headquarters at a moment's call.

Describing Wal-Mart's impact on the U.S. economy as "almost beyond calculation," Environmental Defense Executive Vice President David Yarnold said he and his colleagues "really believe that Wal-Mart can create a race to the top for environmental benefits."[4]

The Sierra Club refused to work with Wal-Mart because of concern about its labor policies, but Executive Director Carl Pope said Wal-Mart managers "deserve the chance to show that their business model is compatible with high standards, not just low prices."[5]

Nu Wexler, a spokesman for Wal-Mart Watch — which was created to challenge the company's business practices — said his organization is "encouraged by Wal-Mart's new environmental initiatives because they could, if implemented, change the way American businesses approach environmental sustainability."[6]

The Cornucopia Institute, an advocate for small organic farms, attacked the company for purchasing from "industrial-scale factory farms" and from China. Pressure to cut prices could destroy family farms and reduce some of the environmental benefits of organic farming, said Mark Kastel, Cornucopia's senior farm-policy analyst.

"Food shipped around the world — burning fossil fuels and undercutting our domestic farmers — does not meet the consumer's traditional definition of what is truly organic," Kastel said.[7]

Ronnie Cummins, national director of the Organic Consumers Association, questioned the authenticity of organic food grown in China, where "organic standards are dubious, and farm-labor exploitation is the norm."[8]

Wal-Mart replied that it would not compromise organic standards.[9] In addition, a spokesman said, "whenever possible, as with all fresh merchandise, we try to purchase fresh organic products from local suppliers for distribution to stores in their areas. This is good for the surrounding communities and helps to generate savings on distribution costs that we can pass on to our customers."[10]

---

[1] Lee Scott, presentation to Wal-Mart employees, Bentonville, Ark., Oct. 24, 2005; www.walmartstores.com/Files/21st%20Century%20Leadership.pdf.

[2] "Experimental Wal-Mart Stores One Year Later," Wal-Mart; www.walmartfacts.com/FactSheets/11132006_Experimental_Stores.pdf.

[3] Marc Gunther, "The Green Machine," *Fortune*, Aug. 7, 2006. p. 42. Michael Barbaro, "Wal-Mart Effort on Health and Environment Is Seen," *The New York Times*, June 22, 2006, p. 2.

[4] "Environmental Defense Will Add Staff Position in Bentonville, Arkansas," Environmental Defense, July 12, 2006; www.environmentaldefense.org/pressrelease.cfm?ContentID=5322.

[5] Abigail Goldman, "Wal-Mart goes 'green,'" *Los Angeles Times*, Nov. 13, 2006.

[6] *Ibid.*

[7] Mark Kastel, "Wal-Mart Declares War on Organic Farmers, the Cornucopia Institute, Sept. 28, 2006; www.cornucopia.org/WalMart_News_Release.pdf.

[8] Ronnie Cummins, "Open Letter to Wal-Mart," the Organic Consumers Association, July 4, 2006; www.organicconsumers.org/2006/article_1009.cfm.

[9] Tom Daykin, "Wal-Mart threatens farmers, report says," *The Milwaukee Journal Sentinel*, Sept. 28, 2006.

[10] Mya Frazier, "Critics' latest beef with Wal-Mart is . . . organics?" *Advertising Age*, Oct. 16, 2006, p. 47.

"There is no substitute for having clear national goals," Sierra Club spokesman Eric Antebi agrees. "It's great to have over 300 mayors doing their part. It's critical that states are taking the lead. But there are still too many gaps."

"There are some places where voluntary business actions will offer the greatest opportunities," says Denis Hayes, president and CEO of the Bullitt Foundation, and one of the key organizers of the first Earth Day. "But it's nice to have a regulatory basement beneath which you're not allowed to sink."

U.S. energy consumption is like a giant ocean liner that can't change direction quickly, says Americans for Balanced Energy Choices Executive Director Joe Lucas. "We don't want draconian measures," says Lucas, whose advocacy group is funded by coal producers and

The Rainforest Action Network's Jumpstart Ford campaign urges Ford and other corporations to reduce their dependence on oil. The campaign claims Ford has the worst fleetwide fuel efficiency and the highest average vehicle greenhouse-gas emissions of major U.S. automakers.

consumers. "Don't force the ocean liner to do a U-turn immediately."

The federal government should continue to fund efforts to develop technologies that burn coal more efficiently and with fewer emissions, he says. And the government should offer incentives for farmers and foresters to adopt practices that absorb more greenhouse gases from the atmosphere.

Similarly, the auto industry opposes higher fuel-efficiency standards but favors tax breaks for those who buy fuel-efficient cars. "Competition among the automakers will drive this process far better and with fewer

disruptions to the marketplace than any regulations that can be adopted," said Frederick Webber, president and CEO of the Alliance of Automobile Manufacturers.[24]

American businesses and individuals have become much more energy efficient since the emergence of the modern environmental movement and the 1973 Arab oil embargo. Today coal emits 70 percent less pollution per unit of energy produced than it did 30 years ago, Lucas says. Compared with the growth in gross domestic product, the United States puts a declining amount of greenhouse gases into the air, he adds.

America's new cars and light trucks average about 24 miles per gallon now, up from 15 in 1975. The typical refrigerator uses less than half as much electricity as its counterpart in 1972.[25]

Population growth, economic expansion and consumer tastes, however, have driven total energy consumption up by a third since 1973, and it is expected to jump another 30 percent by 2025.[26] Americans burned 75 percent more coal in 2005 than in 1980, and the coal industry says consumption will increase more than 30 percent over the next two decades.[27]

This doesn't surprise Joel Schwartz, a visiting fellow at the American Enterprise Institute (AEI), who doubts the need for, or effectiveness of, government regulations. "When you make things more efficiently," he explains, "you free up resources to make something else. Pound for pound, cars are more energy efficient now. Because of consumer demand, the efficiency benefits have gone into creating bigger cars that get about the same fuel economy."

If the United States did import less oil, Schwartz adds, "it would get used somewhere else. Developing countries would use that energy."

Nevertheless, environmentalists want the federal government to impose tougher restrictions on the use of fossil fuels. Cars began getting better gas mileage after federal corporate average fuel economy (CAFE) standards were enacted in 1975, they note. But the standard for passenger cars has not been raised since 1990, and the average fuel efficiency of cars and light trucks has actually declined since 1987. Over the last two decades, the auto industry has focused technology on getting heavier vehicles to run faster, and the growing American population has driven more miles.

The Union of Concerned Scientists wants CAFE standards increased to more than 40 miles per gallon (mpg) by 2015 and 55 mpg by 2025. Boosting mileage standards would not require U.S. auto companies to reinvent the wheel, the organization contends. For instance, Ford could apply existing technology to boost the Explorer SUV's fuel efficiency to 36 miles per gallon from 21.[28]

Environmental organizations also want restrictions on greenhouse-gas emissions, which are not regulated because they are not legally classified as pollutants under the Clean Air Act.[29] One often-advocated plan would assign every company an emissions allowance and let those that emit less sell their excess allowance to others. This so-called "cap-and-trade" scheme has been used successfully to reduce the sulfur emissions that cause acid rain.

Sens. John R. McCain, R-Ariz., and Joseph I. Lieberman, D-Conn., introduced legislation to do that in early 2005, and Maryland Republican Rep. Wayne T. Gilchrest did the same in the House. Neither bill got out of committee.

Recently some conservatives, concerned about U.S. reliance on imported oil, have suggested raising taxes on fossil fuels. "That's the way to get consumption down," said Alan Greenspan, former chairman of the Federal Reserve Board. "It's a national-security issue." Joining him have been such prominent conservative economists as Gregory Mankiw, former chairman of President Bush's Council of Economic Advisors, and Andrew Samwick, the council's former chief economist.[30]

While he doesn't agree that it's needed, Schwartz says a tax would be the most effective way to curb fossil-fuel use, as long as it were combined with other tax cuts so it didn't depress the economy.

Can the industrial world switch from fossil fuels to other forms of energy?

Environmentalists argue the only way to stop global warming is to stop burning fossil fuels. But switching from coal and oil is no easy task, and alternative energy sources have their own drawbacks — including damage to the environment.

"No energy source is perfect," says David Hamilton, director of the Sierra Club's global warming and energy program, using words echoed by Lucas, the coal-industry advocate.

For Hamilton, that means accepting the shortcomings of alternative fuels in the near term while conducting the research and development needed to make them

work over the long haul. For Lucas, it means environmentalists have to accept that fossil fuels will be the world's primary energy source for the foreseeable future.

Eliminating coal and oil is "a pipe dream," that could occur only in "science-fiction land," Lucas says. "For the next 30 to 50 to 100 years, folks are going to have little choice but to use coal."

Currently, nearly 80 percent of the world's energy comes from burning fossil fuels.[31] In the United States, it's 86 percent.[32] Coal produces 52 percent of the electricity consumed in the United States,[33] and oil powers nearly all U.S. transportation.[34]

The coal producers and their customers project that America will continue to get a majority of its electricity from coal in 2025. They also say they will steadily reduce coal emissions during that time and will begin building "ultra-low-emissions plants" in the decade following 2025. Those plants could eliminate more than 99 percent of sulfur, nitrogen oxide and particulate emissions, along with 95 percent of mercury, they say. They also aim to be able to capture and sequester carbon dioxide, fossil fuels' primary contributor to global warming.[35]

The Rainforest Action Network's Brune acknowledges that "we have massive amounts of coal in the United States and around the world. If we want to extract every bit of fossil fuel, we could go for a couple hundred more years. But the planet wouldn't be able to survive."

Industry has not proven that it can capture and sequester greenhouse gases on a commercial scale, he says, and coal mining itself does terrible damage to the environment.

Even if factories could capture greenhouse gases in the future, Hamilton says, "scientists say we need to actually reduce emissions now, not just get on a path to reducing emissions in 10 years."

That would require a variety of methods for conserving and switching to alternative sources of energy, environmentalists say. "There is no silver bullet," Sierra Club spokesman Antebi says. "I heard someone say that you need silver buckshot.

"We're going to need to make our cars go further on a gallon of gas," he continued. "We're going to need solar and wind power and biofuels. We're going to need to design our buildings to operate more efficiently. We're going to need to clean up our power plants and use new technologies to reduce their impact on global warming."

Wind power has been the fastest-growing U.S. source of energy, jumping by 160 percent from 2000 to 2005. But it accounts for less than two-tenths of a percent of American energy consumption.[36] And it is not without its problems.

Jesse Ausubel, director of Rockefeller University's human-environment program, terms wind one of environmentalism's "false gods." To replace a typical, traditional power plant, he said, a windmill farm would have to cover 300 square miles. Other environmentalists oppose windmill farms because they endanger birds and can clutter the landscape.[37]

Similarly, U.S. use of ethanol — a fuel made from corn and other plants — increased by 145 percent from 2000 to 2005. Like wind power, however, it supplies a tiny fraction of America's energy — about a third of a percent.[38] Spurred by government incentives, annual ethanol production may more than double from 4.5 billion gallons now to more than 10 billion by 2010.[39] But that still would represent less than 1 percent of U.S. energy sources, and ethanol, too, carries environmental baggage. (*See sidebar, p. 250.*)

Despite problems posed by some alternative-energy sources, Hamilton says, "we're going to need almost every tool in the shed for a while.

"Scientists are saying we won't have the luxury to go back and stop global warming if we reach some of these biological tipping points," he continues. "We need to solve this problem now, and if we do we will then have the opportunity to make technological improvements later.

"You can always take the wind turbines down because some people think they're ugly. You can't take the carbon dioxide out of the air — it stays there for 200 years."

Many environmentalists place hope in solar energy, even though it currently produces less than a tenth of a percent of U.S. power. A handful of environmentalists are calling for more use of nuclear power. A growing number of environmental organizations are acknowledging that nuclear shouldn't be rejected out of hand. But most argue that nuclear's downsides will not be overcome in the foreseeable future.

Pro-nuclear environmentalists, such as British scientist Lovelock, contend it offers the only realistic alternative to fossil fuels. Other alternatives are "largely gestures," Lovelock said. "If it makes people feel good to shove up a windmill or put a solar panel on their roof, great, do it.

It'll help a little bit, but it's no answer at all to the problem."[40]

Bruce Babbitt — Clinton administration Interior secretary and one-time head of the League of Conservation Voters — described nuclear power as "the lesser [evil] of the only two alternatives that are on the table right now. One is to fry this planet with continuing use and burning of fossil fuels, and the other is to try to make nuclear power work."[41]

Environmentalists can't "just say 'no way, no how,' " Environmental Defense's Yarnold says. "That's one reason some people look at a caricature of environmentalists and say, 'There they go again.' "

But he also says the nuclear industry must answer tough questions about reactor safety, waste disposal and weapons proliferation before new plants should be opened.

The industry might be able to address some concerns about safety, the Bullitt Foundation's Hayes says, "but the one I can't think of any way to make progress on is nuclear proliferation. I'm pretty terrified of a world in which 60 countries have nuclear stockpiles, and if they all have nuclear power I can't think of any way to avoid that."

BACKGROUND

Early Warnings

American environmentalists can trace their roots to distinguished writers — and some obscure bureaucrats — of the mid-19th century.[42]

Students still read Henry David Thoreau's *Walden* (published in 1854) and his other paeans to nature. In 1857, after the discovery of the California redwoods, poet James Russell Lowell proposed establishing a society for the protection of trees.

But even earlier, the U.S. commissioner of patents warned in 1849 about "the folly and shortsightedness" of wasting timber and slaughtering buffalo. Other commissioners of patents and of agriculture issued similar warnings about environmental destruction throughout the 1850s and '60s.

Congress had gotten the message by 1864, when it gave Yosemite Valley to California to establish a state park. Eight years later, it made Yellowstone the world's first national park.

CHRONOLOGY

1870-1900 *Environmentalists organize, and Congress begins to act.*

1870 Congress passes law to protect Alaska wildlife.

1872 Yellowstone becomes world's first national park.

1891 Congress empowers president to create national forests.

1900-1969 *Teddy Roosevelt leads crusade to protect the environment. Modern environmental movement is born.*

1901 President Theodore Roosevelt makes conservation a priority.

1906 Congress passes Antiquities Act; Roosevelt creates the first national monuments — Devil's Tower in Wyoming and Petrified Forest in Arizona.

1916 National Park Service created.

1962 Writer and biologist Rachel Carson warns of the dangers of pesticides in her landmark book *Silent Spring*.

1970-1979 *Modern environmental movement soars into prominence; Congress responds with landmark laws.*

1970 Some 20 million Americans celebrate first Earth Day. . . . Clean Air Act passed. . . . Environmental Protection Agency created.

1972 Clean Water Act passed; DDT is banned.

1973 Endangered Species Act passed.

1974 Safe Water Drinking Act enacted.

1975 Fuel-economy and tailpipe-emission standards are established.

1980-1987 *Environmental activism slows, but Congress passes significant legislation, and international agreements target global environmental challenges.*

1980 Superfund created to clean hazardous-waste sites. . . . Landmark Alaska Lands legislation sets aside more than 100 million acres, doubling U.S. parks and refuge acreage

1987 Two-dozen nations agree to phase out chlorofluorocarbons, which damage Earth's ozone layer.

1990-1999 *Climate change becomes top global environmental issue.*

1992 U.N. convention calls for greenhouse-gas reductions.

1994 Republican takeover of Congress diminishes environmentalists' power in federal government.

1995 Attack on acid rain launched.

1997 Kyoto Protocol mandates greenhouse-gas reductions; U.S. fails to ratify.

2000-2006 *Republican control of Congress and White House further weakens environmentalists' voice. Environmentalists increase efforts to influence business. More businesses go "green."*

2000 Republican George W. Bush wins White House; GOP holds Congress. . . . Thirty-five institutional investors with several trillion dollars in assets launch Carbon Disclosure Project to pressure corporations to address global warming.

2001 Vermont Sen. James Jeffords, an environmentalist, leaves Republican Party mid-year, giving Democrats control of Senate.

2002 GOP regains control of Senate.

2006 Environmentalists celebrate Democratic capture of Congress but don't expect great success while Bush occupies White House and Senate is nearly evenly divided. . . . Carbon Disclosure Project grows to 225 investors with $31.5 trillion in assets. . . . Tyson Foods warns meat prices to rise because ethanol production is driving up cost of corn.

The Promise — and Problems — of Ethanol

For environmentalists, ethanol wields a double-edged sword. It replaces oil-based fuels, reducing emissions of greenhouse gases and other pollutants. But it poses its own threats.

Tyson Foods, the world's largest meat processor, recently underscored one ethanol worry — that increased production of ethanol, almost all from corn, will drive up the price of that widely used grain. Rising corn prices will lead to higher chicken, beef and pork prices in 2007, the company announced in November.

"The American consumer is making a choice here," Tyson President and CEO Richard Bond said. "This is either corn for feed or corn for fuel. That's what's causing this."[1]

Critics also worry that devoting more land to expanded corn production could damage the environment by increasing harmful runoff of pesticides and fertilizers and by discouraging the preservation of land for conservation reserves, wetlands, wildlife preserves and wilderness.[2] According to Friends of the Earth, corn requires nearly six times more fertilizer and pesticide than most crops.[3]

Ethanol enjoys substantial government subsidies, in no small part because of farm-state lawmakers whose constituents grow corn. Ethanol production consumed about 14 percent of U.S.-grown corn in 2005 and was projected to run as high as 19 percent this year. America's entire corn crop would supply just 3.7 percent of the energy demanded by the U.S. transportation sector, however, researchers at the Polytechnic University of New York estimated.[4]

Corn ethanol contains less energy than gasoline, so an ethanol-fueled vehicle gets lower fuel efficiency. *Consumer Reports* magazine compared gasoline with an ethanol fuel burned in a Chevy Tahoe sport utility vehicle, a so-called "flexible fuel" model that can run on gasoline or a mixture of up to 85 percent ethanol and 15 percent gas. The ethanol blend delivered 27 percent lower gas mileage.[5]

According to a team of researchers from the University of California at Berkeley, corn ethanol can make a real, but relatively small, contribution to reducing greenhouse-gas emissions. They compared the energy in the ethanol with the fossil fuels used to make it — powering farm machinery and production equipment, for instance. The ethanol contained 20 percent more energy than was used to make it, and it reduced greenhouse-gas emissions by 13 percent.[6]

Most modern cars can run on a 10 percent ethanol blend, and about a third of U.S. motor fuel uses that mixture to reduce pollution. But only about 5 million of America's 230 million passenger vehicles can run on 85-percent ethanol, called E85, and many of them are gas-guzzlers like the Tahoe.[7] The United States had 70 percent more E85-dispensing service stations in August than it did at the beginning of last year, but that's still just 850 of 169,000 stations nationwide.[8]

Ethanol proponents hope other crops will prove to be more efficient energy sources.

Ethanol from sugarcane has eight times the energy of corn ethanol.[9] It delivers 40 percent of Brazil's automobile fuel, costs less than half as much as gasoline there and helps to generate electricity as well.[10] But the United States doesn't have much land suitable for the crop. In addition, federal laws keep sugar prices artificially high and restrict imports of cheaper sugar from overseas.[11]

Entrepreneurs and scientists are trying to produce ethanol from more economical plant matter, such as farm waste, municipal trash, grass, leaves and wood. Corn ethanol is made from the corn's starch. Ethanol also can be made — with greater difficulty — from cellulose, which is the main component of plant-cell walls.

Not only can cellulosic ethanol be made from more materials, it also can reduce greenhouse-gas emissions by

During the 1870s, Congress passed legislation to protect fur-bearing animals in Alaska, fisheries in the Atlantic Ocean and Eastern lakes and trees on government lands. Environmental organizations also began to sink roots. Botanists and horticulturalists created the American Forestry Association (now known as American Forests), and New Englanders founded the Appalachian Mountain Club.

The 1890s also proved to be "green." Congress established Sequoia and General Grant (now part of Kings Canyon) national parks, and brought Yosemite back under federal control. Congress also gave the president power to create national forests, and President Benjamin Harrison issued a proclamation that created the first national wildlife refuge, in Alaska. In the private sector, John Muir and some friends on the West Coast founded

67 to 89 percent, according to the U.S. Energy Department's Argonne National Laboratory.[12]

The economies of tropical and subtropical countries, with year-round growing seasons, could benefit from the growing demand for sugarcane ethanol. "The risk," Earth Policy Institute President Lester Brown warned, "is that economic pressures to clear land for expanding sugarcane production . . . in the Brazilian cerrado and Amazon basin . . . will pose a major threat to plant and animal diversity."[13]

The Rainforest Action Network is "very concerned about biofuel's impact on rain forests," Network Executive Director Michael Brune says. Ethanol can contribute to reducing fossil-fuel consumption, he says, but only as part of a comprehensive approach that includes more efficient motor-vehicle engines and clean generation of electricity.

"If we replaced gas-guzzling internal-combustion engines with a similar engine that uses biofuel, we'll just be replacing one problem with another," Brune says. "If we use more advanced auto technology and 'green' the electricity grid, then the impact of an appropriate use of biofuels would be revolutionary."

More Corn Used for Ethanol

Nearly 20 percent of the corn grown in the United States this year — a five-percentage-point increase over 2005 — was used for ethanol production. If the nation's entire corn crop were used for ethanol, it would supply just 3.7 percent of the energy needed for transportation alone.

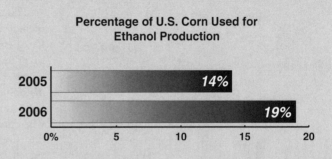

Percentage of U.S. Corn Used for Ethanol Production

2005	14%
2006	19%

Source: Polytechnic University of New York

[1] Marcus Kabel, "Tyson Foods Sees Higher Meat Prices," The Associated Press, Nov. 13, 2006.

[2] Brad Knickerbocker, "Why the Next Congress Will Be 'Greener,' But Only by a Few Shades," *The Christian Science Monitor*, Nov. 15, 2006, p. 2.

[3] Mike Nixon, "Skepticism Rides along with Gasoline Ethanol Requirement," *St. Louis Daily Record*, July 15, 2006.

[4] Adriel Bettelheim, "Biofuels Boom," *CQ Researcher*, Sept. 29, 2006, pp. 793-816.

[5] "The Ethanol Myth," *Consumer Reports*, October 2006, p. 15.

[6] Elizabeth Douglass, "Report Challenges Claims about Ethanol," *Los Angeles Times*, Jan. 27, 2006, p. C2.

[7] Elizabeth Douglass, "A Future Without Oil?" *Los Angeles Times*, April 16, 2006, p. C1; "Annual Vehicle Distance Traveled in Miles and Related Data 2004," Federal Highway Administration, www.fhwa.dot.gov/policy/ohim/hs04/htm/vm1.htm.

[8] Alexei Barrionuevo, "An Alternative Fuel Is Scarce, Even in the Farm Belt," *The New York Times*, Aug. 31, 2006, p. C1.

[9] Jerry Taylor and Peter Van Doren, "California's Global Warming Dodge," *The Arizona Republic*, May 7, 2006.

[10] Marla Dickerson, "Homegrown Fuel Supply Helps Brazil Breathe Easy," *Los Angeles Times*, June 15, 2005, p. 1.

[11] "Sugar's sweet deal," *Sarasota Herald-Tribune*, Aug. 15, 2006, p. A10.

[12] Barbara McClellan, "Biofuel Crossroads," *Ward's Auto World*, Nov. 1, 2006, p. 30.

[13] Lester R. Brown, "Rescuing a Planet Under Stress," *The Futurist*, July 1, 2006, p. 18.

the Sierra Club to preserve wilderness. Back East, creation of the Massachusetts Audubon Society touched off the Audubon movement, which led to the National Association of Audubon Societies in 1905.

President Theodore Roosevelt (1901-1909), an avid outdoorsman, doubled the acreage in national parks and established 53 wildlife sanctuaries. Following congressional passage of the American Antiquities Act in 1906,

Roosevelt created the first national monuments — Devil's Tower in Wyoming and Petrified Forest in Arizona. The early-20th century also spawned Western opposition to federal environmental-protection activities, notably when Western business and government representatives met at the Denver Public Lands Convention and demanded that federal lands be turned over to the states.

Getty Images/Sandy Huffaker

The Kumeyaay wind farm on the Campo Indian Reservation serves 30,000 customers in San Diego. Wind power is the fastest-growing U.S. source of energy but accounts for less than two-tenths of a percent of American energy consumption. Replacing a typical, traditional power plant with wind power would require a 300-square-mile wind farm, according to one expert.

While most early 20th-century environmentalism focused on preserving pristine nature, public officials also began to take note of a growing side effect of urbanization — pollution of waters near big cities. Congress responded in 1910 by passing legislation that restricted dumping refuse into Lake Michigan in or near Chicago.

In something of a harbinger of current partnerships between environmental organizations and businesses, conservationists and sportsmen found allies within railroads and travel agencies. Together, they promoted creation of a federal bureau to look after the national parks. Congress responded in 1916 by establishing the National Park Service.

Three years later, supporters of the parks founded the National Parks Association (which was renamed the National Parks and Conservation Association in 1970). The organization sought to build public backing for the parks through educational activities and by encouraging Americans to visit.

The roaring '20s became better known for environmental exploitation than environmental protection, as Congress opened federal lands to mining and drilling for small fees, authorized federal hydroelectric projects and set the U.S. Army Corps of Engineers to dredging and damming inland waters.

In the 1930s, the Great Depression was worsened when poor agricultural practices contributed to massive dust storms that turned formerly bountiful farmland on the Plains into the Dust Bowl. In efforts to fight the Depression, President Franklin D. Roosevelt's New Deal policies created the Civilian Conservation Corps, through which unemployed workers planted trees, built roads, erected fire towers and carried out other public works.

The environmental costs of industrialization commanded increasing attention during the 1930s, '40s and '50s. Offshore oil drilling began. Smog episodes in St. Louis led to the nation's first smoke-control ordinance. Los Angeles established the first air-pollution control bureau. California adopted the first automobile-emissions standards. Congress passed laws — that would be strengthened after the '60s — to address water and air pollution.

The political and counter-culture ferment of the 1960s spurred interest in environmentalism that emphasized personal responsibility. This manifested itself in movements to encourage recycling, organic gardening and farming, cooperatives and purchases of "green" products.

Mimicking the violent political activists of the era, a few organizations and individuals began engaging in "ecoterrorism," destroying property that they viewed as encroaching on nature and setting booby traps to threaten loggers. Their legacy included trials and guilty pleas this year from alleged members of the Earth Liberation Front and Animal Liberation Front who were charged with firebombing ranger stations, corrals, lumber mill offices, ski resorts, slaughterhouse and federal plant-inspection facilities throughout the West between 1996 and 2001.[43]

Era of Activism

Taking an entirely different tack, biologist Rachel Carson wrote *Silent Spring*, highlighting the dangers posed by DDT and other pesticides and foreshadowing the coming era of massive environmental activism.

That era was kicked off by the first Earth Day, on April 22, 1970. The event was conceived by Democratic Sen. Gaylord Nelson of Wisconsin as a way to "shake up the political establishment and force this issue onto the national agenda."[44] He modeled it after the teach-ins that built opposition to the Vietnam War on college campuses, and it succeeded beyond his wildest dreams.

An estimated 20 million Americans — including 10 million students from 2,000 colleges and 1,000 high schools — participated in a wide variety of activities throughout the country. There were marches, rallies, songfests, mock funerals for the internal-combustion engine, mock trials of polluters, trash pickup drives, protests against aircraft noise and polluting companies. New York City closed Fifth Avenue for Earth Day events. Congress shut down because so many members were out participating. Earth Day speakers ranged from famed anthropologist Margaret Mead to liberal Sen. Edward M. Kennedy, D-Mass., to conservative Sen. Barry Goldwater, R-Ariz., to Nixon administration Cabinet officers.[45]

At the same time, according to organizer Hayes, Attorney General John R. Mitchell ordered the FBI to investigate the organizers of Earth Day.[46] In addition, a Georgia gubernatorial candidate called Earth Day a communist plot because it was held on Russian revolutionary Vladimir Lenin's birthday, and the Daughters of the American Revolution denounced it as "subversive."[47]

But lawmakers heard loud and clear that Earth Day was above all an expression of national will. Later in 1970, Congress passed the Clean Air Act, and President Richard M. Nixon established the Environmental Protection Agency. These were followed in subsequent years by a flood of landmark laws, including the Clean Water Act, the Endangered Species Act, the Marine Mammal Protection Act, the Safe Drinking Water Act, the Toxic Substances Control Act, the Resource Conservation and Recovery Act to regulate hazardous waste, fuel-economy standards, tailpipe-emission and lead-paint restrictions, bans on DDT, the phasing out of leaded gasoline, PCBs and ozone-destroying chlorofluorocarbons and a U.S.-Canada agreement to clean up the polluted Great Lakes.

The '70s also witnessed the birth of Green political parties, which eventually wielded significant influence in Europe but not in the United States. While the first Green parties were organized in New Zealand and Australia, the first Green Party candidate won election to a national legislature in Switzerland, in 1979. Green parties contributed to some of the movements that overthrew communist regimes in former Soviet-bloc countries. The German Green Party joined the governing coalition in 1998, and its leader served as foreign minister. Greens also have been mayors of Dublin, Rome and other major European cities.

In the United States, although Congress passed environmental legislation at a slower pace in the 1980s and '90s, some of the new laws were highly significant. The Superfund program began to clean up hazardous-waste sites in the '80s, for example, and the attack on acid rain began in the following decade.

Global warming has been the world's top environmental issue since the 1990s. Most — though not all — scientists believe that fossil-fuel emissions are causing the planet to heat up. Scientists can't make specific predictions about how much or how fast. Worst-case scenarios are truly catastrophic, forecasting drought, famine, floods, animal and plant extinctions, destruction of island and coastal communities — even massive human death.

The 1992 U.N. Framework Convention on Climate Change called on industrialized nations to reduce their emissions of "greenhouse gases," which are released when coal, oil and other fossil fuels are burned. The reduction was voluntary, however, and countries soon realized that the convention's goal — to stabilize emissions at 1990 levels by 2000 — would not be met.

The Kyoto Protocol, negotiated in 1997, set mandatory emissions reductions. But the United States — the world's largest greenhouse-gas emitter — has refused to ratify it, arguing that compliance would damage the economy. Critics warn that countries that have ratified may not meet the cuts because they aren't making sufficient changes in their consumption of fossil fuels. And rapidly industrializing countries — notably China and India — are expected to make major increases in their emissions.

CURRENT SITUATION

Democrats Take Over

Environmentalists celebrated the Democratic takeover of Congress on Nov. 7, 2006, and can point to growing signs of public support for environmental protection. But many environmental leaders remain focused on businesses for solutions to environmental problems, especially global warming.

Meanwhile, environmental groups are reporting recent increases in membership and financial contributions. The Sierra Club now has 800,000 members, a one-third rise in the last four years.[48] Between 2003 and 2006, membership jumped from 400,000 to 550,000 in the Natural Resources Defense Council and from 300,000 to 400,000 at Environmental Defense. Both reported substantial budget hikes as well.[49]

Overall, giving to environmental organizations increased by 7 percent from 2003 to 2004 and by 16.4 percent the next year — greater growth in both years than any other category of nonprofit organization tracked by the Giving USA Foundation.[50]

The Gallup Organization reports that the percentage of Americans who worry about the environment "a great deal" or "a fair amount" increased from 62 to 77 percent between 2004 and 2006. Since 1984, Gallup has asked Americans to choose between two sides in a mock debate: whether "protection of the environment should be given priority, even at the risk of curbing economic growth," or "economic growth should be given priority, even if the environment suffers to some extent." (*See graph, p. 240.*)

The pro-environment side has always prevailed, usually by a large margin. After falling precipitously during the early years of the Bush administration — from a 43-percentage-point pro-environment margin in 2000 to 5 percentage points in 2003 and 2004 — the pro-environment gap began widening again. Pro-environment respondents outnumbered pro-economy respondents by 17 percent in 2005 and 15 percent this year.[51]

Despite such positive signs, environmental activists don't expect major legislation to work its way through the House and Senate and survive presidential vetoes during the next two years. They also believe businesses are essential to the solutions, with or without government action.

Democratic congressional leaders tend to be more supportive of environmentalists' positions than Republicans.

But Democrats didn't win large enough majorities to override vetoes or break GOP filibusters in the Senate. Indeed, the agenda Democratic leaders announced for the opening days of the next Congress, in 2007, does not include environmental legislation.

The loss of Republican power means environmentalists won't have to battle attempts to roll back environmental protections, such as California Rep. Richard Pombo's efforts to weaken the Endangered Species Act, sell national park land in Alaska, open the Arctic National Wildlife Refuge to oil drilling and increase drilling off the nation's coasts. Pombo, who chaired the House Resources Committee, was defeated.

Individual representatives and senators will introduce environmental bills, including some to address global warming. But, said Sierra Club Executive Director Carl Pope, "I don't think we're going to see, at a national level, major progress, because Bush is still going to be there."[52]

Environmentalists "can't wait for the federal government, which is why you're seeing all these other players take the first steps," Sierra Club spokesman Antebi says.

Focus on Business

Environmentalists are drawing more sympathy from corporate executives, Public Affairs Council President Pinkham says, because "we've reached a tipping point where most business people agree that global warming is an issue that can't be ignored. Even companies with doubts are coming to realize you can't sit on the sidelines."

Environmental organizations are working with companies on a wide range of environmental challenges. Some relationships are cooperative, others confrontational. Environmentalists seek to apply pressure by winning support from companies' customers, employees and investors. They also appeal to executives' sense of social responsibility.

"We attempt to appeal to the most core, basic values that remind us that we're all human, that we all need to live on a healthy Earth together, and that some of us have far more decision-making power than others," says the Rainforest Action Network's Hogue. "If you're the CEO of a major bank or a government official or a logging executive, you are a human being first, and you don't want to do anything that you can't explain in good faith to your children and grandchildren."

In addition to its partnerships with FedEx, UPS and DuPont, Environmental Defense has struck agreements with numerous firms, including Wegmans Food Markets and Bon Appétit Management Company on implementing health and environmental standards for farmed salmon, McDonald's on reducing antibiotics in chicken, Compass Group food services on limiting antibiotics in pork and chicken, Bristol-Myers Squibb on incorporating environmental considerations into pharmaceutical development and packaging, and with other companies on other topics.

Having negotiated accords on environmentally friendly lending policies with Citigroup, JPMorganChase and Goldman Sachs, the Rainforest Action Network (RAN) now is running campaigns against Wells Fargo's investments in oil, coal, logging and mining operations. Among RAN's other campaigns to change corporate policies, it's pressing for revisions in Weyerhaeuser's logging practices and for increases in the fuel-efficiency of Ford vehicles.

"You're seeing tremendous leadership from the private sector right now," Environmental Defense's Yarnold says. But environmentalists continue to press for government action because "businesses alone can't solve the global-warming problem."

Environmental groups want the federal government to require companies to meet environmental standards and to help them do so. New regulations are needed, environmentalists argue, not only to force recalcitrant companies to act but also to encourage corporations that want to act but can't afford to do more than their competitors.

"Many corporations, especially those active in international areas, are realizing they need to be more environmental and more progressive to stay competitive in the international arena," Oklahoma State University's Dunlap says. "A lot of American firms are caught in a bit of a dilemma. In some ways, they like having an administration that seems friendly to the market and keeping regulations minimal. On the other hand, they're not

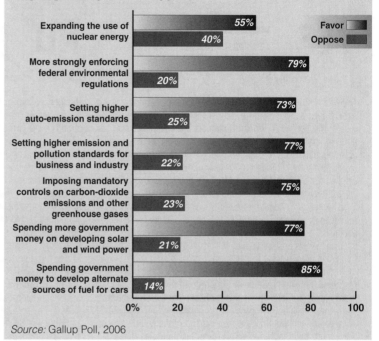

Public Strongly Favors Action on Environment

Americans strongly favor environmental initiatives by both industry and government to cut pollution and increase energy efficiency.

Do you generally favor or oppose:

Expanding the use of nuclear energy — Favor 55%, Oppose 40%

More strongly enforcing federal environmental regulations — Favor 79%, Oppose 20%

Setting higher auto-emission standards — Favor 73%, Oppose 25%

Setting higher emission and pollution standards for business and industry — Favor 77%, Oppose 22%

Imposing mandatory controls on carbon-dioxide emissions and other greenhouse gases — Favor 75%, Oppose 23%

Spending more government money on developing solar and wind power — Favor 77%, Oppose 21%

Spending government money to develop alternate sources of fuel for cars — Favor 85%, Oppose 14%

Source: Gallup Poll, 2006

getting the incentives and the regulatory push to stay on the cutting edge."

Brune, of the Rainforest Action Network, describes companies that are "trying to lead by example and trying to pressure the government to wake up and step up to the plate."

The Sierra Club's Hamilton says he knows corporate executives "who have almost begged Congress to tell them what to do to reduce emissions, so they know how to plan for it. But companies are reluctant to take action on their own for fear of losing competitive advantage, because they don't know what is going to be required of them" when Congress finally does act.

"Businesses crave certainty," Yarnold explains. "Global businesses in particular crave certainty. To be operating in one regulatory environment in Europe and another in the United States is crazy. It's not good for business." Conflicts in state laws also will increase

Are businesses better equipped than governments to address 21st-century environmental challenges?

YES
Margery Kraus
President and CEO,
APCO Worldwide*

Written for *CQ Researcher*, November 2006

There is no doubt the environment is on people's minds: Used hybrid cars can fetch more than the original sticker price at resale; the *Oxford American Dictionary*'s word of the year for 2006 is "carbon neutral." However hip it may be, environmental responsibility is more than just the "flavor of the month," it is our future. And businesses not only can be the most efficient catalyst for creating a more sustainable planet but they also are increasingly expected to play that role.

A recent study conducted by APCO Worldwide reveals that the American public holds businesses to a higher standard on environmental issues than it does the U.S. government. There is a belief that business is less encumbered by politics and bureaucracy and has more resources to act and influence others to do so.

Today's progressive companies already know they have this responsibility and embrace it. Big corporations are larger than many nations. Major companies' global reach and standards allow them to directly impact environments beyond the boundaries of any one country. As they expand globally, businesses are able to build factories with proven technologies that often exceed the requirements of local governments.

Corporations have a tremendous opportunity to influence individual behavior. Employees can be offered incentives to use public transportation, recycle and contribute time to community environmental efforts. More broadly, businesses can sway consumer bases to adopt environmentally responsible behavior.

Finally, an increased number of businesses see sustainable products as a new part of their business. They are engineering or re-engineering those products to be recyclable and to incorporate recycled materials; they are employing clean production processes to create less waste and pollution.

Down the road, these forward-looking businesses will have a healthy, sustainable work force, clean water and quality of life that will enable them to have good employees and more consumers. Their ultimate incentive: You can't run a successful business in a failed world.

Obviously, safeguarding our environment is best accomplished by governments, businesses and individuals working together. However, businesses, especially multinational corporations, are well-positioned to take decisive leadership and have the infrastructure and resources to achieve measurable results — and consumers are expecting nothing less.

* The public-relations and strategic-communications firm represents many of the world's largest corporations.

NO
Michael Brune
Executive Director,
Rainforest Action Network

Written for *CQ Researcher*, November 2006

Businesses and governments both have a vital role to play in addressing environmental challenges. We are beginning to see strong policies from a select number of high-profile businesses on issues such as forest protection and climate change. Meanwhile, state and local governments are responding to widespread public support for environmental protection, compensating for a disturbing lack of leadership in the White House and Congress.

One test for either businesses or governments is to determine to which constituency they are the most loyal. Most companies are guided by the old business axiom, "The customer is always right." These businesses realize that not only do consumers want to do business with companies that exhibit strong environmental values but also their own employees want to feel good about their employer's environmental record. Indeed, it is this view that has helped Home Depot, Lowe's, FedEx Kinko's and others to work with Rainforest Action Network to help protect endangered forests, and for Citigroup, Bank of America, JP Morgan Chase and Goldman Sachs to take principled stands on climate change and forest protection.

Conversely, many officials in Washington are stuck in the past, guarding the status quo. Within the last few years, the federal government has failed to enact, protect or enforce strong environmental policies, as evidenced by the attempted rollback of the Forest Service's "Roadless Rule" and the gutting of the Clean Water Act. Our politicians have fallen into the trap of believing they must choose between prosperity and the environment. Consequently, neither political party has stood up to the corporations whose policies are destabilizing and devastating our environment.

By leveraging public opinion and consumer choice to publicly stigmatize companies that refuse to adopt responsible environmental policies, environmental organizations are able to positively influence corporations' policies. This tactic strengthens marketplace democracy and empowers the consumer. It also has created significant progress and dramatic successes for environmental preservation. It gives consumers the ability to influence companies, stepping in where government has failed.

The reality is there is a new voice of business that shows how it is possible to do well by doing good, earning profits while upholding environmental principles. These businesses have shown a strong interest in working with government to meet the pressing environmental challenges of the 21st century. It's time for officials in Congress and the White House to listen and get to work.

pressure for federal legislation, says Robert Brulle, an associate professor of sociology and environmental science at Drexel University, who is researching the 21st-century history of the environmental movement.

Environmentalists' top legislative goals are the cap-and-trading scheme for greenhouse gases and significant increases in vehicle fuel-economy standards. California Democrat Barbara Boxer, in line to chair the Senate Environment and Public Works Committee, said she plans "to roll out a pretty in-depth set of hearings on global warming. It isn't going to help any business, it isn't going to help anybody, if we do nothing" about the issue, she insisted.

Sen. McCain said he and Sen. Lieberman will re-introduce their global-warming bill and "absolutely" will push for a floor vote. McCain, a potential 2008 presidential candidate, also expressed optimism that President Bush would sign the legislation before he leaves the White House in January 2009.

"I think the president is coming around," McCain said. "He made a statement recently where he said that climate change is a significant issue. To tell you the truth, I'm worried more about [other] people in the administration than the president himself."[53]

In the past, Bush has said he agrees that human activity has contributed to climate change, but he has consistently rejected the idea of imposing mandatory curbs on carbon-dioxide emissions. Bush also has resisted calls to impose tougher standards on vehicle fuel economy, household appliances and building insulation — measures that could sharply reduce America's oil consumption.

Those Bush positions — plus opposition from other GOP lawmakers — lead other legislators to suggest that action is less likely than McCain predicts.

California Democrat Henry A. Waxman, incoming chair of the House Government Reform Committee, said environmentalists need to understand that "President Bush would veto any bill that ever got to him."[54] Oklahoma Republican James M. Inhofe, outgoing chair of the Senate Environment and Public Works Committee, expressed confidence that he can round up the 41 votes needed to sustain a filibuster against global-warming legislation.

Inhofe said he is seeing "an awakening" to his argument that harmful global warming is a myth. "People are realizing that [environmentalists] are saying things that are just flat not true," Inhofe said.[55]

Gov. Arnold Schwarzenegger, R-Calif., discusses his environmental initiatives as New York City Mayor Michael Bloomberg looks on at fuel-cell maker Bloom Energy in Sunnyvale, Calif., on Sept. 21, 2006. The mayor announced he is launching a citywide greenhouse-gas inventory and appointing an environmental advisory board. California just mandated cuts in motor vehicles' carbon-dioxide emissions.

Boxer, Inhofe's successor, acknowledged that passing legislation will be difficult. "Maybe I want to take the ball 50 yards," she said, "but I can take it only 30."[56]

OUTLOOK
Entrepreneurs in Spotlight

Environmentalists are counting on entrepreneurs to produce a future green world. Once governments impose restrictions on greenhouse-gas emissions, leaders of environmental organizations say, entrepreneurs will supply the technology that makes the restrictions work.

"It's going to look much the way it did during the information-technology gold rush at the advent of the Internet Age," Greenpeace Executive Director Passacantando says. "A whole new generation of entrepreneurs is going to lead us into the new era, and eventually we will have an economy that's built on low carbon-dioxide emissions or no carbon-dioxide emissions."

Environmental Defense's Yarnold sees hope in different pro-environment precedents — such as the restrictions on emissions that cause acid rain and deplete the ozone layer.

"Things were invented," he says. "Processes were created. People rise to the challenge. Investments get made. It creates economic activity. It creates jobs.

"Will there be solar panels made with nanotechnology? Are there chemical compounds that are better at conducting electricity than the materials we now have? I don't know. But I do know the circumstances under which those will be carried out. Efficient markets find low-cost, highly efficient solutions, and that's what will happen if the government puts a hard cap on carbon dioxide."

As Passacantando puts it, the choice of technologies "is not going to be Greenpeace's pick. It's going to be the entrepreneurs.' "

Environmentalists are most optimistic about conservation and renewable energies such as solar and wind.

"We have enough sunlight hitting the state of California every day to fulfill the country's energy needs," Oklahoma State's Brune says. "Enough wind flows through the Midwest to fulfill the country's energy needs. Both forms of energy are clean, create more jobs and have no greenhouse-gas emissions. Neither creates the environmental legacy of nuclear waste or the national-security problems associated with nuclear plants."

Some environmentalists acknowledge the possibility that new technology could make coal, oil and nuclear energy acceptable as well.

"There's great hope in low-carbon coal," Yarnold says, "and nuclear has to be on the table." Before new nuclear plants can be built, he adds, the industry must prove it can dispose of waste safely and prevent nuclear materials from being turned into weapons — obstacles that many environmentalists believe are insurmountable. Others caution that the transition away from fossil fuels won't be so simple. Envisioned solutions can be double-edged swords: windmill farms that deface the landscape and injure birds that fly too close; hydropower projects that dam waterways and injure fish; agriculture-based fuels that levy their own environmental costs and drive up the cost of food.

Critics from the left and the right warn against succumbing to pressure to take actions that don't really provide long-term solutions.

"You'll probably find that promises to do something about global warming will become more popular over time," the Cato Institute's Taylor says. "Politicians will make those promises, and voters will embrace politicians who make those promises. But the public doesn't seem to be willing to pay anything to reduce greenhouse gases. So politicians are going to find it's popular to propose programs but not popular to impose programs with costs, and I don't think greenhouse gases will be reduced much at all."

While Europe appears to be ahead of the United States in protecting the environment, Drexel University's Brulle says, Europe really is practicing "simulation of environmentalism. We have symbolic responses. But, when you look at carbon-dioxide emissions in Europe, they have not significantly gone down."

Brulle fears the United States will follow the same path. "We're not going to just stop using coal any more than we're going to destroy the economy of West Virginia," he says. Neither are Americans about to abandon a consumer culture that requires ever-higher energy consumption, he says.

"The way to reduce greenhouse-gas emissions now is to conserve big time, but I don't see any political will to do that," Brulle says. That leaves increased use of nuclear power as the only alternative for the foreseeable future, he argues.

"The question," he says, "is which is the worst poison. One will be absolutely fatal — climate change. One might be fatal, but is not always fatal — nuclear power.

"I'm not a fan of nuclear power, by any means. But, given the alternative of destroying the global eco-system for thousands of years, we have to seriously consider putting nuclear power into the mix."

NOTES

1. "Corporate Innovation: Changing the Way Business Thinks About the Environment," Environmental Defense; environmentaldefense.org/corporate_innovation.cfm. See also Jia Lynn Yang, "It's Not Easy Being Green — But Big Business Is Trying," *Fortune*, Aug. 7, 2006.

2. "For the Health of the Nation: An Evangelical Call to Civic Responsibility," National Association of Evangelicals, Oct. 7, 2004; www.nae.net/images/civic_responsibility2.pdf.

3. Elizabeth Keenan, "Plugging Into Nuclear," *Time*, June 19, 2006, p. 46; Andrew C. Revkin, "Updating Prescriptions for Avoiding Worldwide Catastrophe,"

The New York Times, Sept. 12, 2006, p. F2. For background, see Marcia Clemmitt, "Climate Change," *CQ Researcher*, Jan. 27, 2006, pp. 73-96.

4. Accessed at people-press.org/reports/display .php3?ReportID=280.

5. Accessed at www.pewtrusts.com/pdf/pew_research_ economy_012506.pdf.

6. Accessed at www.harrisinteractive.com/harris_poll/ index.asp?PID=607.

7. Accessed at www.foe.org/camps/intl/corpacct/wall-street/handbook/index.html and rockpa.org/ wp-content/uploads/2006/06/Power%20of%20 Proxy.pdf.

8. The Carbon Disclosure Project, "The $31.5 Trillion Question: Is Your Company Prepared for Climate Change?" www.cdproject.net/viewrelease.asp?id=8/.

9. Juliet Eilperin, "Cities, States Aren't Waiting For U.S. Action on Climate," *The Washington Post*, Aug. 11, 2006, p. A1.

10. *Ibid.* See also Karen Matthews, "States To Lower Greenhouse Gas Emissions," The Associated Press, Oct. 16, 2006.

11. Accessed at www.apolloalliance.org.

12. Accessed at www.apolloalliance.org/strategy_ center/a_bold_energy_and_jobs_policy/ten_point_ plan.cfm. For background on hydrogen, see Mary H. Cooper, "Alternative Fuels," *CQ Researcher*, Feb. 25, 2005, pp. 173-196.

13. Michael Schneider, "Leo's Green Builds Skein," *Daily Variety*, Oct. 17, 2006, p. 1.

14. Karen Krebsbach, "The Green Revolution: Are Banks Sacrificing Profits for Activists' Principles?" *US Banker*, Feb. 6, 2005.

15. Marc Gunther, "The Green Machine," *Fortune*, Aug. 7, 2006, p. 42.

16. *Ibid.*

17. Yang, *op. cit.*

18. Accessed at fedex.com/us/about/responsibility/ environment/hybridelectricvehicle.html?link=4.

19. Steven Mufson, "As Power Bills Soar, Companies Embrace 'Green' Buildings," *The Washington Post*, Aug. 5, 2006, p. A1.

20. General Electric, press release, "GE Launches Ecomagination to Develop Environmental Technologies"; http://home.businesswire.com/portal/ site/ge/index.jsp?ndmViewId=news_view&ndmConf igId=1002373&newsId=20050509005663&newsLa ng=en&ndmConfigId=1002373 &vnsId=681.

21. "2005 Report on Socially Responsible Investing Trends in the United States," Social Investment Forum, Jan. 24, 2006; www.socialinvest.org/areas/ research/trends/sri_trends_report_2005.pdf.

22. "Proxy Season Preview — Spring 2006," As You Sow Foundation and Rockefeller Philanthropy Advisors; www.asyousow.org/publications/2006_proxy_ preview.pdf.

23. Carol Hymowitz, moderator, "Corporate Social Concerns: Are They Good Citizenship, Or a Rip-Off for Investors?" *The Wall Street Journal Online*, Dec. 6, 2005; http://online .wsj.com/public/article/SB113355105439712626 .html?mod=todays_free_feature.

24. Testimony before U.S. House Energy and Commerce Committee, May 2, 2006.

25. Barbara Mantel, "Energy Efficiency," *CQ Researcher*, May 19, 2006, pp. 433-456.

26. *Ibid.*

27. The Coal Based Generation Stakeholders Group, "A Vision for Achieving Ultra-Low Emissions from Coal-Fueled Electric Generation," January 2005; www .nma.org/pdf/coal_vision.pdf.

28. Mantel, *op. cit.*

29. *Ibid.*

30. Daniel Gross, "Raise the Gasoline Tax? Funny, It Doesn't Sound Republican," *The New York Times*, Oct. 8, 2006.

31. Worldwatch Institute, *Vital Signs 2006-2007* (2006), p. 32.

32. U.S. Energy Department, "Annual Energy Review 2005," Energy Information Administration, July 27, 2006, Table 1.3; www.eia.doe.gov/emeu/aer/pdf/ pages/sec1_9.pdf.

33. *Ibid.*, Table 8.4a; www.eia.doe.gov/emeu/aer/pdf/ pages/sec8_17.pdf.

34. *Ibid.*, Table 2.1e; www.eia.doe.gov/emeu/aer/pdf/ pages/sec2_8.pdf.

35. The Coal Based Generation Stakeholders Group, *op. cit.*

36. "Annual Energy Review 2005," *op. cit.*, Table 1.3.

37. Peter Schwartz and Spencer Reiss, "Nuclear Now! How Clean, Green Atomic Energy Can Stop Global Warming," *Wired*, February 2005.

38. U.S. Energy Department, *op. cit.*, Table 10.1; www .eia.doe.gov/emeu/aer/pdf/pages/sec10_3.pdf.

39. Adriel Bettelheim, "Biofuels Boom," *CQ Researcher*, Sept. 29, 2006, pp. 793-816.

40. Revkin, *op. cit.*, p. 2.

41. Frank Clifford, "Alarmed by 'Cycle of Anti-Environmentalism,'" *Los Angeles Times*, Nov. 15, 2005, p. B2.

42. Unless otherwise noted, this "Background" section is based on "The Evolution of the Conservation Movement," Library of Congress; lcweb2.loc.gov/ ammem/amrvhtml/conshome.html; Lorraine Elliott, "Environmentalism," *Encyclopaedia Britannica*, 2006; www.britannica.com/eb/article-224631; *History of the Environmental Movement*, Glen Canyon Institute; www.glencanyon.org/library/movementhistory.php; "History," U.S. Environmental Protection Agency; epa.gov/history/index.htm; Tom Arrandale, "National Parks Under Pressure," *CQ Researcher*, Oct. 6, 2006, pp. 817-840; Mary H. Cooper, "Environmental Movement at 25," *CQ Researcher*, March 31, 1995, pp. 273-296, and William Kovarik, "Environmental History Timeline," www.radford .edu/~wkovarik/envhist.

43. The Associated Press, "3 Plead Guilty to Ecoterror Charges," *Los Angeles Times*, July 21, 2006, p. A19.

44. "History of Earth Day," Earth Day Network; www .earthday.org/resources/history.aspx.

45. Beverly Beyette, "Earth Observance: The Day Politics Stood Still," *Los Angeles Times*, May 23, 1985, p. 5-1. Joanne Omang, " 'Sun Day,' Slated in May," *The Washington Post*, Sept. 19, 1977, p. A20.

46. Beyette, *op. cit.*

47. The Associated Press, April 23, 1970 (Lenin's birthday); Dan Eggen, "Earth Day: From Radical to Mainstream," *The Washington Post*, April 22, 2000, p. B1 (Daughters of the American Revolution).

48. Jerry Adler, "Going Green," *Newsweek*, July 17, 2006, p. 42.

49. *Encyclopedia of Associations*, 2003 and 2006.

50. *Giving USA 2006: The Annual Report on Philanthropy for the Year 2005*, published by the Giving USA Foundation.

51. The Gallup Organization, 2006.

52. Bettina Boxall, "Conservationist Clout," *Los Angeles Times*, Nov. 9, 2006. p. 27.

53. Darren Samuelsohn, "Sen. McCain Pledges Push for 'Long-Overdue' Emissions Bill," *Environment and Energy Daily*, Nov. 17, 2006.

54. *Ibid.*

55. *Ibid.*

56. Charles Babington, "Party Shift May Make Warming a Hill Priority," *The Washington Post*, Nov. 18, 2006, p. A6.

BIBLIOGRAPHY

Books

Bailey, Ronald, ed., *Global Warming and Other Eco Myths: How the Environmental Movement Uses False Science to Scare Us to Death*, Prima Publishing, 2002.
In this collection of essays the writers argue that many warnings about threats to the environment are way overblown.

Gore, Al, *An Inconvenient Truth: The Planetary Emergency of Global Warming and What We Can Do About It*, Rodale Books, 2006.
Former Vice President Al Gore urges action on global warming in this book written to accompany his surprisingly popular movie of the same name.

Savitz, Andrew W., and Karl Weber, *The Triple Bottom Line: How Today's Best-Run Companies Are Achieving Economic, Social and Environmental Success — and How You Can Too*, Jossey-Bass, 2006.
A business consultant and a freelance writer offer practical advice on how companies can profit from responding to environmental and other public needs.

Articles

Adler, Jerry, "Going Green," *Newsweek*, July 17, 2006, p. 42.
Adler looks at how individual Americans are taking action to protect the environment.

Gunther, Marc, "The Green Machine," *Fortune*, Aug. 7, 2006, p. 42.
Gunther reports on Wal-Mart's ambitious plans to become the world's greenest retailer and increase profits at the same time.

Holstein, William J., "Saving the Earth, And Saving Money," *The New York Times*, Aug. 13, 2006, p. 9.
Gwen Ruta, director of corporate partnerships for Environmental Defense, explains how her organization works with businesses.

Hymowitz, Carol, moderator, "Corporate Social Concerns: Are They Good Citizenship, Or a Rip-Off for Investors?" *The Wall Street Journal Online*, Dec. 6, 2005. Available online at http://online.wsj.com/public/article/SB113355105439712626.html?mod=todays_free_feature.
Debaters about corporations' environmental responsibility included Benjamin Heineman Jr., then senior vice president of GE; Ilyse Hogue, director of the Rainforest Action Network's Global Finance Campaign; and Fred Smith Jr., president and founder of the Competitive Enterprise Institute.

Pollan, Michael, "Mass Natural," *The New York Times*, June 4, 2006, p. 15.
Pollan fears Wal-Mart's plan to become an organic grocer and its massive purchasing power and lust for low prices will hurt organic farmers and consumers.

Schwartz, Peter, and Spencer Reiss, "Nuclear Now! How Clean, Green Atomic Energy Can Stop Global Warming," *Wired*, February 2005.
The authors argue that nuclear power can end global warming and the other environmental degradations associated with extracting and burning coal and oil.

Reports and Studies

Coal Based Generation Stakeholders Group, "A Vision for Achieving Ultra-Low Emissions from Coal-Fueled Electric Generation," January 2005; www.nma.org/pdf/coal_vision.pdf.
The coal industry and its customers tell how they plan to meet America's energy and environmental needs by cleaning up their acts.

Friends of the Earth, "Confronting Companies Using Shareholder Power: A Handbook on Socially-Oriented Shareholder Activism;" www.foe.org/camps/intl/corpacct/wallstreet/handbook/index.html.
The environmental organization urges corporate shareholders to press their companies to adopt environmentally friendly practices.

Hayward, Steven F., "Index of Leading Environmental Indicators 2006," *American Enterprise Institute*, 2006; www.aei.org/books/bookID.854/book_detail.asp.
The think tank's annual analysis of environmental statistics contends Earth is in much better shape than leading environmental organizations say.

National Association of Evangelicals, "For the Health of the Nation: An Evangelical Call to Civic Responsibility," Oct. 7, 2004; www.nae.net/images/civic_responsibility2.pdf.
Conservative religious leaders admonish believers that faith requires acting to relieve social ills and to protect the environment.

Price, Tom, "Activists in the Boardroom: How Advocacy Groups Seek to Shape Corporate Behavior," *Foundation for Public Affairs*, 2006.
The author examines how advocacy organizations influence companies' policies through both confrontation and cooperation.

Worldwatch Institute, *State of the World 2006: A Worldwatch Institute Report on Progress Toward a Sustainable Society*, W. W. Norton, 2006.
The environmental group reports on developments important to environmental protection and sustainability, including renewable alternatives to oil and the special challenges posed by rapid economic development in China and India.

For More Information

American Enterprise Institute, 1150 17th St., N.W., Washington, DC 20036; (202) 862-5800; www.aei.org. Conservative think tank that studies environmental and other issues.

Bullitt Foundation, 1212 Minor Ave., Seattle, WA 98101-2825; (206) 343-0807; www.bullitt.org. Philanthropic organization working to protect, restore and maintain the natural environment of the Pacific Northwest.

Cato Institute, 1000 Massachusetts Ave., N.W., Washington, DC 20001; www.cato.org. Libertarian think tank that questions environmental-protection measures that interfere with free markets.

Ecomagination, ge.ecomagination.com. Web site where General Electric explains its plans to profit from making environmentally friendly products.

Environmental Defense, 257 Park Ave. South, New York, NY 10010; (212) 505-2100; www.environmentaldefense.org. The advocacy group forms partnerships with corporations to promote environmentally friendly business practices.

League of Conservation Voters, 1920 L St., N.W., Suite 800, Washington, DC 20036; www.lcv.org. Advocacy group that reports on government officials' actions on environmental issues.

Natural Resources Defense Council, 40 West 20th St., New York, NY 10011; www.nrdc.org. Advocacy group that studies and acts on a wide range of environmental issues, with special focus on wildlife and wilderness areas.

Pew Center on Global Climate Change, 2101 Wilson Blvd., Suite 550, Arlington, VA 22201; (703) 516-4146; www.pewclimate.org. Funded by Pew Charitable Trusts.

Rainforest Action Network, 221 Pine St., 5th Floor, San Francisco, CA 94104; (415) 398-4404; www.ran.org. The activist group protests corporate practices that harm the environment and helps design pro-environment business practices.

Resources for the Future, 1616 P St., N.W., Washington, DC 20036; www.rff.org. Independent scholarly organization that analyzes energy, environment and natural-resources issues.

Rockefeller Philanthropy Advisors, 37 Madison Ave., 37th Floor, New York, NY 10022; (212) 812-4330; www.rockpa.org. Studies and offers advice about shareholder activism by nonprofit organizations.

Sierra Club, 85 Second St., Second Floor, San Francisco, CA 94105; www.sierraclub.org. Founded in 1892 to protect wilderness but now active on many environmental issues.

Social Investment Forum, 1612 K St., N.W., Suite 650, Washington, DC 20006; (202) 872-5319; www.socialinvest.org. The socially responsible investing industry's trade association.

Wal-Mart Sustainability, www.walmartfacts.com/featuredtopics/?id=1. Web site where Wal-Mart showcases its efforts to become environmentally friendly.

Worldwatch Institute, 1776 Massachusetts Ave., N.W., Washington, DC 20036; (202) 452-1999; www.worldwatch.org. Studies environmental and economic trends.

Confronting Warming

12

Can States and Localities Prevent Climate Change?

Alan Greenblatt

Solar panels cover the Staples Center arena in Los Angeles. As a national leader in anti-pollution and energy-saving efforts, California adopted the first statewide "green" building code and vehicle fuel-efficiency standards.

From *CQ Researcher*,
January 9, 2009.

John Coleman concentrates on cutting energy use for the city of Fayetteville, Ark., as if his job depended on it. In fact, it does.

"I got the City Council to let me hire this person based on the promise that we would reduce our energy consumption to more than cover his or her salary," recalls Fayetteville Mayor Dan Coody.

Coleman has found easy pickings all over town — even at City Hall: inefficient thermostats, wasteful light-bulbs, computers that are left on all night. In 2007, Fayetteville budgeted $1.9 million for utility costs, but thanks to Coleman ended up spending about $180,000 less than that. "You just barely covered my salary," Coleman joked at an end-of-year meeting. "I get to stick around for another year."[1]

Actually, they more than covered his salary of $57,000. Coleman is one of dozens of so-called sustainability directors now employed by cities around the country. (Coody got the idea from a similar program in Seattle.) By switching police departments from paper tickets to electronic ones, or looking for dramatic savings by putting municipal utilities on an energy diet, these environmental specialists are helping city officials like Coody make good on their promise to cut down on emissions that cause global warming.

Scientists say a buildup of six types of heat-trapping gases in the Earth's atmosphere are beginning to cause potentially dramatic climate changes, such as planetary warming, melting ice caps, rising sea levels and intensified droughts, floods and hurricanes. The gases — called "greenhouse" gases (GHG) because they act as a greenhouse by

Many States Set Energy-Efficiency Standards

Energy efficiency standards are in place in 21 states, including all the Northeast states except New Hampshire and Rhode Island. Some standards encourage greater efficiency in generation, transmission and use of electricity and natural gas. Others require utilities to generate a fixed percentage of their power from renewable sources such as wind and solar.

States With Energy-Efficiency Standards
(As of August 2008)

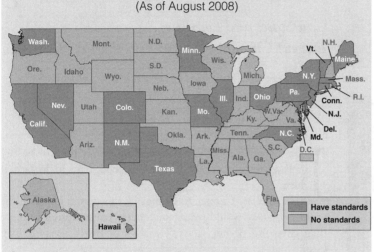

Have standards
No standards

Sources: World Resources Institute; Environmental Protection Agency

During the Bush years, global warming became an increasingly pressing topic — yet growing public concern never translated into serious policy breakthroughs in Washington. While Congress and the White House slept, however, state and local governments throughout the country have come up with their own methods for limiting pollutants that scientists believe are contributing to climate change.

"I was one of many Americans who were outraged when my country would not sign the Kyoto Protocol," says Minneapolis Mayor R. T. Rybak. "The federal government dropped the ball on a critical environmental issue."

Cities are not only tightening their own energy belts but increasingly issuing new rules, such as stricter building codes, to make sure that residents and businesses cut back as well.

Among states, California has been leading the way. A 2006 law imposed the first statewide cap on carbon emissions. California also adopted the first statewide green-building code last summer, and the state has long been the leader in setting fuel-efficiency standards for vehicles.[3]

retaining the sun's heat in Earth's atmosphere — are emitted when carbon-based fossil fuels like oil, coal and natural gas are burned. Under the 1997 Kyoto Protocol, industrialized countries were asked to reduce their GHG emissions — often referred to as "carbon" emissions because carbon dioxide (CO_2) is the most abundant greenhouse gas — by 5.2 percent below 1990 levels by 2012. The U.S. reduction target was set at 7 percent.*

Although the U.S. government is not bound by the treaty, hundreds of mayors, including Coody, have pledged to abide by the protocol, even though it was never ratified by the Senate and has been explicitly rejected by President George W. Bush. But local officials believe it still provides a good guidepost for their own efforts in the fight against climate change.[2]

---

* The six types of greenhouse gases are carbon dioxide, methane, nitrous oxide, hydrofluorocarbons, perfluorocarbons and sulfur hexafluoride.

Numerous states — but not all — have engaged in other serious efforts to address climate change. About half the states, for instance, require utilities to generate a significant share of their power from renewable, non-carbon-based sources such as wind and solar. And many states are encouraging greater use of biofuels, such as ethanol. Groups of states in the Northeast, Upper Midwest and interior West have formed regional compacts to create "cap-and-trade" systems.

Under cap and trade, large polluters such as power plants are issued permits for each ton of carbon they emit. Companies that reduce the amount of pollution they spew are able to sell, or "trade," permits they don't need.

"States have been tripping all over themselves to show national leadership on this issue," says Barry G. Rabe, a professor of environmental policy at the University of

Michigan. "California, I would argue, has made as heavy an investment in time and treasury into climate change as any government on Earth, including the European Union."

President-elect Barack Obama has said he will approve a waiver for California and 19 other states to regulate greenhouse gas emissions from vehicles. California passed a law in 2002 to do just that, and it has been widely imitated by other states. But states have not been able to enforce the policy absent a waiver from the Environmental Protection Agency (EPA), which the Bush White House has blocked.[4]

Obama has promised to do more than just sign off on state actions, though. "When I am president, any governor who's willing to promote clean energy will have a partner in the White House," Obama said in a videotaped address to state leaders gathered at a climate change summit in California in November. "Any company that's willing to invest in clean energy will have an ally in Washington. And any nation that's willing to join the cause of combating climate change will have an ally in the United States of America."[5]

As a candidate, Obama pledged to pursue a national cap-and-trade system to limit carbon emissions. Prominent supporters of cap and trade now hold key committee posts in Congress, including Henry A. Waxman, the new chair of the House Energy and Commerce Committee, and Barbara Boxer, chair of the Senate Environment and Public Works Committee. Both are California Democrats.

But attempts to pass cap-and-trade legislation have failed four times over the last five years, and it's not clear the outcome will be different this year or next. Even if federal lawmakers do act, so much momentum has built up in this area among state and local leaders that it's unlikely they'll suddenly concede the issue to Washington.

At the November climate change summit, California Republican Gov. Arnold Schwarzenegger and leaders of more than a dozen other states and provinces from other countries pledged to work together to slash greenhouse gas emissions. Fighting global warming, Schwarzenegger declared, couldn't be just a matter of national policy but must go "province by province."[6]

Not everyone has climbed on board the limited-carbon bandwagon, however. In November, Gov. Rick Perry, R-Texas, argued strongly against a national cap-and-trade policy, warning that it would "cripple the Texas energy sector, irreparably damaging both the state

and national economies and severely impacting national oil and gas supplies."[7]

And not everyone who supports limiting greenhouse gases believes state and local efforts are effective. "Carbon dioxide is a naturally occurring gas that is fairly well blended in the atmosphere around the world," says Myron Ebell, director of energy and global warming policy at the Competitive Enterprise Institute, a free-enterprise advocacy group. "If California does something and China and India don't, then what we do is virtually useless."

Ebell and other critics also argue that the efforts undertaken thus far may have been good public relations but are not effective at reducing carbon emissions. Often, public officials have done little more than pledge to reduce emissions or increase use of alternative fuels at some distant date in the future. In a way, Ebell suggests, their actions have been reminiscent of a famous prayer of Saint Augustine: "Give me chastity and continence, but not yet."

But the policies pursued by state and local leaders have been evolving rapidly. A decade ago, few people thought they even had a role in addressing an issue that was global in scope. State and local laws, however, have quickly changed from being mainly symbolic to having real teeth, with penalties for noncompliance for entities ranging from utilities to developers, all in the span of a few short years.

As state and local leaders continue to contemplate ways of addressing climate change, here are some of the issues they are debating:

Should states regulate carbon emissions?

In the absence of federal action, states are making ambitious efforts to cut down on carbon usage. In the last few years, they have sought to regulate auto tailpipe emissions, required utilities to generate significant shares of their power from renewable energy sources and denied permits to coal-fired power plants. (*See sidebar, p. 276.*)

Several states in the Northeast, West and Midwest have formed regional compacts to create cap-and-trade systems, setting limits on emissions from major polluters. A few have even set overall limits on carbon emissions on a statewide basis. California led the way in 2006 with a law that would reduce the state's total carbon emissions to 1990 levels by 2020.

"The political will to do something about climate change has grown substantially," says Patrick Hogan, a

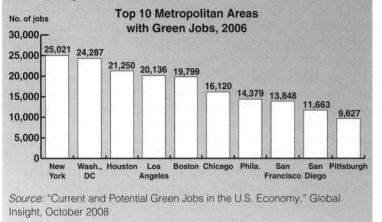

New York Offers Most 'Green' Jobs

More than 25,000 "green" jobs were available in the New York metropolitan area in 2006, the most of any metropolitan area in the country. Three of the top 10 cities were in California — totaling more than 45,000 jobs.

Top 10 Metropolitan Areas with Green Jobs, 2006

No. of jobs

- New York: 25,021
- Wash., DC: 24,287
- Houston: 21,250
- Los Angeles: 20,136
- Boston: 19,799
- Chicago: 16,120
- Phila.: 14,379
- San Francisco: 13,848
- San Diego: 11,663
- Pittsburgh: 9,627

Source: "Current and Potential Green Jobs in the U.S. Economy," Global Insight, October 2008

regional policy coordinator at the Pew Center on Global Climate Change. "An important thing to bear in mind is that several actions that states are taking, like renewable energy portfolio standards, will deliver economic and environmental benefits beyond anything related to climate change."

But not everyone applauds the state action. There was considerable internal debate within the Bush administration about granting California a waiver to regulate tailpipe emissions — a regulatory course more than a dozen other states stand ready to follow. California's tailpipe law has also been the subject of several lawsuits.

Despite a Supreme Court decision that appeared to bolster California's argument and advice from some Environmental Protection Agency officials to grant the waiver, the White House was concerned that a waiver could lead states to impose varying fuel-economy standards that would create a burden for the automobile industry.[8]

The incoming Obama administration is expected to approve the waiver for California and the other states. But even if that argument is about to be settled, there are endless debates about whether state actions will help or hurt their economies.

Margo Thorning, senior vice president of the American Council for Capital Formation, a Washington think tank, argues that the various state actions necessarily will increase energy costs. "Over the past 15 years, I've participated in or seen many of the analyses of the economic impact of reducing greenhouse gases," she says. "In every case there is a slower economy and less overall employment, even though new green jobs are created. The reason that happens is that renewables are more expensive."

Ebell, at the Competitive Enterprise Institute, agrees that state efforts on climate change will lead to higher energy costs and that various industries will look to Washington to create a single standard rather than having to satisfy a patchwork quilt of competing regulations.

Some of the state requirements are not realistic anyway, argues Rabe, the University of Michigan professor. He notes that California set a renewable-energy standard for utilities of 20 percent by 2010, which the state clearly won't meet. (It's at 11 percent now.) Legislators this year debated raising the standard to 33 percent by 2020. Rabe calls it "hubris" to create ever-tougher but elusive standards for the future.

"State regulators and state legislatures are putting a lot of pressure onto utilities to invest in alternative energy like windmills that are very expensive but are not viable power, by which I mean they're not available at times of peak demand," Ebell says.

But John Cahill, an attorney who helped design the Regional Greenhouse Gas Initiative, the Northeast's cap-and-trade program, as an aide to former Republican New York Gov. George E. Pataki, says complaints that such programs could hurt the economy are missing the point.

"The fact is that carbon is having a long-term impact on our country's and the world's natural resources," Cahill says. "What we're trying to do with cap and trade is capture the cost of our emissions, rather than making future generations pay for it."

And Ron Burke, Midwest climate change director at the Union of Concerned Scientists, says states and localities are trying to "get ahead of trends" that point to lower usage of carbon in the future, whether due to declining oil supplies or environmental concerns.

"Every city and state that does a greenhouse gas inventory gets a step ahead," Burke says. "They'll be better prepared to deal with a low-carbon economy in the future."

Burke also argues that state efforts to require utilities to turn to renewable energy sources is part of a long tradition of environmental activism. He notes that California's law seeking to regulate tailpipe emissions is in keeping with the state's historic role in promoting more efficient cars.

Due to its smog problems, the state was granted special status under the Clean Air Act of 1970 to set air-quality standards that are stricter than federal limits. California's subsequent standards have often been adopted by other states, and thus by carmakers.

"If not for California's leadership, I think it's fair to say that cars wouldn't be as clean today as they are," Burke says. "We would have suffered through more bad air days over the last 30 years."

Can local governments prevent global warming?

Seattle Mayor Greg Nickels still recalls his concern as he looked out over the Cascade Mountains during the winter of 2005. The snowpack his city relies on for both drinking water and hydroelectric power had just about failed to materialize.

"At that point, it was sort of an 'Aha' moment," he says. "Climate change went from being an esoteric issue affecting someone else in the near future to hitting us here, now."

Nickels has since spearheaded an effort among local officials to abide by the Kyoto Protocol, even though it hasn't been ratified by the U.S. Senate. More than 900 mayors have signed on from cities that are home to a total of more than 81 million Americans, according to the U.S. Conference of Mayors. "We as mayors recognize the threat of hurricanes, drought and the lack of snowpacks" that have been linked to global warming, Nickels says. "It's our obligation to take action."

But there are limits on what local officials can do. They lack the authority to regulate the dominant sources of greenhouse gas emissions — power plants and vehicles. The mayors' efforts, as a result, have mostly been

Minneapolis Mayor R. T. Rybak says people thought he was "flaky" when he replaced the city's gas-guzzling Ford Crown Victoria with a Prius like the one above. "I was not considered as flaky by the time I switched from a Prius to a plug-in," he adds. Many cities are not only tightening their own energy belts but increasingly issuing new rules to force residents and businesses to cut back as well.

small-bore affairs. Many local officials lack the ability even to measure their cities' total emission levels, let alone reduce them.

In many instances, their actions appear more symbolic than substantive. Critics say it's going to take more than door-to-door promotion of new lightbulbs, to cite one Minneapolis initiative, or replacing inefficient streetlights, to prevent global warming.

"Virtually all of the actions that have been taken at the local level are symbolic," says Ebell, of the Competitive Enterprise Institute. "They are meant to gain immediate public approval for the current incumbent and put all the responsibility for achieving those future goals on some future officeholder."

Even some environmentalists concede that the mayors' efforts, while obviously well-intentioned, won't put a serious dent in carbon emissions as yet.

"It's a mixed bag," says Teri Shore, a campaign director with Friends of the Earth in San Francisco. "You've got a lot of cities and counties that have signed up and set goals, but the harder part comes with actually implementing those goals."

The University of Michigan's Rabe notes that because of the lack of standardized emissions reporting, it's hard to know whose efforts have been successful and which haven't. For example, it was only in September that

Chicago put forward models of the first city-specific climate-change projections.

At that time, Chicago Mayor Richard M. Daley announced a plan to reduce the city's greenhouse gas emissions by 25 percent in 2020, compared with 1990 levels, through tougher building codes, improved transportation, reduced industrial pollution and use of clean and renewable energy sources.

"We can't solve the world's climate change problem in Chicago," Daley said, "but we can do our part."[9]

Chicago had already drawn praise for its green rooftops program, which boasts plantings on more than 200 buildings, including City Hall and the Target and Apple stores. But not even the cities that have been most ambitious about trying to meet their reduction targets have succeeded. Promises by big-city mayors to plant a million trees each have run into obstacles such as cost and lack of usable land. And New York City Mayor Michael Bloomberg's plan to charge cars a "congestion pricing" fee for driving into parts of Manhattan was rejected by the state legislature in April.

"Every locality is really good about talking about the virtues of their programs, but I don't think we've seen careful analysis and scrutiny about what works and doesn't," Rabe says. "What you have is a lot of self-celebration and claiming of success."

But Rabe notes that the municipal experiments are just

Midwest Has Most Wind Potential

North Dakota has the potential to produce more than 1.2 trillion kilowatt hours of wind energy annually — more than any other state. Most of the 20 states with the greatest potential are in the West and Midwest.

States With the Most Wind Energy Potential
(in billions of kilowatt hours annually)

North Dakota	1,210
Texas	1,190
Kansas	1,070
South Dakota	1,030
Montana	1,020
Nebraska	868
Wyoming	747
Oklahoma	725
Minnesota	657
Iowa	551
Colorado	481
New Mexico	435
Idaho	73
Michigan	65
New York	62
Illinois	61
California	59
Wisconsin	58
Maine	56
Missouri	52

Source: "Current and Potential Green Jobs in the U.S. Economy," Global Insight, October 2008

getting under way. And Shore says that cities are trying to remake themselves into "green incubators" and engaging in a friendly competition to find the best ways of limiting their local carbon "footprints."

"Having hundreds of cities across the country doing a test-run of innovations is a good thing," says Kathleen Casey Ridihalgh, a Sierra Club regional representative in Seattle. "It kind of gives us a huge pilot test of what we need to do at the federal level."

Toward this end, mayors are reducing municipal electricity use, planting thousands if not millions of trees, promoting car and bike sharing and purchasing more environmentally friendly vehicle fleets themselves — and, in New York, requiring cabbies to do the same.[10]

"People thought I was flaky when I took office and got rid of the city's Crown Victoria that was getting 10 miles per gallon and replaced it with a Prius," says Minneapolis Mayor Rybak. "I was not considered as flaky by the time I switched from a Prius to a plug-in."

James Brainard, the mayor of Carmel, Ind., and co-chair of a climate change task force for the U.S. Conference of Mayors, says that local officials can have an enormous impact due to their influence over building codes and transportation planning. He points out that metropolitan areas since World War II have been designed around automobile driving.

Cutting down on vehicle miles traveled, or VMT, has become a top goal of environmental activists and land-use planners. "Mayors are the ones who decide how planning and zoning are going to take place," Brainard says. "We have to train our planning commissioners and others to insist on good city design where one is not forced to drive from place to place."

Even a prominent advocate of local action such as Seattle's Nickels concedes federal action will be necessary not only to meet the Kyoto standards but also to surpass them. But cities can still have considerable influence over transportation and land-use planning.

Perhaps as important, cities have helped spark and keep alive a dialogue about translating concerns about climate change into tangible action. "Mayor Nickels getting various mayors to sign off on climate change predates what we did at the state level," says Terry Tamminen, who served as an energy and environment adviser to California Gov. Schwarzenegger. "It's a great way to stimulate action at the next level of government."

Should state and local governments do more to prepare for the consequences of climate change?

While she was still running for vice president, Gov. Sarah Palin, R-Alaska, said during a September interview with Katie Couric of CBS News that she wasn't "going to solely blame all of man's activities" for climate change, arguing that "the world's weather patterns are cyclical."

"But," she added, "[it] kind of doesn't matter at this point, as we debate what caused it. The point is, it's real, we need to do something about it."[11]

Palin received some criticism during the campaign for these remarks and others that suggested she denied a link between human activity and global warming. How could she address the problem, critics asked, if she wouldn't examine the underlying cause?

New Jobs Accompany 'Green' Strategies

Many new jobs are expected to be created if certain "green" economic initiatives — such as retrofitting buildings and harnessing wind and solar power — are launched. Many of the jobs are engineering-related, but blue-collar jobs would be created as well.

Potential 'Green' Investments and Jobs

Building Retrofitting — Electricians, heating/air conditioning installers, carpenters, construction equipment operators, roofers, insulation workers, carpenter helpers, industrial truck drivers, construction managers, building inspectors

Mass Transit/Freight Rail — Civil engineers, rail track layers, electricians, welders, metal fabricators, engine assemblers, bus drivers, dispatchers, locomotive engineers, railroad conductors

Smart Grid — Computer software engineers, electrical engineers, electrical equipment assemblers, electrical equipment technicians, machinists, team assemblers, construction laborers, operating engineers, electrical power line installers and repairers

Wind Power — Environmental engineers, iron and steel workers, millwrights, sheet metal workers, machinists, electrical equipment assemblers, construction equipment operators, industrial truck drivers, industrial production managers, first-line production supervisors

Solar Power — Electrical engineers, electricians, industrial machinery mechanics, welders, metal fabricators, electrical equipment assemblers, construction equipment operators, installation helpers, laborers, construction managers

Advanced Biofuels — Chemical engineers, chemists, chemical equipment operators, chemical technicians, mixing and blending machine operators, agricultural workers, industrial truck drivers, farm product purchasers, agricultural and forestry supervisors, agricultural inspectors

Source: Robert Pollin, et al., "Green Recovery: A Program to Create Good Jobs and Start Building a Low-Carbon Economy," Center for American Progress, Sept. 2008

That argument aside, Palin's stance — skepticism about global warming's roots but acceptance of it as real — reflects an increasingly important part of the larger debate: If climate change is already having real impacts — and will continue to do so, even if efforts to reduce greenhouse gas emissions succeed — how should governments begin to adapt to the resulting problems, such as flooding, coastal erosion and species loss? Should they, for example, build higher seawalls to offset rising sea levels?

"Alaska has been thinking about adaptation certainly more than it has been thinking about reducing emissions, and that's because it's on the front lines of climate change," says Hogan of the Pew climate change center.

Up until the last year or two, most environmentalists dismissed talk about adaptation. Their concern seemed to be that shifting the policy debate away from efforts to prevent climate change by cutting down on carbon emissions amounted to Palin-style denials that human activity causes global warming.

They also felt that planning for the effects brought about by climate change was defeatist. "It was seen as a potential smokescreen behind which high-emission countries could hide so they wouldn't have to make binding agreements to reduce," said Nathan Hultman, a professor of science, technology and international affairs at Georgetown University.[12]

The notion that adaptation is just a smokescreen seems to be changing. The Intergovernmental Panel on Climate Change, which shared the 2007 Nobel Peace Prize with former Vice President Al Gore, has been stressing the importance of adaptation in recent reports, while a group of scientists published an article in *Nature* in 2007 called "Lifting the Taboo on Adaptation."[13]

There are still advocates who argue that discussion about how to adapt to climate shifts amounts to a distraction from the larger project of reducing emissions. "There are people out there working on adaptation, but I have to say the overwhelming effort is to try to reduce our emissions," says Tom Adams, president of the California League of Conservation Voters. "At this point, some fairly significant climate impacts are inevitable, but a lot of us feel that this is a genuine planetary emergency, and it's imperative that we cut emissions."

Cahill, the former aide to New York Gov. Pataki, makes a similar point. "My concern is about using adaptation as a diversion program from a national cap-and-trade program," he says. "I would just be wary of something talking about adaptation without national cap and trade."

Still, Cahill and other environmentalists recognize that, even if all carbon emissions ceased tomorrow, changes are already occurring, and there is already enough carbon dioxide in the air to guarantee more changes to come. For that reason, policy makers are increasingly concerned about how to plan for the changes.

Not surprisingly, the issue has drawn the most attention in areas along coastlines, such as Maryland and Oregon. But because climate change will manifest itself differently in different locales, adaptation questions are drawing attention all over. For instance, Republican Gov. James Douglas of Vermont has been working with the state university to begin crafting plans to help the forestry and farming industries cope with climate change's local effects.

And Seattle Mayor Nickels' concerns about diminishing snowpack are increasingly shared in the Puget Sound area. In parts of the nearby Cascade Range, snowpack has declined by as much as 60 percent. In response, King County, which includes Seattle, has begun planning backwards from 2050, formulating plans to adapt to climate change effects seen as likely to occur even if carbon emissions are significantly cut between now and then.

Officials expect coastal-erosion problems associated with rising sea levels, health effects such as new infectious diseases and heat stroke, increasing numbers of forest fires and ecological issues affecting salmon. In 2007, the county council agreed to a tax inspired by such looming dangers, part of County Executive Ron Sims' $335 million plan to bolster river levees and reduce flood risks.

The county is now building climate-change risks into all of its long-term planning and policy development. "We're learning to define ourselves not in 2009 terms but in 2050 terms," Sims said. "We're making decisions based on something that has not occurred yet."[14]

Like most environmentalists, Burke of the Union of Concerned Scientists says that both responses to climate change — reduction of carbon emissions, or "mitigation," and adaptation — are important.

Still, he says, "If you had to argue one versus the other, which I don't think is really helpful, I think mitigation is a higher priority given the urgency with which we need to create these reductions.

"You see that reflected in how most cities and states are going about their planning," Burke continues. "They're definitely doing the mitigation piece first and then moving onto adaptation."

Relatively few jurisdictions have turned full-scale attention to adaptation and planning questions. Even normally proactive California has barely paid attention to adaptation issues, according to a recent study, and is unprepared for flooding, coastal erosion and loss of wildlife habitat predicted to occur in coming decades due to higher temperatures.[15] Last Nov. 14, Gov. Schwarzenegger issued an executive order to identify the state's biggest vulnerabilities to rising sea levels and draft an "adaptation strategy."[16]

States and local governments face a practical challenge when it comes to crafting adaptation plans. Much of the science in this area has been, not surprisingly, global in scope. Thus, planning for climate change's local impacts will require experts to "downscale" large-scale data to make them applicable and useful for communities.

But Sims argues that it's imperative for states, cities and counties to accept the need to make decisions based on scientific modeling rather than historical experience.

"With all the discussion we've had on global warming, I am stunned that people haven't realized that it's actually going to occur," he says. "The ice caps are melting now. They're not going to refreeze next year because we reduce our emissions. We're going to live in that world. So plan for it."

BACKGROUND

States Take Charge

Climate change has become such a hot issue among state and local officials that it's worth remembering they have taken it seriously only for a few years. "We're still very much at the embryonic stage of dealing with climate change in this country," says Cahill, the former aide to Gov. Pataki. "But at the same time, the train has left the station."

Although environmentalists deride President Bush for not squarely addressing global warming, the Clinton administration's record was not notably better. Congress rejected President Bill Clinton's 1993 proposal to impose a tax on energy, and the Senate passed a unanimous resolution in 1997 that it would reject the Kyoto Protocol if it harmed the U.S. economy.

At first, states expressed skepticism about Kyoto, with 16 passing legislation opposing its ratification in 1998 and 1999. Most were resolutions simply stating an opinion, but some states forbade their agencies from any unilateral steps to reduce greenhouse gases.[17]

But it soon became clear that many states were eager to address the problem of global warming, particularly after Bush's formal rejection of Kyoto in 2001. "Ironically . . . American states may be emerging as international leaders at the very time the national government continues to be portrayed as an international laggard on global climate change," the University of Michigan's Rabe wrote in 2004.[18]

Most initial state-level efforts were largely symbolic, lacking specific mandates or resources. As early as 1989, New Jersey Gov. Thomas Kean, a Republican, signed an executive order instructing all state agencies to take the lead in reducing greenhouse gases.

But New Jersey and other states soon put real teeth into their efforts. In 2001, Massachusetts Gov. Jane Swift, also a Republican, issued a rule limiting a variety of pollutants from six major power plants, including the nation's first carbon dioxide standards. "The new, tough standards will help ensure older power plants in Massachusetts do not contribute to regional air pollution, acid rain and global warming," Swift said.[19] Her action was soon copied in New Hampshire.

But California quickly emerged as the leader among states in addressing the issue. As the only state allowed to set air pollution controls stricter than those mandated by federal law (thanks to a provision in the Clean Air Act), California is an almost constant environmental battlefield. There was strong pressure from environmental forces to move on the issue of greenhouse gases at the start of this decade, with both the legislature and governor's mansion in Democratic hands for the first time in two decades.

California lawmakers responded in 2002, enacting a measure to regulate tailpipe emissions — greenhouse gases released from vehicles — which in 1999 accounted for 37 percent of carbon dioxide emissions in the state.[20]

The idea came from Bluewater Network, a San Francisco environmental group that has since become part of Friends of the Earth, a global organization. They found their sponsor in then-state Rep. Fran Pavley, a Democratic freshman willing to take on the fight when more prominent legislators were avoiding it. "We were happy at that point to find any progressive author,

CHRONOLOGY

1980s-1990s *Despite growing scientific concern, U.S. officials make mostly symbolic efforts to address global warming.*

1988 The United Nations and the World Meteorological Organization create the International Panel on Climate Change (IPCC) to assess scientific information related to global warming.

1989 New Jersey Gov. Thomas Kean directs state agencies to start cutting greenhouse gas emissions (GHG).

1990 Amendments to the Clean Air Act introduce states to emissions trading.

1992 Delegates to World Environmental Summit in Rio de Janeiro adopt U.N. Framework Convention on Climate Change, calling on industrialized nations to voluntarily reduce emissions to 1990 levels by 2000.

1997 The Kyoto Protocol is adopted in Kyoto, Japan, on Dec. 11, committing industrialized countries to cut GHG emissions by an average of 5 percent below 1990 levels by 2012. The treaty goes into effect in 2005; 183 countries have ratified it so far, but not the United States. The Clinton administration signed it in 1997, but the Senate had voted unanimously in July to oppose any treaty that would harm the U.S. economy and exempt developing countries.

1998-1999 Sixteen states pass legislation and resolutions critical of the Kyoto treaty and GHG reduction efforts.

1999 A law deregulating electricity in Texas includes a provision promoting renewable energy, sparking large-scale efforts to harvest wind energy in the state.

2000s *Federal inaction spurs local action to cut GHGs.*

2002 California regulates GHG emissions from vehicles.

2005 Governors from seven Northeastern states form Regional Greenhouse Gas Initiative to create a cap-and-trade system limiting emissions. . . . U.S. Conference of Mayors encourages cities to abide by Kyoto Protocol emission limits.

2006 California enacts first statewide cap on carbon emissions as part of a landmark global warming law. . . . Washington is first major U.S. city to mandate green construction for all large private buildings.

2007 In response to a case brought by Massachusetts and other states, Supreme Court rules Environmental Protection Agency can regulate carbon dioxide as a pollutant. . . . Regulator in Kansas denies permits for two 700-megawatt power plants due to GHG pollution concerns.

2008 April 7: New York State Assembly kills a plan by Mayor Michael Bloomberg to charge drivers an $8 "congestion pricing" fee for entering parts of Manhattan. . . . April 22: Los Angeles City Council approves ordinance requiring developers to meet tougher environmental building standards. . . . June 6: Senate rejects a vote to consider federal greenhouse gas legislation that includes a national cap-and-trade system. . . . July 18: California Building Standards Commission approves first statewide "green building codes," requiring greater energy efficiency in both commercial and residential properties. . . . Sept. 18: Chicago Mayor Richard M. Daley announces a plan to reduce GHG emissions by 25 percent by 2020, compared with 1990 levels, through tougher building codes and improved transportation. . . . Sept. 30: California Gov. Arnold Schwarzenegger signs bill that will award increased state and federal transportation funds to regions that encourage dense development. . . . Nov. 19: Governors of Illinois, Wisconsin and California sign agreement with counterparts in Indonesia and Brazil to address forestry issues pertaining to global warming. . . . Canada reverses course and expresses support for a North American cap-and-trade system. . . . Dec. 8: Local government groups urge Congress and the incoming Obama administration to devote $10 billion to their efforts to create green jobs and promote energy efficiency as part of an economic stimulus plan. . . . Dec. 11: California Air Resources Board moves to implement the state's 2006 global warming law, approving a plan to cut emissions 25 percent by 2020.

2009 Jan. 1: Northeast's multistate limits on carbon emissions take effect. . . . March 3: Los Angeles voters will decide whether to require Department of Water and Power to install solar collectors on roofs of government, commercial and industrial buildings by 2014.

because we knew it would be a difficult bill," said Bluewater Executive Director Russell Long.

The legislation survived a committee challenge and was ready to reach the floor by the middle of 2001, but Pavley held off on a vote until 2002 so she could broaden her backing. Car makers and oil companies spent an estimated $5 million attempting to sink it, and she was ardently attacked by talk-radio hosts for impinging on the freedom of Californians to drive SUVs and other large vehicles.

Pavley responded with polls demonstrating overwhelming popular support for the bill, even among SUV owners. She also got help from water-quality districts, religious leaders, technology executives from Silicon Valley and celebrities such as Paul Newman, Tom Hanks and former President Clinton, who called wavering lawmakers. Her bill's progress was helped immeasurably, however, by legislative leaders who showed the former

California state Sen. Fran Pavley sponsored legislation in 2002 to regulate tailpipe emissions. In 2006, another law she authored called for reductions in industrial carbon dioxide emissions from power plants, oil refineries and other plants by 25 percent by 2020. The law includes penalties for noncompliance.

civics teacher some parliamentary tricks to ensure its passage.

Her law required the state's Air Resources Board to adopt "cost-effective" and "reasonable" restrictions on carbon dioxide emissions from cars and light trucks by 2005, with automakers having until 2009 to comply. Not surprisingly, carmakers have fought the law through numerous court challenges.

A total of 19 other states have since enacted laws saying they will abide by California's rules once they are approved, but the Bush administration has refused to grant California the necessary waiver.

"All we asked for was permission to enforce, because the rules were all in place," California Air Resources Board spokesman Stanley Young said in a recent interview. "We've been ready for two years on Pavley. The rules were fully fleshed out. They were formally adopted back in 2005, and we're ready to move on them as soon as we get the green light."

Pavley was back in 2006 with another piece of legislation designed to address global warming. The measure to address stationary sources of pollution aims to reduce industrial carbon dioxide emissions by 25 percent by 2020. It affects not only power plants but also other polluters such as oil refineries and cement plants.

The legislation was the first in the nation to require a cap-and-trade system. It also served to codify limits on future greenhouse gas emissions that Schwarzenegger had outlined in 2005. The 2006 law represented the first imposition of statewide, enforceable limits on GHG emissions that include penalties for noncompliance.

States Challenge the EPA

States have been exploring numerous other avenues toward curbing emissions in recent years. In 2007, first Western and then Midwestern states joined together in regional compacts meant to mirror and build on the Northeast's Regional Greenhouse Gas Initiative, which aims to set up cap-and-trade systems to limit emissions. Various states have taken steps to encourage use of high-efficiency vehicles, either through purchases for their own fleets or tax incentives for individuals to purchase them. States such as New Mexico, New Jersey and Minnesota have recently crafted and adopted plans for reducing their overall greenhouse gas emissions.

'Green' Jobs Counted on to Revive Economy

But critic says stimulus program won't help.

In October, Progressive Insurance announced the winner of its $10 million Automotive X Prize, a competition to encourage students to develop designs for safe, low-emission, "production capable" cars. Among the finalists were engineering students from West Philadelphia High School.

"Our team has built four cars, including a hybrid Jeep that gets double the mileage it's supposed to get," said Lawrence Jones-Mahoney, 18. "If we can do it as high school students, why can't the major auto companies?"[1]

Amid the nation's current economic doldrums, many people see green manufacturing projects as a hopeful sign. Investment in alternative energy and more efficient automobiles and buildings was high and growing rapidly over the past year, at least until the price of oil began to drop.

Many still are counting on "green collar" jobs to revive the economy, restoring the manufacturing sector in places where it's long been in decline. "American cities have suffered more than anyone from the loss of manufacturing jobs," says Minneapolis Mayor R. T. Rybak. "Cities have become the green incubators for America."

Every month seems to see another study released suggesting that there will be an explosion of investment and job creation in the green sector. The Center for American Progress estimates that a government-funded $100 billion green stimulus package would create 2 million jobs in the next two years for engineers, machinists, construction workers and others.[2]

The Apollo Alliance, a coalition of business, labor and environmental groups, estimates that a $300 billion investment over 10 years will create 3.3 million jobs in renewable energy, hybrid cars and infrastructure replacement.[3] The U.S. Conference of Mayors forecasts 4.2 million green jobs by 2038 and suggests that cities and towns prepare to compete for them.[4]

"Everything that is good for global warming is good for jobs," says Van Jones, author of the 2008 book *The Green Collar Economy*. "Buildings do not weatherize themselves, wind turbines do not construct themselves, solar panels do not install themselves. Real people are going to have to get up in the morning and do these things."

This is one of the central premises of *New York Times* columnist Thomas Friedman's 2008 bestselling book, *Hot, Flat and Crowded* — that energy-technology jobs will serve as a cornerstone of economic revival in this country, in large part because they mostly cannot be done by workers overseas.

President-elect Barack Obama has pledged to make green jobs and manufacturing a centerpiece of any economic-stimulus package. "President-elect Obama did a great job on the campaign trail [communicating] that this is an opportunity, an economic opportunity for America, and that if we miss it, other countries in the world will be way ahead of us," Kansas Gov. Kathleen Sebelius, a Democrat, said at a November climate-change summit in California. "Jobs are clearly part of this."[5]

For all the apparent promise, however, the interest in green technology has not yet translated either into mass employment or a huge economic windfall. "People are talking about this in the future, but it's not happening today," says Eric Crawford, president of Greenman Alliance, a Milwaukee-based recruiting firm. "Everyone wants a green job," but the demand for such jobs totally outstrips the supply.

And government investment in clean technology has not always reaped large dividends. Under New Jersey's

But environmentalists and state officials alike have been hoping the federal government would take action. In the face of its reluctance to regulate greenhouse gas emissions, several environmental groups as early as 1999 had petitioned the EPA to use its authority under the Clean Air Act to regulate the gases. The agency denied it had such authority and also argued that the link between greenhouse gases and climate change was not firmly established.

Massachusetts and 11 other states appealed the EPA's denial. In April 2007, the Supreme Court ruled, 5-4, in the states' favor, noting that they had standing to bring such a case due to the "risk of catastrophic harm" they faced as sovereign entities. Justice John Paul Stevens wrote that the EPA had provided "no reasonable explanation for its refusal to decide whether greenhouse gases cause or contribute to climate change." In his dissent, Chief Justice energy master plan, solar power should account for more than 2 percent of the Garden State's electricity by 2020. But solar systems now generate only 0.07 percent of current energy needs.

That's despite the fact that the state has already handed out more than $170 million in rebates to encourage their installation. To meet its 2020 goal, the state would have to spend $11 billion more. "We need to do things differently because ratepayers can't keep paying for rebates indefinitely," says Jeanne M. Fox, president of New Jersey's Board of Public Utilities.[6]

"This idea that we're going to have a massive environmental WPA — it's not going to help the economy, it's going to hurt the economy," says Myron Ebell, director of energy and global warming policy at the Competitive Enterprise Institute, referring to the Depression-era jobs program, the Works Progress Administration.

Putting government money into green energy would not create great economic returns, Ebell suggests, because — at least so far — renewable energy is more expensive than dirty fuels such as coal. It also means directing dollars away from other fields entirely, he says.

"I believe just on a very simple analysis that there is no question it will take net jobs out of the economy and it will be a net economic harm," Ebell says.

Even if Ebell's right, however, the goal of green investment is not only to stimulate the economy but also to help

About half the states require utilities to generate a portion of their power from renewable sources, such as wind and solar. Above, wind turbines near Palm Springs, Calif.

Getty Images/David McNew

clean up the environment. In a column published in *The New York Times* just after the November election, former Vice President Al Gore called for large governmental investments in clean energy as the optimum way to address climate change — a shift from his traditional focus on increased regulation of carbon pollution.[7]

"With his op-ed, Gore has reversed the longstanding green-lobby prioritization of regulation first and investment second," wrote Michael Shellenberger and Ted Nordhaus for *The New Republic Online.*[8]

[1] Jim Motavalli, "Upstart Team Eyes the X Prize," *The New York Times*, Sept. 7, 2008, p. AU6.

[2] Robert Pollin, *et al.*, "Green Recovery: A Program to Create Good Jobs and Start Building a Low-Carbon Economy," Center for American Progress, September 2008.

[3] "The New Apollo Program: Clean Energy, Good Jobs," The Apollo Alliance, September 2008.

[4] "Current and Potential Green Jobs in the U.S. Economy," *Global Insight*, October 2008.

[5] "Governors Say Climate Change Programs Can Aid Economic Recovery," *Carbon Control News*, Nov. 24, 2008.

[6] Anthony DePalma, "New Jersey Dealing With Solar Policy's Success," *The New York Times*, June 25, 2008, p. B1.

[7] Al Gore, "The Climate for Change," *The New York Times*, Nov. 9, 2008, p. WK10.

[8] Michael Shellenberger and Ted Nordhaus, "A New Inconvenient Truth," *The New Republic Online*, Nov. 17, 2008, www.tnr.com/politics/story.html?id=971eed4b-1dc8-4afd-a8fe-193c373286ac.

John G. Roberts Jr. argued that it was an issue better decided by Congress and the executive branch.[21]

But the court's majority determined that carbon dioxide was indeed an air pollutant under the federal Clean Air Act, and that law gives California the authority to regulate any such pollutant, as long as the state can get a waiver from the EPA. Other states are then allowed to follow California's rules.

The Supreme Court decision set the political stage for Congress to set a new mileage standard for cars and light trucks. In December 2007 President Bush signed into law requirements that a car manufacturer's entire fleet average 35 miles per gallon by 2020.

But just hours after that bill was signed, EPA Administrator Stephen L. Johnson dashed hopes that the *Massachusetts v. EPA* decision would lead the agency to

Kansas Regulator Blocks Coal-Fired Plants

Project is among 60 canceled in 2008 to protect environment.

Many people would be surprised to find Kansas at the epicenter of a nationwide environmental debate. Yet the decision by Rod Bremby, secretary of the Kansas Department of Health and Environment (KDHE), to block a pair of massive coal-fired power plants has set off one of the nation's fiercest political and legal environmental battles.

Several other states have blocked coal-fired plants over the past year, but Bremby is the only regulator to have done so strictly out of concern for climate change and without getting specific statutory cover from the legislature. "To approve the permit didn't seem a reasonable option, given that carbon dioxide is a pollutant," he said in an interview, "and we're talking about 11 million tons of carbon."

Bremby delayed making his coal-plant decision until after the U.S. Supreme Court's ruling in a case (*Massachusetts v. EPA*) brought in 2007 by Massachusetts and other states seeking to force the federal Environmental Protection Agency to regulate greenhouse gases.

The states' victory — along with an opinion from the Kansas attorney general that Bremby had the authority to block the permit — allowed him to overrule his own staff and refuse Sunflower Electric Power Corp.'s application to build its $3.6 billion power-plant project outside Holcomb.

The project is one of roughly 60 coal-fired plants canceled over the past year due to environmental concerns. Florida Gov. Charlie Crist asked a utility to cancel two projects in his state. The Texas energy giant TXU Corp. has shelved eight out of 11 planned coal plants, investing heavily in wind energy instead. Only three out of 10 plants once planned for southern Illinois remain active.[1] Nowadays, wherever a coal-fired plant is proposed, the Sierra Club or an allied group steps forward with a lawsuit to block it.[2]

"There have been other decisions in which state public utility commissions or environmental regulators have blocked construction or operation of coal-fired plants on the basis of climate change," says Robert Glicksman, a University of Kansas law professor, "but those have been based on legislation designed to minimize pollution or used climate change coupled with other factors."

In Washington state, for instance, the legislature in 2007 limited the amount of greenhouse gases coal plants could emit. To obtain construction permits, energy companies must show they can capture or sequester any carbon dioxide above strict limits.

Because Kansas lacks such legislation, and despite the attorney general's opinion, many critics say Bremby overstepped his authority. Kansas law gives the secretary authority to block emissions found to endanger health or the environment. But that power, according to the health department's own testimony, applies only to emergencies, says Jay Emler, who chairs the state Senate Utilities Committee.

Legislators — their attention focused by a million-dollar lobbying campaign by Sunflower and its allies — voted

approve California's waiver application for enforcement of the Pavley bill. "The Bush administration is moving forward with a clear national solution, not a confusing patchwork of state rules, to reduce America's climate footprint from vehicles," Johnson said in a statement. Congress has since investigated the circumstances surrounding Johnson's decision.[22]

CURRENT SITUATION

Limiting Land Use

American governors are now working with partners from around the world, as well as with each other, to combat environmental threats. On Nov. 19, governors from 13 states and regional leaders from four other nations signed a declaration to work together to combat global warming. The statement was the capstone of a climate summit organized by California's Schwarzenegger.

Under a separate agreement, Illinois, California and Wisconsin pledged to work with the governors of six provinces within Indonesia and Brazil to help slow tropical deforestation and land degradation through joint projects and incentive programs.

"When California passed its global warming law two years ago, we were out there on an island, so we started forming partnerships everywhere we could," Schwarzenegger said.[23]

three times to ban Bremby's department from regulating greenhouse gases. Each time, Democratic Gov. Kathleen Sebelius sided with Bremby and vetoed their efforts. The legislature came close to overriding her, but fell short.

The battle is now left to the state and federal courts, which are weighing a half-dozen lawsuits. Environmentalists, needless to say, are delighted by the outcome so far, believing that delays, and their concomitant costs, can only serve to move power generation away from coal. "Each time you step back and reassess the politics and economics of coal," says Bob Eye, a Sierra Club attorney and former KDHE counsel, "things are more difficult for the coal-plant proponents."

Plant advocates, of course, make exactly the opposite argument, saying the protracted fighting will simply cause Sunflower to look to friendlier states. Uncertainty about permitting — as well as the state's general regulatory climate — has caused problems for the business community, which put energy costs at the top of its list of concerns in a Kansas Chamber of Commerce survey last fall. "We've heard people saying that because of what happened last session they feel that the state has hung a big 'We're not open for business' sign out," said Kent Eckles, the chamber's vice president for government affairs.[3]

Action by Rod Bremby ignited fierce battle in Kansas.

U.S. House Select Committee on Energy Independence and Global Warming

"His decision, which I say is nothing but a political decision, has had a disastrous effect on the economy of Kansas," says Sen. Emler, "and will until it's rectified."

Bremby and his allies have pointed out that Sunflower was the only applicant not to receive a clean-air permit, out of more than 3,100 applications received during the six years Sebelius has been governor. But the issue is expected to be front and center again during the upcoming legislative session.

"I anticipate a full-blown debate until we get this fixed," says Senate President Steve Morris, who strongly supports Sunflower's project.

Then again, Bremby always suspected he couldn't win many friends with his decision. "We knew going in that we were in a no-win situation," he says, "There would be litigation either way we went."

---

[1] Michael Hawthorne, "How Coal Got a Dirty Name," *Chicago Tribune*, July 9, 2008, p. 1.

[2] Judy Pasternak, "Coal at Heart of Climate Battle," *Los Angeles Times*, April 14, 2008, p. A1.

[3] Jeannine Koranda, "Climate Cleanup Costs Could Trickle Down," *The Wichita Eagle*, Nov. 10, 2008, p. A1.

On Dec. 11, the California Air Resources Board approved a set of regulations designed to implement the state's 2006 greenhouse gas law. It aims to reduce carbon emissions to 1990 levels by 2020, which would amount to a 25 percent cut. The plan will allow businesses to buy and sell emission credits, impose fees on water use and require utilities to generate a full third of their power from renewable sources — about three times as much as they do currently.

California estimates that about 30 percent of its greenhouse gas emissions come from cars. The new vehicle regulations would account for 18 percent of the state's overall reduction goal, according to the new state plan. The air board's plan also includes a "feebate" proposal,

which would give rebates to people buying fuel-efficient cars, while adding fees to the purchase of gas-guzzlers.[24]

The Air Resources Board will almost certainly have to revisit some of these issues in response to a major land-use bill Schwarzenegger signed last September, known as SB 375, which directed the board to come up with regional greenhouse gas reduction targets by September 2010. The next step under the law calls for regional planning boards to rewrite their master plans in ways that seek to meet those targets. The ones that come closest will be rewarded with extra federal and state transportation dollars.

The best way to meet the standards, argues Adams at the California League of Conservation Voters, is to cut

Getty Images/Tim Boyle

The rooftop garden atop Chicago's City Hall is one of about 200 such green roofs in the city. Mayor Richard M. Daley announced in 2008 the first city-specific climate-change projections in the nation along with plans to reduce greenhouse gas emissions by 25 percent in 2020, compared with 1990 levels.

down on sprawl. He points out that the number of miles traveled per vehicle is still growing at one-and-a-half times the rate of population growth. It's only by creating more compact and energy-efficient communities, Adams believes, that the state's long-term environmental goals can be achieved.

It's no surprise that environmentalists backed SB 375, but it also had the support of home builders, who liked the prospect of more predictability in the zoning process. One of the bill's main goals is inducing localities to coordinate their major planning tasks — transportation, land use and housing. Few have been able to do that up to now.

In addition, SB 375 provides relief from certain air-quality standards that had, perversely, discouraged developers from undertaking "infill" projects that use small plots of undeveloped land within existing communities. "Builders thrive on certainty, knowing what the rules are," says Tim Coyle, a senior vice president at the California Building Industry Association. Local governments also supported the law. Although it provides incentives and creates a policy-making framework, it doesn't create specific mandates for any individual regions.

SB 375 will take years to implement, but it already has received lots of attention from other states. "It's really a very important piece of legislation," says Peter Kasabach, executive director of New Jersey Future, a smart-growth group. "How we develop our land is going to impact our greenhouse-gas targets.

"A lot of folks think that if we drive hybrids or change our lightbulbs, we'd be OK," he says. "But a significant amount of our greenhouse gas targets will be met by how we get around and reduce vehicle miles traveled."

Green Building

The number of local governments attempting to shrink their carbon footprints continues to grow, with more than 900 mayors having signed a pledge to bring their cities in line with the Kyoto Protocol's carbon reduction targets.

In 2007, Congress authorized up to $2 billion a year in block grants for state and local programs designed to save energy. "If we reflect back on the mayors' initiative, it was such a powerful vehicle to establish the voice of local action," says Michelle Wyman, executive director of the American affiliate of the international group ICLEI-Local Governments for Sustainability. "There's increasing sentiment that local climate action is where the real work is being done in the United States."

In September, Chicago Mayor Daley unveiled what *The New York Times* described as "perhaps the most aggressive plan of any major American city to reduce heat-trapping gases."[25] The plan, which aims to cut Chicago's carbon output by 25 percent by 2020, focuses on tougher building codes.

Green building codes have drawn the most attention among local governments seeking to cut back on carbon. Buildings account for 40 to 50 percent of a city's energy demands. They use a fourth of the drinking water and produce 35 percent of the solid waste, mostly in the form of construction materials. And buildings make up anywhere from 30 to 70 percent of municipal carbon emissions, according to the American Institute of Architects (AIA).

Many cities have received grants from former President Clinton's foundation to rewrite their codes, but far more are pursuing such strategies on their own. In November, more than 25,000 local officials attended the "Greenbuild" conference in Boston sponsored by the U.S. Green Building Council.[26]

The trend has exploded in recent years. From 2003 to 2007, the number of cities with green building programs grew by 418 percent, from 22 to 92, according to the AIA. By mid-2008, 14 percent of municipalities with populations of more than 50,000 had adopted such programs, with many more cities planning programs soon.

AT ISSUE

Can "green" jobs revive the U.S. economy?

YES

Bracken Hendricks
Senior Fellow, and

Benjamin Goldstein
Research Associate,
Center for American Progress

From "A Strategy for Green Recovery," Nov. 10, 2008

There is a growing consensus in Washington and on Main Streets across the country that the economy needs a jump-start. There are compelling reasons why the infrastructure and work-force components of the economic stimulus and recovery package should be "green."

Confronting the mounting energy and global warming crises represents an extraordinary opportunity to reinvigorate the economy through investment in clean, sustainable, low-carbon energy sources. Investment in new, clean technologies and improving energy efficiency can drive immediate spending into some of the hardest-hit sectors of the economy, such as construction and manufacturing, and can ensure that this infusion flows directly into job creation and domestic investment. Further, smart policies for energy efficiency can reduce household utility bills and free up income for consumer spending.

There are many ways that government spending can boost the economy and create jobs as part of a stimulus and recovery program. Yet dollars directed toward renewable energy and energy efficiency would result in more jobs than spending in most other areas, including, for example, rebates for increasing household consumption, which was the primary aim of the $168 billion stimulus program last April. "Green" investments, on average, create more than twice as many jobs per dollar invested as traditional, fossil fuel-based generating technologies by redirecting money previously spent on wasted energy and imported fuel toward advanced technology, modern infrastructure and skilled labor.

Green investments also pave the road for sustained economic recovery. Larger, capital-intensive, green infrastructure projects such as renewable-energy generating facilities may take two years to get fully up and running but will be good job creators with a dependable economic-multiplier effect. About 22 percent of total household expenditures go to imports. But only about 9 percent of a green infrastructure investment program purchases imports. This is another critical advantage of a green economic-recovery program: Investments are focused primarily on increasing domestic productive capacity, improving national infrastructure and making the entire economy more efficient over the long term.

Confronting energy and climate challenges will require a sustained commitment and long-term policy framework. But near-term green investments can immediately stimulate the economy, create millions of good jobs and put a solid down payment on the low-carbon future vital for our economic growth.

NO

Margo Thorning
Senior Vice President and
Chief Economist, American
Council for Capital Formation

Written for *CQ Researcher*, January 2009

The U.S. economy has slowed markedly in recent months, prompting some to suggest putting even more taxpayer dollars into subsidized renewable energy in the United States. Advocates claim lots of new "green collar" jobs would be created, and the threat of global warming would be lessened. Both claims are unlikely to be realized.

Despite many years of tax credits and taxpayer-funded research and development, most forms of renewable energy are still not competitive with electricity generated by coal, natural gas or nuclear power. Wind-powered electricity is estimated to cost as much as 50 percent more than coal-fired generation, and solar generation up to 700 percent more.

Both wind and solar must be backed up by conventional generation capacity, which adds greatly to their cost, because the wind does not always blow, and the sun is available only 12 hours a day. Furthermore, renewable resources are often geographically remote, and building transmission lines to large metropolitan areas is expensive.

Proposals like that of the Center for American Progress to invest $100 billion-$200 billion of taxpayer money in green infrastructure are based on the flawed premise that raising the price of conventional energy through a tax on carbon emissions and using the money to pay for more expensive renewable energy will promote economic recovery. In fact, substituting higher-cost energy for lower-cost conventional energy will slow U.S. economic and job growth.

A study by the American Council for Capital Formation and the National Association of Manufacturers shows that if the U.S. had adopted the Senate's Lieberman-Warner global warming bill last year, overall U.S. employment would have been reduced by 850,000 to 1,860,000 jobs in 2014. This figure includes gains from new green jobs. The high energy prices required to curb greenhouse gas emissions cause net job loss even after taking into account increased employment in renewable energy.

What's more, a recent EPA report concluded that even if the United States achieved the emission-reduction targets in the Lieberman-Warner bill, it would make virtually no difference in global greenhouse gas concentrations unless developing countries also adopt stringent reduction targets.

Although renewable energy has a role to play in the U.S. economy, the Obama administration should consider policies to promote U.S. energy supplies of all types and avoid unrealistic climate change policies.

Getty Images/Justin Sullivan

A motorist in San Rafael, Calif., checks his tailpipe exhaust level. California passed a law in 2002 to regulate tailpipe emissions, and 19 other states followed suit. The Bush White House has blocked the other states from enforcing their laws, but President-elect Barack Obama has said he will approve a waiver allowing enforcement.

By and large, cities' green building programs are based on the standards of the council's rating system, known as LEED (Leader in Energy and Environmental Design). To encourage developers to build green, cities are offering tax incentives, reductions in permit fees and access to grants for projects that meet certain environmental benchmarks. Some cities offer bonus density allowances — a green building project might be exempt from height restrictions, for example. But the most popular incentive by far is expedited permitting for green projects. Cities can implement such a policy at virtually no cost to themselves, which has proven extremely attractive.

Some cities are going further and actually requiring energy-efficient construction through their building codes. Washington, D.C., in 2006 became the first major U.S. city to mandate green construction for all private buildings of at least 50,000 square feet, beginning in 2012. But in 2007, Boston became the first city actually to implement a green requirement for private construction and renovation projects.

Since then, a handful of other cities have adopted similar mandates. San Francisco last August adopted the strictest codes of any U.S. city so far, requiring green standards for any residential buildings taller than 75 feet and commercial buildings of more than 5,000 square feet.

Last July, California became the first state to require certain environmental standards in its statewide building code.

Cap-and-Trade

In September, 10 Northeastern states concluded their first auction selling the right to emit carbon dioxide from power plants. The idea, as explained by the plan's architect, former Pataki aide Cahill, is to translate everyone's awareness that carbon emissions have a price into an actual cost.

Cap-and-trade auctions have taken place for years as a means of reducing acid-rain-causing sulfur dioxide, and the European Union runs a cap-and-trade program for carbon. But the Northeastern effort — known as the Regional Greenhouse Gas Initiative, or RGGI (pronounced "Reggie") — was the first CO_2 auction in the United States.

RGGI, which went into force on Jan. 1, places an overall regional limit on the amount of carbon that power plants can emit. The cap-and-trade plan is the central mechanism for regulating and limiting carbon emissions. Each utility has a permit for each ton of carbon it is allowed to emit — and the number of permits will steadily shrink over time. Utilities that emit less than their quota can sell their excess permits. (That's the "trade" part of cap and trade.)

The Northeastern states aren't the only ones interested in such an approach. In the West, seven states and four Canadian provinces are developing a similar regime, with negotiators having drawn up a blueprint for their governors in September. In the Midwest, six other states are working on a regional carbon-trading program. Florida is developing its own program, although it may join forces either with the Western effort or RGGI.

The history of RGGI, in particular, includes many touch-and-go moments when states dropped out of or rejoined the program. But the effort has stayed afloat based on the hope that once carbon emissions carry a price, utilities will burn less coal, oil and natural gas because it's in their economic interest, while carbon-free alternatives will become comparatively more attractive.

Not everyone agrees that such a scenario will play out. Wind power, for instance, is already heavily subsidized yet still can't compete on price with coal. And the region-by-region approach that's now in place leaves plenty of opportunities open for undermining the system.

In the Northeast, for example, it would be easy enough for a big industrial customer in New York, which is part of RGGI, to look for cheaper power generated by coal plants in Pennsylvania or Ohio, which are not part of the initiative. If that occurs, said Kenneth Pokalsky, a regulatory analyst for the Business Council of New York State, "We'll have the worst of both worlds: higher energy costs in New York to implement a program that has no discernible impact on worldwide greenhouse gas emissions."[27]

Nevertheless, hoping to build on the RGGI model and benefit from lessons learned there and from the troubled European model, the system being developed in the West is even bolder. The Western Climate Initiative is targeting not just carbon dioxide but five other greenhouse gases as well. And the WCI isn't limiting its scope to power plants. Instead, it's trying to bring all major industries, transportation fuels and residential furnaces, stoves and hot-water heaters into its system.

Such an ambitious approach may represent the logical evolution of cap and trade, but it nonetheless has made business groups, local governments and unions nervous about the potential impact on their costs and the economy. Officials involved in WCI are tweaking their plans, looking at giving away a good share of emission allowances rather than auctioning them off. They're also seeking other ways to protect entities that would be affected if the system takes effect.

Focus on Renewables

Even as the regional cap-and-trade systems get under way, more than half the states are trying to cut down on coal as a share of their power sources individually. Twenty-seven states now require utilities to rely on renewable sources such as wind and solar to generate a significant share of electricity — up to 25 percent in future years. That's nearly twice as many states as had renewable portfolio standards in place just five years ago.

"It's an important step in the process of weaning ourselves from foreign oil," said Rhode Island state Sen. David E. Bates, who helped push through legislation in 2004 that requires a 20 percent renewable energy portfolio in his state by 2020. "We provided incentives for companies to produce renewable energy. We also took great pains to make it a workable formula. You can't tell a national grid to produce green energy in 20 years without making sure the energy is available."[28]

Meeting the required targets remains quite a challenge, however, especially in coal-dependent regions such as the South and Midwest. Coal generates about half the nation's electricity.

Joe Manchin, the governor of West Virginia, has touted wind energy but noted in a recent interview that his state's coal production is key for the entire Eastern Seaboard. "Economists and scientists . . . will tell you that coal is going to be the primary factor that's going to power this nation and most of the world for the next 30 to 50 years."[29]

According to the American Wind Energy Association, wind energy capacity has been growing rapidly, with wind turbines installed in 2008 capable of generating 7,500 megawatts of additional electricity. That's up from 5,249 megawatts installed in 2007. But 7,500 megawatts is still only enough electricity to power about 2 million homes.[30]

OUTLOOK

Will Washington Help?

If California has been a leader in state-level efforts to prevent climate change, two Californians are likely to have a profound effect on the national response to the issue. Sen. Barbara Boxer, who chairs the Senate Environment and Public Works Committee, has pledged to introduce legislation to create a national cap-and-trade program in this Congress. Henry A. Waxman, another California Democrat, will be Boxer's counterpart in the House, having ousted legendary Rep. John D. Dingell, D-Mich., as chairman of the Energy and Commerce Committee in November.

Dingell, who has been in Congress for a half-century and had been the panel's top Democrat since 1981, represents the Detroit area and has been a leading champion of the auto industry in Congress. His replacement by Waxman was widely seen as a signal that House Democrats will favor a more aggressive approach on climate change.

President-elect Obama, for his part, has also promised to make climate change a priority — a switch from the outgoing Bush administration. Obama is expected to approve the EPA waiver to allow California and 19 other states to regulate greenhouse gas emissions from vehicles.

But even if new leadership in Washington appears ready to tackle an issue long left to states and localities, does that mean national policy will trump the efforts of lower levels of government?

A lot will depend, of course, on what form congressional action will take. Plenty of people are skeptical, despite the changed circumstances in Washington, that Congress will actually act on cap and trade or any equally ambitious responses to global warming. There has been a lot of talk that caution will remain a watchword, given the fragile state of the economy. Further regulation may be seen as more than the economy — and the tottering auto sector in particular — can bear.

"Yes, there will be concerns about the current economic climate," says former Pataki aide Cahill, who helped design the Regional Greenhouse Gas Initiative (RGGI). "But it will take several years to develop the regulatory framework to go ahead and implement a national cap and trade. We all have enough confidence in the economy that it won't still be where it is now."

But the Competitive Enterprise Institute's Ebell points out that a Senate vote to consider last year's major climate-change legislation received only 48 votes — far short of the 60 needed under Senate rules to formally consider the bill. Although Democrats picked up seven seats in the November elections, some of them replaced Republicans who had voted in favor of the bill.

"I think there will be somewhat more enthusiasm for cap and trade in the 111th Congress than in the 110th," Ebell says, "but I don't know that it will translate into actual legislation."

If Congress does manage to overcome its own procedural hurdles and economic concerns to move major greenhouse gas legislation, one of the biggest challenges for lawmakers will be how to balance competing desires among states. Some, such as California, Massachusetts and New Jersey, will want to be rewarded for their pioneering efforts. Others in the South and Midwest, though, will not want to be penalized for not having acted sooner. It will be tough to create a national system that balances those different interests.

Rabe, the University of Michigan policy professor, says Congress has only recently taken into account the role that states and localities are playing. He says states will lobby to ensure that any federal system allows them maximum flexibility to set their own courses, while demanding that any money generated by a cap-and-trade

system be shared generously with them. "States and localities are going to want it both ways," Rabe says.

But the fact that states and localities will be very much part of the national debate demonstrates how well-established their role in addressing climate change has already become. They may have gotten into the game due mainly to federal inaction. Still, many observers predict that states, cities and counties will continue to address this challenge even if Congress and the White House agree on climate change legislation.

"Even if we get federal climate change legislation — or when we get it — that doesn't eliminate the need for states and cities to have their own strategies, their own plans," says the Union of Concerned Scientists' Burke.

Given the growing understanding that global warming is misnamed — that climate change will play out very differently around the world, with some regions heating up and others cooling down and some getting drier while others get wetter — states and localities should continue their work, suggests Hogan at the Pew Center on Global Climate Change.

"There should be a substantial role for the states," Hogan says. "The history of environmental regulation teaches us that the states do some things well, and the feds do some things well.

"Environmental goals are typically best achieved when all levels of government are doing their part."

NOTES

1. Ellen Perlman, "Mister Sustainability," *Governing*, April 2008, p. 36.

2. For background, see the following *CQ Researcher* reports: Marcia Clemmitt, "Climate Change," Jan. 27, 2006, pp. 73-96; Mary H. Cooper, "Global Warming Treaty," Jan. 26, 2001, pp. 41-64; Mary H. Cooper, "Alternative Fuels," Feb. 25, 2005, pp. 173-196, and Thomas J. Billitteri, "Reducing Your Carbon Footprint," Dec. 5, 2008, pp. 985-1008; and the following *CQ Global Researcher* reports: Colin Woodard, "Curbing Climate Change," February 2007, pp. 27-50, and Jennifer Weeks, "Carbon Trading," November 2008, pp. 295-320.

3. Michael Grunwald, "Arnold Schwarzenegger," *Time*, Oct. 6, 2008, p. 60.

4. For background, see Mary H. Cooper, "Bush and the Environment," *CQ Researcher*, Oct. 25, 2002, pp. 865-896.

5. Samantha Young, "Schwarzenegger Opens Climate Summit With Obama," The Associated Press, Nov. 19, 2008.

6. Margot Roosevelt, "California Offers to Lead on Climate Change Fight," *Los Angeles Times*, Nov. 20, 2008, p. A22.

7. Kate Galbraith, "Texas Worries About a Carbon Cap," *The New York Times Green Inc. Blog*, http://greeninc.blogs.nytimes.com/2008/12/04/texas-worries-about-a-carbon-cap/, Dec. 4, 2008.

8. Juliet Eilperin, "Ex-EPA Official Says White House Pulled Rank," *The Washington Post*, July 23, 2008, p. A4. The case is *Massachusetts v. EPA*.

9. Dirk Johnson, "Chicago Unveils Multifaceted Plan to Curb Emissions of Heat-Trapping Gases," *The New York Times*, Sept. 19, 2008, p. A13.

10. Alan Greenblatt, "Cities vs. Carbon," *CQ Weekly*, Nov. 19, 2007, p. 3474.

11. Alec MacGillis, "Palin Gives Beliefs, Demurs on Policies," *The Washington Post*, Oct. 1, 2008, p. A7.

12. Alan Zarembo and Thomas H. Maugh II, "U.N. Says It's time to Adapt to Warming," *Los Angeles Times*, Nov. 17, 2007, p. A1.

13. Roger Pielke Jr., *et al.*, "Lifting the Taboo on Adaptation," *Nature*, Feb. 8, 2007, p. 445.

14. Christopher Swope, "Local Warming," *Governing*, December 2007, p. 25.

15. Louise Bedsworth and Ellen Hanak, "Preparing California for a Changing Climate," Public Policy Institute of California, November 2008.

16. Chris Bowman, "California Bulks Up Defenses Against Tide of Global Warming," *The Sacramento Bee*, Nov. 24, 2008, p. A1.

17. Barry G. Rabe, *Statehouse and Greenhouse* (2004), p. 20.

18. *Ibid.*, p. xiv.

19. *Ibid.*, p. 77.

20. Alan Greenblatt, "Fran Pavley: Legislative Prodigy," *Governing*, September 2002, p. 80.

21. Linda Greenhouse, "Justices Say EPA Has Power to Act on Harmful Gases," *The New York Times*, April 8, 2007, p. A1.

22. John M. Broder and Felicity Barringer, "EPA Says 17 States Can't Set Greenhouse Gas Rules for Cars," *The New York Times*, Dec. 20, 2007, p. A1.

23. John M. Broder, "Obama Affirms Climate Change Goals," *The New York Times*, Nov. 19, 2008, p. A4, www.nytimes.com/2008/11/19/us/politics/19climate.html.

24. Michael Gardner, "Emissions Plan Calls for Tougher Rules, Fees," *The San Diego Union-Tribune*, Nov. 21, 2008, p. A1.

25. Dirk Johnson, "Chicago Unveils Multifaceted Plan to Curb Emissions of Heat-Trapping Gases," *The New York Times*, Sept. 19, 2008, p. A13.

26. David Beard, "At Least 25,000 at Greenbuild Conference in Boston," *The Boston Globe Greenblog*, Nov. 19, 2008, www.boston.com/lifestyle/green/greenblog/2008/11/at_least_25000_at_greenbuild_c.html.

27. Tom Arrandale, "Carbon Goes to Market," *Governing*, September 2008, p. 26.

28. Chelsea Waugaman, "Voltage Charge," *Governing*, November 2005, p. 76.

29. Mannix Porterfield, "Manchin Wants Aggressive Renewable Energy Policy," Beckley [West Virginia] *Register-Herald*, Oct. 20, 2008.

30. Dirk Lammers, "US Wind Energy Adds 1,400 MW of Capacity," The Associated Press, Oct. 22, 2008.

BIBLIOGRAPHY

Books

Linstroth, Tommy, and Ryan Bell, *Local Action: The New Paradigm in Climate Change Policy,* **University of Vermont Press, 2007.**

An environmental consultant and a planner use case studies to illustrate how local governments are fighting global warming.

Rabe, Barry G., *Statehouse and Greenhouse: The Emerging Politics of American Climate Change Policy,* **Brookings Institution Press, 2004.**

A political scientist explains how states came to be lead actors in the fight against climate change and what their initial strategies were.

Articles

Arrandale, Tom, "Carbon Goes to Market," *Governing*, **September 2008, p. 26.**
Many states, especially those in the Northeast, are moving ahead with regional cap-and-trade systems to cut down on carbon emissions.

Davidson, Paul, "Utilities Shrink the Role of Coal," *USA Today*, **Sept. 22, 2008, p. 4B.**
Power companies are shifting away from coal-fired electricity amid increased regulatory hurdles due to global warming concerns.

Gerstenzang, James, and Janet Wilson, "White House Puts Warming Threats on Back Burner," *Los Angeles Times*, **July 12, 2008, p. A1.**
The Bush administration rejects the Environmental Protection Agency's conclusions about global warming threats.

Gore, Al, "The Climate for Change," *The New York Times*, **Nov. 9, 2008, p. WK10.**
The former vice president emphasizes the need for direct government investments in clean energy technology.

Johnson, Dirk, "Chicago Unveils Multifaceted Plan to Curb Emissions of Heat-Trapping Gases," *The New York Times*, **Sept. 19, 2008, p. A13.**
Following 18 months of research, Chicago Mayor Richard M. Daley releases a plan to reduce greenhouse gas emissions by 25 percent by 2020.

McGreevey, Patrick, and Margot Roosevelt, "Sprawl Measure OKd, Smog Bill Dies," *Los Angeles Times*, **Oct. 1, 2008, p. B1.**
The California legislature has approved a bill that rewards communities that take urban sprawl and global warming into account in their development planning.

Perlman, Ellen, "Mr. Sustainability," *Governing*, **April 2008, p. 36.**
The new sustainability coordinator in Fayetteville, Ark., is succeeding in his efforts to get city departments to cut down on energy usage.

Roosevelt, Margot, "California Offers to Lead on Climate Change Fight," *Los Angeles Times*, **Nov. 20, 2008, p. A22.**
Led by California, a dozen U.S. states have agreed with counterparts in five countries overseas to reduce greenhouse gas emissions.

Swope, Christopher, "Local Warming," *Governing*, **December 2007, p. 25.**
Many communities throughout the country, particularly those in the Seattle area, are starting to plan for the consequences of climate change.

Reports and Studies

"Analysis of the Lieberman-Warner Climate Security Act (S. 2191)," *American Council for Capital Formation, National Association of Manufacturers*, **March 2008, www.accf.org/pdf/NAM/fullstudy031208.pdf.**
Examining a congressional cap-and-trade proposal, a study underwritten by two business groups finds that it would severely undermine economic growth.

Aulisi, Andrew, *et al.*, **"Climate Policy in the State Laboratory: How States Influence Federal Regulation and the Implications for Climate Change Policy in the United States,"** *World Resources Institute*, **August 2007, pdf.wri.org/climate_policy_in_the_state_laboratory.pdf.**
An environmental organization provides a report on states' aggressive climate change policies, with particular attention to those in California and the Northeast's Regional Greenhouse Gas Initiative.

Bedsworth, Louise, and Ellen Hanak, "Preparing California for a Changing Climate," *Public Policy Institute of California*, **November 2008, www.ppic.org/content/pubs/report/R_1108LBR.pdf.**
A leading think tank finds that California is not prepared to cope with global warming.

Pollin, Robert, *et al.*, **"Green Recovery: A Program to Create Good Jobs and Start Building a Low-Carbon Economy,"** *Center for American Progress*, **September 2008, www.americanprogress.org/issues/2008/09/pdf/green_recovery.pdf.**
Economists at the University of Massachusetts find that a $100 billion initiative would both lower greenhouse gas emissions and provide an economic stimulus for the country.

For More Information

American Council for Capital Formation, 1750 K St., N.W., Suite 400, Washington, DC 20006; (202) 293-5811; www.aacf.org. A business research group that promotes economic growth and "cost effective environmental policies."

Climate Change Division, U.S. Environmental Protection Agency, 1200 Pennsylvania Ave., N.W., Washington, DC 20460; (202) 343-9990; www.epa.gov/climatechange. Provides comprehensive information about science, health effects, regulations and policies concerning global warming.

Climate Communities, 1130 Connecticut Ave., N.W., Suite 300, Washington, DC 20036; (202) 261-6011; www .climatecommunities.us. A national coalition of cities and counties that lobbies and educates federal policy makers in support of local efforts to address climate change.

Competitive Enterprise Institute, 1899 L St., N.W., 12th Floor, Washington, DC 20036; (202) 340-4034; www.cei .org. A think tank and advocacy organization that promotes free enterprise and limited government.

Environmental Council of the States, 444 N. Capitol St., N.W., Suite 445, Washington, DC 20001; (202) 624-3660; www.ecos.org. The association of state environmental agencies, provides a clearinghouse of information for members and lobbies federal authorities.

Heartland Institute, 19 S. LaSalle St., Suite 903, Chicago, IL 60603; (312) 377-4000; www.globalwarmingheartland .org. A conservative think tank that presents conferences and issues publications skeptical about the role of humans in causing climate change.

ICLEI-Local Governments for Sustainability, 436 14th St., Suite 1520, Oakland, CA 94612; (510) 844-0699; www .iclei.org/us. An international organization that provides grants and technical assistance to local governments seeking to increase energy efficiency.

Mayors Climate Protection Center, U.S. Conference of Mayors, 1620 I St., N.W., Washington, DC 20006; (202) 861-6700; http://usmayors.org/climateprotection. Provides assistance to mayors attempting to reduce greenhouse gas emissions.

Pew Center on Global Climate Change, 2010 Wilson Blvd., Suite 1550, Arlington, VA 22201; (703) 516-4146; www.pewclimate.org. Supports and disseminates research related to climate change.

U.S. Climate Change Science Program, 1717 Pennsylvania Ave., N.W., Washington, DC 20006; (202) 223-6262; www .climatescience.gov. Integrates research on climate change performed by 13 federal agencies

13

Carbon Trading

Will it Reduce Global Warming?

Jennifer Weeks

A worker pours chemicals into a vat of molasses used to make ethanol in Simbhaoli, Uttar Pradeshi, India. Replacing gasoline with ethanol in cars can reduce emissions of carbon-based "greenhouse gases" (GHGs), created by burning fossil fuels, which contribute to climate change. Projects in developing countries that produce such alternative fuels are part of an international carbon trading scheme that allows polluters in industrialized countries to "offset" some of their GHG emissions by buying pollution credits from companies in developing countries.

From *CQ Researcher*,
November 2008

It's little wonder that Tirumala temple in Tirupati, in the south Indian state of Andhra Pradesh, prepares 30,000 meals for visiting Hindu pilgrims daily. The shrine is among the busiest religious pilgrimage sites in the world. In years past, cooks fired up pollution-spewing diesel generators to power their stoves to boil water in massive cauldrons. But today there's a new, clean energy source: the sun. Curved solar collectors heat water up to 280 degrees Centigrade, creating steam to cook foods such as rice, lentils and vegetables.[1]

"With most businesses, the first question is of economics," says engineer Deepak Gadhia, whose company built the system. "But spiritual organizations look at larger issues. They want energy that is spiritually positive."[2]

In fact, the temple does quite well financially, too, and so do many other temples, schools and government offices throughout India that use energy-saving systems built by Gadhia and his wife. The energy they save enables them to amass credits that can be used in a process called "carbon trading" — buying and selling rights to emit greenhouse gases.

Two years ago, the energy-saving systems at those sites were approved as carbon credit sources under the Kyoto Protocol.[3] The international agreement is designed to stem global warming, and — among other things — allows some developing countries to profit from projects that reduce emissions of greenhouse gases (GHGs) that cause climate change. (*See sidebar, p. 292.*)

Under the protocol, most of the world's wealthy countries agreed to reduce their GHG emissions by fixed percentages between 2008 and 2012, mainly by reducing energy use and switching to

Which Countries Emit the Most Carbon Dioxide?

Australia and major oil producing countries like the United States, Norway, Russia, Canada, Saudi Arabia, Kuwait and other Gulf states emit the most carbon dioxide (CO_2) per capita. Carbon dioxide is the most abundant greenhouse gas — one of several blamed for causing global warming.

Carbon Dioxide Emissions Per Capita, 2004
(in metric tons*)

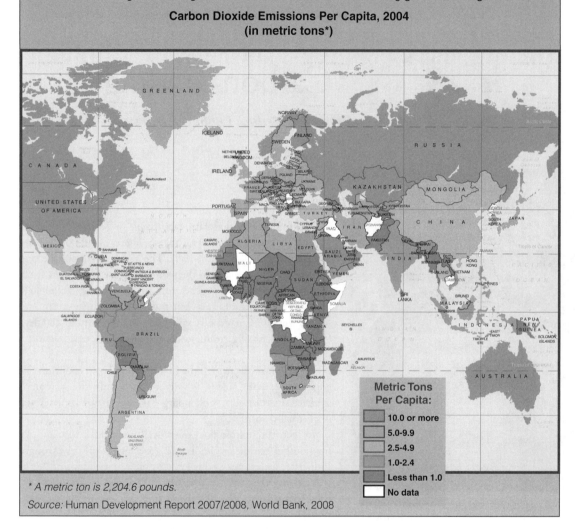

Metric Tons Per Capita:

- 10.0 or more
- 5.0-9.9
- 2.5-4.9
- 1.0-2.4
- Less than 1.0
- No data

* A metric ton is 2,204.6 pounds.

Source: Human Development Report 2007/2008, World Bank, 2008

low-carbon fuels. But if they can't reach the required reductions, rich nations can also "offset" some of their GHG emissions by buying credits from energy-saving projects — like the Gadhia solar cookers — in developing countries.

If U.N. officials certify that those projects reduce GHG emissions beyond levels that would have occurred otherwise, they can sell "certified emission reductions," each representing one avoided metric ton of carbon dioxide (CO_2). Companies in industrialized nations buy these credits to help reach their GHG reduction targets.

Virtually all scientists agree that human use of carbon-based fossil fuels such as oil, coal and natural gas is raising concentrations of heat-trapping gases in the atmosphere to the highest levels in at least 650,000 years.[4] The gases are called "greenhouse" gases because their heat-trapping properties warm the Earth's surface, much as the glass walls of a greenhouse retain the sun's heat. Unless countries sharply reduce their GHG emissions by mid-century, the buildup of greenhouse gases — often referred to as "carbon" emissions since carbon dioxide (CO_2) is by far the most abundant GHG in Earth's atmosphere — could cause dramatic planetary warming. Climate scientists predict that higher temperatures will cause melting of the polar ice caps, rising sea levels and more intense droughts, floods and hurricanes.[5]

The Kyoto Protocol, which was signed in 1997 and went into effect in 2005, requires major industrialized countries (except for the United States, which failed to ratify the agreement) to reduce their GHG emissions, on average, by 5.2 percent below 1990 levels.[6] Members of the European Union vowed to reduce their emissions even farther — to 8 percent below 1990 levels by 2012. At the same time, the EU launched the world's largest mandatory carbon emissions trading system, in which governments cap national emissions and allow polluters to buy and sell permits to emit carbon dioxide. Australia, Canada and Japan are developing their own emission reduction systems, which will likely include some form of carbon trading.

Global interest in carbon trading is part of a gradual movement toward market-based environmental policies — strategies that give polluters economic incentives to clean up instead of simply telling them how much pollution they can release and what kinds of controls to install. The approach makes sense because climate change is what scholars refer to as a "commons problem" — in which a resource (in this case, Earth's atmosphere) is held in common by everyone. Individual polluters profit more by using and degrading a common resource than by cleaning it up while their competitors continue polluting.

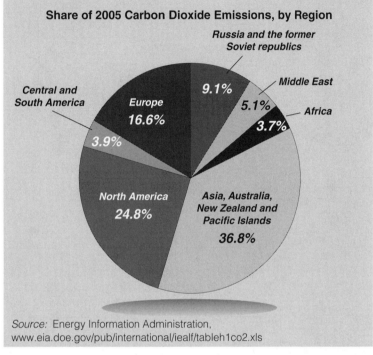

Most Emissions Come From Asia, North America

Nearly two-thirds of the world's carbon dioxide emissions — the main pollutant blamed for global warming — came from Asia and North America in 2005.

Share of 2005 Carbon Dioxide Emissions, by Region

Russia and the former Soviet republics 9.1%
Middle East 5.1%
Africa 3.7%
Europe 16.6%
Central and South America 3.9%
North America 24.8%
Asia, Australia, New Zealand and Pacific Islands 36.8%

Source: Energy Information Administration, www.eia.doe.gov/pub/international/iealf/tableh1co2.xls

"The rational man finds that his share of the cost of the wastes he discharges into the commons is less than the cost of purifying his wastes before releasing them," wrote biologist Garrett Hardin in a famous 1968 essay that identified commons problems as a central challenge for modern societies. "Since this is true for everyone, we are locked into a system of 'fouling our own nest,' so long as we behave only as independent, rational, free-enterprisers."[7]

Climate experts agree that one of the best ways around the commons problem is to "put a price on carbon" by making factories, power plants and other large GHG sources pay for their emissions. Hitting them in the pocketbook gives them more incentive to clean up — for example, by imposing a tax so that every source pays for its own GHG emissions at some set rate per ton.

However, an alternative approach — trading emission allotments — has become increasingly popular in

Europe Leads the World in Carbon Trading

The European Union accounted for 70 percent of the 40 billion ($60 billion) spent worldwide to buy carbon emission allowances in 2007. The Clean Development Mechanism, which allows companies in industrialized countries to buy emission credits from companies in the developing world, accounted for 29 percent.

Distribution of Carbon Trading Contracts, by Financial Value, 2007

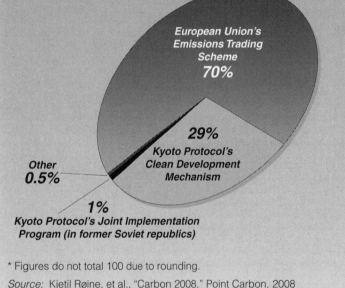

European Union's Emissions Trading Scheme **70%**

29% Kyoto Protocol's Clean Development Mechanism

Other **0.5%**

1% Kyoto Protocol's Joint Implementation Program (in former Soviet republics)

* Figures do not total 100 due to rounding.

Source: Kjetil Røine, et al., "Carbon 2008," Point Carbon, 2008

them decide how, it will stimulate research and development into a wide range of new, clean technologies. "It puts an infrastructure in place that releases capital for long-term investments," Hasselknippe explains.

Global carbon markets have grown quickly since the Kyoto Protocol entered into force in 2005. The total value of international carbon trades increased more than 80 percent between 2006 and 2007, from €22 billion ($33 billion) to €40 billion ($60 billion).[8] The market is expected to grow still larger as Europe lowers its cap on GHG emissions, and new trading systems gear up in some U.S. states and in other countries.[9]

Moreover, public support is growing for the U.S. government to act on climate change. President George W. Bush rejected the Kyoto treaty shortly after taking office in 2001, claiming that capping GHG emissions would harm the U.S. economy. But since then 23 states have joined regional carbon trading schemes, and the United States is widely expected to participate in a post-Kyoto agreement

recent decades. It is usually enacted through so-called cap-and-trade policies, in which regulators set an overall cap on emissions and then issue quotas that limit how much pollution each company can release. If a company wants or needs to emit more than its allowance, it must buy permits from cleaner companies that don't need all their allotments. Over time, regulators can lower a country's cap to further reduce total pollution.

Advocates say carbon emissions trading encourages companies to use clean fuels and technologies because firms that reduce their own emissions can then sell their unneeded allowances. "The carbon market gives companies an incentive to reduce emissions so they can make money," says Henrik Hasselknippe, global carbon services director for Point Carbon, an international market research firm in Oslo, Norway. Moreover, he predicts, since carbon trading tells companies to limit their emissions but lets

to limit GHG emissions after 2012.[10] Many U.S. political leaders, including both major presidential candidates, say the United States should create a cap-and-trade system similar to Europe's to cut GHG emissions in the United States far below 1990 levels by 2050.[11]

Ironically, several market-based elements were included in the Kyoto agreement at U.S. insistence in hope of convincing the United States to sign on to the treaty. They included two programs that let companies in industrialized countries offset some emissions by investing in carbon reduction projects elsewhere. The Clean Development Mechanism (CDM) paves the way for projects in developing countries, such as Gadhia's steam cookers at the temples in India, while Joint Implementation (JI) supports projects in other industrialized countries, mainly former Soviet satellite countries that are transitioning to market economies.

However, offset projects are controversial for several reasons. First, companies in industrialized countries can emit more carbon than is allowed under their countries' total allowable levels under the Kyoto Protocol by buying credits from developing countries, which have no emission caps. In effect, offsets allow industrialized countries to outsource reductions to places where they can be done more cheaply.

Supporters say offsets are primarily designed to lower the cost of meeting Kyoto targets, and that it shouldn't matter where reductions take place because a ton of CO_2 causes the same amount of warming whether it's released in Germany or Malaysia. But others worry that if rich countries rely on offsets too heavily, they will have little incentive to reduce fossil fuel use or develop cleaner technologies. Ultimately, they argue, developing countries will refuse to make deep cuts in their own emissions if they see little change in rich countries.

"The developed world is responsible for the majority of greenhouse gas emissions," the World Wildlife Fund warned in 2007. "If the [European Union] is to maintain its status as a major player in global climate change negotiations, then it must put its own back yard in order first and ensure that Europe is placed firmly on a path towards a low carbon economy."[12]

Moreover, say critics, offset projects sometimes credit "anyway tons" — reductions from projects that would have gone forward anyway, even without extra revenue from selling emission reductions. Reductions are supposed to be "additional" to business as usual, but that concept can be hard to prove.

As governments, corporations and advocacy groups weigh the pros and cons of carbon trading, here are some issues they are debating:

Are current trading systems working?

Global carbon markets are booming, but some experts question whether carbon trading systems are making emission reductions affordable or reducing GHG emissions at all.

Two markets dominated world carbon trading through 2007. The European Union's Emissions Trading Scheme (EU ETS) accounted for 70 percent of trades by value, followed by the Clean Development Mechanism, which accounted for 29 percent. Joint Implementation projects and all other carbon trading forums generated less than 2 percent.

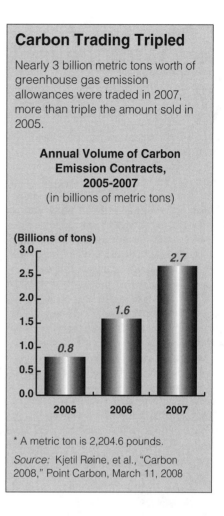

Carbon Trading Tripled

Nearly 3 billion metric tons worth of greenhouse gas emission allowances were traded in 2007, more than triple the amount sold in 2005.

Annual Volume of Carbon Emission Contracts, 2005-2007
(in billions of metric tons)

(Billions of tons)

- 2005: 0.8
- 2006: 1.6
- 2007: 2.7

* A metric ton is 2,204.6 pounds.

Source: Kjetil Røine, et al., "Carbon 2008," Point Carbon, March 11, 2008

During its trial phase from 2005 through 2007, the EU ETS produced mixed results. Carbon allowances initially traded for €20-30 (about $30-$45) per ton of CO_2, but in April 2006 the Czech Republic, Estonia, the Netherlands, Switzerland and France announced that their 2005 GHG emissions had been lower than expected. Demand for allowances fell sharply. Share prices plunged to €10-15 ($15-23) within a few days. And prices for allowances that were valid only for the trial period — and hence not usable after 2007 — fell to almost zero in early 2007. Allowances then stabilized at €15-25 ($23-38) for the second trading period.[13]

Some observers called the price gyrations a sign that the ETS was failing. Open Europe, a London think tank, charged that ETS had failed to provide either a "workable

How Greenhouse Gases Are Measured

When discussing greenhouse gas (GHG) emissions, businesses and government agencies often use shorthand terms, like "carbon" or "carbon dioxide," to refer to the various gases emitted when carbon-based fuels are burned.

The Kyoto Protocol and other schemes to regulate greenhouse gases cover six major types of emissions that remain in the atmosphere for a significant time, trapping heat that is reflected back to Earth, which warms the planet's surface. Most are caused by various human activities.

Climate scientists have assigned each gas a global warming potential (GWP), based on its heat-trapping properties. A GWP value measures the impact a gas has on the climate over a given time period (usually 100 years) compared to the heat-producing impact of a ton of carbon dioxide (CO_2) — the most abundant greenhouse gas. For example, methane's GWP value is 25, which means that a ton of methane released into the atmosphere will cause as much warming as 25 tons of CO_2 over a 100-year period.[1] Thus, the higher the GWP, the more global warming the gas causes.

Carbon trading schemes allow emitters to trade allowances to release some or all of the six types of gases, whichever are covered by a particular system. For example, under the Kyoto Protocol, so-called Clean Development Mechanism (CDM) projects in developing countries can generate credits that they can then sell abroad by reducing their own emissions from any of the six GHG categories. Each credit certifies that the project has reduced greenhouse gas emissions by the equivalent of one metric ton (2,205 pounds) of carbon dioxide per year.

Under the European Union's Emissions Trading System (EU ETS), an electric power company in Italy might buy credits to cover excess CO_2 emissions created by its coal- or oil-fired power plants. These credits could come from

Types of Greenhouse Gases

GHG Categories	GWP Value*	Major Sources
Carbon dioxide (CO_2)	1	Fossil fuel combustion, deforestation
Methane (CH_4)	25	Landfills, rice paddies, digestive tracts of cattle and sheep
Nitrous oxide (N_2O)	298	Fertilizer, animal waste
Hydrofluorocarbons (HFCs)	Varies (up to 14,800)	Semiconductor manufacturing and other industrial processes
Perfluorocarbons (PFCs)	Varies (up to 12,200)	Same as HFCs, plus aluminum smelting
Sulfur hexafluoride (SF_6)	22,800	Electrical transmission systems, magnesium and aluminum production

* Global warming potential

Source: U.S. Environmental Protection Agency

CDM projects that reduced other GHG emissions through such actions as collecting methane emissions from landfills or reducing hydrofluorocarbon leakage at aluminum-smelting plants. Using the GWP values for these gases, project owners can calculate how many tons of CO_2 equivalent the project releases or avoids, and then sell the reduction credits easily across international borders.

[1] U.S. Environmental Protection Agency, "Inventory of U.S. Greenhouse Gas Emissions and Sinks: Fast Facts," April 2008.

market in carbon" or reduced emissions.[14] Others said market volatility was not surprising for the trial phase of a new system without historical data to guide it.

"Since companies had not previously been required to track and disclose emissions, there were no hard numbers on which to base allocations," wrote Annie Petsonk, an attorney for the New York-based Environmental Defense Fund. "So companies were asked how much they'd need to emit, and naturally they said, 'A lot!'

When emissions data became available and companies saw that cutting emissions was easier than they anticipated, the price of allowances plummeted."[15]

In a detailed assessment, Massachusetts Institute of Technology (MIT) economists A. Denny Ellerman and Paul Joskow pointed out that ETS was not intended to deliver big emissions cuts during its trial run, and that estimating emissions for any given year is difficult because weather patterns and fuel prices affect fossil fuel use.

Similar fluctuations occurred when the United States launched a trading program for sulfur dioxide (SO_2) allowances in the late 1990s, they noted, and as in the SO_2 program, ETS allowance prices settled down once policy makers had some real emissions data to work with.[16]

In its second trading period, which runs from 2008 through 2012, the EU's total emissions cap is 6.5 percent below the 2005 level. "Leaders learned their lesson after they over-allocated allowances in Phase I, and the cap is more stringent now. They have definitely done a better job in Phase 2," says Anja Kollmuss, an analyst at the Stockholm Environment Institute (SEI).

EU leaders now are grappling with new challenges for Phase 3, which starts in 2013, including bringing more emitters under the pollution cap. Currently the ETS only covers six sectors — energy, iron and steel, cement, glass, ceramics and pulp and paper — which produce about 45 percent of EU emissions. The European Parliament voted in July 2008 to include aviation emissions, beginning in 2012, and EU government ministers formally approved the policy in October over industry resistance.[17] Airlines assert that their industry has been hit hard by high oil prices and that the EU does not have legal authority to regulate emissions from flights, regardless of where airlines are based. (*See "At Issue," p. 305.*) European leaders also propose to include emissions from petrochemicals, aluminum and ammonia production in Phase 3.

Another critique points up flaws in both the ETS and CDM systems. In a 2007 report, the World Wildlife Fund warned that many EU countries might allow emitters to use offset credits from CDM and JI projects to meet most or all of their Phase 2 EU emission limits. Because they are not buying allowances from other EU sources, that would mean they aren't really cutting carbon among EU emitters.[18]

That prospect raises two problems, says Kollmuss. First, the Kyoto Protocol and EU directives say offsets should be "supplemental" to direct reductions. "When emitters can use a high fraction of offset credits, some sectors may not have to actually cut their emissions at all," she says.

Second, some offsets fail the "additionality" test, critics say, which occurs when the GHG reductions they produce are not additional to what would have happened anyway. For example, if local law already requires landfill owners to collect methane emissions instead of venting them into the air, they should not be able to market that action as a CDM project and sell the emission credits to a company in an industrialized country. Conversely, they say, if there is no clear financial reason to carry out a project unless it can produce CDM credits that can be sold, then the project is probably additional.

"Additionality is a simple concept, but it often comes down to subjective decisions," says Kollmuss. "And it's very easily fudged."

As one example, Stanford University law professors Michael Wara and David Victor pointed out in a 2008 paper that nearly all new renewable and gas-fired power plants in China are applying for CDM credits, even though China's energy sector is growing rapidly and the Chinese government has asked companies to invest in non-coal energy sources. Given these trends, they contend, China would probably be moving toward lower-carbon fuels even without CDM credits for new power plants. "[I]n practice, much of the current CDM market does not reflect actual reductions in emissions, and that trend is poised to get worse," the authors argued.[19]

Such controversies have spurred development of an entirely new industry of consultants and third-party certifiers who screen and verify claims from "green" development projects and help buyers find high-quality offset sources. (*See sidebar, p. 300.*)

U.N. officials acknowledge that additionality is a key challenge but argue that the CDM has effective rules for measuring it. They also point out that that the CDM has generated three times more funding for climate-friendly technology transfers to developing countries than direct foreign aid programs.

"Has the Kyoto Protocol's Clean Development Mechanism met the goal for which it was designed?" Yvo de Boer, executive secretary of the U.N. Framework Convention on Climate Change, asked in October. "In my view, the answer is yes."[20]

The EU has barred using reforestation projects in developing countries as offsets because regulators say reductions from these projects are hard to measure and can be quickly reversed (for example, if a forest plantation burns down). Ironically, developing countries without large industrial sectors would have a better chance of earning money through the CDM if the EU accepted forestry credits, since farming and forestry projects are among their best options for slowing climate change.

Carbon marketers generally see the CDM as an important tool despite its flaws. "CDM has the strictest review and approval process for emission reduction projects in the world," says Point Carbon's Hasselknippe. "Some offset projects in North America [where companies are experimenting with emission reductions and trading] are even more questionable than CDM projects. Without a regulated market, anything goes."

Are there better ways to cut emissions?

Creating carbon markets and trading carbon emission allowances is the best way to speed the transition to a low-carbon world, say proponents, because it puts a limit on carbon pollution and creates big profit incentives for cutting emissions. But critics see it as a complicated scheme that isn't guaranteed to deliver innovative energy solutions. Instead, some say, carbon taxes would be a simpler and more direct way to slow climate change.

Both approaches make polluters pay for carbon emissions, which spurs investments in cleaner technologies — with one important difference. In cap-and-trade schemes regulators specify how much pollution can be emitted, but they can't predict exactly how much allowances will cost once trading starts. Many factors, including weather, economic conditions and the discovery of new technologies influence fossil fuel use, which can drive demand for carbon allowances either up or down.

Economists can model what allowance prices may look like, but experience can be quite different from predictions, as the U.S. acid rain trading program of the 1990s (*see p. 302*) and the trial phase of EU ETS both showed.

Carbon taxes, on the other hand, charge polluters a set rate for each ton of greenhouse gases released, so there are no surprises about compliance costs. Regulators can't be sure, however, how taxes will affect pollution levels because they don't know how businesses will handle those costs. Some companies may pay taxes on their emissions and pass the expense on to consumers, while others clean up their operations to avoid the extra charge. In other words, carbon taxes offer more certainty for businesses, but cap-and-trade systems provide more certainty that the environment will improve.

"A tax doesn't put any legal limits on how much pollution can be released, so it's like a blind bet," says Fred Krupp, president of the Environmental Defense Fund

(EDF). "You know what the ante is, but not what the payoff will be. Only a cap guarantees results."

Norway has achieved mixed results since it imposed a $65-per-ton carbon tax on oil and gas companies in 1991. The tax prompted StatoilHydro, one of Norway's largest energy companies, to sharply cut its carbon emissions, largely by pumping them into an undersea reservoir. Today the firm is one of the world's few companies doing large-scale geologic storage of CO_2 emissions.[21]

But StatoilHydro also has expanded drilling operations since the tax was levied. So, even though the company is more carbon efficient than many other big energy producers, its net emissions have increased as world demand for oil has grown. Today Norway's total GHG emissions are 15 percent higher than in 1991. Norway still has the tax in place, but it also has joined the EU ETS, even though it is not an EU member.

Cap-and-trade supporters also argue that carbon trading generates larger investments in new technologies than taxes do, because polluters can turn emissions into income by cleaning them up and selling their unneeded allowances. "A tax creates no such market and, so, fails to enlist the full range of human potential in a struggle where every bit of creativity is needed," writes Krupp.[22] But many energy experts say a whole suite of measures is needed to commercialize new energy technologies and that the process shouldn't be left up to market forces. Rather, they argue, a combination of big governmental investments and other measures like tax credits and clean energy targets are needed to help ensure that clean technologies are put to use.

"Emissions trading won't do much to stimulate investment in research and development of technologies that may be able to deliver deep cuts in emissions in the future," says Chris Riedy, research director at the CAP Institute for Sustainable Futures at the University of Technology in Sydney, Australia. "Markets are very good at meeting short-term goals but not so good at looking many years ahead."

Australia is developing a national carbon trading plan, Riedy notes, but it also has established a national target to generate 20 percent of its energy from renewable fuels by 2020. "That will ensure that renewable energy is developed over time until it can establish itself in the market," says Riedy. "We need to give the industry some long-term certainty."

The challenge is even larger in fast-growing countries like China, India and Brazil, which are just now industrializing and have not yet accepted binding caps on GHG emissions. As those countries raise their living standards over the next several decades, they will account for a rising share of world energy consumption. It is crucial to help those countries move onto clean energy pathways in order to slow climate change.

For instance, carbon trading could become an important option for China at some point, says Yang Fuqiang, chief representative in Beijing for the U.S.-based Energy Foundation. "China is now the top CO_2 emitter in the world, and we expect that its emissions will be much larger by 2030, perhaps as much as 20 percent of world emissions," he says. "If carbon becomes a commodity that is traded in the market, and China is the biggest source, trading can help China make more cuts because businesses will see value in carbon."

But several things must happen before carbon trading becomes a useful tool for cutting Chinese GHG emissions, Yang continues. First, Beijing must make a political commitment to reducing emissions. Then the Chinese government must fund development of clean energy sources. Carbon trading will not work, however, without a strong legal system to ensure trades are protected and penalties enforced if partners violate the rules.

"China's legal systems aren't strong enough for carbon trading yet," says Yang.

Does carbon trading help developing countries?

Global climate change policy has been complicated by the need to create strategies that enable countries to share the burdens fairly. Because developed nations got rich from fossil-fueled growth and produced most of the human-driven warming that has occurred to date, the framers of the Kyoto Protocol decided that developed countries should make the deepest GHG emissions cuts. However, large developing countries like China and India are rapidly becoming the world's biggest carbon sources, so it is also crucial to limit their emissions while allowing their citizens to enjoy rising standards of living, say climate experts.

"[W]e need to provide resources to see that the developing countries don't get hooked onto the same path of development that we have," said Rajendra K. Pachauri,

China's booming growth has made it one of the world's top emitters of carbon dioxide, the most abundant greenhouse gas (GHG). Advocates of carbon trading say that if China were to set formal limits on its GHG emissions, polluters would have an incentive to cut emissions in order to trade their allowances for cash.

chairman of the Intergovernmental Panel on Climate Change (IPCC), which advises governments on climate science.[23]

The Clean Development Mechanism was designed as a first step to help poor countries grow while reducing their emissions. But critics argue that CDM projects primarily benefit the rich nations that sponsor them and that some actually damage the environment in the host countries.

For instance, the environmental advocacy group International Rivers charged in a 2007 report that awarding carbon reduction credits to numerous hydropower projects resulted in "blindly subsidizing the destruction of rivers, while the dams it supports are helping destroy the environmental integrity of the CDM." The study contended that the CDM has few standards to block projects that harm nearby ecosystems and that many hydropower projects applying for CDM credit would clearly be built in any case. As examples it cited a 60-megawatt dam in Kenya that started construction in 1999 (before the CDM was established) and an 880-megawatt dam in Brazil that applied for CDM validation six months after it began generating power in May 2007.[24]

Funding is not the only yardstick, replies U.N. spokesman David Abbass. "A company might have the ability to undertake an emission-reduction improvement, but not the incentive," he says. "If CDM was a motivating factor, then the project could potentially qualify, regardless of when construction was begun. In most hydro projects, CDM is providing incentives for efficiency improvements such as installing more efficient turbines. Such a decision could be undertaken after dam construction has begun or even after the dam has entered operation."

Forest carbon credits are also controversial. Under the CDM program, carbon credits can be granted for planting trees on formerly forested land that is either being reforested or used for other purposes. Many early CDM forestry projects were commercial tree plantations that were popular because planting swathes of fast-growing tree species absorbs large quantities of carbon. But opponents complained that such projects sometimes ended up clearing large areas of native forest, expelling local populations and damaging the environment.

"The fact that eucalyptus absorbs carbon dioxide to grow . . . can never be used to justify the environmental, social, economic and cultural damage that has occurred in places where large-scale monoculture tree plantations have been implemented in our country," wrote 53 unions and nonprofits in 2003 opposing a tree plantation proposed by a company called Plantar in the Brazilian state of Minas Gerais. The project ultimately was approved by the CDM board after three tries, not for absorbing carbon into the trees but for using a low-carbon process to turn those trees into charcoal.[25]

"The CDM is riven with fraud, just like other government-to-government aid programs, and it doesn't save any carbon," says Michael Northcott, a divinity professor at Scotland's Edinburgh University who views carbon trading as a route by which governments can avoid imposing hard limits on GHG emissions. Citing projects like the Plantar venture, Northcott writes, "The new global carbon market is not incentivizing real reductions in emissions. But it has created tremendous, new trading opportunities and new opportunities for fraud and injustice."[26]

Now, however, awarding credits for forest protection is gaining new support from tropical countries and conservation experts, who say forests can soak up carbon emissions, protect biodiversity and provide economic benefits to developing nations. Advocates are proposing some new approaches to make this method more rigorous. For example, avoided emissions would be measured

at the national level instead of project by project, so it would be harder for a host country to claim credit for saving one forest while it cut down others.[27]

Advocates say the new approach would reward countries that preserve their forests instead of cutting them down and then seeking carbon credits for new tree plantations. "Central African countries consider that their efforts made in managing forests deserve to be recognized and supported, because they are positive for climate," the 15-member Coalition of Rainforest Nations contended in 2007.[28] More than 300 national leaders, research institutes and conservation groups have signed a policy statement urging governments to include tropical forests in global carbon markets.[29]

As negotiations on a post-Kyoto climate treaty proceed, CDM officials say the program needs to be scaled up. "Carbon markets and market-based mechanisms, like the [CDM], are essential for achieving the large shifts in investment required . . . to put the world on a clean path to development," said the U.N.'s de Boer.[30]

For the long term, some experts are thinking beyond the CDM model. "The CDM only lets developing countries trade credits if they prove additionality project-by-project, which is a nightmare. It's cumbersome, it leads to endless arguments and small countries have been squeezed out by big projects in China, India and Brazil," says EDF's Krupp. "We should . . . offer all developing nations technical assistance and more generous emissions targets if they agree to cap their emissions quickly. We need a global system where everyone agrees to a cap that's fair, given their level of development."

Even CDM advocates agree that benefits have been spread unequally up to now. About three-quarters of all CDM projects to date are located in China, Brazil, India and South Korea.[31] Many poor regions like sub-Saharan Africa, which are extremely vulnerable to the negative impacts of climate change, have seen little benefit from carbon trading.

"So far, the poorest developing countries have been bypassed — and there have been limited benefits for broad-based sustainable development" from carbon trading, the U.N. Development Programme observed in its 2007/2008 *Human Development Report.* "Marginal women farmers in Burkina Faso or Ethiopia are not well placed to negotiate with carbon brokers in the City of London."

However, the report noted, new approaches, such as "bundling" many small, rural projects together for CDM credit, could help poor countries participate.[32] Under a 2006 initiative called the Nairobi Framework, the U.N. is working to channel CDM projects to countries in sub-Saharan Africa. In 2008 the U.N. Environment Programme estimated that CDM projects in Africa could generate nearly $1 billion worth of credits by 2012.[33]

BACKGROUND

Who Pays for Pollution?

The fledgling global carbon trading industry represents the intersection of two complex debates that stretch back for more than a century. Scientists have worked since the early 1800s to understand how Earth's climate systems function and whether human actions affect them. And for nearly as long, economists who study the environment have sought cost-effective ways to control pollution.

Climate science has been international from its earliest days. In 1859 Irish physicist John Tyndall showed that certain gases in the atmosphere absorbed heat. Svante Arrhenius, a Swedish chemist, built on this idea with his calculation in 1896 that doubling the quantity of CO_2 in the atmosphere would raise Earth's average by 5 to 6 degrees Centigrade. Other researchers have shown that natural processes also influence climate cycles. For example, in 1860, Scottish physicist James Croll theorized that regular variations in Earth's orbit could trigger ice ages. Eighty years later Milutin Milankovic, a Serbian geophysicist, calculated these variations more precisely and developed a theory of glacial periods, now known as Milankovic cycles.

Other environmental issues were more urgent in the early 1900s. Air and water in industrialized countries were already heavily polluted from factory operations and urban growth, but governments had little power to respond. In Britain and the United States the nuisance doctrine — an historic concept of English common law — held that people should not use their property in ways that infringed heavily on their neighbors and that injured parties could sue those responsible for noise, odors and toxic discharges. Noxious facilities such as metal smelters were frequent early targets for nuisance lawsuits in the United States.

Indonesian environmental activists at the U.N. climate change conference in Bali, Indonesia, last December demonstrate against a proposal to award carbon credits to tropical countries that join the Reducing Emissions From Deforestation and Degradation (REDD) program. The protesters say the Indonesian government can't handle the delicate and complicated carbon trading scheme and that the program will benefit developed countries and large corporations at the expense of indigenous communities. Delegates agreed to include forest conservation in future discussions on a new global warming treaty.

However, nuisance law was ineffective at controlling harmful discharges and emissions from large-scale industrial production. With pollution coming from many sources, it was hard to prove direct connections between discharges and impacts. Moreover, by the early 1900s, U.S. courts had come to view pollution as an unavoidable result of economic activity. Rather than shutting down dirty factories, they generally weighed harms against benefits and compensated plaintiffs for serious damages while allowing polluters to keep operating.[34]

Governments then developed new approaches, like zoning, which established rules for using large areas of land. City and state agencies enforced a growing body of public health laws barring practices such as dumping untreated waste into waterways. In 1920, British economist Arthur Pigou proposed a new option: pollution taxes. Pollution, he argued, was a "negative externality" — a production cost that polluters did not have to pay for. If

CHRONOLOGY

1900s-1960s *As scientists study Earth's climate, experts debate controlling pollution efficiently.*

1920 British economist Arthur Pigou suggests taxing polluters for the indirect costs of their emissions.

1945 Researchers start developing models to test atmospheric behavior.

1957 American geochemist Charles David Keeling begins measuring atmospheric carbon dioxide (CO_2) levels in Hawaii, where readings are not skewed by pollution.

1960 British economist Ronald Coase proposes tradable emission allowances.

1970s-1980s *Scientists warn that humans may be causing global warming. Stricter pollution controls are enacted.*

1970 Congress creates Environmental Protection Agency, expands Clean Air Act.

1972 First major global environmental conference — held in Stockholm, Sweden — spurs creation of United Nations Environment Programme.

1976 Scientists identify deforestation as a major cause of climate change.

1980 U.S. President Ronald Reagan's election signals a backlash against technology-specific regulations.

1987 Montreal Protocol sets international limits on ozone-destroying gases.

1988 U.N. creates Intergovernmental Panel on Climate Change (IPCC) to provide expert views on global warming.

1990 IPCC says global temperatures are rising and likely to keep increasing. . . . U.S. adopts emissions trading to reduce acid rain.

1990s *Governments pledge to tackle climate change, but worry about costs.*

1992 The United States and over 150 nations pledge to cut greenhouse gas (GHG) emissions below 1990 levels by 2000.

1995 IPCC finds that global warming has a "human-driven" signature.

1997 Kyoto Protocol is adopted after intense negotiations, requiring developed countries to cut GHG emissions 5.2 percent, on average, below 1990 levels by 2012. U.S. Senate refuses to ratify it until developing nations also are required to make cuts.

2000s-Present *Carbon emissions trading begins, primarily in Europe. Support grows in United States for action to reduce GHGs.*

2001 IPCC says major global warming is "very likely."

2002 Clean Development Mechanism (CDM) — which allows industrialized countries to partly fulfill their carbon-reduction commitments by purchasing GHG reductions in developing countries — begins.

2003 Chicago Climate Exchange launches voluntary GHG trading system for selected U.S. companies and nonprofits.

2005 Kyoto Protocol enters into force with only the United States and Australia as non-participating developed countries. . . . EU Emissions Trading Scheme begins trials. . . . Seven Northeastern states agree to form GHG cap-and-trade system for electric power plants.

2006 EU carbon allowance prices plummet after emissions are lower than expected. . . . Global carbon trading reaches $30 billion, triple the previous year's level. . . . California promises to cut CO_2 emissions 25 percent by 2020 and to start trading emissions in 2012.

2007 IPCC says climate warming is mostly due to human activities. . . . Australia joins Kyoto Protocol. . . . Three more states join Northeastern cap-and-trade system. . . . 180 countries agree to negotiate a post-Kyoto climate change treaty.

2008 EU emissions trading scheme enters Phase 2, with tighter caps. . . . U.N. proposes stricter standards for CDM projects.

CARBON TRADING **299**

manufacturers were taxed for their pollution they would have an incentive to pollute less, according to the theory.

Economists generally agreed with Pigou's approach, but environmental regulation did not gain a serious foothold until after World War II. Economic growth expanded worldwide in the 1950s and '60s, first in the United States and then in post-war Western Europe and Japan. Governments began to limit industrial pollution, but instead of taxing it they applied so-called command-and-control standards, which told polluters how much pollution they could release and often specified what kind of technologies had to be used to clean up their operations. The same standards applied to all producers, whether their operations were relatively clean or dirty. As a result, these laws imposed much larger costs on some sources than on others.

In 1960 University of Chicago economist Ronald Coase proposed a way to control pollution with lower total costs to society. If rights to pollute could be bought and sold, he argued, polluters could bargain and find an efficient way to distribute those rights. Other economists took up his idea and called for government regulators to limit total quantities of pollutants and then create markets for pollution rights.

"[N]o person, or agency, has to set the price — it is set by the competition among buyers and sellers of rights," wrote Canadian economist John Dales in 1968.[35] This approach was more effective, proponents contended, because producers (who knew more about their own costs and production methods than regulators) could decide who would clean up and find the best ways to do it.

International Cooperation

By the 1960s, protecting the environment was a national political issue in many industrialized countries. Social Democrat Willy Brandt campaigned for chancellor in West German in 1961 with a promise to clean up air pollution. Japanese activists began suing large polluters in the mid-1960s, pressuring regulators and industrialists into adopting tighter controls. In 1970 two versions of Earth Day were launched: an international celebration on the date of the spring equinox, formally endorsed by the United Nations, and a U.S. observance on April 22 that drew millions of Americans to rallies and teach-ins.

National governments began setting standards for air and water quality, waste management and land conservation. Then a 1972 international conference on the environment, held in Stockholm, set lofty goals for international cooperation and led to the formation of the United Nations Environment Programme. The conferees declared that most environmental problems in the developing world were caused by poverty and underdevelopment, and that rich countries should try to reduce the gap between rich and poor countries.[36]

Meanwhile, international cooperation was growing in the field of climate science. In the 1950s and '60s, international research groups in the United States, England, Mexico and elsewhere developed circulation models to simulate climate processes and began testing theories about how the system might change in response to natural or manmade events. French, Danish, Swiss, Russian and U.S. scientists drilled into ice sheets in Greenland and Antarctica and analyzed air bubbles trapped thousands of years earlier to determine how the atmosphere's composition had changed over time. A growing body of climate studies showed that many processes shaped global climate patterns, and that human actions could disrupt the system.

In 1976, frustrated with the slow pace of pollution reductions under the Clean Air Act, U.S. policymakers began experimenting with market-based measures. As a first step, companies were permitted to build new factories in polluted areas if they bought credits from nearby sources that had reduced emissions below legal limits. In 1977 Congress amended the act to allow policies like banking credits (saving them for use or sale in the future). In 1982 the Environmental Protection Agency (EPA) used a trading program to phase out lead from gasoline. Refiners were issued tradable lead credits that they could sell if they were already blending unleaded gasoline or use while retooling their plants. Lead, which had been outlawed from U.S. gasoline, was finally eliminated by 1987.

Other nations also tried market-based environmental policies, primarily pollution taxes. Many European countries — including West Germany, the Netherlands, Czechoslovakia and Hungary — taxed water pollution discharges to help fund sewage treatment and bring water quality up to healthy standards.[37] France and Japan imposed charges for air pollution emissions. China also

Nonprofit Auditors Keep Projects 'Honest'

Gold Standard projects provide jobs, help the environment.

Power outages and voltage fluctuations once plagued the Honduran city of La Esperanza, and many rural residents in the surrounding countryside had no electricity at all.

Now a small hydroelectric project on the nearby Intibuca River reliably produces 13.5 megawatts of electricity — enough to power 11,000 households for a year — while avoiding 37,000 tons of annual carbon dioxide emissions from diesel generators previously used to produce electricity. And because it is a so-called run-of-river project, it generates electricity without damming the river.

The La Esperanza Hydroelectric Project is the first to be certified as reducing greenhouse gas (GHG) emissions under the Kyoto Protocol's Clean Development Mechanism (CDM). The CDM allows Third World developers whose projects reduce carbon emissions to sell "emission credits" — equal to the emissions they avoid — to polluting companies in industrialized countries.

The project also will provide a variety of other sustainable benefits in the community, such as reducing local residents' use of carbon-consuming trees for fuel, encouraging reforestation and providing reliable jobs and technical skills for the dam construction, maintenance and operating staffs, providing running water for households near the project and engaging more women in work and community life.

How can La Esperanza's developers prove their facility will provide all those benefits? The project is being evaluated by Gold Standard, an independent, nonprofit organization in Basel, Switzerland. Founded by the World Wildlife Fund and other nongovernmental organizations and funded by public and private donors, Gold Standard accredits high-quality CDM projects that benefit the local community and cut carbon emissions. Gold Standard approval gives carbon-credit buyers extra assurance that the carbon credits they are purchasing come from measurable GHG reductions that have clearly benefited the host countries where they were carried out.

Nonprofits like Gold Standard have emerged to provide extra certification for carbon offset projects because of concerns that private verification companies, which are paid by project developers, have a financial incentive to certify that the projects they are auditing reduce carbon emissions just to get them approved. And the CDM Executive Board, which reviews CDM applications, does not have enough staff to verify all of the information submitted by auditors.

"Right now, good auditors get their projects approved, but that shouldn't be the only incentive," says Stanford University law professor Michael Wara. The CDM board has "done the best it can, but it's in an untenable situation," he contends, because it is understaffed and facing a growing demand for offset credits.

---

adopted air and water pollution taxes in the early 1980s, although these levies were quite low, and a large share of the funds were distributed back to pollution sources as subsidies.[38]

Then, in an important milestone for global environmental cooperation, 23 nations signed the Montreal Protocol in 1987, agreeing to restrict production and use of industrial chemicals that were damaging Earth's protective ozone layer. Over the next decade, as science showed that damage was still occurring, more nations joined, and members amended the agreement to eliminate the substances completely. Several nations used allowance trading systems to phase out domestic use of ozone-depleting chemicals, including the United States, Canada, Mexico and Singapore.

The protocol established some other important precedents: It relied on expert advice from scientists, forced governments to act in time to prevent serious environmental harm and required developed nations to help developing countries adjust to the ban without harming their living standards.[39]

Confronting the Evidence

By the late 1980s many environmentalists and scientists believed human activities were affecting Earth's climate and that policy makers needed to act. In 1988 the United Nations established the Intergovernmental Panel on Climate Change (IPCC) to advise national governments about climate science and potential impacts from global warming. But critics, including large

Some critics have claimed that as a result of these conflicts of interest and other problems, carbon markets, in effect, are generating "rights to pollute."

"We require project developers to make positive contributions to local communities in two out of three categories — economic, social and environmental — and our screening process gives them numbers they can use to rate what they're delivering in each area," says Caitlin Sparks, U.S. marketing director for Gold Standard. "We monitor those promises through the full life of the project. U.N.-accredited auditors validate and verify all of the documents, and the information is re-verified after the project starts."

For instance, all CDM projects are supposed to promote "sustainable development," but it's usually left up to the host country to define what that means. However, Gold Standard makes its own judgment.

"They are doing the sorts of things that should be applied wholesale to CDM," says Wara. "They dig in and do better verification, which costs more and makes the process more time-consuming, but that needs to happen. We need more scrutiny of these projects."

Gold Standard projects have three key features: They must focus on renewable energy or energy efficiency to help promote a transition to a clean-energy economy; developers must prove that the carbon reductions will be "additional" to business as usual (this test is optional when projects go through CDM review but is required by Gold Standard); and they must show that their projects will make measurable economic contributions to sustainable development in host communities.

"A free market for credits will tend to focus on quantities of tons," says Sparks. "The Gold Standard is meant to focus on quality" of emission reductions.

Gold Standard projects in India and South Africa reflect the program's diversity and focus on quality:

- The Shri Chamundi biomass co-generation power plant in Karnataka, India, will generate 16 megawatts of electricity from biomass fuels such as eucalyptus branches, coconut fronds, rice husks and cashew shells. It will also use waste heat to produce steam for manufacturing, replacing boilers that run on heavy fuel oil. The plant will create more than 800 jobs, including collecting and preparing biomass, converting previously useless crop residues into fuel. It also will reduce open burning of crop wastes in fields, which pollutes the atmosphere and local water supplies.
- In Cape Town, South Africa, the Kuyasa housing service upgrade project installed ceiling insulation, solar hot water heaters and energy-efficient lighting in a low-income housing development and will install similar improvements in future developments. Making homes more energy-efficient will reduce CO_2 emissions, local air pollution and the danger of household fires.[1]

---

[1] Information about these projects comes from validation reports in the Gold Standard Registry, http://goldstandard.apx.com; and "Reducing the Carbon Footprint of the UN: High-Level Event on Climate Change," U.N. Headquarters, Sept. 24, 2007, www.un.org/climatechange/2007highlevel/climatefriendly.shtml.

corporations and President George H. W. Bush, argued that the scientific evidence was uncertain and that reducing GHG emissions would seriously harm economic growth.

Other nations, led by Western European countries with strong Green parties, wanted a binding agreement to limit greenhouse emissions. The Framework Convention on Climate Change (FCCC), signed at the 1992 Earth Summit in Rio de Janeiro, Brazil, amounted to a compromise: It called only for voluntary reductions in greenhouse gases to 1990 levels but laid out a path for further action. Some countries — including the Netherlands, Sweden, Finland, Norway and Denmark — passed domestic carbon taxes to reduce their emissions. But total GHG emissions from industrialized nations kept

rising, making it clear that mandatory targets and timetables would be needed.

In 1997 FCCC members adopted the Kyoto Protocol, which required signatories to make specific reductions (averaging 5.2 percent below 1990 levels) by 2012. U.S. President Bill Clinton supported the goal, but his administration was worried about costs. A U.S. carbon tax was not an option: The administration had suffered an embarrassing defeat in 1993 when it proposed a BTU tax (a levy on the energy content of fuels), only to be blocked by fellow Democrats in Congress. Instead, U.S. negotiators at Kyoto pushed to include emissions trading and credits for funding offset projects in developing countries and former Eastern Bloc nations.

> "Marginal women farmers in Burkina Faso or Ethiopia are not well placed to negotiate with carbon brokers in the City of London."
>
> — *U.N. Human Development Report 2007/2008*

Although the final agreement included these policies and the Clinton administration signed the treaty, the Senate voted 95-0 for a resolution against ratifying it unless developing countries also had to make binding reduction pledges. President George W. Bush, who had promised during his campaign to limit carbon dioxide emissions, repudiated the Kyoto agreement shortly after taking office, arguing that mandatory GHG reductions (even through market-based mechanisms) would harm the U.S. economy.

Nonetheless, President Bush embraced the idea of emissions trading to address domestic air pollution issues and sought to build on a successful program initiated a decade earlier under the first Bush administration. In 1990 Congress had amended the Clean Air Act to create an emissions trading program for sulfur dioxide (SO_2) and nitrogen oxide (NO_x), two pollutants from fossil fuel-fired power plants. These emissions formed acids in the atmosphere that fell back to Earth in rain and snow, damaging forests, soils and buildings. The so-called acid rain trading program, which began in 1995, capped emissions of SO_2 (with looser limits for NO_x) and set up a trading market for emission allowances.

The program was widely viewed as a success. EPA reported in 2004 that a decade of emissions trading had reduced the power sector's SO_2 and NO_x emissions 34 and 38 percent, respectively, below 1990 levels.[40] Economists estimated trading had saved $1 billion or more per year over command-and-control approaches.[41] Touting these results, President Bush proposed emissions trading initiatives to cut U.S. SO_2 and NO_x emissions even further and suggested using a trading scheme to control mercury emissions. But congressional critics argued that these measures did not cut far or fast enough and that emissions trading was the wrong way to reduce toxic pollutants like mercury.[42]

As the Bush administration continued to oppose cutting GHG emissions, other U.S. leaders grew increasingly worried about climate change. Sens. John McCain, R-Ariz., and Joseph Lieberman, D-Conn., offered carbon cap-and-trade legislation in 2003 and 2005 and reintroduced the bill in 2007. Seeing the political handwriting on the wall, large U.S. corporations began to endorse carbon controls.

"We know enough to act on climate change," said the U.S. Climate Action Partnership, an alliance of major corporations including Alcoa, Dupont and General Motors. The group called on Congress to pass mandatory GHG limits and create a cap-and-trade system to attain them.[43]

CURRENT SITUATION

A New Player?

As Americans increasingly worry about climate change, many observers expect the United States to limit its greenhouse gas emissions and create a domestic carbon trading system after the 2008 elections. Multiple cap-and-trade bills were introduced in both houses of Congress in 2007 and 2008, including several with bipartisan support.[44] And the two major-party presidential candidates, Sens. McCain and Barack Obama, D-Ill., both pledged to set up a cap-and-trade system and to pursue deep cuts in U.S. GHG emissions.

Since the United States is one of the world's largest GHG emitters, U.S. entry into carbon trading would dramatically expand global carbon markets. New Carbon Finance, a market research firm in London, estimated in October that the total value of world carbon trading would reach $550 billion by 2012 and just over $2 trillion by 2020, even without U.S. participation. If the United States introduces a federal cap-and-trade system, however, those figures would increase to $680 billion by 2012 and more than $3 trillion by 2020.[45] By way of comparison, $3 trillion is roughly the size of the combined world markets for oil, coal, natural gas and electricity today.[46]

Two legislative proposals — one debated by the Senate in mid-2008 and a House Energy and Commerce committee proposal released on Oct. 7 — offer some indication of what national cap-and-trade legislation might look like. Both bills would cap U.S. greenhouse gas emissions and set up a trading system to reduce them.

The House bill would require a 6 percent cut below 2005 levels by 2020, and the Senate bill calls for a 19 percent cut. By 2050, however, the House measure would reduce emissions by 80 percent below 2005 levels, compared to 71 percent under the Senate bill.

Along with public concern and growing scientific evidence that human activities are warming the planet, another factor pushing U.S. policy makers to act is a 2007 Supreme Court ruling which held — contrary to the Bush administration's position — that carbon dioxide was a pollutant under the Clean Air Act and that the EPA had authority to regulate it.[47] "CO_2 controls are clearly coming. The only remaining questions are when and who is going to do the controlling," said Rep. Rick Boucher, D-Va., chair of the House Energy and Commerce Committee's Subcommittee on Energy and Air Quality, in late 2008. A coauthor of the committee's cap-and-trade proposal, Boucher said he thought Congress rather than the EPA should lead on regulating carbon and that he planned to hold hearings on cap-and-trade legislation early in 2009.[48]

If Congress does pass such legislation, its effectiveness will depend on which sectors it covers, how quickly it cuts emissions and whether it compensates businesses and consumers for higher costs. Carbon marketers will watch closely to see how strictly the U.S. limits the use of offset credits from foreign sources such as CDM projects.

Some states are launching regional cap-and-trade schemes to show the approach can work and to build support for national action. In September, 10 Northeastern states, stretching from Maryland to Maine, launched the Regional Greenhouse Gas Initiative (RGGI) — the first mandatory U.S. carbon cap-and-trade system. RGGI is designed to reduce GHG emissions from electric power plants 10 percent below current levels by 2018. Unlike systems that have given polluters emission allowances for free, RGGI auctioned off its first batch of allowances and will invest the proceeds — $38.5 million, at a final price of $3.07 per ton of CO_2 — in energy efficiency and renewable energy programs.

State officials called the first RGGI auction a success. "Demand was high, and fears of low-ball bidding did not come to pass," said Democratic New York Gov. David Paterson. "Instead, RGGI has used market forces to set a price on carbon."[49]

River waters crash into a Buddhist temple during high tide on the outskirts of Bangkok, Thailand. Climatologists say higher global temperatures are causing polar ice caps to melt, raising sea and river levels in low-lying coastal areas. Carbon trading schemes are the world's current answer to the question of how to control global warming.

AP Photo/Sommuk Attipanyo

At nearly the same time, seven Western states and four Canadian provinces agreed on the basics of a broader regional cap-and-trade program that would cover emissions from electricity generation, industry, transportation and residential and commercial energy use. The initiative would cut members' GHG emissions to 15 percent below 2005 levels by 2020. Trading is scheduled to start in 2012, with a second phase beginning in 2015.[50]

"The Western Climate Initiative is increasingly the system that many observers see as a possible precursor to a U.S. federal system because of its size and design features. They've received input from some key experts who were involved in setting up the EU system," says Hasselknippe of the Point Carbon research firm. However, if Congress enacts national GHG controls, that system would almost certainly replace regional cap-and-trade programs.

Beyond Kyoto

Global negotiators are working on a follow-on agreement to the Kyoto Protocol, which only limits signatories' emissions through 2012, although some countries have made longer-term commitments. For example, in 2007 EU countries pledged to cut their total GHG emissions 20 percent by 2020 and to increase this target to 30 percent if other nations sign a post-Kyoto treaty.

Getty Images/Jeff J. Mitchell

Thousands of planes will be required to cut their carbon emissions now that the European Union has decided that airliners should be included in EU carbon emission caps under Phase 3 of the Kyoto Protocol climate change treaty, beginning in 2012. Airlines are resisting, saying that their industry has been hit hard by high oil prices and that the EU does not have legal authority to regulate emissions from flights that originate in other countries. Above, planes in Glasgow, Scotland.

At a contentious international conference in 2007 in Bali, Indonesia, negotiators agreed on basic principles for crafting a post-Kyoto agreement. The plan calls for finalizing a new treaty in 2009 (to take effect in 2013) that includes deep cuts in developed countries' greenhouse emissions and unspecified "mitigation actions" by developing countries. It also pledges to develop policies that reward tropical countries for protecting their forests and creates a fund using a surcharge on CDM projects to help poor countries adapt to climate change impacts.[51]

Many developed countries wanted emissions cuts of 25 to 40 percent in rich countries by 2020, but the United States refused to approve an agenda with specific targets. U.S. representatives were booed during the talks, and at one point Papua New Guinea's representative was cheered when he told them, "If you're not going to lead, get out of the way." Ultimately, however, the U.S. supported the principles — the first time that the Bush administration had agreed to negotiate climate targets with other nations.[52]

It is not yet clear what shape a post-Kyoto agreement may take. It could set binding national emissions targets, like the Kyoto treaty, or build on pledges by individual countries or groups of countries. Some nations have already made significant commitments outside the Kyoto framework. The European Parliament, for example, is already setting emissions caps and planning to auction some carbon allowances in the third phase of EU ETS, to start in 2013.[53]

Some developing countries have also pledged to reduce their contribution to climate change. China's current five-year plan, which runs through 2010, calls for reducing the energy intensity of gross domestic product (the amount of energy used to produce each unit of income) 20 percent below 2005 levels by 2010. Beijing is also working to generate 10 percent of national energy demand with renewable sources by 2010 and 15 percent by 2020; by contrast, the U.S. currently gets about 7 percent of its energy from renewables. And Costa Rica has pledged to become carbon-neutral, as have New Zealand, Monaco, Norway and Iceland.[54]

Beyond these steps, however, experts warn that unless large developing countries like China, India, Indonesia and Brazil accept binding carbon caps soon, it will be impossible to avoid disastrous climate change. "If China and India keep doing what they're doing, their emissions will be tremendous," says Kollmuss of the Stockholm Environment Institute. "At the same time, these countries need to develop, so we need to find a just and equitable climate solution that will get them to buy in."

The U.N. Development Programme seconded this view in its 2007/2008 *Human Development Report*, which urged large developing countries to accept emissions targets proportional to what they could accomplish. "Any multilateral agreement without quantitative commitments from developing countries will lack credibility," the report asserted. However, it also argued that it would be impossible to negotiate such an agreement unless wealthy countries provided money and technology to help poorer nations adopt low-carbon strategies.[55]

Some advocates in developing countries worry that they will be asked to take on GHG reduction commitments when many rich nations have not cut their emissions significantly (or, in the case of the United States, at all).

"The message from Bali is that the fight against climate change will be brutal and selfish," says Sunita Narain, director of the Centre for Science and Environment in New Delhi. She agrees that India is "devastatingly vulnerable" to climate change impacts like floods and heat waves. By signing an action plan in Bali without hard reduction targets or timetables, she argues,

Should the European Union cap aviation carbon emissions?

YES

Joao Vieira
Policy Officer, European Federation for Transport and Environment

From *T&E Bulletin*, July 22, 2008

After years of us and others highlighting the environmental damage caused by aviation, the [European Union] has finally done something to try and counteract its impact. It has shown courage, in particular, in standing up to threats from the USA and against a background of abysmal inaction from the International Civil Aviation Organisation, the body charged with regulating emissions from aircraft under the Kyoto Protocol. . . .

So why are we at *T&E* so reluctant to be happy about this? There are two reasons. The terms on which aviation has entered the ETS [Emissions Trading Scheme] will mean very limited reductions in emissions from aircraft [which] might create the illusion that other measures that would do much more to reduce emissions . . . are no longer needed. And . . . the ETS might now be seen as a "silver bullet" solution for emissions from transport. . . .

Airlines will be allowed to buy permits from other sectors without restrictions, so their emissions will continue to grow. Instead of changing to greener technologies and operations, the aviation sector is likely to limit its climate efforts to buying permits in the carbon market. In addition, this directive only addresses CO_2 [carbon dioxide] emissions, ignoring the fact that NO_x [nitrogen oxides] is emitted from aircraft . . . and aviation-induced clouds also have climatic impact. It will mean aviation remains the least-efficient and most climate-intensive mode of transport.

The limitations of a cap-and-trade system's ability to effectively reduce emissions from transport should be a lesson for EU decision-makers, some of whom seem tempted by the idea of emissions trading for road transport.

The ETS is . . . for large, fixed-emission facilities. Transport . . . has numerous operators of mobile emissions sources, which do not face international competition [since] transport is a geographically bound activity.

T&E has said all along that including aviation in the ETS can only be a first step. If the transport sector is to reduce its emissions, other measures to address the climatic impacts of all modes of transport will be needed.

Without the courage to apply fuel taxation, fair and efficient infrastructure charging and strict emission standards, applying emissions trading to transport will simply allow transport to keep growing its emissions. . . . That is unfair to [other] industries, and irresponsible to future generations.

NO

Giovanni Bisignani
Director General and CEO, International Air Transport Association (IATA)

From remarks at the Farnborough [England] International Air Show, July 18, 2008

Today, airlines are in crisis. Oil is above $140. Jet fuel is over $180. In five years fuel went from 14 percent of operating costs to over 34 percent. If oil averages $135 for the rest of the year, the industry bill will be $190 billion. And next year it could be over $250 billion. . . .

IATA's environment leadership is delivering results. We worked with our members to implement best practices in fuel management. In 2007 this saved 6.7 million tonnes of CO_2 and $1.3 billion in cost.

We also worked with governments and air navigation service providers. Optimising 395 routes and procedures in 81 airports saved 3.8 million tonnes of CO_2 and $831 million in costs.

We could save up to 73 million tonnes of CO_2 with better air traffic management, but, while painting themselves green to win votes, governments are slow to deliver results. . . .

IATA supports emissions trading, but it must be global, fair and effective. Europe's approach could not be more wrong.

First, it's not an effective incentive. Developed when oil was $55 per barrel, it was meant to be an economic stick to force airlines to become more fuel-efficient. Europe's politicians had not foreseen the giant club of $140 oil.

It has beaten the life out of 25 airlines already this year, and we expect many more to follow into bankruptcy protection if they can afford it or straight into liquidation if they cannot. To survive, airlines are doing everything possible to reduce fuel burn. The [Emissions Trading Scheme] will add costs but will not improve the results. . . .

Second, the timing is wrong. Why make long-range policy decisions in the moment of a crisis when the future is completely uncertain — even five years out. And why make fuel more expensive when it is at its highest level ever — an 87 percent increase in the last year? Clearly, green politics has got in the way of good policy. . . .

How can Europe expect to charge an Australian airline for emissions over the Middle East on a flight from Asia to Europe? This will be challenged at [the International Civil Aviation Organisation] and in the International Court of Justice. And a responsible industry could easily be caught in a trade war of a layering of punitive economic measures.

Instead of cleaning up the environment, Europe is creating an international legal mess.

Growers burned down a dense forest in Sumber, Kalimantan, Indonesia, to make way for a palm oil plantation. Deforestation accounts for about 20 percent of human-generated greenhouse gas emissions worldwide. Environmentalists point out that forest preservation is one of the most cost-effective ways to address climate change.

"The world powers have reneged on all of us. Now developing countries will be even more reluctant to engage. Hardliners will say, 'We told you so.' "

In September U.N. Secretary-General Ban Ki-moon announced a cooperative program to test ways of managing tropical forests to keep them healthy and store large amounts of carbon. Norway donated $35 million for the first phase, which will involve at least nine countries in Africa, Asia and Latin America. The program seeks to pave the way for including forest conservation in a post-Kyoto treaty.

"This initiative will not only demonstrate how forests can have an important role as part of a post-2012 climate regime," said Ban, "it will also help build much needed confidence that the world community is ready to support the implementation of an inclusive, ambitious and comprehensive climate regime, once it is ratified."[56]

OUTLOOK

Cost of Inaction

As world leaders struggle to address this fall's global financial meltdown, some policy makers say now is the wrong time to impose further limits on greenhouse gas emissions. Putting a price on carbon, they worry, will raise energy costs when economies are already sputtering.

In October, for example, some East European countries tried unsuccessfully to delay the auctioning of EU ETS emission allowances, and conservative U.S. legislators questioned whether the economy could handle the added impact of cap-and-trade legislation.[57] If the world goes through a prolonged recession, energy prices are likely to fall, which would ease the financial crunch somewhat but would also reduce some of the imperative to shift away from fossil fuels.

Indeed, controlling carbon emissions won't be cheap. The total cost of controlling global warming could cost 1-2 percent of world gross domestic product — or roughly $350 to $700 billion — per year over the next few decades, according to several prominent economists, including Nicholas Stern of Great Britain and Jeffery Sachs of the United States.[58]

But advocates say it's more urgent than ever to act on climate change. Since renewable fuels like wind, solar and geothermal energy are free or low-cost, investing in them now will not only reduce GHG emissions but also make nations less dependent on oil and gas. And, they argue, green technologies can generate thousands of new, high-paying jobs.

Supporting this view, a 2008 study by David Roland-Holst, an economist at the University of California, calculated that energy efficiency policies in California from 1976 through 2006 had saved households some $56 billion and created about 1.5 million jobs.[59]

"The longer we wait to cap our emissions, the farther we fall behind in the remaking of a $6 trillion economy," says Environmental Defense Fund President Krupp.

Moreover, the cost of inaction is likely to be much higher than those of cutting emissions. Climate change will have major impacts worldwide, especially in poor countries that have few resources to protect people or move them out of harm's way. Global policy experts warn that recent progress against poverty in developing countries could be wiped out by climate change impacts like crop failures, water shortages and catastrophic flooding in river deltas that could leave millions hungry and homeless.

"If we are to avoid the catastrophic reversals in human development that will follow in the wake of climate change, we need to more than halve emissions of greenhouse gases," wrote Kevin Watkins, lead author of the U.N.'s *Human Development Report*, during the Bali climate conference. "That will not happen without a global accord that decarbonises growth and extends access to affordable energy in the developing world: a shake-up in energy policy backed by a programme similar to the post-Second World War Marshall Plan."[60] Under that initiative, the United States spent about $13 billion from 1947 through 1951 to rebuild war-torn Western Europe. The price tag for a program on the same scale, measured in 2007 dollars, would be roughly $740 billion.[61]

Rising concerns about costs make it increasingly likely that carbon trading will be a central part of the climate change solution, since it offers the opportunity to make cuts where they are most affordable. But cap-and-trade programs alone will not be enough. Government also must fund energy research and development; tighten energy efficiency standards and create markets for new technologies by setting national renewable energy targets. The overall goal, says IPCC Chair Pachauri, is to create a cleaner, less resource-intensive development path.

Pachauri often recalls Mahatma Gandhi's quip when asked whether India's people should have the same standard of living as the British. "It took Britain half the resources of the planet to achieve this prosperity," Gandhi replied. "How many planets will a country like India require?"[62]

NOTES

1. Mamuni Das, "Germany To Buy Carbon Credits From TTD Solar Kitchen," *The Hindu Business Line. com*, Aug. 24, 2005, www.thehindubusinessline .com/2005/08/24/stories/2005082402960100.htm; "Solar Amenities Way Above Sea Level," *The Statesman*, Oct. 15, 2006, www.thestatesman.net/ page.arcview.php?clid=30&id=161337&usrsess=1; Madhur Singh, "India's Temples Go Green," *Time*, July 7, 2008, www.time.com/time/world/article/ 0,8599,1820844,00.html.

2. Singh, *ibid.*

3. http://cdm.unfccc.int/UserManagement/File Storage/ 4WZXEVUUTRCJDV4AC6SY7VSL0KBFC5.

4. David Adam, "World Carbon Dioxide Levels Highest for 650,000 Years, Says U.S. Report," *The*

Guardian, May 13, 2008, www.guardian.co.uk/ environment/2008/may/13/carbonemissions.climate change.

5. For background, see Colin Woodard, "Curbing Climate Change," *CQ Global Researcher*, February 2007, pp. 27-52.

6. For background, see Mary H. Cooper, "Global Warming Treaty," *CQ Researcher*, Jan. 26, 2001, pp. 41-64.

7. Garrett Hardin, "The Tragedy of the Commons," *Science*, Dec. 13, 1968, pp. 1243-1248.

8. "Carbon 2008" Point Carbon, March 11, 2008, p. 3.

9. Fiona Harvey, "World Carbon Trading Value Doubles," *Financial Times*, May 7, 2008, http://us.ft.com/ ftgateway/superpage.ft?news_id=fto05072008 2214562909.

10. "Regional Initiatives," Pew Center on Global Climate Change, www.pewclimate.org/what_s_ being_done/in_the_states/regional_initiatives.cfm.

11. Sen. Barack Obama (D-Ill.) endorsed cutting U.S. emissions 80 percent below 1990 levels by 2050, while Sen. John McCain (R-Ariz.) called for reducing at least 60 percent below 1990 levels on the same timetable. "Science Debate 2008," www.sciencedebate2008.com.

12. "Emission Impossible: Access to JI/CDM Credits in Phase II of the EU Emissions Trading Scheme," World Wildlife Fund-UK, June 2007, p. 10, http:// assets.panda.org/downloads/emission_impossible__ final_.pdf.

13. A. Denny Ellerman and Paul Joskow, "The European Union's Emissions Trading System in Perspective," Pew Climate Center, May 2008, figure 1, p. 13, www.pewclimate.org/docUploads/EU-ETS-In-Perspective-Report.pdf.

14. "Europe's Dirty Secret: Why the EU Emissions Trading Scheme Isn't Working," *Open Europe*, 2007, p. 16, www.openeurope.org.uk/research/etsp2.pdf.

15. "What's Really Going On in the European Carbon Market," Environmental Defense Fund, June 27, 2007, http://blogs.edf.org/climate411/2007/06/27/ eu_carbon_market/.

16. Ellerman and Joskow, *op. cit.*, pp. 12-15.

17. James Kanter, "Europe Forcing Airlines to Buy Emissions Permits," *The New York Times*, Oct. 25, 2008, p. B2.

18. "Emission Impossible . . . ," *op. cit.*, pp. 3-4.

19. Michael W. Wara and David G. Victor, "A Realistic Policy on International Carbon Offsets," *Working Paper #74*, Program on Energy and Sustainable Development, Stanford University, April 2008, p. 5, http://pesd.stanford.edu/publications/a_realistic_policy_on_international_carbon_offsets/.

20. Yvo de Boer, "Prepared Remarks for Public Debate on the Kyoto Mechanisms," New York, Oct. 9, 2008.

21. Leila Abboud, "An Exhausting War On Emissions," *The Wall Street Journal*, Sept. 30, 2008, p. A15.

22. Fred Krupp and Miriam Horn, *Earth: The Sequel: The Race to Reinvent Energy and Stop Global Warming* (2008), p. 247.

23. "A Conversation with Nobel Prize Winner Rajendra Pachauri," *Yale Environment 360*, June 3, 2008, http://e360.yale.edu/content/print.msp?id=2006.

24. Barbara Haya, "Failed Mechanism: How the CDM is Subsidizing Hydro Developers and Harming the Kyoto Protocol," *International Rivers*, November 2007, http://internationalrivers.org/files/Failed_Mechanism_3.pdf.

25. Oliver Balch, "Forests: A Carbon Trader's Gold Mine?" ClimateChangeCorp.com, May 7, 2008, www.climatechangecorp.com/content.asp?Content ID=5305; for project details and review documents, see "Project 1051: Mitigation of Methane Emissions in the Charcoal Production of Plantar, Brazil," United Nations Framework Convention on Climate Change, http://cdm.unfccc.int/Projects/DB/DNV-CUK1175235824.92/view.

26. Michael S. Northcott, *A Moral Climate: The Ethics of Global Warming* (2007), p. 136.

27. William F. Laurance, "A New Initiative to Use Carbon Trading for Tropical Forest Conservation," *Biotropica*, vol. 39, no. 1 (2007), pp. 20-24, www.globalcanopy.org/themedia/NewCarbonTrading.pdf.

28. Keya Acharya, "Rainforest Coalition Proposes Rewards for 'Avoided Deforestation,'" Environmental News Network, Aug. 15, 2007, www.enn.com/ecosystems/article/21854.

29. "Forests in the Fight Against Climate Change," www.forestsnow.org.

30. De Boer, *op. cit.*

31. "CDM Experiences and Lessons" (presentation), slide 5, U.N. Development Programme, April 1, 2008, http://unfccc.meta-fusion.com/kongresse/AWG_08/downl/0401_1500_p2/Krause%20UNDP%20JI_CDM1.pdf.

32. "Fighting Climate Change: Human Solidarity in a Developed World, *Human Development Report 2007/2008* (2008), United Nations Development Programme, p. 155.

33. " 'Global Green Deal' — Environmentally-Focused Investment Historic Opportunity for 21st Century Prosperity and Job Generation," United Nations Environment Programme, press release, Oct. 22, 2008.

34. Richard N. L. Andrews, *Managing the Environment, Managing Ourselves: A History of American Environmental Policy* (1999), pp. 127-128.

35. J. H. Dales, *Pollution, Property and Prices* (1968), p. 801.

36. The final conference declaration is online at www.unep.org/Documents.Multilingual/Default.asp?DocumentID=97&ArticleID=1503.

37. See Thomas H. Tietenberg, *Environmental and Natural Resource Economics*, 5th ed. (2000), pp. 454-455.

38. Randall A. Bluffstone, "Environmental Taxes in Developing and Transition Economies," *Public Finance and Management*, vol. 3, no. 1 (2003), pp. 152-55.

39. Richard Elliot Benedick, *Ozone Diplomacy: New Directions in Safeguarding the Planet* (1998), pp. 314-320.

40. "Acid Rain Trading Program, 2004 Progress Report," U.S. Environmental Protection Agency, October 2005, pp. 2, 10, www.epa.gov/airmarkt/progress/docs/2004report.pdf.

41. Robert N. Stavins, "Lessons Learned from SO2 Allowance Trading," *Choices*, 2005, p. 53, www.choicesmagazine.org/2005-1/environment/2005-1-11.htm; Nathaniel O. Keohane and Sheila M. Olmstead, *Markets and the Environment* (2007), p. 184.

42. For background see Jennifer Weeks, "Coal's Comeback," *CQ Researcher*, Oct. 5, 2007, pp. 817-840. The Bush administration then issued regulations through EPA to promote emissions trading, but in 2007 the D.C. Circuit Court held that the EPA did not have authority under the Clean Air Act to develop such broad trading programs.

43. "A Call for Action," Jan. 22, 2007, U.S. Climate Action Partnership, p. 2, www.us-cap.org/Climate Report.pdf.

44. For a summary of bills pending in September 2008, see "Comparison of Legislative Climate Change Targets," World Resources Institute, Sept. 9, 2008, www.wri.org/publication/usclimatetargets.

45. "Carbon Market Round-Up Q3 2008," *New Carbon Finance*, Oct. 10, 2008; www.newcarbonfinance.com/download.php?n=2008-10-10_PR_Carbon_Markets_Q3_20082.pdf&f=fileName&t=NCF_downloads.

46. Simon Kennedy, " 'Carbon Trading' Enriches the World's Energy Desks," *Marketwatch*, May 16, 2007.

47. *Massachusetts v. Environmental Protection Agency*, 549 U.S. 497 (2007).

48. Rep. Rick Boucher, remarks at the Society of Environmental Journalists annual conference, Roanoke, Va., Oct. 17, 2008.

49. "Governor Paterson Hails Nation's First Global Warming Cap and Trade Auction A Success," Sept. 29, 2008, www.ny.gov/governor/press/press_0929083.html.

50. For details see www.westernclimateinitiative.org/.

51. Robert N. Stavins and Joseph Aldy, "Bali Climate Change Conference: Key Takeaways," Harvard Project on International Climate Agreements, Dec. 18, 2007, http://belfercenter.ksg.harvard.edu/publication/17781/bali_climate_change_conference.html.

52. Daniel Howden and Geoffrey Lean, "Bali Conference: World Unity Forces U.S. to Back Climate Deal," *The Independent*, Dec. 16, 2007, www.independent.co.uk/environment/climate-change/bali-conference-world-unity-forces-us-to-back-climate-deal-765583.html; Gary LaMoshi, "Bumpy Ride Ahead for Bali Road Map," *Asia Times*, Dec. 18, 2007, www.atimes.com/atimes/Southeast_Asia/IL18Ae01.html.

53. Ian Traynor and David Gow, "EU Promises 20% Reduction in Carbon Emissions by 2020," *The Guardian*, Feb. 21, 2007, www.guardian.co.uk/environment/2007/feb/21/climatechange.climatechangeenvironment; Pete Harrison and Gerard Wynn, "EU Lawmakers Watch Credit Crisis in Climate Fight," Reuters, Oct. 7, 2008.

54. Stefan Lovgren, "Costa Rica Aims to Be 1st Carbon-Neutral Country," *National Geographic News*, March 7, 2008, http://news.nationalgeographic.com/news/2008/03/080307-costa-rica.html.

55. "Fighting Climate Change, . . ." *op. cit.*, pp. 27-28.

56. " 'Redd'-Letter Day for Forests: United Nations, Norway United to Combat Climate Change from Deforestation, Spearheading New Programme," U.N. press release, Sept. 24, 2008.

57. Pete Harrison and Gerard Wynn, "EU Lawmakers Watch Credit Crisis in Climate Fight," Reuters, Oct. 7, 2008, www.reuters.com/article/rbssIndustryMaterialsUtilitiesNews/idUSL711408420081007?sp=true; Dina Cappiello, "Economic Woes Chill Effort to Stop Global Warming," The Associated Press, Oct. 12, 2008, http://ap.google.com/article/ALeqM5jFaQmoLWbpKq8HH1AAQ5GoGZjz0gD93OTVC00; James Kanter, "Europe's Leadership in Carbon Control at Risk in Credit Crisis," *The New York Times*, Oct. 21, 2008, p. B10.

58. Juliette Jowit and Patrick Wintour, "Cost of Tackling Global Climate Change Has Doubled, Warns Stern," *The Guardian*, June 26, 2008, www.guardian.co.uk/environment/2008/jun/26/climatechange.scienceofclimatechange; Jeffrey D. Sachs, *Common Wealth: Economics for a Crowded Planet* (2008), pp. 308-311.

59. David Roland-Holst, "Energy Efficiency, Innovation, and Job Creation in California," Center for Energy, Resources and Economic Sustainability, University of California, Berkeley, October 2008.

60. Kevin Watkins, "Bali's Double Standards," *The Guardian*, Dec. 14, 2007, www.guardian.co.uk/commentisfree/2007/dec/14/comment. bali.

61. Niall Ferguson, "Dollar Diplomacy: How Much Did the Marshall Plan Really Matter?" *The New Yorker*, Aug. 27, 2007, p. 81.

62. "A Conversation with Nobel Prize Winner Rajendra Pachauri," *op. cit.*

BIBLIOGRAPHY

Books

Krupp, Fred, and Miriam Horn, *Earth: The Sequel,* *Norton,* **2008.**

The president and senior staff writer, respectively, at the U.S.-based Environmental Defense Fund describe innovators who are leading a clean-energy revolution and argue that the United States should adopt a carbon cap-and-trade system to boost investments in innovative energy technologies.

Northcott, Michael S., *A Moral Climate: The Ethics of Global Warming,* *Orbis,* **2007.**

An Episcopal priest and divinity professor at the University of Edinburgh views climate change as an ethical issue and criticizes carbon trading as biased toward rich countries and large greenhouse gas emitters.

Tietenberg, Thomas H., *Emissions Trading: Principles and Practice,* **2nd edition,** *Resources for the Future,* **2006.**

An environmental economist shows how emissions trading became popular as an alternative to command-and-control regulation and assesses successes, failures and lessons learned in 25 years of application.

Zedillo, Ernesto, ed., *Global Warming: Looking Beyond Kyoto,* *Brookings,* **2008.**

Authors from around the globe examine how to structure a post-Kyoto climate change agreement that can reduce emissions quickly enough to avert disastrous warming.

Articles

"C is for Unclean," *Down to Earth,* **Dec. 15, 2007.**

A critique of the Clean Development Mechanism (CDM) by India's Centre for Science and Environment argues that the program has been taken over by carbon entrepreneurs and turned into a financial tool instead of fighting climate change.

"First Africa Carbon Forum Fosters Clean Climate Projects," *Environment News Service,* **Sept. 4, 2008.**

Only a fraction of CDM projects are in Africa, but African leaders and international development officials want to increase the continent's share.

Arrandale, Tom, "Carbon Goes to Market," *Governing,* **September 2008, p. 26.**

As Congress debates cap-and-trade policies, nearly half the states are working on their own carbon trading schemes.

Scott, Mark, "Giant Steps for Carbon Trading in Europe," *Business Week,* **Jan. 23, 2008.**

The EU Emissions Trading Scheme is setting stringent, new targets, which will make carbon credits more valuable.

Szabo, Michael, "Problems Plague Canada's Emissions Trading Plans," *Reuters,* **May 8, 2008.**

Canada wants to start carbon trading, but some of its provinces have already adopted their own schemes, and emissions from the Canadian oil industry are rising.

Turner, Chris, "The Carbon Cleansers," *Canadian Geographic Magazine,* **October 2008, p. 3.**

Norway's carbon tax on the oil and gas industry, adopted in 1992, has spurred research into cleaner energy technologies, as well as carbon capture and storage.

Reports and Studies

"Carbon 2008," *Point Carbon,* **March 11, 2008, www .pointcarbon.com/polopoly_fs/1.912721!Carbon_ 2008_dfgrt.pdf.**

An international market research firm focusing on carbon markets provides an overview of global carbon trading and major carbon policy trends.

"Fighting Climate Change: Human Solidarity in a Developed World," *Human Development Report 2007/2008,* **2008,** *United Nations Development Programme,* **http://hdr.undp.org/en/media/ hdr_20072008_en_complete.pdf.**

Climate change is a major threat to human development and is already undercutting global efforts to reduce poverty in some parts of the world. This report calls for urgent action on a post-Kyoto agreement and policies to help poor countries adapt to unavoidable climate change impacts.

Ellerman, A. Denny, and Paul Joskow, "The European Union's Emissions Trading System in Perspective," *Pew Center on Global Climate Change,* **May 2008,**

www.pewclimate.org/docUploads/EU-ETS-In-Perspective-Report.pdf.

Two economists from the Massachusetts Institute of Technology conclude that the EU ETS is still a work in progress but has successfully set a European price for carbon emissions and offers important lessons for U.S. leaders as they debate cap-and-trade policies.

Wara, Michael W., and David G. Victor, "A Realistic Policy on International Carbon Offsets," *Working Paper #74, Program on Energy and Sustainable Development, Stanford University,* **April 2008, http://iis-db.stanford.edu/pubs/22157/WP74_final_final.pdf.**

Two Stanford University law professors recommend major reforms to the Kyoto Protocol's Clean Development Mechanism, which they say awards credits for projects that don't really reduce emissions, and argue the United States should not rely on offsets to lower the cost of reducing carbon emissions.

For More Information

Centre for Science and Environment, 41 Tughlakabad Institutional Area, New Delhi, India; (+91)-11-29955124; www.cseindia.org. An independent public interest organization that works to increase awareness of science, technology, environment and development issues.

China Sustainable Energy Program, The Energy Foundation, CITIC Building, Room 2403, No. 19, Jianguomenwai Dajie, Beijing, 100004, P.R. China; (+86)-10-8526-2422; www.efchina.org. A joint initiative funded by U.S. foundations to support China's policy efforts to promote energy efficiency and renewable energy.

The Gold Standard, 22 Baumleingasse, CH-4051, Basel, Switzerland; (+41)-0-61-283-0916; www.cdmgoldstandard.org. A nonprofit that screens carbon offset projects and certifies initiatives that provide measurable economic, environmental and social benefits.

Institute for Sustainable Futures, University of Technology, L11, 235 Jones St., Broadway, Sydney, Australia; (+61)-2-9514-4590; www.isf.uts.edu.au. Research institute that works with Australian businesses and communities to promote sustainable environmental and design policies.

Intergovernmental Panel on Climate Change, 7bis Ave. de la Paix, C.P. 2300, CH-1211 Geneva 2, Switzerland; (+41)-22-730-8208; www.ipcc.ch. A U.N.-sponsored organization created to advise national governments on climate change science.

Regional Greenhouse Gas Initiative, 90 Church St., 4th Floor, New York, NY 10007; (212) 417-7327; www.rggi.org. A joint venture launched in 2008 by 10 Northeastern states to reduce greenhouse gas emissions from the electric power sector through carbon emissions trading.

U.N. Development Programme, One United Nations Plaza, New York, NY 10017; (212) 906-5000; www.undp.org. Works to cut poverty and use aid effectively.

World Wildlife Fund — UK, Panda House, Weyside Park, Godalming, Surrey GU7 1XR, United Kingdom; (+01)-483-426444; www.wwf.org.uk. The British arm of an international conservation organization

14

Ecotourism

Does It Help or Hurt
Fragile Lands and Cultures?

Rachel S. Cox

Marine iguanas show little fear of visitors to the Galapagos Islands, where the Ecuadorian government tightly controls tourism. Ecotourism supporters say such "sustainable" travel brings environmental and economic benefits to isolated communities, but critics warn that even well-managed ecotourism can destroy the very attractions it promotes.

From *CQ Researcher*,
October 20, 2006.

A week-long cruise to the fabled Galapagos Islands last summer took members of the Sturc family of Washington, D.C., back into history. As they clambered out of their rubber landing raft, boobies and penguins, iguanas and sea lions greeted them as nonchalantly as their forebears had greeted British naturalist Charles Darwin when he arrived in 1835 to collect evidence that led to his theory of natural selection.

"It was beautiful in a very stark way," Susan Sturc recalls. "We were impressed at how clean everything was. There was no trash anywhere." But, she adds, the islands 600 miles off the coast of Ecuador were "not as untouched as I had thought they would be. I was surprised at how much development there was. I thought it would be pristine."

The Sturcs' experience typifies the paradox of ecotourism, a relatively new and increasingly popular form of tourism that The International Ecotourism Society defines as "responsible travel to natural areas that conserves the environment and improves the well-being of local people."

To its supporters, ecotourism offers a model with the potential to remake the travel industry, bringing environmental and economic benefits to destination communities while providing tourists with more meaningful experiences than conventional tourism offers. But critics warn that the environmental and social changes that accompany even well-managed ecotourism threaten to destroy the very attractions it promotes.

Over the last 25 years, travelers have enjoyed expanding opportunities to visit locations once considered impossibly remote. Even

Hotels Going 'Green' Around the World

Many tourism companies are trying to reduce their impact on the environment — and save money — by cutting consumption of water, energy and other resources and improving the disposal of waste.

Hotel "Greening" Success Stories

Hilton International

The chain saved 60 percent on gas costs and 30 percent on both electricity and water in recent years, cutting waste by 25 percent. Vienna Hilton and Vienna Plaza reduced laundry loads by 164,000 kilograms per year, minimizing water and chemical use.

Singapore Marriott and Tang Plaza Scandic

Efforts to save some 40,000 cubic meters of water per year have reduced water use by 20 percent per guest. The chain pioneered a 97 percent "recyclable" hotel room and is building or retrofitting 1,500 rooms annually.

Sheraton Rittenhouse Square, Philadelphia

Boasts a 93 percent recycled granite floor, organic cotton bedding, night tables made from discarded wooden shipping pallets, naturally dyed recycled carpeting and nontoxic wallpaper, carpeting, drapes and cleaning products. The extra 2 percent 'green' investment was recouped in the first six months.

Inter-Continental Hotels and Resorts

Each facility must implement a checklist of 134 environmental actions and meet specific energy, waste and water-management targets. Between 1988 and 1995, the chain reduced overall energy costs by 27 percent. In 1995, it saved $3.7 million, reducing sulfur dioxide emissions by 10,670 kilograms, and saved 610,866 cubic meters of water — an average water reduction of nearly 7 percent per hotel, despite higher occupancies.

Forte Brighouse, West Yorkshire, United Kingdom

Energy-efficient lamps reduced energy use by 45 percent, cut maintenance by 85 percent and lowered carbon emissions by 135 tons. The move paid for itself in less than a year.

Hyatt International

Energy-efficiency measures in the United States cut energy use by 15 percent and now save the chain an estimated $15 million annually.

Holiday Inn Crowne Plaza, Schiphol Airport, Netherlands

By offering guests the option of not changing their linens and towels each day, the hotel reduced laundry volume, water and detergent — as well as costs — by 20 percent.

Source: Lisa Mastny, "Traveling Light, New Paths for International Tourism."

Indeed, eco/nature tourism is growing three times faster than the tourism industry as a whole, according to the World Tourism Organization.[1]

Tourism activist Deborah McLaren, the founder of Indigenous Rights International, says many tourists are no longer interested in the fantasy tourism culture of "sand, sun, sea and sex" offered by packaged tours to beach resorts and cruise ships.[2] Many travelers now prefer what the industry calls "experiential" tourism — encounters with nature, heritage and culture. Many also want a sense of adventure and discovery or philanthropic activities, such as restoring historic buildings or teaching.[3]

While ecotourism has brought new income to isolated parts of the world, it has come at a price, critics say. When archeologist Richard Leventhal, director of the Museum of Archaeology and Anthropology at the University of Pennsylvania, began his field work in 1972 in Cancun, Mexico, grass huts bordered the island's white-sand beaches. Today, Cancun's 20,000 hotel rooms attract more than 2.6 million visitors a year, and a sprawling shanty town houses the 300,000 workers drawn to the new industry.[4]

"Ecotourism has brought a lot of attention to a lot of places that wouldn't have gotten it otherwise," Leventhal observes. "That's generally good, because the economies are so fragile." But "tourism is one of the most fickle stimuli that exist. A hurricane comes, and the tourists are gone."

"Ecotourism is not the cost-free business option that its supporters suggest," argues Rosaleen Duffy, a senior lecturer at the Centre for International Politics at Manchester University in England. "Because ecotourism often takes place in relatively remote

Antarctica is now visited by more than 10,000 travelers per year. Tourism in general is considered by many to be the world's largest industry, and one of the fastest growing.

areas and small communities, the effects of establishing a small-scale hotel or food outlet can have the same impact as building a Hilton in a large town or city."[5]

As a Maya scholar, Leventhal has worked closely with communities throughout Central America, especially in Belize — considered a leading ecotourism success story similar to nearby Costa Rica. "What I always ask," he says, "is, 'Does it really benefit local people?' "

Development economists call the problem "leakage." Studies have shown that up to half of the tourism revenue entering the developing world reverts to the developed world in profits earned by foreign-owned businesses, promotional spending abroad or payments for imported labor and goods.[6]

And, as "ecotourism" has become a popular gimmick in travel marketing, another sort of leakage has emerged. "Ten years ago, I could tell you what ecotourism was," Leventhal says. "Today, everyone's trying to claim it, because it's a hook people really like."

Ron Mader, a Mexico-based travel writer and founder of the ecotourism Web site Planeta.com, agrees. "Look at national travel Web sites," he says. "Even Cancun has a page on ecotourism," with a picture of a contented drinker lounging at a pool bar, suggesting that just getting a sunburn is "practicing ecotourism."

Partly to clarify such public misperceptions, some ecotourism advocates support creation of a certification system reflecting a destination's environmental and cultural sensitivity. Conservation groups like the Rainforest Alliance and Conservation International see the plan as a way to encourage responsible ecotourism and sound environmental practices.

"'Eco-travel' can come in many shades of green," senior editor Rene Ebersole writes in *Audubon* magazine. "Without a global certification label — something as recognizable as, say, the [U.S. Department of Agriculture] 'Organic' sticker on produce —- it's hard to be sure" which trips qualify as genuine ecotourism.[7]

Critics contend, however, that ecotourism certification will further diminish the involvement of indigenous people and exacerbate many of the problems ecotourism already creates for its communities. "It really pits people against each other," says McLaren.

Conservation International and other major nongovernmental conservation organizations (NGOs) say ecotourism can give indigenous people a stake in

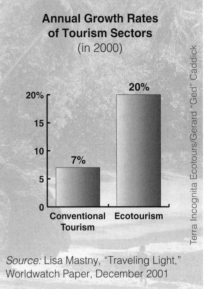

'Green' Travel Outpaces Conventional Tourism

Ecotourism is one of the fastest-growing segments of the tourism industry, generating $154 billion in 2000.

Annual Growth Rates of Tourism Sectors
(in 2000)

- Conventional Tourism: 7%
- Ecotourism: 20%

Terra Incognita Ecotours/Gerard "Ged" Caddick

Source: Lisa Mastny, "Traveling Light," Worldwatch Paper, December 2001

protecting their environment, with income from tourism compensating for the loss of traditional lifeways, such as hunting and slash-and-burn agriculture.

"Carefully planned and implemented tourism can . . . offer a powerful incentive to conserve and protect biodiversity," says Conservation International. "People who earn their living from ecotourism are more likely to protect their natural resources and support conservation efforts."[8]

But Luis Vivanco, an anthropology professor at the University of Vermont who has studied the effects of ecotourism in Costa Rica, is skeptical. "For elites and people with the ability to make money, it's a great opportunity," he says. But in real life, "ecotourism is redefining people's lives and landscapes. It's impossible not to wonder if they could be destroying what they love."

As conservationists, tourism operators, development banks and anthropologists evaluate ecotourism, here are some of the key questions in the debate:

Does ecotourism threaten fragile ecosystems?

Traveling in Nepal in the early 1980s, Steve Powers, a tour operator in Long Beach, N.Y., witnessed the effects of uncontrolled tourism. "Nepal was a prime example of how not to do tourism in the Third World," he says. "The government policy was to let everybody in with no controls. Tourists just trashed the trekking sites, and backpackers living on $2 a day really weren't benefiting the community."

Even the native porters contributed to the problem. He remembers seeing them conscientiously collect all the trash at a campsite, then dump it in a river.

By 2003, more than 25,000 trekkers were visiting the Khumbu Valley near Mt. Everest. Much of the area that Sir Edmund Hillary described as being superbly forested in 1951 had become "an eroding desert."[9]

The main culprit in the area's massive deforestation was the tourists, and the demand they created not only for fuel to warm themselves and their porters but also to build the "teahouses" where they stayed.

"Do tourists who come here consider what their need for hot water costs in terms of wood?" asked Gian Pietro Verza, field manager at an Italian environmental research station near a Sherpa village. "One trekker can consume an average of five times more wood per day than an entire Sherpa family uses — and the porters and guides they bring with them need firewood, too."[10]

Other ecotourism skeptics tell the story of Brazil's first "eco-resort," Praia do Forte, a 247-room hotel whose developer bought thousands of acres of rain forest on a spectacular beach, then leveled much of the forest to build his hotel.[11]

In Africa, uncontrolled "nature" tourism has been linked to a decline in cheetah survival rates. As tourists clamor to watch the cats up close, according to Costas Christ, Sr., director of ecotourism at Conservation International, they frighten the cheetahs and their young away from hard-won kills, the food is scavenged by hyenas and the cubs go hungry.[12]

The Third World Network, a Malaysia-based coalition that supports development in developing countries, recently reported that tourism was destroying the "World's Eighth Wonder" — the Banaue rice terraces, a UNESCO World Heritage site in the northern Philippines. The group said timber cutting in the Banaue watershed to provide wood for handicrafts for tourists was reducing water flow to the terraces and encouraging giant earthworms to bore deeper into their banks.

In addition, a recent study by the Tebtebba Foundation, a Philippines-based indigenous peoples' advocacy and research center, found the terraces also were being damaged by the water demands of hotels, lodges and restaurants, as well as the conversion of rice paddies into lots for lodges and shops. At the same time, the study said, rice farmers are giving up their traditional livelihoods to take jobs in tourism.[13]

Similarly, the development in the Galapagos Islands that surprised ecotourist Susan Sturc reflected social changes brought about by increased tourism. The Ecuadorian government tightly controls Galapagos tourism, limiting the number of cruise ships, requiring visitors' groups to be accompanied by guides and prohibiting the carrying of food onto the islands.[14]

Nonetheless, the influx of tourists has attracted many Ecuadorians from the mainland who seek better economic opportunities. Between 1974 and 1997 the population of the Galapagos grew by almost 150 percent, and today there are about 27,000 year-round residents. In 2004, a study about the future of the Galapagos warned "tourism is the main economic driver, yet the migration it induces threatens the future of tourism."[15]

These and many other environmental impacts are being addressed by governments and NGOs. Tour operator Powers helped to establish Nepal's Kathmandu Environmental Education Project, now being run by Nepalis. It educates both tourists and locals by conducting eco-trekking workshops, encouraging trekking companies to be environmentally responsible and even paying porters for the trash they bring home. "It's better now," he says, but finding funds for such educational efforts is a perennial problem.

Powers believes organizations like the American Society of Travel Agents (ASTA) can help educate businesses, especially since its code of conduct includes respecting destination cultures and environments. But in-country operators — the local hotels and guides with whom travel agents arrange tours — also should be held accountable, he says.

But defining and measuring practices that promote environmental sustainability is a very new field, says David Weaver, a professor of tourism management and an ecotourism expert at the University of South Carolina in Columbia. "We're working to pin down the variables and criteria you would need to measure to determine whether an operation is sustainable," he says, but "we still have a long way to go. There aren't a lot of mature programs, and a lot of it is learn as you go."

For instance, a recent study of Magellanic penguins nesting at Punta Tombo, in Argentina, found that the birds adjusted relatively quickly to tourists. To study stress in the birds, researchers measured their number of head turns when humans approached and the level of stress-related hormones they secreted.

Greg Wetstone, U.S. director for the International Fund for Animal Welfare, calls the findings encouraging. "We still have a lot to learn, but this study reinforces the sense that responsible ecotourism can be a low-impact way to create economic pressure for protecting threatened wildlife." The study's authors cautioned, however, that "long-term consequences are much harder to document, especially in long-lived animals."[16]

Ecotourism consultant Megan Epler Wood, the first executive director of the Ecotourism Society (now The International Ecotourism Society), sees the problem of managing environmental effects more in terms of money than methodology. "With the participation of large conservation agencies, it has been shown that as long as an ecotourism project is appropriately planned, zoning the infrastructure well away from protected areas, people can visit without harming," she says.

But even in the United States, Epler Wood notes, the National Park Service has trouble implementing new methodologies because of funding gaps, a situation that is even more dire in developing countries.[17] "You may have one or two staff overseeing hundreds or thousands of acres," she says. "The idea of them controlling and managing so much requires a budgetary level that many can't approach."

Even the best-managed ecotourism facility can pave the way for less-benevolent permanent development, say other observers. In the remote Canadian province of Newfoundland, for instance, the tourism infrastructure gradually improved as the fishing industry gave out. "There has always been the hook and bullet crowd," says Larry Morris, president of the Quebec-Labrador Foundation/Atlantic Center for the Environment. "Now it's 'non-consumptive use.'"

Declining survival rates of African cheetahs have been linked to heavy tourism in game preserves. According to Conservation International, clamoring tourists frighten adult cheetahs and their young away from their kills, allowing hyenas to scavenge the food and forcing cubs to go hungry.

The sophistication of the outfitters has increased dramatically, Morris notes, and the province is capitalizing on concerns about global warming by promoting itself as a reliable destination for snow lovers. Now some of the visitors are purchasing permanent homes — a trend the industry labels "amenity migration." The province just got its first gated community, in Deer Lake, and its "wilderness cottages" — next to a new golf course — are attracting buyers from the United Kingdom.

The University of South Carolina's Weaver suggests that environmental damage caused by ecotourism can be diminished if it is practiced in areas that are already heavily altered. In downtown Austin, Texas, for instance, crowds gather every night at the Congress Street Bridge between March and November to watch up to 1.5 million Mexican free-tailed bats — North America's largest urban bat colony — emerge from their nests in deep crevices.

"You can have very high-quality ecotourism in highly disturbed areas," he says. "People go to see whooping cranes in the stubble of farmers' fields in Saskatchewan."

Others view peregrine falcons roosting in Pittsburgh skyscrapers, and even in the much-maligned New Jersey Meadowlands — just five miles from Manhattan — a bird-watching and fishing guidebook now promotes ecotourism.[18]

"The perception that [ecotourism] is a threat comes mostly from indigenous groups," says anthropologist Vivanco. "When you don't have control over tourism in your community, things leave." About five years ago, he points out, "bioprospecting" — in which pharmaceutical companies send people into the rain forest to see if they can find useful plants — became identified as ecotourism.

"Indigenous groups felt that things were being taken from them," he says, and it made them "very politicized," even though the evidence of biological theft was mostly anecdotal. "There is the notion that this is yet another effort to bring us into the modern world, to get control of our land — the latest version of the white man telling us what we should do with our land."

Some indigenous peoples involved with ecotourism projects are simply calling it quits. In Santa Maria, Costa Rica, where for several years Vivanco took his students on field trips, the community-based tourism project that sent paying guests to stay in local homes began to arouse resentment because not all families got guests. Recently, the villagers decided to end the program. "People are saying, 'We've had enough. It's causing division in the community,'" Vivanco says. "Their own conflicts play out in tourism."

Does ecotourism offer a realistic alternative to more traditional commercial development?

In the early 1990s, archeologist Leventhal worked with a group of Mayan Indians studying the future of their communities in southern Belize. At the time Belize — following Costa Rica's lead — was in the process of transforming itself into a major ecotourism destination. The group went on a tour of Mexico's popular Yucatan Peninsula.

"They were fascinated by being waited on by other Maya," Leventhal recalls. But not all the encounters were positive. When they'd walk into the big hotels, the Mayan security guards would immediately stop them.

"They really understood the impact of tourism," Leventhal says. "Yes, it brought money in, but they got very worried about certain aspects of it. They got involved with the idea that these were their cousins. Living in a subsistence economy in their own villages, they basically controlled the show. They didn't need to borrow money. When you borrow money, you have to pay it back." In the end they rejected ecotourism.

A 1999 study commissioned by the environmental group Greenpeace and conducted by American resource economist Christopher LaFranchi, however, suggests that while ecotourism may not be perfect, it is far more advantageous for indigenous peoples than "industrial" options such as logging and plantation-style agriculture. The study compared such traditional development tactics with small-scale development options, including ecotourism in the forest lands of the Marovo lagoon area in the Solomon Islands. It found negative long-term repercussions despite "rapid and considerable cash returns available from abruptly selling the forest for logging" and potential governmental revenues derived from taxing the timber industry.

"The rapid exploitation of tropical forests, although very profitable for international timber companies, has produced only limited long-term economic gain for the nations of the Pacific, and at great environmental and social cost," the study said.[19]

In comparing the costs and benefits of exploiting the reef and forest resources of the area, the study found that "the economic benefits of the small-scale options considerably exceed those of the industrial options. Moreover, they leave landowners in more direct control of their resources, distribute benefits more equitably and do not expose them to the high risks of fluctuations in international commodity markets."[20]

The present value of industrial options — mainly logging and palm oil — to landowners was estimated at $8.2 million, while small-scale options were valued at $29 million.

Tourism Professor Weaver calls this advantage the "one shot" angle. With traditional development, he says, "You get a lot of money in a limited time, but then it's done. With ecotourism, it's never exhausted."

Within the world of international aid agencies and development banks, says ecotourism consultant Epler Wood, ecotourism is "increasingly gaining credibility as a development tool because of its clear economic statistics and because there aren't that many other tools." Proposed development projects must now be sustainable, she says. "The economic growth potential is on a par with textiles. The reception is growing, and all the statistics have been clearly presented."

Often, she points out, the poorest countries stand to gain the most from ecotourism. Many studies show that traditional development strategies "have created a gap between rich and poor and between urban and rural," she explains. "Rural people have been left out of grand development schemes. But as long as they are an ecotourism attraction, rural people can get a nice growth trend."

Ecotourism has other advantages over traditional development schemes, she adds. Start-up takes a much lower investment and, thanks to the Internet, projects can be marketed directly to consumers, allowing the benefits to be delivered directly to the producer.

"It's very viable," says Benjamin Powell, a managing partner of Agora Partnerships, an American NGO that promotes Nicaraguan entrepreneurship. "Certain countries have completely branded themselves as ecotourism destinations to great effect. If it is done right, people are often willing to pay, and it often does trickle down to the locals."

Traditionally, institutional and cultural barriers have prevented native people from owning local businesses. Besides lacking a cultural tradition of entrepreneurship, Powell explains, "Most aspiring entrepreneurs in poor countries are caught in a development blind spot: They're too big for microfinance, yet too small for traditional lending."

'Green' Certification on the Rise

Tourism companies increasingly are participating in voluntary certification programs that provide a seal of approval to businesses that demonstrate environmentally or socially sound practices.

Selected Tourism-Certification Efforts Worldwide

Green Globe 21 — Has awarded logos to some 500 companies and destinations in more than 100 countries. Rewards efforts to incorporate social responsibility and sustainable resource management into business programs. But may confuse tourists by rewarding not only businesses that have achieved certification but also those that have simply committed to undertake the process.

ECOTEL® — Has certified 23 hotels in Latin America, seven in the United States and Mexico, five in Japan and one in India. Assigns hotels zero to five globes based on environmental commitment, waste management, energy efficiency, water conservation, environmental education and community involvement. Hotels must be reinspected every two years, and unannounced inspections can occur at any time. A project of the industry consulting group HVS International.

European Blue Flag Campaign — Includes more than 2,750 sites in 21 European countries; being adopted in South Africa and the Caribbean. Awards a yearly ecolabel to beaches and marinas for their high environmental standards and sanitary and safe facilities. Credited with improving the quality and desirability of European coastal sites. Run by the international nonprofit Foundation for Environmental Education.

Certification for Sustainable Tourism, Costa Rica — Has certified some 54 hotels since 1997. Gives hotels a ranking of one to five based on environmental and social criteria. Credited with raising environmental awareness among tourism businesses and tourists. But the rating is skewed toward large hotels that may be too big to really be sustainable.

SmartVoyager, Galapagos, Ecuador — Since 1999, has certified five of more than 80 ships that operate in the area. Gives a special seal to tour operators and boats that voluntarily comply with specified benchmarks for boat and dinghy maintenance and operation, dock operations and management of wastewater and fuels. A joint project of the Rainforest Alliance and a local conservation group.

Green Leaf, Thailand — Had certified 59 hotels as of October 2000. Awards hotels between one and five "green leaves" based on audits of their environmental policies and other measures. Aims to improve efficiency and raise awareness within the domestic hotel industry.

Source: Lisa Mastny, "Traveling Light, New Paths for International Tourism."

Powell promotes the advantages to small investors of small investments in local businesses. "From an investment perspective, you have more leverage if you invest in a local operation because you can put some corporate-responsibility standards in place," he says. "There's no correlation with the stock market at all. It's a very specific market, very local. It's not affected by anything macro. But still, it is very risky."

Should ecotourism businesses and programs be certified?

As ecotourism has become highly marketable, numerous schemes have sprung up that offer a "green" imprimatur for businesses. Some certification proposals require high standards while others set the bar lower; some are operated for profit, others are run by nonprofit organizations; some can be purchased, others are awarded.

"We're seeing nearly 100 different programs," says Katie Maschman, a spokeswoman for The International Ecotourism Society. Some programs are worldwide, national or regional in scope and others relate to specific resources, such as Blue Flag certification for healthy beaches. Other examples include the worldwide program Green Globe 21 and the World Wildlife Fund's PAN Parks network in Europe. The American Hotel & Lodging Association lets its most energy-efficient members display a Good Earthkeeping logo. The association estimates 43 million domestic travelers each year are "environmentally minded."

In recent years, the Rainforest Alliance and the ecotourism society have spearheaded an effort to regularize certification, supported by the Inter-American Development Bank, foundations and other development groups. Now they are studying how to develop and judge standards and certify eco-ventures that practice sustainable tourism, inspired by successful certification programs in other industries — such as the Forest Stewardship Council's approval of sustainably harvested lumber and the fair trade movement's certification of "green" coffee beans and bananas.

Advocates argue that a more coherent certification system is the only way to protect the market advantages of genuine ecotourism and encourage development of sustainable practices in the broader marketplace.

But critics say certification programs now being discussed raise more questions than they answer. For one thing, deciding who qualifies is not a simple matter. At an ecolodge in Australia, for example, visitors can buy packets of seeds to feed the colorful, parrot-like lorikeets, which will then flock around and alight on tourists' arms and heads.

"It's a paradox that this park lodge has advanced accreditation," says tourism professor Weaver. "They do a lot of fantastic things," but the bird feeding is a "demonstrable ecological problem." It keeps a lot of weak birds alive, which spreads diseases, he explains, and when the birds, gorged on seeds, return to the wild and defecate, weeds and other invasive species are introduced.

Nonetheless, a good ecolabel or certification "would give the public some confidence in what they're buying," Weaver says.

The difficulties lie in deciding how such a system would be monitored, he says, and what penalties should be levied for violations. To Planeta.com founder Mader, certification based on sustainability does not address questions many travelers are concerned about. "Most of the travelers I talk to would love certification if it would tell them where there's a clean bathroom," he says. Mader sees a far greater need for certification in safety- and service-related areas such as scuba diving, rock climbing or massage therapy.

Certification efforts so far have been "prioritized far too ahead of the curve, before we have reliable information, let alone communication," Mader argues. "In countries that are developing rural travel, there are usually six to 12 state or federal entities involved — none of whom ever want to talk to one another. The tourism section and the environmental, labor, agriculture and forestry sections each want to protect its place in the pipeline. Communication that could improve the marketability of the ecotourism product is all too rare. They're not sharing information, and none is very transparent or public."

McLaren, of Indigenous Rights International, questions the parallel being drawn between products like lumber and ecotourism. "It's really hard, because tourism is a service instead of a product. You can follow the trail from farm to market with a potato, but it's much more difficult to certify all these different parts" of tourism.

McLaren says the certification process so far looks to some observers like "another grab at money and control" that has left the local communities out of the process.

"We need to talk to the businesses," says Mader, echoing her concern. "There's a lot of discussion at the consultancy level, but at the operator level we're just not speaking their language."

Martha Honey, executive director of The International Ecotourism Society and a leader of the certification effort, says that while many certification programs came into being without consultation with indigenous people, those involved in current efforts are "extremely concerned about and sensitive to" the issue. Last September, she notes, the first meeting in an effort to bring indigenous peoples to the table was held in Quito, Ecuador, and future meetings are scheduled in Fiji and Norway. She cites as a possible model the Respecting Our Culture program in Australia, run by indigenous peoples through a program called Aboriginal Tourism Australia.

Critics of certification also worry that it will be too costly. "The field is not ready for certification," says Epler Wood. "There's no identifiable market for it, and without a market driver you get a lot of investment in systems that are not selling with the public."

"Ecotourism is a small, micro-business phenomenon," she continues. "The profit margins barely justify staying in business." While certification could have a viable role in developing a bigger market, she says, until the companies are more stable and profitable, they cannot afford it.

Honey agrees that cost is an issue. "Certification cannot be so expensive that it sets the bar too high for small-scale operators," she says, but she feels the problem is surmountable. One solution would be scaled fees, with larger operators paying more. Another might be government subsidies drawn from revenues such as airport taxes or "negative taxes" on less eco-friendly businesses, such as the cruise industry.

Honey explains that existing certification programs failed to develop a large market because most of them had virtually no marketing budget. And, she says, what marketing they did was misdirected. The key to greater success, she believes, is to market the label not to travelers — the ultimate consumers — but to the tourist industry's equivalent of dealers or middle men — tour operators who stand to save money by not having to investigate individual accommodations and attractions for themselves.

Honey also argues that a reliable certification program also would be extremely useful to guidebook publishers, national parks — which must evaluate the reliability of concessionaires — and development agencies like the U.N. Development Programme, the U.S.

The Karawari Lodge in Papua New Guinea's East Sepik Province sits on the edge of a lowland rain forest in one of the country's most remote regions. Visitors can explore the area's varied flora and fauna and visit villages on the Karawari River.

Terra Incognita Ecotours/Gerard "Ged" Caddick

Agency for International Development and the World Bank.

But Xavier Font, a lecturer in tourism management at Leeds Metropolitan University in England, says "certification is most suited to those countries with well-established infrastructures and the finances to support industry to reduce its negative impacts. It is not the best tool for livelihood-based economies or sectors, be it tourism, forestry, agriculture or any other at the center of attention of certification today."[21]

Brian Mullis, president of Sustainable Travel International, a nonprofit organization that is developing the first certification program in North America, disagrees. "Having spent a good part of the last four years looking at the problem," Mullis says, "I don't think it is premature. At the end of the day, the only way sustainable travel can really be defined is to have verification that companies are doing what they say they're doing.

"More and more consumers are supporting businesses that define themselves as green," he continues. "But if they're not doing what they say they're doing, it doesn't really matter what they say."

BACKGROUND

Tourism Is Born

Travel for pleasure came on the world scene with the emergence of wealth and leisure. Affluent Greeks and Romans vacationed at thermal baths and visited exotic locales around Europe and the Mediterranean. The first guidebook for travelers is credited to the French monk Aimeri de Picaud, who in 1130 wrote a tour guide for pilgrims traveling to Spain. In the 18th and 19th centuries, European and British aristocrats as well as wealthy Americans took the "grand tour" of continental Europe's natural and cultural attractions, including the Swiss Alps, and health spas became popular destinations.[22]

Until the Industrial Revolution, travel had more to do with its etymological root — the French word for "work," travailler — than with pleasure. The development of railroads, steamships and, later, the automobile and airplane, made travel easier and faster. The Englishman Thomas Cook set up a travel agency in 1841 and organized tourist excursions by train to temperance rallies in the English Midlands. By the mid-1850s he was offering railway tours of the Continent.

In the United States, the American Express Co. introduced Travelers Cheques and money orders, further easing the logistics of tourism. By the end of the 19th century, the tourism industry had fully emerged, complete with guidebooks, packaged tours, booking agents, hotels and railways with organized timetables.[23]

Earlier, the dawning of the Romantic era in around 1800 had fired a new passion for the exotic among Europeans and an upwelling of scientific curiosity that fueled journeys of exploration and discovery. Beginning in 1799, Alexander von Humboldt, a wealthy German, spent five years exploring in the uncharted reaches of Central and South America, gathering data and specimens. Three decades later, a young British aristocrat keen on biology, Charles Darwin, sailed to the Galapagos Islands and developed the foundations of his revolutionary theory of evolution.[24]

Armchair adventurers avidly sought reports of explorers supported by the British Royal Geographic Society, founded in 1830. Among them were the legendary missionary/explorer David Livingstone in Africa and the man who went to find him, journalist Henry Stanley, in the mid-19th century; Antarctic explorers Robert Scott, the British naval officer who perished on his journey to the South Pole, and Ernest Shackleton in the early 20th century; and Sir Edmund Hillary, the New Zealander who in 1953, with his Nepalese guide Tensing Norgay, first climbed Mt. Everest.

By the late 19th century, the beauty of unspoiled nature was attracting more and more ordinary visitors. In the United States, Congress set aside more than 2 million acres in 1872 to create Yellowstone National Park, the world's first national park. Reserving public lands for "public use, resort and recreation," became a guiding principle of the National Park Service, established in 1916.

Private tourism promoters also played a large role in the creation and expansion of the National Park System, with the Northern Pacific Railroad urging the creation of Yellowstone as a draw for its passengers. The railroads later played similar roles in promoting the creation of Sequoia and Yosemite (1890), Mount Rainier (1899) and Glacier (1910) national parks.[25]

Beginning in Australia in 1879, other countries also set aside protected areas for parks, including Mexico (1898), Argentina (1903) and Sweden (1909). The Sierra Club began its Outings program in 1901 with an expedition for 100 hikers, accompanied by Chinese chefs, pack mules and wagons, to the backcountry wilderness of the Sierra Nevada Mountains. The trips not only provided healthful diversion for the members but also encouraged them to "become active workers for the preservation of the forests and other natural features" of the area.

The political implications behind the early trips would continue to motivate nonprofit organizations to sponsor travel outings in the years ahead.

In the 1950s, big-game hunters began flocking to luxury safari lodges in Kenya, South Africa and, later, Tanzania. The creation of national parks and wildlife

CHRONOLOGY

1860s-1960s *Interest in nature travel grows after first being limited largely to the wealthy.*

1916 U.S. National Park Service is founded.

1920s "Bush walker" movement in Australia increases the popularity of wilderness excursions.

1953 Sir Edmund Hillary and Tenzing Norgay are the first to climb Mount Everest.

1970s *Tourism spreads into remote and fragile regions after wide-bodied jets make travel cheaper.*

1970 First cruise ship visits Antarctica.... First Earth Day on April 22 signals birth of environmental movement.

1980s *Environmental and cultural impact of tourism sparks concern.*

1980 Manila Declaration on World Tourism declares that "tourism does more harm than good" to people and societies in the Third World. . . . Ecumenical Coalition on Third World Tourism takes shape to fight such negative impacts as poverty, pollution and prostitution.

1989 Hague Declaration on Tourism calls on states "to strike a harmonious balance between economic and ecological considerations."

1990s *Ecotourism is promoted as a "win-win" for economic development and the environment. Tourism increases 66 percent in 10 years on the Galapagos Islands.*

1990 The Ecotourism Society (later renamed The International Ecotourism Society) is founded.

1992 First World Congress on Tourism and the Environment is held in Belize.

1995 *Conde Nast Traveler* magazine publishes its first annual "Green List" of top ecotourism destinations.

1996 World Tourism Organization, World Travel & Tourism Council and Earth Council draft Agenda 21

for the travel and tourism industry, outlining key steps governments and industry need to take for sustainability.

1997 Governments and private groups from 77 countries and territories pledge in the Manila Declaration on the Social Impact of Tourism to better involve local communities in tourism planning and to address social abuses.

1999 World Bank and World Tourism Organization agree to cooperate in encouraging sustainable tourism development.

2000s *"Sustainable travel" is embraced by governments and the travel industry. The number of tourists visiting Antarctica tops 10,000 a year.*

2000 Mohonk Agreement sets out terms for international ecotourism certification. . . . One-in-five international tourists travels from an industrial country to a developing one, compared to one-in-13 in the mid-1970s.

2002 U.N. celebrates International Year of Ecotourism; more than 1,000 participants at World Ecotourism Summit approve Quebec Declaration on Ecotourism — stressing the need to address tourism's economic, social and environmental impacts.

2003 The once heavily forested base of Mt. Everest has become an "eroding desert" due to 10,000 trekkers a year burning trees for fuel.

2004 A study about the Galapagos Islands warns that tourism-induced human migration "threatens the future of tourism."

2005 Between 1950 and 2004, the number of tourist arrivals worldwide grows by more than 3,000 percent — from 25 million arrivals to some 760 million in 2004.

2006 International tourist travel jumps 4.5 percent worldwide in the first three months. The fastest-growing destinations are Africa and the Middle East, each rising about 11 percent.

Taking the Guilt Out of Ecotravel

Travel — even by the most dedicated ecotourists — invariably takes a toll on the environment. But now environmentally sensitive travelers are finding ways to compensate.

When the World Economic Forum sponsored a meeting of its Young Global Leaders Summit this year in Vancouver, British Columbia, the forum offered attendees the opportunity to "offset" the negative environmental effect of the emissions generated by their plane flights by contributing to the rehabilitation of a small hydropower plant in Indonesia.

Concerns about the negative impact of their own airplane emissions also prompted conservationists and community-development activists who gathered in Hungary in April 2006, to offset their emissions by planting trees on a Hungarian hillside.

Airplanes contribute 3 to 5 percent of global carbon dioxide emissions — 230 million tons in the United States alone in 2003 — and air transport is one of the world's fastest-growing sources of emissions of carbon dioxide and other so-called greenhouse gases, according to the Worldwatch Institute.[1]

The only sure-fire way to eliminate negative environmental impacts is to stay home — an option some travel writers actually are promoting.[2] But short of that, say those promoting ecotourism, travelers can "give back" to Mother Nature by donating "carbon offsets."

At the Web site for ClimateCare.org, a British organization started in 1998, travelers can learn how many tons of carbon dioxide their trip will produce and donate money to underwrite renewable-energy projects, energy-efficiency improvements and reforestation efforts in developing countries to produce a comparable reduction in carbon emissions.

A round trip between New York and Chicago, for example, produces the equivalent of 0.27 tons of CO_2, which the organization translates into a \$3 donation per traveler to renewable-energy projects.

A 2004 German program, atmosfair (www.atmosfair .de/index.php?id=08L=3) converts carbon emissions into euros, then contributes donated sums to climate-protection projects in India and Brazil. Its installation of solar power instead of diesel- and wood-fired equipment in 10 industrial kitchens in India, for example, will save roughly 570 tons of CO_2 — the equivalent of 2,000 round-trip flights between New York and Chicago.

The Portland, Ore.-based Better World Club claims it's "the first travel company in the world to offer a carbon-offset program." Its TravelCool! Program offers offsets in \$11 increments, which it equates to roughly one ton of CO_2, or a tenth of the emissions produced annually by the typical automobile. The funds collected have helped replace old oil-burning boilers in Portland public schools.

The Web site nativeenergy.com, based in Charlotte, Vt., will calculate all the carbon dioxide emissions from an entire vacation, including hotel stays. The Native American group supports American Indian and farmer-owned wind, solar and methane projects. Contributions to offset automobile and other travel emissions can be made in the form of regular monthly contributions.

---

[1] Lisa Mastny, "Traveling Light: New Paths for International Tourism," Worldwatch Paper 159, December 2001, p. 29; and Esther Addley, "Boom in green holidays as ethical travel takes off, *The Guardian*, July 17, 2006; and P. W. McRandle, "Low-impact vacations (Green Guidance)," *World Watch*, July-August 2006.

[2] See Ian Jack and James Hamilton-Paterson, "Where Travel Writing Went Next," *Granta*, Summer 2006.

sanctuaries by Kenya's British colonial government, however, forced the nomadic Maasai people from their ancestral lands. The resulting resentments led to poaching and vandalism, problems that to this day complicate conservation efforts.

Rise of Ecotourism

The powerful combination of the labor movement and 20th-century industrialization brought tourism within reach of a vast, new universe — the burgeoning population of middle-class wage earners seeking diversion for their annual vacations.

In 1936, the International Labor Organization called for a week's paid vacation every year. A 1970 ILO convention expanded the standard to three weeks with pay.

But it was the rise of the aviation industry after World War II that sparked mass, intercontinental tourism. In 1948 Pan American World Airways introduced tourist class, and the world suddenly grew smaller. In 1957 jet engines made commercial travel faster still.

The introduction of wide-bodied jets in the 1970s made international travel between developed and developing nations practical for holiday travelers. By 1975, international tourist arrivals had surpassed 200 million annually — and double that number by 1990.[26]

In the mid-1970s, 8 percent of all tourists were from developed countries traveling on holidays to developing countries. By the mid-1980s the number had jumped to 17 percent.

Developing countries and international aid institutions initially welcomed the burgeoning source of foreign exchange sparked by the spurt in tourism. The World Bank's first tourism-related loan was made in 1967 for a hotel in Kenya that was partly owned by a subsidiary of Pan American Airways. In the 1970s the bank loaned about $450 million directly to governments for 24 tourism projects in 18 developing countries, and other international aid and lending institutions followed suit.

But the bank's support of conventional tourism and large hotel projects provoked criticism that it encouraged indebtedness while failing to address the problems of poverty in Third World countries. Concern about the environmental effects of resort development, along with a string of financial failures, caused the bank to close down its Tourism Projects Department in 1979.

As the emergence of the environmental movement in the 1960s and '70s pushed international aid agencies to re-examine their commitments, other forces were also pushing the development of a less intrusive, more eco-friendly form of travel.

Despite setbacks among local operators and growing discontent among indigenous peoples, by the turn of the millennium the notion that tourism could be both more lucrative and less resource-intensive than heavy industry or plantation-style monoculture was gaining currency in the international community. In 1998 it was reported to be the only economic sector in which developing countries consistently ran a trade surplus. It represented roughly 10 percent of developing-world exports and accounted for more than 40 percent of the gross domestic product in some countries.[27]

In 2002, more than 1,000 participants from 132 countries gathered in Quebec, Canada, to attend the World Ecotourism Summit, organized by the U.N. Environment Programme and the World Tourism Organization. In adopting the Quebec Declaration on

Watched by local experts, an ecotourist gives a blowgun a try in Peru's Amazon rain forest. Tour groups now flock to the Amazon for trips up the river and forays into the forest in search of the region's animals and colorful birds.

Ecotourism, they embraced "the principles of sustainable tourism, concerning the economic, social and environmental impacts of tourism" — which would come to be seen as the "triple bottom line" in development circles.

The declaration also pointed out that ecotourism differed from the broader concept of "sustainable tourism" by four key characteristics:

- contribution to the conservation of natural and cultural heritage;
- inclusion of local and indigenous communities;
- interpretation of natural and cultural heritage; and
- affinity for independent and small-group travelers.[28]

The summit also boosted ecotourism certification efforts by endorsing "the use of certification as a tool for measuring sound ecotourism and sustainable tourism" while also stressing that certification systems "should reflect regional and local criteria."[29]

Giving native peoples a stake in conservation outcomes was a prime force behind the development of ecotourism, says Harold Goodwin, director of the International Centre for Responsible Tourism at the University of Greenwich in England. To win the support of indigenous peoples, international conservation organizations began creating environmentally responsible tourist accommodations near private conservation areas

G.A.P Adventures

Terra Incognita Ecotours/Gerard "Ged" Caddick

G.A.P Adventures

Mixing People and Nature

Penguins in Antarctica show no fear of humans (top); tourists in Baja, Calif., watch a blue whale (middle); and a visitor gets acquainted with giant turtles in the Galapagos Islands (bottom).

that would provide some income to native peoples. Foundations were established to return earnings to the community in the form of water projects and other physical improvements, educational opportunities, even clinics and health services. Besides being altruistic, the program had practical outcomes as well.

"You have to give the local community economic benefits so they don't poach," Goodwin says.

Ecotourism also opened up new marketing possibilities, Goodwin says. Costa Rica, for example, unable to compete in the world tourism market on the quality of its beaches, began promoting its rich, unspoiled biodiversity as an attraction — with great success. Belize followed suit.

Ecotourism also introduced a new type of competition, he says, because "there are only so many places to go and things to do," and only so much elasticity in pricing. Introducing the values of environmentalism, conservation and education, he says, "avoids competing on price. You can compete on interpretation."

But many of the first small, local ecotourism endeavors that sprang up in the 1990s failed because there was a disconnect between the international market and the local entrepreneurs, Goodwin says. Those that succeeded, however, transformed their surroundings.

"In the early 1990s, everybody was talking about ecotourism," says anthropologist Vivanco, who did his field research at that time near the private Monte Verde Cloud Forest Preserve, considered the jewel in the crown of Costa Rica's extensive park system. "Over 10 years ago, there were about 45,000 to 50,000 tourists a year in an area of about 3,500 to 4,000 inhabitants," he says. But as the number of visitors increased and new facilities went up, hundreds of Costa Rican workers moved to the area, creating a negative environmental impact on the fringe of the preserve — a problem that has afflicted ecotourism sites as remote as the Galapagos Islands.

"Nowadays, there are at least 140,000, and as many as 200,000 visitors, "and it's grown up in a completely unmanaged way at the edge of the park," he says.

"The population explosion has an impact on their whole way of life," Vivanco continues. "Class differences emerged that didn't exist before. Locally, many people were saying, 'It's a bit out of hand, we need to get greater control.' "

CURRENT SITUATION
Global Presence

Growing awareness of the environmental costs of travel, such as its contribution to global warming, increasingly

Making Sure Your Travel Is Really 'Green'

The term ecotourism is used so loosely by marketers these days that tourists may be getting "ecotourism lite," not a truly "green" experience, says Katie Maschman, a spokeswoman for The International Ecotourism Society.

"It's great to see ecotourism principles incorporated from a mass-tourism perspective," Maschman says, "but there is a lot of green-washing going on. A hotel simply advertising that they only change the sheets every three days does not, by any means, suggest they've given it real attention."

Research is vital to planning a trip that minimizes negative environmental and cultural impacts, experts say. And while a variety of Web sites and guidebooks focus on "green" travel, nothing substitutes for direct questioning of tour and facility operators and of other travelers. [1]

"The best thing to do is to ask to speak to former clients," says Steve Powers, of Hidden Treasure Tours, in Long Beach, N.Y. Like many other tour packagers, Powers tries to support small, grassroots programs. But it can be difficult to determine whether operators at a far-off destination are actually doing what they say.

A tourist also can ask travel companies for their policies, which may already be codified and thus easily communicated. "If you want to book a tour," says Ron Mader, founder of the ecotourism Web site planeta.com, "ask [tour operators] if they support conservation or local development projects. Many agencies and operators are very proud of their environmental conservation and community-development work." [2]

Helpful Web sites featuring ecotourism destinations are operated by nonprofit organizations, travel marketers and for-profit online travel clubs and information exchanges, including www.sustainabletravelinternational.org, ecoclub.com, responsibletravel.com, eco-indextourism.org, ecotourism.org, ecotour.org, tourismconcern.org, travelersconservationtrust.org, and visit21.net.

Travel-award programs are another good source of ideas, such as the Tourism for Tomorrow awards of the World Travel & Tourism Council at www.tourismfortomorrow.com; the annual ecolodge award of the International Ecotourism Club, available at ecoclub.com; and the First Choice Responsible Tourism Awards from responsibletravel.com.

In addition to consulting those and similar sites, adding terms such as "green travel" or "ecotourism" to a country- or destination-based Internet search can bring results.

Here are the questions experts say travelers should ask their tour firm or the operator of the destination:

- Do you have an ethical ecotourism policy?
- What steps have you taken to reduce waste and water use?
- Do you practice recycling?
- How do you minimize damage to wildlife and marine environments?
- What community members do you employ and do they have opportunities for advancement? What local products do you purchase, and do you use local produce whenever possible? What community projects are you involved in?
- Do you donate to community organizations and/or conservation programs?
- What energy-saving activities do you practice?
- Are your buildings built with locally available materials?
- Do you use environmentally friendly products?

---

[1] P. W. McRandle, "Low-impact Vacations (Green Guidance)," *World Watch*, July-August 2006; and Esther Addley, "Boom in Green Holidays as Ethical Travel Takes Off," *The Guardian*, July 17, 2006.

[2] Quoted in Clay Hubbs, "Responsible Travel and Ecotourism," *Transitions Abroad*, May/June 2001, www.transitionsabroad.com/publications/magazine.

---

affects travel decisions. More than three-quarters of U.S. travelers "feel it is important their visits not damage the environment," according to a study by the Travel Industry Association of America and *National Geographic Traveler* magazine. The study estimated that 17 million U.S. travelers consider environmental factors when deciding which travel companies to patronize.[30]

A survey by the International Hotels Environmental Initiative found that more than two-thirds of U.S. and Australian travelers and 90 percent of British tourists consider active protection of the environment — including support of local communities — to be part of a hotel's responsibility.[31] Another industry study found that 70 percent of U.S., British and Australian travelers

Tourism is threatening the Philippines' ancient Banaue rice terraces, created 2,000 years ago by Ifugao tribesmen. The naturally irrigated paddies are endangered by deforestation to supply wood for tourist handicrafts and by the water demands of hotels and restaurants.

would pay up to $150 more for a two-week stay in a hotel with a "responsible environmental attitude."[32]

Overall, the travel industry employs 200 million people, generates $3.6 trillion in economic activity and accounts for one in every 12 jobs worldwide.[33] Between 1950 and 2004, the number of tourist arrivals worldwide grew by more than 3,000 percent — from 25 million arrivals in 1950 to some 760 million in 2004.[34]

Moreover, travelers' destinations have shifted, with visits to the developing world increasing dramatically while travel to Europe and the Americas has dropped. By 2000, one-in-five international tourists from industrial countries traveled to a developing nation, compared to one-in-13 in the mid-1970s.[35] The fastest-growing areas for international travel in the first quarter of 2006 were Africa and the Middle East, with estimated increases of 11 percent each.[36]

For example, Wildland Adventures conducts tours to Central America, the Andes, Africa, Turkey, Egypt, Australia, New Zealand and Alaska. The Seattle-based tour operator created the nonprofit Traveler's Conservation Trust, which contributes a portion of the firm's earnings to community-improvement projects and conservation organizations in the countries they visit.

In the Ecuadorian Amazon rain forest, Yachana, an eco-lodge constructed in 1995 by the Foundation for Integrated Education and Development, attracts nearly 2,000 visitors a year — but limits the number to 40 at a time — who reach the lodge by canoe. Visitors spend time with indigenous families, participate in traditional rituals and visit the foundation's model farm and tree nursery. The lodge has generated more than $3.5 million for the foundation's programs in conservation, poverty reduction, health care and community development.

International Development

"Nearly every country with national parks and protected areas is marketing some type of ecotourism," according to the Center on Ecotourism and Sustainable Development. "Lending and aid agencies are funneling hundreds of millions of dollars into projects that include ecotourism; major environmental organizations are sponsoring ecotourism projects and departments; and millions of travelers are going on ecotours."

"It's absolutely excellent," says ecotourism consultant Epler Wood. "I used to tell people I was a consultant on ecotourism, and they'd give me a blank stare. Now they are, like, 'Wow, you are so lucky.' It's been one of our greatest goals to make it an accepted, mainstream profession."

Moreover, many of the basic tenets of ecotourism are being embraced by the international development world as goals for economic development generally. In choosing which development projects to fund, the new "triple bottom line" adds environmental and social/cultural effects to the longstanding criterion of profitability — at least on paper.

At a tourism policy forum at George Washington University in October 2004 — the first of its kind — Inter-American Development Bank (IDB) President Enrique Iglesias and World Bank Vice President James Adams joined delegates from donor agencies, developing countries and academia in endorsing tourism's potential as a sustainable-development strategy. They also agreed, however, that the complex nature of the industry presents special challenges.

The IDB, after being involved with tourism projects for 30 years, has changed its focus from big infrastructure projects to more community-based projects, Iglesias said. Adams reported the World Bank had undertaken approximately 100 projects, including tourism in 56 countries — 3 percent of the bank's total investment.[37]

Will improved certification make ecotourism more marketable?

YES
Martha Honey
Executive Director, The International Ecotourism Society

Written for *CQ Researcher*, October 2006

Reputable "green" certification programs that measure environmental and social impacts will promote ecotourism — but it will take time to educate consumers. It took some 30 years to build the U.S. market for certified organic foods, and now consumer demand for organics is booming. In tourism, AAA and 5 Star quality-certification programs for hotels and restaurants have been around for nearly a century and are part of the "fabric" of the tourism industry.

U.S. consumers want to travel responsibly. But they are not yet actively asking for "green" certification, in part because there is no national program.

Around the world, my colleague Amos Bién notes there are some 60 to 80 "green" tourism-certification programs, but most are less than 10 years old. Costa Rica's Certification for Sustainable Tourism (CST) program, launched in 1998, awards one to five green leaves to hotels and tour operators. Lapa Rios Eco-lodge is one of only two hotels there to have earned five leaves. Owner Karen Lewis sees a link between certification, improved sustainability and increased marketability. "Certification is the best internal audit out there, for any owner and/or management team," she says.

Adriane Janer, of EcoBrazil, who has been involved in creating Brazil's new Sustainable Tourism Program, says "certification has been very successful in improving quality and reliability of products and services." In Guatemala, the Green Deal program principally certifies small businesses at a minimal cost of $300. In Costa Rica, certification is free, and the CST cannot keep up with all the hotels wanting to be audited.

In tourism, as in retailing, we're beginning to see the successful use of "retailers" — tour operators — who are choosing to use certified hotels and other "green" supplies. The Dutch tour operators association, which represents over 850 travel companies, requires all members to use hotels and other businesses that have a credible sustainability policy. In Costa Rica, seven leading tour operators are giving preference to CST-certified hotels, and at least two are hoping within three years to be using only certified hotels.

Indeed, without certification, the danger of 'greenwashing' — businesses that use "eco" language in their marketing but don't fit any of the criteria of ecotourism — greatly increases. Certification provides a necessary tool to separate the wheat from the chafe, the genuine ecotourism businesses from the scams and the shams.

As Glenn Jampol, owner of the Finca Rosa Blanca Inn, the other Costa Rican hotel to have earned five green leaves, puts it, "I envision a day when guests will routinely check for Rosa Blanca's green leaf rating as well as our star rating."

NO
Ron Mader
Founder, Planeta.com

Written for *CQ Researcher*, October 2006

Indigenous peoples, tour operators and others claim that many certification programs for ecotourism and sustainable travel do not deserve support. I agree.

Certification has a number of serious problems, starting with the lack of consumer demand. Moreover, most stakeholders have been left out of the process, including indigenous people, community representatives and owners of travel businesses. When invited to participate, many of these leaders opt out, reminding organizers they have other priorities.

Stakeholders around the world confided during the International Year of Ecotourism that certification does not enhance business. In fact, some leading tour operators believe certification and accreditation schemes are a scam that creates a cottage industry for consultants.

In short, ecotourism certification is not a "market-driven" option.

Said one tour operator during the Ethical Marketing of Ecotourism Conference: "First, get consumers to care, then worry about rating and certification. Doing it any other way is not only putting the cart before the horse, it is putting the wheel before the cart, the spoke before the wheels."

Much more effective are industry awards. They are conducted in the public eye and cost a fraction of formal certification programs. Likewise, an investment in Google ads pays better dividends than certification.

In 2006 Planeta.com invited tourism professionals — particularly those at the forefront of ecotourism — to participate in a candid review of tourism promotion. Respondents gave government marketing campaigns around the world a low mark. Comments indicate that in-country and outbound travel operators do not know the PR agencies that represent the country.

These are alarming results for those interested in ecotourism and responsible travel as they indicate that rather than promoting what's available, the promotion departments are seen as an obstacle, particularly for small- and medium-sized in-country businesses.

If our collective goal is to improve the marketing of ecotourism, the solution is simply to improve the dialogue among operators and national tourism campaigns. The reality is that by far the most "eco" and "community-focused" services are the ones that receive the least promotion.

While little or no consumer demand may exist for certified "eco" vacations, we should not accept the status quo. The emphasis needs to be placed on evaluating the industry and offering training and promotion for local providers who strive toward sustainability and ecotourism.

Terra Incognita Ecotours/Gerard "Ged" Caddick

Visitors can come within a few yards of wild mountain gorillas in Volcanoes National Park, on the Rwanda side of the Virunga Volcanoes. "I just about burst open with happiness every time I get within one or two feet of them," said naturalist Dian Fossey, who studied the gorillas for years.

USAID Administrator Andrew Natsios similarly stressed the need for community involvement to ensure tourism is sustainable. "Properly planned tourism requires good natural-resource management and good local governance to protect and enhance the resources on which it depends," he said.[38]

Until recently, says Epler Wood, ecotourism funds typically were funneled through conservation-oriented NGOs, which often lacked the business experience needed to make new enterprises succeed. Another handicap was the paucity of small-scale loans. In 1995, she recalls, the International Finance Corp., profit-making arm of the World Bank, was investing no less than $500 million per project. Now, she says, they're down to about $1 million — still high for community-based ecotourism undertakings. And they're looking for partners with expertise in business development, not conservation.

"We're at the very beginning phase in a new era of enterprise development," Epler Wood says. "It's still a new paradigm. Economic growth still gets the big players and the big money, while the environmental and humanitarian development goals tend to be evaluative afterthoughts, instead of being integral to the projects."

But, she says, the big players are taking an interest. "The donor architecture is still not quite built to accommodate the potential of ecotourism as a sustainable-development tool. It's a very big, slow-moving world, but you do see change happening within it."

Variations on a Theme

As ecotourism joins the tourism mainstream, it is spinning off numerous new tourism genres. In Europe, especially, so-called pro-poor tourism, responsible tourism and ethical tourism aim to extend the benefits of tourism to developing countries while improving its effects on destination communities and the environment.

Evidence is mounting that travelers are embracing the concept's values. In England this past summer, ethical holidays reportedly were the fastest-growing travel sector. According to a recent survey, by 2010 the number of British visitors going on "ethical" holidays outside England will have grown to 2.5 million trips a year, or 5 percent of the market. The Web site ResponsibleTravel.com has seen bookings double in the last year.[39]

Other variations of ecotourism are viewed less favorably by ecotourism advocates. Adventure travel to exotic and often physically challenging destinations — "ecotourism with a kick," ecotourism society executive director Honey calls it — has been a particularly fast-growing style of nature tourism.

Adventure travel proponents argue that adventurers, like ecotravelers, have an interest in protecting the resources they enjoy, but critics blame them for a wide range of damaging intrusions — helicopter trips causing noise and air pollution while taking skiers to pristine mountain tops; growing numbers of tourists struggling to ascend Mt. Everest (and risking their lives and the lives of others in the process); polar bear watchers who ride bus-like vehicles on monster-truck tires along the south shore of Hudson Bay in Manitoba in the fall, dangerously stressing the bears when they should be building up fat reserves for the long winter season.[40]

"Whereas nature, wildlife and adventure tourism are defined solely by the recreational activities of the tourist," Honey explains, "ecotourism is defined as well by its benefits to both conservation and people in the host country."

'Green' Chic

An essay in *The New York Times* fall travel magazine, "Easy Being Green," portrays ecotourism as the latest fashion trend. "In luxury resorts, eco is the flavor du jour," proclaims author Heidi S. Mitchell.[41]

"There has been a real movement toward high-end ecotourism," Honey said. A 2004 survey found that 38 percent would be willing to pay a premium to patronize travel companies that use sustainable environmental practices.[42]

But as green travel goes upscale, environmentalists worry that the original goals of environmental conservation paired with community betterment will be lost under a misleading "greenwash."

"Ecotourism has been watered down from the beginning," says Planeta.com founder Mader. "The NGOs have watered it down. They're even participating in Antarctic travel."

But others, like Honey, see the upscale trend as a sign that environmental sustainability — a key aspect of ecotourism — is having a real effect on the travel industry as a whole. In a less glamorous example, the Rainforest Alliance, with support from the Inter-American Development Bank, is working with small- and medium-sized travel businesses in Latin America to improve sustainable practices, whether or not the businesses meet all the requirements of classic ecotourism.

In Costa Rica, Guatemala, Belize and Ecuador, more than 200 tourism operations in or near sensitive or protected areas are receiving training in the "best practices" of sustainable tourism, including waste management and water and electricity conservation, as well as such social factors as paying adequate salaries and including local and indigenous people in decision-making.

Businesses that adopt best practices become eligible for certification by existing national programs and gain access to marketing networks and trade-show appearances organized by the Rainforest Alliance. The program has had two benefits, says Alliance marketing specialist Christina Suhr: "It has let people know what we do, and they have gained confidence in us."

OUTLOOK
Setting Limits

The latest worry for travelers who care about the Earth's environment is global warming, especially since air transport is one of the world's fastest-growing sources of emissions of carbon dioxide and other greenhouse gases. If global warming continues unabated, many of the attractions most favored by eco-travelers will be among the most vulnerable. A report for the United Kingdom's World Wide Fund for Nature warned of soaring temperatures, forest fires and other consequences that could drive wildlife from safari parks in Africa, damage Brazil's rain forest ecosystems and flood beaches and coastal destinations worldwide.[43]

Some observers say the costs of global travel in environmental damage, cultural homogenization and economic displacement are so serious that would-be travelers should just stay home.

"The more we flock to view the disappearing glaciers, the faster they will vanish," mused novelist James Hamilton-Paterson.[44]

Similarly, travel writer Anneli Rufus observes ruefully, "Colonialism isn't dead. Colonialism is alive and well every time you travel from the First World to the Third and come home bearing photographs of sharks and storms and slums . . . and then you tell your friends and co-workers, 'Oh man, it was so great, you gotta go.' "

But the quandary Rufus faces as she considers ending her travel writing is common to affluent travelers visiting poor countries: "Am I saving some tribe from extinction by not looking for it, much less telling you about it? Or am I starving some shopkeeper by not buying his sandals? Both. Neither. I am out of that [travel writing] game now."[45]

But indigenous-rights activist McLaren feels that the interpersonal connections and first-person impressions derived from independent travel are more important than ever. "In an age where the media dominates and shapes our views of the world," she writes, "it is imperative to utilize tourism as a means to effectively communicate with one another. In fact, there is no better way to understand the global crisis that we face together than through people-to-people communication."[46]

McLaren finds hope in the growing number of successful projects that blend tourism, environmentalism and sustainability, like Elephant Valley eco-resort in India. "There are lots of good examples, though not everybody calls them ecotourism," McLaren says. "A lot of workable projects tend to be more regional, more of public-private partnerships. Elephant Valley, she says, is "a beautiful, low-impact place. Money is really being used to conserve the area, employ local people, produce food, teach about sustainability and work with schools in the region."

In Tasmania, ecotourism has been proposed as an alternative to logging in Australia's largest temperate rain forest, the Tarkine.[47]

In the Patagonia region of southern Chile, environmentalists are seeking to block plans to build a series of hydro-electric dams that would flood thousands of acres of rugged, pristine lands that, they say, could better serve as ecotourism attractions and ranchland.[48]

And in Puerto Rico, environmentalists and other groups are fighting the proposed development of resorts and residential complexes in one of the territory's "last remaining pristine coastal areas," seeking to preserve it "for wildlife, the citizens of Puerto Rico and ecotourism." According to the Waterkeeper Alliance, an organization leading the fight, the developments threaten local water supplies and also mean that "tourists who flock to Puerto Rico to enjoy its cultural and natural resources...will have one less reason to visit the island."[49]

NOTES

1. The International Ecotourism Society, Fact Sheet, June 2004, p. 2.

2. Deborah McLaren, "Rethinking Tourism," Planeta Forum, updated June 16, 2006, www.planeta.com/planeta/97/1197rtpro.html; Martha Honey, *Ecotourism and Sustainable Development: Who Owns Paradise?* (1999), p. 9.

3. A 2003 study by the Travel Industry Association of America and *National Geographic Traveler* found that 55.1 million U.S. travelers could be classified as "geo-tourists" interested in nature, culture and heritage tourism; see The International Ecotourism Society, *op. cit.*

4. Jacob Park, "The Paradox of Paradise," *Environment*, October 1999. For a detailed discussion of the environmental costs of resort development, see Polly Patullo, *Last Resorts: the Cost of Tourism in the Caribbean* (1996).

5. Rosaleen Duffy, *A Trip Too Far: Ecotourism, Politics & Exploitation* (2002), pp. x-xii.

6. Lisa Mastny, "Traveling Light," *Worldwatch Paper 159*, Worldwatch Institute, 2001, p. 10.

7. Rene Ebersole, "Take the High Road," *Audubon Travel Issue*, July-August 2006, p. 39.

8. Conservation International Web site; www.conservation.org/xp/CIWEB/programs/ecotourism/.

9. Finn-Olaf Jones, "Tourism Stripping Everest's Forests Bare," *National Geographic Traveler*, Aug. 29, 2003.

10. *Ibid.*

11. Simon Davis, "So Can Tourism Ever Really Be Ethical?" *The* [London] *Evening Standard*, July 19, 2006, p. 51.

12. Costas Christ Sr., "A Road Less Traveled," Conservation International Web site; www.conservation.org/xp/frontlines/partners/focus32-1.xml.

13. Maurice Malanes, "Tourism Killing World's Eighth Wonder," Third World Network, www.twnside.org.sg/title/mm-cn.htm.

14. An exception to the low-impact policy was recently permitted, allowing small kayaking groups to camp in preapproved sites on some islands.

15. Juliet Eilperin, "Despite Efforts, Some Tours Do Leave Footprints," *The Washington Post*, April 2, 2006, p. A1.

16. Juliet Eilperin, "Science Notebook," *The Washington Post*, Jan. 30, 2006, p. A5.

17. For background, see Thomas Arrandale, "National Parks Under Pressure," *CQ Researcher*, Oct. 6, 2006, pp. 817-840.

18. Janet Frankston, "State to push unlikely site for eco-tourists: the Meadowlands," The Associated Press, Aug. 8, 2006.

19. Christopher LaFranchi and Greenpeace Pacific, "Islands Adrift: Comparing Industrial and Small-Scale Economic Options for Marovo Lagoon Region of the Solomon Islands," Greenpeace, 1999, p. 4; www.greenpeace.org/international.

20. *Ibid.*

21. Xavier Font, "Critical Review of Certification and Accreditation in Sustainable Tourism Governance," www.Planeta.com.

22. Unless otherwise noted, background drawn from Honey, *op. cit.*, pp. 7-8.

23. Mastny, *op. cit.*, p. 10.

24. For background, see Marcia Clemmitt, "Intelligent Design," *CQ Researcher*, July 29, 2005, pp. 637-660.

25. Rachel S. Cox, "Protecting the National Parks," *CQ Researcher*, June 16, 2000, p. 521-544.

26. Mastny, *op. cit.*, p. 13.

27. *Ibid.*

28. See "Ecotourism: a UN Declaration," *The Irish Times*, Aug. 5, 2006.

29. Martha Honey, "Protecting Eden: Setting Green Standards for the Tourism Industry," *Environment*, July-August, 2003.

30. *Ibid.* For background, see Marcia Clemmitt, "Climate Change," *CQ Researcher*, Jan. 27, 2006, pp. 73-96.

31. Zoe Chafe, "Consumer Demand and Operator Support for Socially and Environmentally Responsible Tourism," CESD/TIES Working Paper No. 104, Center on Ecotourism and Sustainable Development and The International Ecotourism Society, revised April 2005, p. 4.

32. *Ibid.*, p. 6.

33. Mintel report cited in The International Ecotourism Society, Ecotourism Fact Sheet, "Eco and Ethical Tourism-UK," October 2003.

34. Mastny, *op. cit.*, and "Ecotourism Fact Sheet," The International Ecotourism Society and World Tourism Organization, *World Tourism Barometer*, January 2005, p. 2.

35. Martha Honey, *Ecotourism and Sustainable Development: Who Owns Paradise?* (1999), p. 8.

36. World Tourism Organization, news release, *op. cit.*

37. Cited in www.dantei.org/wto.forum/background-papers.html

38. Theodoro Koumelis, "WTO Policy Forum: Tourism is top priority in fight against poverty," Oct. 22, 2004, TravelDailyNews.com.

39. Simon Davis, "So Can Tourism Ever Really Be Ethical?" *The* [London] *Evening Standard*, July 19, 2006, p. A51.

40. Mark Clayton, "When Ecotourism Kills," *The Christian Science Monitor*, Nov. 4, 2004, p. 13.

41. Heidi S. Mitchell, "Easy Being Green," *The New York Times Style Magazine*, fall travel 2006, Sept. 24, 2006, p. 14.

42. Christopher Solomon, "Where the High Life Comes Naturally," *The New York Times*, May 1, 2005, Sect. 5, Travel, p. 3.

43. Mastny, *op. cit.*, p. 29. The report is by David Viner and Maureen Agnew, "Climate Change and Its Impact on Tourism," 1999.

44. James Hamilton-Paterson, "The End of Travel," *Granta*, summer 2006, pp. 221-234.

45. Anneli Rufus, "There's No Such Thing as Eco-Tourism," AlterNet; posted Aug. 14, 2006; www.alternet.org/story/40174/.

46. McLaren, *op. cit.*

47. Leisa Tyler, "Next Time You're In . . . Tasmania," *Time International*, Dec. 27, 2004, p. 120.

48. Larry Rohter, "For Power or Beauty? Debating the Course of Chile's Rivers," *The New York Times*, Aug. 6, 2006, p. 3.

49. Waterkeeper Alliance Web site, "Marriott and Four Seasons: Do Not Disturb PR"; www.waterkeeper.org/mainarticledetails.aspx?articleid=262.

BIBLIOGRAPHY

Books

Buckley, Ralf, ed., *Environmental Impacts of Ecotourism, CABI Publishing*, 2004.
This collection of articles analyzes the cost of various types of ecotourism and what is being done to mitigate negative impacts of the industry.

Duffy, Rosaleen, *A Trip Too Far: Ecotourism, Politics and Exploitation, Earthscan*, 2002.
Based on her field work in Belize, a senior lecturer at the Centre for International Politics at the University of Manchester in England critiques positive assumptions about ecotourism by examining its place in the complex web of "green capitalism."

Honey, Martha, *Ecotourism and Sustainable Development: Who Owns Paradise? Island Press*, 1999.
Using a clear, engaging writing style, Honey outlines the history and development of ecotourism, including a country-by-country study of the industry.

Weaver, David B., ed., *The Encyclopedia of Ecotourism*, *CABI Publishing*, 2001.
Papers by leading experts cover a range of ecotourism issues — from defining the term and its impact on host destinations to the practicalities of business planning and management.

Articles

Boynton, Graham, "The Search for Authenticity," *The Nation*, Oct. 6, 1997.
Paradoxes and compromises emerge when tourists search for "the real thing" in the developing world.

Duffy, Rosaleen, ed., "The Politics of Ecotourism and the Developing World," *Journal of Ecotourism*, Vol. 5, Nos. 1 and 2, September 2006.
An ecotourism scholar explores the range of issues raised by the politics of ecotourism in the developing world — from abstract theories to specific cases.

Ebersole, Rene, "Take the High Road," *Audubon Travel Issue*, July-August 2006, p. 39.
Without a globally recognizable certification label, travelers cannot be sure which trips and hotels qualify as genuinely ecologically friendly.

Honey, Martha, "Protecting Eden: Setting Green Standards for the Tourism Industry," *Environment*, July-August, 2003.
The writer provides an excellent overview of the background and rationale for creating a regularized certification program for ecotourism.

Jones, Finn-Olaf, "Tourism Stripping Everest's Forests Bare," *National Geographic Traveler*, Aug. 29, 2003.
As of 2003, more than 25,000 trekkers were visiting the Khumbu Valley near Mt. Everest, turning into "an eroding desert" much of the area described by Sir Edmund Hillary in 1951 as being superbly forested.

Nicholson-Lord, David, "The Politics of Travel: Is Tourism Just Colonialism in Another Guise?" *The Nation*, Oct. 6, 1997.

The writer offers a negative take on the cultural, political and economic conundrums posed by ecotourism.

Vivanco, Luis A., "The Prospects and Dilemmas of Indigenous Tourism Standards and Certification," in R. Black and A. Crabtree, eds., *Quality Control and Ecotourism Certification, CAB International*, in press.
An anthropologist examines ecotourism certification from the point of view of native peoples.

Reports and Studies

Chafe, Zoe, "Consumer Demand and Operator Support for Socially and Environmentally Responsible Tourism," *CESD/TIES Working Paper No. 104, Center on Ecotourism and Sustainable Development/ The International Ecotourism Society*, revised April 2005.
Statistics and trends are presented from a range of studies focusing on the U.S., Europe, Costa Rica and Australia.

Christ, Costas, Oliver Hillel, Seleni Matus and Jamie Sweeting, "Tourism and Biodiversity: Mapping Tourism's Global Footprint," *Conservation International*, 2003, p. 7.
The authors document the overlap between biodiversity "hotspots" and tourist destinations, making a case for carefully managed, sustainable tourism.

LaFranchi, Christopher, and Greenpeace Pacific, "Islands Adrift? Comparing Industrial and Small-scale Economic Options for Marovo Lagoon Region of the Solomon Islands," *Greenpeace*, March 1999; www.greenpeace.org/international/press/reports/islands-adrift-comparing-indu.
An analysis of the subsistence-based economy of a small but biologically rich region illuminates the complex issues that arise when ecotourism is chosen over more conventional, extractive development routes.

Mastny, Lisa, "Traveling Light: New Paths for International Tourism," *Worldwatch Paper 159, Worldwatch Institute* 2001.
A well-documented study examines the environmental implications of global travel in light of the massive economic forces it entails and considers the challenges and opportunities of achieving sustainable travel.

For More Information

Center on Ecotourism and Sustainable Development, 1333 H St., N.W., Suite 300, East Tower, Washington, DC 20005; (202) 347-9203; www.ecotourismcesd.org. Designs, monitors, evaluates and seeks to improve ecotourism practices and principles.

Conservation International, 1919 M St., N.W., Suite 600, Washington, DC 20036; (202) 912-1000; www.conservation .org. Seeks to protect endangered plants and animals around the world.

EplerWood International, www.eplerwood.com. Consultancy that offers insights into the challenges and opportunities of ecotourism from specific projects to broader economic and organizational issues.

The International Ecotourism Society, 1333 H St., N.W., Suite 300, East Tower, Washington, DC 20005; (202)

347-9203; www.ecotourism.org. Works to foster responsible travel to natural areas that conserves the environment and improves the well-being of local people.

Planeta.com, www.planeta.com. An ecotourism Web site featuring news, blog articles and links to other relevant Internet sites.

Transitions Abroad, P.O. Box 745, Bennington, VT 05201; (802) 442-4827; www.transitionsabroad.com. Web site offering information on working, studying, traveling and living abroad.

World Tourism Organization, Calle Capitan Haya, 42, 28020 Madrid, Spain; (34) 91 567 9301; www.unwto.org. United Nations agency that promotes economic development through responsible, sustainable tourism.

Philanthropy in America

Are Americans Generous Givers?

Peter Katel

Billionaire investor Warren Buffett and his wife Susan arrive for a state dinner at the White House in February 2005. Buffett, who recently pledged to give away most of his $44 billion fortune, urges other wealthy Americans to more generously support philanthropic causes.

From *CQ Researcher*, December 8, 2006.

In a world where wealth and conspicuous consumption often get big headlines, Warren Buffett's June 25 announcement made front pages around the world. Often called the world's second-richest man, the 76-year-old investment wizard from Omaha declared he would give away most of his $44 billion fortune.* And in keeping with his unassuming manner — he still lives in the same modest house he's been occupying for more than 40 years — he said most of the money would go to a foundation named for someone else. In fact, it's going to the vast foundation started by Microsoft co-founder Bill Gates and his wife Melinda.

Buffett, who has five children, pointedly rejected the standard rich man's practice of leaving most of his fortune to his family. "When your kids have all the advantages anyway . . . I would say it's neither right nor rational to be flooding them with money," he told *Fortune* magazine. . . . Dynastic mega-wealth would further tilt the playing field that we ought to be trying instead to level."[1]

"Never in my career have I seen as much attention focused on philanthropy as in the two or three weeks after [Buffett's] announcement," says James A. Smith, a professor of philanthropy at Georgetown University's Public Policy Institute. "We had [the German newspaper] *Die Zeit*, here, and a film crew from Singapore."

Astounding as it was, Buffett's jaw-dropping donation was just the latest in a long line of recent mega-gifts, many from real-estate

---

* Buffett structured his donation as a yearly gift of stock in his firm, Berkshire Hathaway Inc. The approximately $6 billion in shares not going to the Gates Foundation is being given to four philanthropic foundations that his children operate.

Donations Have Doubled Since 1966

Philanthropic contributions have more than doubled since 1966, with individuals giving most of the total. Donations increased dramatically during the 1996-2000 economic boom.

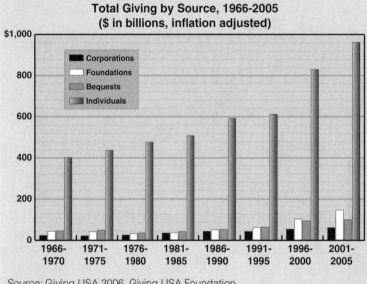

Total Giving by Source, 1966-2005
($ in billions, inflation adjusted)

Legend:
- Corporations
- Foundations
- Bequests
- Individuals

Source: Giving USA 2006, Giving USA Foundation

consortium to treat 100,000 more children in 40 poor countries next year. In addition, Clinton and former President George H. W. Bush — who first teamed up to raise funds for tsunami relief efforts in Southeast Asia — raised $80 million after Hurricane Katrina for reconstruction projects in the U.S. Gulf Coast region.[4]

Last year U.S. corporations, foundations and individuals donated $260.3 billion — slightly below their all-time high of $260.5 billion at the height of the dot-com bubble in 2000.[5] Individuals gave $199 billion of the total. (*See graph, p. 339.*) Although 67 percent of all American households give to charity, rich Americans have the biggest impact: Nine percent of households with incomes over $100,000 provided 43 percent of all charitable donations in 2003, according to the most recent data from the Giving USA Foundation.[6]

If donations following the tsunami, the India-Pakistan earthquake and Hurricanes Katrina, Rita and Wilma are excluded, however, charitable giving increased only nominally in 2005, from $245.22 billion to $252.99 billion — actually a 0.2 percent drop after adjusting for inflation.[7]

Viewed over the past 40 years, however, philanthropic contributions from Americans have soared. In 1965, total donations amounted to about $91 billion. Since then, inflation-adjusted donations have risen 185 percent.

Poor people who donate to charity give a greater percentage of their incomes than those in other income groups. That share runs as high as 4.7 percent for the poor (who favor religious causes) and no higher than 3.4 percent for the wealthy. But the better-off are more likely, as a group, to contribute in the first place.[8]

Historically, American philanthropy has compiled a record of achievement that no one disputes. Philanthropic foundations funded development of the Salk polio vaccine, drought- and plague-resistant strains of corn and wheat and modern medical-school curricula. Foundations also kept black colleges and universities alive throughout the Jim Crow era.[9]

and high-tech billionaires. Many of the givers have been much younger than big donors of the past, like 19th-century steel magnate Andrew Carnegie. Even the 51-year-old Gates — who stoked his foundation with $21.8 billion — seems like an elder statesman next to improbably youthful billionaires like Google co-founders Sergey Brin and Larry Page — both 33 — whose philanthropic ventures include the $90-million Google Foundation.[2]

Still, many big givers today are older Americans like Buffett and currency trader George Soros, who specializes in political philanthropy. He has donated hundreds of millions of dollars beginning in the 1990s to pro-democracy and educational programs throughout the former Soviet bloc and poor countries (as well to justice-reform projects in the United States). Former President Bill Clinton — who turned 60 in August 2006 — got donors to pledge $2.5 billion last year to his foundation for programs to cut pollution and fight HIV/AIDS and other diseases.[3] On Nov. 30, Clinton announced that his foundation had persuaded anti-AIDS drugmakers to discount their prices by 45-60 percent to enable a new international

"Individual American citizens have been for over 270 years the most generous people in the world — [particularly] to people we've never met," says Claire Gaudiani, a professor of philanthropic history at the George H. Heyman Jr. Center for Philanthropy and Fundraising at New York University and author of a book on American philanthropy.[10]

Philanthropy has woven itself so deeply into the fabric of American life that some observers, including many conservatives, say charities should provide many social services, instead of the government. But philanthropy's big players say charitable giving alone can't carry the ball.

"There's not a single problem that the Gates Foundation is confronting that we can solve with our own resources — or with our resources combined with those of other foundations," says Lowell Weiss, a senior program and advocacy officer at the foundation. "The problems we are confronting depend on [joint] government and private-sector participation."

Meanwhile, with Congress set to shift in January from Republican to Democratic control, some critics want the government to ratchet up its oversight to ensure that philanthropies are meeting their obligations to sponsor good works — and not underwriting high living by charity executives.

In recent years, the Senate Finance Committee under outgoing Chairman Charles E. Grassley, R-Iowa, has focused on exposing abuses by philanthropies and other nonprofit organizations. His Democratic successor, Sen. Max Baucus of Montana, is likely to take a different tack, says Steven

Most Donations Come From Individuals

Individuals accounted for more than three-quarters of the $260 billion in U.S. charitable contributions in 2005 (top). Religious organizations received the largest share — more than a third of the total — followed by educational organizations (bottom).

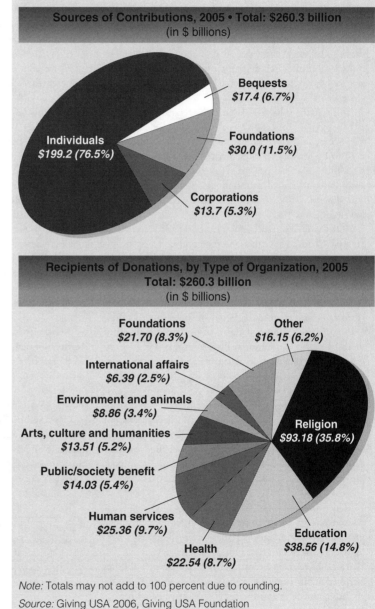

Sources of Contributions, 2005 • Total: $260.3 billion
(in $ billions)

Bequests $17.4 (6.7%)

Individuals $199.2 (76.5%)

Foundations $30.0 (11.5%)

Corporations $13.7 (5.3%)

Recipients of Donations, by Type of Organization, 2005
Total: $260.3 billion
(in $ billions)

Foundations $21.70 (8.3%)

Other $16.15 (6.2%)

International affairs $6.39 (2.5%)

Environment and animals $8.86 (3.4%)

Arts, culture and humanities $13.51 (5.2%)

Religion $93.18 (35.8%)

Public/society benefit $14.03 (5.4%)

Human services $25.36 (9.7%)

Education $38.56 (14.8%)

Health $22.54 (8.7%)

Note: Totals may not add to 100 percent due to rounding.
Source: Giving USA 2006, Giving USA Foundation

Watchdog Groups Spotlight Efficient Charities

Due diligence. That's the term used to describe the process of investigating the soundness of a company, typically before one buys or invests in it. In the business world, armies of analysts and shelves of publications offer just such determinations. Those wishing to give money to charity, however, have far less information to go on before writing their checks.

But resources do exist. Charity Navigator, a Mahwah, N.J.-based nonprofit, operates a free Web site designed to fill in some of the blanks. Executive Director Trent Stamp says his 11-person staff rates charities based on various criteria, including what percent of proceeds are spent on philanthropic work rather than administration and fundraising. The data all come from forms filed with the Internal Revenue Service (IRS).

"Our primary focus is as a donors' advocate," says Stamp. "Charities have their interest groups, charity recipients often have their interest groups and Congress has its groups, but there isn't anyone speaking for the rights of donors."

A similar organization, Ministry Watch, analyzes Christian charities. And the Better Business Bureau's Wise Giving Alliance gathers detailed information from hundreds of charities, granting seals of approval (for a fee) to organizations that meet its standards on finances and performance. More than 350 charities have earned the seal.

Unlike the Wise Giving Alliance, Charity Navigator does not seek information directly from the 5,000 organizations it evaluates. Relying solely on IRS data means not only that the same standards are applied to all charities, but that they are evaluated whether they welcome the scrutiny or not, Stamp says. "We want to keep an eye on people who don't necessarily want to participate in the process," he says.

The biweekly *Chronicle of Philanthropy* also keeps readers abreast of news about charities. And two organizations provide information on charities for a fee. Guidestar maintains a massive nonprofit database and a separate archive on charities. The American Institute of Philanthropy publishes a report on 500 charities.

Navigator began as the brainchild of philanthropists John and Marion Dugan, who found themselves stymied by a lack of data when searching for worthy charitable recipients. In 2001, the Dugans provided a start-up grant of $5 million to launch Navigator, which now receives money from foundations and corporate philanthropy programs at Cisco Systems Inc., and Tyco.[1]

However, using only financial data raises a question about whether charities that work to ensure efficient operations get unfairly downgraded for putting too much money into administration — a longstanding issue in the philanthropy world. "People want high-impact nonprofit organizations and no administrative costs," says Eugene Tempel, executive director of Indiana University's Center on Philanthropy. "They don't recognize that money needs to go into planning, administration and evaluation if you want effective programs."

Navigator tries to allow for reasonable administrative spending. It gives organizations a low score for "organizational efficiency" if they spend less than one-third of their budgets on services. These organizations "are simply not living up to their missions," the site says. Seven in 10 charities on the Navigator list spend at least 75 percent of their budgets on programs, and nine in 10 spend at least 65 percent.[2]

A former vice president of Teach for America, which recruits new college graduates to teach in poor neighborhoods and rural areas, Stamp has become a member of the philanthropy community's small corps of in-house critics. In a recent posting on his blog, he cites a recent survey showing declining public confidence in charities.[3]

"It's anything but surprising," he writes. "We're one Enron-like scandal away from an entire generation of donors taking their money and going home. As a sector, we can embrace these findings and push for real reforms in an effort to restore public trust, or we can stick our heads in the sand and hope it goes away."

---

[1] For background, see Robert Barker, "Charity Begins with a Fiscal Checkup," *BusinessWeek online*, Nov. 11, 2002, www.businessweek.com/magazine/content/02_45/b3807134.htm.

[2] Quoted in "Our Ratings Tables," Charity Navigator, undated, www.charitynavigator.org/index.cfm/bay/content.view/catid/2/cpid/48.htm.

[3] Trent Stamp, "Some Tasty Tidbits," Trent Stamp's Take [blog], Nov. 22, 2006, http://trentstamp.blogspot.com.

Gunderson, president and CEO of the Council on Foundations. "I think Baucus will focus much more on the role of philanthropy in addressing social needs," Gunderson says.

Doubts about oversight of philanthropies intensified after 1995, when United Way Executive Director William Aramony was imprisoned for stealing from the organization. According to a recent poll, only 10 percent of Americans strongly agreed that charitable organizations handle donated money honestly and ethically.[11]

Many experts credit Americans' generosity to the U.S. tax system, which allows tax deductions for gifts. In additon, relatively low U.S. tax rates enable wealthy Americans to keep more of their money than people in higher-tax countries.

"Some other countries have higher tax rates, so some of the common good that we care for through philanthropy is cared for through the tax system," such as health care for all citizens, says Eugene Tempel, executive director of Indiana University's Center on Philanthropy.

By contrast, Americans in recent years have become increasingly interested in applying business principles and techniques to charitable giving. " 'Strategic philanthropy' is a term that's thrown around loosely," says Mark Kramer, founder of FSG-Social Impact Advisors, a nonprofit Boston consulting firm that advises foundations and governments on their projects and grants. "Increasingly, serious efforts are being made to be more accountable and to be able to demonstrate effectiveness."[12]

Modern philanthropists often cite the development of the New York public library system as a model of the public-private partnership. In 1901, retired steel baron Carnegie began paying for 39 free public libraries in New York City on the condition that the city government come up with operating funds. Carnegie eventually built 1,679 libraries nationwide — and many more worldwide.[13]

The self-made Scottish immigrant forged a philosophy of wealth that has guided Buffett and others. Carnegie argued that the rich owed a debt to society, and that paying it off demanded giving away much of what they had earned. The money should go to institutions and projects that give people at the bottom of the socioeconomic scale the chance to climb the ladder of success, he said.

"Man does not live by bread alone," Carnegie once wrote in explaining his support of libraries. . . . "There is no class so pitiably wretched as that which possesses money and nothing else."

Carnegie's philosophy lives on. In 1997, as he pledged $1 billion for U.N. human-services projects, CNN founder Ted Turner exhorted his fellow billionaires to strive to be America's most generous citizens. And he's been haranguing them ever since. Before Buffett announced his planned donation to the Gates Foundation, Turner called him a "Scrooge" for waiting until his death to give away most of his wealth.

More recently, Turner dubbed fellow communications tycoon Rupert Murdoch a tightwad. The chairman and CEO of News Corp. (holdings include the Fox TV channels and Twentieth Century Fox) has agreed to help finance a $3 million program to help cities around the world lower pollution. But Murdoch's contribution represents only a tiny fraction of his assets, estimated at $7.7 billion.[14] "He gives nothing to charity," Turner said.[15]

As citizens, lawmakers and philanthropists consider the role of charitable giving, here are some of the questions being asked:

Are Americans more generous than citizens of other countries?

The charitable impulse knows no borders. It is encouraged by virtually all the world's religions and predates the founding of the United States by millennia. Still, Americans tend to believe they are more generous than people in other countries.

Americans indeed are No. 1 in giving when charitable donations alone are considered. But when the value of volunteered work and cash and property gifts are calculated together, the United States ranks below the Netherlands and Sweden. (*See chart, p. 343.*) In the Netherlands, the combined value of donated time and money amounted to 4.95 percent of gross domestic product (GDP) in 1995-2002. Sweden stood at 4.41 percent of GDP vs. the United States at 3.94 percent.[16]

Despite the universality of charitable giving, some scholars of philanthropy and members of the charity community point both to donations and to America's unparalleled record of philanthropically financed

Catholic Charities USA/Frank Methe

Catholic Charities volunteers clean out flooded houses in New Orleans after Hurricane Katrina. Thousands of volunteers flocked to the city to help, and Americans donated more than $5 billion for hurricane relief on the Gulf Coast in 2005.

scientific and educational achievements to conclude that nowhere else has philanthropy been so widespread and so successful.

"We're by far the most charitable country on Earth," says Adam Meyerson, president of the Philanthropy Roundtable and former vice president for educational affairs at the conservative Heritage Foundation.

"We have a can-do spirit, a conviction that individuals can and should make a difference, a long tradition of neighbor helping neighbor, of not looking to government or the local nobleman to look out for us. That's part of why charity and philanthropy have been such a big part of the American experience."

But Pablo Eisenberg, a fellow at Georgetown University's Public Policy Institute, rejects that view. "A lot of it is myth," he says, arguing that Americans' philanthropy grows less out of their inherent generosity than out of the U.S. tax system. "Take away the tax deduction, and how much will people give, especially major donors? I'm willing to bet they wouldn't give half of what they give now. I agree it's probably good to have that incentive, but let's admit it's the incentive and not just the generosity."

But Meyerson points out that Carnegie, oilman John D. Rockefeller and the other pioneers of big-scale

American philanthropy took up their roles before the advent of income-tax deductions for charitable contributions, in 1917; tax deductions for corporations' philanthropic donations were allowed in 1935.

"Massachusetts General Hospital, the Chicago Symphony, Stanford University — all of these great institutions of American life were started in the 19th century, before there were charitable tax incentives," says Meyerson.

Still, Eisenberg asks, how much philanthropy actually benefits the needy — as opposed to the well-endowed universities where the donors graduated? "The overwhelming number gave to universities, colleges, medical schools and hospitals," he says, citing surveys by *The Chronicle of Philanthropy* and Indiana University's Center on Philanthropy of major American donors. "They give to those institutions they know well, which saved their mother, which educated their kids and maybe an environmental group or two and cultural organizations that they know."

Some experts point out that comparisons between educational philanthropy in the United States and other societies often fail to account for the fact that other governments provide many educational services for which Americans must rely on themselves, financial aid or charity. In Western Europe, for instance, university education and health care are financed by much higher taxes than Americans pay — and cover all citizens.

"When you look at those types of things, the need for private philanthropy is quite different," says economist Patrick Rooney, research director at the Center on Philanthropy at Indiana University. "In Germany, even religion is financed through taxation. This is a whole different economy and set of values. While it's important to celebrate the generosity of Americans, we need to not get the horse riding too fast — this horse of righteous morality."

In fact, author Gaudiani argues that Europe's system of virtually free public universities loses much of its appeal on closer examination. The kinds of elementary and high schools available to low-income students in Europe do not prepare them for top-flight universities as well as the schools attended by wealthier students, says Gaudiani, who headed Connecticut College from 1988 to 2001.

Philanthropy scholars say that data on donations can provide material to both sides in the comparative-generosity debate. "When you look at [U.S.] giving as a share of GDP or national income, I'm struck by how stable it is — around 2 percent," says Smith of Georgetown's Public Policy Institute. "The fact that it hasn't moved would suggest we're not growing more generous."

But another conclusion is possible, says Smith, noting that the percentage of giving didn't drop following tax cuts the Bush administration pushed through Congress. Theoretically, as the tax obligations of rich people drop, they have less incentive to shelter earnings with tax-deductible contributions. "That would mean that we have sustained our levels of generosity even as the incentives for remaining generous have dropped," Smith says.

Dutch Donate the Most to Charity

The Dutch give the most to philanthropic pursuits as a share of their country's gross domestic product (GDP), mostly in the form of volunteering. Americans donate the most cash and other property gifts.

Top 10 Countries in Philanthropy
(As a percentage of GDP, 1995-2002)

Country	All Private Philanthropy (volunteering and giving)	Country	Private Giving (cash and property gifts)
The Netherlands	4.95%	United States	1.85%
Sweden*	4.41	Israel	1.34
United States	3.94	Canada	1.17
Tanzania	3.78	Argentina	1.09
United Kingdom	3.70	Spain*	0.87
Norway	3.42	Ireland	0.85
France	3.21	United Kingdom	0.84
Germany	2.56	Uganda	0.65
Finland	2.43	Hungary	0.63
Canada	2.40	Tanzania	0.61

* Data on volunteering/giving to religious worship organizations not available.

Source: Johns Hopkins Comparative Nonprofit Sector Project

Do increases in private philanthropy lead to cuts in government funding for social programs?

A left-right divide underlies the debate on whether government or private charity is the best provider of social services. The conservative view that helping the unfortunate is a duty of charities — not government — has deep roots in American political culture.

For instance, when the Great Depression began to sweep the country, President Herbert Hoover declared that philanthropies — not the government — should relieve Americans' suffering. However, his hands-off policy wilted in the face of massive unemployment and hunger.

Franklin D. Roosevelt, Hoover's successor, reversed his policy. Roosevelt's New Deal became the liberals' rallying cry, with the government establishing employment and welfare programs ranging from the Civilian Conservation Corps to the Social Security system.

Now that memories of the Depression have faded and philanthropy is booming, the debate over government services vs. charity has revived. For conservatives, the billions of dollars pouring into philanthropies strengthen the case for shifting much of the burden of providing social services to charitable organizations.

President Bush has long insisted that faith-based organizations and charities do a better job of helping the needy than government-provided services. "Governments can hand out money," he told the first White House Conference on Faith-Based and Community Initiatives in 2004, "but governments cannot put love in a person's heart, or a sense of purpose in a person's life."[17]

Consistent with that view, Bush has pushed for cutting funding to such traditional anti-poverty programs as Medicaid, housing vouchers for low-income renters and community-development block grants.[18] He also called for eliminating a $93.5 million education program designed to promote small classes ("learning communities") in large high schools.

Rick Cohen, former director of the National Committee for Responsive Philanthropy, says the administration's main justification was that some major philanthropies had become active in the small-class movement. The administration's budget document said: "Non-federal funds for such purposes has [sic] become readily available through the Carnegie Corporation of New York and the Bill & Melinda Gates Foundation."[19]

Cohen, who now writes for *Nonprofit Quarterly*, argues that the administration overstates the level of service charities and other nonprofits can provide. "The reality is that they can supplement some of what government does, but shouldn't substitute for government," he says.

Some conservative philanthropy experts acknowledge that asking private organizations to replace the government is out of the question — for now. "At the moment," says Meyerson, of the Philanthropy Roundtable, "the philanthropic infrastructure is not there to replace large parts of what government currently does."

Along with other conservatives, he takes a long view and advocates a wide-ranging discussion on whether the federal government should end — or reduce its role in — such social services as providing legal representation for people without adequate funds and health care for the uninsured. The Federal Emergency Management Agency's (FEMA) monumentally botched response to Hurricane Katrina indicates that government services can be overrated, Meyerson says. "We can't say FEMA has been doing a distinguished job."[20]

Other voices in the nonprofit world, however, argue that so-called small-government conservatives disregard the fact that the federal government helps pay nonprofits to provide the services they offer. Although nonprofits get an average of 20 percent of their funding from private and corporate donations, about 31 percent comes from government, says Diana Aviv, executive director of Independent Sector, an alliance of charities, foundations and corporate philanthropy programs. Dues and fees provide most of the rest of nonprofit funding.

"We would need many, many Warren Buffets before we came near to the 31 percent of the nonprofit-sector budget that government funding supports," she says.

In fact, says Leslie Lenkowsky, director of graduate studies at Indiana University's Center on Philanthropy, ever since the Reagan administration the government has been pouring a growing amount of money into nonprofits because they deliver services more cheaply than the government.

Lenkowsky, a former CEO of the Corporation for National and Community Service, which encourages volunteerism, argues that liberals are more worried that federal funding of nonprofits increasingly takes the form of vouchers to service recipients, rather than grants to service providers.[21]

"When I get a Pell Grant" for higher education, Lenkowsky says, "I don't have to take it to the Ivy League, I can take it to a for-profit university; just as I can pick the hospital or day-care center I like. There's more competition, which means more uncertainty" for nonprofits. In the past, he says, many had mastered the bureaucracy of getting grants, hence assuring their organizations a secure existence.

Should Congress get tougher on charities?

A series of scandals that began in the mid-1990s focused attention on the almost complete lack of state and federal oversight of spending by philanthropic organizations. More recently, the *Los Angeles Times* in 2005 disclosed unusually high-end salaries, perks and insider deals at the J. Paul Getty Trust, considered one of the world's richest arts organizations.

"Charities shouldn't be funding their executives' gold-plated lifestyles," said Senate Finance Committee Chairman Grassley, as his panel prepared to consider reining in such spending.[22]

Some restrictions were eventually enacted in the Pension Protection Act of 2006, which doubles to $20,000 the amount foundation managers can be fined for "self-dealing" — making property deals or other advantageous arrangements with board or staff members and their relatives. The penalty would also double to 30 percent of the amount of money that foundations failed to distribute in grants, if the foundations didn't meet a requirement to distribute at least 5 percent of their assets each year.[23]

The legislation left intact, however, an IRS exemption allowing payments to foundation insiders who provide "reasonable and necessary" foundation work, such as investment advice.[24] Eisenberg of Georgetown University's Public Policy Institute says the exception effectively permits big fees to trustees for fundraising, investment guidance and legal work.

"One simple regulation — no self-dealing and no exceptions to self-dealing — would kill 100 percent of that," says Eisenberg, a former director of the foundation-supported anti-poverty organization, Center for Community Change, and a co-founder of the National Committee for Responsive Philanthropy.

At Georgetown Eisenberg directed a 2003 study of payments to trustees at large and small foundations. Researchers found that the 238 foundations surveyed paid insiders $44 million in 1998 (then the most recent year for which full records were available) for board membership and professional services. "The self-dealing provisions in IRS regulations have neither been a deterrent to large trustee fees nor served adequately as a tool by which to punish foundations and trustees guilty of providing excessive compensation," the report concluded.[25]

Tempel of Indiana University acknowledges that the Getty Trust scandal raises questions about how well some foundation boards run their organizations. "There may be other cases like that out there that we don't know about," he says. But Tempel believes — as do most foundation managers — that no new laws or regulations are needed. "There are regulations on the books that could use better enforcement, but there are few resources at the IRS to enforce them."

But philanthropy-community watchdogs say the present regulatory structure is nowhere near adequate. For one thing, says Trent Stamp, executive director of Charity Navigator, a New Jersey-based nonprofit that helps donors select charities, existing law delegates considerable enforcement authority to states, but many of today's philanthropies cross state lines.

"We are continuing to regulate nonprofits in a way that might have worked in 1954," he says, "but nonprofits are a big business that they weren't in 1954." And while the Securities and Exchange Commission (SEC) oversees for-profit organizations, he explained, influential nonprofit boards of directors investing billions of dollars in the stock market represent "a parallel universe that we are not paying attention to."

Stamp, in fact, advocates establishing an SEC counterpart to oversee the entire nonprofit sector. Short of that, philanthropies should have to justify keeping their tax-exempt status, he argues. "The IRS gives out tax-exempt status and doesn't see those charities ever again," except in a handful of cases, he says.

Lenkowsky agrees that the IRS only "lightly" keeps an eye on organizations to ensure that they still adhere to the standards for tax exemption. But he and others in the philanthropy community argue that stepped-up government oversight would cause more problems than it would solve.

"Let's get the nonprofit sector to take responsibility for its own behavior and to set its own standards," says Joel Fleishman, director of the Samuel and Ronnie Heyman Center for Ethics, Public Policy and the Professions at Duke University. "We don't need new legislation."

While Fleishman concedes that no amount of self-regulation can deal with willful violations of the law, he thinks nonprofit organizations themselves can deal with "inadvertent actions that amount to something less than the willful intention to defraud," such as excessive or improper compensation, or perks.

BACKGROUND

Biblical Roots

Since ancient times, charity has stood as a pillar of Judaism, Christianity and Islam. *The Book of Deuteronomy* (Deut. 26:12) instructs the faithful to tithe — donate 10 percent of their earnings — "to the stranger, to the fatherless, and to the widow, that they may eat within thy gates, and be satisfied." In the *New Testament*, Jesus tells his followers: "Sell that ye have, and give alms" (Luke 12:33). Every Muslim who can afford it is obligated to make a donation — the *zakat* — to charity. Islam's holy book, the *Koran*, tells the faithful: "Devote yourself to prayer [and] pay the *zakat*." (2:43). Countless Web sites help Muslims calculate what they should pay, depending on their occupations, incomes and assets.

In the United States, some wealthy early Americans embraced the admonition to share their wealth. In 1847, when businessman and former U.S. congressman Abbott Lawrence donated $50,000 to Harvard College, his brother Amos, a merchant and industrialist, told him his gift "enriches your descendants in a way that mere money never can do and is a better investment than any you have ever made."[26] Similarly, said 19th-century educator Horace Mann, inheriting a fortune saps "the muscles out of the limbs, the brain out of the head and virtue out of the heart."[27]

CHRONOLOGY

Early 1900s *Americans' charitable contributions expand after onset of Industrial Age.*

1889 Steel tycoon Andrew Carnegie preaches that dying immensely wealthy is disgraceful.

1901 Oil magnate John D. Rockefeller suggests fellow millionaires establish foundations to ensure effectiveness of their donations.

1902-1931 Many of America's wealthiest citizens establish foundations.

1910 The Carnegie Foundation for the Advancement of Teaching publishes *Medical Education in the United States and Canada*, which transforms medical curriculum.

1913 Rockefeller Foundation established.

1932-1969 *During the Great Depression, President Franklin D. Roosevelt establishes an active social role for government.*

1949 President Harry S Truman declares a worldwide campaign against poverty.

1956 American philanthropies spend $535 million — 8 percent of all charitable spending — on foreign projects.

1968 Foundations direct nearly 20 percent of their grants to fight poverty and improve race relations.

1970s-1980s *Philanthropies are challenged to take over social programs.*

Aug. 1, 1971 Ex-Beatle George Harrison mounts "Concert for Bangladesh" in New York's Madison Square Garden.

1973-74 Study of the nonprofit sector counts 6 million organizations receiving a total of $25 billion in donations and $23 billion in government funding.

1981 President Ronald Reagan urges more "voluntarism" and less government.

1985 Since Reagan became president, nonprofits have lost $30 billion in government funding.

1989 President George H. W. Bush declares that private charities, rather than government, should step up social-service work.

1990s *The dot-com boom fosters the first philanthropic ventures by a new class of young millionaires.*

1992 Microsoft co-founder Bill Gates donates $12 million to the University of Washington.

1996 Billionaire financier George Soros pledges $100 million to set up Internet connections for regional Russian universities — part of hundreds of millions of dollars in democracy-building projects in the former Soviet Union and elsewhere.

1997 Desktop-publishing tycoon Paul Brainerd founds Social Venture Partners as a grant-making vehicle for himself and fellow high-tech success stories. . . . CNN founder Ted Turner commits $1 billion to the United Nations and challenges other billionaires to give their fortunes away.

1999-2000s *Bill Gates, Warren Buffett and Bill Clinton energize big-league philanthropy; newspaper exposés reveal foundation abuses.*

1999 Bill and Melinda Gates kick their foundation into higher gear with a $6 billion contribution.

2001 Turner pledges $50 million to eradicate weapons of mass destruction.

2003 Newspapers in Massachusetts and California expose insider deals and lavish spending at some foundations.

2004 ebay founder Pierre Omidyar sets up a philanthropy dedicated to both nonprofit and for-profit ventures.

2005 Natural disasters in Asia and the U.S. Gulf Coast generate more than $7 billion in charitable donations.

June 25, 2006 Buffett announces he will give away 85 percent of his $44 billion fortune.

Charitable giving in the nation's early years was linked to helping to cure society's ills. For instance, activists collected donations from philanthropists to build reformatories for children being held in adult prisons. The first was the New York House of Refuge, built in 1825. Philadelphia and Boston soon followed suit, with a prominent Bostonian, Theodore Lyman, donating nearly $75,000 to build the first state reformatory, in Westborough.

Abolitionist ministers raised money to send escaped slaves to Canada, and some wealthy foes of slavery helped anti-slavery settlers move to Kansas in the early 1850s so they could vote against expansion of human bondage to the Western frontier.

The Civil War further spurred the growth of charities, as hundreds of noncombatants on both sides of the conflict formed organizations offering hospitality or medical care for soldiers and their families. Clara Barton, who went on to found the American Red Cross, began her public-health career tending to the war's wounded. But it was in the post-war era of vast industrial expansion that modern American philanthropy flowered. By the 1880s, railroads, steelworks and automated manufacturing were transforming American society — and creating enormous fortunes. Between the 1870s and 1916, the number of millionaires in America exploded from 100 to about 40,000.[28]

Carnegie helped lead the transition from charity to philanthropy, with its more ambitious goals than just helping the poor on an individual basis. As a young Scottish immigrant, the young Carnegie began work in the United States as a bobbin boy in a textile factory. He later gave away $350 million for projects aimed at helping people help themselves and at raising professional standards in various fields. In addition to building public libraries throughout the United States, he created a new medical-education system and established a pension system for college professors that spurred the development of pensions throughout the economy.

Carnegie also advocated taxing wealth, in part because it would encourage the wealthy to make big donations rather than see their assets taxed away. The wealthy should set an example of "unostentatious living," Carnegie argued. "The man who dies leaving behind him millions

of available wealth, which was his to administer during life, will pass away 'unwept, unhonored, and unsung,' " he wrote. "Of such as these the public verdict will then be: 'The man who dies thus rich dies disgraced.' "[29]

The scale of the fortunes accumulated by the likes of Carnegie, Rockefeller and banker Andrew Mellon and others made plain that they couldn't simply give away money without a plan and hope to achieve meaningful results. "Let us erect a foundation, a trust, and engage directors who will make it a life work to manage, with our personal co-operation, this business of benevolence properly and effectively," said Rockefeller, the founder of the Standard Oil Co., in 1901.[30]

Many of the foundations created in the years immediately following Rockefeller's call are still operating today, including the Rockefeller Foundation, Rockefeller Institute for Medical Research (which later became Rockefeller University), the Carnegie Foundation for the Advancement of Teaching, Carnegie Endowment for International Peace and the Russell Sage Foundation.

New Directions

During the Great Depression, the Rockefeller Foundation and other big charitable organizations had limited success in preventing the ravages of unemployment and its ripple effects on health, housing and education.

President Hoover, who had built and directed pioneering famine-relief projects in post-World War I Western Europe and Russia, tried to enlist philanthropies in fighting the Depression's effects. In 1931, Hoover reminded Americans of the "God-imposed individual responsibility of the individual man and woman to their neighbors."[31]

In 1933 Roosevelt took office as president with a radically different agenda. Roosevelt believed the government should sustain unemployed workers "not as a matter of charity but as a matter of social duty." Under the New Deal forged during his presidency, government took responsibility for ensuring that the basic needs of citizens were met, effectively freeing philanthropies to pursue more far-reaching objectives.[32]

Although philanthropies had long worked hand in hand with the government, that relationship deepened during and after World War II, as American philanthropy

In Poor Nations, 'Philanthropy' Is Cost of Doing Business

In Kazakhstan Chevron Corp. spent $35 million last year to help build 430 new houses and a school for families displaced by expansion of the vast Tengiz oil field.[1]

In Nigeria's oil-rich Niger Delta, a Chevron-operated river-boat clinic provides free health care to 2,500 patients a month along the Benin and Escravos rivers.

In oil-rich Venezuela and Angola, Chevron is working with the Discovery Channel to install televisions, VCRs and satellite dishes in isolated rural classrooms and teach educators how to incorporate educational video programming into their curricula.

U.S.-based Chevron may be in the oil business, but last year it spent $73 million on social projects in many of the 180 countries where it operates. As part of the company's corporate-philanthropy arm, the projects are designed to create long-term, sustainable programs that serve specific local needs — indirectly benefiting the company's bottom line in the process.[2]

Stimulating economic growth and enabling communities to prosper "is fundamental to the broader success we seek to achieve as a business," says the company's annual Social Responsibility report.[3] For example, in HIV/AIDS-ravaged countries — including South Africa, Nigeria and Angola — the company runs voluntary testing, counseling and treatment programs for employees and their families, as well as awareness programs for the broader communities.[4]

"It's not being done for the intrinsic good that these programs bring, but to support our business goals and operations," says Chevron spokesman Alex Yelland. "We rely on a large, healthy employment pool, and a policy that supports our business operations, as well as being for the good of all, is helpful."

However, corporate philanthropy today is not only designed to achieve social benefits that indirectly benefit companies' bottom lines. Some charitable programs end up as investment opportunities. "There are actually business opportunities developing around social issues," says Mark Kramer, managing director of FSG-Social Impact Advisors, a Boston-based consulting firm for nonprofits. "You're beginning to see the merging of economic and social interests."

Microfinance projects — in which as little as a few dollars are loaned to very poor people to start or expand businesses — are a prime example, he says. Devised in 1976 by Bangladeshi economist Muhammad Yunus, microfinancing originated as a purely philanthropic enterprise, though it was designed to be self-supporting through interest

became, in effect, an arm of U.S. foreign policy. In his inaugural speech on Jan. 20, 1949, President Harry S Truman declared a worldwide campaign against poverty in which the United States would furnish technical assistance and capital investment.

By 1956, U.S. donations for foreign philanthropic projects amounted to $535 million, or 8 percent of U.S. charitable spending. The Rockefeller and Ford foundations were especially active in international programs, along with religious organizations, such as the American Friends Service Committee, Church World Service and Catholic Relief Services.

Cooperation between the government and philanthropic organizations grew closer on the domestic front as well. In 1968, during the height of the civil-rights struggle, about 18 percent of foundation grants were going to programs aimed at poverty, race relations and urban problems. The Great Society programs of President Lyndon B. Johnson began channeling government funds to community social-service programs, including Community Action Boards in various cities. Money was being spent so fast that many wondered whether government money was undermining philanthropic independence and initiative.

Also in 1968, the Ford Foundation announced that it would invest part of its assets in minority-owned businesses and in low-income and racially integrated housing. "Never in the history of American philanthropy had anything comparable in scale and aggressiveness to the Ford Foundation's assault on the problem of race and payments. Then it attracted the attention — and dollars — of conventional investors. Citigroup set up a microfinance pilot program in Hyderabad, India, and the Netherlands-based venture-capital firm Goodwell has raised $10 million to invest in Indian microfinance operations.[5]

It's all part of a philanthropy-business synthesis that has been emerging for years, says Kramer. In 2002, he co-authored an article with Harvard Business School Professor Michael Porter arguing that the traditional distinction between the profit motive and philanthropy was disappearing. "There is no inherent contradiction between improving competitive context and making a sincere commitment to bettering society," they wrote. "Improving education, for example, is generally seen as a social issue, but the educational level of the local work force substantially affects a company's potential competitiveness. The more a social improvement relates to a company's business, the more it leads to economic benefits as well."[6]

Apple Computer, for instance, has been donating computers to U.S. schools for years — a practice that helped them introduce new generations of users to Apple products, they pointed out.[7]

In a new wrinkle, however, partly to appease critics who claim their countries' resources are being pillaged, some developing countries have begun demanding that foreign companies — especially oil and mining companies — pay so-called "social bonuses" as a prerequisite to doing business. For instance, in 2004 the Angolan government sought and received a promise of $80 million from Chevron for school construction and other development projects if it wanted its lease extended on an offshore oil field.[8]

Chevron considers such bonuses as business expenses, not part of the company's philanthropic endeavors. "If you want to operate in Angola as an extractive industry, a 'social bonus' is going to be part and parcel of doing business," says Yelland.

---

[1] For more details, see "Corporate Responsibility Report 2005," Chevron Corp., [undated], p. 17, http://chevron.com/cr_report/2005.

[2] *Ibid.*, pp. 16-17, 3. For background, see Kathy Koch, "The New Corporate Philanthropy," *CQ Researcher*, Feb. 27, 1998, pp. 169-192.

[3] *Ibid.*, p. 16.

[4] For the complete policy, see "Policy 260, HIV/AIDS," 2005, http://chevron.com/social_responsibility/hiv_aids/docs/policy_260.pdf.

[5] Yunus received a Nobel Prize this year for his creation of the microfinance model. For details, see "A Short History," Grameen Bank, www.grameen-info.org/bank/hist.html. For more on conventional investment in microfinance see Amy Yee, "A serious business not charity," *Financial Times* [London], Nov. 15, 2006, p. 12.

[6] Michael E. Porter and Mark R. Kramer, "The Competitive Advantage of Corporate Philanthropy," *Harvard Business Review*, December 2002, p. 56.

[7] *Ibid.*

[8] For background on the Angola production deal, see "ChevronTexaco Awarded Extension of Block O Concession in Angola," press release, May 13, 2004, www.chevron.com/news/press/2004/2004-05-13.asp; "Angola Fact Sheet," Chevron Corp., updated November, 2006, http://chevron.com/operations/docs/angola.pdf. Also see John Reed, "A peace dividend is elusive as Angola embraces 'petro-diamond capitalism,' " *Financial Times* [London], Nov. 14, 2005, p. 15.

---

poverty been seen," wrote Waldemar A. Nielsen, a philanthropy scholar and former Ford Foundation staffer.[33]

Rockers and Volunteers

The conservative era that began with President Ronald Reagan's election in 1980 fostered a view of the relationship between philanthropy and government different from the partnerships of the 1960s and '70s that grew out of the 1930s New Deal.

"Voluntarism is an essential part of our plan to give the government back to the people," Reagan said in 1981.[34]

Reagan wanted to cut back government social-service programs and let philanthropies pick up the slack. Indeed, Reagan's first budget included deep cuts in child welfare, day care, nutrition for the elderly, services for the mentally ill and developmentally disabled, food stamps, school lunches and aid to poor people with high energy bills.

But the notion that nonprofit organizations could fill the resulting gaps in services proved misguided, because the private groups depended heavily on government funding. In 1981-85 alone, nonprofit service providers' government receipts declined by $30 billion due to the Reagan budget cuts.

His successor, President George H. W. Bush, also thought that charities were better at helping the poor, the ill and the disabled. "The old solution, the old way, was to think that public money alone could end these problems," Bush said in his 1989 inaugural address. "We

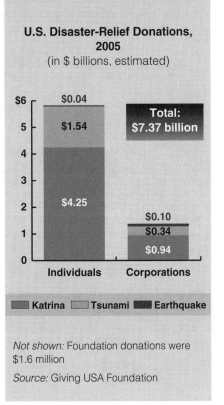

Katrina Relief Efforts Received $5.3 Billion

Americans donated more than $5 billion for Gulf Coast hurricane relief.

U.S. Disaster-Relief Donations, 2005
(in $ billions, estimated)

Total: $7.37 billion

Individuals: $0.04, $1.54, $4.25
Corporations: $0.10, $0.34, $0.94

Katrina   Tsunami   Earthquake

Not shown: Foundation donations were $1.6 million

Source: Giving USA Foundation

will turn to the only resource we have that in times of need always grows — the goodness and the courage of the American people.

"I have spoken of a thousand points of light, of all the community organizations that are spread like stars throughout the nation, doing good," he continued. "We will work hand in hand, encouraging, sometimes leading, sometimes being led, rewarding."[35]

Celebrities who support charitable efforts today are following in the footsteps of earlier entertainers, such as silent-film stars Douglas Fairbanks and Mary Pickford, who promoted the Red Cross during World War I. But new generations of music and movie stars have opted for somewhat deeper involvement.

In 1971, former Beatles lead guitarist George Harrison sparked the new age of celebrity involvement in campaigns against poverty and disease in poor nations when he organized the Concert for Bangladesh to benefit victims of flooding, famine and warfare in the newly independent nation.[36]

A long line of music and film stars have followed Harrison's example. In 1984 Irish rocker Bob Geldof recruited famous singers to help him record a song he'd co-written, "Do They Know It's Christmas?" — raising $10 million for famine relief in Ethiopia. The following summer, he organized "Live Aid" concerts in London and Philadelphia, which were televised worldwide and raised $80 million in pledges, also destined for Ethiopia.[37]

Also in 1985, singer Harry Belafonte used Geldof's model to assemble an all-star cast to record "We Are the World," a song written by Michael Jackson and Lionel Richie to raise funds for famine and hunger relief in Africa. The project drew in more than $40 million.[38]

More recently, Bono, frontman for the Irish band U2, has taken a different approach: Using his celebrity to focus public and government attention on poverty in Africa. Bono organized the "Live 8" concerts in Philadelphia and London last year, timed to coincide with a meeting of leaders of the G-8 — the world's eight industrial powers — to discuss aid to Africa and champion debt relief and effective aid in Africa. He also touts the work of Columbia University development-aid guru Jeffrey Sachs, who argues that ending deep poverty is a realistic worldwide goal.

Although Bono focuses more on encouraging foreign aid than individual philanthropy, his mastery of development issues and relentless lobbying of politicians and international institutions such as the World Bank have won him respect not usually accorded to entertainers who take up social causes. A new philanthropic venture shows that he has embraced the trend of business-savvy charity. The singer helped devise a multi-brand campaign in which Apple Computer, The Gap, Nike and American Express sell red-colored products (a red leather jacket from The Gap, for instance) and donate part of the revenue to projects fighting AIDS, malaria and other illnesses.[39]

Billionaires and Scandals

In a 1995 *Newsweek* interview with Bill Gates, the topic of giving away money never came up. Nor did Gates seem preoccupied by social problems. When one of the interviewers mentioned that many Americans lacked medical insurance, Gates shot back: "Don't joke around. Medical treatment across the board at every income level is dramatically better today than in the past."[40]

The only hint of Gates' future involvement in school reform came in the context of remarks he made about America's ranking in the global economy: "Our education system isn't as good as it needs to be. Our universities are very, very strong. The top 10 percent do pretty well, but...it's not as good as many, many other countries."[41]

Only three years earlier, Gates had made his first philanthropic donation — $12 million to the University of Washington in his hometown of Seattle to found a molecular biotechnology department. He also recruited a leader in the field to head the department.

"You've got to put in the same amount of work and exercise the same degree of judgment in giving money away as you do in making it," Gates told *Fortune*.[42]

None of today's other high-tech celebrity donors were even mentioned in the *Fortune* article, some because they weren't rich yet. For instance, Google founders Brin and Page were 19-year-old college students when the article appeared.[43]

Likewise, Paul Brainerd hadn't yet sold the desktop-publishing software company he founded, Aldus Corp., for $450 million. After that 1994 deal, Brainerd helped start Social Venture Partners, a philanthropic grant-maker that draws from the ranks of high-tech millionaires. And when Gates made his first big donation, Pierre Omidyar had not yet founded eBay, which catapulted him into the billionaire class. In 2004, Omidyar set up the Omidyar Network, which funds nonprofits and invests in some for-profit businesses with socially responsible aims and methods.

"I really believe everyone has the power to make a difference," Omidyar told the *Financial Times* of London. "And by working together we can help make the world a better place."[44]

In the mid-1990s a series of scandals — primarily exposed by investigative journalists — focused a harsh glare on philanthropic foundations.

In 1995, the United Way's Aramony was sentenced to seven years in federal prison for diverting charitable donations to subsidize personal expenses — a case brought to light by *The Washington Post*.[45] Then in 2003 the *Boston Globe* reported that nonprofit foundations across the country were spending lavishly and promoting insider dealing. Some had bought private aircraft, while others had paid hundreds of thousands of dollars in fees to their trustees — some of them lawyers who also billed at their top rates for legal work.[46]

At about the same time, the *San Jose Mercury-News* reported that the James Irvine Foundation of San Francisco — well-known in California for its grants to colleges, social welfare programs and arts organizations — had paid its ex-president more than $700,000 a year, plus perks, at a time when economic recession had prompted the foundation to cut its grant making by $20 million. And some grant recipients and applicants had hired an executive-search firm owned by the president's wife, the newspaper reported.[47]

Then, in 2005, the *Los Angeles Times* began publishing details of high living by the $1.2 million-a-year president of the $9.6 billion J. Paul Getty Trust, one of the world's richest cultural organizations, named for the oil tycoon who bequeathed his estate to the trust, which received it in 1982.[48]

In October, California Attorney General Bill Lockyer named an outside overseer for the trust after concluding that its board had approved hundreds of thousands of dollars' worth of improper spending. Payouts included first-class travel costs for the wife of trust President Barry Munitz; initial installments of a $300,000 fee for a 25th-anniversary book on the trust by its outgoing board chairman and high-end perks for Munitz, including a $72,000 Porsche Cayenne SUV.

As the articles continued, Munitz resigned under pressure in February 2006, after repaying $245,000 and forgoing more than $2 million in severance benefits.[49]

CURRENT SITUATION

Legislative Outlook

The Council on Foundations' Gunderson is among the philanthropy world's best-placed players for analyzing

Charitable Giving at a Glance

The 5 Largest Private Foundations
(As of May 1, 2006, based on total assets)

1. Bill & Melinda Gates Foundation ($31 billion)
2. The Ford Foundation ($11.6 billion)
3. J. Paul Getty Trust ($9.6 billion)
4. The Robert Wood Johnson Foundation ($9.0 billion)
5. Lilly Endowment ($8.6 billion)

The 5 Largest Corporate Grantmakers
(As of May 1, 2006, based on total given)

1. Wal-Mart Foundation ($154.5 million)
2. Aventis Pharmaceutical Health Care Foundation ($114.7 million)
3. Bank of America Foundation ($80.7 million)
4. Ford Motor Company Fund ($77.9 million)
5. The Wells-Fargo Foundation ($64.7 million)

The 5 Largest Nonprofit Organizations
(As of November 2005, based on total income)

1. YMCAs in the United States ($4.8 billion)
2. Catholic Charities USA ($3.2 billion)
3. Salvation Army ($3.1 billion)
4. American Red Cross ($3.1 billion)
5. United Jewish Communities ($2.9 billion)

The 5 Largest Gifts to Charity, 2005

1. Cornelia Scaife May ($404 million bequest to Colcom Foundation, others)
2. Bill & Melinda Gates ($320 million to Bill & Melinda Gates Foundation)
3. Eli & Edythe Broad ($300 million to the Broad Foundations and others)
4. George Soros ($240 million to Central European University and others)
5. T. Boone Pickens ($229 million to Oklahoma State University, others)

Sources: National Philanthropic Trust; Chronicle of Philanthropy; NonProfit Times

are the key panels for philanthropy-related legislation.

"There was a consistent theme in what each of these individuals talked about," Gunderson says. It was: "We will work with you, the sector, to help grow philanthropy if you will partner with us to address issues of concern within our communities." For example, Baucus insisted that philanthropies focus attention on the problems of rural America. "We've offered to co-host a conference in Montana on that very topic," Gunderson adds.

Lenkowsky of Indiana University says he's been hearing talk for some time that lawmakers want to ensure that their constituents see the benefits of what foundations and other philanthropies do. Some have suggested, for example, assuring continuation of tax-exempt status for philanthropies that could demonstrate their work on behalf of low-income citizens.

That idea may resonate more with Republicans, however. Incoming Ways and Means Chairman Charles Rangel, D-N.Y., "has much more sympathy with the charitable sector" than his predecessor, Rep. Bill Thomas, R-Calif., a committee staffer told *The Chronicle of Philanthropy.* "He thinks there's a broad rationale for charitable tax exemption."[50]

Nevertheless, Gunderson acknowledges that the Democrats may get interested in tougher oversight if they perceive philanthropies as uninterested in producing palpable results for lawmakers' constituents. "There is always that risk," he says. "But if we start out with the premise that the mission of philanthropy is to enhance the common good, why would we not want to constructively participate with them?"

Indeed, before the election, Gunderson warned that the oversight issue remains potent. In an October speech

what the new Congress may have in store for the nonprofit sector. A veteran of 16 years in the House as a Wisconsin Republican, Gunderson and his colleagues cultivated ties with prominent Democrats before the Nov. 7 elections.

Over the past year, council members have met with Sen. Max Baucus, D-Mont., incoming chairman of the Senate Finance Committee, and Reps. John Lewis, D-Ga., and Xavier Becerra, D-Calif., both members of the new majority on the House Ways and Means Committee. The two committees, which have jurisdiction over tax matters, to the National Association of State Charity Officials, he said, "If Capitol Hill doesn't believe we're serious about ethical conduct, we will see significantly more legislation coming from the Hill."[51]

Red Cross Shake-up

Following a string of upheavals — the resignations of two presidents in a row, revelations of failures in delivering emergency aid and pressure from a powerful Senate committee — the American Red Cross has just proposed sweeping changes in the operation of America's most high-profile charity.

The country's premier disaster-response agency received more than $2.2 billion in donations after Hurricanes Katrina, Rita and Wilma in 2005, but operational problems have raised questions about how effectively that money was used.[52] In the past five years, many of the agency's problems have centered on conflicts between the presidents of the organization and its huge 50-member Board of Directors. In October, the board agreed — among other things — to reduce its own size to no more than 20 members by 2012. In addition, board members' role in day-to-day management would diminish, and internal auditing would be strengthened.[53]

The changes show how complicated the politics of philanthropy can become, even in an organization dedicated mainly to the straightforward task of relieving suffering after disasters. Politics can be even more tricky for the Red Cross because — while not a federal agency — it is chartered by Congress, and the president chooses the board chairman and seven other board members from among federal officials whose jobs involve working with the Red Cross.[54] That interlocking relationship — designed to ensure coordination between government agencies and the Red Cross — also guarantees a higher level of congressional interest when problems crop up.

"It's good news that the Red Cross' board recognized that a Band-Aid won't do, and that the American people expect the best from an organization that so many people have supported with time and money," Sen. Grassley said in a written statement responding to the proposed changes. Grassley, who will be stepping down as Finance Committee chairman in January because Republicans lost control of the Senate on Nov. 7, has taken the lead on Red Cross oversight.[55]

His investigation began after the 2001 resignation of Bernadine Healey, widely viewed as a divisive figure during her brief tenure as Red Cross president (1999-2001), who was forced out after repeatedly clashing with the board. Controversy erupted after it was revealed that she received a $1.9 million severance package. Then in 2005, President Marsha J. Evans resigned after three years, during which she, too, clashed with the board. Her severance package came to $780,000.[56]

In 2005, the Red Cross' internal problems became a national issue after a breakdown — visible to millions of TV watchers — in providing emergency aid to hurricane victims in New Orleans and the Gulf region. The Red Cross is supposed to work hand-in-hand with FEMA, but that relationship didn't materialize after the hurricanes, the Government Accountability Office (GAO) concluded earlier this year.[57]

"The agencies spent time during the response effort trying to establish operations and procedures, rather than focusing solely on coordinating services," the agency report said.[58]

In a written response in May, the Red Cross said the GAO had mischaracterized the agency's role under the federal emergency plan. Although in smaller-scale emergencies the Red Cross provides shelter and other necessities to victims, in massive emergencies like the Katrina disaster its primary function is "to help bring federal resources to state and local governments," the letter said. The Red Cross acknowledged, however, that the difference in the two roles caused "much confusion" after Katrina.[59]

Earlier, in March, the Red Cross dismissed three volunteers in the hurricane relief operation who had been accused by fellow volunteers of having diverted supplies. The Red Cross referred allegations of what it called "waste and abuse" to the FBI.[60]

Grassley praised the Red Cross for designing new procedures to encourage whistleblowers to step forward with reports of improprieties. "I want to make certain that the Red Cross also has in place reforms that will contribute to greater transparency and openness to the Congress and the public."[61]

Bonds for Vaccines

A bond issue on behalf of the Global Alliance for Vaccines and Immunization (GAVI) in London this month raised

Are tougher philanthropy laws needed?

YES
Rick Cohen
*Former Executive Director,
National Committee for
Responsive Philanthropy*

Written for *CQ Researcher*, December 2006

Nonprofits and the public need better protection against financial predators who misuse tax-exempt resources without suffering legal consequences. Current laws are not sufficient for today's nonprofit sector, where the number of nonprofits and foundations has doubled over the past two decades. The recent boom in nonprofit revenues and assets — philanthropy accounts for more than 5 percent of the nation's GDP — and new organizational structures that mix nonprofit and for-profit models and practices all point to a need to review and augment nonprofit-sector laws, which have not been comprehensively updated in nearly three decades.

Take, for example, philanthropic foundations — institutions that have no market accountabilities to speak of and are now collectively sitting on more than a half-trillion dollars. Half a dozen new laws are needed in this subsector alone. For instance, private foundations should be required to spend at least 6 percent of their assets — instead of the 5 percent they spend now. And they should not be allowed to count their often extravagant administrative expenditures toward their required payouts. Trustees should be prohibited from paying themselves five- and six-figure fees for their board service, and loopholes that allow foundation executives and trustees to engage in self-dealing and conflicts of interest should be closed. Meaningful standards need to be established for determining what constitutes excessive compensation and what should be done about it.

The opponents of additional government oversight say new laws will kill the goose that lays the golden egg. Apparently, preventing abuses, closing loopholes and mandating more accountability will drive away philanthropic donors and nonprofit workers. These same opponents, or their ideological predecessors, proclaimed the same doomsday scenario for philanthropy after the Tax Act of 1969. That prognostication didn't come to pass and neither will the panicked predictions of today's anti-regulatory leaders.

Tax-exempt funds are not the private funds of foundations and nonprofits. Tax-exempt resources are public funds entrusted to the stewardship of foundations and nonprofits for the public benefit. The media understands this, as reflected in its increasing coverage of accountability deficiencies. It is past time this sector's representatives get with the program.

What is needed? Three things: a new commitment to accountability by nonprofits and their associations, significant additional state and federal resources for oversight and new laws and regulations to address the growth and diversity of the nonprofit sector.

NO
Adam Meyerson
*President, The
Philanthropy Roundtable*

Written for *CQ Researcher*, December 2006

In January 2005, The Philanthropy Roundtable established the Alliance for Charitable Reform (ACR) as an emergency initiative to respond to legislative proposals on Capitol Hill that would affect private foundations and public charities. The mission of the ACR is to offer common-sense solutions for abuses in the charitable sector while protecting the freedom of donors and foundations to use their best judgment in carrying out their charitable objectives.

Government should vigorously enforce existing laws before announcing sweeping new ones. We recognize that new, narrowly targeted laws may be necessary to correct specific abuses not covered by current rules, and several provisions in new laws enacted in 2004 and 2006 are quite reasonable.

But most of the transgressions in our sector are violations of existing law. Some wrongdoers have already been subject to severe financial penalties and public humiliation, and their example is a powerful deterrent to future law-breakers. To catch more wrongdoers, state attorneys general and the Internal Revenue Service should devote more resources to policing charities and foundations — beginning with the excise tax revenues already assessed on foundations for this purpose.

There is no need to rewrite the fundamental public policy framework governing philanthropy, which historically has given private philanthropic organizations wide discretion in how they use their resources.

We expect that the big battle over philanthropic freedom will take place in 2007. We will do everything in our power to resist requirements for foundation accreditation, five-year reviews of tax-exempt status, arbitrary limits on trustee and staff compensation, federal micromanagement of the boards of private organizations, limits on the compensation of family members who sit on family foundation boards and other freedom-threatening measures proposed in the last three years by Senate Finance Committee and/or Joint Tax Committee staff.

As it becomes ever clearer that the Sarbanes-Oxley anti-corporate fraud law has imposed significant costs on small companies and is responsible for keeping new businesses from listing on American stock exchanges, it is also important to resist applying the Sarbanes-Oxley mindset to charities and foundations.

When existing laws are not being vigorously enforced, it makes no sense to add sweeping new regulations that will add costs and diminish freedom for the law-abiding majority without improving the likelihood that wrongdoers will be brought to justice.

$1 billion to vaccinate children in the world's poorest countries against polio, hepatitis B, yellow fever and other preventable illnesses. The event not only linked philanthropy and business but also tightened the ties between philanthropy and government.

"It's a great example of how we're hoping to show people the way to bring in new resources from government," says Weiss, at the Bill & Melinda Gates Foundation.

The foundation committed an additional $1.5 billion to GAVI, an organization the foundation helped establish in 2000.[62] The bond issue, which will allow GAVI to expand its activities, was promoted by Gordon Brown, the United Kingdom's Chancellor of the Exchequer (the equivalent of the U.S. secretary of the Treasury).[63]

The program now will be able to immunize "500 million children against vaccine-preventable diseases before 2015, saving some 10 million lives," Gates and Brown wrote in the British newspaper *The Independent*, bringing the world "one step closer to eradicating polio."[64]

The funding scheme differs from traditional approaches to financing health initiatives in poor countries through grants, in that bond buyers expect a financial return — not just moral uplift. The five-year bonds were designed to yield about 0.32 percentage points more than equivalent U.S. Treasury bonds. Donor countries are helping to make the bond issue possible by pledging development aid to the countries where the immunizations will be carried out — pledges that amount to collateral on the bonds.[65]

Governments felt secure in making those pledges because the foundation had made an early leap into the mass-immunization program and was working to ensure that the money would be spent effectively, says Weiss. "New commitments to immunization are coming from governments in part because we were willing to be the first dollars in," he says.

Britain, Italy, France, Spain, Sweden and Norway made a total of $4 billion in commitments, along with the Gates Foundation. The United States — which has adopted a strategy of linking development aid to progress in fighting corruption and meeting other governance standards — was not among the pledging countries.[66]

Although the bond issue received virtually no news coverage in the United States, Brown and his colleagues showed a flair for grabbing headlines — at least in Europe. The bonds' first buyers were Pope Benedict XVI,

the Archbishop of Canterbury, Britain's chief rabbi, the Muslim Council of Britain, the Hindu Forum of Britain and rock star development-aid advocates Bono and Geldof.[67]

OUTLOOK

Wealth Transfer?

The decades-long growth in American philanthropic contributions leads many experts to believe that U.S. donors' generosity will continue for the foreseeable future. In fact, some philanthropy scholars have predicted a major uptick in contributions as a result of the inter-generational "wealth transfer" from baby boomer parents to their children.

Paul Schervish, a sociologist and director of the Center on Wealth and Philanthropy at Boston College, co-authored a controversial study in 1999 that projected a minimum transfer of $41 trillion during the 55 years from 1998 to 2052. Of that amount, they calculated that about $6 trillion would be donated to philanthropies.

Defending the theory in a 2003 article, Schervish and a colleague wrote, "The $41 trillion estimate of wealth transfer is not affected by short-term economic fluctuations, and if wealth continues to grow in the next 51 years as it has in the past 51 years, the transfer amount will be less than a quarter of the total value of personally held wealth in 2052."[68] In other words, a philanthropy boom seems likely, because donors tend to give when they feel that their assets are secure.

But *The Chronicle of Philanthropy* recently quoted experts saying that the transfer had yet to show up in donation volume. And *The Journal of Gift Planning* published a symposium showing a range of views about the wealth-transfer theory. "I have far more confidence in the overall wealth-transfer figures . . . than in the amount projected to transfer to charity," said Kathyrn W. Miree, a consultant to nonprofits and foundations.[69]

Schervish acknowledges that gauging the future level of donations is tricky, even though his predictions about the family-to-family bequests appear to be panning out. "The wealth transfer and the growth in transfer is taking place," he says. The fact that it's not reflected in philanthropic donations, he explains, could reflect a drop in individuals' assets that makes them less willing to give, "or they're just not giving, or we're missing some other forms of giving."

In any event, most philanthropy experts predict the high-tech industry will continue to produce young success stories who will feel not only a moral obligation to spread their wealth but also a drive to produce fast results. "These are people in their 30s and 40s who are very impatient," says Fleishman of Duke University. "They'll say, 'I created an instant company, why can't we turn the same skills to solving persistent problems?' "

Former National Council on Responsive Philanthropy Director Cohen thinks a new donor class that rose to the top by developing new ways of doing business will likely create new forms of philanthropic development, such as eBay founder Omidyar's strategic focus on both non-profit and for-profit beneficiaries.

But these new forms of philanthropy are likely to raise questions of where profit-taking stops and charity begins, and of who makes decisions about where to draw lines between business and philanthropy, Cohen says. As a result, "Questions of accountability and transparency are going to be even more troubling 10 years from now," he says.

Georgetown's Eisenberg agrees, pointing out that no one is establishing methods to examine accountability. "There's no debate, no discussion," he says. "We're supposed to be so happy that all these mega-wealthy folks are giving money. Everybody is patting each other on the ass. There are no critical faculties operating in philanthropy."

But Lenkowsky of Indiana University's philanthropy center thinks state attorneys general will become more aggressive in overseeing philanthropy, in part because the federal government has all but abandoned the field. Journalists, as well, are likely to keep digging, having seen the fruitful results of recent investigations of the Getty Trust and other foundations. "The big story of the last few years is not what Congress has enacted but that charitable organizations now wear, if not black hats, gray hats," he says.

Optimism remains, however, in part because of the greater sensitivity inculcated in today's high school and college graduates, many of whom have had to perform community-service projects as a prerequisite for graduation. "We are headed for a dramatic increase in giving" among that group, says New York University's Gaudiani.[70]

"The group under age 32 has done more volunteer work during its academic training than any other group in the nation's history," Lenkowsky says. "They are seeing what needs to be done, and as they graduate they have a much livelier commitment to making the world better."

NOTES

1. Quoted in Carol J. Loomis, "Warren Buffett Gives It Away," *Fortune*, July 10, 2006, p. 56. For details on the Buffett gift and its effects on the Gates Foundation's asset base, see Charles Pillar and Maggie Farley, "Buffett Pledges Billions to Gates," *Los Angeles Times*, June 26, 2006, p. A1; Timothy L. O'Brien and Stephanie Saul, "Buffett to Give Bulk of Fortune to Gates Charity," *The New York Times*, June 26, 2006, p. A1. For additional information on the Gates Foundation's assets and grants, see "Fact Sheet," Bill & Melinda Gates Foundation; www.gatesfoundation.org/MediaCenter/FactSheet.

2. For details on the Google Foundation, see Katie Hafner, "Philanthropy Google's Way: Not the Usual," *The New York Times*, Sept. 14, 2006, p. A1. For details on the Gateses' first contributions, see Juan Forero, "$5 Billion Puts Gates Fund in First Place," *The New York Times*, Jan. 25, 2000, p. A14.

3. For more details on Clinton, see Bethany McLean, "The Power of Philanthropy," *Fortune*, Sept. 18, 2006, p. 82. For more details on Soros, see his Open Society Institute Web site; www.soros.org. Also see Lee Hockstader, "U.S. Financier Gives Russia $100 Million for Internet Link," *The Washington Post*, March 16, 1996, p. A21; Mary Beth Heridan, "'Oracle' Prefers Giving Away Millions," *Los Angeles Times*, Aug. 24, 1993, p. D8.

4. For more details, see McLean, *ibid.*, p. 82. For additional details on the Bush-Clinton fund, see "Bush-Clinton Katrina Fund," http://bushclintonkatrinafund.org. For details of the new AIDS drug deal, see Celia W. Dugger, "Clinton Helps Broker Deal for Medicine to Treat AIDS," *The New York Times*, Dec. 1, 2006, p. A6.

5. *Ibid.*, p. 30.

6. For detailed statistics and analysis see *Giving USA 2006*, Center on Philanthropy at Indiana University, 2006, pp. 2-3, 56-77.

7. The calculation assumes that post-disaster contributions were "new money" that wouldn't otherwise have been donated to charity. For details, see *ibid*, p. 11.

8. For a detailed study, see Paul G. Schervish, "Explaining the Curve in the U-Shaped Curve," *Voluntas: International Journal of Voluntary and Nonprofit Organizations*, August 1995, p. 202, http://www.bc.edu/research/swri/meta-elements/pdf/ucurve1.pdf. For further analysis, see Arthur C. Brooks, "Charitable Explanation," *The Wall Street Journal*, Nov. 27, 2006, p. A12.

9. For details, see Roy E. Finkenbine, "Law, Reconstruction, and African American Education in the Post-Reconstruction South," and Gary R. Hess, "Waging the Cold War in the Third World," in Lawrence J. Friedman and Mark D. McGarvie, eds., *Charity, Philanthropy and Civility in American History* (2004), pp. 161-178; 329-330.

10. See Claire Gaudiani, *The Greater Good: How Philanthropy Drives the American Economy and Can Save Capitalism* (2003).

11. For more details, see "While a Third of Adults Think the Nonprofit Sector in the United States is Headed in the Wrong Direction, a Vast Majority of Households Have Donated to Charities in the Past Year," The Harris Poll, No. 33, April 27, 2006; www.harrisinteractive.com/harris_poll/index.asp?PID=657. See also Sharon Hoffman, "For U.S. charities, a crisis of trust," MSNBC.com, Nov. 21, 2006, www.msnbc.msn.com/id/15753760.

12. For background, see Kathy Koch, "The New Corporate Philanthropy," *CQ Researcher*, Feb. 27, 1998, pp. 169-192.

13. Robert H. Bremner, *American Philanthropy* (1988), p. 232. A higher number, 2,509, is cited in Gaudiani, *op. cit.*, p. 84. For more detail on the private-public partnership that Carnegie devised, see "The Carnegie Libraries," New York Public Library, undated, www.nypl.org/press/carnegielibraries.cfm.

14. For details on Murdoch's assets, see Matthew Miller, "The Forbes 400," *Forbes*, Oct. 9, 2006, p. 194. Also see McLean, *op. cit.*, p. 82.

15. Quoted in Aldo Svaldi, "Media mogul Turner takes a meaty poke at Murdoch," *Denver Post*, Nov. 16, 2006, p. C1.

16. For the complete data, see "Private Philanthropy Across the World," the Comparative Nonprofit Sector Project, Center for Civil Society Studies, December 2005, www.jhu.edu/~cnp/pdf/comptable5_dec05.pdf.

17. Remarks at the First White House National Conference on Faith-Based and Community Initiatives, June 1, 2004, http://usinfo.state.gov/usa/faith/s060104.htm.

18. For more detail, see Ronald Brownstein, "Katrina's Aftermath; Floodwaters Lift Poverty Debate Into Political Focus," *Los Angeles Times*, Sept. 13, 2005, p. A1.

19. Cohen's unsigned article on the Education Department cut and related administration moves is available on the National Coalition for Responsive Philanthropy Web site; www.ncrp.org/Bush_FY2007_Federal_Budget.asp. The administration's proposal is available in a White House budget document, "Major Savings and Reforms in the President's 2007 Budget," The White House, February 2006, p. 28, www.whitehouse.gov/omb/budget/fy2007/pdf/savings.pdf.

20. For background, see Pamela M. Prah, "Disaster Preparedness," *CQ Researcher*, Nov. 18, 2005, pp. 981-1004.

21. For background, see Sarah Glazer, "Faith-Based Initiatives," *CQ Researcher*, May 4, 2001, pp. 377-400.

22. Quoted in Jason Felch and Robin Fields, "Senator Rebukes Getty," *Los Angeles Times*, June 23, 2005, p. B1.

23. For details on the legislation, see "Analysis of Charitable Reforms & Incentives in the 'Pension Protection Act of 2006,'" Oct. 16, 2006; www.independentsector.org/programs/gr/Pension_Bill_Summary.pdf; "What Does the Pension Protection act of 2006 Mean for Private Foundations," Association of Small Foundations, Aug. 17, 2006; www.smallfoundations.org/legislative_update/pension_protection_act/pension_protection_act/file; "Self-Dealing: A Concise Guide for Foundation Board and Staff," Forum of Regional Associations of Grantmakers, 2006; www.ctphilanthropy.org/o/page-content/self_dealing_edie.pdf.

24. For details see "Self-Dealing," *op. cit.*, p. 4; "Exceptions — self-dealing," Internal Revenue Service, undated; www.irs.gov/charities/foundations/article/0,,id=137700,00.html.

25. Christine Ahn, Pablo Eisenberg and Channapha Khamvongsa, "Foundation Trustee Fees: Use and Abuse," Center for Public and Nonprofit Leadership, Public Policy Institute, Georgetown University, September 2003; http://cpnl.georgetown.edu/doc_pool/TrusteeFees.pdf.

26. Quoted in Bremner, *op. cit.*, pp. 41-42. Unless otherwise indicated, material in this section is based on this book.

27. *Ibid.*, p. 41.

28. For more details, see Judith Sealander, "Curing Evils at Their Source: The Arrival of Scientific Giving," in Friedman and McGarvie, *op. cit.*, p. 218.

29. http://alpha.furman.edu/~benson/docs/carnegie.htm.

30. Quoted in Bremner, *op. cit.*, p. 111.

31. Quoted in *ibid.*, p. 139.

32. Quoted in *ibid.*, p. 144.

33. Quoted in *ibid.*, p. 188.

34. Quoted in *ibid.*, p. 206.

35. For the full text of Bush's speech, see "Inaugural Address of George Bush," Jan. 20, 1989; www.yale.edu/lawweb/avalon/presiden/inaug/bush.htm.

36. Caryn James, "Megastars Out to Save the World," *The New York Times*, Nov. 13, 2006, p. E1. George Harrison's project lives on in the form of the "George Harrison Fund for UNICEF," which aids children in Bangladesh as well as other regions afflicted by natural disaster and human cruelty. For more details, see www.unicefusa.org/site/c.duLRI8O0H/b.934081/k.20A2/The_George_Harrison_Fund_for_UNICEF_US_Fund_for_UNICEF.htm.

37. For background, see, Mark Donnelly, "New Faces of Charity," *CQ Researcher*, Dec. 12, 1986, available at *CQ Researcher Plus Archives*, www.cqpress.com.

38. For amount raised, see Robert Hilburn, "28th Annual Grammys a 'World'-Class Event," *Los Angeles Times*, Feb. 26, 1986, Part 5, p. 1.

39. For background, see Peter Katel, "Ending Poverty," *CQ Researcher*, Sept. 9, 2005, pp. 733-760; and Josh Tyrangiel, "The Constant Charmer; the inside story of how the world's biggest rock star mastered the political game and persuaded the world's leaders to take on global poverty," *Time*, Dec. 26, 2005, p. 46. For information on the Red Brand campaign, see Candace Lombardi, "Red iPod supports AIDS charity," News.com[cnet], Oct. 19, 2006; Mike Hughlett and Sandra Jones, "One brand, but they're not the same," *Chicago Tribune*, Oct. 13, 2006, p. C1.

40. For the full interview, see "Software Is My Life," *Newsweek*, Nov. 27, 1995, p. 73.

41. *Ibid.*

42. For more details, see Alan Farnham, "The Billionaires; How They Give Their Money Away," *Fortune*, Sept. 7, 1992, p. 92.

43. For background on Google, see Adam Lashinsky, "Who's The Boss," *Fortune*, Oct. 2, 2006, p. 93, and Hafner, *op. cit.*, p. A1.

44. For background on Omidyar and Brainerd, see Kristina Shevory, "When Charity Begins in a Circle of Friends," *The New York Times*, Oct. 9, 2005, Sect. 3, p. 1; and Fergal Byne, "Auction man: eBay made Pierre Omidyar billions overnight. Now he's starting to spend it," *Financial Times* [London], March 25, 2006, p. A16. See also the Omidyar Network's Web site, www.omidyar.net.

45. Charles E. Shephard, "Power, Perks and Privileges in a Nonprofit World," *The Washington Post*, Feb. 16, 1992. For details of Aramony's sentencing, see Charles W. Hall, "Ex-United Way Chief Sentenced to 7 Years," *The Washington Post*, July 23, 1995, p. A1.

46. Beth Healy, *et al.*, "Charity Begins at Home," Oct. 9, 2003, Nov, 9, 2003, Dec. 3, 2003, Dec. 17, 2003, Dec. 21, 2003, Dec. 29, 2003, *The Boston Globe*, p. A1 (all); www.boston.com/news/specials/nation.

47. Eric Nalder, "CEO's Rewards at Nonprofit," *San Jose Mercury-News*, April 27, 2003, p. A1.

48. "About the J. Paul Getty Trust," [undated] www.getty.edu/about/trust.html.

49. Jason Felch, *et al.*, "State Names Monitor for Getty Trust," *Los Angeles Times*, Oct. 3, 2006, p. B1; Randy Kennedy and Carol Vogel, "President of Getty Trust Resigns Under Pressure," *The New York Times*, Feb. 10, 2006, p. A14; Jason Felch, *et al.*, "The Munitz Collection; Getty's Chief Executive Has Been Highly Compensated During a Time of Austerity," *Los Angeles Times*, June 10, 2005, p. A1.

50. Quoted in Elizabeth Schwinn, "Congress' New Outlook," *The Chronicle of Philanthropy*, Nov. 23, 2006.

51. For full text of Gunderson's speech, see Steve Gunderson, "A Delicate Balance: The Growth of Philanthropy and Its Regulation," Oct. 16, 2006, www.cof.org/Council/content.cfm?ItemNumber=7240&navItemNumber=2131.

52. Statistic cited in "American Red Cross, Governance for the 21st Century, Report of the Board of Governors," October 2006, p. 14; www.redcross.org/static/file_cont5765_lang0_2176.pdf.

53. For more details, see Suzanne Perry and Elizabeth Schwinn, "The Red Cross's new limitations on governance get mixed reviews," *The Chronicle of Philanthropy*, Nov. 9, 2006, p. 29. For the Red Cross board's own account of its proposals, see "American Red Cross, Governance for the 21st Century," *op. cit.*

54. "American Red Cross," *ibid.*, p. 18.

55. For Grassley's statement, see "Memorandum, To: Reporters and Editor[s]," U.S. Senate Committee on Finance, Sen. Chuck Grassley, of Iowa — Chairman, Oct. 20, 2006, www.senate.gov/~finance/press/Gpress/2005/prg103006.pdf.

56. For details, see Jacqueline L. Salmon, "Red Cross Gave Ousted Executive $780,000 Deal," *The Washington Post*, March 4, 2006, p. A9; Jacquelin L. Salmon and Manny Fernandez, "Red Cross President Resigns Amid Conflict," *The Washington Post*, Oct. 27, 2001, p. A2.

57. For details, see "Hurricanes Katrina and Rita: Coordination between FEMA and the Red Cross Should Be Improved for the 2006 Hurricane Season," Government Accountability Office, June 2006, pp. 1-2, www.gao.gov/new.items/d06712.pdf.

58. *Ibid.*, pp. 12-13.

59. The Red Cross response is included in the GAO report. For full text see, *ibid.*, pp. 26-30.

60. For details, see "Red Cross Fires 3rd Volunteer Amid Inquiry," *The New York Times*, March 26, 2006; Adam Nossiter, "F.B.I. to Investigate Red Cross Over Accusations of Wrongdoing," *The New York Times*, March 31, 2006, p. A14.

61. Quoted in "Memorandum," *op. cit.*

62. Sebastian Boyd and John Glover, finance vaccines for the poor," *Inte Tribune*, Nov. 8, 2006, p. A19.

63. Johanna Chung and Andrew Jack, "V delayed by late investor interest," *Fina* [London], Oct. 14, 2006, p. 4.

64. For the full text, see Gordon Brown and Bil "How to help the world's poorest children *Independent* [London], Nov. 7, 2006, http://com .independent.co.uk/commentators/article1961419.e

65. Boyd and Glover, *op. cit.*

66. *Ibid.*, and see also Johanna Chung, "New bond raises Dollars 1 bn for child jabs," *Financial Times* [London], Nov. 8, 2006, p. 45.

67. Chung, *op. cit.*

68. John J. Havens and Paul G. Schervish, "Why the $41 Trillion Wealth Transfer Estimate Is Still Valid: A Review of Challenges and Questions," Boston College Social Welfare Research Institute, Jan. 6, 2003, www.bc.edu/research/swri/meta-elements/pdf/41trillionreview.pdf.

69. For details, see Holly Hall, "Much-Anticipated Transfer of Wealth Has Yet to Materialize, Nonprofit Experts Say," *The Chronicle of Philanthropy*, April 6, 2006; and "Wealth Transfer: A Digest of Opinion and Advice," *Journal of Gift Planning*, 2nd Quarter, 2006; www.bc.edu/research/swri/meta-elements/pdf/jogpvol102.pdf.

70. For background, see John Greenya, "National Service," *CQ Researcher*, June 30, 2006, pp. 577-600.

BIBLIOGRAPHY

Books

Bremner, Robert H., *American Philanthropy, University of Chicago Press*, 1988 (2nd edition).
Written for the lay reader, this survey of a centuries-old American tradition by a veteran historian provides an overview of events and persistent debates.

Brooks, Arthur C., *Who Really Cares: The Surprising Truth About Compassionate Conservatism, Basic Books*, 2006.
A professor at Syracuse University's Maxwell School of Public Affairs interprets a variety of data to show that

...AMERICA

"Buying bonds to...
...national Herald
...cines bond
...cial Times

359

...Gates,
..." The
...ent
...e.

Americans tend to be

...w Philanthropy
...ve Capitalism,
...03.

...lanthropy scholar

... Carnegie, Penguin Press,

...y of perhaps the single most influential
...he history of American philanthropy delves
... contradictions embodied in a ruthless business
...on who advocated giving away of riches — and practiced what he preached.

Articles

Hafner, Katie, "Philanthropy Google's Way: Not the Usual," *The New York Times*, Sept. 14, 2006, p. A1.
A journalist specializing in the high-tech industry explores the business-oriented approach to philanthropy embraced by Google's young billionaire founders.

Katz, Stanley N., "What Does it Mean to Say that Philanthropy is 'Effective?'" *Proceedings of the American Philosophical Society, Vol. 149*, No. 2, June 2005, www.aps-pub.com/proceedings/1492/490201.pdf.
A Princeton University historian of philanthropy argues that foundations' growing emphasis on measurable, short-term results threatens basic research at universities long dependent on foundation grants.

Kramer, Mark R., "Foundation Trustees Need a New Investment Approach," *The Chronicle of Philanthropy*, March 23, 2006, p. 43.
A business veteran who now consults for philanthropies argues that foundations should look for investments that reflect their social missions, not ones that simply ensure financial return.

Nasaw, David, "Looking the Carnegie Gift Horse in the Mouth," *Slate*, Nov. 10, 2006, www.slate.com/id/2152830/.
The author of a new biography of Andrew Carnegie deplores widespread acceptance of the idea that society should have to depend on rich peoples' generosity for the solutions to critical problems.

Salmon, Jacqueline L., "With a Hefty Education Grant Come Equally Great Expectations," *The Washington Post*, Dec. 4, 2006, p. A1.
The Bill & Melinda Gates Foundation's mission to improve high schools is proving complicated and demanding.

Serwer, Andy, "The Power of Philanthropy, Robin Hood," *Fortune*, Sept. 18, 2006, p. 102.
The magazine's managing editor reports on a group of rich, young, hedge-fund executives who are applying business techniques to their donation strategy.

Smith, Douglas K., "Market Magic: Nonprofits could access needed capital by turning donors into investors," *Slate*, Nov. 13, 2006, www.slate.com/id/2152801/.
A management consultant lays out a way to restructure philanthropic donations as investments.

Reports and Studies

"Study on High Net Worth Philanthropy," *Bank of America [prepared by the Center on Philanthropy at Indiana University]*, October 2006.
A research team found that wealthy donors tend to favor educational and cultural institutions as recipients.

Ahn, Christine, *et al.*, "Foundation Trustee Fees: Use and Abuse," *The Center for Public and Nonprofit Leadership, Georgetown University*, September 2003.
A research team finds wide differences among large and small foundations in whether and how much trustees are paid.

Hope, Hollis, *et al.*, "Philanthropy in the News: An Analysis of Media Coverage, 1990-2004," *Foundationworks*.
A detailed examination of press reports shows a steady increase in the volume of coverage, with most articles favorable and focused on big gifts and individual projects, rather than on analyses of goals and whether they're met.

Ostrower, Francie, and Marla J. Bobowick, "Nonprofit Governance and the Sarbanes-Oxley Act," *The Urban Institute Center on Nonprofits and Philanthropy*, Sept. 19, 2006.
Requiring nonprofits to meet new corporate-behavior legal standards would make more of a difference to small foundations, say two Urban Institute scholars, because large foundations have already adopted many of the norms.

For More Information

Center for the Advancement of Social Entrepreneurship, Fuqua School of Business, Duke University, Box 90120, Durham, NC 27708; (919) 660-7823; www.fuqua.duke.edu/centers/case/index.html. Sponsors research and offers an MBA program geared toward managing social-improvement projects.

Center on Philanthropy at Indiana University, 550 West North St., Suite 301, Indianapolis, IN 46202; (317) 274-4200; www.philanthropy.iupui.edu. Produces "Giving USA," a widely cited annual report on charitable donations.

Center on Wealth and Philanthropy, Boston College, McGuinn Hall 515, 140 Commonwealth Ave., Chestnut Hill, MA 02467; (617) 552-4070; www.bc.edu/cwp. Focuses on the moral aspects of philanthropy and intergenerational "wealth transfer."

Charity Navigator, 1200 MacArthur Blvd., 2nd Floor, Mahwah, N.J., 07430; (201) 818-1288; www.charitynavigator .org/index.cfm. A Web-based service that offers fr ations of charities for donors investigating pros beneficiaries.

Independent Sector, 1200 18th St., N.W., Suite 2 Washington, DC 20036; (202) 467-6100; www .independentsector.org/index.htm. Advocacy organization for nonprofits supports legislation that provides incentives for donating.

National Committee for Responsive Philanthropy, 2001 S St., N.W., Suite 620, Washington, DC 20009; (202) 387-9177; www.ncrp.org. Encourages foundations and other donors to fight for economic and social justice.

Philanthropy Roundtable, 1150 17th St., N.W., Suite 503, Washington, DC 20036; (202) 822-8333; www .philanthropyroundtable.org. Serves politically conservative charities that tend to favor a reduced government role in social services.